THE CHURCH AND CISTERCIANS IN MEDIEVAL POLAND

EAST CENTRAL EUROPE, 476–1795

VOLUME 2

*Editorial Board under the auspices of Australian Catholic University
and Adam Mickiewicz University, Poznań*

General Editor
Darius von Güttner-Sporzyński, Australian Catholic University

Assistant Editors
Magdalena Biniaś-Szkopek, Adam Mickiewicz University
Matthew Firth, Flinders University
Robert Tomczak, Adam Mickiewicz University

Editorial Board
Daniel Bagi, University of Pécs
Richard Butterwick-Pawlikowski, University College London
Józef Dobosz, Adam Mickiewicz University
Emilia Jamroziak, University of Leeds
Adrian Jones, La Trobe University
David Kalhous, Masaryk University
Krzysztof Skwierczyński, University of Warsaw
Talia Zajac, University of Manchester

The Church and Cistercians in Medieval Poland

Foundations, Documents, People

by
JÓZEF DOBOSZ

translated by
AGNIESZKA TOKARCZUK

edited by
DARIUS VON GÜTTNER-SPORZYŃSKI *and*
MATTHEW FIRTH

with the assistance of
MAGDALENA BINIAŚ-SZKOPEK *and*
ROBERT TOMCZAK

BREPOLS

© 2023, Brepols Publishers n. v., Turnhout, Belgium.

All rights reserved. No part of this publication
may be reproduced, stored in a retrieval system, or
transmitted, in any form or by any means, electronic,
mechanical, photocopying, recording, or otherwise
without the prior permission of the publisher.

D/2023/0095/23
ISBN 978-2-503-59802-4
eISBN 978-2-503-59803-1
DOI 10.1484/M.ECE-EB.5.127204

Printed in the EU on acid-free paper.

Table of Contents

List of Illustrations — 7

Abbreviations — 9

Introduction — 11

Translation of Names and Conventions Used in This Volume — 15

Chapter 1: The Church and Christianity in Poland before 1300 — 17

Part I
Foundations

Chapter 2: The Piasts, the Premonstratensians and Other Religious Orders of Canons Regular in the Twelfth Century — 45

Chapter 3 The Earliest Evidence for Kazimierz II as Patron and Founder — 57

Chapter 4: The Foundation of Łekno Abbey in the Context of Twelfth-Century Polish Cistercian Institutions — 75

Chapter 5: The Foundation Process and the Early Endowment of Jędrzejów Abbey — 89

Chapter 6: The Circumstances of the Founding of the Cistercian Monastery at Sulejów — 123

Chapter 7: The Founder and the Beginnings of the Cistercian Monastery at Wąchock — 133

Chapter 8: Churches in the Endowments to Polish Cistercian Monasteries in the Twelfth and Early Thirteenth Centuries — 145

Chapter 9: The Foundation of Owińska Abbey in the Light of the Earliest Written Records — 153

Part II
Documents

Chapter 10: The Written Document in Medieval Poland — 163

Chapter 11: Research on the Documents and Scriptoria of the Polish Cistercians — 173

Chapter 12: Forgeries as a Subject of Research of Polish Diplomatics of the Middle Ages — 189

Chapter 13: Legitimisation of Forged Documents in Twelfth- and Thirteenth-Century Poland — 199

Chapter 14: The False Thirteenth-Century Documents of the Cistercian Abbeys at Sulejów and Jędrzejów — 207

Chapter 15: The Diploma of Mieszko III for the Canons Regular in Trzemeszno (28 April 1145) — 219

Chapter 16: The Foundation Charter of the Cistercian Abbey at Łekno — 235

Part III
People

Chapter 17: Maur, Bishop of Kraków — 263

Chapter 18: Archbishop Janik and His Successors: Preparation for the Reform of Henryk Kietlicz — 269

Chapter 19: Thirteenth-Century Abbots of the Cistercian Abbey at Wąchock — 283

Chapter 20: The Cistercians in Małopolska and their Position in the Economy and Culture of Thirteenth-Century Poland — 291

Bibliography — 299

Index — 333

List of Illustrations

Charts

Chart 1. Early Piasts (selected dynasty representatives). 26
Chart 2. The genealogy of the Łabędzie Clan (the Wszebor line). 139

Figures

Figure 1. Location of Jędrzejów Abbey. Prepared by A. Wyrwa, drawn by L. Fijał and M. Bucka. 96
Figure 2. The Cistercian abbey at Jędrzejów. Drawn by M. Bucka. 97
Figure 3. Late twelfth-century copy of the foundation charter of Łekno Abbey. AAG, ref. Dipl. Gn. 4. From the collection of the Cistercians. Photo P. Namiota. 178
Figure 4. The charter issued by dukes Bolesław the Pious and Przemysł II on 6 January 1278 to confirm Voivode Benjamin's endowment for the Cistercian monastery at Paradyż. APP, Cystersi Paradyż ref. D.I. From the collection of the Cistercians Photo P. Namiota. 181
Figure 5. Charter of Kazimierz III from 12 October 1334 for the Cistercian Abbey at Mogiła. Archive of the Cistercian Abbey at Mogiła, ref. 67. From the collection of the Cistercians. Photo P. Namiota. 184
Figure 6. The 1464 diploma of the general chapter of the Cistercians to the Abbot of Mogiła authorising him to engage other Polish abbots in the construction of a house for the students of the monastery. Archive of the Cistercian Abbey at Mogiła, ref. 6. From the collection of the Cistercians. Photo P. Namiota. 187
Figure 7. The Scheme of the Production of the Jędrzejów Forgeries. 215
Figure 8. The Scheme of the Production of the Sulejów Forgeries. 216
Figure 9. The Origin of the Trzemeszno Forgery (28 April 1145). 227
Figure 10. Poznań foundation charter of Łekno Abbey (end of twelfth century). Photo P. Namiota (MPP, table vi). 236
Figure 11. Characteristics of the script of the foundation charter of Łekno Abbey. Fragment of the Poznań original. Photo P. Namiota (MPP, table iv). 243
Figure 12. Script in the original Poznań foundation charter of Łekno Abbey. Photo P. Namiota (MPP, table iv). 243
Figure 13. Seal of Archbishop Janik. Photo P. Namiota. 244
Figure 14. The interior of the Cistercian monastery at Wąchock. Photo P. Namiota. 294

Maps

Map 1.	Tribes of Polish lands before 966.	18
Map 2.	Early Expansion of the Piast Realm.	24
Map 3.	Church Administrative Structures by 1138.	30
Map 4.	The Act of Succession of 1138.	36
Map 5.	The Settlement of 1146.	38
Map 6.	Religious Orders in Poland before 1200.	40

Tables

Table 1.	1153 (and earlier) grants for Jędrzejów Abbey	104
Table 2.	1166/67 grants for Jędrzejów Abbey	106
Table 3.	The property status of Jędrzejów Abbey in the final stage of the foundation process	112
Table 4.	The Economic Foundations of the Monastery in Trzemeszno (considering the forgery of 28 April 1145, bull of Eugene III of 31 May 1147, diploma of Hubaldus of 2 March 1146)	228
Table 5.	Twelfth-century grants for Łekno Abbey	256

Abbreviations

AU/PAU	Akademia Umiejętności/Polska Akademia Umiejętności
Chronica Polonorum	Mistrz Wincenty (tzw. Kadłubek), *Kronika Polska* (1992)
RPD	Repertorjum polskich dokumentów doby piastowskiej, Kozłowska-Budkowa (1937)
KDM	Kodeks dyplomatyczny Małopolski, Piekosiński (1878–1886)
KDP	Kodeks dyplomatyczny Polski, Ryzszczewski et al. (1847–1858)
KDŚ	Kodeks dyplomatyczny Śląska, Maleczyński (1956)
KDW	Kodeks dyplomatyczny Wielkopolski, Zakrzewski (1877)
KKK	Kodeks dyplomatyczny katedry krakowskiej, Piekosiński (1874)
LB	Liber beneficiorum dioecesis Cracoviensis, Długosz (1863–1864)
MCP	Monasticon Cisterciense Poloniae, Wyrwa et al. (1999)
MGH	Monumenta Germaniae Historica
MPH	Monumenta Polaniae Historica (1866–1888)
MPP	Monumenta Poloniae Paleographica
PSB	Polski Słownik Biograficzny
PTPN	Poznańskie Towarzystwo Przyjaciół Nauk
PWN	Państwowe Wydawnictwo Naukowe
UAM	Uniwersytet im. Adama Mickiewicza
WP	Wydawnictwo Poznańskie
WUW	Wydawnictwo Uniwersytetu Wrocławskiego
ZDK	Zbiór dokumentów katedry i diecezji krakowskiej, Kuraś (1965)
ZDŚ	Zbiór dokumentów średniowiecznych, Piekosiński (1897)
ZNO	Zakład Narodowy im. Ossolińskich

Introduction

The studies of the history of the development of the Church in Poland contained in this volume focus on the establishment and dynastic endowment of ecclesiastical institutions and their operations in the twelfth and thirteenth centuries. My research published over the course of the last forty years in Polish is in this volume for the first time translated and, in several instances, significantly edited. I believe it represents the first major overview in the English language of Cistercian foundations in Poland in the twelfth and early thirteenth centuries.

As the subtitle of the books suggests, the chapters are grouped thematically into three parts. The first of these focuses on the ecclesiastical establishments (mainly monasteries) of the Piast dynasty and their founders. The second is devoted to the major sources (charters and other documents) related to such institutions, while the third examines the pre-eminent representatives of the Church (bishops and abbots) in Poland.

This book reflects my special interest in the Cistercians, who enjoyed a very strong patronage of the Piast dynasts in the twelfth and thirteenth centuries, as well as the various areas of canonry, on both micrographic and monographic levels. The outcomes of that research relate to specific issues: the origins of the establishments, their foundation, the composition of individual monasteries, their architecture, and so on. I am hopeful that by presenting these thematic studies together in this one volume a broader, worldwide audience will be able to experience the rich world of Polish academic research.

The volume opens with my introduction to the history of early Piast Poland and the progress of Poland's Christianisation. The rest of the book is then divided into three parts, each containing a number of chapters. The chapters included in Part I of this volume draw on research into the beginnings of monasteries based on St Augustine's order (Canons Regular of the Lateran and the Premonstratensians) and the Cistercian abbeys. Both the Cistercians and the Canons Regular emerged within the Piast domain as early as in the first half of the twelfth century. In the second half of the century, they gradually established their position and became a regular element of Polish religious, social, cultural, and economic life.

Chapter 2, in Part I, is dedicated to the relations between the Piast dynasty and the Premonstratensians (the Norbertines) and other forms of the Canon Regular in the twelfth century. The Piast dynasts became involved with the Canons Regular in the early twelfth century and brought them to Trzemeszno, and perhaps also to Czerwińsk. These foundations were initiated by Bolesław III Krzywousty (the Wrymouth). His sons turned their interest to the reformed branch of this stream of Christian communities — the Norbertines — by supporting the foundations of the local magnates, such as the monastery in Zwierzyniec near Kraków, various Silesian monasteries, and the Busko monastery. The Chapter 3 turns to the foundations of Kazimierz II Sprawiedliwy (the Just) or, to be more precise, the extant sources for such. Kazimierz founded and supported the Cistercian houses; he showed interest in various canon groups as well as the Kraków bishopric with which he closely cooperated. At present, there is little evidence from that time that illustrates these interests. At our disposal are predominantly documents, which include many forgeries prepared in the thirteenth or fifteenth centuries, and the remains of sacral architecture. In many cases, such as Wiślica — and perhaps Sulejów, Jędrzejów, and Opatów — the remains of the architecture can be traced back to the reign of Kazimierz II. There is some information about Kazimierz's foundations in chronicles and annals, although they were also mainly in the thirteenth to fifteenth centuries.

The subsequent chapters in Part I of this volume are related to the establishment of the Cistercian monasteries in Poland in the twelfth century. First, I present the foundation of the two oldest Cistercian monasteries in Poland: the abbeys of Łekno and Jędrzejów, which were established around the mid-twelfth century. The two subsequent chapters present the beginnings of the monasteries in Sulejów and Wąchock, established in the 1170s. The discussion of these monasteries is supplemented by a chapter focused on the specific form that support of Cistercian monasteries took — namely, the donations of existing small churches in a duke's or a magnate's estate together with property. The final chapter of Part I turns again to the foundation of monasteries, particularly the early years of the convent in Owińska, a thirteenth-century establishment of the Polish branch of the Cistercians.

Such detailed studies of the oldest Cistercian and canon foundations in Poland, accompanying the shift in the nature of the Piast rule from a patrimonial monarchy to a polyarchy, have provided the basis for further research into the subject. I have published a more comprehensive study of the foundations of Kazimierz II, whom I consider one of the most interesting rulers of the early Piast Poland.[1] In that study I included a comprehensive review of the duke's ecclesiastical foundations, as well as the reasons for and circumstances of these actions. It also presented an analysis of the entire source basis, including annals, chronicles, hagiographies, and archaeological and architectural evidence. Polish historian Roman Michałowski has previously followed a slightly different path as he presents, in an analytical synthesis, the Polish rulers in the early Middle Ages as generous founders and protectors of the Church. In his opinion, the religious foundations were an element

---

1 Dobosz, *Działalność fundacyjna*, p. 253.

of the political culture of the time.[2] Other historians, including Halina Manikowska and Tomasz Ginter agree with that argument. The former has written extensively on Piotr Włostowic († 1153), one of the most illustrious Polish magnates, and his large-scale endowment of the Church, especially his foundations in Silesia before the reign of Henry Brodaty (the Bearded) († 1238).[3] The latter has focused on the foundations of Mieszko III Stary (the Old) († 1202).[4] To complement these studies, Leszek Wetesko has presented an in-depth analysis of the contribution of the Piast rulers to the Church foundations established in Wielkopolska.[5]

Part II of this volume is related to early medieval Polish documents or, to be more precise, the early period of their reception in Poland in the twelfth and thirteenth centuries. All the charters discussed were produced for various ecclesiastical institutions. They are most typically foundation diplomas enumerating each foundation's endowment or inventory records. The first chapter in this part is dedicated to the general topic of the history of Polish medieval documents. The subsequent chapters are dedicated to providing overviews of research into scriptoria and Polish Cistercian documents, document falsifications, and documents (or series thereof) issued for the monasteries in Sulejów, Jędrzejów, Trzemeszno, and Łekno. To a large extent, these analyses refer to primary written testimonies of a pragmatic nature that show the economic, organisational, and legal bases upon which Polish Church institutions, chiefly monasteries, rested.

In Part III of this volume, I focus on the people in the Church. The opening chapter is dedicated to Maurus († 1118), a relatively unknown bishop of Kraków who most probably came from Italy and who, during the reign of Bolesław III, oversaw the diocese of Kraków for approximately ten years. Then, I devote attention to the archbishops of Gniezno who, in the second half of the twelfth century, laid the foundation for the revival of the Polish Church in the wake of the Gregorian reform movement brought about in the thirteenth century by Archbishop Henryk Kietlicz († 1219). In the next chapter, I focus again on the Cistercians, examining the oldest and least studied abbots of the monastery in Wąchock. Finally, the book's closing chapter considers the cultural and economic role of the Małopolska Cistercians in the thirteenth century.

---

2 See Michałowski, *Princeps fundator*.
3 Manikowska, 'Princeps fundator', pp. 37–57.
4 Ginter, *Działalność fundacyjna*.
5 Wetesko, *W służbie państwa i Kościoła*.

Translation of Names and Conventions Used in This Volume

For the English reader not familiar with Polish, names can appear daunting. Place names can be a minefield, particularly as there is not always an established convention for the translation of a place name into English. Also, a German translation of the name may also be in popular use. The following naming conventions are used in this book:
  Wielkopolska – Greater Poland (Latin: Polonia Maior)
  Małopolska – Lesser Poland (Latin: Polonia Minor)
  Sandomierz – (Latin: Sandomiria, German: Sandomir)
  Pomorze Gdańskie – Pomerelia (Latin: Pomerelia, German: Pommerellen)
  Pomerania (Latin: Pomerania, Polish: Pomorze, German: Pommern, Latin: Pomerania or Pomorania)
  Prussia (Latin: Prussia, Borussia, or Pruthenia, Polish: Prusy, German: Preußen).

References to 'Poland' and 'Polish' in this book are meant to refer to the region of Europe inhabited by a Slavic peoples known to others and themselves as *Polanie* and ruled by the Piast dynasty. The use of the name Piast as the name of the first recorded ruling dynasty of *Polanie* is a matter of convention. The first documented Polish monarch Mieszko I and his descendants certainly did not use this name to denote their house. The term seems to have emerged only in the seventeenth century.

In this book the term *princeps* is used as established by Bishop Vincentius of Kraków in reference to the first member by precedence of the Piast dynasty. Thus, *princeps* denote the suzerain of Poland after 1138. Other terms used in the historiography for the *princeps* are senior duke, duke of Kraków or high duke.

For the Polish rulers, on first use I provide their full Polish name together with their sobriquet in Polish, which is then translated, and on subsequent use only their translated byname is used. Thus on the first use 'Bolesław I Chrobry (the Brave)' and thereafter 'Bolesław the Brave' or 'Bolesław I'. The only exception is Henryk Sandomierski who, after his first use in this book, is thereafter referred to as Henryk of Sandomierz.

There are two other conventions of Polish historiography that also need to be explained here. The author of the *Gesta principum Polonorum* is almost always referred to by Polish authors as 'Gall Anonim' (Gallus Anonymous). This is simply a matter of convention as the author has never been convincingly identified. This established convention is followed in this volume and this author has referred to him as Gallus. Similarly, the author of the *Chronica Polonorum* is referred to in Polish historiography as 'Mistrz Wincenty zwany Kadłubkiem' (Master Vincentius called Kadłubek) or 'Mistrz Wincenty Kadłubek' (Master Vincentius Kadłubek). In this volume, he is referred to using the Latin name 'Vincentius' with which he signed the extant charters and, as he was canonically elected Bishop of Kraków, he is referred to as 'Bishop Vincentius of Kraków'. In my view, the use of the highly dubious patronymic Kadłubek only complicates the issue of the author's identity.

Polish Language

Polish names and words may appear difficult but their pronunciation is consistent. All vowels are simple and of even length, as in Italian, and their sound is best rendered by the English words 'sum' (a), 'ten' (e), 'ease' (i), 'lot' (o), 'book' (u), 'sit' (y). Most of the consonants behave the same way as in English, except for 'c' (which is pronounced 'ts'), 'j' (which is soft as in 'yes'), and 'w' (which is equivalent to the English 'v'). As in German, some consonants are softened when they fall at the end of a word and 'b', 'd', 'f', 'w', 'z' became 'p', 't', 'k', 'f', 's' respectively.

There are also several accented letters and combinations peculiar to Polish of which the following is a rough list:

ó u, as in 'cook', hence Kraków is pronounced 'krakooff'.
u as 'ó'.
ą nasal a, approximating to 'om' or 'on', hence sąd is pronounced 'sont'.
ę nasal e, approximating to 'em' or 'en',
hence Łęczyca is pronounced 'wenchytsa'.
ć soft ch as in 'cheese'.
cz hard ch, as in 'chalk' or 'catch'.
ch guttural h as in 'loch'.
ł English w, as in 'wood', hence Bolesław becomes 'Boleswaf', Władysław 'Vwadiswaf'.
w v as in 'virago'.
ń soft n as in Spanish 'mañana' or 'news'.
rz French j as in 'je', or hard zh as in 'measure'.
ś soft sh as in 'sheer' or 'sheep'.
sz hard sh as in 'bush' or 'shot'.
ż as rz.
ź a similar sound, but sharper as in French 'gigot'.

CHAPTER 1

The Church and Christianity in Poland before 1300

The introduction of Christianity to Poland was followed or perhaps accompanied by a gradual establishment of its institutional forms in the realm of the Piasts in the early second half of the tenth century. The Christianisation of the communities of the Piast realm, as well as the emergence and development of the major structures of the institutional Church, was a process that took place over a long period of time, and was plagued by various difficulties and crises. It is safe to say that the spread of the Christian religion and the establishment of the Church commenced with the decision of Mieszko I in 966. Much more difficult to ascertain, however, is when these two phenomena ended. The baptism of Mieszko I and the elites of his realm marked the beginning of a stage of Christianisation that can be deemed extensive. Within a short time, the people in the territories ruled by the Piasts were considered to be Christianised but, in truth, this needs to be understood as the acceptance of the new religion by the magnate elites than all of the inhabitants of the lands under Mieszko's control. There is no doubt that the intensification of new religious activity depended on access to Christian practices that, in turn, relied on the number of priests and churches. A breakthrough must have come in the late twelfth and early thirteenth centuries, when the diocesan organisation, successfully established since 1000, was further strengthened. A new link was added to the ecclesiastical structures with the establishment of archdeaconries, followed by parishes at the lowest levels of the institutional structure. This likely signalled the end of the phase of early Christianisation, when the new religion was spread rather superficially among large groups within the population, giving way to intensive and ingrained Christianisation.

Over two centuries, the population in the territory ruled by the Piasts grew. The borders changed and so did the political and economic conditions, accompanied by a growing number of church and residential clerical buildings. In favourable conditions, protected by the ruler and the elites, Christianity reinforced its position across the realm of the Piast dynasty. The Church's institutional structures were supported by a diocesan organisation that subsequently expanded, with archidiaconal (and, later, parochial) districts and numerous monasteries, particularly from the twelfth century. This was a breakthrough of not just a religious nature, as paganism was abandoned for Christianity, but also a cultural nature. Brick churches appeared and Latin

Map 1. Tribes of Polish lands before 966.

became the language not only of liturgy and diplomacy (visible in letters and documents) but also of memory and tradition (written chronicles). The Church instituted by the first Piasts became a part of the local economic and social structures, and an important part of the monarchy, as well as a significant partner and pillar of the dynasty. In this chapter, I will make an attempt to present how this happened over the span of several generations of the Piast dynasty.

The Church under protection of the ruler

In the mid-tenth century, following the territorial development of Piast realms, the Church quite unexpectedly became a part of written history. As a result of Piast expansion to the north-west, the people ruled by the Piasts, the Polans, entered the sphere of influence of Polabian politics, indirectly Czech politics and, first and foremost, German politics. The Piast efforts of expansion, aimed at seizing Pomerania with Szczecin and Wolin, led to conflict with the Veleti, politically supported by the Czech Přemyslid dynasty. When Lubusz was seized in 963, Mieszko I changed his politics in the aftermath of the defeat. His goal, as early as 965, was to break the alliance between the Czechs and the Veleti by forging political bonds with the Přemyslid dynasty. Sources attest to this fact in the form of the arrival of Dobrava, daughter of Boleslav I, Duke of Bohemia, at the Piast court. She married Mieszko, probably to service as a guarantor of the new political alliance. Irrespective of the picture that emerges from the scant and hard-to-interpret sources (often written many decades after the events), in 966 Mieszko made a momentous and far-sighted decision. He adopted the new religion, as most chroniclers suggest, at the suggestion of his Christian spouse. This breakthrough event has triggered a wide-ranging discussion in Polish historiography, which is beyond the scope of this chapter. It is enough to be aware that historians continue to argue about the major related issues, like the motivation and circumstances of Mieszko's baptism, its location, the role of the duke's spouse, and even the exact date (only the year seems to be undisputable).

The crucial thing seems to be that, in 966, the pagan ruler of the Polans accepted the new faith himself, and seems to have involved his immediate, or even less immediate, entourage in the process. It is hard to determine whether this was done for reasons of politics and prestige, because of Dobrava's influence, or because it was a way to provide a more effectively centralised governmental apparatus. There must have been many factors at play. Most importantly, a group of clergy arrived in the Piast realm with Dobrava, and another after Mieszko's baptism, and embarked on a program of Christianisation. The baptism of the Piast ruler must have taken place in a prominent location, although there have been suggestions that it was outside of immediate Piast control, such as Prague, Magdeburg or Regensburg. The study of the historical circumstances and the archaeological research have led to a conclusion that it must have happened in the 'triangle' marked by Gniezno, Ostrów Lednicki and Poznań. While each of these locations has avid supporters among historians, it seems to me that Mieszko could have been baptised in Poznań. The latest archaeological discoveries in Poznań's Ostrów Tumski provide an argument in favour of this theory in the form of the discovery of a church and palace complex that dates back to the mid-tenth century. It has been suggested this may have been the seat of Dobrava and Mieszko's court. Bearing in mind that pagan worship was still practiced in Gniezno, and that the interpretation of the oldest remains of the church and palace in Ostrów Lednicki is inconclusive, we can assume that the duke chose Poznań as the home for his Christian spouse. The first ecclesiastical buildings were raised in Poznań to host the baptism of the duke and his immediate political supporters; after some time, construction of the first cathedral in the Piast realm began.

The years 965–966 marked the beginning of a sequence of events that led to the Christianisation of the Piast dynasty's subjects and, consequently, to establishing ecclesiastical structures and incorporating them into the existing system of government. This had a number of consequences, including the young Piast realm's introduction to the sphere of Western (Latin) culture. The cultural impact of Christianity on Mieszko's realm was enormous. The new religion also ushered in a political and systemic change, followed by social and economic transformations. Poland was becoming an important part of the *Respublica Christiana*.[1] In the tenth century, it became tied to Rome by religion and in the realm's active search for its position in the emergent political system of the new Central European monarchies.

Mieszko I's decision to adopt Christianity in 966 had far-reaching consequences and resulted in the rapid establishment of the first bishopric, with certain chroniclers indicating it took place in 968. It is hard to ascertain whether Mieszko was assisted by emperor Otto I, who was grateful for Mieszko's defeat of Wichmann II the Younger in 967, as it has been suggested, or whether there was a different reason for sending a bishop to the lands of the Polans. We can only be certain of the year of the arrival in 968 of the first Polish bishop, a man named Jordan who may have come from an area of Greek or Celtic cultural influence. The date of his death or of his stepping down as bishop is not as certain, though sources suggest 982 or 984. Similarly, the circumstances of his arrival in the Piast realm remain unknown, while the legal basis for his status has kept Church historians busy for many decades. Without dissecting the various intricacies of the scholarly disputes, we can state with certainty that a decision was made to appoint a bishop for the Piast realm as a result of Mieszko's baptism and the favourable political makeup of the papal and imperial courts in the years that followed. It is impossible to say, in the present state of historical knowledge, whether Jordan was a missionary or a territorial bishop, or if he reported directly to the Holy See. There is every indication that Jordan's ecclesiastical jurisdiction in 968 covered all of Mieszko's realm: Wielkopolska, Gdańsk Pomerania, Lubusz, Mazovia, central Poland (Sieradz and Łęczyca), and most probably West Pomerania.

---

1 Experts in the history of the Church use this phrase, 'the Christian Republic', to refer to the emerging community of Christian Europe.

Therefore, he was a bishop in a broader sense of the title, and the entire Piast dominion was his territorial diocese. Mieszko was undoubtedly the founder of the first bishopric in his realm; we can also assume that Dobrava had an important role in the appointment of Jordan. As a result, the introduction of the Christian faith was accompanied by laying the foundations of the institutional Church.

For at least two centuries, historiographical discussion — and sometimes dispute — about the location of the first ecclesiastical see has been ongoing. The discussion intensified as new archaeological discoveries at Ostrów Tumski in Poznań opened the way for new interpretations. Since the decision to adopt Christianity was made relatively quickly — there is no indication of lengthy preparations for the baptism in 966 — it should not be assumed that Mieszko managed to provide the required facilities, such as a cathedral, for Jordan's arrival in 968. Notably, the Piast ruler reigned over a large territory, but not from a single location. Rather, he exercised power by touring the country, which marked the emergence of the *rex ambulans* system. Therefore, the ruler's 'capital city' was wherever he and his entourage were, with a special role played by the largest strongholds: Gniezno, Poznań, Giecz, Ostrów Lednicki, Grzybowo and others. The ruler must have been accompanied by his bishop, who had just started the mission of converting the pagans to Christianity with the ruler's protection. Nonetheless, it is certain that the itinerant Piast duke had his 'special place', with sources from the latter half of Mieszko's rule pointing to *Gnezdun Civitas* or *Civitas Schinesghe*: Gniezno where St Adalbert's body was buried during the reign of Mieszko's son, Bolesław I Chrobry (the Brave). There is every indication that when Dobrava was still alive, the major residence was in Poznań where, most probably, Bishop Jordan was stationed and where a church and a palace were raised together with the first Polish cathedral. After Dobrava's death in 977 and Mieszko's next marriage (to Oda of Haldensleben in 980), the situation changed, and the centre of gravity shifted to Gniezno. This must have been the reason why, when recounting Otto III's arrival into Gniezno in the year 1000, Thietmar of Merseburg wrote that, 'After being received with veneration by Bishop Unger, he was led into the church'.[2] The chronicler emphasised that before 1000, the diocese of Unger included 'the realm in its entirety', meaning Mieszko's and later Bolesław's lands. It seems that the first two bishops, Jordan from 968 and his successor Unger from 982/84, were territorial bishops for all lands under Piast rule in the late tenth century. Initially, they were headquartered in Poznań in the stronghold in Ostrów Tumski. Later, it seems, Gniezno gradually took over that role. The bishops' major task was to propagate Christianity together with the ruler and with his protection, as Thietmar meaningfully stated,

---

2   Thietmar Merseburgensis, *Chronicon* iv.45. Thietmar refers to Bishop Unger as the Bishop of Poznań later in the *Chronicon*, but in the context of the changes that took place after the Congress of Gniezno.

'Jordan, their first bishop, laboured much with [the peoples of Mieszko's lands] while he diligently invited them by word and deed to the cultivation of the heavenly vineyard'.[3]

Therefore, Mieszko I, the first historically documented Piast ruler, adopted Christianity and established a bishopric. It was not until the reign of his son, Bolesław the Brave, however, that a complete ecclesiastical organisation was built. Gallus Anonymous wrote that 'King Bolesław was deeply devoted to religion, building churches and establishing episcopal sees and granting endowments, so much indeed, that in his days Poland had two metropolitans along with their suffragans'.[4] It must be said that the chronicler did not exaggerate much in his assessment of Bolesław the Brave's contribution to the Church in Poland. Bolesław made an excellent use of Bishop Adalbert of Prague's mission in Prussia in the spring of 997 and his martyr's death on 23 April. Adalbert's body, bought back for its weight in gold, became the founding relic of the first Polish church archbishopric in Gniezno. The developments of 997 soon led to the canonisation of the martyr bishop and the pope's appointment to the Adalbert's archbishopric. These decisions were solemnly confirmed and announced during the Congress of Gniezno in 1000 when emperor Otto III made a pilgrimage to the new martyr's relics. Thietmar of Merseburg described the event in the spring that year in the following way:

> Without delay, [emperor Otto III] established an archbishopric there, as I hope legitimately, but without the consent of the aforementioned bishop [Unger] to whose diocese this whole region is subject. He committed the new foundation to Radim, the martyr's brother, and made subject to him Bishop Reinbern of Kolberg, Bishop Poppo of Kraków, and bishop John of Wrocław.[5]

As a result of Bolesław the Brave's efforts, a Polish archbishopric was established in Gniezno, headed by Radim Gaudentius, half-brother of Adalbert of Prague. Three suffragan dioceses were subordinated to it, in Kraków, Kołobrzeg, and Wrocław; and Unger, the bishop of all Poland, was ultimately based in Poznań. For a long time, Gallus' mention of the second Polish archbishopric during the reign of Bolesław the Brave was a puzzle to historians. However, lately it has been assumed that on a temporary basis, the south of Poland, incorporated into the Piast domain in the last years of Mieszko I's reign (988–990), reported to the bishoprics in Prague and Olomouc. The ecclesiastical land was subordinated to the archbishopric in Mainz. Following the establishment of the Gniezno archbishopric in 999–1000, for a short time the lands of Bolesław the Brave were under the influence of two archbishoprics: Gniezno and Mainz, most probably to settle the ecclesiastical and legal issues.

---

3 Thietmar Merseburgensis, *Chronicon* iv.56.
4 MPH s.n. ii p. 55.
5 Thietmar Merseburgensis, *Chronicon* iv.45.

Despite this considerable success, Bolesław the Brave did not stop strengthening the Church that two generations of the Piast dynasty had created. The first religious orders appeared relatively quickly. The Camaldolese most certainly settled in Międzyrzecz, and the Benedictine order and a small congregation of nuns were possibly established. The Piast ruler started to raise cathedrals, as well as big and smaller churches that were typically located in the state's major political centres such as Giecz and Kałdus. In the church in Gniezno, the remains of Adalbert of Prague were soon joined by other relics, most certainly those of the Five Martyred Brothers, perhaps also those of Bruno of Querfurt, though it remains unclear whether his relics were brought to Gniezno or Giecz. The latter died with his comrades during a mission among Sudovians in 1009. Thietmar reported that the saint's body and the bodies of his comrades were bought by Bolesław the Brave who 'thereby secured the solace of his house for the future'.[6] There is some suggestion of plans to collect the relics of the martyrs in the heart of the expanding Piast realm, a foundation upon which the Church and its structures were to be built, and through which the Piast dynasty would be protected.

It did not take the Piasts long to provide their domains with a fully functional diocesan Church organisation, securing its ideological bases with the relics of the recently martyred saints. The Piasts were not only founders of churches but, more importantly, of bishoprics supported financially by founders not only of churches but also by the tithing arrangements of subsequent rulers. What resulted was the creation of a Piast Church, capable of quick Christianisation, strongly supported by the monarch and the political elites. The Church would rapidly become a mainstay of the throne and, owing to the rulers' support, could effectively conduct its mission while expanding and maintaining its economic bases.

The development of the Polish Church was suddenly curtailed by events late in the reign of Bolesław the Brave and during that of his son, Mieszko II. As a result of long-term wars with Germany, West Pomerania gained independence and the Kołobrzeg diocese ceased to function around 1013. Thus, one of the links in the painstakingly-built Piast Church structure broke. The situation only deteriorated after Bolesław's death in 1025, the same year he was crowned king. During the rule of his son, Mieszko II, the Piast monarchy was faced by an acute crisis caused by Bolesław's expansionist politics, as well as an internal dynastic feud when Bolesław's sons fought to seize power. In the 1030s, internal rebellions broke out in the Piast realm, perhaps including a 'pagan reaction', coupled with external invasions. Following the death of Bezprym in 1031 after a short reign, and of Mieszko II in 1034, and the departures of queen Richeza of Lotharingia and later Kazimierz I Odnowiciel (the Restorer), the dynasty was no longer in power. The act of destruction was completed by this invasion of Břetislav I, Duke of Bohemia who, most

---

6 Thietmar Merseburgensis, *Chronicon* vi.95.

Map 2. Early Expansion of the Piast Realm.

probably in 1039, ravaged Wielkopolska, destroyed the strongholds in Gniezno and Poznań, plundered the relics of Adalbert of Prague, the Five Martyred Brothers and Radim Gaudentius and, on his way back to Prague, seized Silesia. As the Piast monarchy fell apart, the still-fragile Church structures were destroyed. According to Gallus Anonymous, those who 'escaped the clutches of the foe or their rebellious fellow-countrymen fled over the river Vistula into Mazovia'.[7] There, a magnate called Miecław, the cup-bearer of Mieszko II according to Gallus Anonymous, tried to establish a small realm independent of the Piasts. Of all the bishoprics established by Bolesław the Brave, only Kraków continued.

In 1039, Kazimierz I, rightly nicknamed 'the Restorer' by posterity, was on his way back to Poland, accompanied by German knights and assisted by his mother, Richeza, and his uncle, Herman II, archbishop of Cologne. He must have settled in Małopolska, not affected by the events of the 1030s, planning from there to restore the work of his predecessors. The task he faced was no mean feat: the structures of the country and the slightly younger Church organisation had fallen into ruin. The entire rule of this king was dedicated to regaining the old territories of the Piast monarchy, by introducing required changes and slowly restoring the Church as an institution on the basis of the Kraków diocese. This program of restoration was made possible by a new system of alliances, predominantly with Yaroslav the Wise, the Grand Prince of Kyiv, whose sister, Maria Dobroniega, Kazimierz married. He was supported also by his mother, who had settled in the Rhineland where she died. As for his ecclesiastical work, Kazimierz accomplishments boiled down to providing continuity of the Church investiture. As a result, the pope appointed Aaron, Bishop of Kraków, as metropolitan bishop, giving the duke a free hand as far as appointing new bishops was concerned. After regaining Silesia from Bohemia in 1050, he also managed to restore the bishopric in Wrocław. He probably also founded the Benedictine monastery in Tyniec near Kraków in 1044, although some historians attribute the foundation to his son, Bolesław II Śmiały (the Bold). When Kazimierz died in 1058, he left an integrated monarchy where order was restored, the Church had been once more raised high, but his work was not completed. He failed to restore the Gniezno metropolitan bishopric, although he must have taken some steps to re-establish the position of Poznań and Gniezno.

Bolesław II the Bold followed in his father's footsteps and completed the work. He was the third Polish ruler who was crowned (1076) but in order to claim it, he had to be anointed by the pope and restore the Gniezno archbishopric. He did that in close cooperation with the pope in 1075. What is more, he founded a bishopric in Płock to coexist with the establishments in Kraków, Poznań and Wrocław, this perhaps undertaken jointly with his younger brother, Władysław I Herman who ruled Mazovia. The restored metropolitan bishopric in Gniezno again had four suffragan dioceses, as it had been the case during the rule of Bolesław the Brave. Bolesław II the Bold also raised impressive cathedral buildings on an unprecedented scale in Gniezno and Płock, and probably Poznań and Kraków; and founded new Benedictine abbeys, including the monastery in Mogilno. He also had a say

---

7 MPH s.n. ii p. 81.

Chart 1. Early Piasts (selected dynasty representatives).

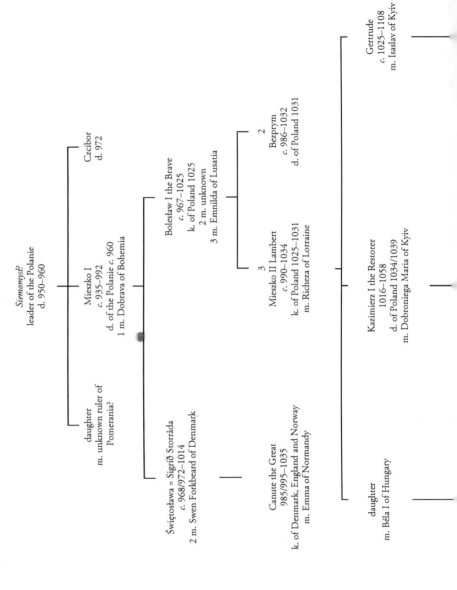

THE CHURCH AND CHRISTIANITY IN POLAND BEFORE 1300

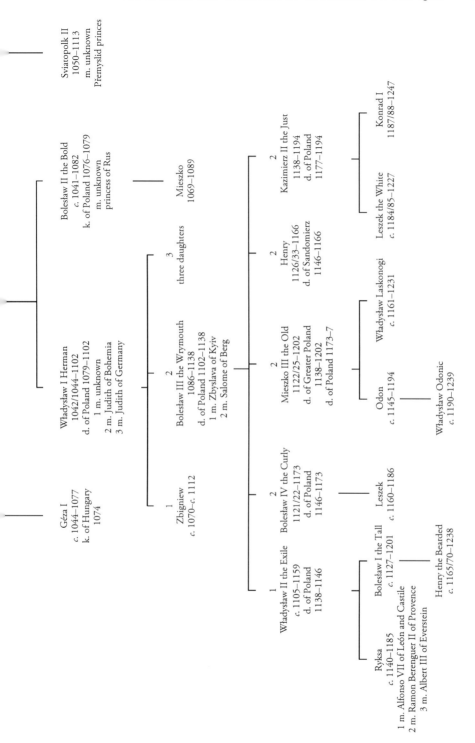

in the first stage of the establishment of the abbey in Lubiń. He continued the reforms to the system of support for ecclesiastical institutions commenced by Kazimierz. The old system of direct financing of the Church with stronghold tithes, introduced by Bolesław the Brave, was regularly substituted with grants of land and income, and probably people tied to the land. This led to gradual economic independence of the Church establishments that were transforming into landowners as a form of economic feudalisation. The Church under the rule of Kazimierz and Bolesław II was a royal institution, and the completion of the restoration of its structures and the bestowal of lands opened up path to independence.

The rule of Bolesław II the Bold, so favourable to the Polish Church, ended rather unexpectedly at its peak with a rebellion that dethroned the king and exiled him in 1079. Bolesław's brother, Władysław Herman, assumed power, but not much is known about his ecclesiastical activity. He must have restored order in internal affairs after his brother had had bishop Stanisław executed, and he put significant effort into raising a Romanesque cathedral on Wawel Hill in Kraków. He maintained contacts with Bamberg Cathedral. To some extent, he contributed to the continuing construction of the Romanesque cathedral in Gniezno and restoring the cult of Adalbert of Prague. Most probably, cathedral chapters emerged during his rule, gaining in importance in the centuries to come. Perhaps some small churches outside the major power centres can also be attributed to him, but the condition of the remnants of sacral architecture and the dating thereof render any suppositions uncertain. What we do know, however, is that Władysław Herman's second wife, Judith of Swabia, bestowed the chapter village of Chropy in central Poland upon Kraków Cathedral, and made some provisions for Tyniec Abbey. Gallus Anonymous informs that, together with his first wife, Judith of Bohemia, the duke sent a written request to Odilo, abbot of the Abbey of Saint Gilles in Provence, for the saint's pleading 'in hope of offspring'.[8] Envoys were sent with generous gifts, including a gold statue of a boy and a gold chalice, as well as liturgical robes, gold and silver. Soon, the royal couple welcomed a son, the later duke Bolesław III the Wrymouth.

Bolesław III the Wrymouth and his support of the Church

Władysław Herman's successor, Bolesław, the third of the great Bolesławs, rulers of Poland, largely continued the ecclesiastical work of his uncle and father. He continued construction of the cathedrals in Kraków and Gniezno, promoted the cult of Adalbert of Prague, took care of the Tyniec foundation, and contributed to the restitution of Lubiń. First and foremost, he made efforts

---

8 MPH s.n. ii p. 107.

to extend the diocesan organisation within his realm. To a large extent, this involved its expansion into Pomerania, where he proved very successful in the first half of his rule. The conquest and Christianisation of Pomerania, first entrusted to Bernard the Spaniard and then to Otto of Bamberg, required extending Polish Church organisations into these areas. Around 1124, cardinal Gilo of Toucy, Bishop of Tusculum, a papal legate, arrived in Poland. The goal of his visit to the lands lying along the Vistula, the Oder, and the Warta must have been to establish new bishoprics subordinated to the Gniezno metropolitan and to propagate Christianity in Pomerania.[9] The bishoprics in Kruszwica and Włocławek were erected for Gdańsk Pomerania, and the bishoprics in Lubusz, Wolin, and Szczecin for West Pomerania. Bolesław III had a broad outlook; the new dioceses were to cover all the new territories stretching from the Vistula in the east to the Oder in the west. As is so often the case with grand plans, practice does not always match theory: only a part of the planned and perhaps established bishoprics survived. Two Kuyavia bishoprics, Kruszwica and Włocławek, serving Gdańsk Pomerania and perhaps, to some extent, to planned conquests in Prussia, soon merged into a single entity. In the second half of the twelfth century and thereafter, it was referred to as the Kuyavia bishopric (Włocławek, sometimes also Kruszwica). The project of establishing a bishopric in Szczecin failed completely. The diocese in Wolin, established and assumed, after much trouble, by Bishop Adalbert, was transferred in the 1170s to Kamień. The bishopric in Lubusz survived in a basic form but could not develop any further when the plans to seize the Elbe territory went awry.

Bolesław Wrymouth's ecclesiastical plans broke down following the actions of Norbert, Archbishop of Magdeburg, in the early 1130s. The Archbishop of Magdeburg decided to take advantage of the situation and subordinate at least a part of the Church in Poland under his jurisdiction. In 1133, Norbert received a papal bull from Innocent II that subordinated all the dioceses in the lands ruled by Bolesław to his authority. Opposed to these developments, Bolesław aided the archbishop of Gniezno to put an end to these plans. The archbishop received a protection bull from Pope Innocent II, issued on 7 July 1136 in Pisa. With this papal sanction, the Church in Poland remained independent of any authority outside the Piast realm. But with the death of Bolesław III in 1138, a gradual separation of the Wolin/Kamień diocese commenced from the Gniezno archbishopric, coupled with the West Pomeranian duchies separation from the authority of Piast dynasty. Back in the early twelfth century, the Polish-Pomeranian relations had been quite normalised, but at the end of the century the Kamień bishopric had received a papal bull (1188) that subordinated it directly to the Holy See, which further emboldened the local Griffin dynasty to work towards gaining independence from the Piasts.

---

9 For more hypothesis about this visit see von Güttner-Sporzyński, *Poland, Holy War, and the Piast Monarchy*, pp. 60–64.

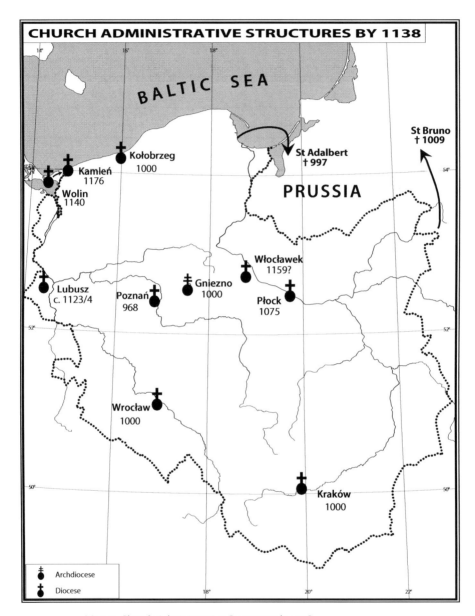

Map 3. Church Administrative Structures by 1138.

Throughout his reign, Bolesław Wrymouth maintained close relations with the Church. He was the last Piast who founded a new bishopric, and he capped this with the founding of a Benedictine monastery in Św. Krzyż (Świętokrzyskie Mountains). At the end of his reign, he probably established

St Gilles Church in Inowłódz. When he died in October 1138, the Gniezno archbishopric was comprised of the Poznań, Wrocław, Kraków, and Płock bishoprics, and perhaps the already merged bishopric of Kuyavia, the bishopric in Lubusz, and the still vacant bishopric in Wolin. The plans of establishing five new dioceses could only be compared with the achievements of the first great Bolesław in 999–1000.

The Church in Poland after the death of Bolesław the Wrymouth

When Duke Bolesław died and his succession disposition became effective, the Piast patrimony was gradually divided politically among the Piast dynasts. Centralised power was declining, and the realm's system of government was progressively shifting from a patrimonial monarchy to a polyarchy. None of Bolesław's heirs and successors managed to put a stop to these processes, probably because they were favoured by the magnates and Church authorities. These elites accumulated wealth as a result of the generosity of the Piast dynasts, and the territorial division allowed for the reinforcement of their growing economic power and political influence. The magnates were increasingly bolder in challenging the royal monopoly of Church foundations, establishing their own churches and monasteries. Although Piast rulers remained generous benefactors and protectors of the Church and the clergy, increasingly they faced competition from magnates and, over time, knights, from the late eleventh century through the twelfth. The power of the elites grew as these social classes extended their economic base through lands and people and imitated the ruler's actions.

Bolesław Wrymouth's sons established new monasteries, small churches, and large collegiate churches with the residing groups of canons, and also supported existing establishments. However, they also experienced competition on the part of famous magnates like Jaksa of Miechów and Piotr Włostowic, and bishops like Gedko of Kraków. At the threshold of the period of political division of Poland, the Church was changing rapidly. It had already enjoyed a well-developed economic base of land, people, legal immunity, and income from ducal monopolies. In the last quarter of the twelfth century, the Church created an organisation of archdeacons and provosts, established contacts with the Holy See, and enjoyed papal privileges. It was ready for independence from lay power. Following that path, the Church was ready in the early thirteenth century to receive the Gregorian Reform. The importance of cathedral chapters was growing, including new chapters near collegiate churches. The work of many generations of Piasts took on a life of its own.

The Piast rulers from the tenth to the twelfth centuries seem to have been powerful founders, generous donors, and protectors of the Church. Just as in the west, a pious foundation of an ecclesiastical building — a chapel, a church, a monastery, the highest form of alms — was an important instrument of ideological power. An ideal monarch must not neglect the Church in his country. In this respect, the Piast dynasty was preoccupied with Christianising the country, ensuring that the process was developed and reinforced in order to create an organisation fit for purpose. As a result, the ecclesiastical structures that emerged in Poland first assumed the form of a bishopric covering an entire region, then a diocesan organisation within the Gniezno metropolitan bishopric. In the late twelfth century, the dioceses were also incorporated into archdiocesan structures. The Piasts — and, later, the magnates cooperating with them — funded the numerous churches built in strongholds and in rural areas, as well as the entire network of Christian communities, predominantly based on the Rule of Benedict of Nursia and the Rule of Saint Augustine. In the early stage of the Piast-led Christianisation, the institutional foundations of the Church were laid to construct the so-called intensive Christianisation that could have only taken place following the Gregorian Reform, with new trends in communal life and the emergence of parochial structures.

Around the mid-twelfth century, the Polish metropolitan archdiocese, restored by Bolesław the Bold and strengthened at the end of the reign of Bolesław Wrymouth, had in total eight dioceses: the Gniezno archbishopric and the bishoprics in Poznań, Kraków, Wrocław, and Płock, plus the bishoprics in Lubusz, Wolin, and Kuyavia, established earlier around 1124. The numbers of clergy were growing, operating from larger collegiate churches and small rural churches, founded either by the monarch or private donators. Initially they had the form of small canon groups and monastic communities — the older Benedictine and the younger Cistercian — and various formations of regular canons following the Rule of St Augustine.[10]

The division of the Piast patrimony

The twelfth century is now perceived as an extremely interesting time in Poland for historical research for many reasons. One of these is undoubtedly the important change to the political system of the Piast dominion in the course of its transformation from a patrimonial monarchy to polyarchy. The twelfth century serves as a bridge and a transition period between the former and the other forms of governance. Another reason for this interest is the sources. While these remain scarce, they suffice to give us a good understanding of the history and politics of this time. A third reason is the extraordinary dynamics of Poland's political, economic, and social processes, along with its flourishing intellectual culture. Finally, the period abounds in many persisting stereotypes and myths.

After the death of Bolesław Wrymouth in October 1138, and in accordance with his disposition regulating the succession of the throne, the Piast monarchy

---

10 On the Polish Church at that time, see Dobosz, *Monarcha i możni*, pp. 293–438.

was divided into several parts, probably under the overall governance of the duke's oldest son. This decision made by the third of the great Bolesławs has resulted in a 200-year-long, heated historiographical dispute.[11] Its intensity is reminiscent of discussions of other important medieval developments in Poland, such as Mieszko I's baptism, the puzzle of *Dagome iudex*, the conflict between Bolesław the Bold and Bishop Stanisław, the Teutonic Knights, and the Battle of Grunwald. Looking at the events of the first half of the twelfth century, from the perspective of nearly 900 years later, we can see that the political reality of the Piasts realm appears as extremely dynamic, full of twists and surprising endings. There must have been many factors at play, some of which cannot be identified today. Nonetheless, the major reason for these dynamics was surely the political system, that is, the formulation of the patrimonial monarchy. The state, treated as the ruler's patrimony and divided by the monarchs among their male offspring, was thus prone to decentralisation.

Bolesław Wrymouth divided his dominion, large by Central European standards, before his death in October 1138.[12] While this is not the place for an analysis of the nature of this fragmentation or the subsequent events that affected the Piast realm, it is worth mentioning at least a few important facts. To the forefront comes the first division of the realm, completed after Bolesław Wrymouth's death, followed by the scope of the division and delineation of the provinces, and the fight for the territorial inheritance amongst Bolesław's sons and their offspring from the 1140s until the end of the century. All this affected the political milieu of a period in which the patriarchal monarchy was slowly yet inevitably transforming into a polyarchy, forming a bridge to developments of the thirteenth century.

Much has been written about Bolesław Wrymouth's so called 'last will and testament' or the act of succession.[13] Let me simply refer to the only

---

11 Extensive, strictly academic research into the fragmentation of Poland, dates back at least to Joachim Lelewel, including the reasons behind Bolesław's decision, the first fragmentation, the new quality of the political system when the testament of Bolesław Wrymouth became effective, rebellions and internal fights. There have been attempts, more or less successful, to sum up the findings by academics like Stanisław Smolka, Tadeusz Wojciechowski, Henryk Łowmiański, Gerard Labuda and many others, but this article is not the right place for them. See for example Łowmiański, *Rozdrobnienie feudalne Polski*, pp. 7–34; A. Gąsiorowski, *Spory o polskie*, pp. 115–22; Derwich, 'Testament Bolesława Krzywoustego', pp. 113–52; Jurek, 'Nowsze badania historyków', pp. 7–19.

12 In Polish historiography, it has been a popular opinion that Bolesław made the decision before his death (perhaps around 1136). Janusz Bieniak draws attention to the fact that the very idea of the establishment of the appanages for Bolesław's younger sons could have emerged as the consequence of the duke's second marriage to Salomea of Berg, Bieniak, 'Polska elita polityczna XII w., Part I', p. 29.

13 Labuda, 'Testament Bolesława Krzywoustego', pp. 171–94, collects older literature on the subject. Cf. Jurek, 'Nowsze badania historyków', pp. 7–19, and Dobosz, *Kazimierz II Sprawiedliwy*, pp. 255–56, 12–18.

source from a time close to the events, albeit only a general introduction to the issue, written by Vincentius, Bishop of Kraków in the late twelfth and early thirteenth centuries. Other chroniclers scarcely knew anything more, although they often supplemented their narrations with various suppositions.[14] Vincentius reports that when Bolesław felt that his death was approaching, he ordered that his last will be written. His disposition provided inheritance for four of his five male descendants. His eldest son, Władysław, was to succeed as the suzerain of Poland and rule as the *princeps* of the Piast dynasty over the whole of the patrimony. In addition he received Silesia as his hereditary province. The other three sons, and Władysław's half-brothers, received a province each. The fifth and youngest son, Kazimierz, was not specifically provided for. Vincentius' account of Bolesław's decision as to succession is rather vague. It stipulates that 'the succession would always be secured by seniority and the right of primogeniture'.[15] According to this account, Bolesław made the decision about the division of the Piast patrimony in writing and as late as on his deathbed. Right away, four provinces were delineated, with the province of the *princeps* who ruled as suzerain of the whole Piast monarchy (Kraków) at the centre of the realm was established, together with the rules of secession to the dignity of *princeps* which served as the means of executing supreme power over the entire Piast domain. Following this logic, in 1138 separate provinces were set for Władysław (Silesia), Bolesław (Mazovia, probably with Kuyavia), Mieszko (Wielkopolska) and Henryk (Sandomierz). Bolesław's eldest son, Władysław, born of Bolesław's first wife, Zbysława, received Kraków and its territories as the *princeps*. This model of succession ignored Kazimierz, Bolesław's youngest son. Vincentius explained it enigmatically, placing in Bolesław's mouth words to the effect that he had 'long remembered and included him' and foretold that the boy would in fact inherit all of his brothers' possessions' because it is only just that minors' provinces are bestowed on the guardians, not the minors'.[16] In the chronicler's narration, Kazimierz was born when his father was still alive but was intended to be taken into the care of his elder brothers (probably until he reached maturity).

Vincentius, a close ally of Kazimierz II Sprawiedliwy, presented the youngest son in Bolesław's disposition in the form of a prophetic vision of his future greatness, predestined to achieve the greatest distinctions in the land, clearly meaning the throne of the *princeps*.[17] It was probably an oblique reference to the legitimisation of Kazimierz's power seizure in 1177 as a result of a coup d'état that deposed his elder brother, Mieszko III Stary (the Old).

---

14 More about Bolesław's testament in Dobosz, *Kazimierz II Sprawiedliwy*, pp. 18–24.
15 *Chronica Polonorum* iii.26.
16 Ibid.
17 See Wiszewski, 'Piąte koło i złoty dzban', pp. 479–95; Dobosz, *Kazimierz II Sprawiedliwy*, pp. 18–32.

Vincentius' writings — viewed with other chronicle accounts, medieval Polish and foreign annals, and the resulting models and hypotheses on the territorial division after Bolesław's death put forward by academics as part of critical historiography — leads to the conclusion that the late 1130s marked the beginning of the long-term disintegration of the Piast monarchy.[18] Of course, the decentralisation processes were not rapid, and originally they covered mainly government of the realm divided into provinces as appanages, only gradually extending to the economy, the society and culture. Around the mid-twelfth century, the political situation did not seem very complicated: in the autumn of 1138, the principate and the Kraków lands were bestowed on Władysław II, later called the Exile. We know that he also ruled Silesia, while his stepbrothers Mieszko and Bolesław, the sons of Bolesław Wrymouth's second wife Salomea of Berg, ruled in Wielkopolska, Małopolska, and Mazovia (including Kuyavia).[19] The question of whether the young Henryk, only 6–8 years old in 1138, ruled his province right away, and how the dowager duchess Salomea was provided for, have long been matters of some debate. If we accept Vincentius' account, Henryk should have come to the government of his province immediately. Because he was a minor, however, he must have been in the care of either his eldest brother (as the head of the family) or his mother for some time. It is difficult to resolve this dilemma now, and there are two competing hypotheses at play. The first one came to prominence as a result of Tadeusz Wojciechowski's research that advanced a historical concept of the fragmentation (*podział dzielnicowy*). In his opinion, the dowager duchess received a widow's dower scattered throughout the strongholds, villages, and churches in the lands of Sieradz and Łęczyca, and in Sandomierz. Kazimierz, the youngest son of Bolesław Wrymouth was born posthumously; Henryk inherited Sandomierz back in 1138; while the *princeps* had at his disposal Silesia and the central provinces stretching longitudinally from Pomerania to Kraków.[20]

An alternative theory was proposed by Gerard Labuda, who adopted an altogether different view. Following an in-depth analysis of the sources and the accompanying interpretations of Bolesław Wrymouth's testament, he concluded that the fragmentation took place in two stages. Stage one related

---

18 For the sources of these issues see Labuda, 'Testament Bolesława Krzywoustego'; on the status of research and various opinions and concepts related to the fragmentation of Poland as a result of the patrimonial system, see the above quoted works by Janusz Bieniak, Tomasz Jurek and Antoni Gąsiorowski, also M. Biniaś-Szkopek, *Bolesław IV Kędzierzawy* and Dobosz, *Kazimierz II Sprawiedliwy*.

19 It is of some debate as to whether the provinces as defined by Bolesław Wrymouth were inherited from the outset, in accordance with the account of Vincentius of Kraków, or if the sons served as some sort of viceroys of the *princeps*. Irrespective of the different scholarly positions, it seems that every province rapidly became a *patrimonium* assigned to a male offspring or transferred in line with the wishes of Piasts who died without issue.

20 Wojciechowski, *Szkice historyczne*, pp. 297–302.

CHAPTER 1

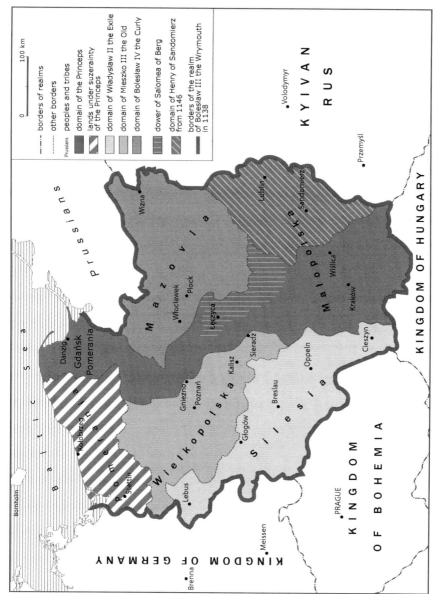

Map 4. The Act of Succession of 1138.

to the time immediately after Bolesław's death and offered the following solutions: Władysław, the eldest, received Silesia and the principate province, which included, putting it in a slightly simplified way, Małopolska and the dignity of the *princeps*; Mazovia and Kuyavia were taken over by Bolesław IV Kędzierzawy (the Curly) while Mieszko III the Old received Wielkopolska. Duchess Salomea's dower included a province consisting of the Łęczyca and Sieradz land as well as custody of two juvenile sons, Henryk and Kazimierz, who were to receive their appanages upon gaining their majority. The events of 1144–1146, coupled with the fact that Henryk reached maturity, resulted in significant corrections to this planned distribution of the inheritance. In July 1144, Salomea died. In 1146, Władysław was removed from the principate when Henryk was at least 14 years old and probably no longer required a formal guardian. Bolesław, the new *princeps*, took over Władysław's Silesia and the widow's dower, leaving Sandomierz to Henryk. Kazimierz seems to have been in the *princeps*' guardianship.[21] This theory shows a very different shape of the principate and different dower of the widow, as well as a slightly different role for the two youngest sons in the developments of 1138–1146. This hypothesis has received in-depth analysis in historiography. Attempts have been made to correct some of the details, specifically by Karol Buczek and Janusz Bieniak, which have been to some extent adopted by historians.[22] However, Tadeusz Wojciechowski's interpretation has also received broad uptake among historians and in popular literature, specifically by journalists and in schoolbooks.[23]

The time between the death of Bolesław Wrymouth in October 1138 and the deposition and exile of his eldest son Władysław from Poland in the spring of 1146, was very dynamic. It seems that right after her husband's death, dowager duchess Salomea started to forge an alliance of her sons' supporters. Among them, Bolesław IV the Curly and Mieszko III the Old became natural leaders. The other members included prominent secular and ecclesiastical figures from the realm's northern provinces of Mazovia and Kuyavia, Wielkopolska, and perhaps Łęczyca and Sieradz. They represented a strong political base for Salome's sons, often referred to as 'the younger Piast brothers' in the decisive fight for power in 1144–1146.[24] We do not know if among them was Piotr Włostowic, one of the most prominent Polish magnates in the twelfth century, blinded and muted by order of Władysław II in 1145. Perhaps this accelerated Władysław's decline, tipping the balance and attracting the powerful magnate's next of kin and enthusiasts to the camp of the younger Piasts.

---

21   This is how Labuda viewed these issues. Labuda, 'Testament Bolesława Krzywoustego'; Labuda, 'Zabiegi o utrzymanie', pp. 1147–67.
22   See Buczek, 'Jeszcze o testamencie', pp. 621–39. See also, Dobosz, *Kazimierz II Sprawiedliwy*, pp. 255–56.
23   For an overview of older trends, see Dobosz, *Kazimierz II Sprawiedliwy*, pp. 255–56.
24   More on the subject in Dobosz, *Kazimierz II Sprawiedliwy*, pp. 24–28, cf. Bieniak, 'Polska elita polityczna XII w., Part I'.

38 CHAPTER 1

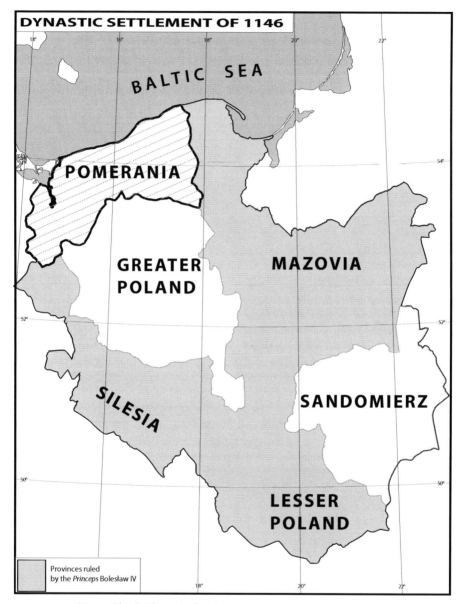

Map 5. The Settlement of 1146.

The years of Bolesław IV's principate are not well covered in the sources; a large part of our knowledge comes from Vincentius' chronicle. Unlike his father and two younger brothers, Mieszko and Kazimierz, the princeps does not seem to have enjoyed a charismatic personality, nor did he attract as much attention as Henryk, the third of his younger brothers. However, he must have adjusted to the internal and external political conditions well enough to hold power until his death in January 1173. The subsequent years resulted in a growing rivalry among the sons and, later, the grandsons of Bolesław Wrymouth, mainly over Kraków, and lands and influence, providing historians with ample opportunity for fascinating deliberations about the nature of early Polish monarchy. During the reign of the first generation of the descendants of Bolesław Wrymouth, Poland changed gradually yet distinctly from a patrimonial monarchy to a polyarchy, with the process at its peak in the thirteenth century in Silesia, Mazovia, and Kuyavia.[25]

Of great importance to the history of early medieval Poland is the nature and organisation of the realm that developed under the rule of the Piast dynasty, on political, social, and economic levels alike, taking into consideration the scope of Piast power and the methods of exercise. As a result of the emerging and gradually developing patrimonial monarchy, members of the dynasty seized what we would call today legislative, executive and judicial powers.[26] The prevailing independent economy based on agriculture, initially supplemented to a small degree by an exchange of goods and trade of slaves on a scale hard to identify, required specific fiscal forms. In order to fulfil his jurisdictional duties and to support himself, the ruler and his entourage had to be on the move all the time. Of course, that system, referred to in historiography as *rex/dux ambulans*, was not invented by the Piasts, but it was extensively and effectively used in the early stages of the Piast realm to ensure the good use of the region's economic resource, and that executive and judicial power was exercised as desired.[27] In the twelfth century, the monarch's power still relied on his progress throughout his realm, but the role of the symbolic centre of the state must have grown gradually. After Břetislav's invasion, Kraków assumed the role of the centre, together with the ruler's governors residing in numerous strongholds. Without going into detail, it is worth emphasising that, in the first half of the twelfth century, the Piast realm was divided into provinces and stronghold districts, headed by province and stronghold *comes* or castellan. Therefore, the ruler had at his disposal the central supply base in the form of a more-or-less extended court and the still developing

---

25 The history of the early division of the Piast patrimony is best covered in biographies of Bolesław Wrymouth and his sons. See, Rosik, *Bolesław Krzywousty*; Dworsatschek, *Władysław II Wygnaniec*, Teterycz-Puzio, *Henryk Sandomierski*; Przybył, *Mieszko III Stary*; M. Biniaś-Szkopek, *Bolesław IV Kędzierzawy*.
26 The most complete Polish work on the subject remains Łowmiański, *Początki Polski*, pp. 101–26.
27 In Poland, the local travelling monarchy has been discussed in Skierska and Gąsiorowski, 'Średniowieczna monarchia objazdowa', pp. 67–80, including the crux of the *rex ambulans* system.

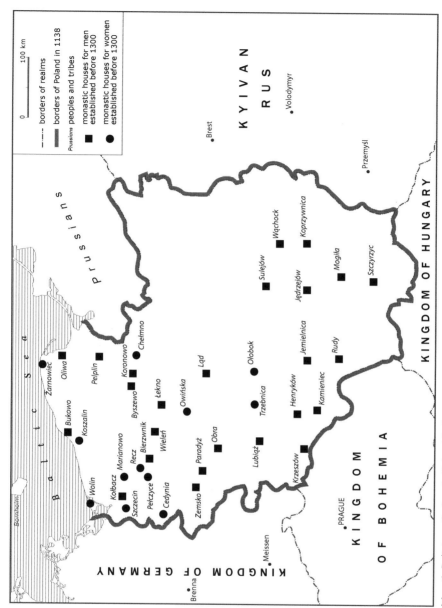

Map 6. Religious Orders in Poland before 1200.

territorial base of a dynamically growing group of local officials, built around the stronghold organisation. Quite certainly, after 1138, the system of the provinces was replaced by the newly emergent appanage duchies as a result of the subsequent divisions.[28]

At the core of this realm, organised and ruled by the Piasts, was its population. Society was essentially divided into the social, economic, and political elite; and the rural population. The former, referred to as the gentry and knights, came predominantly from the royal officials and their families. Their elitist nature was based, especially at the beginning, on the proximity of the ruler and the related advantages. The rural population included all free peasants who owned land and hence provided the monarchy with some benefits, and unfree people who were under the direct rule of the monarch or representatives of the secular elites and the Church. Gradually, another social category emerged: the clergy, which grew in numbers in the twelfth century and reinforced and developed the organisational structures of the Polish Church. The people and the orders of the Church, as the studies in this volume demonstrate, played an important role in the structures of the Piast realm as it developed from a patrimonial monarchy to a polyarchy.

---

28 For the organisation of strongholds, see Zajączkowski, 'Uwagi nad terytorialnym', pp. 285–323; Lalik, 'Organizacja grodowo-prowincjonalna', pp. 5–51; Bardach, *Historia państwa i prawa Polski*, vol. I; Dąbrowski, *Studia nad organizacją*.

PART I

Foundations

CHAPTER 2

The Piasts, the Premonstratensians and Other Religious Orders of Canons Regular in the Twelfth Century*

The twelfth century appears not so much as a breakthrough in the history of the Piast state and the Church but as a period preparing the ground for a truly revolutionary thirteenth century. It was probably then that a hitherto superficial Christianisation became decidedly more intense and penetrating. On the one hand, Church institutions developed to the extent that they could demand more and more independence, and on the other, that the Piast rulers progressively introduced the idea of a model monarch as a protector and an extraordinarily generous benefactor to the Church. The nobles followed suit, with the result being not only the intensification of aspirations for foundations of ecclesiastical institutions as such, but also hopes of being dealt a fresh hand. While the foundation of bishoprics remained the exclusive domain of the Piast dynasty, the broader monastic life or smaller church institutions could also have been the work of both the lay and ecclesiastical nobility. Among several monastic and canonical communities established in the twelfth century, most significant were different varieties of canons regular, both in its older and reformed shape. In some way, canons regular faced competition with the Cistercians, whose activity during the time when Bernard was the provost of Trzemeszno was unmatched.[1] This was usually a no-contact competition, focusing on increasing popularity of the Cistercians

---

* Original publication: Józef Dobosz, 'Piastowie wobec premonstratensów i innych form kanonikatu regularnego w XII wieku', in *Premonstratensi na ziemiach polskich w średniowieczu i epoce nowożytnej*, ed. by Jerzy Rajman (Kraków: Wydawnictwo Naukowe Akademii Pedagogicznej, 2007), pp. 6–18.
1   The Cistercians in Poland have received much attention. Materials from four Cistercian symposiums that took place in 1985 (Błażejewko), 1987 (Gniezno), 1993 (Poznań) and 1998 (Kraków-Mogiła) have appeared in print: Strzelczyk, ed., *Historia i kultura cystersów*; Strzelczyk, ed., *Cystersi w kulturze średniowiecznej Europy*; Strzelczyk, ed., *Dzieje, kultura artystyczna*; Wyrwa and Dobosz, eds, *Cystersi w społeczeństwie Europy Środkowej*. A conference devoted to the Cistercians was also held in Trzebnica in 2002: Wyrwa, Kiełbasa and Swastek eds, *Cysterki w dziejach i kulturze ziem polskich*. A more complete 'state of the field' overview can be found in the two volumes of MCP. The Benedictine communities, which settled in lands under Piast rule have also been widely investigated, see for example Derwich, *Monastycyzm benedyktyński*, from p. 175; cf. Derwich, 'Fundacja lubińska', pp. 12–23; Derwich, 'Studia nad początkami monastycyzmu', pp. 77–105.

among the rulers, the lay nobles and local hierarchs of the Church; that is, those who had something to offer (or rather, donate). Over time, the rivalry turned to direct conflict over the economic basis of existence, which is to say property: mainly land, tithes or other income. This, however, was rather more a phenomenon typical of the following century, when Polish institutions of common life solidified both in terms of economics and demography. Whether any side emerged victorious from this generally positive competition is very difficult to say. Painstakingly, and with variable luck, modern scholars have attempted to tease out even the modest scraps of the unknown past. So, let us try it now and examine how different religious orders of canons regular, gradually gained a foothold in the cultural landscape of the Oder, Warta and Vistula rivers, by winning favour of the Piast dynasts, and how popular they became in their circles.

In the period starting with the death of Władysław I Herman in 1102 and ending with the death of the last of his grandsons, Mieszko III Stary (the Old), in 1202, at least a dozen communities of canons were established in the Piast realm.[2] Most of them were somehow related to the Premonstratensian order, but the first to reach the areas under the Piast rule were the Canons Regular of the Lateran. Without going into the often-complicated disputes about the chronology of their arrival, it can be generally said that it occurred during the reign of Bolesław III Krzywousty (the Wrymouth) (1107–1138). At that time, the Canons Regular of the Lateran settled in Trzemeszno,[3] Wielkopolska (Greater Poland, *Polonia Maior*), perhaps also in the immediate vicinity of the Wrocław stronghold,[4] and only a little later in Czerwińsk,

---

[2] There is as yet no single study bringing together research on the different orders of canons regular. Derwich has catalogued the Norbertine institutions, Derwich, 'Die Prämonstratenserorden', pp. 311–47. Nor is there yet a study on Canons Regular of the Lateran. Noteworthy is a paper by Mrozowicz, 'Kanonicy regularni św. Augustyna', pp. 401–13, which summarises the state of research on Silesian institutions, and the study by Pobóg-Lenartowicz, *Kanonicy regularni*. Important works on the history of canons regular foundations in Poland have been published by Jerzy Rajman (Zwierzyniec), Anna Pobóg-Lenartowicz (Piasek), and Dariusz Karczewski (Strzelno). Earlier, several extensive dissertations and contributions were published by Czesław Deptuła.

[3] The monastery in Trzemeszno has not been the subject of a comprehensive monograph, excepting the partial and largely outdated study by Józefowiczówna, *Trzemeszno*; see also Józefowiczówna, 'Trzy klasztory romańskie', pp. 165–207. For the interpretation of the early history of the canonry, see particularly Labuda, 'Najstarsze klasztory w Polsce', pp. 187–93; Kürbis, 'O początkach kanonii w Trzemesznie', pp. 337–43.

[4] Originally located on Mt Ślęża, the House of Canons Regular of the Order of St Augustine of the Blessed Virgin Mary on Piasek was founded by Piotr Włostowic. The historical sources are vague as to the origins of this institution, which gives rise to debate on the date of its establishment. It has been argued that the canonry was founded shortly before 1138, see Mrozowicz, 'Kanonicy regularni', pp. 403–04, or in the first half of the 1140s, see Pobóg-Lenartowicz, *Kanonicy regularni*, pp. 28–29. For the dislocation of the monastery from Mt Ślęża to Piasek, see Pobóg-Lenartowicz, *Kanonicy regularni*, pp. 33–35. See also Dobosz, *Monarcha i możni*, pp. 271–72.

Mazovia.[5] The Premonstratensians came to Poland later, probably around the mid-twelfth century, but they quickly gained momentum and were likely successful in replacing their 'older brothers'.[6] The settlement of the chapter of the Canons of the Holy Sepulchre in Miechów was a separate incident.[7] The fundamental question of who brought them, erected their abodes, and looked after them during the initial phases of establishing the convent and property structure is fairly easy. In most cases, these were Polish nobles, although the representatives of the dynasty also appear to show some activity in this field. The Piasts' alignment with the newly established institutions in that difficult early period of their activity, especially during the initial years of their functioning, is a more troublesome issue.

Since Bolesław III (or probably anybody else during his lifetime) did not bring the Premonstratensians into the Piast realm, it seems unlikely that he was in any way engaged in their promotion. And yet, Bolesław took interest in the canons regular, for whom he founded a monastery in Trzemeszno, Wielkopolska. It is difficult to determine whether canons regular replaced an unspecified earlier community that had purportedly functioned there since the second half of the eleventh century.[8] In light of the Trzemeszno forgery dated 28 April 1145, we only know that Bolesław III endowed the canons regular with two villages with taverns; income from custom tolls at the crossings of the Pilica River in Przedbórz, Sulejów and Inowłódz; and the local church of St Giles, probably also in Trzemeszno.[9] This is what the sources tell us

---

5 Earlier literature assumed that the canonry was founded before 1138 by Bolesław III himself, see for example Bachulski, 'Założenie klasztoru', pp. 51–76. This idea was rejected by Gębarowicz, 'Mogilno–Płock–Czerwińsk', pp. 112–74, who suggested a slightly later chronology. Deptuła's thesis that Czerwińsk was established between 1148 and 1155 by Alexander of Malonne, Bishop of Płock has received wide acceptance, Deptuła, 'Krąg kościelny płocki', from p. 96, which accords with Gębarowicz's hypothesis. Only Żebrowski seems to perceive the issue differently, Żebrowski, 'Kościół (X–XIII w.)', p. 157. See also Dobosz, *Monarcha i możni*, pp. 412–13.
6 The origins of the Norbertine monasteries in Poland have been explored in several studies, see for example Rajman, 'The origins of the Polish Praemonstratensian Circary', pp. 203–19; Rajman, 'Norbertanie polscy', pp. 71–105, cf. Derwich, 'Die Prämonstratenserorden', from p. 313.
7 The settlement of the Canons of the Holy Sepulchre in Miechów founded by Jaksa has been the subject of several studies, among which the most noteworthy are Pęckowski, *Miechów*, pp. 40, 304; Piłat, 'Fundator i fundacja', pp. 11–43. See also Dobosz, *Monarcha i możni*, pp. 371–73.
8 Henryk Łowmiański advocated a theory whereby the monastery in Trzemeszno was founded by Bolesław II and was first run by the Benedictines, Łowmiański, *Początki Polski* vi, pp. 324–29. This idea was based on the Trzemeszno forgery dated 28 April 1145. Gerard Labuda opposed to the idea, arguing that the canonry, or more broadly the monastery in Trzemeszno, was founded by Bolesław III, Labuda, 'Najstarsze klasztory w Polsce', p. 187, cf. Dobosz, 'Dokument Mieszka III Starego', pp. 87–106; Chapter 14 in this volume; Dobosz, *Monarcha i możni*, pp. 147–49, 194–96. See also Józefowiczówna, 'Trzy klasztory romańskie', pp. 165–207; Wojciechowski, 'Początki immunitetu w Polsce', pp. 53–58.
9 *Inoulodz ecclesia beati Egidij cum duabus uillis cum thabernis, cum theloneis per ipsum fluuium, Predbor, in Sulugev, in ipso in Inoulodz*. ZDŚ i.10.

about the relations between Bolesław III and the canons regular. It seems that the events took place in the second phase of Bolesław's reign, after 1124, when his foundation policy gained momentum.[10] Excavations at the site of the monastery showed that the first buildings forming the monastery in Trzemeszno must have been erected during the reign of Bolesław III (rather closer to his death), perhaps thanks to his patronage.[11]

The contact between the Piasts and the canons of Trzemeszno became closer a few years after Bolesław's death. The ground prepared by Bolesław was cleverly exploited to its fullest extent by his wife Salomea of Berg after his death in 1138. Salomea made the local canons part of a wide coalition of the secular and ecclesiastical nobles gathered around her and her sons and directed against Władysław, her stepson and Bolesław's heir and successor. Apart from Bernard the provost of Trzemeszno, the essential links of this alliance included Boguchwał (I), Bishop of Poznań, Alexander, Bishop of Płock; Jakub, the Archbishop of Gniezno; and probably also the Abbot of Mogilno. Following Salomea's death in 1144, the connections were inherited and efficiently exploited by Bolesław IV Kędzierzawy (the Curly) and Mieszko III, the leaders of the coalition of so-called younger Piasts, in their struggle against their stepbrother Władysław.[12] Bolesław and Mieszko probably settled their debt to the provost around 1146, when they gave some estates in the Łęczyca District and then a privilege to the monastery in Trzemeszno.[13] The grants of the younger Piasts were preceded by generous donations by Salomea, the traces of which are contained in the Trzemeszno forgery, which records that the canons received Waśniów (including a marketplace, taverns and a church, salt) and Kwieciszewo.[14] It was probably thanks to Salomea and then Mieszko III that the canons of Trzemeszno attracted the interest of a throng of nobles, who hurried in with generous endowments for the abbey.[15]

10 For more detail, see Dobosz, *Monarcha i możni*, p. 194.
11 The archaeological and architectural research of the early construction phase of Trzemeszno Abbey has been surveyed in Świechowski, *Architektura romańska w Polsce*, pp. 258–60; Świechowska and Mischke, *Architektura romańska w Polsce. Bibliografia*, pp. 128–30. Noteworthy are papers summarising excavations conducted by Jadwiga Chudziakowa: Chudziakowa, 'Kościół opacki w Trzemesznie', pp. 133–44; Chudziakowa, 'Romański kościół Kanoników Regularnych w Trzemesznie', pp. 55–60; Świechowski, 'Romańskie bazyliki Wielkopolski północno-wschodniej', pp. 105–14. Cf. Holas, 'Dwie bazyliki romańskie w Trzemesznie', pp. 107–28.
12 See Dobosz, *Monarcha i możni*, from p. 295. Cf. Bieniak, 'Polska elita polityczna XII w., Part III B', from p. 28.
13 This is suggested by both the Trzemeszno forgery dated 28 April 1145 (ZDŚ i.10), and the diploma of Cardinal-Legate Hubaldus (ZDŚ i.12). See Dobosz, *Monarcha i możni*, from p. 296; Dobosz, *Działalność fundacyjna*, pp. 114–17.
14 ZDŚ i.10, which reads: *Salome quoque ducissa contulit Wasnou forum cum thabernis et ecclesia ad supplementum salis ecclesie predicte.* For further discussion, see Dobosz, *Monarcha i możni*, pp. 199, 196, 296; Dobosz, 'Dokument Mieszka III Starego'; Chapter 15 in this volume.
15 The grants are listed in the Trzemeszno forgery (ZDŚ i.10). For discussion, see Dobosz, *Monarcha i możni*, pp. 401–02; Dobosz, 'Dokument Mieszka III Starego'; Chapter 15 in this volume.

The question of Bolesław III's endorsement of the Wrocław foundation of Palatine Piotr Włostowic, the canons from the convent of the Blessed Virgin Mary on Wyspa Piasek (an island known as Piasek), will probably remain unanswered.[16] It is possible to point, albeit with great caution, to an interesting chronological coincidence between the Wrocław and Trzemeszno foundations: both institutions were established more or less at the same time. Yet it can only be speculated whether Bolesław III's activity inspired Piotr Włostowic, or if it happened the other way round. Who can provide final answers to those questions? Perhaps both foundations provided an impetus for Alexander, Bishop of Płock, to establish a congregation of the canons regular in Czerwińsk, which is known to have been founded a little later, in the second half of the 1140s.

The short reign of Władysław II Wygnaniec (the Exile) as suzerain of Poland left no significant traces in the historical record that would hint at his interest in any variety of the canons regular, except perhaps that Władysław granted farmsteads to a few people and one village to the monastery on Piasek Island.[17] The speculations of Czesław Deptuła, who saw Władysław as the founder of Brzesko-Hebdów, should be abandoned once and for all.[18] Things were different, however, between his half-brothers and the canons regular. It has already been noted that Mieszko III maintained contacts with the Trzemeszno canonry right after Władysław was expelled, but a clearer Premonstratensian thread can also be traced in his actions. This applies to as many as three centres of this branch of the canons regular: Kościelna Wieś near Kalisz, Ołbin and Strzelno. The first two cases, however, are extremely uncertain and to a large extent their interpretation depends on the imagination of the

---

16   See Pobóg-Lenartowicz, *Uposażenie i działalność*, who does not see the participation of Bolesław III in the foundation of the monastery. See also, Pobóg-Lenartowicz, *Kanonicy regularni*, from p. 26. There are few traces of contact between the monastery and Bolesław III in the extant historical sources, and if we accept that the monastery was founded after 1138, they are even more difficult to find.
17   The inventory of the monastery's estates dating from 1180/90s reads: *Dux Wlodislaus dedit ad montem Bezdad cum uilla, Abrinicoy cum filiis suis Solay et Tossoz* (KDŚ i.68). See also Pobóg-Lenartowicz, *Uposażenie i działalność*, pp. 14–15. How is this grant related to the conflict between the founder, Piotr Włostowic, and Duke Władysław II is hard to tell, though it must have taken place before 1145. It is also difficult to respond to suggestions from some scholars on the possible confiscation of monastic property by Władysław II after the fall of Piotr Włostowic. See for example, Deptuła, 'Przyczynek do dziejów Ślęży', pp. 30–31; Łowmiański, *Początki Polski* vi, pp. 275–80. Korta opposed this position, Korta, *Tajemnice góry Ślęży*, p. 318. See also Pobóg-Lenartowicz, *Uposażenie i działalność*, p. 12, though cf. Pobóg-Lenartowicz, *Kanonicy regularni*, p. 33. The paucity of evidence recommends Bieniak's scepticism about the forfeiture of property, Bieniak, 'Polska elita polityczna XII w., Part III A', p. 47. It is hard to imagine, given his political circumstances, that Władysław would have consciously opposed such an important institution of the Church as the convent of canons regular.
18   Deptuła, 'O niektórych źródłach', p. 198; Deptuła, *Monasterium Bethleem*, from p. 34. See Dobosz, *Monarcha i możni*, p. 404, on Brzesko Abbey's foundation date. Cf. Derwich, 'Die Prämonstratenserorden', pp. 330–31.

interpreter. Likely taking advantage of the political turmoil in Wielkopolska at that time, the Norbertines of Kościelna Wieś forged a document around 1232,[19] in light of which Mieszko purportedly endowed the local St Lawrence Abbey with considerable land estates, incomes and an extensive immunity.[20] The forgery may have had some historical basis, but so far scholars have been bogged down in speculation from which little can be derived, except for the fact that Mieszko did patronise the Premonstratensians of St Lawrence Abbey.[21] It seems that Mieszko did not establish the monastery, but was its benefactor at best, and perhaps not even a very generous one at that.[22]

We know even less about Mieszko's endowments for the Premonstratensians of Ołbin (after the Benedictines were replaced and removed), as suggested by some scholars on the basis of the information contained in the 1193 bull of Pope Celestine III: *Dux Mesco dedit forum Kenese, tabernam, libertatem foro et hominibus.*[23] The presumption that this fragment describes endowments in Gniezno must be rejected.[24] It probably refers to the donations of Mieszko IV Plątonogi (Tanglefoot) in Księże Wielkie.[25] The presence of entries referring to Mieszko III and his wife Eudoxia and their offspring in the local obituary[26] suggest that the contacts between Mieszko III and the Premonstratensians in Strzelno should be looked at differently.[27] Though the simple fact that the ducal couple are mentioned in no way determines the nature of the relationships, it clearly suggests that they indeed existed. The matter become

---

19 KDW i.34. The document is commonly considered a forgery, see Matuszewski, *Immunitet ekonomiczny*, p. 357, note 1. Stanisław Trawkowski suggests that the inventory of property was drawn up around 1232, perhaps on some historical basis, Trawkowski, 'Młyny wodne w Polsce', p. 66. See also Rajman, 'Norbertanie polscy', p. 74. It seems possible that the document was forged around 1232 given the upheaval in Wielkopolska at the time, see relevant chapters of Topolski, *Dzieje Wielkopolski*.

20 KDW i.35, for discussion of the immunity see Matuszewski, *Immunitet ekonomiczny*, pp. 357–58.

21 See Trawkowski, 'Młyny wodne w Polsce', p. 66.

22 See by Rajman, 'Norbertanie polscy', pp. 76–79; Dobosz, *Monarcha i możni*, p. 348. For a different perspective on the issue, see Karczewski, *Dzieje klasztoru norbertanek w Strzelnie*, pp. 83–87. See also Derwich, 'Die Prämonstratenserorden', pp. 335–36.

23 KDŚ i.70.

24 KDW i.31; in the editor's commentary on the bull of Pope Celestine III, it is posited that the expression *in Kenese* refers to Gniezno.

25 KDŚ i.70; the editor was probably right to recognise the name Księże Wielkie in the expression *in Kenese* but was unable to resolve the question whether it was donated by Mieszko III or Mieszko IV; cf. Dobosz, *Monarcha i możni*, p. 348.

26 *Liber mortuorum monasterii Strzelnensis Ordinis Praemonstratensis*, MPH v, pp. 719–67, where under 13 March is a commemorative entry for Mieszko and Eudoxia, his second wife; under 2 January, his daughter Wierzchosława, and under 17 September his son Bolesław. For an extensive analysis of the source see Jasiński, 'Nekrolog klasztoru norbertanek w Strzelnie', pp. 7–44.

27 A comprehensive study of this institution has been published by Dariusz Karczewski, *Dzieje klasztoru norbertanek w Strzelnie*, who also pointed out its relations with Duke Mieszko III, pp. 81–95.

clearer when we take a look at the document issued by Konrad of Mazovia, which recounts that Mieszko III confirmed his son Bolesław's endowment of the village of Węgierce to the Norbertine Sisters.[28] The 1193 bull of Pope Celestine III mentions considerable donations of income from the tavern and the ninth part of the income in Kujawy, although it does not disclose the benefactor.[29] This could have been Mieszko III, who might have also granted the Norbertines possession of Sarbick and Kłodawa.[30] The Kujawy donations of the Duke to the magnate foundation of the Premonstratensian sisters of Strzelno must be considered in the political context of the border between Kujawy and Wielkopolska. In the face of Mieszko's efforts to win Kujawy from the hands of Kazimierz II Sprawiedliwy and his successors, such donations may have had a propagandist overtone, being intended to send a clear message as to who actually governed this territory.[31] We may wonder whether this was not simply an extension or renewal of the old dispute over Kwieciszewo, but in a much wider scale, not only over the village, but over the entire Kujawy region.[32]

Although the members of the Canons of the Holy Sepulchre, brought by Jaksa to Miechów, may not have obtained great financial benefit from the Piast dynasts, they clearly gained their support, most likely very soon after their house was founded. The immunity for the commandery of the Order in Miechów, most likely granted by Bolesław IV, was subsequently confirmed by Mieszko III and Kazimierz II as suzerains of Poland.[33] In addition, the contacts between Kazimierz, his wife Helena and the community are evidenced in the entries in the *Liber fraternitatis* or a diploma issued by the Duke.[34] The same

---

28 Ulanowski, 'Dokumenty kujawskie i mazowieckie', p. 117. For more information on the grants, see Kürbis, 'Pogranicze Wielkopolski i Kujaw', p. 349; Karczewski, *Dzieje klasztoru norbertanek w Strzelnie*, pp. 124–25.
29 KDW i.32. The bull mentions a tavern in Strzelno, the ninth part of income from markets in Kwieciszewo and Inowrocław, a tavern in Mątwy and the ninth part of income in Kruszwica, without indicating the benefactor. The grants have been analysed by Karczewski, *Dzieje klasztoru norbertanek w Strzelnie*, pp. 124–25, 135.
30 See for example, by Karczewski, *Dzieje klasztoru norbertanek w Strzelnie*, p. 134.
31 See Dobosz, *Monarcha i możni*, p. 349; Karczewski, *Dzieje klasztoru norbertanek w Strzelnie*, pp. 115–36.
32 The ownership of Kwieciszewo was a contentious issue for Mieszko III and his older brother Bolesław IV (it was probably located on the border of their realms) during the lifetime of their mother, Salomea of Berg (died 27 July 1144). Salomea had settled the dispute between her sons. Knowledge about these events comes from the Trzemeszno forgery of 1145 (ZDŚ i.10).
33 This information is provided by the earliest Miechów documents, the diploma of Patriarch Monachus of 1198 and the so-called *album patriarchale* (KDM ii.375–76). For commentary on the rights granted by dukes Bolesław IV, Mieszko III and Kazimierz II, see Dobosz, *Działalność fundacyjna*, pp. 104–07. For discussion of the documents see RPD i.143–44; Oblizajek, 'Najstarsze dokumenty', pp. 97–108.
34 Both the entries from the *Liber fraternitatis* and the detail that Kazimierz II issued a document concerning the Skaryszew grants are contained in the earliest Miechów documents, KDM ii.375–76. See also Dobosz, *Działalność fundacyjna*, pp. 108–11, 29–30.

happened to Mieszko III, whose wife Eudoxia granted Grodzisk, Wielkopolska to the monastery; both Mieszko's wives and sons were accepted into the prayer fraternity.[35]

Though not particularly active in the foundation of churches, Bolesław III did grant several villages to the canons regular of Czerwińsk in 1161, and issued an appropriate diploma together with his younger brother Henryk of Sandomierz.[36] He may also have supported the efforts of the Czerwińsk monastery to attain a protection bull in 1155,[37] and most likely also endowed it with the village of Łomna with its *adscriptici* and the immunity.[38] Later, in the time of Kazimierz II and Konrad I those clever peasants attempted to escape the dependence. This was probably a conscious support for the foundation of its former ally, Alexander of Malonne, Bishop of Płock (died 1156). This magnate's ties with Trzemeszno and Miechów were rather weak, in the latter case probably connected with the duties of the *princeps*, not strong enough to be noticed by any of his contemporaries.

Despite being the last to engage in founding church institutions, the two youngest sons of Bolesław III achieved the greatest success in this venture. It appears that Henryk did not cooperate with the Norbertine movement but rather supported the canons of Czerwińsk, as we are informed by the bull of Pope Hadrian IV of 18 April 1155 and a diploma issued in May 1161 at the Łęczyca convention.[39] The monastery received a marketplace in Kochów from Henryk, another one in the village of Zuzela, a considerable income from a tavern and a crossing, and three farmsteads with people settled there.[40] He also cooperated with his brothers in some way in the endowments for Trzemeszno in the years 1144–1146, but his early death interrupted this very

---

35   On Duchess Eudoxia's grant (Grodzisk with a tavern) and the commemoration of Mieszko III's family, see KDM ii.375–76.

36   Bolesław IV's grants for Czerwińsk are described in a document he issued in May 1161 together with his brother Henryk in Łęczyca on the occasion of the consecration of the Collegiate Church in Łęczyca: *Zaskowi cum omnibus suis appendenciis, Pomnichow cum omnibus pariter appendenciis, Komsina cum omnibus suis appendenciis, Parlin cum Radossewicze et Nedan cum suis filiis in pistrinum*, KDM ii.373.

37   The monastery received a bull from Pope Hadrian IV on 18 April 1155, KDŚ i.22. See also Dobosz, *Monarcha i możni*, p. 343.

38   These events are described in documents issued by Konrad of Mazovia on the occasion of a convention held in Trojanów in 1222, Kochanowski, *Zbiór ogólny przywilejów*, 211–12, pp. 208–13. For details of the immunity see Kaczmarczyk, *Immunitet sądowy i jurysdykcja poimmunitetowa*, pp. 298–99. For discussion on the *adscriptici*, see Dobosz, *Działalność fundacyjna*, pp. 118–21.

39   For more details about Henryk's engagement in matters of the Church in Poland see Dobosz, *Monarcha i możni*, pp. 355–58; cf. Teterycz, 'Rządy księcia Henryka', pp. 259–62.

40   The bull of 18 April 1155 contains the following reference to Henry: *forum in Cohov ex dono Henrici ducis* (Kochanowski, *Zbiór ogólny przywilejów*, 78), whereas the document of May 1161 lists the following endowments for the canons regular of Czerwińsk: *dedi forum, scilicet Zuzela cum thabernariis et transitu, Sdziwi cum sorte sue at aliis sortibus duabus cum appendenciis* (KDM ii.373).

promising cooperation with the Church.[41] Kazimierz II, in contrast, was a relatively generous patron, and various elements among the canons regular also benefited from his largesse.[42] Grants for Trzemeszno, as in the case of Henryk, are a side issue, as he was only eight years old at the time.[43] Both younger sons of Salomea were under the influence of Bolesław and Mieszko who, desiring to demonstrate the unity of their political faction, entered them into charters, thus enabling their debut on the political scene of the time. Perhaps in the face of a civil war and a serious conflict within the dynasty, this demonstration of the concerted cooperation of the four junior princes was of propaganda value, directed especially to external opposition, but also for those among the nobility who were undecided. Kazimierz established his own contacts with the canons regular in Czerwińsk, but whether he was an active party or only performed the duties of the head of the Masovian district is unclear.[44] From the later Trojanów documents (after 1222) of his son Konrad, we know only that the fugitives from the monastery village of Łomna tried to find shelter with Kazimierz, yet the Duke ordered them to return, and that he had granted, or confirmed, the monastery an immunity.[45] No other examples of Kazimierz having contact with the canons in Czerwińsk were recorded, and his engagement with foundations in Mazovia was obviously episodic. Nevertheless, there is no doubt that the grants to two of Jaksa's foundations, the Canons of the Holy Sepulchre in Miechów and the Norbertine Sisters at Zwierzyniec, were not a one-off event. I have already mentioned the former, and the latter was also a significant economic boost for the new Premonstratensian canonry. It consisted of donations from a few villages in the Skowieszyn District on the Vistula River that, although distant from the main seat of the monastery at Zwierzyniec near Kraków, were economically viable.[46] Jaksa was undoubtedly one of the main associates of Kazimierz at a key period of his political career as he gradually acquired land and power, first in Wiślica,

---

41 Henryk's role in the endowment of the Chapel of the Blessed Virgin Mary in Góra Małgorzaty near Łęczyca along with several villages and immunity for Trzemeszno Abbey is unclear. It is likely that Henryk, together with Kazimierz II, assisted his older brothers, Bolesław IV and Mieszko III. For more detail, see Dobosz, *Działalność fundacyjna*, pp. 90–95.
42 For more detail of actions undertaken by Kazimierz II for the benefit of the Church, see Dobosz, *Działalność fundacyjna*.
43 Dobosz, *Działalność fundacyjna*, pp. 90–95. The grants of the younger Piasts for Trzemeszno Abbey are reported by the forged document of Mieszko III of 28 April 1145 and the diploma of Cardinal-Legate Hubaldus.
44 For more detail, see Dobosz, *Działalność fundacyjna*, from p. 118.
45 Kochanowski, *Zbiór ogólny przywilejów*, pp. 211–12.
46 Zwierzyniec Abbey received the following villages in the vicinity of today's Kazimierz Dolny on the Vistula River: Skowieszyn, Wietrzna Góra, Krępa, Wojszyn, Rzeczyca, Jaworzec, which are detailed in LB iii, p. 59. For further discussion, see Dobosz, *Działalność fundacyjna*, pp. 121–23; Rajman, 'Nadanie dóbr skowieszyńskich', pp. 23–33; Rajman, *Klasztor norbertanek na Zwierzyńcu*, p. 50.

then Sandomierz.[47] He did not live to see the throne in Kraków taken over by the youngest son of Bolesław III, but Bolesław was introduced to the throne by, among others, Jaksa's brother-in-law, Świętosław Piotrowic. The contacts with the Canons of the Holy Sepulchre and the Norbertine nuns were certainly the result of cooperation between the young Duke and an experienced magnate, and perhaps a form of repaying political obligations on the part of the former.

Among the grandsons of Bolesław III, only two fit in the frames we have set for the thirteenth century: Bolesław I Wysoki (the Tall) and Leszek Biały (the White), son of Bolesław IV. It seems that apart from some unspecified ties with Czerwińsk and Dobiechna's church in Płock, the latter did not support the community of the canons regular. In any case, both his life and his sole rule were short. We know slightly more about Bolesław the Tall but that still does not mean we know much. Bolesław granted a general privilege to the canons of Piasek confirming their property status even before 1193, approving the endowment of his father and adding a few people who were settled there.[48] He also participated in a program at St Vincent's Abbey at Ołbin associated with the removal of the Benedictines and the introduction of the Premonstratensians from Kościelna Wieś. According to the bull of Pope Celestine III of 7 April 1193, he was the patron of this undertaking, probably together with the descendants of its founder, the Archbishop of Gniezno and Bishop of Wrocław.[49]

Although we are able to extract some information from extant sources on the connections between the Piast dukes and the canons regular, and the Norbertines, what we have is little diversified and often singular in nature. We can formulate some ideas if we look into those sources more closely, but these certainly remain far from satisfactory. The foremost conclusion is that we rarely learn anything more than about the economic protection of the dukes, including the endowments of land, people, regalia or immunity. In many cases, the dukes' custody was not comprehensive or ongoing, having been frequently limited to one-time or temporary actions. Due in part to the small number of written records, our reconstructions of the connections between the Piasts and the religious communities are in fact mere speculation. Having that in mind, close political liaison between Salomea, her sons and Trzemeszno Canonry can hardly be questioned. They seem so unambiguous that they can be referred to as a historical fact. The fact that the dukes supported the foundation for canons established by loyal nobles on the basis of reciprocation for political favours seems an important observation. This

---

47 For both the portrayal of Jaksa and his cooperation with Kazimierz II, see Dobosz, *Działalność fundacyjna*, pp. 193–96; Dobosz, *Monarcha i możni*, pp. 368–78.
48 KDŚ i.68; see also Pobóg-Lenartowicz, *Uposażenie i działalność*, pp. 14–15.
49 KDŚ i.69. See also Dobosz, *Monarcha i możni*, p. 316, note 385; Rajman, 'Norbertanie polscy', pp. 79–80; Karczewski, *Dzieje klasztoru norbertanek w Strzelnie*, p. 83.

is how I perceive the relationship between Kazimierz II and Jaksa. Here we observe an additional Bohemian theme, especially in the context of the birth of Helena, Kazimierz's wife and the fact that she was included in the obituary of Zwierzyniec.[50] There is something specific about the frame of reference that was created in the case of Jaksa's foundation in Miechów, which was supported by three successive suzerains of Poland: Bolesław IV, Mieszko III and Kazimierz II. It may be possible to connect some threads of cultural contact between Mieszko III and Trzemeszno and Czerwińsk, but this is a task, first of all, for an art historian (which has already been undertaken).[51]

The preserved historical sources rarely show us other forms of contact or cooperation between the convents of the canons regular and the Piast dukes. Their help in the efforts to obtain protection bulls for Trzemeszno, Czerwińsk or some Norbertine institutions such as Strzelno is mere suggestion, if not speculation. The interference in the internal operation of the monastery at Ołbin and the undertaken changes are a notable exception, although it was undertaken jointly with the descendants of the founder and national ecclesiastical factors.

To conclude, it seems that in the twelfth century, the Piasts were not heavily engaged in the founding of monasteries for the canons regular and Premonstratensians. Only the monastery in Trzemeszno was founded exclusively by the Piasts, and a few other communities received considerable economic support (Zwierzyniec, Czerwińsk, Miechów). In other cases, we read about minor interventions or donations. In these matters, the Piasts were definitely giving way to the leading Polish nobles, such as Piotr Włostowic, Jaksa, Piotr Wszeborowic, Wit and Dzierżek of the Janina clan, or the Strzegomiów clan. Thus, unlike the Cistercians, who also arrived at the Polish lands in the twelfth century, or the Benedictines, the canons regular were certainly not favoured by the Polish dukes. It seems that this period saw no coherent policy of the dynasty towards the canons regular and the Norbertines, despite a certain number of source references and some interesting contexts. Should it be inferred from this then, that this form of religious life initially went unnoticed or underestimated by the Piasts? Or rather that the path to a broader understanding of these problems is blocked by the weakness and fragility of the source base? Today, it is impossible to give an unequivocal answer to these questions, although I am inclined to believe that on the threshold of the increasing decentralisation of the region, the dukes were more interested in monk foundations than in the canons. It is also likely not fully possible to answer the question as to why this was the case either. Perhaps the former,

---

50 The fact that Helena, the wife of Kazimierz II, came from the family of the dukes of Znojmo was convincingly demonstrated by Wasilewski, *Helena księżniczka znojemska*, pp. 115–20. For more information on Helena, see Dobosz, *Działalność fundacyjna*, pp. 198–201. Her name is mentioned in the Obituary of Zwierzyniec, Rajman, 'Średniowieczne zapiski', p. 52, note 110.
51 These issues are explored by Wetesko, *Historyczne konteksty*.

to frame it in a modern way, were more skilled at advertising and promoting themselves, and the Piasts, slightly conservative, were used to the old forms of communal life. In any case, a field for discussion opens up here. One that, even if not always fertile and profound, is nevertheless often colourful.

CHAPTER 3

The Earliest Evidence for Kazimierz II as Patron and Founder*

Some aspects of the religious foundations of Kazimierz II, who reigned as Duke of Wiślica from 1166/67 and subsequently as the *princeps* between 1177 and 1194, have already been subject to a comprehensive analysis in my other publications. The establishment of religious institutions by the Duke is well illuminated by written sources and critical studies of the documents relating to individual foundations. In this study I would like to examine the earliest sources of his endowments for the Church in Poland. In analysing Kazimierz and his reign primarily in the context of the competition for the *princeps'* throne in Kraków, historians have focused on the scope and nature of his power as well as his attitude towards his brothers (mainly Mieszko III) and nephews. Much attention has been paid to Kazimierz's achievements, particularly his foreign political relations with Rus'. The attitudes toward the Church and its hierarchy during Kazimierz's reign has mainly been assessed through the prism of the Statute of Łęczyca (1180) and in the context of the political landscape in progressively territorially divided Poland.

When Vincentius, Bishop of Kraków, portrayed Kazimierz in the pages of his chronicle, he justified the Duke being nicknamed 'the Just' by referencing his rigorous attitude towards his subordinates.[1] The chronicler made no reference to the fact that the sobriquet 'the Just' could have been earned through the benefits he provided to the Church. Kazimierz's reign allows for his inclusion among those medieval rulers who fulfilled the doctrinal postulate of taking responsibility for the development and prosperity of churches and monasteries. Being responsible for his subjects obliged a Christian monarch to show mercy towards the needy. These included the clergy in its entirety who, together with their communities, constituted a place of worship and exemplar of Christian life.[2] In the early Piast period, rulers assumed material responsibility for the development of church institutions. The co-participation of the knighthood is primarily known to us only from the turn of the twelfth century, particularly from the mid-twelfth century. However, this did not

---

* Original publication: Józef Dobosz, 'Najstarsze świadectwa działalności fundacyjnej Kazimierza Sprawiedliwego', *Studia Źródłoznawcze*, 35 (1994), 65–77.
1 *Chronica Polonorum* iv.5.
2 The theological and feudal model of the ruler as a protector of the Church in Poland has been examined by Michałowski, *Princeps-fundator*.

happen without the will and consent of the dukes, who remained the main initiators of new foundations, as well as the powerful patrons of old foundations.

A comprehensive assessment of the foundations of Kazimierz II must be preceded by an attempt to revise the entire source base: documents, historiography, and material culture. This study is devoted to diplomas as the oldest and most important testimonies of the broadly understood (as a resultant *fundatio* and *dotatio*) engagement of the Duke in the foundation of religious houses. Among the documents issued by the end of the thirteenth century, some of them unpreserved in their original form, as many as twenty-seven mention Kazimierz's foundations and endowments. These documents show the Duke as the founder or co-founder, or they serve to confirm his earlier endowments. There is no question of the foundational importance of the twelfth-century diplomas issued by Kazimierz himself, whilst the later documents (mainly of thirteenth-century origin) which confirmed the Duke's endowments, are of auxiliary significance.

The twelfth-century diplomatic legacy contains six documents issued in the name of Kazimierz and testifying to his activities for the benefit of the Church. The authenticity of some of them has aroused considerable controversy over time. If we aim for the most complete reconstruction of the range of the Duke's endowments our most important task is, therefore, to review the credibility and usefulness of the sources.

The Cistercian abbey at Sulejów was the first and probably the most important foundation of Duke Kazimierz. The earliest history of this monastery can be reconstructed on the basis of three documents. Two of them show Kazimierz II as the issuer (1176 and 1178), and the third was issued by Piotr, Archbishop of Gniezno (1176). The documents have been the subject of an almost 100-year-long debate, in the course of which the authenticity of Sulejów's documents were extensively discussed by such scholars as Wojciech Kętrzyński, Stanisław Krzyżanowski, Zofia Kozłowska-Budkowa, Józef Mitkowski and Władysław Semkowicz.[3] This multi-faceted discussion led to the conclusion that all the above-mentioned Sulejów documents were forgeries.

The alleged act of foundation from 1176 emerged during a dispute over the village of Bałdrzychów between Sulejów Abbey and the descendants of Knight Bałdrzych between 1260 and 1261, over which Kazimierz of Kujawy sat as a judge. In the first phase of the trial, in which Bałdrzych's family hoped to retrieve Bałdrzychów from the monastery, Abbot Piotr attempted to defend himself with a bull of Honorius III of 1218, but the Duke considered it to be insufficient evidence and adjourned the hearing until a more reliable source was presented.[4] Such a source, in the form of a foundation charter, was provided and the Duke dismissed the claims of the descendants of Bałdrzych on 6

---

3 A discussion of the earliest Sulejów diplomas can be found in RPD i.80–81, 91; Mitkowski, *Początki klasztoru cystersów*, pp. 3–14, 32–49.
4 Mitkowski, *Początki klasztoru cystersów*, pp. 317–18.

February 1261.⁵ Thus, it may be concluded that the foundation charter was drawn up shortly before 6 February 1261. The following facts speak against its authenticity:
1) inconsistency regarding the persons and the date (Pełka became Bishop of Kraków only at the end of 1185, and Archbishop Piotr assumed his office around 1190),
2) duality of stylisation (parts of the text in the form of *pluralis* and *singularis*, alternatively),
3) parts in *pluralis* display a striking similarity to Sulejów diplomas dating from 1236 to the beginning of the third quarter of the thirteenth century, in which the recipient's *dictatus* is present,
4) the parts written in *singularis* are similar in form to Jędrzejów diplomas from 1167, and these are thirteenth-century falsifications based on older monastery records,
5) the form of immunity clearly shows its thirteenth-century character,
6) the speedy confirmation of the 1262 document issued by Bolesław V Wstydliwy (the Chaste), and its subsequent disappearance.⁶

The forgery was based on some unknown monastery records, either a *notitia* or an inventory of goods endowed to the monastery in the twelfth century. The fragments written in *singularis* were taken from the records along with those sections of the document about the endowment of Comes Radosław and the marketplace in Sulejów, including the freedoms granted to it. The rights to tithes granted to the monastery by Archbishop Piotr were recorded separately. The second part of the document, which deals with the donation of tithes for the monastery of Sulejów, was derived from these notes. The forger stylised the document as a whole, added the information about Bałdrzychów and developed the immunity clause, enriching it with judicial immunity, *ius ducale* (*narzaz*) and one of its forms, the right to being provided with a horse-drawn vehicle (*powoz*). The *corroboratio* of the document is undoubtedly of thirteenth-century origin, while the invocation and dating do not raise any objections.⁷

Another of the Sulejów documents (the diploma issued by Archbishop Piotr regarding the tithing) was also considered to be a forgery, primarily due to the fact that it is known only from the forged transumpt of Archbishop Pełka from 1232.⁸ In the Sulejów cartulary, there is a document of Pełka with the same date and content but does not include the transumpt of Archbishop Piotr's grant.⁹ However, the forged transumpt of Pełka was certified by Cistercian

---
5 KDP i.49.
6 KDP i.50.
7 Cf. Mitkowski, *Początki klasztoru cystersów*, pp. 3–14.
8 KDW i.587 (21a).
9 Mitkowski, *Początki klasztoru cystersów*, pp. 319–20.

abbots in Lubiąż in 1289, before then being lost.¹⁰ It can be assumed that the document was forged because the monks needed a written substantiation for the tithes that had been granted to the monastery; Archbishop Jakub Świnka had issued a statute in 1285 that required a document with the seal of the bishop and patron be issued when endowing churches and monasteries with tithes. This decree caused concern among the Sulejów monks, who made a false transumpt of Piotr's document using the monastery records, the authentic document of Pełka in which he endowed the abbey with new tithes on the occasion of the consecration of the second church at the Abbey, and the transumpt of the alleged foundation charter. The forger contributed the stylisation of the whole document and the *corroboratio*, which, in accordance with the requirements of Archbishop Jakub, mentioned the appropriate seals. Composed between 1285 and 1289, it was therefore a typical diplomatic (formal) forgery, aimed at guaranteeing rights to the property to which the monks had perfectly good title.¹¹

The monastic tithes listed in the false document were indeed endowed by Archbishop Piotr, but certainly not on 10 August 1176, because at that time the archbishop's seat was probably occupied by Zdzisław. Piotr did not take over the seat of Gniezno until around 1190,¹² and he most likely endowed the monastery with the tithes in 1191. On 8 September of the same year Archbishop Piotr was in Sandomierz, where, in the presence of numerous bishops, he consecrated the Collegiate Church of the Blessed Virgin Mary.¹³ Assuming that he set off for Sandomierz territory from Gniezno, he could have travelled via Sulejów, which was located on the route from Wielkopolska to Kraków and Sandomierz, and consecrated the first monastery church on 10 August 1191. It was on this occasion that the abbey received the right to the tithes. The proposal presented here is based on the following premises:

1. The forger took the date of the endowment of the tithes from the monastic records and the purported foundation charter, and linked the year of the abbey foundation found in that diploma to the day noted in the record that the tithes were endowed; hence 10 August 1176.
2. In the west façade of the monastery church there is a side tympanum, a relic of the twelfth-century church, which was taken over by the Cistercians, remodelled and consecrated by Archbishop Piotr. Originally, the church was consecrated and dedicated to St Blaise, at which time the foundation charter was most likely composed.
3. By way of example, the Jędrzejów accounts from 1167 indicate that tithes were given on the occasion of the consecration of the monastery church.¹⁴

---

10 This document has not been printed in its entirety, see Mitkowski, *Początki klasztoru cystersów*, pp. 305, 311.
11 Cf. Mitkowski, *Początki klasztoru cystersów*, pp. 32–35.
12 See Trawkowski, 'Piotr', in PSB xxvi, pp. 361–62.
13 KDM i.2.
14 See KDM ii.374.

4. The consecration of the monastery church was one of the last stages of the foundation process of the Cistercian abbey.[15]
5. These facts coincide with the beginning of Piotr's pontificate and his stay in the Sandomierz district.

The acceptance of the proposed date of the endowing of the tithes reconciles the diploma with the plea for tithes from Duke Kazimierz and Pełka, Bishop of Kraków, and thus eliminates the inconsistency between the people and the date in the forged document.

The third of the Sulejów forgeries, a Kazimierz diploma dated to 1178, is the least problematic. The year 1178 as the endowment and issue date is unacceptable due to its incompatibility with the people mentioned (Pełka, Piotr and Kazimierz) and the striking resemblance of the ductus of this diploma to the style of writing of a diploma of Bolesław Konradowic from 1237.[16] As in the case of the previous document, the confirmation formulary and the seal marks are anachronistic. The forgery was drawn up because of a legal dispute over the tithes and the village of Milejów with the Premonstratensian monastery at Witów, which started around the mid-thirteenth century. It follows that the document was produced between 1237 and the mid-thirteenth century. Noteworthy is the elaborate form of the note on which the false document was based and included in the forgery in its entirety. The note was enriched with a witness list mixed with a *corroboratio* and details about the tithing.[17] The monastery received the endowments listed in the note and subsequent forgery during the process of the abbey's establishment between 1176 and 1191.[18] The date 1178 may refer to the exchange of the villages or rather its approval by Duke Kazimierz. It follows from the above arguments that:
1. All the Sulejów documents are forgeries.
2. The forgeries were produced for purely materialistic reasons: the need to protect property that lacked legal guarantees, such as diplomas and charters, which were becoming increasingly necessary in the thirteenth century.
3. The forgeries were drawn up because of various crises at Sulejów Abbey resulting from the constant struggle between the monastery and aristocracy over the property.

---

15 Cf. Zawadzka, 'Procesy fundowania opactw cysterskich', from p. 121.
16 KDP i.27.
17 Cf. Mitkowski, *Początki klasztoru cystersów*, pp. 35–49.
18 Bieniak, 'Polska elita polityczna XII wieku, Part I', p. 23, suggests that the record and endowments date to 1191. However, it cannot be ruled out that the diploma dated 1178 may evidence two or more endowment phases: the villages were exchanged in 1177 (before the removal of Mieszko from Kraków), the tithes granted by 1191. Thus, a series of events that took place between 1176 and 1191 were merged into a single document by the forger.

Thanks to the Sulejów forgeries, it is possible to determine what the foundation process of the local abbey looked like and its property status in its first years of operation. It seems that Kazimierz came to the idea of establishing a new Cistercian monastery around 1176 and implemented it gradually. He first applied for the permission of the Archbishop of Gniezno to establish a foundation, then brought monks from Morimond and endowed them with Sulejów, several villages with immunity, and regalia. The Duke's initiative was supported by Comes Radosław; Knight Bałdrzych; Gedko and Pełka, Bishops of Kraków; Archbishop Piotr; and Mieszko III, who granted rights to new estates and tithes to the monastery. The consecration of the monastery church on 10 August 1191 was the final act of the process.[19]

The Zagość diploma draws attention to Kazimierz's other undertakings. At the congress in Milica on 29 August 1191, the Duke confirmed, through a writ, that the Knights Hospitallers Abbey at Zagość had been founded by his brother Henryk. At the same time, Kazimierz provided specificity to the very generally worded immunity granted by Henryk. Research on Kazimierz's diploma to date has been surveyed by Kozłowska-Budkowa, who convincingly validated its authenticity.[20] However, since the date formulary contains only the phrase *ad. colloquium in Milice IIII kalendas Septembris*,[21] the year of composition remains a controversial element of the text. Although some possible hypotheses have been put forward, the problem remains unresolved.[22] An attempt to establish the year can be made with the help of the document witnesses, primarily Lupus, Bishop of Płock and Jaksa, and by including Bolesław IV in considerations. Since Lupus, Bishop of Płock, does not appear in Kazimierz's diploma as merely a witness, but also as one who performs certain duties of office, as evidenced by the phrase *dominus Lupus episcopus Plozensis, per cuius manum elemosina data est*,[23] it may be assumed that he was one of Kazimierz's most trusted collaborators. Such close liaison between Duke Kazimierz and the Bishop of Płock might only have been established after the death of Bolesław IV when, according to Bishop Vincentius of Kraków, Kazimierz was taking care of Bolesław's son, Leszek.[24] Prior to this, such close liaison between the Bishop of Płock, whose diocese

---

19   The grants obtained by the monastery during the foundation process (1176–1191) have been compiled in Dobosz, 'Uwagi o fundacji opactwa cystersów', p. 90 (table).
20   RPD i.78.
21   ZDŚ i.29.
22   According to Kętrzyński, *Studia nad dokumentami XII w.*, pp. 298–300, the date of Kazimierz's diploma and the convention in Milica was determined by the death of Bolesław IV and the appointment of Lupus as Bishop of Płock, hence the dates 1172–1173. Following Kętrzyński, this dating of the document was accepted by F. Piekosiński, S. Krzyżanowski, R. Grodecki, K. Tymieniecki and others. Zachorowski, 'Colloquia w Polsce', p. 53, was inclined to date the Milica convention to 1173. RPD i.78 suggests it took place between 1170 and 1175.
23   ZDŚ i.29.
24   *Chronica Polonorum*, pp. 173–74.

was part of Bolesław's district, and Kazimierz, was basically impossible. The death of Bolesław IV therefore marks the *terminus post quem* of Kazimierz's document. Perhaps the Milica convention was held in connection with the annexing of the remainder of the Sandomierz territories. It is commonly assumed that Bolesław died in 1173, but the month and day that this happened is more difficult to determine. There are three competing options: 3 April, 30 October and 5 January. Following the *Kalendarz katedry krakowskiej*, Oswald Balzer advocated the first date;[25] Kozłowska-Budkowa supported the second date, relying on another entry from the same calendar;[26] while Kazimierz Jasiński convincingly argued that the correct date of the death for the Duke is included in the obituary of St Vincent's Abbey (5 January).[27] Assuming that Bolesław's death took place on 5 January 1173, Kazimierz's document could have been issued (and the convent held in Milica) on 29 August 1173. According to the sources, Jaksa of Miechów died between 24 and 27 February 1176,[28] hence the diploma would have been written on 29 August 1175 at the latest.

An (undated) diploma of Kazimierz II concerns the donation of thirteen carts of salt from the Sandomierz chamber and the confirmation of immunity exemptions for the Cistercian monastery at Jędrzejów. In his detailed analysis of this text, Semkowicz distinguished its individual parts, drawing attention to the similarity of Kazimierz's salt grants for Jędrzejów and Sulejów, and confirmed the authenticity of the witness list. In his opinion, this document is authentic; its content does not raise any objections, and it exhibits features typical of twelfth-century diplomatics. He argued that Kazimierz's charter and the corresponding document issued by Mieszko III were produced from monastic records containing the bestowal, curse, names of the benefactors, and a list of witnesses, in the late twelfth or the early thirteenth century, as evidenced by their form and content. The lack of the date was due to the fact that it was not included in the monastery records.[29]

Kozłowska-Budkowa took a different position. On the basis of monastic records, she concluded that the charter was forged and was partly intentionally dishonest. The fabrication concerned mostly the immunity clause. Kozłowska-Budkowa believed that the document had been drawn up before 1245, as evidenced by a diploma of Bolesław V from that year.[30] Two documents of

---

25 Balzer, *Genealogia Piastów*, pp. 155–56.
26 Kozłowska-Budkowa, 'Który Bolesław?', pp. 81–89. See also *Kalendarz katedry krakowskiej*, MPH v, p. 181 (after 30 October); however, in note 442 the author withdraws from the hypothesis she put forward in the cited study.
27 Jasiński, review of Kozłowska-Budkowa, 'Który Bolesław?', pp. 182–84. See also *Nekrolog opactwa św. Wincentego we Wrocławiu*, MPH ix.1, p. 4, note 13, which endorses Jasiński's statement.
28 *Nekrolog opactwa św. Wincentego*, MPH v, pp. 20–21. See also *Rocznik kapituły krakowskiej*, v, p. 62, which gives the year of Jaksa's death.
29 Semkowicz, 'Nieznane nadania', pp. 70–97, with the text of the document on pp. 69–70.
30 RPD i.63–64. The author's position was contested in Maleczyński, review of RPD, pp. 581–82, in which he argued that the document was genuine. However, Kozłowska-Budkowa's view has become commonly accepted.

thirteenth-century origin prove that the Jędrzejów document is a forgery. the first, issued by Duchess Grzymisława in 1228, mentions the endowments of Bolesław IV, Kazimierz and Grzymisława's husband, Leszek, for the Cistercians of Jędrzejów. However, there is no evidence here that Kazimierz issued a diploma on the occasion of his grants.[31] The other diploma, issued in 1245 by Bolesław V, settled a dispute between Jędrzejów Abbey and Michał, Castellan of Kraków, around the exercise of certain powers of the castellan's authority over the monastery property. In this dispute, it was alleged that the monastery documents were inauthentic, and that Duke Bolesław therefore ordered the incriminating diplomas to be presented to him. Having examined the documents (of Kazimierz and Leszek the White), Bolesław approved them.[32] There is every reason to believe that Kazimierz's charter was produced between 1228 and 1245. It was created from the monastic records and perhaps repeats their content in full. It seems, however, that not all of Kazimierz's grants were made at the ceremonial congress on the occasion of the consecration of the Cistercian monastery church in Jędrzejów. Only a decision to grant salt was made at the time, while the immunity waivers were confirmed later. The right to immunity was granted to the abbey by Bolesław IV (before 1173), and this fact was then confirmed by Mieszko (between 1173 and 1177), and later by Kazimierz, who probably did it right after assuming the throne in Kraków, perhaps even in 1177. When confirming the immunity, the dukes did the same with regard to the of the monastery's property, hence the corresponding phrase in Kazimierz's (and Mieszko's) document.

Contrary to Kozłowska-Budkowa, and in agreement with Semkowicz, I do not see any elements of factual forgery in Kazimierz's document. The authenticity of salt grants has already been vigorously defended by Semkowicz, and his position confirmed by subsequent research.[33] Neither does the immunity clause raise doubts; similar or even more developed examples from other, undisputed documents of twelfth-century origin are known to exist.[34] Kozłowska-Budkowa's suggestion that the young dukes could not have confirmed the immunity in the Duchy of Bolesław in 1166/67 results from the erroneous assumption that all the grants contained in the documents of Kazimierz and Mieszko were made at the convention held on the occasion of the consecration of the monastery church. As noted above, when they drew up the document on the basis of the notes stored in the monastery, the monks of Jędrzejów combined the two phases of grants into one whole. However, they paid especial attention to the accuracy of the facts and the appropriate form of the text. Its form is close to that of a *notitia*, a brief record of the transaction. It

---

31 KDM i.11.
32 KDP iii.24.
33 Semkowicz, 'Nieznane nadania', pp. 78–79. Cf. Grzesiowski and Piotrowicz, 'Sól małopolska w nadaniach', pp. 84–85.
34 For example, the Zagość diploma of Kazimierz II (ZDŚ i.29) or the diploma of Patriarch Monachus (KDM ii.375).

consists of an invocation, *intitulatio, inscriptio*, poorly developed disposition, penal formulary, and a relatively extensive list of witnesses, typical for the twelfth-century documents.[35]

Determining the date of the summit at which the described events took place is another matter. The position of Semkowicz — that the convention in Jędrzejów took place between 18 October 1166 and 2 March 1167 — has gained wide acceptance. Only Janusz Bieniak questioned these findings, believing that monks of Jędrzejów received the endowments in 1168.[36] Important for the dating of the Jędrzejów convention are Henryk of Sandomierz, Kazimierz Kazimierzowic and Gedko, Bishop of Kraków. The death of Henryk of Sandomierz marks the beginning of the independent rule of Kazimierz II in Wiślica, which happened on 18 October 1166.[37] Kazimierz Kazimierzowic, the firstborn son of Kazimierz II, appears in the Jędrzejów document as a witness. According to *Kalendarz katedry krakowskiej*, he died on 1 March,[38] and the year of his death was given by *Rocznik Traski* and the *Rocznik krakowski* as 1167 and 1168, respectively.[39] Balzer, followed by Semkowicz, found the information provided by the former annals to be more credible,[40] but it seems that it is difficult to settle the issue with any clarity. Errors and date shifts can be found in both sources, and it is not easy to judge which of them is more credible in this case. A deciding factor in this case may be the episcopacy of Gedko, who became Bishop of Kraków after 18 October 1166 (Mateusz's death), though his consecration by Pope Alexander III took place in Rome as late as on the day of Saints Gervasius and Protasius (19 June) in 1167. He could have set out to Rome in the spring of 1167 and left the city in the summer of the same year. It seems that Gedko took part in the solemn congress in Jędrzejów as the accepted and ordained Bishop of Kraków, the more so because he granted several tithes to the Cistercians there. This would indicate that the convention must have taken place in the second half of 1167, pushing the date of Kazimierz Kazimierzowic's death to 1 March 1168, making the information provided by *Rocznik krakowski* more credible. It seems that the aforementioned congress could have taken place in the early autumn of 1167, and certainly before 1 March 1168. Two dates are probable: 14 September 1167, the Feast of the Exaltation of the Holy Cross (one of the most important Cistercian holidays), or Christmas 1167.

---

35 Compare the analysis of the formulary conducted by Semkowicz, 'Nieznane nadania', pp. 71–74.
36 See Semkowicz, 'Nieznane nadania', p. 71; Bieniak, 'Polska elita polityczna XII w., Part III A', p. 49, announced that he would substantiate his hypothesis in a separate study.
37 This date is set by a Złocka document of 31 December 1167, which reports that Bishop Mateusz and Duke Henryk died on the same day and in the same year (ZDŚ i.27) and the *Kalendarz katedry krakowskiej*, MPH v, p. 179, which states that Mateusz died on 18 October.
38 *Kalendarz katedry krakowskiej*, MPH v, p. 128.
39 MPH ii, p. 834.
40 Balzer, *Genealogia Piastów*, pp. 261–62; Semkowicz, 'Nieznane nadania', pp. 73–74.

Subsequent diplomas issued by Kazimierz are indicative of his strong ties with the chapter of Kraków Cathedral. Two documents have been preserved: the 1189 charter from Opatów and an undated charter drawn up probably in the same year.[41] The research on both was surveyed by Kozłowska-Budkowa, who considered them authentic. In her opinion, they were drawn up in 1189 in the following order: first the Opatów document (12 April), and then the hunting act in Kalina.[42] We learn from them that the Chropy *opole* was returned to the Kraków chapter, with a tavern and a right to the saltern being granted on this occasion (the Opatów document), and that the Duke maintained for life the right to hunt in Kalina along with benefits from the inhabitants of Chropy. This is the only trace of Kazimierz's material support for the cathedral chapter in Kraków, although he is known to have cooperated for several years with the Bishops of Kraków (Gedko and Pełka).

Source analysis and a study of the extensive literature on the subject suggest that there were at least three more diplomas of Kazimierz II referencing his activities relating to religious foundations. The first of these was issued for the Collegiate Church of St Florian in Kleparz, the second concerned the Canons of the Holy Sepulchre in Miechów, and the third the Cistercians of Jędrzejów. The information preserved in the first of these documents was published by Stanisław Kuraś.[43] According to the record, the diploma was issued by the Duke on the occasion of the establishment of a canon group in Kleparz with the intent of building a church in honour of St Florian. It happened *sexto calendas novembris* (27 October) 1184 with the participation of Gedko, Bishop of Kraków, who endowed the new institution with tithes.[44] There is nothing more we can say about this document. The short note only gives the reason for the issue, the Duke's title and the date. None of these elements is in doubt. The document may still have existed in the second half of the fifteenth century, as it was used by Jan Długosz, but whether the chronicler had access to the original or a copy is unknown.[45] The document's information concerning the foundation of the Collegiate Church of St Florian verifies the data from later sources.

Enumerating the grants of Duke Kazimierz for the Canons of the Holy Sepulchre in Miechów, Patriarch Monachus provided the details about the exemptions previously granted to the marketplace in Skaryszew.[46] Based on this information, it was suspected that the Duke must have issued a document, which was subsequently lost through unknown causes. Kozłowska-Budkowa

---

41 KKK i.4–5.
42 RPD i.118–19.
43 ZDK i.3.
44 ZDK i.3.
45 Jan Długosz, *Annales*, p. 135; LB i, p. 477.
46 *Eandem eciam libertatem coram Sdislauo archiepiscopo in Pascha Domini in Spirzou multis ibidem nobilibus astantibus, domino Kasimiro iubente dominus Lupus episcopus in communi predicauit, tunc etiam scripto et sigillo suo confirmauit.* KDM ii.375.

was inclined to believe that there were in fact two documents — one issued by Kazimierz and the other by Lupus — although she did not reject the idea that there was only one document, issued by the Duke but sealed by Lupus and with a relevant clause by Lupus.[47] It seems that only one document was issued in connection with the Skaryszew privileges, and that its issuer was Kazimierz. At that time, Lupus carried out activities of the ducal office and most likely signed the document with his seal (or perhaps his and the Duke's). He probably played a similar role at the Milica convention (1173–1175), where he performed chancellery functions at Kazimierz's side, as evidenced by the passage in the Zagość document stating that the alms has been given 'by his hand'.[48] The bull of Innocent III of 14 October 1208, issued for the Canons of Holy Sepulchre in Miechów, testifies to the existence of Kazimierz's diploma, which confirmed the immunity for the monastic property.[49] It is doubtful whether the Pope's approval was intended for the diploma concerning Skaryszew, but it is possible that the Canons of the Holy Sepulchre supplied the privilege from Kazimierz, prepared on the basis of monastic records (perhaps Monachus' document?), for the Pope to confirm, especially since Innocent III confirmed Mieszko III's diploma also concerning immunity with a bull almost identical in content.[50]

The third of Kazimierz's lost documents concerning the Cistercian monastery at Jędrzejów confirmed the exchange of the monastery village of Buszków for the village of Niegosławice. The only trace of the charter is preserved in an 1192 diploma of Pełka, Bishop of Kraków, and it seems that it was also issued that year or close to that date.[51] Perhaps, when approving the Buszków–Niegosławice transfer, the Duke gave the tenants settled in Tarszawa to the Cistercians of Jędrzejów at the same time.[52]

In addition to the documents issued by Kazimierz II, or forged using his name, further corroboration of these grants can be found in other twelfth- and thirteenth-century documents. The two oldest Trzemeszno diplomas from 1145 and 1146 should certainly be mentioned. The first, issued by Mieszko III, shows the Duke's share in the endowments made to the monastery of canons regular in Trzemeszno. It states that Kazimierz and his brothers granted certain rights to the chapel in Góra Małgorzaty near Łęczyca, including

---

47 RPD i.113.
48 *Dominus Lupus episcopus Plozensis, per cuius manum elemosina data est.* ZDŚ i.29.
49 *Specialiter autem libertates domui et hominibus uestri a bone memorie Casimiro Polonie duce concessas, sicut eas iuste ac pacifice possidetis, et in ipsius ducis scripto autentico continetur, uobis et per uos domui uoestre auctoritate apostolica confirmamus, et presentis scripti patrocinio communimus.* KDM ii.377.
50 KDM ii.378.
51 KDM i.3.
52 KDM i.32 (the document of Bolesław V from 3 August 1250 claims that Tarszawa was granted by Kazimierz II. However, the village was in fact granted by Archbishop Jan before 1153, and the Duke settled it with his subjects who paid him tithes, likely after 1177).

villages, immunity, salt, and immunity for the village of Kwieciszewo, to the canons from Trzemeszno.[53] The other diploma, issued by Cardinal Hubaldus, confirms the credibility of the previous act in regard to the grants relating to the villages near Łęczyca.[54]

The research on the Trzemeszno diploma of Mieszko III was summed up by Kozłowska-Budkowa. Having concluded that the document was false, Kozłowska-Budkowa identified the fragments of the thirteenth-century original: the script, the formulary, and the immunity provision. She considered the twelfth-century elements to be a fairly faithful reflection of the monastery records. In her opinion, the forger also made use of Hubaldus's diploma and the list of monastic property from an old inventory compiled between 1216 and 1223.[55] Mieszko's charter has been inspected by Brygida Kürbis, Henryk Łowmiański, and Jarosław Wenta, but there are no significant differences between their conclusions and those of Kozłowska-Budkowa. The most significant revelation is that of Wenta, who dated the donation of the villages near Łęczyca to the second half of 1144.[56]

Mieszko's diploma was probably forged at the monastery in order to secure the status of its property by giving it written substantiation. To make up for the lack of a diploma issued by a member of the ruling dynasty, the monks decided to use the monastic records and Hubaldus's charter to add greater immunity provisions and an extensive introductory formula of the *arenga*. Noteworthy are certain similarities in the forged Trzemeszno document to the 1198 diploma issued by Monachus, which also enumerates the possessions of the Canons of the Holy Sepulchre in Miechów, starting with the rulers and ending with the grants of the nobility.[57]

Hubaldus's charter is consistently recognised as authentic, and research on it has been summarised several times.[58] It remains unknown when the document was issued. Kozłowska-Budkowa recognised the separability of *actum* and *datum*. She believed that the events presented in the text took place in April 1145 during the cardinal's stay in Poland, while the citation was composed in the Roman curia on 2 March 1147 (per the Florentine style of 1146).[59] This position was challenged by Wenta, who asserted that the convention during which decisions were made to grant the chapel in Góra Małgorzaty to the canons of Trzemeszno took place in Płock. The donation was made at the funeral ceremonies of Duchess Salomea, widow of Bolesław III, in the summer of 1144, and then the decisions were confirmed in Gniezno.

---

53 KDW i.11.
54 ZDŚ i.12.
55 RPD i.42.
56 Kürbis, 'Pogranicze Wielkopolski i Kujaw', pp. 91–92; Łowmiański, *Początki Polski* v, pp. 32–59; Wenta, 'Na marginesie dokumentu', pp. 101–14.
57 KDM ii.375.
58 See RPD i.44; Kowalska, 'Dokument Humbalda, kardynała', pp. 27–47.
59 RPD i.44.

Hubaldus stayed in Poland in the second half of 1144 and composed the document confirming his donation, though it was not drawn up in Rome until 1146. According to Wenta, the document was witnessed by the participants of the convention in Płock.[60]

Both Trzemeszno documents show the first examples of Kazimierz, then only a boy, engaging with grants for the Church. It seems that Kazimierz's participation in these events was primarily related to the conflict between the younger Piasts and the *princeps* Władysław II. The joint presence at the rallies and conventions of all the junior brothers was a staged demonstration of unity for both their supporters and opponents. It seems likely that the endowments to the Church were meant to gain supporters, and it is in this context that we should consider the joint donation from all the brothers of the villages near Łęczyca to the abbey at Trzemeszno.

The relationship between Kazimierz and the members of the Canons of the Holy Sepulchre in Miechów are evidenced in the earliest monastery documents: the Monachus' document and the so-called *album patriarchale*. The former states that the Duke sanctioned the immunity for the monastery property and bestowed privileges to the marketplace in Skaryszew; the latter describes only the first event.[61] Both documents are believed to be entirely authentic, their composition based on unknown monastery records.[62]

The fragment of the grant issued by Monachus, concerning the forum in Skaryszew, indicates that Kazimierz offered the endowments on Easter of an unknown year at the congress in Świerże Górne. At the same time, documents from Miechów inform us that Skaryszew — together with the marketplace, church, and adjoining areas — had been granted to the monastery by Comes Radosław, who belonged to Kazimierz' close circle, and that Gedko, Bishop of Kraków, offered the tithe from these goods. At the congress in Świerże — which was attended by Zdzisław, Archbishop of Gniezno — Lupus, Bishop of Płock, performed the duties of the ducal office.[63] The sequence of events can therefore be reconstructed as follows: first, Radosław granted Skaryszew to the Canons of the Holy Sepulchre, then he arranged the immunity from the Duke and the tithe from the Bishop of Kraków. The presence of Lupus in Świerże indicates that the convention took place in 1173 (the death of Bolesław IV) at the earliest, when the Bishop of Płock became a close associate of Duke Kazimierz. The meeting between the Duke of Kraków and the Archbishop of Gniezno could have taken place in connection with laying the groundwork for the Łęczyca convention. This would imply that the marketplace in Skaryszew was granted immunity in the Easter of 1180.

---

60 Wenta, 'Na marginesie dokumentu', pp. 107–14.
61 KDM ii.375–76.
62 Research on the earliest Miechów documents was summarised in RPD i.14–144, pp. 135–36 and Oblizajek, 'Najstarsze dokumenty', pp. 97–108.
63 KDM ii.375–76. Kozłowska-Budkowa cautiously dated the Świerże Górne convention to the years 1170–1187 (RPD i.112–13).

Some further information on Kazimierz's endowments for the Church in Poland can be gleaned from certain thirteenth-century documents. Two of these were issued by Konrad I of Mazovia at a convention in Trojanów in 1222. They direct our attention to the ties between Duke Kazimierz and the canons regular of Czerwińsk. The written records discussed earlier concerned grants in Sandomierz and Kraków territories (with the exception of some donations to Sulejów and Trzemeszno), and the Trojanów diplomas show the Duke's donation activities in Mazovia. Their content reveals that Kazimierz confirmed the endowments his brother Bolesław had given to the canons from Czerwińsk, which consisted of *adscriptici* from Łomna along with judicial (possibly also fiscal) immunity.[64] The grants were confirmed between 1186 and 1194.

Konrad's diplomas are similar in content and form and should be considered authentic.[65] The similarities in their formulation and content stems from the fact that a legal action was taken at the same convention. This is evidenced by the date and place of the issue, and, above all, by the list of witnesses. The monastery wanted to protect itself against escapes by ascribed villagers (twice certified by the second document), hence the first document — which generally confirmed the privileges bestowed by Konrad's predecessors — was probably not sufficient. In the second document, therefore, an attempt was made to identify the ascribed villagers by name.

In 1250, Bolesław V issued a document in which he confirmed the village of Tarszawa, together with ten serfs, to the Cistercians of Jędrzejów granted by his grandfather Kazimierz.[66] The content and form of this document do not raise any suspicions, although the account of the donation of the village of Tarszawa by Duke Kazimierz is puzzling, since in the Jędrzejów foundation diploma we read that the village was granted by Archbishop Jan, the founder of the monastery.[67] It seems that the Duke merely confirmed the settlement of the estate bestowed by Jan, but the later tradition remembered him as the one who granted the entire estate.

The 1260 document issued by Kazimierz's grandson Bolesław V provides the earliest evidence of ties between Kazimierz and the Cistercian monastery at Wąchock. That part on the Duke's endowments is admittedly very general, not permitting any detailed conclusions; however, it can be said that the monastery at Wąchock had been granted some (probably very generally formulated) immunity by Kazimierz.[68] Mieczysław Niwiński suggested that it was a forgery made around 1318, based on the authentic document of Bolesław V

---

64 Kochanowski, ed., *Codex diplomaticus* 211–12.
65 Konrad's documents have been examined in Bachulski, 'Założenie klasztoru', p. 55; Grodecki, *Początki immunitetu w Polsce*, pp. 62–65; Wolfarth, *Ascripticii w Polsce*, pp. 44, 78, 87.
66 KDM i.32.
67 See Bobowski, 'Ze studiów nad dokumentami', pp. 29–65. KDM ii.372.
68 KKK i.61, for a more accurate edition, see Niwiński, *Opactwo cystersów w Wąchocku*, pp. 158–63.

from 1260 and the monastery records. The reason for the forgery was the need to repeal the burden of the knight's communication service (*conductus militibus, przewód*) and for the monastery to free itself from the patronage of the Bishops of Kraków. This is probably why the founder, Gedko, Bishop of Kraków, was left out and the role of the ducal family (Kazimierz, Leszek the White), which aided in attempts to remove the patronage of bishops, was emphasised instead.[69]

The forged document of 1260 for Wąchock is the last that provides new information about the foundations and endowments of Kazimierz II. Any others merely confirm previous records. There is also a number of charters that relate to three monasteries: the Cistercians of Sulejów, the Cistercians of Jędrzejów, and the Canons of the Holy Sepulchre at Miechów. Grants to the monastery at Sulejów made by his father were confirmed by Leszek the White in three diplomas. The first is dated 1206, the others to 1208 and 1222; their various problems have been discussed by Mitkowski.[70] He also proved the inauthenticity of another Sulejów document that mentions Kazimierz's foundations: the 1242 document by Konrad.[71] The remaining diplomas concerning Sulejów Abbey are related to the forged foundation charter. These include the transumpt of Bolesław V from 1262, and the diplomas of Kazimierz of Kujawy from 1261 and Leszek Czarny (the Black) from 1279.[72] Kazimierz II's participation in the founding of the monastery at Sulejów is further confirmed by the bull of Gregory IX of 1234.[73] The Duke's grants to the Cistercian monastery at Jędrzejów are confirmed by two previously mentioned authentic diplomas: one issued by Grzymisława in 1228[74] and the other issued by Bolesław V in 1245.[75] Kazimierz's participation in the endowments to the Canons of the Holy Sepulchre in Miechów is confirmed by a 1208 bull of Innocent III[76] and a 1256 diploma of Bolesław V.[77] The thirteenth-century documents listed above show that the Church institutions granted by Kazimierz enjoyed considerable support from his successors. It is clear that Sulejów Abbey, Kazimierz's grandest and most favoured foundation, was of the greatest importance for the Duke's descendants.

---

69 Niwiński, *Opactwo cystersów w Wąchocku*, pp. 7–17.
70 For the diplomas of Leszek the White from 1206 and 1208, see Mitkowski, *Początki klasztoru cystersów*, p. 302 (reg. 4–5). The 1222 document was published and annotated by Mitkowski, 'Nieznane dokumenty Leszka Białego', pp. 653–58. See also Mitkowski, *Początki klasztoru cystersów*, pp. 86–87.
71 KDP i.31. For analysis of the document see Mitkowski, *Początki klasztoru cystersów*, pp. 16–24.
72 KDP i.50 (diploma of Bolesław V); KDP i.49 (diploma of Kazimierz of Kujawy); KDP i.61 (diploma of Leszek the Black).
73 Mitkowski, *Początki klasztoru cystersów* 11, pp. 324–25.
74 KDM i.11.
75 KDP iii.24.
76 KDM ii.377.
77 KDM ii.449.

The analysis of documents related to the foundations and donations of Kazimierz II to the Church represent the development of Polish administrative documents. During the initial phase of church and monastery establishment, endowments were given orally at conventions and rallies, in the presence of the gathered nobility and knights. These were later confirmed by subsequent founders or benefactors. Widespread in the eleventh century, this practice continued until the end of the following century. The twelfth century saw the emergence of the first documents with seals and witness lists. This new phenomenon was most likely related to the arrival of new orders in Poland from around the mid-twelfth century, who were more concerned about legitimising their claims on property through legal evidence. The increasing role of the bishoprics and cathedral chapters was not without significance. In 1153, the two oldest Cistercian abbeys in Poland, Jędrzejów and Łekno, received foundation charters. The efforts undertaken by the monasteries to obtain papal bulls provide further evidence of how important it was for them to have evidence documenting their accumulated property. A redacted form of diploma, an objective record or a *notitia*, functioned in parallel to the sealed document. In the second half of the twelfth century, this were frequently used in place of diplomas, which were still fairly uncommon. The review of the twelfth-century documents concerning Kazimierz's foundations and grants shows that such writs were used by monasteries (mainly Cistercian), which in the next century drew up formal forgeries of endowment from such dukes as Kazimierz or Mieszko III. In addition to these records, the abbeys kept various lists of goods and benefactors, whether in the form of *album*, *liber traditionum*, or lists of property. These were also used to fabricate diplomas in monastic *scriptoria*. With the increased use of documentation in the thirteenth century, the lack of legal evidence for the rights to the property acquired through grants and exchanges became evident, especially in monasteries. This was the main reason for the wave of forgeries (mainly formal ones) that passed through Polish monasteries at that time (led by Cistercian abbeys, such as Sulejów and Ląd). The period between the mid-twelfth century and the mid-thirteenth century saw an intensified development of local ducal chancelleries. Rare at the beginning of this period, royal documents were most often drawn up by the representatives of the recipients. In the thirteenth century, the ducal chancelleries had already become well-organised and were producing documents with a developed formulary, although the recipient's chancellery still retained the advantage.

The diplomatic material reveals that Kazimierz II was actively involved in the establishment and endowment of a considerable number of monastic and Church institutions, mainly in Kraków and Sandomierz territories. Kazimierz was one of the founders and benefactors of Cistercian monasteries (Sulejów, Jędrzejów, Wąchock) of the Kraków chapter (he was bound by ties of close political cooperation with the Bishops of Kraków); numerous canon institutions (Miechów, Trzemeszno, Czerwińsk); and finally Knights Hospitaller at Zagość. In many cases, he continued the work of others, suh as his brother Henryk, or showed his generosity towards the foundations established by bishops and the nobility, such as Jędrzejów and Wąchock. The Duke's efforts were also supported by the nobles from his closest circle: Lupus, Bishop of Płock; Gedko, Bishop of Kraków; Comes Radosław; or Knight Bałdrzych.

Among the dozens of documents discussed in this chapter, seven are undoubtedly forgeries, with this conclusion based mostly on earlier, authentic records. They are therefore reliable sources (in many cases the *only* sources) on which to found analysis of the activity of Kazimierz II as a patron and benefactor of religious foundations. The forgeries were most often honest; they were not intended to increase the number of privileges or land estates but to defend the property owned by a monastic centre. It is characteristic that the Cistercians of Sulejów resorted to forgery five times, while the Cistercian monks from Jędrzejów and Wąchock did so only once (one document was forged by canons regular from Trzemeszno), which would prove that the Polish branch of this order favoured documentary evidence in the court proceedings.

Among the issuers of the documents analysed here, Kazimierz II comes in as the leader, followed by his immediate successors Bolesław V, Leszek the White, and Konrad I of Mazovia. The Cistercian monasteries were most often the recipients of diplomas — sixteen documents in total. Most far-sighted in this matter were the monks from Sulejów, who obtained eleven documents. This would confirm the hypothesis presented above that the order attached great importance to securing legal evidence confirming their possessions. It also indicates that the Cistercians were significant contributors to the reception and development of the administrative document in Poland.[78]

The revision of the documentary sources for the scope of grants and foundations of Kazimierz II undertaken in this study allows the following propositions to be put forward:
1. The proposed date of the granting of the right to the tithes to Sulejów Abbey (10 August 1191);
2. An attempt to establish the date of the Jędrzejów forged document to the last months of 1167 and the indication that the endowments for the monastery were made in two phases;
3. An attempt to define a new time frame for Kazimierz's Zagość diploma;
4. The hypothesis linking the convention in Świerże Górne with the convention in Łęczyca in 1180;
5. A suggestion that Kazimierz II could not have granted the village of Tarszawa to the Cistercians of Jędrzejów.

That would be as much as critical consideration of the documents relating to Kazimierz as Church benefactor will allow to be said at this time.

---

78 Kętrzyński, *Zarys nauki o dokumencie*, p. 156.

CHAPTER 4

The Foundation of Łekno Abbey in the Context of Twelfth-Century Polish Cistercian Institutions*

The tenth and eleventh centuries brought but few monastic foundations in the Piast realm, all of which were, without exception, established by representatives of the ruling dynasty.[1] The twelfth century, however, effected considerable changes in this regard. Not only did the number of religious communities expand but so too did their forms, as well as the recruitment base of prospective founders. The Piast realm became home, in addition to the Benedictines, to the Cistercians, who also grew up from the rule of St Benedict of Nursia, and the canons regular of various provenance, rooted in the rule of St Augustine.[2] This period saw the collapse of the dynasty's monopoly on the founding of Church institutions or monastic and canon communities. The magnates and prelates began to follow the path marked out by the Piast dynasts.[3] It was then that such great founders as Piotr Włostowic and Jaksa of Miechów appeared on the stage.[4] Although the Piast dynasty still maintained a lead in the field of activities for the benefit of the Church and retained its position as its primary benefactor and protector, one of the most active orders in Christian Europe at that time, the Cistercians, was brought to Poland by Polish knighthood. Despite some speculation about the participation of the *princeps* Władysław II

---

* Original publication: Józef Dobosz, 'Założenie klasztoru w Łeknie na tle dwunastowiecznych fundacji cysterskich na ziemiach polskich', in *Cystersi łekneńscy w krajobrazie kulturowym ziem polskich w 850-lecie fundacji opactwa cysterskiego w Łeknie. 1153–2003*, ed. by Andrzej Marek Wyrwa (Wągrowiec: Wydawnictwo M-Druk, 2004), pp. 69–81.

1 These were most often Benedictine communities, see Derwich, *Monastycyzm benedyktyński*, from p. 175; Derwich, 'Fundacja lubińska', pp. 12–23; Derwich, 'Studia nad początkami monastycyzmu', pp. 77–105. The most important publication on the earliest monastic communities in Poland was written by Gerard Labuda, 'Szkice historyczne XI wieku', pp. 7–73; on its basis Derwich modified some of his views.

2 Research on the Cistercians in Poland has been recently systematised in MCP ii, pp. 394–501, which cites extensive scholarship. The canons regular have not been a subject of such a comprehensive study thus we necessarily refer to general surveys: Szymański, 'Kanonikat', pp. 356–59 and *Encyklopedia katolicka*. Among the monographs of individual abbeys see particularly Karczewski, *Dzieje klasztoru norbertanek w Strzelnie*, or Pobóg-Lenartowicz, *Uposażenie i działalność*. See also Mrozowicz, 'Kanonicy regularni', pp. 401–13.

3 For this issue see Dobosz, *Monarcha i możni*, pp. 250–92, 367–420.

4 Dobosz, *Monarcha i możni*, pp. 264–77, 368–86; Bieniak, 'Polska elita polityczna XII wieku, Part III A', pp. 13–107.

and his wife Agnes of Austria based on the interpretation of the extant sources, it seems certain that both the initiative and generosity in this regard came from Janik Gryfita, an unquestionably outstanding man of the Church, and Zbylut, a lay noble of the Pałuki clan.[5] Janik and Zbylut decided to bring the Grey Monks to their familial estates and made contact with the authorities of the Cistercian Order. (Here, it is perhaps necessary to note that in the Piast realm, the Cistercian monks became known as the Grey Monks because they wore habits made of undyed wool that distinguished them from the Black Monks, the Benedictines.) Judging from the texts of the foundation charters of Cistercian institutions they established, they must have worked together to realise their aspirations.[6]

Who of these two leading figures came up with the idea to bring the Cistercians to the Piast monarchy? Whether it was a faithful Janik Gryfita as the archbishop or a representative of the Pałuki clan is hard to say. Nor is it easy to provide a definite answer to the question of whether the abbey at Łekno, Pałuki or the abbey at Jędrzejów near Kielce is the older.[7] The most reasonable thing is to assume a simultaneous foundation initiative for Łekno and Jędrzejów. The turning point came in the spring of 1147, when each of the prospective Cistercian foundations was visited by, as it seems, Master Achard, probably the envoy of the general chapter of the Cistercians and also a student of Bernard of Clairvaux.[8] Achard came to Poland, then under the rule of the younger Piasts, as an emissary of St Bernard, most likely in order to promote the idea of the Second Crusade, though at the same time he also explored the possibility of Cistercian settlement in Łekno and Jędrzejów.[9]

Zbylut made his mark as a founder of ecclesiastical institutions even before the Cistercians were brought to Łekno in Pałuki. According to the

---

5 Wyrwa, 'Powstanie zakonu cystersów', in MCP i, pp. 37–38; Wyrwa, 'Rozprzestrzenianie się cystersów', pp. 46–48; Dobosz, 'Arcybiskup Janik i jego następcy', pp. 82–88; Dobosz, *Monarcha i możni*, pp. 387–89, 407–08; Dobosz, 'Dokument fundacyjny', pp. 70–72; Wyrwa, *Procesy fundacyjne*, pp. 60–64. See also Chapters 16 and 18 in this volume.

6 For the Łekno foundation charter see Dobosz, 'Dokument fundacyjny', pp. 53–55; Chapter 16 in this volume; Wyrwa and Strzelecka, *Dokument fundacyjny*, pp. 39–52. An analogous diploma for Jędrzejów can be found in KDM ii.372. For the analysis of these documents see also RPD i.53, 149, 150 (Łekno) and 55 (Jędrzejów). Both nobles are listed as witnesses to the charters, confirming their foundation of the Cistercian monastery and, in addition, Janik authenticated the Łekno charter with his archbishop's seal: *Iohanne sanctę Gneznesis ęcclesię uenerabili archipresule, cuius ętiam sigilli inpresione signatę sunt*, Dobosz, 'Dokument fundacyjny', p. 54.

7 Here, contrary to the unequivocal position of Wyrwa, who argues for the earlier chronology of Łekno. Compare also the slightly unclear position of Zdanek, 'Pierwsze opactwo', pp. 31–32, and Jurek's arguments relating to the date of Ląd's foundation, Jurek, 'Dokumenty fundacyjne', *Roczniki Historyczne*, 66 (2000), pp. 7–51.

8 Plezia, 'List biskupa Mateusza', pp. 123–40; cf. Dobosz, *Działalność fundacyjna*, pp. 135–39. Kürbis, 'Cystersi w kulturze polskiego', pp. 223–27; RPD i.43.

9 von Güttner-Sporzyński, *Poland, Holy War, and the Piast Monarchy*, pp. 162, 178–79.

account provided by the Mogilno forgery, he founded St James' Church in Mogilno, which he bestowed, together with the village of Boguszyno (today probably Baba), on the local Benedictines.[10] The settlement has not survived; according to the forged document, it is known to have been located in Mogilno, and therefore its remains most likely lie somewhere in the area of the former village of Mogilno, probably near the monastery.[11] A similar church, this time dedicated to St Peter, was built by Zbylut on the site of the former Łekno stronghold at the spot of an earlier eleventh-century rotunda, possibly with the intention of settling Grey Monks next to it.[12] Noteworthy are the apostolic patron saints of both churches founded by Zbylut, yet whether the twelfth-century church was a direct continuation of the Piast rotunda and it inherited its patron saint remains undetermined. Zbylut also served as witness to pious endowments made by others — such as the donation of Radziejów Stary to the Benedictines of Mogilno by Salomea of Berg, wife of Bolesław III — between October 1138 and July 1144.[13] It can be presumed that the 1130s, 1140s and early 1150s saw the peak of Zbylut's political activity and his association with the generation of Piotr Włostowic. Inspired by the activity of Bolesław III, his second wife Salomea, or the aforementioned comes Piotr of the Łabędzie clan, Zbylut established an independent and greater foundation in the early 1140s and, for reasons unknown to us today, his choice fell on the Cistercians.[14] Whether, as Władysław Semkowicz argued, the Archbishop of Gniezno (Jakub of Żnin, whom Semkowicz placed alongside Zbylut as a member of the Pałuki clan) played an inspiring role in this foundation is difficult to determine.[15] More obvious were relations between the Cistercians, the West and Jakub's successor in the archbishop's capital in Gniezno, Janik of the Gryfici family. Probably educated somewhere in the West, though clearly associated with the younger Piasts, Janik was firmly anchored in the politics of the time. His rapid progression through his Church career likely also contributed to broadening his horizons, and he is also known to have brought Grey Monks to his family estate in Brzeźnica. This undoubtedly makes him a more conceivable inspirer (or collaborator) for Zbylut than Archbishop Jakub, especially since everything points to the fact that it was Janik who dictated

---

10 *Ecclesiam sancti Iacobi in Mogilna quam fundavit Sbyluth miles, addens eidem ecclesie hereditatem Bogussino cum consesu amicorum suorum*, KDW i.3; RPD i.8; Kürbis, 'Najstarsze dokumenty', pp. 27–61; Bieniak, 'Polska elita polityczna XII wieku, Part III B', p. 28 and note 88. Cf. Dobosz, *Monarcha i możni*, pp. 140, 300. The information contained in the document can be considered reliable and it must be assumed that it refers to the period directly following the exile of Władysław II (the spring of 1146).
11 For more detail see Dobosz, *Monarcha i możni*, pp. 281–82.
12 Wyrwa, *Procesy fundacyjne*, pp. 69–71; Wyrwa, 'Badania archeologiczno-architektoniczne', from p. 109; cf. Wyrwa, *Badania archeologiczno-architektoniczne*, from p. 109.
13 For Salomea's diploma see KDW i.9, and for its analysis see RPD i.38.
14 On the title of *comes* (later to be replaced by castellan) see Bogucki, *Komes w polskich źródłach średniowiecznych*.
15 Semkowicz, *Ród Pałuków*, pp. 38, 50.

and issued a foundation charter for the Cistercians of Łekno, affixing his own archbishop's seal despite Zbylut having formal role as the issuer.[16]

Eventually, after a dozen or so years of preparation, the Cistercians arrived in Łekno sometime around 1153 and in this year received a charter confirming the foundation of a new monastic institution.[17] Zbylut, its founder and protector, granted the new religious community a part of his free patrimony (for which he probably did not have to seek permission) in the form of the villages of Rgielsko, Straszewo, and Panigródź. He likely also added the area of the former Łekno stronghold with St Peter's Church, a marketplace, and a tavern in the village of Łekno (on the other side of Lake Łekneńskie), as well as Lake Rgielskie.[18] Thus, the Cistercians were placed within an established infrastructure from the outset: they obtained a seat with a church and most likely provisional monastery buildings from the founder, and secured the bases of their material existence, which was confirmed by the foundation charter. The process of the new abbey's foundation, it can be assumed, was completed but, according to the analysis of the foundation charter, this view must be slightly modified. Around the seal affixed to the presumed original of the charter, the so-called Poznań original, there is an annotation imitating the original *ductus* and enumerating grants offered to the abbey after 1153, mainly by the magnates.[19] The *princeps* Bolesław IV heads the list of benefactors with his donation of the village of Mątwy. Following that, we read of Przecław (possibly Pomian), who offered the village of Głojkowo; Prędota (undoubtedly of the Odrowąż Clan), who granted the village of Wierzenica; Przedwój (Awdaniec), who gave the village of Łoskuń; and Brodzisław, who endowed the village of Oleszno (Olesno). Next, is Zbylut's unnamed wife (*uxor Zbiluti*), identified in the Łekno-Wągrowiec obituary as Zofia, who donated the villages of Gościsław (Gościsławie) and Kaczkowo; Zbylut's sons gave Pokrzywnica and his brothers Piotr and Sławnik gave Mokronosy. Finally, Ogierz of the Poraj Clan or Niałek-Jeleń Clan gave the village of Turza, and Filip (a Cistercian) granted Dębogóra.[20] In addition to the immovable property already granted by Zbylut after 1153, Łekno Abbey

---

16 The document contains *intitulatio*: ego Zbilud Polonię ciuis, but below this read: Iohanne ... cuius ętiam sigilli inpressione signatę sunt hęc litterę sub priuilegiali cautione. See Chapter 16 of this volume for the text of the charter.

17 For an extensive study on the foundation process of Łekno Abbey see Wyrwa, *Procesy fundacyjne*, pp. 53–59 and other works by this author, particularly 'Łekno-Wągrowiec', in MCP ii, pp. 230–50.

18 Dobosz, 'Dokument fundacyjny', pp. 54, 80–83; Chapter 16 in this volume. See also Przybysz, 'Fundacja i pierwotne', pp. 56–72; Wyrwa, *Procesy fundacyjne*, pp. 74–76; Wyrwa, 'Łekno-Wągrowiec', pp. 231–33.

19 Dobosz, 'Dokument fundacyjny', pp. 54, 80–83; Chapter 16 in this volume; Wyrwa, *Procesy fundacyjne*, from p. 23.

20 Dobosz, 'Dokument fundacyjny', pp. 55, 62–65. For the identification of villages and people see Wyrwa, *Procesy fundacyjne*, pp. 47–50; Dobosz, 'Dokument fundacyjny', pp. 78–80; Chapter 16 in this volume, especially table 5.

received eleven more villages, one of them from Bolesław IV. The founder's immediate family added at least four villages from their family estates, while others were donated by other representatives of the Polish nobility.

The annotation on the Poznań original also contains a list of tithes received by the monastery: Bartodzieje, Słosin (Słosim), Bukowiec, Dąbrowa (Dambrouici), Slachowo (Załachowo, Załachów, Słuchowo?), Danabórz, Ochodza, Morakowo, Bliskowice, Łekno, Czerlin, Koninek, Krosno, Mokronosy and Pokrzywnica. This amounts to a total of fifteen tithe villages, but who granted them is unknown. According to the extended version of the annotation on the late twelfth-century imitation copy, three of these — Czerlin, Mokronosy and Pokrzywnica — were given to the monastery by Piotr, Archbishop of Gniezno.[21]

Assuming that the three tithe villages were granted to Łekno Abbey by Archbishop Piotr (in office around 1190 to August 1198), others must have given by one of his predecessors, Bogumił, Zdzisław or Janik.[22] The most probable hypothesis holds that Janik Gryfita was the mysterious benefactor. Janik was a close ally of Zbylut, who offered a similar endowment to the Cistercian monastery at Brzeźnica/Jędrzejów that he had established. We know almost nothing about Zdzisław's activities; Bogumił was probably his successor and a direct predecessor of Piotr. He is known mainly for giving the Cistercians his own property around Dobrowo to support their Christianisation mission in Prussia.[23] While the identity of the benefactor remains open to debate, it must be emphasised that these fifteen tithes perfectly complemented previous or parallel donations of villages, lakes or income. The name of an abbot who administered Łekno Abbey sometime after 1153 is known, however, appearing for the first time in the Jędrzejów forgeries, which describe authentic events unfolding around the autumn of 1167.[24] In these we find a witness listed alongside the other abbots of the Polish Benedictine and Cistercian monasteries, as *Simon abbas de Lukna*.[25] Whether this Szymon was the first superior of the house of Grey Monks in Łekno is again difficult to ascertain. The foundation charter overlooks all names of the Cistercians residing at Łekno, and other sources are silent in this respect. It can therefore be assumed that, if Szymon was the first abbot of the Cistercian outpost in Pałuki, it was he who brought his confreres to Poland and that he managed the monastery for at least a dozen years.

---

21 Dobosz, 'Dokument fundacyjny', p. 55; Wyrwa, *Procesy fundacyjne*, pp. 51–52 for the identification of the villages.

22 Dobosz, 'Arcybiskup Janik', pp. 92–94; Chapter 18 in this volume.

23 Dobosz, 'Arcybiskup Janik', pp. 88–92; Chapter 18 in this volume.

24 Bieniak dates the events related to the Jędrzejów convention on the occasion of the consecration of the local Cistercian church to 2 February 1168, Bieniak 'Polska elita polityczna XII wieku, Part III C', pp. 44–45). In my opinion, they took place in the autumn of 1167; the documents relating to these events were drawn up as late as the thirteenth century. Dobosz, *Działalność fundacyjna*, pp. 25–28; Dobosz, 'Trzynastowieczne falsyfikaty', pp. 225–37.

25 Semkowicz, 'Nieznane nadania', pp. 69–70; KDM ii.374.

In summary, the new monastery was founded on Zbylut's initiative, although we need to emphasise his collaboration with Archbishop Janik and perhaps the inspiring role of other noble founders of that time, such as Zbylut's contemporary, Piotr Włostowic. Thus, Zbylut initiated work that lasted nearly 700 years, and its existence commenced with the not very generous, though promising, grant of four villages, a lake, a marketplace and a tavern, a church and an old Łekno stronghold, which he designated as the seat of a new monastery. It seems that, after the death of the founder, the abbey's original grants were multiplied, perhaps on the initiative of his family members, by the addition of eleven villages and fifteen tithes (before the 1190s). Such additional endowments can be regarded as at least enough to provide sufficient economic bases for the Cistercian monks residing at Łekno.

The foundation of the Łekno community of Grey Monks did not turn out to be an exception in the areas ruled by the Piast dukes. We know that Janik of the Gryfici clan decided to bring the Cistercians to his family estate in Brzeźnica in Sandomierz territory at the same time as Zbylut began his patronage of the order. The foundation process of the abbey was fairly extended, beginning in the 1140s as evidenced by the first records in the Polish annals.[26] It seems that it was still not completed when Janik issued a foundation charter in 1153, but rather as late as in 1167 when the monastery church was consecrated. The consecration was celebrated with a great gathering, attended by Mieszko III and Kazimierz II with their sons, as well as noble clergy and laity. That is why the source literature equates this solemn consecration convention, organised by Archbishop Janik, with a rebellion against the *princeps* Bolesław IV.[27] Regardless of the political overtone of the Jędrzejów meeting of dukes and nobles, most important for the new Cistercian community were its effects in the form of numerous grants of estate, tithes and income. Prior to 1153, the Cistercians received the original *fundum* centred around Brzeźnica/Jędrzejów, which consisted of eight villages and sixteen tithes.[28] We can see right away that Janik's generosity (and the economic possibilities) was enormous, more than twice that offered by Zbylut. In 1167, the founder significantly enlarged these estates, adding sixteen more villages and nineteen tithes, some of the latter given by Janik in his capacity as the Archbishop of Gniezno, the rest obtained from Gedko, Bishop of Kraków.[29] In total, the Cistercians received twenty-four villages and thirty-five tithes during the process of its foundation, and this was complemented by salt grants offered by Mieszko III and Kazimierz II

---

26 Dobosz, 'Proces fundacyjny', pp. 40–79. Cf. Zdanek, 'Pierwsze opactwo', pp. 31–32, and so-called Cistercian sources collected by Janauschek, *Originum cisterciensium*, p. 117. See also Winter, *Die Cistercienser* i, p. 332.
27 Bieniak, 'Polska elita polityczna XII wieku, Part III C', pp. 31–52. Cf. Dobosz, *Monarcha i możni*, pp. 301–02.
28 The foundation charter of Jędrzejów Abbey: KDM ii.372; Dobosz, 'Proces fundacyjny', pp. 56–58, 66.
29 Dobosz, 'Proces fundacyjny', pp. 58–62, 66.

(Wieliczka, customs house in Sandomierz),[30] fiscal immunity of unknown scope, a marketplace in Jędrzejów, and a number of serfs.[31]

Thus, with the space of a little over ten years Janik had constructed a powerful centre of communal life and endowed it with considerable goods, enabling its self-sufficient economic functioning. He also organised grants for his foundation from both princes and Gedko, Bishop of Kraków (perhaps also Radost). Dedicated, importantly, to St Adalbert and the Blessed Virgin Mary, Jędrzejów Abbey received extraordinary endowment and was well anchored within the political landscape of the mid twelfth century, no doubt at least in part due to the prominent role and position of its founder.

The first two Cistercian foundations in Poland were thus the work of noble clergy and laity from local family clans boasting a long tradition (the Pałuki, the Gryfici). The Piast dynasty barely supported the monasteries in Łekno and Brzeźnica/Jedrzejów, having granted merely one village to the former (Bolesław IV),[32] and immunity, the proceeds from the marketplace, and salt to the latter.[33] The situation changed only in the 1170s, when the Piasts increased their support for the Cistercians. A major breakthrough came, perhaps, with the activities of Bolesław the Tall, the Duke of Silesia, son of Władysław II, and with those of the youngest of the Bolesław III's sons, Kazimierz II. They were the first representatives of the ruling dynasty to establish new settlements of Grey Monks on their estates.

Bolesław the Tall must have taken the decision to bring the Cistercians to Lubiąż before 1175, because that is the year in which the monastery obtained a foundation charter from him.[34] Whether the new monastery of Grey Monks was erected on the site where the Benedictine monks had previously had their outpost is hard to say.[35] Perhaps after an unsuccessful attempt to settle the Black Monks in Lubiąż, Bolesław opted for the Cistercian chapter. In any case, the new abbey was settled by monks who had already arrived from Pforta by 1175.[36] In light of the foundation charter, the new community received the original *fundum* in the form of sixteen villages, four of which

---

30 Dobosz, 'Proces fundacyjny', p. 62. See also J. Grzesiowski and Piotrowicz, 'Sól małopolska w nadaniach', pp. 84–85; Semkowicz, 'Nieznane nadania', pp. 69–70; Wyrozumski, *Państwowa gospodarka solna*, and Keckowa, *Saliny ziemi krakowskiej*.

31 Semkowicz, 'Nieznane nadania', pp. 69–70; Dobosz, 'Proces fundacyjny', pp. 62–64. For discussion of the serfs of Tarszawa, given by Kazimierz II see KDM i.32, and Dobosz, *Działalność fundacyjna*, pp. 30, 33–34, 66.

32 Dobosz, 'Dokument fundacyjny', p. 55.

33 See Semkowicz, 'Nieznane nadania', pp. 69–70.

34 KDŚ i.55. For analysis of the act see RPD i.74, pp. 78–81, and Matuszewski, 'Jeszcze o treści dokumentu', pp. 171–85. Accounts of the monastery's origins have been compiled in Dobosz, *Monarcha i możni*, pp. 360–62 and Harc, Harc and Łużyniecka, 'Lubiąż', in MCP ii, pp. 202–03. Cf. Wielgosz, *Wielka własność cysterska*.

35 Derwich, *Monastycyzm benedyktyński*, p. 184; Derwich, 'Zarys dziejów benedyktynów', pp. 444, notes 67–75, p. 439, note 31. Cf. Harc, Harc and Łużyniecka, 'Lubiąż', p. 202.

36 See Harc, Harc and Łużyniecka, 'Lubiąż', pp. 201–02; KDŚ i.55.

were granted by Bolesław the Tall himself, and the others by nobles whose estates were located in Silesia. The land endowments were complemented by the grants of three churches with income, immunity, people and income from crossings, slaughterhouses, taverns, and other such benefits.[37] By 1201 (the protection bull), the Cistercians of Lubiąż acquired a further nine villages and significant lands on the Stradunia and Osobłoga rivers.[38] The donations of villages and incomes were accompanied by tithes from a further nine villages.[39] All this considered, the Cistercian abbey at Lubiąż was a considerable royal foundation, only slightly smaller than Brzeźnica/Jędrzejów, with a clear admixture of patronage from the Silesian nobility. During Bolesław I's lifetime, comfortable living conditions were created for the new monastic community, along with which came promising prospects for its future development.

Most likely acting only a little later than Bolesław I, the youngest of Bolesław III's sons, Kazimierz II, took the initiative to bring the Cistercians to the duchy he ruled. Kazimierz's endeavours to bring a convent of the Grey Monks to Sulejów on the Pilica River probably began right after he strengthened his political position in the Sandomierz territories, but some time before the coup d'état of 1177 that brought him to the throne of Kraków.[40] It seems likely that 1176 was the turning point; this year appears on the forged foundation charter of Sulejów Abbey.[41] If the information provided by another forgery, drawn up before the mid-thirteenth century and bearing the year 1178, is to be trusted, the convent must have been established on the Pilica in 1177 at the latest, because in 1178 the monks exchanged villages in order to consolidate land holdings.[42] The foundation process of the new abbey must have stretched over quite some time, ending only after Mieszko III's unsuccessful attempt to seize Kraków in 1191, and most likely related to the subsequent settlement between the brothers Kazimierz II and Mieszko III. It was then, perhaps, that Mieszko III enriched the foundation of his younger

---

37 See KDŚ i.55 and Harc, Harc and Łużyniecka, 'Lubiąż', *Lubiąż*, pp. 203–04; Dobosz and Wyrwa, 'Działalność gospodarcza cystersów', in MCP i, pp. 203–04 (Table). Cf. Wielgosz, 'Początki wielkiej własności', pp. 61–124. For discussion of the church grants, see Dobosz, 'Kościół jako element', pp. 190–92.

38 KDŚ i.86 (Bull of Pope Innocent III of 10 August 1201).

39 KDŚ i.55 (1175) and KDŚ i.86 (1201); Wielgosz, 'Początki wielkiej własności', pp. 113–14.

40 Dobosz, *Działalność fundacyjna*, pp. 30, 33–34, 66; Dobosz, *Kazimierz II Sprawiedliwy*.

41 The most accurate text of the forgery is given in Mitkowski, *Początki klasztoru cystersów*, pp. 313–15, with discussion of the forgery itself at pp. 3–14. See also Dobosz, *Działalność fundacyjna*, p. 19; Dobosz, 'Trzynastowieczne falsyfikaty', p. 225; Chapter 14 in this volume.

42 This involved the exchange of the villages of Cienia and Ścibor, most likely granted by Kazimierz, for Straszów, which in turn was exchanged for the villages of Skąpice and Tomisławice. For the most accurate version of the document dated 1178 see Mitkowski, *Początki klasztoru cystersów*, pp. 315–16. For analysis of the text see pp. 35–49; Dobosz, *Działalność fundacyjna*, p. 19; Dobosz, 'Trzynastowieczne falsyfikaty', p. 225.

brother with endowments,[43] and that Piotr of the Łabędzie clan — the Archbishop of Gniezno and mediator in concluding the settlement — granted tithes to the monastery.[44] Between 1176 and 1191, the monastery of Sulejów received the original endowment, which consisted in total of fourteen villages (and farmsteads, the so-called *źreby*), one village granted in 1191, twelve tithe villages, two churches in Bałdrzychów, and probably the church of St Blaise in Sulejów, which is non extant. The grants of lands and tithes were supplemented by rich gifts — a marketplace in Sulejów, beavers, and salt from Sandomierz and Wieliczka — extensive immunity, and serfs.[45] Most of the immovable grants were offered by Kazimierz II, but he was greatly assisted by comes Radosław, who donated five villages along the Ner River; a knight named Bałdrzych, who gave a village called Bałdrzychów (with a church); and Mieszko III who gave a village later called Milejów.[46] The tithe was granted by Archbishop Piotr, known to us from an analogous grant for Łekno.[47]

Sulejów was thus a significant dynastic foundation that also enjoyed extensive support from the nobility. The individual who inspired Kazimierz II to establish the abbey and the reasons behind his decision to do so remain unclear.[48] In any case, as a result of the initiative and generosity of an important representative of the Piast dynasty at that time, the Cistercians of Morimond, Burgundy came to Sulejów on the Pilica River, and took over large and ostensibly well-organised estates. In the decades that followed, out of the property they had received from their founder, they constructed one of the largest Cistercian institutions in Poland.[49]

---

43 The grants endowed by Mieszko III are mentioned in the forgery dated 1178, where we read: *Contuli etiam Mileo et f[ratres] eius cum hereditate eorum [S]uemingala quoque et fratres eius cum hereditate eorum de voluntate et consensu fratris mei Mesconis*. Mitkowski, *Początki klasztoru cystersów*, p. 315.

44 A document relating to these tithes, forged in the name of Archbishop of Gniezno, is dated 10 August 1176, KDW i.587 (21a). For discussion of the forgery, see Mitkowski, *Początki klasztru cystersów*, pp. 32–35 and Dobosz, *Działalność fundacyjna*, p. 19; Dobosz, 'Trzynastowieczne falsyfikaty', p. 225; Chapter 14 in this volume.

45 For more detail on the endowment for Sulejów Abbey, see Mitkowski, *Początki klasztoru cystersów*, pp. 163–201 and Dobosz, *Działalność fundacyjna*, pp. 66–74; Dobosz, 'Okoliczności i motywy', pp. 177–87.

46 For discussion of Radosław and Bałdrzych's grants see Dobosz, 'Okoliczności i motywy', pp. 177–87; Chapter 6 in this volume. Cf. the discussion of the forged foundation charter in Mitkowski, *Początki klasztoru cystersów*, p. 314. For the detailed outline of the life of Radosław see Bieniak, 'Polska elita polityczna XII w., Part III C', pp. 21–23; Bieniak, 'Polska elita polityczna XII wieku, Part III D', pp. 24–25 and Dobosz, *Działalność fundacyjna*, pp. 186–93.

47 See KDW i.587 (21a).

48 Cf. Dobosz, *Działalność fundacyjna*, pp. 127–57 (chapter Motywy i okoliczności działań fundacyjnych księcia Kazimierza).

49 Mitkowski, *Początki klasztoru cystersów*, pp. 202–87; Dobosz, 'Kryzys w opactwie cysterskim', pp. 133–46.

Among the early Cistercian foundations in the territories subordinate to the Piasts, the outpost in Ląd on the Warta River is another story. This is mainly due to problems with written records. Virtually all early monastic documents are forgeries,[50] and the information provided by so-called Cistercian sources, often drawn up outside Poland, tend to confuse the picture rather than provide unambiguous answers.[51] We can say with certainty that Mieszko III launched the initiative to bring the Cistercians to Ląd, although it is possible that he only made the local Cistercian outpost independent, where it had previously been subordinate to Łekno. Earlier research on the origins of the Cistercian convent at Ląd has since been competently compiled and examined, so there is little need to go over the analyses again.[52] There are two competing hypotheses on the dating of the foundation, with Andrzej Wyrwa's pointing to the 1170s,[53] and Tomasz Jurek's giving a more exact date for the foundation: 17 or 18 March 1146.[54] I am not convinced by Tomasz Jurek's arguments, however, despite his erudite presentation of the argument and the use (partially at least) of so-called Cistercian sources that date to a notably later period. The spring of 1146 witnessed the initial stages of the foundation processes of the two oldest Polish Cistercian abbeys, Łekno and Jędrzejów. The younger Piasts had just emerged victorious from the battle for power over the legacy of Bolesław III and did not engage in these undertakings. Mieszko III himself was busy with the process of buttressing the canons regular of Trzemeszno and granting the village of Lusowo to the Church of Poznań.[55]

Mieszko III did not materially support the Zbylut foundation in Łekno, neither do we observe his interest in other Church institutions at that time (apart from those mentioned above). It seems that Mieszko turned to the Cistercians only when he held the dignity of the *princeps*, and probably under the influence

---

50   See RPD, by dates: 1145, 1173, 1181, 1186, 1188, 1174; Jurek, 'Dokumenty fundacyjne', pp. 7–51; Wyrwa, *Procesy fundacyjne*, pp. 83–86, 110–18.

51   These written records were collected and used in Leopold Janauschek's foundational work on the history of the Cistercian Order, *Originum cisterciensium*, in which see pp. 90, 291, 318 for Ląd. Cf. Winter, *Die Cistercienser* i, pp. 81, 332, 336, 342; ii, pp. 383–84. These contain written records drawn up sometime between the thirteenth and eighteenth centuries in various Cistercian circles, with a predominance of modern accounts, distant from the times they describe. They have never been subjected to a comprehensive study, neither has the full relationship between them been established and it seems that in such a case priority should be given to native sources.

52   See Wyrwa, *Procesy fundacyjne*, p. 83; Wyrwa, 'Ląd', in MCP ii, p. 190; cf. Jurek, 'Dokumenty fundacyjne', p. 7; Waraczewski, *Proces fundacyjny*, pp. 151–68.

53   Wyrwa, *Procesy fundacyjne*, p. 83; Wyrwa, 'Ląd', p. 190.

54   Jurek, 'Dokumenty fundacyjne', from p. 7.

55   The engagement of Mieszko III in patronage has not been a subject of comprehensive analysis; neither the studies of Stanisław Smolka nor Maciej Przybył meet these are sufficient for this purpose. Smolka, *Mieszko Stary i jego wiek*; Przybył, *Mieszko III Stary*. Some consideration on the topic was given in Piechowicz, 'Działalność fundacyjno-donacyjna'. See also Dobosz, *Monarcha i możni*, pp. 344–55, on the donations of Mieszko III to the Church in Poznań and the monastery in Trzemeszno.

of the foundation initiatives of Bolesław I and Kazimierz II, thus only after 1173, or even as late as 1175. Probably then, as *dux totius Poloniae*, the suzerain of Poland, he sought to raise his prestige with a new and large Church foundation. Unfortunately, there is nothing certain that we know about this, although it must be acknowledged that, at the time of the competition for the Kraków throne, the Cistercian Charter could have proved a useful tool. Perhaps it was then that Mieszko III attempted to establish a new Cistercian outpost on the basis of the already established Łekno, but the events of 1177–1179 (his removal from Kraków and expulsion from Wielkopolska) must have seriously shaken this initiative. Mieszko might have returned to it after 1181, when he regained control over Wielkopolska. We can cautiously conclude that, on Mieszko's initiative, the settlement in Ląd had initially been a branch of Łekno or that, as a result of Mieszko's removal, Łekno Abbey administered Ląd after 1177. The establishment of the new abbey was probably not very successful, since in 1191 it was earmarked for closure by the general chapter of the Cistercians.[56] It was only this threat of closure that motivated Mieszko III to more vigorous action. He sent a petition to the religious authorities in defence of the monastery, as a result of which the earlier decision was cancelled.[57] The abbey survived, perhaps also thanks to the participation of Piotr, Archbishop of Gniezno, who donated tithes from three villages as compensation for Łekno, as the Cistercians of Łekno were forced to give up their rights to Ląd.[58]

The above construction is a mere hypothesis that seeks to position the foundation of the Ląd monastery in a wider historical context. It can also be supported by the fact that Mieszko III only became deeply engaged in the activities of the Church in Poland in the second phase of his reign, once he had assumed the principate and faced the challenge of retaining it. Previously, his activities had been purely *ad hoc* or focused on the preparation of his position to set out for Kraków and make his claim on the principate. Ultimately, therefore, we must accept that the monastery at Ląd originated in the 1170s, retaining ties with Łekno in the first phase and, once having gained its independence, with Cologne (Altenberg). At first, Mieszko endowed his foundation with few villages, but later granted rights to a further fifteen estates.[59] The abbey's early endowment was thus comparable to that of Łekno, but generally smaller than the foundation of Bolesław I or Kazimierz II.

The end of the twelfth century brought fresh Cistercian noble foundations, this time in Małopolska (Lesser Poland, *Polonia Minor*). A close associate of Kazimierz II, Gedko of the Powała clan and Bishop of Kraków, brought the Cistercians to the property of the Kraków bishopric.[60] Around 1179, he handed

---

56 Canivez, ed., *Statuta Capitulorum Generalium* i, p. 137.
57 Canivez, ed., *Statuta Capitulorum Generalium* i, p. 168.
58 Trawkowski, 'Piotr', in PSB xxvi, pp. 361–62.
59 Wyrwa, *Procesy fundacyjne*, from p. 110; Wyrwa, 'Ląd', p. 190.
60 Dobosz, *Działalność fundacyjna*, pp. 161–72; Dobosz, *Monarcha i możni*, pp. 414–15.

over a few villages (as farmsteads, *źreby*) to the Grey Monks, a large amount of the Radom Forest in the vicinity of Wąchock, as well as tithes from nearly twenty villages.[61] Kazimierz endowed the new institution with immunity.[62] However, this initially modest foundation received such significant economic stimulus from the Polish nobles and the *princeps* Leszek the White in the first decades of the thirteenth century that it became one of the most important monastic communities in the Sandomierz territories.[63]

Another nobleman from Małopolska, Mikołaj of the Bogoria clan, settled Cistercians in his village of Koprzywnica, probably in 1185. The founder handed over vast goods to the new community (twelve villages),[64] while Kazimierz II granted considerable immunity waivers.[65] Pełka, Bishop of Kraków, added extensive tithes from eight villages[66] and thus the new Cistercian community gained a strong economic foundation, with lands extending as far as Jasło in the Podkarpacie region. Both abbeys in Małopolska benefited from the engagement of the *princeps* Kazimierz II in the patronage of ecclesiastical foundations, and their founders were his close associates. Apart from bearing the invocation of Blessed Virgin Mary, the monastic churches of both communities were dedicated St Florian, a saint whose relics were brought to Kraków by Kazimierz and the Bishop Gedko in 1184, most likely as part of the promulgation of the new cult.[67]

In addition to the princes and the Polish nobility, two new dynasties that had just developed or were just emerging in the northern fringes of the Piast hegemony expressed interest in the Cistercians. All the Grey monastic foundations discussed so far were directly or indirectly anchored in Morimond Abbey. It was different in Pomerania, where we see the emergence of intermediate branches of the great abbey of Clairvaux via Denmark (Esrøm).[68] This was most likely related to Denmark's increased political activity in the area during the reign of King Valdemar I, and the desire to free the local dynasties from the incumbent overlordship of the Piast dukes. At the time,

---

61 For analysis of the foundation and endowment of Wąchock Abbey, see Dobosz, 'Wokół fundatora', pp. 37–49 and Chapter 7 in this volume, which puts forward the theory that the monastery was founded by Otto of Wierzbica. See also Dobosz and Wetesko, 'Wąchock', in MCP ii, pp. 329–31; Niwiński, *Opactwo cystersów w Wąchocku*, pp. 35–38, 42–45. That Bishop Gedko granted tithes was further supported by Jan Długosz, LB iii, pp. 417–20.
62 See Dobosz, *Działalność fundacyjna*, pp. 75–76.
63 For the text and analysis of the forged 1260 document, see Niwiński, *Opactwo cystersów w Wąchocku*, pp. 158–60; 42–45; cf. Dobosz, 'Wokół fundatora', pp. 46–48; Chapter 7 in this volume.
64 Wdowiszewski, 'Ród Bogoriów', from p. 2; see also Kozłowska-Budkowa and Szczur, 'Dzieje opactwa cystersów'; Dobosz and Wetesko, 'Koprzywnica', in MCP ii, pp. 150–51.
65 See Dobosz, *Działalność fundacyjna*, pp. 78–80.
66 Jan Długosz, LB iii, p. 376; see also Dobosz and Wetesko, 'Koprzywnica', p. 151; Dobosz, *Działalność fundacyjna*, p. 176; Kozłowska-Budkowa and Szczur, 'Dzieje opactwa cystersów'.
67 Dobosz, *Działalność fundacyjna*, pp. 86–90.
68 Wyrwa, 'Powstanie zakonu cystersów', pp. 27–54.

the West Pomeranian Duke Wartislaw II decided to bring the Cistercians to his estate in Kołbacz, probably in 1173. It was, however, actually his successor, Bogusław I, who organised the foundation.[69] In the course of the foundation process, between 1173 and 1185, the new monastery received twelve villages (the thirteenth was bought by the Cistercians themselves), fifteen tithe villages, as well as extensive immunity and monopolies (customs, forests, taverns).[70] These were relatively generous donations that put Kołbacz Abbey on an equal footing with Lubiąż or Sulejów; in terms of economic bases, it was inferior only to Jędrzejów in Małopolska.

The other Pomeranian foundation, the monastery at Oliwa, was the work of the emerging East Pomeranian dynasty of Sobiesław. It seems that it was founded by Duke Sambor I, although the foundation charter dated 18 March 1178 (probably forged) points to Sobiesław.[71] Contrary to some claims,[72] the case that Oliwa Abbey received the confirmation of Kazimierz II, or that he had any other form of participation in its founding, is unconvincing. The influence of the *princeps* in the 1180s did not reach so far north. The Oliwa foundation should rather be considered as an independent initiative of the Pomeranian Sobiesławowice, who sought to subject the entire Pomeranian region to their power and, through such actions, attempted to strengthen their position and prestige. Oliwa Abbey, which it is worth emphasising in the context of the above-mentioned argument, became a branch of the young Kołbacz Abbey, unrelated to Kazimierz II. It received six villages, an extensive immunity, and monopolies (tithes from taverns, customs duties, the right to fish) as the primary endowment.[73] Compared to the previously considered endowment of the monasteries in Lubiąż, Jędrzejów, Sulejów or Kołbacz, the donations appear frankly mediocre.

The twelfth century brought major changes for the Church in the lands ruled by the Piasts; the introduction of new institutions of common life, particularly the Cistercians, undoubtedly ranked among the most important of them. Nine Cistercian abbeys in total were established in Poland, including seven in the lands under Piast rule. The other two were established in the area more loosely connected with the Piast realm, where two new ducal dynasties, the Houses of Griffin and Sobiesław, were maturing. The new foundations were probably motivated by a collection of religious, political, economic and cultural reasons, of which only the devotional aspect is fully

---

69 Jarzewicz and Rymar, 'Kołbacz', in MCP ii, pp. 136–37, and the now-classic study, Chłopocka, *Powstanie i rozwój*.
70 See Chłopocka, *Powstanie i rozwój*; Jarzewicz and Rymar, 'Kołbacz', pp. 150–51; Wyrwa and Dobosz, 'Działalność gospodarcza', pp. 203–04.
71 Perlbach, *Pommerellisches Urkundenbuch* 6, and for its analysis see RPD i, pp. 92–93. Cf. Dekański and Wetesko, 'Oliwa', in MCP ii, pp. 268–70, which provides overview of the historiographical debate on the authenticity of the foundation charter for Oliwa.
72 For example, Śliwiński, 'Na marginesie fundacyjnej', pp. 174–75.
73 Dekański and Wetesko, 'Oliwa', p. 270.

readable in the sources.[74] Most important, however, is the fact that, in the Piast state — on the verge of fragmentation into districts — the social and economic situation had matured enough for new religious communities to obtain generous founders and benefactors not only among dynasts, but also the economically and politically braced nobility. Individuals sought to receive the newcomers, most often from the West, and to establish appropriate conditions for their development, and those newcomers wanted to settle in areas located far beyond the Elbe.

All seven abbeys established in the territories under the direct control of the Piasts were related to Morimond; four of them were founded by the noble clergy and laity (most of them received family goods that could be alienated). The remaining three benefited from the generosity of the Piasts (sometimes receiving additional grants from the nobles), whose interest in the Cistercians increased starting from the 1160s. We note an interesting geographical aspect of abbeys of Grey Monks at the time: two were located in Wielkopolska (Łekno, Ląd), three in Sandomierz (Jędrzejów, Wąchock, Koprzywnica), one in Silesia (Lubiąż), and one on the border of Małopolska and Central Poland (Sulejów). One monastery was founded in Western Pomerania and one in Pomerelia. At that time, the Cistercian foundations did not cross the Vistula line, and only Koprzywnica Abbey owned estates beyond this border. One of the two oldest monasteries in Poland (along with Jędrzejów), Łekno Abbey could not have originally been counted among the wealthiest foundations. Considering the Polish realities, Łekno Abbey should be considered a medium-sized, yet promising institution that reached its peaked in the thirteenth century. The monastery at Jędrzejów was without doubt the wealthiest of the Cistercian Abbeys in the Piast realm.

Several new phenomena found their way into Poland with the Cistercians. It should be acknowledged that they were among the pioneers of the administrative document in the Piast state and, consequently, of the introduction of new legal formulae. The situation was similar with the new patterns of architecture that accompanied the monastic houses, although this phenomenon is more fully noticeable in the thirteenth century. The Grey Monks also brought tried and tested models of organisation, not only internal, related to *vita contemplativa*, but also economic organisation. Contrary to what has been previously believed, the Cistercians were not pioneers of settlement but settled in developed areas. And yet, they were among the first to employ new economic patterns, such as land consolidation, exchange or sale of estates or mining, and introduced the Magdeburg rights in their estates (the founding of villages and, from the thirteenth century, towns). The Cistercians quickly blended into local society and the cultural mosaic, becoming a permanent element and leaving their mark on the regional landscape.

---

74   Dobosz, *Działalność fundacyjna*, pp. 127–57. Cf. Wyrwa, *Procesy fundacyjne*, pp. 168–78, and also R. Michałowski, *Princeps-fundator*.

CHAPTER 5

The Foundation Process and the Early Endowment of Jędrzejów Abbey*

Research on the history of the Cistercian Order and its convents in Poland has a long record, one that starts in the mid-nineteenth century.[1] Although scholars were fairly quick to notice that the foundation of a monastery was not a one-off event but a dynamic process that stretched over time,[2] there was an observable tendency in Polish historiography to present the foundation of a monastery or Church institution as a static event. A number of Cistercian abbeys were made the subject of valuable monographs, but the state of research on the foundation processes remained far from satisfactory. This was due to the lack of any theoretical models or indisputable written records for the earliest history of the Cistercian abbeys in Poland, especially those established in the twelfth century. A breakthrough came in the mid-twentieth century in the form of a paper written by Józefa Zawadzka, in which she comprehensively laid out the principles underlying the foundation of medieval Cistercian monasteries based on analysis of *Charta Charitatis* and the statutes of the Cistercian General Chapter, the basic sources concerning the order. These principles were presented by the author in the form of diagrams or models according to which the foundation processes of Cistercian monasteries in the twelfth and thirteenth centuries were carried out. Zawadzka emphasised that the foundation of Cistercian abbeys was explainable as a process that ran over time and space, consisting of a number of elements and drawing various interested people into its orbit. In the light of Zawadzka's research, the theoretical model of the foundation process of Cistercian abbeys in the twelfth century, which is the focus of this chapter, seems to have consisted of the following stages:

1. Arriving at the decision to establish an abbey;
2. Obtaining the approval of the bishop or archbishop;
3. Efforts to establish a convent by an existing Cistercian abbey or general chapter;
4. Visit to the foundation site;

---

* Original publication: Józef Dobosz, 'Proces fundacyjny i pierwotne uposażenie opactwa cystersów w Jędrzejowie', in *Cystersi w Polsce. W 850-lecie fundacji opactwa jędrzejowskiego*, ed. by Daniel Olszewski (Kielce: Wydawnictwo Jedność, 1990), pp. 40–79.

1 Helcel, 'O klasztorze jędrzejowskim', pp. 125–228.
2 This is how the matter was put in Winter, *Die Cistercienser*.

5. Arrival of the convent;
6. Commencement of the construction of the church and monastery;
7. Issuing a foundation charter;
8. Consecration of the church.[3]

Obviously, the above scheme cannot be treated rigidly, as the author herself pointed out.[4] Not every Cistercian abbey in Poland received a foundation charter. The monks were frequently satisfied with a note, which remained in the monastery, enumerating the grants offered at the *veche* or convention. Particular stages in the scheme could also have taken a different order.

It follows from the above that a detailed theoretical model to discuss the process of founding a Cistercian abbey has existed for some decades now, but it has been rather modestly used. What follows is an attempt to reconstruct the foundation process of the Cistercian abbey at Jędrzejów based on the above scheme.

The course of Jędrzejów Abbey's foundation can be reconstructed in the first instance based on Polish and Cistercian annals. Furthermore, there is some diplomatic material as well as that information provided by Jan Długosz. These sources provide different dates for the year Jędrzejów Abbey was founded, with the following Polish annals placing it in 1140: *Rocznik Traski* (*1140. claustrum Andreow edificatur*);[5] Codex of Szamotuły and Codex of Königsberg of the *Rocznik małopolski* (which read, respectively: *1140. Claustrum Andrzeiow edificatum*;[6] *1140. Clastrum in Andreow hoc anno edificatur*).[7] The Codex of Kuropatnicki of Annals of Małopolska contains a similar record placing the foundation between 1139 and 1141,[8] which probably equates to 1140. The *Lubiń Codex* of *Annals of Małopolska* contains the following entry between the years 1138 and 1145: *Claustrum in Andreow edificatur*.[9] *Spominki Koprzywnickie* places Jędrzejów Abbey's foundation in the year 1143,[10] while *Rocznik krakowski* and the *Annals Sandivogii* report it under the year 1149.[11] This brief overview of the Polish annals demonstrates how difficult it is to determine the exact date of foundation. Discrepancies in the interpretation of Jędrzejów Abbey's foundation date can be attributed to the fact that the annals were written at different times, in different places, and benefitted from different sources of information transmission, among other contributing

---

3 Zawadzka, 'Proces fundowania opactw cysterskich', pp. 121–50.
4 Ibid., p. 125.
5 *Rocznik Traski*, MPH ii, p. 833.
6 *Rocznik Małopolski: kodeks szamotulski*, MPH iii, p. 155.
7 *Rocznik Małopolski: kodeks królewiecki*, MPH iii, p. 155.
8 *Rocznik Małopolski: kodeks Kuropatnickiego*, MPH iii, p. 154.
9 *Rocznik Małopolski: kodeks lubiński*, MPH iii, p. 154.
10 *Spominki Koprzywnickie*, MPH iii, p. 134, which states: *MCXLIII Andrzeow fundatur*.
11 *Rocznik krakowski*, MPH ii, p. 833: *1149 abbacia fundatur in Andreow*; *Rocznik Sędziwoja*, MPH ii, p. 875: *1149 Abbacia fundata in Indrzejow*.

factors. Indeed, the Cistercian records generally do not provide unequivocal evidence in this regard.[12]

In addition to the relatively sparse information of the annals, diplomatic material and chronicle records can, to some extent, facilitate the reconstruction of the foundation process of Jędrzejów Abbey. The foundation charter issued in 1153 by Janik, Archbishop of Gniezno, is obviously the most fundamental of these sources.[13] In addition to information on the foundation of the abbey and its endowment, the document furnishes details of the consecration of the church in Jędrzejów, which Archbishop of Gniezno offered to the Cistercians along with the tithes.[14] This information is significant inasmuch as it directs attention to the fact that the Cistercians did not establish the abbey at *cruda radice* but that there was already a church in Jędrzejów with considerable tithes. Important also are the so-called formal forgeries of Jędrzejów, which recount the events of 1166/67. These are the documents of Archbishop Janik and Gedko, Bishop of Kraków (text in two editions), Mieszko III, and Kazimierz II.[15] They all list the grants offered at the solemn convention on the occasion of the consecration of the monastery church.[16] In turn, a 1210 formal forgery of Vincentius, Bishop of Kraków (which is a kind of compilation of the foundation charter and the above-mentioned false documents), provides information about the church that had previously existed in Jędrzejów and had been consecrated by Maur. It also places the foundation of the monastery in 1154 and mentions rights granted by Gedko on the occasion of the consecration of the new monastery church.[17]

The establishment of Jędrzejów Abbey is also mentioned in Edition III of the *Katalog biskupów krakowskich*.[18] The catalogue does not give the exact date of the foundation but points out that this event took place during the lifetime of Bishop Radost.

Apart from the above-mentioned sources, some interesting information about the foundation and the early history of Jędrzejów Abbey was furnished by Jan Długosz. A brief portrayal of the founder of the monastery at

---

12 See Janauschek, *Originum cisterciensium*, p. 117; cf. Winter, *Die Cistercienser* i, p. 333.
13 KDM ii.372; RPD i.55.
14 *preterea episcopus bone memorie Maurus, qui eandem ecclesiam consecravit, et Radosth succesor suus decimas super villas has addiderunt*. KDM ii.372.
15 KDM ii.374, the document of Janik and Gedko. Here the publisher provides the wrong date 1174–1176. For discussion of this document, forged in the second half of the thirteenth century, see RPD i.65, 66. See also Semkowicz, 'Nieznane nadania', p. 69 (diploma of Mieszko), pp. 69–70 (diploma of Kazimierza); RPD i.63, 64.
16 KDM ii.374 contains phrases: *in consecracione eiusdem ecclesie* (Jan); *in consecratione ecclesie* (Gedko).
17 KDM ii.380. For discussion of the document's authenticity, see Mieszkowski, *Studia nad dokumentami katedry krakowskiej*, pp. 105–06.
18 *Radost. XIII. Hic anno domini M°CXVIII ordinatur in episcopum Cracoviensem. Sedit autem annis — vigitiquinque et anno domini MCCXLII moritur. Huius tempore fundatum est monasterium Andrzeioviense*. *Katalogi biskupów krakowskich*, Edition III, MPH x, pp. 46–47.

Jędrzejów, Archbishop Janik, included by Długosz in his *Vitae archiepiscoporum Gnesnensium*, acknowledges the Archbishop of Gniezno's contribution to the establishment of Jędrzejów Abbey.[19] In his other, more renowned, work, *Annales Poloniae*, Długosz refers to the founding of the abbey twice: first, under the year 1140[20] then under 1154.[21] Under the same year, Długosz also mentions that the Jędrzejów church had previously been endowed by Bishops Maur and Radost.[22] However, the most extensive information on the origins of the Jędrzejów Cistercians was included in Długosz's work describing the endowment of the Kraków diocese. He stated that, in 1140, the brothers Janik and Klemens of the Gryfici clan founded, established, and endowed a Cistercian monastery on their estate called Brzeźnica, and that, in 1154, the monastery received further grants from the brothers.[23] He also wrote that the church in Brzeźnica was endowed with tithes by Maur, Bishop of Kraków, with the intention of founding a monastery, and that his successor Radost confirmed the endowment for the abbey and added tithes from three villages.[24] This suggests that Jan Długosz must have seen the foundation charter (or a copy), that he may have known the 1210 document of Bishop Vincentius (likely already forged), and that he likely made use of other sources still unknown.[25] It bears recalling, however, that information provided by Jan Długosz is not always precise, having been largely based on the author's own deductions.

This tangle of dates and information makes it difficult to formulate an unambiguous hypothesis concerning the date of the Jędrzejów foundation. The discrepancies stem from the complexity of the abbey's foundation process and the fact that it was extended over time. The individual dates given by the sources seem to be related to one among the various stages in the process and it is only reasonable to seek to establish which phase of the process they concern (allowing of course for the possibility of chronological error in the sources). To do this, it is necessary to provide some familiarity with the

---

19 Jan Długosz reports the date of the foundation of the abbey: *Vir devotus et religiosus, et ad augendas res divinas plurimum intentus: qui Anno Domini Millesimo centesimo quinquagesimo quarto, in pago et fundo patrimonii sui Brzesznicza Cracoviensis diocesis, fundavit coenobium Ordinis Cisterciensis, et illud Andrzeoviense appelavit.* Jan Długosz, *Vitae episcoporum Poloniae*, p. 348.

20 *Cum illis temporibus Cisterciensis ordo floridus et celebris haberetur, nobiles de domo Griffonum, videlicet Johannes alias Ianyk, vir venerabilis [...] cum germano suo Clemente eius devotione attracti, in praedio suo Brzesznicza vocato [...] monasterium Cisterciensium erigunt.* Jan Długosz, *Annales*, p. 12.

21 *Cum Andrzeoviense coenobium Cisterciensis ordinis in fundo Nobilium Griffonum Brzesznicza vocato, Cracoviensis diocesis, tenuibus reditibus provisum esset, nec numerus fratrum in eo Deo militantium subsistere illic posset, Johannes Gnesnensis archiepiscopus, qui illius primarius extitit, dum adhuc minor illum haberet status, fundator.* Ibid., p. 53.

22 Ibid., pp. 53–54.

23 LB iii, p. 361: *fundant, erigunt et dodant.*

24 See Semkowicz, *Krytyczny rozbiór*. On this work, see the controversial monograph, Matuszewski, *Annales seu cronicae Jana Długosza*.

25 Semkowicz, *Krytyczny rozbiór*, pp. 361–62.

results of research on Jędrzejów Abbey in such areas as archaeological and architectural history. The superimposition of source data and the results of such research carried out by scholars over the last two centuries allows for an approximate reconstruction of the process of the abbey's foundation.

Although the Cistercian monastery at Jędrzejów has enjoyed some considerable interest in Polish historiography, it has rarely been the subject of comprehensive studies. Such research as was undertaken focused mostly on the origins of the monastery. Scholarly discussion was initiated by Antoni Helcel in his 1852 monograph on the abbey. Helcel found himself unable to take a position on the date of foundation of the monastery. He quoted the year 1140 (after Długosz) and 1149 (after the Polish annals), believing that either the date 1149 referred to the later founding of the abbey, or one of them was incorrect.[26] Franz Winter, a German researcher of the Cistercian Order who wrote some time later, was already aware that the founding of an ecclesiastical institution was a dynamic process (an idea not very favourably received in later Polish literature).[27] He, therefore, believed that Jędrzejów Abbey was founded in 1146/49, that a convent arrived on 30 September 1164, and that the monastery church was consecrated in 1167.[28] In the entry on Jędrzejów Abbey, the *Słownik geograficzny* confuses the consecration of the local church by Bishop Maur with the establishment of the abbey, and hence suggests the Cistercians were brought by Janik and Klemens in 1111, with the monastery founded in 1149.[29] Franciszek Piekosiński, who both published the foundation charter and wrote some analysis of the monastery, described a fairly probable course for the foundation process. He stated that the first church in Jędrzejów was consecrated and endowed with tithes by Bishop Maur in the early twelfth century. The first phase of the foundation of the monastery falls on the period when Radost was Bishop of Kraków (1140) and it slowed down when the founder, Janik, became Bishop of Wrocław. With Janik becoming Archbishop of Gniezno, the initiative was revived, and the foundation resolved. Around 1153/54, Janik issued a foundation privilege and, together with Bishop Gedko, consecrated the monastery church between 1174 and 1176 as the church consecrated by Maur was no longer sufficient for the needs of the convent.[30] Similar to the authors of *Słownik geograficzny*, Jan Korytkowski quoted false information in his biography of Janik concerning his bringing the Cistercians to Jędrzejów when Maur sat on the bishop's throne in Kraków. At the same time, he posited the following question: why did as many as thirty years pass before

---

26 Helcel, 'O klasztorze jędrzejowskim', pp. 131–32.
27 See Mitkowski, *Początki klasztoru cystersów*, pp. 151–52. In his analysis of the foundation of Sulejów Abbey, Mitkowski concluded that while Winter successfully reconstructed the course of the foundation, his dating was suspect.
28 Winter, *Die Cistercienser* ii, p. 391 (on p. 81 of volume 1, Winter stated that Jędrzejów was founded between 1149 and 1164).
29 Chlebowski and Walewski, eds, *Słownik geograficzny Królestwa* iii, p. 588.
30 KDM ii.374, 380.

Archbishop Janik made the foundation legally valid?[31] In his brief consideration of the topic, Wojciech Kętrzyński opted for the year 1149 as the date of the foundation of the abbey.[32] Antoni Małecki was of a similar opinion, adding that, after 1149, the foundation was complete and the church consecrated, all of this occurring prior to 1154. The monastery church was consecrated in 1154 in the place of the previous one that was extended — although the new church might have been erected in a different place, hence the change of the name of the village from Brzeźnica to Jędrzejów.[33] In following decades, the problem of the dating of the Jędrzejów foundation failed to attract new research, and only Tadeusz Manteuffel pointed out that the discrepancies in the dates given by various sources were in no way unexpected. Each new foundation had to be carefully examined by the representatives of the general chapter before a convent was dispatched.[34] Zofia Kozłowska-Budkowa had fewer doubts as to the foundation date, arguing that Jędrzejów Abbey was established in 1146.[35] Having analysed the results of research on the history of the monastery, Andrzej Wędzki, concluded that the abbey was founded in 1140, and in 1149 a convent was brought from Morimond.[36]

This, in a nutshell, is the state of the historical research about the early history of Jędrzejów Abbey. In addition, archaeological and architectural research of several dozen years, mainly concerning the oldest church in Jędrzejów, yielded equally interesting data. This can be used by historians as comparative material for the verification of hypotheses based on source analyses. The research on the earliest church architecture of Jędrzejów brought about certain discrepancies and discussions. Earlier studies were compiled in the monumental work *Sztuka polska przedromańska i romańska*.[37] It is worth quoting the views of at least a few scholars who investigated the architecture of the oldest church in Jędrzejów and participated in the debate before 1970. For example, Tadeusz Szydłowski concluded that the church in Jędrzejów was related to St John the Baptist's Church in Prandocin. In his opinion, the church in Jędrzejów was an early twelfth-century stronghold structure handed over to the Cistercians and consecrated in 1166/67. In Szydłowski's interpretation, the church in Jędrzejów had supposedly been the prototype of the Prandocin church.[38] In several studies devoted to the church, Zygmunt Świechowski dated it to the first quarter of the twelfth century, based on written records and the spatial arrangement and construction of the body

---

31 Korytkowski, *Arcybiskupi gnieźnieńscy*, pp. 251–52.
32 Kętrzyński, *Studia nad dokumentami XII w.*, pp. 290–91.
33 Małecki, 'W kwestii fałszerstwa dokumentów', p. 2.
34 Manteuffel, *Papiestwo i cystersi*, p. 71.
35 Kozłowska-Budkowa, 'Jan', in PSB x, p. 428.
36 Wędzki, 'Jędrzejów', p. 336.
37 Walicki, ed., *Sztuka polska przedromańska i romańska*, p. 697.
38 Szydłowski, 'Architektoniczny palimpsest jędrzejowski', pp. 229–34. Cf. Szydłowski, 'O cysterskich budowlach', pp. lxvii–lx.

of the building, reversing the chronology of the churches in Prandocin and Jędrzejów.[39] A similar interpretation was presented by the authors of the relevant volume of the *Katalog zabytków*.[40] A different hypothesis was presented by Michał Walicki, who concluded that the church dates from the first half of the twelfth century, around 1140. It was purportedly funded by the nobility, Janik and Klemens of the Gryfici clan, to service their residence, and then handed over to the Cistercians around 1149. A certain formal similarity to the Prandocin Church is again emphasised.[41] This phase of the discussion on the architecture of the original church in Jędrzejów was summed up by Andrzej Tomaszewski, who stated that the dimensions of the church in Jędrzejów are close to the size of the church in Prandocin, and that it was impossible to date the former based on stylistic premises. Tomaszewski argued that there were no grounds for inferring that the clan abode of the Świebodzice-Gryfici was located in Brzeźnica. Ultimately, he concluded that the church had been the work of the brothers Janik and Klemens and built with the foundation of a Cistercian monastery at mind. It was handed over to the monks upon their arrival and consecrated in 1166/67. The stylistic similarity of the building in Jędrzejów to the Collegiate Church in Tum near Łęczyca, with Jędrzejów being a miniature copy of Tum, suggests a connection to Archbishop Janik.[42]

A new stage in the discussion on the architecture of Jędrzejów Abbey began with archaeological and architectural research carried out by Zbigniew Lechowicz in 1977. Prior to this, only the remains of the western part of the church had been known. At this time, the eastern end of the church was uncovered and documented. It turned out that it was a rectangular single-space building with a gallery on the western side, two apses on the east and west, with a tower over the west apse.[43] Having carried out a detailed analysis, Lechowicz stated that the Cistercian monastery was preceded by settlement in the area of the former village, and the architectural details of the church suggested that it was constructed around the early twelfth century in the years 1109–1118.[44] The results of this archaeological and architectural research were summarised by Jerzy Splitt, who accepted the thesis of Lechowicz without reservation.[45] The last voice in the discussion was again that of Świechowski, who returned to the matter of the architecture of the church in Jędrzejów. Świechowski re-emphasised the analogues with the Prandocin church and drew attention to the information provided by Jan Długosz that the church in Jędrzejów was consecrated and endowed by Maur, Bishop of Kraków. In his opinion, the church was erected

---

39 Świechowski, 'Znaczenie kościoła', pp. 13–26; Świechowski, *Budownictwo romańskie w Polsce*, p. 64.
40 See Przypkowski, *Katalog zabytków sztuki w Polsce*.
41 Walicki, ed., *Sztuka polska przedromańska i romańska*, pp. 137–38 (part 1), p. 697 (part 2).
42 Tomaszewski, *Romańskie kościoły*, pp. 124–28.
43 Gąssowski and Lechowicz, 'Jędrzejów, woj. Kieleckie', p. 169.
44 Lechowicz, 'Wyniki badań archeologicznych', pp. 223–32.
45 Splitt, 'Stan badań archeologiczno-architektonicznych', pp. 229–32.

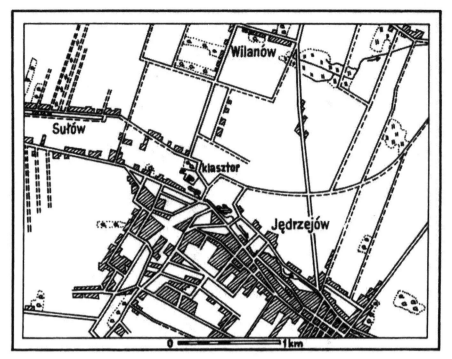

Figure 1. Location of Jędrzejów Abbey. Prepared by A. Wyrwa, drawn by L. Fijał and M. Bucka.

between 1109 and 1118. This is evidenced by the fact that the church with its feudal gallery and tower could not have been built for the Cistercians. He also pointed out that the church did not function *in cruda radice*. Świechowski expressed the opinion that the consecration of 1166/67 refers to another building, perhaps the initial phase of the Cistercian basilica that still exists today.[46]

The above review of sources and literature plainly show the multitude of opinions regarding the date the Cistercians were brought to Jędrzejów and the chronology of the oldest church. What follows is an attempt to reconcile these contradictions by combining the data obtained from the review of sources and literature with Zawadzka's model of the foundation of Cistercian abbeys.

The first church in Jędrzejów had been consecrated long before the arrival of the Cistercian convent. This is clearly evidenced by the information provided in the foundation charter, the document of Bishop Vincentius dated 1210, and Jan Długosz. These sources state that the church was consecrated by Bishop Maur, who endowed it with tithes on this occasion, and that this decision

---

46 Świechowski, 'Pierwotny kształt', pp. 212–15.

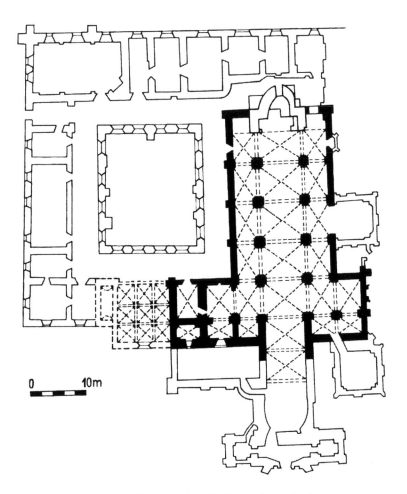

Figure 2. The Cistercian abbey at Jędrzejów. Drawn by M. Bucka.

was confirmed by his successor Radost.[47] At this point, the question arises as to whether the first church consecrated by Maur was a stone structure or a wooden building. The question was first posed by Szydłowski in 1928,[48] but it still remains unanswered. It seems not unreasonable to assume, especially in light of Lechowicz's research, that the church was made of stone from the very beginning. Without getting into the intricate problems of the history of architecture, it must be acknowledged that Jędrzejów Abbey was not built

---

47   KDM ii.372; KDM ii.380; LB iii, pp. 361–62; Długosz, *Annales*, p. 54. For the portrayals of Maur and Radost see *Katalogi biskupów krakowskich*, MPH x; Kozłowska-Budkowa, 'Radost', in PSB xxix, p. 747; Kozłowska-Budkowa, 'Maur', in PSB xx, pp. 261–62.
48   Szydłowski, *Pomniki architektury epoki piastowskiej*, p. 183, note 30.

in cruda radice, but in an area with developed settlement, most likely in one of the seats of the Gryfici clan, explaining the function of the church's feudal gallery. It would thus have been funded by the Gryficis at the turn of the twelfth century and consecrated by Maur sometime between 1109 and 1118.[49]

The foundation initiative, most probably undertaken by Janik Gryfita I, and the arrival of the Cistercians marked a turning point in the history of the church. According to the above-cited sources, it seems that the foundation idea was conceived sometime before 1140, thus the references in the annals to the foundation of the monastery in that year, and that it rapidly took on more definite shape during the lifetime of Radost, Bishop of Kraków. The foundation charter details that the bishop confirmed the tithes given by his predecessor, Maur, to the church in Brzeźnica;[50] similar information is given in the forged 1210 document of Bishop Vincentius.[51] Jan Długosz recounts matters in a similar vein, although he divides the grants of Maur and Radost into two phases.[52] It seems that the foundation was initiated by Janik, who asked the Bishop of Kraków for permission to establish a Cistercian abbey at his estate sometime around 1140 and certainly before 1142. At that time, he obtained not only the approval for the foundation, but the future congregation of monks who were to obtain the tithes granted to the church in Brzeźnica. Thus, the first two stages of the process of founding Jędrzejów Abbey took place between 1140 and 1142, although both probably occurred in 1140. The references in the Polish annals, which place the establishment of a Cistercian monastery at Jędrzejów under this year, seem to echo these events.

There is every reason to believe that in the years that followed, the abbey's foundation process experienced some disturbances. Several reasons seem to account for this. First, Janik became Bishop of Wrocław. Second, the political situation in Poland was fairly fraught with the case of Piotr Włostowic, the rebellion of the younger Piasts, and the civil war. After the complex political situation had more or less normalised around 1146, the founder probably started making efforts to arrange a visit to the site of the future foundation and to bring the convent. In the sources, these efforts are reflected in the Cistercian annals, which place the foundation of Jędrzejów Abbey at 1145, 1146 or 1147. A letter written by Mateusz, Bishop of Kraków, to St Bernard (with Piotr Włostowic as the co-responder) is an important source of information in this regard. It demonstrates the contacts between Polish nobility and the Cistercian Patriarch. In response to Bernard's letter, Bishop Mateusz and Piotr Włostowic invited him to Poland and informed him of the possibilities of converting schismatic

---

49 A different opinion was voiced in Tomaszewski, *Romańskie kościoły*, pp. 124–28, but this position cannot be maintained in the light of Lechowicz's research.
50 KDM ii.372.
51 KDM ii.380.
52 LB iii, pp. 361–62; Jan Długosz, *Annales*, p. 54. Długosz recounts that Maur consecrated the church and granted tithes from five villages and Radost approved the endowment and added tithes from three more villages.

Ruthenians.[53] The letter directs attention to a *magister* A., who is mentioned in it as Bernard's 'beloved son', who 'served in your place, were any able to do so'.[54] Thus, the letter evidences the visit of a mysterious man, who can be identified as Master Achard, to Poland. Master Achard had acted as a sort of courier overseeing the establishment of new Cistercian abbeys several times before.[55] The time of his stay in Poland, more or less contemporary with the letter itself, was determined by Marian Plezia as the years 1146–1148. The letter to St Bernard was written in the spring of 1147.[56] Master Achard probably came to Poland to accomplish two tasks assigned to him by St Bernard and the general chapter: to deliver to Poland the crusade manifesto issued by Bernard of Clairvaux to the peoples of Christian Europe,[57] and to visit the site where the Polish magnate began to erect a new monastery. Likely sent by the general chapter, or perhaps from Morimond, the latter mission was to investigate the possibility of the development of the future abbey at Brzeźnica (Jędrzejów), taking economic conditions and the security of performing God's service into account. Master Archard may have also visited Łekno, Wielkopolska, the foundation process of which was chronologically consistent with the construction of the abbey at Brzeźnica-Jędrzejów.[58] It seems that this event took place in 1147, the written records reporting the fact of the foundation of Jędrzejów Abbey this year may echo this fact. Contrary to Plezia's opinion, however, this was not necessarily connected to Cardinal-Legate Hubaldus's stay in Poland.[59] These were probably two different missions taking place at different times.

Another stage in the model of the foundation process, the visit to the foundation site, seemingly occurred in 1147, and it was probably at that time that the general chapter decided to send a convent to Jędrzejów. The very moment of the monks' arrival is difficult to determine. It probably happened between 1147 and 1153, the date of the issue of the foundation charter. The most probable date is 1149, often quoted by the sources as the date of the abbey's foundation. As observed, the convent arrived to find an already-developed settlement in Brzeźnica, including a church, which the Gryfici were likely already attempting to prepare for the arrival of the monks from the distant

---

53   The letter was printed in MPH ii, pp. 15–16, and KDŚ i.17. It has been analysed by Brygida Kürbis, who published the letter again, together with a translation into Polish, Kürbis, 'Cystersi w kulturze polskiego', pp. 324–27. Earlier research on the letter has been summarised in RPD i.43.
54   Per Kürbis, 'Cystersi w kulturze polskiego', p. 324: *Dilectus filius vester; ex parte vestra consultuit, si quis posset.*
55   See Plezia, 'List biskupa Mateusza', p. 135; Kürbis, 'Cystersi w kulturze polskiego', p. 323.
56   Plezia, 'List biskupa Mateusza', pp. 136–40; MPH ii, pp. 15–16 dates the letter to *c.* 1150; RPD i.43 to 1143–1145; KDŚ i.17 to 1146/47, as does Kürbis, 'Cystersi w kulturze polskiego', pp. 323–24.
57   The opinion of Plezia, 'List biskupa Mateusza', p. 138 and Kürbis, 'Cystersi w kulturze polskiego', p. 324.
58   See Dobosz, 'Dokument fundacyjny', pp. 80–82, and Chapters 4 and 16 in this volume.
59   Plezia, 'List biskupa Mateusza', p. 139.

Morimond. However, having arrived, the Cistercians began to erect an abbey, probably with the help of the founder and the endowments granted to the monastery, while instigating the remodelling of the existing church. The ownership and property relations of the new ecclesiastical institution were legally regulated by the foundation charter issued by Janik, at that time already Archbishop of Gniezno, in 1153.[60] Attempts to locate a ducal foundation charter are inevitably fruitless, though earlier historiography wilfully indulged in this search.[61] The abbey was founded by Janik and it was also he who issued the document, which had a legal force and all the characteristics of a dispositive and public document, similar to the one he had issued for the Cistercians of Łekno.[62] The endowment included Janik's own ancestral property to which the charter refers as 'free share' of his inheritance,[63] as well as the tithe from the estates belonging to the Archbishops and Bishops (Table 3).

The solemn consecration of the monastery church, which took place late in 1166 was the crowning achievement of the foundation of the new abbey. The occasion was celebrated with a convention that was graced by the presence of Dukes Mieszko III and Kazimierz II, along with numerous clergy and lay dignitaries.[64] Some scholars have assumed that the congress was related to the rebellion against the *princeps* Bolesław IV.[65] The Cistercians of Jędrzejów were endowed with a number of new grants by the founder, Gedko, Bishop of Kraków, and Dukes Mieszko and Kazimierz. The church consecrated in 1166/67 was probably the one donated by Janik to the Cistercians and initially consecrated by Maur. The Cistercians only rebuilt the structure, perhaps pulling down the western gallery at this time, in a spirit corresponding to the

---

60 KDM ii.372.
61 For example, Semkowicz, 'Nieznane nadania', p. 73, who writes of the possible existence of Bolesław IV's foundation charter.
62 See Dobosz, 'Dokument fundacyjny', p. 70, and Chapter 16 in this volume for the text of the Łekno document of 1153.
63 KDM ii.372: *patrimonii mei liberam portionem*.
64 See KDM ii.374; Semkowicz, 'Nieznane nadania', pp. 69, 70; KDM ii.380. Edition I of Jan and Gedko's document (no. 374) states that the convention was attended by *dominus Mezeco, d. Kazimirus, domini terre, abbates multi, comites, nobiles, capellani, quorum nomina scribere longum esset*; Edition II (no. 374) provides a more detailed list: *d. dux Mesco. d. Kazimirus, abbas Tinecensis Hildebrandus, abbas de Caluo monte Miluanus, abbas de Seciechow Arnoldus, abbas de Lokna Simon, dominus Aiax, d. Zetozlaus, Gneomirus, Stephanus, Iacobus, Iohannes, Clemens*. An identical list of witnesses to the ceremony is given by the 1210 forgery (no. 380). The diplomas of Mieszko and Kazimierz provide an even more extensive list of witnesses: *Mesco dux, et filii eius Stephanus Boleslaus Mesco Wladizlaus filius Kazimiri Kazimirus Joannes Archiepiscopus Gedeo Cracouiensis episcopus Simon Abbas de Lukna Hildebrandus ticensis Abbas Miluanus Abbas de Clauo monte Arnoldus Abbas de Zetechow Jaczo Zantozlaus Leonardus filius eius Gneomirus et filii eius Venzeslaus et Emmeramus Stephanus et filii eius Staphanus et Vincencius Nicolaus frater Stephani Clemens Joannes Cherubin Cancellarius Stephanus Cancellarius*. Quotation is per Kazimierz's document; the list in Mieszko's document is identical except that Kazimierz and his son are mentioned first in place of Mieszko.
65 See Deptuła, 'Wokół postaci arcybiskupa', p. 39.

needs of the contemplative order.[66] It might also be tentatively hypothesised that a Marian dedication typical of this order was added to St Adalbert, who had previously been adopted as the sole patron saint of the church. This hypothetical chronology of the oldest Jędrzejów church would satisfactorily dispel the doubts of architectural historians.

To conclude, it can be said that the process of the foundation of Jędrzejów Abbey took place between 1140 and 1166/67 and consisted of the following stages:

1. c. 1140 – Janik Gryfita decides to establish an abbey (Janik's initiative might have been taken up by the entire family, headed by his brother Klemens);
2. 1140–1142 – Bishop Radost approves the foundation and the tithes belonging to the Gryfici clan church in Brzeźnica are donated for its use;
3. c. 1146 – efforts are undertaken in the general chapter or in Morimond to visit the foundation site and bring the convent (a delay being caused by the political situation in Poland and the founder's career);
4. 1147 – Magister Achard visits the foundation site;
5. 1147–1149 – the convent arrives, likely closer to the latter date, and the construction of the monastery begins;
6. 1153 – the foundation is legally approved, the foundation charter issued by Archbishop Janik;
7. 1166/67 – the monastery church is consecrated (or rather reconsecrated) and a ceremonial convention is held on this occasion.

In discussing the above matters related to the foundation of Jędrzejów Abbey, it has been repeatedly mentioned that it was founded by Janik Gryfita, who later became the Archbishop of Gniezno. Janik is well-known to Polish historians and it seems unnecessary to relay his biography.[67] In light of the foundation charter, he should be considered the only founder of the Cistercian monastery at Jędrzejów.[68] However, while describing the beginnings of Jędrzejów, Jan Długosz stated that it was a joint foundation of brothers Janik and Klemens.[69] Several historians followed this lead, hence Janik's brother Klemens quite often appears in the subject literature next to Janik as a co-founder.[70] Where Jan Długosz got this information from is hard to say. In the foundation charter, Klemens is included only in the list of witnesses, though his name is found several more

---

66 Małecki, 'W kwestii fałszerstwa dokumentów', p. 2; Semkowicz, 'Nieznane nadania', p. 93, suggests that the Jędrzejów church was reconsecrated in 1166/67.
67 On Archbishop Jan, see Kozłowska-Budkowa, 'Jan', pp. 427–28.
68 KDM ii.372.
69 LB iii, pp. 361–63; Jan Długosz, *Annales*, p. 12, where under 1140 reads: *nobiles de domo Griffonum, videlicet Iohannes alias Ianyk, vir venerabilis [...] cum germano suo Clemente eius devotione attracti in praedio suo Brzesznicza [...] monasterium Cisterciensium erigunt*. Under 1154 (pp. 53–54), in his description of the endowment of the newly-established monastery, Długosz mentions Janik alone as first founder. In *Vitae episcoporum* (p. 348) Długosz recognises Klemens as a co-founder.
70 Helcel, 'O klasztorze jędrzejowskim', p. 131.

times in twelfth-century sources, in 1161 and 1166/67.[71] According to Władysław Semkowicz, the records indeed mention a member of the Gryfici clan, each time together with the Archbishop of Gniezno, but his relation to Archbishop Janik is unclear.[72] In addition, Klemens is also found in a 1149 document of St Vincent's Abbey at Wrocław.[73] The obituary of that abbey reads, *Clemens miles* under 12 March,[74] and Karol Maleczyński identifies this Klemens with Archbishop Janik's brother and considers him to be a co-founder of Jędrzejów Abbey.[75] Whether Klemens really co-founded Jędrzejów Abbey, and if so, what his share in that process was is difficult to say. Original twelfth-century (or slightly later) written records do not confirm this, and the above hypothesis is based on the not always precise information of Jan Długosz. The most that can be said is that Jędrzejów Abbey was founded by Archbishop Janik and that his brother, who participated in the issuance of the foundation charter, sanctioned the decisions and, in this respect, may be considered a co-founder.

In accordance with the decision of Archbishop Janik, the Cistercians received the tithes from Rokoszyno, Pothok, Lyszakowo, Lantczyno, Rakowo, Tharszawa, Chorzewa, and from Brzeźnica for the seat of the monastery.[76] In addition, and as already noted, the abbey also obtained the church in Brzeźnica, erected sometime between 1109 and 1118 and consecrated by Maur, Bishop of Kraków, and on this occasion quite richly endowed with tithes.[77] The church was probably owned by the Gryfici and was handed over to the Cistercians by the founder, perhaps with the consent of his family members and Radost, Bishop of Kraków, who gave his consent for the foundation. With the approval of Radost, the existing endowments granted to the church were transferred into the hands of the new friars. They consisted of the tithes in the following villages: Osarowici, Preneslawe, Konare, Michowo, Bechlowo, Borowa, Prekopa, Linowo, and Holosisze, alongside the tithes from the seven villages mentioned above.[78] Thus, in 1153 the Cistercians of Jędrzejów

---

71 KDM ii.372: *ego Johannes archiepiscopus et Clemens frater meus*. KDM ii.373.
72 Semkowicz, 'Nieznane nadania', p. 83.
73 KDŚ i.25.
74 *Nekrolog opactwa św. Wincentego we Wrocławiu*, MPH ix, p. 26.
75 Ibid.
76 KDM ii.372.
77 KDM ii.372. It is difficult to determine the patron saint of the church. The foundation charter mentions St Adalbert. Kürbis, 'Cystersi w kulturze polskiego', p. 335, note 27 puts forward the hypothesis that the Jędrzejów church was originally dedicated St Andrew the Apostle, hence the name of Andrzejów-Jędrzejów appearing in place of Brzeźnica. This hypothesis is probable, if only because the original church in Brzeźnica was consecrated by Maur, Bishop of Kraków, and a little earlier in Kraków, a church dedicated to St Andrew had been founded. The change of the invocation could have occurred either before 1142, during the church's preparations to receive the monks, or when Jan became Archbishop of Gniezno. The hypothesis follows then that the church's original dedication remained in the area's cultural memory, displacing the original name of the town over time.
78 KDM ii.372.

owned eight villages and had a right to the tithes from sixteen. At this point, it should be noted that the abbey's foundation charter has not been preserved in the original. It is known only from two late seventeenth-century copies.[79] In addition, there are traces of interpolation,[80] especially in the passage concerning the tithes granted by Maur and his successor Radost. However, it seems that the interpolations were purely formal. The tithes belonged to the family church of the Gryfici clan in Brzeźnica and accompanied the donation of the church to the monks of Jędrzejów. Radost, who acceded to this, had probably died before the convent arrived in Brzeźnica-Jędrzejów, as he issued no diploma and no material proof of the donation existed. The Cistercians made up for this by producing their own document, probably in the twelfth century. The details contained in the foundation charter confirm the information provided by Jan Długosz. Długosz claims that the tithes were in fact granted to the Cistercians, or to the church in Brzeźnica, on two different occasions. First, the tithes from several villages were presented by Maur and then they were confirmed by Radost, who added tithes from three further villages.[81] The details of the tithes found in the foundation charter are largely confirmed by the 1210 forgery of Bishop Vincentius. Table 1 below summarises the information contained in the foundation charter, the 1210 forgery and that provided by Jan Długosz.

Janik's donation provided a comfortable economic basis for the development of the new monastic centre, especially when compared with Zbylut's donation to the Cistercians in Łekno, Wielkopolska. The monastery was sanctioned by a document issued in 1153 by Archbishop Janik, receiving only four villages, a marketplace and a tavern in Łekno, and a lake.[82] As observed, the foundation process of Jędrzejów Abbey did not end with the issuance of the foundation charter. The Cistercians of Jędrzejów also had to prepare the church they received for their liturgical needs. The necessary alterations were finally made before 1166/67, when it was re-consecrated. This information has been preserved in several documents issued by Janik, Archbishop of Gniezno, and Gedko, Bishop of Kraków (in two editions), Dukes Mieszko and Kazimierz, and Vincentius, Bishop of Kraków.[83] Jan Długosz provides an extensive narrative on the history of the church.

Unfortunately, diplomatic records have the fundamental drawback of being formal forgeries and being know only from late copies, even though based on authentic monastery records.[84] The credibility of Mieszko's and

---

79 The first is contained in Jędrzejów cartulary A (from 1610) on card 1 (now stored at the University Library, Adam Mickiewicz University, Poznań), the other in Jędrzejów cartulary B (from 1624–1627), now in Kraków.
80 RPD i.55.
81 LB iii, pp. 361–62; Jan Długosz, *Annales*, p. 54.
82 KDW i.18.
83 KDM ii.374; KDM ii.380.
84 See Semkowicz, 'Nieznane nadania', pp. 91–93; RPD i.63–67.

Table 1. 1153 (and earlier) grants for Jędrzejów Abbey

Source / Grant type	According to 1153 document	According to 1210 document	Jan Długosz *Liber beneficiorum*	*Annales*	
Land grants	Rakoszno Pothok Lyszakowo Lantczyno Rakowo Tharszowa Chorzewa Brysinch		Vol. III, p. 361: Brzesznicza Rakoszino Potok Lyszakowo Lanczino Tharschowa Vol. III, p. 365: Chorzewa	1144: opidum Andrzeowiense et septem villas: Brzesznica Rakoszyno Potok Lyszakowo Rachowo Tharschawa Chorzowa	1154: Brzesznica Rakoschino Pothok Lysszakowo Lanczino Rachowo Tharszawa Chorzewa
Tithes	Tithes from the villages mentioned above (except for Brzeźnica?) and: Osarowici Preneslawe Konare Michowo Bechlowo Borowa Prekopa Linowo Holosisze	Rakoszino Pothok Liszakowo Lanczino Rakowo Tharsawa Chorzewa Czaczowo Preneslawe Konare Michowo Gerlowo Borowa Prokopa Lunowo Cholosino	Marowicze Przemyslawe Conari Mychow Wyeglowo Przewyezlanye Borowa Przekopa Lunyowo and tithes from: Brzesznica Rakoszino Potok Lyszakowo Lanczino Rachowo Tharschowa Holuszy	under 1154 tithes from the villages mentioned above and: Marowicze Przemyslawe Conari Michowo Węglewo Borowa Przecopa Lunyowo Holusz	

Kazimierz's documents was defended with great passion and erudition by Semkowicz,[85] and it must be admitted that, when approached with appropriate caution, they constitute extremely valuable sources for the research on the origins of the monastery. This holds true of other documents concerning Jędrzejów. Jan Długosz must have made use of the above-mentioned forgeries when he recounted the early history of Jędrzejów. In examining the scope of the endowment granted by the bishops and dukes on the occasion of the consecration of the church, another obstacle rears its head: the differences

---

85   Semkowicz, 'Nieznane nadania'.

in data from particular written records. This primarily relates to details of the granted estates and tithes in the documents of Janik and Gedko (there are differences between the first and second editions of these documents), Bishop Vincentius, and Jan Długosz's *Liber beneficiorum* and *Annales*. Leaving aside the grants of Mieszko and Kazimierz for the moment, it is worth attempting to list the grants contained in the above-mentioned sources. The documents accord with the information given by Długosz in that the endowments were made on the occasion of the consecration of the church. Table 2 provides the details of the grants.

A comparison of the details of Gedko's and Janik's endowments of 1166/67 reveals significant differences in the two editions of the forgeries. The first edition lists fifteen villages granted by Janik, while the second lists only twelve omitting villages of Pelknice, Krzencino, Zdeccze, Miraue, but adding the village of Lanche. These villages were in part inherited by Janik from his relative Smile, son of Bodzęta (Ed. I 1–6; Ed. II, 1–7), and in part purchased and handed over to the Cistercians (Ed. I 7–15; Ed. II 8–12). In addition to land endowments, the archbishop donated tithes from fifty *pługi* to the monks,[86] which he later assigned in nine villages, and in this case both editions agree. As far as Gedko's endowments are concerned, the tithes listed in Edition I concern a total of eighteen villages, while in Edition II only sixteen (Skroniów and Wazlino are missing).[87] Everything indicates that Edition II preserves more information on the earlier state of endowments than Edition I. It seems that at the 1166/67 convention, the monastery received the property as described in Edition II, but new grants were added shortly after and, at the same time, the village and tithes were exchanged, which was reflected in Edition I. Some errors, especially the variations of place names, can be attributed to the copyist who entered the document into the cartulary, though some may have been made by a forger in the second half of the thirteenth century.

The information contained in Długosz's works basically repeats the details from the above-discussed forgeries. In *Liber beneficiorum*, Długosz leaves Skotniki out, though still lists it when discussing the tithes, and instead of the name Zesie, he lists Zerczicze.[88] Information in Długosz's *Annales* suggest a closer connection with the second edition of the document from 1166/67 (it also lists twelve villages granted by Janik, but instead of Lanche it mentions the name of Mierzewo).[89] It can be assumed that Długosz either made use of the discussed forgeries or the monastery records upon which the basis of the forgeries were drawn.[90] The false document of Vincentius, Bishop of Kraków, based on the records of the monastery, gives a list of tithes granted by

---

86   *Pługi* is a unit of land measurement originally intended to represent the amount of land that a team of two oxen could plough in a single season.
87   KDM ii.374.
88   LB iii, pp. 361–62, 373.
89   Jan Długosz, *Annales*, p. 54.
90   For discussion of Długosz's sources, see Semkowicz, *Krytyczny rozbiór*.

CHAPTER 5

Table 2. 1166/67 grants for Jędrzejów Abbey

Source	Grants by Jan acc. to 1166/67 document		Grants by Gedko acc. to 1166/67 document		Grants by Gedko acc. to 1210 document	Jan Długosz	Annales
Endowment type	Ed. I	Ed. II	Ed. I	Ed. II		Liber benef.	
Land grants	Viazd	Viazd				Jan:	Jan:
	Blonie	Zesie				Ugyazd	Ugyasd
	Zesie	Boloniam				Blonye	Blonye
	Blonika	Blotnici				Zerczicze	Zerzicze
	Skowrodlno	Lachne				Blonycza	Blonicza
	Kamienci	Scowrodne				Skowrodno	Skowrodno
	Gyresinam	Camienci				Kamyenczicze	Kamenczicze
	Buzecow	Dzierezna				Dzerzansznam	Dzerszanszna
	Tropiszowo	Buskow				Buszków	Buszków
	Biala	Tropiszow				Tropiszow	Tropiszow
	Belgen	Beala				Byalya	Byala
	Miraue	Besdin				Byeszden	Beszdin
	Pelkinice					Mirzewa	Mirzewa
	Krzencino					Pelcznica	
	Zdeccze					Krzenczino	
						Sdeczcze	

Source	Grants by Jan acc. to 1166/67 document		Grants by Gedko acc. to 1166/67 document		Grants by Gedko acc. to 1210 document	Jan Długosz Liber benef.	Annales
Endowment type	Ed. I	Ed. II	Ed. I	Ed. II			
Tithes	so *plugi* from the villages: Zlotniki Skotniki Rambiescici Lasochouici Zarczyci Zdanowici Rakowici Brzezno Breghe	so *plugi* from the villages: Zlotnici Skotnici Lasochowici Zarcici Zdanowicand Chacheuici Brzezno Brech	Tithes from the villages granted by Janik in Edition I and: Skroniow Walizno and a village between the village of Budziwoj and the village of Niegoslaw	Tithes from villages granted by Janik in Edition II and: a village between the land properties of Budziwoj and Niegoslaw	Viazd Blonie Senich Blonica Skowrodno Pauenchic Beresznam Buzecow Opatkowo Tropiszowo Bealla Grambalow Besgen Mirawa Branichia Scronow Vaslino and a village between the land properties of Budziwoj and Niegoslaw	Jan: so *plugi* from the villages: Zlothniky Rambyeszicze Lysszakowicze Zarczicze Sdanowicze Czaczow Brzeszna Brzem Skotniki Gedko: tithes from villages granted by Janik (see by land endowments) and: Skronyow Waszlino I Waszlino II Opathkowicze	Jan: so *plugi* from the villages: Zlothniky Skothniky Rambyesszycze Jasszlikowice Zarczicze Szdanowicze Czaczow Brzeszna

Bishop Gedko. Gedko endowed the monastery with tithes from eighteen villages, and the comparison of the information from this source and the 1166/67 documents shows that the number of tithes listed in both is similar (the document of Vincentius and Edition I of Janik and Gedko's diploma). The same number of tithes granted by Gedko was cited by Jan Długosz in his *Liber beneficiorum*. The document dated 1210, however, does not mention the villages of Kamarówka, Krzencino, Zdeccze, which are mentioned in the 1166/67 document and Długosz, and in their place it introduces Opatkowo, Grambalow and Branichia.[91] Długosz mentions the latter three as the tithing villages of the monastery during a detailed discussion of the monastery goods and, in the case of Opatkowo (called here Opathkowycze), he adds that the tithes were granted by Gedko.[92] It seems that the 1210 forgery describes the state of tithe grants after subsequent changes, and perhaps new endowments), and thus reflects matters a dozen or so years later than 1166/67. The changes probably took place before Gedko's death in 1185.

The generosity of the nobles and the dukes towards Jędrzejów Abbey did not end with endowing the villages and tithes. Dukes Mieszko and Kazimierz joined the string of benefactors of Jędrzejów Abbey. They granted: *alueum ad magnum salem* (Mieszko)[93] and *tredecim plaustratas salis de theloneo in Zandemir* (Kazimierz).[94] Thus, Mieszko offered salt deposits near Kraków, or more precisely a saltern in Wieliczka,[95] while Kazimierz endowed the Cistercians of Jędrzejów, like later the Cistercians of Sulejów, with thirteen salt carts from the duty in the Sandomierz chamber (salt imported from Rus').[96]

Not only did the brothers grant salt but they also confirmed the donations of their predecessors.[97] In addition to a very general immunity clause, there here the detail that the monastery owned people (*coloni* — probably serfs) and a marketplace, to which the immunity also applied. Who gave the marketplace and people to the monastery or when this happened is difficult to determine.

---

91 KDM ii.380, 374; LB iii, p. 362. See also ZRPD i.67.
92 LB iii, pp. 368, 375 (the last information from LB seems to be sixteenth or seventeenth century in origin).
93 Semkowicz, 'Nieznane nadania', p. 69.
94 Ibid.
95 See Keckowa, *Saliny ziemi krakowskiej*, p. 50. Semkowicz, 'Nieznane nadania', pp. 78–79, explains that salt deposits were the common property of all district dukes, hence the grants of Mieszko in Wieliczka before assuming the principate. See also Grzesiowski and Piotrowicz, 'Sól małopolska w nadaniach', pp. 84–85.
96 For information on the endowment for Sulejów see Mitkowski, *Początki klasztoru cystersów*, p. 313. The similarity between the Jędrzejów and Sulejów endowments is noted in Semkowicz, 'Nieznane nadania', p. 72.
97 *Confirmo etiam uillis, et colonis, et foro ipsius Ecclesie, quam predecessores mei contulermunt immunitatem et omnis pensionis atque tributarie seruitutis libertatem.* Semkowicz, 'Nieznane nadania', p. 69 (quoted from Mieszko's document in the text, but both diplomas are identical with only slight differences in the spelling of some words.

In any event, the founder himself could certainly have been the benefactor between 1153 and 1166/67 but this seems improbable since the grant would have been mentioned in the foundation charter, and certainly in the 1166/67 forgery. All seems to imply that a certain number of people, though the number is impossible to determine, and the marketplace in Jędrzejów (then still Brzeźnica), along with a fiscal immunity, were granted to the monastery by the princeps Bolesław IV. This event was not commemorated with the issuance of a document. The fact that Bolesław IV granted the immunity is confirmed by a document issued by Duchess Grzymisława (wife of Leszek the White) from 1228.[98] It follows that the first immunity was granted by Bolesław, and his successors on the Kraków throne, Kazimierz and Leszek the White (as well as Grzymisława herself) confirmed the endowment and probably expanded on it. This is a typical situation when the granted immunity was not confirmed by a document, but each subsequent princeps (Bolesław, Mieszko, Kazimierz, Leszek) confirmed the donations of his predecessors. Roman Grodecki interpreted this problem in a similar way,[99] while a completely different interpretation was offered by Józef Matuszewski, who decided that Kazimierz II alone granted the immunity. However, Matuszewski's arguments should be rejected, because he confuses the founder of the monastery with the reigning duke — the duke who granted the immunity was not necessarily the founder of the monastery — and, in terms of the date of the monastery establishment or convent's arrival, he follows the erroneous suggestions of Małecki.[100]

It is difficult to establish the scope of the original immunity granted to the monastery at Brzeźnica-Jędrzejów through the prism of the forgeries drawn up in the second half of the thirteenth century. All researchers that have addressed the issue have been convinced that the immunity must have been economic,[101] but the question remains whether it was full or limited in terms of territorial or factual scope. Following the Sulejów analogy, it can be said that it concerned the marketplace in Brzeźnica and certain burdens of the ducal law though which ones, the sources do not specify. It is even more difficult to say whether the monastery was granted a judicial immunity at that time. On the basis of the diplomas of Grzymisława from 1228 and Bolesław V from 1245,[102] scholars have expressed a cautious view that the monastery received a judicial immunity in the twelfth century, perhaps from Bolesław IV

---

98   *Cum ergo omnimoda libertas, a duce Boleslao, et a bone memorie Kazimiro, et a marito meo Lescone, quondam duce Polonie, omnibus Andrzeiowiensis Abbacie hominibus collata fuerit, eandem libertatem a nobis renouando corroboratam sciatic.* KDM i.11.
99   Grodecki, *Początki immunitetu w Polsce*, pp. 47–49.
100 Matuszewski, *Immunitet ekonomiczny*, p. 232.
101 Grodecki, *Początki immunitetu w Polsce*, pp. 47–49; Matuszewski, *Immunitet ekonomiczny*, p. 232; Wojciechowski, 'Początki immunitetu w Polsce', p. 174.
102 KDM i.11; KDP iii.24.

or Kazimierz II.[103] It seems that if the beginnings of a judicial immunity for Jędrzejów Abbey are moved to the last third of the twelfth century, it must have been related to those *coloni* mentioned in the documents of Mieszko and Kazimierz. Perhaps the judiciary power over them was entrusted by one of the mentioned dukes to the abbot.

The above overview of the early endowment of Jędrzejów Abbey shows that prior to 1166/67 the Cistercians received twenty-four villages; rich tithes (in forty-five villages, or forty-eight including all the exchanges); a fiscal and possibly judicial immunity in a form difficult to determine (in the first phase probably limited and gradually expanded with subsequent grants); the church in Brzeźnica as a place for the monastery's abode; and people and salt grants. The Jędrzejów foundation appears to therefore as impressive, especially when compared to the Łekno foundation, which was being established around this time, or Sulejów Abbey a little later.[104] The abbey was endowed by its main founder Janik and perhaps other members of the Gryfici clan, and in its the first phase by Radost, Bishop of Kraków, then by Bishop Gedko and Dukes Bolesław, Mieszko and Kazimierz. It should be noted here that in the following period, Jędrzejów Abbey enjoyed the protection of both Bishops of Kraków and the dukes ruling in Małopolska.[105] The monastery's property status at the time of the completion of the foundation process is shown in the table below, which also deciphers the names of the villages and towns listed in in written records.

What were the reasons behind the establishment of this first Cistercian institution in Poland and its rich endowments? It seems that the purported long-term political plans of the papacy related to the mission of the Cistercians settled in Poland in Rus', as promoted by Manteuffel, should be excluded as the cause of the foundation. Manteuffel based his argumentation primarily on a letter to St Bernard and the location of Cistercian monasteries on the routes leading to Rus'.[106] The letter to St Bernard has been noted, but it should be emphasised that it was a response to the Crusade Manifesto and had little to do with the mission in Rus'. As for the trade routes, virtually all monastic

---

103 Wojciechowski, 'Początki immunitetu w Polsce', p. 184; Kaczmarczyk, *Immunitet sądowy i jurysdykcja poimmunitetowa*, pp. 133–34. Extreme positions in this regard were taken by Grodecki, *Początki immunitetu w Polsce*, p. 67 (arguing a judicial immunity was certainly granted in the twelfth century) and Tymieniecki, 'Majętność książęca w Zagościu', p. 40, note 8 (arguing that the right to the judicial immunity was granted after the time of Grzymisława and Bolesław IV).
104 See Dobosz, 'Dokument fundacyjny', p. 82; Chapter 15, Table 5 in this volume (listing the early endowment of Łekno Abbey); Dobosz, 'Uwagi o fundacji opactwa cystersów', p. 90 (table listing the early endowment of Sulejów Abbey).
105 For example, the forged document of Vincentius, Bishop of Kraków of 1210, quoted several times: KDM ii.380; KDM i.3 (document of Bishop Pełka of 1192); KDM i.11 (the earlier-quoted document of Grzymisława of 1228); KDP iii.24 (document of Bolesław V of 1245); KDM i.32 (document of Bolesław V of 1250).
106 Manteuffel, *Papiestwo i cystersi*, p. 71.

establishments at that time were located along communication arteries, which were used as internal communication routes.[107] Furthermore, the nature of the Cistercian Order was not conducive to missionary campaigns.[108] In general, a Cistercian abbey was founded for the devotional and prestige reasons so extensively expounded by Archbishop Janik in the foundation charter.[109] It is noteworthy that this is the only factor directly communicated by the historical sources. In line with the ideas of the time, through a pious foundation, the founder entered the circle of *sacrum*.[110] Moreover, the founded ecclesiastical institution became a place of prayers for the founders' family, frequently their resting place or the centre of the church career of their offspring. The foundation could have also been determined by economic, political, social or cultural considerations, which are hard to infer from the sources. In general, there were different factors at play that gave rise to the Jędrzejów foundation, with a devotional element coming to the fore. Most importantly, however, the Cistercians wanted to come to Jędrzejów (or, more broadly, to Poland), they were warmly welcomed and found favourable conditions for their development.

---

107 Tymieniecki, review of Manteuffel, *Papiestwo i cystersi*, pp. 167–73.
108 See Kozłowska-Budkowa and Szczur, 'Dzieje opactwa cystersów', pp. 11–12.
109 KDM ii.372.
110 See Michałowski, 'Święta moc fundatora klasztoru', pp. 3–24.

Table 3. The property status of Jędrzejów Abbey in the final stage of the foundation process[111]

Grant type	Modern village name	Name in sources	Benefactor	Remarks
Land	Brzeźnica	1153: Brysinch Długosz: Brzesznicza	Archbishop Janik	The village of Brzeźnica, granted as the seat of a monastery, later changed its name to Jędrzejów (probably still in the 12th century). Now a city in Świętokrzyskie Province, Jędrzejów Commune.
	Rakoszyn	1153: Rakoszyno 1210: Rakoszino Długosz: Rakoszino, Rakoszyno	Archbishop Janik	Now a village in Nagłowice Commune, Świętokrzyskie Province (*Wykaz* iii, p. 110), to the W of Jędrzejów. Cf. Helcel, p. 142: a parochial village W of Jędrzejów; Jan Długosz, *Annales*, 1140–15 km W of Jędrzejów.
	Potok	1153: Pothok 1210: Pothok Długosz: Potok, Pothok	Archbishop Janik	LB iii, p. 364 – village in the Krzcięcice parish. Also, Helcel, p. 142. KDM ii.372: Potok Wielki and Mały in the Krzcięcice parish. Now Potok, settlement and Potok Wielki, village – Jędrzejów Commune, Świętokrzyskie Province (*Wykaz* iii, pp. 36, 38). Cf. Jan Długosz, *Annales*, 1140: 9 km to the N-W of Jędrzejów.

---

111   Abbreviations of the references in the table:
Helcel: Helcel, 'O klasztorze jędrzejowskim'.
Kamińska, Nazwy: Kamińska, Nazwy miejscowe dawnego województwa sandomierskiego.
KDM:
Rymut: Rymut, Patronimiczne nazwy miejscowe w Małopolsce.
SG: Słownik geograficzny Królestwa Polskiego i innych krajów słowiańskich.
SHG: Słownik historyczno-geograficzny województwa krakowskiego w średniowieczu. = SHGWKwŚ
Wykaz: Wykaz urzędowych nazw miejscowości w Polsce.

Grant type	Modern village name	Name in sources	Benefactor	Remarks
	Łysaków	1153: Lyszakowo 1210: Liszakowo Długosz: Lyszakowo, Lysszakowo	Archbishop Janik	LB iii, p. 364, village in Jędrzejów parish; Helcel, p. 142 – identifies after Długosz, adding that the village is located S of Jędrzejów. KDM ii:372 – Łyszaków in Jędrzejów parish. Jan Długosz, *Annales*, 1140: village 7 km S of Jędrzejów. *Wykaz* ii, p. 370 lists: Łysaków Dziadówki, Łysaków Kawęczyński and Ł. By the forest, villages in Jędrzejów Commune, Świętokrzyskie Province.
	Łączyn	1153: Lantczyno 1210: Lanczino Długosz: Lanczino, Lanczno	Archbishop Janik	LB iii, p. 364, village in Jędrzejów parish. Similar Helcel, p. 142 (S of Jędrzejów); KDM ii:372: Łątczyn in Jędrzejów parish; Jan Długosz, *Annales*, 1140: Łączyn, village 4 km S-E of Jędrzejów; *Wykaz* ii, p. 343 – now in Jędrzejów Commune, Świętokrzyskie Province.
	Raków	1153: Rakowo 1210: Rakowo Długosz: Rachowo, Rakowo Maior	Archbishop Janik	LB iii, p. 364: village in Jędrzejów parish; Helcel, p. 142: village in Jędrzejów parish, E of the town; identical in KDM ii:372; Jan Długosz, *Annales*, 1140: village 7 km E of Jędrzejów. See also *Wykaz* iii, p. 111: Jędrzejów Commune, Świętokrzyskie Province.
	Tarszawa	1153: Tharszowa 1210: Tharszawa Długosz: Tharschova, Tharschwa, Tharszawa	Archbishop Janik	LB iii, p. 365: village in Jędrzejów parish; Helcel, p. 142: in Jędrzejów parish, N of the town. See also KDM ii:372; Jan Długosz, *Annales*, 1140: 5 km N of Jędrzejów; *Wykaz* iii, p. 450 – now a satellite settlement, Jędrzejów Commune, Świętokrzyskie Province.
	Chorzewa	1153: Chorzewa 1210: Chorzewa Długosz: Chorzewa, Chrzowa	Archbishop Janik	LB iii, p. 365: village in Jędrzejów parish; Helcel, p. 142: in Jędrzejów parish, N of the town. See also KDM ii:372; Jan Długosz, *Annales*, 1140: 6 km N-W of Jędrzejów; *Wykaz* i, p. 235: now in Jędrzejów Commune, Świętokrzyskie Province.

Grant type	Modern village name	Name in sources	Benefactor	Remarks
	Ujazd	1166/7: Viazd 1210: Viazd Długosz: Uygazd, Ugyasd	Archbishop Janik (inherited the village after Smil, son of Bodzęta)	Helcel, p. 144: in Iwańska parish; Kamińska, *Nazwy*, p. 209: Opatów District, Iwańska Commune and parish. See also KDM ii.372: Staszów District, Iwańska parish; *Wykaz* iii, p. 495: village in Iwańska Commune, Świętokrzyskie Province.
	Błonie	1166/7: Bloniam 1210: Blonie Długosz, Blonye	as above	Helcel, p. 144: Staszów District, Koprzywnica parish; Kamińska, *Nazwy*, p. 29: Sandomierz District, Koprzywnica Commune and parish; *Wykaz* i, p. 102: Koprzywnica Commune, Świętokrzyskie Province. See also LB iii, p. 365: Blonye Maius, village in Koprzywnica Commune; Jan Długosz, *Annales*, pp. 27, 54: E of Koprzywnica.
	?	1166/7: Blonika, Blotnici Długosz: Blonycza, Blonicza	as above	Helcel, pp. 144–15: supposed villages listed in 1166/67 document as Zesie, Blonika and Zesie, Blotnici could perhaps be identified as Zarzecze Blotniste near Koprzywnica. KDM ii.374 agrees. SG xiv, pp. 429–30 lists: Zarzecze, formerly Blotniste, Sandomierz District.
	?	1166/7: Zesie 1210: Senich Długosz: Zerczicze, Zarzaycze, Zerzicze	as above	See above. Now in Koprzywnica Commune, Świętokrzyskie Province, the village of Zarzecze (*Wykaz* iii, p. 734). Perhaps, as Helcel claims, there were two villages next to each other: Zarzecze (Zesie) and Blotnica (Blonica), which with time grew into one village now called Zarzecze.
	Skowronno	1166/7: Skowrodno, Skowrodlne 1210: Skowrodno Długosz: Skowrodno	as above	Helcel, p. 145: village in Szydłów District, Pińczów parish. After him KDM ii.374; Kamińska, *Nazwy*, p. 181: on the bank of the Nida River, Pińczów District, Commune and parish. Now Skowrodno Górne and Dolne: *Wykaz* iii, p. 234: Pińczów Commune, Świętokrzyskie Province. See also LB iii, p. 366: village in the 'Pyandziczow' parish, and Jan Długosz, *Annales*, pp. 30, 54: N-E of Pińczów.

Grant type	Modern village name	Name in sources	Benefactor	Remarks
	Kamieńczyce	1166/7: Kamienci, Camienci Długosz: Kamyenczicze, Kamienczicze	as above	Helcel, p. 145: village in the Kościelec parish, Skalbmierz District; SG iii, p. 741: Kościelec parish, Pińczów District; KDM, ii:374: as Helcel; Rymut, p. 34: Kazimierza Wielka District; *Wykaz* ii, p. 23: Kazimierza, Wielka Commune, Świętokrzyskie Province.
	Podlęże	1166/7: Lachne	as above	Helcel: no information; KDM ii:374: Podlęcze in Pińczów parish, Szydłów District, see SG viii, p. 332; *Wykaz* ii, p. 814: Pińczów Commune, Świętokrzyskie Province.
	Dzierążna	1166/7: Gyresinam Dzierezna Długosz: Dzerzansznam, Dzerraszna, Dzerszenszna	The village was bought by Archbishop Janik and then granted to the Cistercians	Helcel, p. 145: Dzierząźnia, parochial village near Działoszyce, Skalbmierz District. Similarly, KDM ii:374; Kamińska, *Nazwy*, p. 59: Drożejowice parish, Pińczów District; *Wykaz* i, p. 398: village, Działoszyce Commune, Świętokrzyskie Province (on this page also a satellite settlement bearing this name in Nagłowice-Oksa Commune, closer to Jędrzejów). The name Beresznam from 1210 diploma is most probably Dzierążna.
	Buszków	1166/7: Buzecow, Buskow 1210: Buzecow Długosz: Buszków, Buschkow	as above	LB iii, p. 375: village in Słaboszów parish; Helcel, pp. 145–46; Słaboszów parish, Miechów District; SHG i:2, pp. 299–300 4 km N-W of Działoszyce; *Wykaz* i, p. 200: Słaboszów Commune, Świętokrzyskie Province; Jan Długosz, *Annales*, pp. 34, 54: E of Miechów.
	Tropiszów	1166/7: Tropiszowo Tropiszow 1210: Tropiszowo Długosz: Tropiszow, Tropysszow	as above	Helcel, p. 146: Igołomia parish, Kraków District; KDM ii:374, as Helcel; *Wykaz* iii, p. 468: Igołomia, Wawrzeńczyce Commune, Małopolska Province.

Grant type	Modern village name	Name in sources	Benefactor	Remarks
	Biała Góra(?)	1166/7: Biala, Bella 1210: Bealla Długosz: Byalya, Byala	as above	Helcel, p. 146 lists a few villages with this name but believes that the proper one is Biała Wieś (or Biała Wieża) in Miechów District, Mstyczów parish, 3 miles from Jędrzejów; KDM ii.374 and SHG 1.i, p. 61 do not identify the village. *Wykaz* i, pp. 68–69 lists Biała Góra, part of Dzierążna village, Działoszyce Commune, Świętokrzyskie Province and Biała, part of Kołaczkowice village, Busko Zdrój Commune, Świętokrzyskie Province. This may be the former as Dzierążna was also granted by Jan.
	Bezden	1166/7: Belgen, Besdin 1210: Besgen Długosz: Byeszden Beszdin	as above	Helcel, p. 146 cannot decide; KDM ii.374: Poddzień, Gnojno parish, Szydłów District; SHG 1.i, pp. 39–40: non-extant village, formerly on the Bezden River between Tonie and Krowodrza, now the area of Krowodrza Górka Estate, Kraków.
	Mierzawa	1166/7: Miraue 1210: Mirawa Długosz: Mirzewa Myrzewa	as above	Helcel, p. 146: Krzcięcice parish, Jędrzejów District; KDM ii.374, after Helcel; *Wykaz* ii, p. 442: Wodzisław Commune, Świętokrzyskie Province.
	Piołunka	1166/7: Pelknice 1210: Pauenchic Długosz: Pelcznicza Pelcznycza	as above	KDM ii. 374: perhaps Piołaka in Krzcięcice parish; SG viii, p. 183: Piołunka, Jędrzejów District, Sędziszów Commune, Krzcięcice parish, 12 versts in Jędrzejów; *Wykaz* ii, p. 735: village, Sędziszów Commune, Świętokrzyskie Province. See also Rymut, p. 49: Pełknice, non-existent village near Mierzawa or Krzcięcice, Jędrzejów District (the latter mistakenly).
	Krzcięcice	1166/7: Krzencino Długosz: Krzenczino Krzynyccz	as above	KDM ii.374: parochial village in Jędrzejów District; Rymut, p. 37: village in Jędrzejów District; *Wykaz* ii, p. 224: village in Sędziszów Commune, Świętokrzyskie Province.

Grant type	Modern village name	Name in sources	Benefactor	Remarks
	Deszno	1166/7: Zdeczce Długosz: Sdzeczcze	as above	KDM ii:374: Deszno, Krzcięcice parish, Jędrzejów District; *Wykaz* i, p. 316: Nagłowice Commune, Świętokrzyskie Province. See also SHG i:3 where doubts were expressed: Deszno or Zdzieci; uncertain identification.
Tithes	Brzeźna		Maur and Radost	see above section devoted to land grants (tithes donated by Archbishop Janik)
	Rakoszyn		as above	as above
	Potok		as above	as above
	Łysaków		as above	as above
	Raków		as above	as above
	Tarszawa		as above	as above
	Chorzewa		as above	as above
	Złotniki	1166/7: Zlotniki, Zlotnici Długosz: Zlothniky	Janik	LB iii, p. 373: parochial village on the Nida River; Helcel, p. 147: parochial village in Świętokrzyskie Province; KDM ii:374: parochial village in Jędrzejów District; Kamińska, *Nazwy*, p. 247: Złotniki Commune and parish, Jędrzejów District; *Wykaz* iii, p. 773: Małogoszcz Commune, Świętokrzyskie Province.
	Skotniki	1166/7: Skotniki, Skotnici Długosz: Skothniky	Janik	Helcel, p. 148: unknown, rather closer to Jędrzejów; Similar KDM ii:374; Kamińska, *Nazwy*, p. 180, formerly in Chęciny District, Kielce District.
	Rembieszyce	1166/7: Rambiescici Długosz: Rambyeszicze, Rambyesszycze	Janik	Helcel, p. 147: parochial village in Kielce District; KDM ii:374, as Helcel; Kamińska, *Nazwy*, p. 168: on the Nida River, Jędrzejów District, Złotniki Commune and parish; Rymut, p. 55: village in Jędrzejów District; *Wykaz* iii, p. 120: Małogoszcz Commune, Świętokrzyskie Province.

Grant type	Modern village name	Name in sources	Benefactor	Remarks
	Lasochów	1166/7: Lasochouici Lasochowici Długosz: Lysszakowicze, Lysszakowycze	Janik	KDM ii:374: now Lasochów, Kozłów parish, Kielce District; Kamińska, *Nazwy*, p. 110: Małogoszcz Commune, Jędrzejów District, Kozłów parish; Rymut, p. 39: Jędrzejów District; *Wykaz* ii, p. 272: Małogoszcz Commune, Świętokrzyskie Province. The name Lasszlikowicze (Jan Długosz, *Annales*, p. 54) seems a corrupt form of Lysszakowicze, also used in LB iii, pp. 362, 373).
	Żarczyce	1166/7: Zarczyci, Zarcici Długosz: Zarczicze	Janik	Helcel, p. 148: Złotniki parish, Świętokrzyskie Province; KDM ii:374: Żarczyce W. and M., Jędrzejów District, Złotniki parish; Kamińska, *Nazwy*, p. 248: Jędrzejów District, Złotniki parish; Rymut, p. 73: Jędrzejów District (*małe* and *duże*); *Wykaz* iii, p. 788: Żarczyce Małe and Duże, Commune Małogoszcz, Świętokrzyskie Province.
	Zdanowice	1166/7: Zdanowici Długosz: Sdanowicze, Sdanowycze, Szdanowycze	Janik	Helcel, p. 148: Cierno parish, Jędrzejów District; KDM ii:374, as Helcel; Rymut, p. 71: village in Jędrzejów District; *Wykaz* iii, p. 755: Nagłowice Commune, Świętokrzyskie Province.
	Caców	1166/7: Chacheuici Długosz: Czaczow	Janik	LB iii, pp. 371, 373: village in Jędrzejów parish; KDM ii:374: probably Czaczów in Cierno parish; *Wykaz* i, p. 207: now village consists of three villages: Caców, Caców Dziadowski and Caców Kolonia, Nagłowice Commune, Świętokrzyskie Province. In Edition I of Gedko and Janik's document of 1166/7 the name Rakowici was used, probably a copyist's mistake. The 1210 document mentions Czaczowo, the tithes of which were granted by Maur and Radost; whether this is about the same village or a copyist's mistake is hard to say.
	Brzeźno	1166/7: Brzezno Długosz: Brzeszna	Janik	Helcel, p. 148: Brzegi parish, Jędrzejów District; identically KDM ii:374; Kamińska, *Nazwy*, p. 38: Jędrzejów District, Brzeźno Commune and parish, *Wykaz* i, p. 165: village in Sobków Commune, Świętokrzyskie Province.

Grant type	Modern village name	Name in sources	Benefactor	Remarks
	Brzegi	1166/7: Breghe, Brech Długosz: Brzem	Janik	Helcel, p. 148: parochial village, Jędrzejów District; identically KDM ii.374; Kamińska, *Nazwy*, p. 36: Jędrzejów District, Brzegi Commune and parish; *Wykaz* i, p. 155: Sobków Commune, Świętokrzyskie Province.
	Ujazd		Gedko	see above section devoted to land grants
	Błonie		Gedko	as above
	?	1166/7: Blonica	Gedko	as above
	?	1166/7: Zesie	Gedko	as above
	Skroniów	1166/7: Skroniow 1210: Scronow Długosz: Skronyów	Gedko	Helcel, p. 146: Jędrzejów District and parish; identically KDM ii.380; *Wykaz* iii, p. 236: Jędrzejów Commune, Świętokrzyskie Province. See also LB iii, p. 370: village in Jędrzejów parish.
	?	1153: Osarowici	Maur and Radost	Helcel, pp. 142–43, which suggests Mironice in Rębieszyce parish; KDM ii.380: perhaps in Lelów District, Sączów parish; Most probably Osarowici = Marowicze in Długosz, see also *Wykaz* ii, p. 442: Mieronice, Wodzisław Commune, near Jędrzejów, Świętokrzyskie Province.
	Prząsław	1153: Preneslawe 1210: Prenslawe Długosz: Przemyslawe, Przewyezlanye	as above	Helcel, p. 142: Jędrzejów parish; identically KDM ii.380; *Wykaz* iii, p. 53: Jędrzejów Commune, Świętokrzyskie Province.
	Konary	1153: Konare 1210: Konare Długosz: Conari	as above	Helcel, p. 143; KDM ii.380: Nawarzyce parish; *Wykaz* ii, p. 146: Wodzisław Coomune, Świętokrzyskie Province.

Grant type	Modern village name	Name in sources	Benefactor	Remarks
	Mnichów	1153: Michowo 1210: Michowici, Michowo Długosz: Mychow, Mychowo, Michowo	as above	Helcel, p. 143: parochial village near Jędrzejów; KDM ii,380: now Mnichów, parochial village in Jędrzejów District; Wykaz ii, p. 468: Jędrzejów Commune, Świętokrzyskie Province.
	Węgleniec	1153: Bechlowo Długosz: Wyeglowo, Węglowo	as above	Helcel, p. 144; KDM ii,380: probably Węgleniec in Jędrzejów parish; Wykaz iii, p. 530: Jędrzejów Commune, Świętokrzyskie Province. Gerlowo in the 1210 document is likely a corrupt name for the village.
	?	1153: Borowa 1210: Borowa Długosz: Borowa	as above	LB iii, p. 374: village parish Krzcięcice (record from the 16th/17th c.); Helcel, p. 144: Borowy in Dzierzgów parish or, following LB iii, now lost; KDM ii,380: non-extant village, once in Krzcięcice parish; perhaps Borowiec-Kolonia in Jędrzejów parish, Krzcięcice, Wykaz i, p. 130.
	?	1153: Prekopa 1210: Prokopa Długosz: Przekopa Przecopa	as above	Helcel, p. 144: unknown; KDM ii,380 – not near Jędrzejów.
	Linowo?	1153: Linowo 1210: Lunowo Długosz: Lunyowo	as above	Helcel, p. 144: parish Łoniów, Staszów District, near Koprzywnica; KDM ii,380: not near Jędrzejów; perhaps Linów in Zawichost Commune, Świętokrzyskie Province, Wykaz ii, p. 296.
	Choloszyn	1153: Holosisze 1210: Choloszino Długosz: Holuszy	as above	Helcel, p. 144: Hohudza in Stopnica Commune or Gołuszyn in Wysocice parish, Olkusz District; KDM ii,380: by virtue of the privilege of Bolesław IV incorporated into the town of Jędrzejów in 1271; identically SHG i.iii, pp. 355–56. See also Rymut, p. 76.
	Skowronno		Gedko	see above in the part on the land grants.

Grant type	Modern village name	Name in sources	Benefactor	Remarks
	Kamieńczyce		Gedko	as above
	Podłęże		Gedko	as above (lost probably before 1185)
	Dzierążna		Gedko	see above in the part on the land grants.
	Buszków		Gedko	as above
	Tropiszów		Gedko	as above
	Biała		Gedko	as above
	Bezden		Gedko	as above
	Mierzawa		Gedko	as above
	Piołunka		Gedko	as above
	Krzcięcice		Gedko	as above
	Deszno		Gedko	as above
	Opatkowice	1210: Opatkowo Długosz: Opathkowyczc	Gedko	LB iii, p. 375: village in Smoczygniew parish; KDM ii.380: Jędrzejów District, Mierzwin parish; Rymut, p. 48: village in Jędrzejów District; *Wykaz* ii, p. 632: Działoszyce Commune, Świętokrzyskie Province. It seems that the village was obtained through exchange (Kamieńczyce, Krzcięcice and Deszno for Opatkowice, Brynica and Grębałów – before 1185).
	Brynica	1210: Branichia	Gedko	SHG 1.ii, pp. 224–25: now Brynica Mokra and Sucha 7 km N-W of Jędrzejów. The village probably obtained through exchange (see above).
	Grębałów	1210: Grambalow	Gedko	Helcel, p. 146: near Kraków, Pleszów parish; identically KDM ii.380; SHG 2.i, pp. 46–47: village incorporated into Nowa Huta in 1951, 11 km N-E of the centre of Kraków; *Wykaz* i, p. 545: Kraków, Nowa Huta District, Małopolska Province. The village probably obtained through exchange (see above).

Grant type	Modern village name	Name in sources	Benefactor	Remarks
	Warzyn I	1166/7: Wazlino 1210: Vaslino Długosz: Waszlino primum	Gedko	Helcel, pp. 146–47: doubtfully Warzyn in Cierno parish; KDM iii.380: probably Warzyn, Cierno parish; *Wykaz* iii, p. 320: village in Nagłowice Commune, Świętokrzyskie Province.
	Warzyn II	1166/7: village between the villages of Budziwoj and Niegosław 1210: as above Długosz: Waszlino secundum	Gedko	Helcel, p. 147: between Niegosławice and Budziszowice, Skalbmierz District; *Wykaz*, iii, p. 320: Warzyn II, Nagłowice Commune, Świętokrzyskie Province.

CHAPTER 6

The Circumstances of the Founding of the Cistercian Monastery at Sulejów*

Sulejów Abbey is one of the Cistercian institutions of Poland that has been subject to academic interest for over hundred years. The impetus for the studies in the abbey's history derive from the debate about the authenticity of the oldest monastery diplomas.[1] Scholars have also turned their attention to the material remains of the former abbey, mainly the Romanesque monastery church and the chapter house.[2] The results of these investigations were published in two monographs. The first of these, written by Józef Mitkowski, provides a fairly comprehensive picture of the monastery's origins and its history up to the end of the thirteenth century, alongside an exhaustive critique of the historical sources, which are mainly twelfth- and thirteenth-century documents.[3] The other monograph is Zygmunt Świechowski's extensive dissertation, which presents the results of his research into the abbey's architecture.[4] The following years did not bring further in-depth studies on the history of the monastery, although the research on it was slightly extended when archaeologists began to work in the area of Sulejów-Podklasztorze. Archaeological research has continued until today and has been most fully summarised in Jerzy Augustyniak's 2005 volume on the site.[5]

The source material for Sulejów Abbey's early history is neither extensive nor diverse. There are some documents that are useful mainly for the reconstruction of the asset base of the abbey and a few accounts in chronicles, mainly works by Jan Długosz. Jan Łaski's *Liber beneficiorum* plays an important

---

* Original publication: Józef Dobosz, 'Okoliczności i motywy fundacji klasztoru cystersów w Sulejowie', in *Dzieje, kultura artystyczna i umysłowa polskich cystersów od średniowiecza do końca XVIII wieku. Materiały trzeciego ogólnopolskiego sympozjum naukowego zorganizowanego przez Instytut Historii Uniwersytetu im. Adama Mickiewicza, Poznań 27–30 września 1993 r.*, ed. by Jerzy Strzelczyk (Kraków: Instytut Wydawniczy Księży Misjonarzy, 1994), pp. 177–86.

1 For further detail on this topic, see RPD i.80–81, 91; cf. Mitkowski, *Początki klasztoru cystersów*, from p. 3.
2 For an overview of monastic architecture and its study, see Walicki, ed., *Sztuka polska przedromańska* ii, pp. 761–62 and Świechowski, *Opactwo sulejowskie*.
3 Mitkowski, *Początki klasztoru cystersów*.
4 Świechowski, *Opactwo sulejowskie*.
5 Augustyniak, *Cysterskie opactwo w Sulejowie*. For previous discussion of the archaeological record at Sulejów-Podklasztorze, see Wójcik, 'Sulejów-Podklasztorze, pow. Opoczno', p. 287; Wójcik, 'Sulejów-Podklasztorze, gm. Mniszków, woj. Piotrkowskie', pp. 296–97; Góra, 'Poszukiwania najstarszego Sulejowa', pp. 53–55; Tomala, 'Krótkie podsumowanie wyników', pp. 249–60. See also Splitt, 'Stan badań archeologiczno-architektonicznych', pp. 232–34.

role in the identification of villages associated with the abbey, while annals serve to determine the date of the foundation.[6] Of great importance are the Romanesque, Gothic and later architectural structures preserved in the Podklasztorze area.

On the basis of the information contained in the historical sources, historians established that the abbey was founded by Kazimierz II. The foundation charter was drawn up in 1176–1177, and the convent was brought from Morimond, Burgundy.[7] Mitkowski concluded that the establishment of the new monastic community resulted from a number of devotional, political, and cultural factors.[8] In turn, Tadeusz Manteuffel and later Józef Szymański strongly emphasised the importance of the Rus' mission.[9] The results of such previous research, especially those detailed studies not listed here, do require careful assessment. However, the intent here is to analyse the foundation of Sulejów Abbey not simply through the prism of the monastery itself, but also to take into account its founder and the turbulent political changes unfolding at this time in twelfth-century Poland. Thus, it is just as important to engage in new interpretations of the written records.

The period preceding the foundation of the Cistercian abbey saw the development of settlements in the vicinity of Sulejów.[10] These settlement processes were accelerated due to operation of the ducal customs house at the crossing of the Pilica river.[11] This probably resulted in the establishment of a marketplace, possibly in the immediate vicinity of the crossing and the customs house. It seems that the idea of bringing the monks from the Cistercian Order, which was gaining popularity in Europe, to the vicinity of a fast-developing settlement complex — a village, a marketplace, a crossing, and a customs house — was made between 1167 and 1176. This decision was, then, made under the influence of Kazimierz II, initially as Duke of Wiślica and subsequently as Duke of Sandomierz, and the *princeps*. Kazimierz II first came into contact with the Cistercians in 1167, probably in the autumn of that year. Soon afterwards, he participated in a celebration on the occasion of the consecration of the monastery church of the Cistercians of Jędrzejów, and gave the church thirteen carts of salt from the Sandomierz Chamber, as evidenced by the Jędrzejów forgeries from 1167.[12] This was the time when the young Duke

---

6 For more detail on the historical sources for the history of the monastery see, Mitkowski, *Początki klasztoru cystersów*.
7 The research was summarised by Mitkowski, who introduced new findings into the literature that have received general acceptance, Mitkowski, *Początki klasztoru cystersów*.
8 Mitkowski, *Początki klasztoru cystersów*, pp. 159–62.
9 Manteuffel, *Papiestwo i cystersi*, and Szymański, 'Kanonicy opatowscy', pp. 388–96.
10 See Góra, 'Poszukiwania najstarszego Sulejowa'.
11 ZDŚ 10.
12 The document allegedly issued by Kazimierz II in 1167 was published by Semkowicz, 'Nieznane nadania', pp. 69–70. See also Dobosz, 'Trzynastowieczne falsyfikaty', pp. 225–37, and Chapters 2, 3 and 13 in this volume.

was taking on the legacy of his deceased brother, Henry, and began to lay the foundations of both his economic strength and his political and intellectual base in the form of the court. Reigning in the small principality of Wiślica between 1167 and 1173, it is unlikely that he had a sufficient economic base to carry out this undertaking on his own, especially since he was involved in the reform of the Wiślica community of canons belonging to the diocesan clergy. After January 1173, he extended his reign to the remaining part of the Sandomierz territories with its capital stronghold of Sandomierz, and thus finally implemented the project to establish a new Cistercian community in Sulejów. For this purpose, the Duke made use of his contacts within the Jędrzejów convent and with its founder and patron, Janik Archbishop of Gniezno. Janik granted his consent to the foundation of a new monastery in his diocese, a definitive prerequisite set out by the general chapter regarding any new Cistercian establishments.[13]

Having obtained the consent, likely before 1176, the Duke was then able to instigate efforts to bring the convent to Sulejów. The Cistercians of Jędrzejów and Archbishop Janik probably mediated this undertaking between the Duke and the general chapter. Whether and when the chapter gave its consent is unknown. It is not recounted in the statutes of the Cistercian General Chapter, nor in so-called Cistercian sources, meticulously collected by Leopold Janauschek and Friedrich Winter. Nor is it recorded in the Polish sources. All report only when the monastery was established, giving various dates: 1176, 1177 or 1178.[14] Perhaps echoing the date the consent to the foundation was given, the year 1176 is one that keeps recurring in the sources. It also seems that it was around this year that the site of the future foundation was inspected, with the general chapter possibly appointing an abbot of Jędrzejów. We have no idea when the convent arrived at the location of its new abode. The 1178 document seems to suggest that it happened before that date, because it recounts how the monks exchanged the villages with the Duke.[15]

As we learn from the forged foundation charter, the original charter was ratified by the Duke in 1176 in the yet to be identified St Blaise's Church.[16] Mitkowski assumed that the church must have been located in the immediate vicinity of Sulejów, and perhaps even in Sulejów itself.[17] As previously noted, the western facade of the Romanesque church, which was consecrated in 1232, contains an element that is older than the church itself — the side tympanum.[18] Questions have naturally been asked as to whether it was a relic

---

13 A theoretical model of the foundation process based on the ordinances of the general chapter was developed by Zawadzka, 'Procesy fundowania opactw cysterskich', pp. 121–50.
14 See Janauschek, *Originum cisterciensium*, p. 175 and Mitkowski, *Początki klasztoru cystersów*, pp. 150–55.
15 Mitkowski, *Początki klasztoru cystersów*, pp. 315–16.
16 Mitkowski, *Początki klasztoru cystersów*, pp. 313–15.
17 Mitkowski, *Początki klasztoru cystersów*, p. 177.
18 See Chapter 3 in this volume.

of a pre-Cistercian sacred building, or whether it was an oratory erected by the Cistercians.[19] Świechowski, as the author of the most comprehensive study of the abbey's architecture to date, was in favour of the latter option.[20] It seems unlikely that, having brought a Cistercian convent to the Pilica, the Duke would not have established necessary infrastructure for the community to perform God's service, which was his primary duty as a founder. We may propose a hypothesis that the Church of St Blaise was located in Sulejów and that it was handed over to the Cistercians, together with the village, as their original monastery church, subsequently restored in the years that followed. This was probably a small, one-nave church, most likely founded by a duke before the mid-twelfth century, perhaps in the model of Inowłódz or the noble churches in Brzeźnica or Prandocin.

The Duke endowed the new religious community with seven villages (Sulejów, Strzelce, Dąbrowa, Góra, Byczyna, Tądów, Cienia) and farmsteads (Sgimir Coquelic, Utrosza, Damian), which likely included serfs.[21] In 1176–1177, a close associate of the Duke, Comes Radosław, added five more villages (Kępa, Mianów, Puczniew, Stefanów, Piotrów), all located on the Ner River and thus outside of Kazimierz's authority. Jan Długosz made this mysterious Comes a noble member of the Awdańcy clan and claimed that he granted the village of Sulejów itself.[22] This is an error that probably resulted both from a misinterpretation of the alleged foundation charter, which the chronicler knew and used when describing the foundation of Sulejów Abbey, and from Długosz's occasionally incorrect genealogical assertions. An unknown knight named Bałdrzych also took part in the expansion of the monastic property, donating the village of Bałdrzychów along with a church, again located on the Ner river. The forger of the foundation charter failed to identify the knight as the donor of the village, with Bałdrzyc's name resurfacing only during an attempt to retract the gift that was granted in the years 1260/1261–1267.[23]

The convent that came to Sulejów around 1177 possessed thirteen villages, farmsteads, an unknown number serfs, and two churches in total. The monks started regulating property relations straight away. For example, they consolidated their estates in two regions: in the vicinity of Bałdrzychów (on the Ner River) and Sulejów (on the Pilica River). Located at a considerable distance

---

19 For the description of the Sulejów tympanum see Świechowski, *Opactwo sulejowskie*, pp. 23–28, and Walicki, ed., *Sztuka polska przedromańska* ii, pp. 761–62, where the authors summarise current research on Sulejów architecture.

20 Świechowski, *Opactwo sulejowskie*, from p. 23. For a different interpretation see Augustyniak, Grzybkowski and Kunkel, 'Marginalia Suleioviana', pp. 354–55.

21 See the foundation charter (1176) and the 1178 document printed in Mitkowski, *Początki klasztoru cystersów*, pp. 313–16.

22 Jan Długosz, *Annales*, p. 108.

23 The processes are reported by the following documents: the document issued by Kazimierz of Kujawy in 1261, KDP i.49, and a document issued by Cardinal-Legate Gwido in 1267, Mitkowski, *Początki klasztoru cystersów*, pp. 328–30. See also J. Mitkowski, *Początki klasztoru cystersów*, pp. 146–49.

from the main concentrations of estates, Cienia and Tądów were exchanged for the somewhat better located Straszów, which in turn was finally replaced by Tomisławice and Skąpice. On the occasion of the foundation, the Duke added an immunity, which was probably in force in all the estates under his jurisdiction, though at first probably only on the Pilica river.[24] He also granted the marketplace in Sulejów, nine beaver skins a year, a Kraków saltern, and thirteen carts of Ruthenian salt from the Sandomierz Chamber, this latter being the same quantity previously granted to the Cistercians of Jędrzejów.[25]

To provide more generous grants for his foundation, Kazimierz II obtained tithes from the Archbishop of Gniezno. Information on this matter can be found in the alleged foundation charter and the document purportedly issued by the Archbishop, both of which are formal forgeries.[26] There has been a debate in the subject literature over the date of the endowments, since this event could not have taken place on 20 August 1176. In 1176, either Janik or his successor Zdzisław sat on the archbishop's throne, while Pełka, Bishop of Kraków, who endorsed the Duke's petition, took on the bishop's mantle in the autumn of 1185, being approved by the Holy See in the following year. Mitkowski, and Zofia Kozłowska-Budkowa assumed that the Cistercians of Sulejów must have obtained the tithes between 1186 and 1193/4,[27] yet it seems that the chronological framework established by these scholars can be further refined. In order to do so, we need to take a closer look at the events that took place in Kraków in 1191. At the time, Mieszko III undertook an unsuccessful attempt to regain power in Kraków, in which he was greatly helped by Henryk Kietlicz, the city's castellan. Following Mieszko's unsuccessful attempt, Archbishop Piotr, assumed to have been the grandson of Piotr Włostowic, mediated the settlement between the brothers. These events are recounted by Bishop Vincentius of Kraków.[28] In the early autumn of 1191, Piotr remained in Małopolska performing his mediatory duties; on 8 September he consecrated the Collegiate Church of the Blessed Virgin Mary in Sandomierz, another of Kazimierz's foundations,[29] and was also admitted to the fraternity of the Canons of the Holy Sepulchre at Miechów.[30] As we already know on the basis of monastic records, the document enumerating the tithes states that they were endowed on 10 August 1176. It seems that, on his way to Małopolska,

---

24 That the immunity was granted is mentioned in the alleged foundation charter, Mitkowski, *Początki klasztoru cystersów*, p. 314. The issue has been raised several times by such scholars as J. Widajewicz, Z. Wojciechowski, Roman Grodecki, Zdzisław Kaczmarczyk, Oswald Balzer, Jacek Matuszewski; their research was summarised in Mitkowski, *Początki klasztoru cystersów*, pp. 196–201.
25 Mitkowski, *Początki klasztoru cystersów*, p. 314. The salt grant for Jędrzejów is confirmed by the above-mentioned document purportedly issued by Kazimierz in 1167 — see note 14.
26 KDW i.587 (21 a), the document issued by Archbishop Piotr.
27 Mitkowski, *Początki klasztoru cystersów*, from p. 3, and RPD i.81.
28 *Chronica Polonorum* iv.17.
29 KDM i.2, the so-called Sandomierz record.
30 KDM ii.376.

Archbishop Piotr passed through Sulejów on 10 August, but in 1191, and at that time granted the tithes to the monastery. It can be presumed that it was then that the Cistercians completed the reconstruction of St Blaise's Church and Archbishop Piotr performed the act of consecration. It appears that at the time, St Thomas of Canterbury, whose cult was brought to Poland by the Cistercians, was adopted as the patron saint of the church, which would explain the mysterious disappearance of the church dedicated to St Blaise.

As part of the settlement between Mieszko and Kazimierz, it appears that Mieszko endowed the Cistercians of Sulejów with the farmsteads of Milej and Suemingala, which later assumed the common name Milejów. These events are evidenced in a document dated to 1178.[31] The granting of tithes, the donation of Mieszko, and the consecration of the monastery church constituted the last link in the long-term foundation process, in the course of which the Cistercians received in total fourteen villages (taking account of the exchange of various villages), several farmsteads, serfs (later turned into *adscriptici*), thirteen tithes from the villages, two churches, an immunity, and moveable wealth. I would argue that the immunities for the marketplace in Sulejów turned out to be of utmost importance in the long run.

Neither in light of available written records nor the previous research are Duke Kazimierz's motives behind the establishment of a new Cistercian community in Sulejów clear. In the most comprehensive commentary on the matter, Mitkowski pointed to devotional factors, followed by cultural, political, and economic reasons.[32] Manteuffel followed a different path. He believed that Sulejów Abbey, along with other Cistercian abbeys in Małopolska, was established for the purpose of carrying out missionary activity in Rus', in service to the far-reaching missionary and political plans of the papacy. Sulejów's location along one variant of the Rus' travel and trade routes purportedly corroborates this hypothesis.[33] While Mitkowski's general conclusions do not raise any fundamental problems, the position of Manteuffel needs to be thoroughly revised. The first reviewer of Manteuffel's studies, Kazimierz Tymieniecki, argued that it is inappropriate to draw such far-reaching conclusions from the simple fact that an ecclesiastical institution was located near communication routes. He rightly considered that these were, above all, arteries for internal communication and exchange.[34] Tymieniecki's argumentation is corroborated by the fact that the Duke endowed the marketplace in Sulejów with fairly far-reaching liberties. The monastery was located by an important trade route, and the endowment of a marketplace served to ensure favourable economic conditions for its smooth functioning. The endowment and location provided

---

31 Mitkowski, *Początki klasztoru cystersów*, pp. 315–16.
32 Mitkowski, *Początki klasztoru cystersów*, pp. 159–62.
33 Manteuffel, *Papiestwo i cystersi*, pp. 80–82.
34 Tymieniecki, review of Manteuffel, *Papiestwo i cystersi*, pp. 167–73, and Tymieniecki, review of Manteuffel, 'Rola cystersów w Polsce XII wieku', pp. 214–20.

an excellent basis for the rapid accumulation of assets, offering promising prospects in of the colonisation under German law. This was evidently the Duke's overarching goal as a founder.

Józef Szymanski attempted to provide further arguments to corroborate Manteuffel's position. Based on Sulejów documents from 1206 and 1208, he put forward a hypothesis according to which the Cistercians were to cooperate with the canons of Opatów in missionary activity in Rus'. This was allegedly evidenced by the presence of the representatives of the collegiate chapter from Opatów in the witnesses lists of the aforementioned documents.[35] These conclusions seem to go too far. The question of the role and selection of witnesses in the documents is not necessarily suggestive of close cooperation between the diocesan canons and the Cistercians. The former were included in the list of witnesses as participants of a convention or gathering, with their presence resulting rather from their liaison with Duke Leszek the White, their patron and the founder's successor. It is also the case that, as a religious community, the Cistercians were not well suited to missionary activity due to the limitations of the general chapter.[36] When he recounts Kazimierz's expeditions to Rus', Bishop Vincentius is silent on the Cistercians' participation,[37] even though he was, after all, well positioned to report on their activities. The diocesan canons from Opatów were much better suited than the Cistercians to carrying out missionary activity in such difficult terrain, and it was they who were entrusted with the task of establishing a Latin bishopric in Rus'. This, however, is an entirely different matter, as are the Franciscan and Dominican missions in Rus'.

Let us return to the motives behind the establishment of the monastery at Sulejów. Most studies addressing the origins of pious foundations tend to confuse cause with effect, drawing too far-reaching and unsupported conclusions. In the case of Sulejów, the only contemporary source that hints at reasons why the abbey may have been established is a forged foundation charter.[38] It follows from the text that the most important factor behind the establishment of a new Cistercian institution was religious motivation, devotion. It should also be noted that Sulejów Abbey was founded at a time when Duke Kazimierz's political career and independent rule had barely begun. The idea to raise his prestige through appropriate subsidies for the Church in Poland seems an obvious move. The Duke of Sandomierz, and later the *princeps* of Poland, endeavoured to embody the feudal model of a good ruler,

---

35 Szymański, *Kanonicy opatowscy*, from p. 388, and documents from 1206 and 1208, printed in Kętrzyński, *Biblioteka hr. Raczyńskich*.
36 Canivez, ed., *Statuta Capitulorum Generalium* i, for example Charta Charitatis 1.27.
37 *Chronica Polonorum* iv.14–15.
38 *Ego Casimirus dux Poloniae notum facio praesentibus et futuris, quod ego ob animae meae remedium et omnium tam praedecessorum quam successorum meorum, contuli Deo et Beatae Mariae et fratribus ordinis Cisterciensis ad claustrum construendum cum Dei adiutorio et nostro, villam et fundum* [...]. Mitkowski, *Początki klasztoru cystersów*, pp. 313–14.

which included being a generous benefactor and protector of the Church. If, finally, we accept that Bishop Vincentius' assertion that the Duke took delight in holding scholarly disputes and surrounding himself with people of great learning is an accurate appraisal[39] and not mere rhetoric, we can speculate that cultural factors were also a root cause of the Sulejów foundation. Whether this supposition is substantiated by a phrase from the diploma of 1178, in which the Cistercians of Sulejów are called ducal chaplains, is hard to say.[40] The fact that, as Mitkowski highlights, Kazimierz sought to build a sphere of influence in the border regions of his principality — enlarged after the death of Bolesław IV in January 1173 — was probably not without significance. It was no coincidence that he chose Sulejów on the Pilica River as the place for the new Cistercian outpost. The most important thing, however, was that control was given over to someone who was able to meet the economic requirements of establishing a new community, and that the Cistercians responded positively to his invitation to this end.

Who inspired the Duke to take the trouble to bring the Cistercians to Sulejów and to establish and endow the monastery is a separate question — one, in fact, in the realm of mere hypothesis and conjecture. The broadly understood models for engaging in the foundation of such institutions probably derived from the politics of the milieu in which the Duke grew to maturity: the tradition of his father's foundations, the court of his mother Salomea, or the attitudes of his older brothers (mainly Henry, whose work he continued). Archbishop Janik might have directed Kazimierz's interests to the Cistercians, and it is evident that Jędrzejów provided the foundation model. It is difficult to say to what extent the almost contemporary foundation initiatives in Lubiąż and Ląd, both from around 1175, influenced the Duke's decision, but one thing seems certain: the Cistercians were gaining popularity with the Piasts.

To conclude, the whole process of founding Sulejów Abbey took place between 1176 and 1191 and consisted of the following stages: 1. around 1176 – the birth of the idea, consent of Archbishop Janik and guarantee of support in the Duke's advisory circle; 2. 1176 – consent to send a convent obtained from the general chapter (or from Morimond); 3. around 1177/78 – arrival of the convent, and in 1178 the consolidation of estates; 4. 1191 – consecration of the church, tithes and grants from Mieszko III.

Although the abbey did not receive a foundation charter, the issuance of a false document in the thirteenth century made up for this lack. The grants obtained in the course of the foundation process allowed Sulejów Abbey to retain economic independence, although the monastery did not cease to enjoy the care of Kazimierz's successors into the early fourteenth century, and considerably expanded its estates. It should also be emphasised that, although the Duke bore the main burden of the foundation project, he was

---

39 *Chronica Polonorum* iv.5.
40 Mitkowski, *Początki klasztoru cystersów*, p. 315.

generously backed by his close associates. That, however, is a subject for another paper. This brief analysis has focused on the early history of Sulejów Abbey as glimpsed in the documents of the so-called foundation cycle, and as can be reconstructed from the study on Duke Kazimierz's activities in the areas of pious patronage and foundation.

CHAPTER 7

The Founder and the Beginnings of the Cistercian Monastery at Wąchock*

The monastery at Wąchock was one of the earliest Cistercian congregations in Poland, established in the 1170s. It was a period that saw a wave of new foundations in the lands between the Oder and the Vistula, the abbeys at Wąchock, Kołbacz, Lubiąż, Ląd, and Sulejów all dating to this period. Historians, art historians, architects, and archaeologists have long taken an avid interest in the history of the Cistercian foundation at Wąchock. Indeed, as early the nineteenth century Władysław Łuszczkiewicz had already undertaken a comprehensive survey of the history of the Romanesque monastic buildings.[1] In the early twentieth century, Roman Plenkiewicz in turn sought to reconstruct the history of Wąchock Abbey; however, his insufficient grasp of research methods prevented him from formulating convincing conclusions.[2] Precious information on the early years of Wąchock Abbey can be found in the late nineteenth-century writings of Leopold Janauschek and Franz Winter, but the first serious monograph to cover the abbey's entire medieval history was written by Mieczysław Niwiński in the interwar period.[3] Niwiński focused primarily on the economic history of the abbey as illuminated by written records.[4] Although research on the architecture of the monastery started with Łuszczkiewicz's pioneering dissertation, a more complete view of this topic only came to fruition in the architectural and archaeological studies of the latter half of the twentieth century. Conducted mostly by Krystyna Białoskórska and, to some extent, Olga Lipińska, these brought important insights into the history of the monastic buildings, the relics beneath them, and the development of settlements in the

---

* Original publication: Józef Dobosz, 'Wokół fundatora i początków klasztoru cystersów w Wąchocku', *Scripta Minora*, 2 (1998), 37–49.
1 Łuszczkiewicz, 'Romańska architektura w Wąchocku', pp. 49–71, cf. Sztolcman, 'Nieznane zabytki romańszczyzny', pp. 34–39.
2 Plenkiewicz, 'Opactwo Cystersów w Wąchocku', see also the review of the paper by Zachorowski who identifies the errors and shortcomings of the study. Similarly uncritical remarks on Wąchock Abbey were made in Wiśniewski, *Dekanat iłżecki*, pp. 343–81.
3 Janauschek, *Originum cisterciensium*, p. 178; Winter, *Die Cistercienser* ii, pp. 389–91.
4 Niwiński, *Opactwo cystersów w Wąchocku*, pp. 3–164. Niwiński made some brief comment on previous research on the abbey at pp. 3–4 and also addresses this material in two other papers, Niwiński, 'Średniowieczni opaci klasztoru wąchockiego', pp. 329–43 and Niwiński, 'Ród panów na Wierzbicy', pp. 29–35.

abbey's former monastic estates.[5] The full range of this research has attracted significant commentary and has been surveyed a number of times.[6] In more recent times, analysis of the oldest architecture in Wąchock has been carried out by Zbigniew Pianowski, who verified some of the previous hypotheses.[7] It is regrettable that the systematic investigations of archaeologists and of art and architectural historians, which have brought tangible results and stimulating discussion, have not been accompanied by historical studies. The references to the monastery in the works of Tadeusz Manteuffel, Teresa Dunin-Wąsowicz, Gerard Labuda, and others,[8] or in Białoskórska's dissertation on monastic coins,[9] can hardly be regarded as satisfactory for this purpose. Nor does the edited collection *Z dziejów opactwa cystersów w Wąchocku*, published in the aftermath of the conference held in 1991, provide a complete and up-to-date view of the history of Wąchock Abbey.[10]

For more than a hundred years, researchers primarily sought to establish the provenance of the masons' workshop, to determine the characteristic features of the architecture, and to reconstruct the early endowment of Wąchock Abbey. In regards to the historical aspect of this research, scholars inspected first of all the economic and settlement processes taking place in the monastic estates; the motives behind the foundation or the founders attracted only marginal discussion. The subsequent archaeological and historical research has, however, excited lively debate. First, there has been vigorous debate about the alleged residential complex discovered by Białoskórska and the question of why monks were brought from distant Morimond to Wąchock

---

5   Among the most noteworthy of Białoskórska's publications are, Białoskórska, *Wąchock. Opactwo cystersów*; Białoskórska, 'Problem relacji polsko-włoskich', pp. 249–57; Białoskórska, 'Opactwo cysterskie w Wąchocku', pp. 65–82; Białoskórska, 'Wąchocka rezydencja książęca', pp. 135–78 (see also rhe review of this paper, Gartkiewicz, 'Do redakcji', pp. 98–102); Białoskórska, 'W związku z pismem', pp. 103–10; Białoskórska, 'Kilka uwag', pp. 256–57. Lipińska focused on surveying the estates owned by Wąchock in the Middle Ages. See, Lipińska, 'Badania archeologiczne', pp. 94–97; Lipińska, 'Rola "włości wierzbickiej"', particularly notes 66–68, 71–72, 74–75 for excavation reports on individual structures. A number of interesting observations of the monastery architecture can also be found in Szydłowski, *Pomniki architektury epoki piastowskiej*, pp. 42–60.

6   See Walicki, ed., *Sztuka polska przedromańska* ii, pp. 773–75; Wędzki, 'Wąchock', p. 353; Splitt, 'Stan badań archeologiczno-architektonicznych', pp. 242–47; Lejawa, 'Historia i stan badań archeologicznych', pp. 153–58.

7   Pianowski, 'W sprawie domniemanej rezydencji', pp. 57–66 and Pianowski, *Sedes regni principales*, pp. 103–04.

8   Manteuffel, *Papiestwo i cystersi*, pp. 82–83; Dunin-Wąsowicz, 'Kilka uwag', pp. 167–73; Labuda, 'W sprawie osoby fundatora', pp. 251–55. For summary accounts of the oldest history of the abbey, see also, Wędzki, 'Wąchock', pp. 349–53; Dobosz, *Działalność fundacyjna*, pp. 74–77.

9   Białoskórska, 'Wąchocki skarb', pp. 166–90; cf. Suchodolski, *Moneta możnowładcza*, pp. 98–102. The authors' positions have been summarised in, Brociek, 'Czy cystersi wąchoccy', pp. 3–11.

10 Massalski and Olszewski, eds, *Z dziejów opactwa cystersów w Wąchocku*.

(and other Cistercian abbeys). Second, another discussion was prompted by Stanisław Trawkowski, who questioned the thesis, commonly accepted in historiography, that the abbey was founded by Gedko, Bishop of Kraków.[11] This study seeks to address both these matters of controversy.

From the earliest inquiries into the history of the Cistercian abbey at Wąchock, researchers sought to determine what was happening at the site before the arrival of the Grey Monks. Written sources make no mention of the pre-Cistercian history of Wąchock. According to Jan Długosz, the first monastic buildings and church were erected by Gedko, Bishop of Kraków.[12] In light of Niwiński's research, it should be assumed that the village of Wąchock, originally called Kamienna (*Camina, Camena*), had existed as early as the twelfth century, changing its name to Wielka Wieś at the turn of the fourteenth century. The new settlement that grew up next to it took the name Wąchock.[13] Early studies of the monastic architecture did not reveal any structures earlier than the first half of the thirteenth century.[14] Archaeological and architectural research undertaken from the late 1950s to the 1970s brought sensational results. Białoskórska uncovered architectural relics, which she interpreted as a residential ducal complex consisting of a chapel and a palace dating to the time of Kazimierz I Odnowiciel (the Restorer).[15] The discovery triggered an immediate reaction from architectural historians, who faulted Białoskórska's hypotheses for being inadequately documented.[16] Białoskórska, however, rejected the criticism and held to her views on the earliest history of Wąchock.[17] Her position was partially affirmed by Gerard Labuda. However, having accepted most of Białoskórska's suggestions, Labuda was nevertheless inclined to interpret her discoveries as the remains of a late eleventh-century residence gifted to the Church by Judyta Maria, the wife of Władysław I Herman who was known for her generous patronage. Furthermore, Labuda recognised Wąchock as one of the most important stops on the route from Kraków to Płock, the two main seats of the *princeps* at this time. These hypotheses met with Białoskórska's approval,[18] yet this did not conclude discussion on her vision of the early history of Wąchock. Pianowski, who re-examined the research, questioned the entire interpretation of the residential complex in Wąchock. He considered that the identification of features in the southern part of the monastery as negatives of the walls was unjustified, as they contained no

---

11 Trawkowski, 'Otto z Wierzbicy', in PSB xxiv, pp. 335–37.
12 LB iii, p. 400; Jan Długosz, *Annales*, p. 119.
13 Niwiński, *Opactwo cystersów w Wąchocku*, pp. 28–33.
14 See note 1 and Walicki, ed., *Sztuka polska przedromańska* ii, pp. 773–74, which provides an assessment of research on the architecture and art of the abbey.
15 Białoskórska, 'Wąchocka rezydencja książęca', pp. 135–78.
16 Gartkiewicz et al, 'Do Redakcji', pp. 98–102. See also Konopka, 'List do Redakcji', pp. 245–47.
17 See Białoskórska, 'W związku z pismem', pp. 103–10.
18 Per Białoskórska's hypotheses, Białoskórska, 'Kilka uwag', pp. 256–57, cf. Labuda, 'W sprawie osoby fundatora', pp. 251–55.

building fill or remains. Having analysed the remains of the walls, interpreted by Białoskórska as belonging to the palatial chapel, Pianowski concluded that they were in fact from the foundations of the seventeenth-century cloister, while those features identified as part of the ducal complex turned out to be elements of the thirteenth-century monastery.[19]

Thus, it seems that the settlement in the area of Wąchock must have begun long before the Cistercians arrived there. Yet there are no archaeological or historical grounds on which to suggest that an important ducal residence functioned at the site in the early Piast period. This conclusion forces the discussion of the primary architecture of the Cistercians of Wąchock to come full circle. It is certain, however, that the founder of the new community, not just the Cistercian one, was obliged to make sure, among other things, that God's service could be performed. Given that no church artefacts dating from before the end of the first half of the thirteenth century have been excavated at the site, there are three possible causes of this situation:

a) the original structures were made of wood and no traces of them have survived — a tempting hypothesis considering its simplicity, but probably somewhat deceptive for that;

b) upon their arrival in Poland, the Cistercians were temporarily settled adjacent to a different church, unknown today, though this hypothesis impossible to verify.[20]

The hypothesis of the possible transfer of the Wąchock properties to the bishopric or chapter of Kraków by Judyta Maria is an interesting one, especially as it is substantiated by the analogies of the Chropy and Łagów grants. These goods were also given to the Kraków bishopric thanks to Judyta Maria. The Church of Kraków would have come into possession of the lands on the edge of the Świętokrzyskie Mountains not later than in the early twelfth century and, not having developed intensive settlement in the area, would have transferred them for the seat and endowment of the new Cistercian community in the last quarter of the twelfth century.

The idea of bringing Cistercians to the area must have developed prior to 1179 and was perhaps modelled on the ducal foundation in Sulejów on the Pilica River that in 1176–1177 entered its final stage of development. The so-called Cistercian genealogies (religious sources of various provenance and from different times) most often place the date of the foundation of Wąchock

---

19 See Pianowski, 'W sprawie domniemanej rezydencji', pp. 57–66, and the summary in Pianowski, *Sedes regni principales*, pp. 103–04. See also Pianowski, 'Głos w dyskusji o przedcysterskich', pp. 389–91, 525, and the response, Białoskórska, 'Uwagi o"Głosie w dyskusji"', pp. 393–418; Kurnatowska, 'Głos w dyskusji na temat', pp. 525–27.

20 I argued years ago that archaeological research should precede any further attempt at solving the puzzle of the earliest architecture of the Cistercian monastery at Wąchock. In October 2021 archaeologists commenced work at several sites near Wąchock and may illuminate our understanding of the development of the monastery and its community.

Abbey as 1179, although some mention 1178, 1180, 1181, and even 1166 or 1157.[21] Polish medieval sources provide very little information on this subject. *Spominki koprzywnickie* confuses the foundation of Wąchock Abbey with the date of Gedko's taking over of the episcopal see in Kraków (1166). In turn, the *Katalogi biskupów krakowskich* does not go beyond a general statement that the foundation charter took place at the time when Gedko was Bishop of Kraków.[22] Jan Długosz provides more detailed information, placing the establishment of the new Cistercian community in 1179 and presenting the circumstances of the foundation.[23] The date reported by Długosz has been commonly adopted in historiography; however, the establishment of any church foundation is known to be a long and dynamic process involving the participation of many people. The principles of founding Cistercian institutions were already regulated by the thirteenth-century ordinances of the general chapter. These have been carefully analysed by Józefa Zawadzka, and the models of the foundation processes she reconstructed have subsequently been employed with some success in investigating the origins of the earliest Polish Cistercian communities.[24] This then raises a question as to which stage of the foundation process the date 1179 may refer. It certainly does not refer to the founder's decision or the consent to the foundation granted by the relevant bishop. Rather, the fact that this date is identified in numerous Cistercian genealogies from all over Europe indicates that 1179 refers to a more advanced phase: either the consent to the foundation given by the general chapter or the arrival of the Cistercian convent in Wąchock (Kamienna). Little is either known of the final stages of the foundation process of Wąchock Abbey, the issuing of a foundation charter or the consecration of the monastery church. In accordance with the recommendations of the general chapter, the founder was obliged to create appropriate conditions for the operation of the new institution, and thus provide it material support and enable the *officium divinum* (in short, appropriate church architecture and liturgical books). How this obligation was fulfilled in the case of the Wąchock foundation is, sadly, unknown.

On the basis of the limited sources, all that can be said with certainty is that, around 1179, the work of establishing a new Cistercian mission was fairly advanced and the monks had probably already arrived in the forest land on the edge of the Świętokrzyskie Mountains. The question then arises as to who undertook the endeavour to bring the Cistercian there, and thus took material responsibility for the implementation of this project. The sources are very

---

21 See Janauschek, *Originum cisterciensium*, p. 178.
22 *Spominki koprzywnickie*, MPH iii, p. 134; *Katalogi biskupów krakowskich*, MPH x, pp. 47–48.
23 Jan Długosz, *Annales*, p. 119; LB iii, pp. 400–02.
24 Zawadzka, 'Procesy fundowania opactw cysterskich', pp. 121–50. The frameworks developed by Zawadzka have received wide acceptance, see for example, Wyrwa, *Procesy fundacyjne*; Dobosz, 'Proces fundacyjny', pp. 40–79; Dobosz, *Działalność fundacyjna*, pp. 69–81; Waraczewski, *Proces fundacyjny*, pp. 151–68; Chapter 5 in this volume.

enigmatic about this. A forgery dated 8 May 1260 seems to suggest that efforts to establish the abbey and care for it were undertaken by the Piast dynasty, or more precisely by Kazimierz II.[25] However, in describing the achievements of Gedko, the *Katalogi biskupów krakowskich* notes that: *Hic etiam claustrum in Wanchaczsko consumavit*.[26] In his *Annales*, Jan Długosz clearly states that Gedko was the founder of Wąchock Abbey. This was extended to include details in the *Księga uposażeń diecezji krakowskiej*.[27] Długosz's account was adopted in all early literature and Gedko was generally believed to have been the founder of Wąchock Abbey. Referring to Długosz and the monastic tradition in the monograph of the abbey, Niwiński concluded that 'there is no serious doubt as to who the founder was', and that founder was Gedko.[28] This view was questioned only by Trawkowski who, while preparing his biography of the Małopolska magnate Otto of Wierzbica, took the position that Otto founded the abbey and that Gedko only improved and completed the project. The actual founder was camouflaged by the Cistercians of Wąchock in order to protect themselves against the potential claims of Otto's descendants and family members.[29] Though adopted in some quarters, Trawkowski's position had not otherwise gained much support.[30] Nevertheless, there are here two alternatives: Wąchock Abbey was founded either by Gedko or by Otto of Wierzbica. To settle the question, Otto's genealogy and the false document dated 8 May 1260 require closer examination.

Trawkowski's hypothesis rests on the premise that there was only one Otto of Wierzbica, grandson of Bożen, who died at the turn of the thirteenth century. His family apparently hailed from Bohemia or Moravia. According to Trawkowski, an 1161 document issued at the convention in Łęczyca (or, at least, its better copies), in which Otto and a person named Krystyn appear as witnesses, corroborates the hypothesis. This pair of nobles have usually been considered to be brothers and sons of the Voivode Wszebor. According to Trawkowski, however, this is not an absolute certainty.[31] Having attempted to determine the genealogy of Otto of Wierzbica and Krystyn, Niwiński goes on to state that the two were nobles living in the late-twelfth or early-thirteenth century, and that he believed them to be members of the Gozdawit clan. He

---

25 Niwiński, *Opactwo cystersów w Wąchocku*, p. 158.
26 *Katalogi biskupów krakowskich*, pp. 47–48.
27 *Gedeon Cracoviensis episcopus fundat, construit et dotat monasterium in Wanchoczsko ordinis Cisterciensis supra fluvium Kamyona de bonis sui episcopatus Cracoviensis et plures decimas mense episcopalis illi donat*. Jan Długosz, *Annales*, p. 119; LB iii, p. 400.
28 Niwiński, *Opactwo cystersów w Wąchocku*, pp. 25–27.
29 Trawkowski, 'Otto z Wierzbicy', p. 636.
30 Trawkowski's views have enjoyed wide acceptance. See for example, Lipińska, 'Rola "włości wierzbickiej"', pp. 38–40; Gawlas, *O kształt zjednoczonego Królestwa*, p. 77; Śliwiński, 'Na marginesie fundacyjnej', pp. 174–75.
31 Trawkowski, 'Otto z Wierzbicy', pp. 635–36, argues that the same couple is mentioned in a document dated 8 May 1260: *comes Otto et Cristinus filius Potrconis, frater eius*; Niwiński, *Opactwo cystersów w Wąchocku*, p. 159.

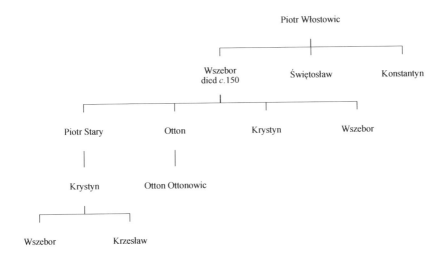

Chart 2. The genealogy of the Łabędzie Clan (the Wszebor line).

was aware, however, of some genealogical contradictions as regards the two nobles, though was unable to explain them in their entirety.[32] A breakthrough came with Janusz Bieniak's pioneering research. Bieniak recognised that there were two pairs of nobles consisting of a Krystyn and an Otto: one in the second half of the twelfth century, and the other in the early thirteenth century. A careful analysis of a 1260 forgery and an 1161 diploma, alongside other source documents, led him to conclude that both pairs of nobles belonged to the same Łabędzie Clan. Based on these findings, the genealogy of the Łabędzie (its Wszebor line) is as follows:

The first Otto-Krystyn pair are the sons of the well-known Voivode Wszebor, a supporter of the younger sons of Bolesław III in the war with Władysław II. The second pair are Krystyn, son of Piotr Stary Wszeborowic, Voivode of Kujawy, and his cousin Otto of Wierzbica, son of Otto.[33] This completely undermines Trawkowski's position because Otto of Wierzbica, the benefactor to the Miechów convent, was Otto's father. It was this Otto Ottonowic, most probably without heirs, who handed over the entire family estate of Wierzbica to the Cistercians of Wąchock.

Arguments against the claim that one of the Ottos was the founder of Wąchock Abbey can be found in the forgeries dated 8 May 1260. The diploma has previously been analysed by Niwiński, who found that the forgery was committed twice, around 1318 and 1440. In the first case, it was done in order to

---

32 Niwiński, 'Ród panów na Wierzbicy', pp. 29–35.
33 Bieniak, 'Polska elita polityczna XII wieku, Part III A', pp. 54–55. See also Bieniak, 'Ród Łabędziów', pp. 9–33, which provides complete source and historiographic documentation.

revoke the bishop's patronage (and probably the knightly obligation to provide transportation), and in the second case, to persuade the nobility to respect the judicial powers of the abbey. Both editions of the false document were later transcribed and copied many times. Niwiński did not find any shortcomings in the matter of the land property enlisted in the document.[34] An authentic charter of Bolesław V issued in Stopnica on 11 June 1275 is a good test of the historicity of much information contained in the forgery. A comparison of the text of both diplomas indicates that the forgery is entirely reliable, and is likely based on monastic records and perhaps an authentic document issued by Bolesław V or Leszek the White. The first possibility is indicated by the seemingly chronologically arranged list of land grants and privileges, while the latter is indicated by the immunity clauses contained therein. For this study, the most important section of the charter is the entry concerning Otto and Krystyn.[35] It was placed between information about the grants of Iwo Odrowąż, which he made while he was still the Leszek's chancellor (hence before 1218), and details of the Princeps' donations (an immunity for the marketplace in Wierzbica), and those of another noble, Mikołaj Repczol, Leszek's chancellor after Iwo Odrowąż. This indicates that Wierzbica was bestowed during Leszek's reign and, since the immunity was granted at the request of his wife Grzymisława, it could have only occurred after their marriage, so in 1207 at the earliest. It should also be noted that the forgery gives details of endowments made by Otto and other members of lay and church nobility, and the name of Gedko is nowhere mentioned. In conclusion, it seems clear that Otto Ottonowic cannot be recognised as the founder of Wąchock Abbey. He granted the estate of Wierzbica with the consent of his closest relative, Krystyn Piotrowic likely between 1207 and 1218, but only as one of his many and generous donations. The claims for patronage over the monastery, put forward by the Łabędzie clan in the times of Jan Długosz, should rather be associated with the Wierzbica estate and the church erected there by their ancestors, probably also by Otto Piotrowic, at the end of the twelfth century.

And so the discussion turns full circle, much as in the case of the pre-Cistercian history of Wąchock. In accordance with the account of Jan Długosz and the monastic tradition, it must be assumed that Wąchock Abbey was founded by Gedko, who probably conceived the idea of bringing the Cistercians to the episcopal estates on the Kamienna River, and was the main organiser of their new institution. The monastery could have been modelled on the Sulejów foundation of Kazimierz II, perhaps also on the earlier foundation of the Gryfici clan in Brzeźnica-Jędrzejów. It cannot be ruled out that Kazimierz

---

34 Niwiński, *Opactwo cystersów w Wąchocku*, pp. 7–17.
35 *Item Wirbicia cum suis pertinentiis et omnibus utilitatibus, mellificio, venatione, castoribus, quam comes Otto et Cristinus filius Potrconis, frater eius dederunt. In qua dux Lestco ad petitionem dominae Grimislauae, uxoris suae, talem costituit libertatem.* Niwiński, *Opactwo cystersów w Wąchocku*, p. 159.

actively participated in this foundation, which could have been related to the joint efforts of the Bishop and the *princeps* to acquire the relics of St Florian, the 1180 convocation in Łęczyca, and the issue of legitimising the rebellion of 1177. The Wąchock foundation was a prestigious reinforcement of the position of the Bishop of Kraków in the rivalry with the Archbishop of Gniezno, and Kazimierz's involvement was connected with gaining and maintaining allies in order to consolidate his position on the Kraków throne. This allows the formulation of a cautious hypothesis that the foundation of Wąchock Abbey took place in the circle of events that followed from the 1177 coup and the church rivalry between Kraków and Gniezno in the last quarter of the twelfth century. It should also be recalled that Gedko belonged to the noble Powała-Wojsławice clan,[36] which from the early twelfth century was known for its generosity towards the Church. Gedko's grandfather, Wojsław, made many donations to the Benedictines of the Holy Cross,[37] while his two sons, Comes Janusz and Trojan, handed some of their properties to the monastery of canons regular in Trzemeszno.[38] Gedko's brother, Wojsław, and his cousin, Żyro, supported the Canons of the Holy Sepulchre in Miechów, as did Gedko himself.[39] The engagement in Church patronage was therefore a family tradition and certainly one of the sources of inspiration for the Bishop of Kraków. Manteuffel's theses about the missionary character of all twelfth-century Cistercian abbeys in Małopolska should be rejected.[40] Grounded in religious (mainly devotional) and prestigious factors, the Cistercian monastic foundation in Wąchock was mostly born of regional and Church politics in Poland at the time.

The original endowment of the newly established monastery is difficult to determine. This is largely due to the attitude of the monks of Wąchock. On the one hand, they sought to avoid the bishop's patronage, so in the fourteenth and fifteenth centuries strove to hide Bishop Gedko's involvement in the foundation, instead emphasising the role of the Piast dynasty.[41] On the other hand, the tradition of Gedko's role was alive and well within the monastery and was echoed in the works of Jan Długosz.[42] The most complete account of the early endowment of the Wąchock Cistercians can be found in the 1260 forgery. Analysis of this source leads to the conclusion that it is a conveniently trumped-up inventory of the abbey's goods (it is difficult to

---

36 Earlier historiography tended to assume that Gedko was a member of the Gryfici clan, see for example, Grodecki, 'Gedko, biskup krakowski', in PSB vii, pp. 366–67. However, Semkowicz argues Gedko should be seen as the son of Trojan, and the grandson of Wojsław, Semkowicz, 'Ród Powałów', pp. 19–20. See also Dobosz, *Działalność fundacyjna*, pp. 361–62.
37 See Derwich, *Benedyktyński klasztor św. Krzyża*, pp. 199–238.
38 This is reported in the forged 1145 diploma of Mieszko III, Piekosiński, *Zbiór dokumentów do objaśniania* 10.
39 KDM ii.375–76.
40 Manteuffel, *Papiestwo i cystersi*, cf. Dobosz, *Działalność fundacyjna*, pp. 130–57.
41 Długosz, *Annales*, p. 119; LB iii, pp. 400–01.
42 Niwiński, *Opactwo cystersów w Wąchocku*, p. 158.

ascertain its original form). The Cistercians probably kept records of the acquired properties, arranged in chronological order, and any changes were scrupulously registered. This material, as suggested above, was used by a monastic forger, perhaps alongside the immunity document. The list of endowments as given in the forged diploma would largely correspond to the chronology of acquisitions. The overwhelming majority of the grants were made during the reign of Leszek the White; only some of them date from the second quarter of the thirteenth century. The description of the monastic property in the forgery suggests that several villages must have developed across this extensive area over time.[43]

As sources attest that Wąchock Abbey was originally called *Camina* (*Camena*), this must be where the village of Kamienna was located. The settlement taking place in this area in the late-twelfth and the early-thirteenth century led to the establishment of the village of Wąchock and the settlement referred to by Jan Długosz as Wielka Wieś, and the disappearance of the name Kamienna. The village of Skarżysko was also close to Wąchock, as were three farmsteads in Mirzec. It follows that Wąchock Abbey was first endowed with regionally compact estates in which settlement was still poorly developed in the twelfth century, but also received extensive forest-covered areas (*cum silvis*) most likely along with beehives and the beavers in the Kamienna river mentioned in the forged charter. This was a good starting point for the development of a new monastic community. The document did not specify who granted the properties to the abbey, but it can be assumed that it was Bishop Gedko who carved them out from the holdings of the Kraków bishopric and handed them over to the Cistercians.[44] The donation was bolstered by Kazimierz II with immunity waivers, the scope of which are impossible to define. They were similar to the grants endowed by the *princeps* to the monasteries in Sulejów, Miechów, and Zagość.[45] It was likely a generally formulated tax exemption concerning the entirety of the abbey's original *fundum*, exempting it from the basic burdens of ducal law. Gedko himself added numerous tithes to further support the foundation, but they are only known from Jan Długosz, who enumerated the following tithe villages of the monastery: Wąchock, Wielka Wieś, Skarżysko, Bzin, Mirzec, Tychowo, Wysocko, Świniów, Jankowice, Zdziechów, Zdziechówek, Zdziechowice, Świerczek, Ziemakowice, Wysoka, Ciepła, Bąków, Guzów, Młodocin, Orońsk, and Ruda.[46] Unfortunately, it

---

43 *In primis ipse locus, in quo est claustrum aedificatum et villae in eodem territorio locatae: villa claustro proxima cum silvis, mellificio, castoribus in Kamena fluvio et omnibus aliis utilitatibus. Item villa, que dicitur Skarsisko, in Merchia tres sortes.* Cf. Niwiński, *Opactwo cystersów w Wąchocku*, pp. 35–42.

44 The participation of Kazimierz II in the foundation is confirmed by a 1260 forgery, Niwiński, *Opactwo cystersów w Wąchocku*, p. 158. See also Dobosz, *Działalność fundacyjna*, pp. 74–77 and 102–03 (Zagość), 104–05 (Miechów), 66–67 (Sulejów).

45 LB iii, pp. 417–20.

46 Cf. Niwiński, *Opactwo cystersów w Wąchocku*, pp. 42–45.

cannot be ascertained which of these twenty-one villages were already in existence in the twelfth century. It is possible that the monastery initially received the land from which it collected tithes, perhaps originally with only a few villages, but subsequent settlement led to the establishment of new population centres, which in turn were listed in full by Długosz.[47]

Gedko's generosity was not particularly impressive: three or four villages with forests and beehives, and tithes from a number of villages that are difficult to identify. Although the endowment was bolstered with fiscal immunity, it was probably still insufficient for the independent operation of the new Cistercian outpost, hence the donations of the rulers, the nobles, and the knights of Małopolska that flowed to the abbey from the thirteenth century through to the reign of Bolesław V. This list begins with Comes Mikołaj, probably Voivode of Kraków, who endowed the village of Bzin, possibly with a tithe, before 1207. Then Iwo Odrowąż, son of Comes Szaweł, at the time still Chancellor of Leszek the White, granted the village of Żyrcin and, if the 1260 forgery is to be believed, the benefits of beehives, hunting grounds, and beavers. This must have happened before 1218, before Iwo was enthroned as Bishop of Kraków. Around the same time, Otto Ottonowic granted the entire estate of Wierzbica. It encompassed Wierzbica and up to three other villages — Łęczany, Pomorzany, and Polany — as well as extensive benefits and a marketplace with a church. At the request of his wife Grzymisława, Leszek endowed the abbey with an extensive immunity and German law for said marketplace. These grants must have taken place after Leszek's marriage in 1207. Further benefactors included: Mikołaj Repczol, chancellor of Leszek the White (Wilczkowice and beavers); Lutogniew, son of Piotr (Bronów); Wszebor, son of Krystyn (Jabłonica with beavers); Knight Krzysz (part of Chronów); Comes Markusz or one of his relatives for his soul (Wawrzyszów with beavers); Lambert, brother of Cherubin of Wysoka (part of Brzezie); Krajek (a farmstead in Krajków); Humbert, Canon of Sandomierz (a farmstead in Prusinowice); and Comes Marek of the Gryfici clan (several farmsteads in Łukawa, in which Leszek later settled tithes). At the end of Leszek's reign the abbey's estate was comprised of several dozen villages (around thirty). Later, it also received tithes, an extensive immunity, and a church with a marketplace in Wierzbica. Thanks to the endowment, the Cistercians were able to commence the construction of a new monastery church with accompanying buildings. It seems that the majority of the grants from the first quarter of the thirteenth century, including the extensive endowment by Otto Ottonowic, were related to the beginning and continuation of the foundation's construction phase, which, perhaps even before 1241, brought about the consecration of the magnificent Romanesque monastery church. The grants were reinforced with benefits that significantly increased the financial capacity of the abbey.

---

47 Niwiński, *Opactwo cystersów w Wąchocku*, pp. 45–56, 158–60. On the matter of the 'Wierzbica estate', see Lipińska, 'Rola "włości wierzbickiej"', pp. 37–50.

The monastery's minting of a coin in the first half of the thirteenth century was probably related to this event.[48]

It follows from the above considerations that the beginnings of the monastery at Wąchock are related to the activities of Gedko, Bishop of Kraków. It is he who brought the first colony of Cistercian monks and allocated them a modest endowment out of the property of the Kraków bishopric. This action was supported by Kazimierz II, who granted the monastery its immunity. The presumption that Otto of Wierzbica was the founder of the monastery at Wąchock should be rejected. Otto's donations to the abbey date to sometime in the early-thirteenth century, and his closest relative, Krystyn Piotrowic, resigned any claims to Wierzbica stemming from his right of proximity. In regards to the oldest monastery buildings, it makes sense to revert to the hypotheses put forward by earlier historiography. Pre-Cistercian Wąchock and Wąchock at the time of the arrival of the first convent of the Cistercian monks are still veiled in mystery, which only renewed archaeological research can illuminate.

---

48   See Białoskórska, 'Wąchocki skarb', pp. 166–90 and Suchodolski, *Moneta możnowładcza*.

CHAPTER 8

Churches in the Endowments to Polish Cistercian Monasteries in the Twelfth and Early Thirteenth Centuries*

The second half of the twelfth century brought significant transformation in the functioning of both the Piast monarchy and the Church in Poland. This period saw the foundations of a market economy begin to emerge as the previous system of internal self-reliance began its slow decline. Gradually, yet systematically, a polyarchy began to prevail over a centralised patrimonial monarchy, and an economically and organisationally strengthened Church started to free itself from ducal power.[1] While this decentralisation of the monarchy served to strengthen the position of the Church, it was also to the benefit of lay elites, and it was within this complex political, economic, and social landscape that the first Cistercian communities appeared in Poland. It remains impossible to unequivocally determine where the initiative to bring Grey Monks to Polish lands came from: court circles (Władysław II and his wife Agnes), magnates (the Pałuki and Gryfici clans), or the bishops (Archbishop Jakub or Janik).[2] Regardless of the answer, the Cistercians quickly settled on the Vistula, Oder, and Warta rivers, gaining support from the church hierarchy, local noble, and knightly structures, as well as from the representatives of the Piast dynasty (or the Pomeranian dukes), who ruled in various districts. The first two foundations were initiated in the 1140s. Established by Zbylut of the Pałuki clan and Archbishop Janik Gryfita, Łekno and Jędrzejów received their foundation charters in 1153. Soon, Cistercian congregations found homes in Kołbacz, Lubiąż, Ląd, Sulejów, Wąchock, Oliwa, and Koprzywnica. The Piast princes followed suit in supporting the foundation

---

* Original publication: Józef Dobosz, 'Kościół jako element uposażenia klasztorów cysterskich w Polsce w XII i początkach XIII wieku', in *Nihil superfluum esse. Studia z dziejów średniowiecza ofiarowane Jadwidze Krzyżaniakowej*, ed. by Jerzy Strzelczyk and Józef Dobosz (Poznań: UAM, 2000), pp. 187–93.

1 See Radzimiński, *Duchowieństwo kapituł katedralnych w Polsce*, pp. 41–57; Szymański, *Kanonikat świecki w Małopolsce*. For the role of the lay nobility in this period, see Bieniak, 'Polska elita polityczna XII wieku, Parts I–IV'.

2 For example, Wyrwa, 'Rozprzestrzenianie się cystersów', pp. 46–48; Wyrwa, 'Powstanie zakonu cystersów', in MCP i, pp. 29–30.

of Cistercian houses, and the monasteries were also regularly patronised by the local clergy, nobles, and knights.³

Founders were obliged to secure the maintenance and livelihoods of the newcomers and enable them to hold *officium divinum*. In addition to adequate economic security (land, people, tithes, income from benefits) and place of residence, they were also required to equip the community with paraments, liturgical books, and a suitable church. Not only was a foundation's first benefactor obliged to donate a part of their immovable and movable property, but they also had to erect a church building or allocate one that already existed.⁴ Setting aside the convent church, Cistercians living across the Polish lands also received additional church or chapel buildings with associated estates, tithes, and incomes as extra endowment. It seems that all newly established Cistercian institutions were granted such additional churches, though in some cases this may have been provisional. The present state of preservation of the buildings or the written records associated with them do not furnish comprehensive information on the construction details of the original churches. Some may have been made of wood, but it is likely that most were made of stone.

A stone church with associated benefits was granted to the Cistercians settled in Jędrzejów by Janik Gryfita. Consecrated sometime between 1109 and 1118 by Maur, Bishop of Kraków, it was a single-nave structure erected in the magnate seat in Brzeźnica and was most likely dedicated to St Andrew. The church may have been modelled on St Andrew's Church in Okół, Kraków, which had been founded by the Toporczyk clan. The church in Brzeźnica had been granted the rights to considerable tithes even before the arrival of the Cistercians, as evidenced by the following passage from its foundation charter:

> these villages with their tithes: Rakoszyno, Pothok, Lyszakowo, Lantczyno, Rakowo, Tharszowa, Chorzewa. Moreover, Bishop Maur of blessed memory, who consecrated this church, and his successor Radosth, added the tithes of the following villages under threat of anathema: Osarowici, Preneslawe, Konare, Michowo, Bechlowo, Borowa, Prekopa, Linowo.⁵

From the words *preterea episcopus*, this passage must be regarded as later interpolation.⁶ At least, this is very likely the case, though it cannot be conclusively

---

3 For more details on each of these tithes, see the entries in MCP ii: Jędrzejów, pp. 90–97; Kołbacz, pp. 135–48; Koprzywnica, pp. 149–57; Ląd, pp. 189–201; Lubiąż, pp. 202–17; Łekno, pp. 230–50; Oliwa, pp. 268–80; Sulejów, pp. 314–23; Wąchock, pp. 328–40.
4 For details on the processes of founding Cistercian abbeys, see, Zawadzka, 'Procesy fundowania opactw cysterskich', pp. 121–50; Dobosz, *Działalność fundacyjna*, pp. 63–81; Wyrwa, *Procesy fundacyjne*, pp. 17–26.
5 *Villas scilicet has: Rakoszyno, Pothok, Lyszakowo, Lantczyno, Rakowo, Tharszowa, Chorzewa cum decimis suis; preterea episcopus bone memorie Maurus, qui eandem ecclesiam consecrauit, et Radosth successor suus decimas super villas has addiderunt sub anathemate: Osarowici, Preneslawe, Konare, Michowo, Bechlowo, Borowa, Prekopa, Linowo.* KDM ii.372; cf. ZDŚ i. 20.
6 See RPD i.55.

verified because the original document is non-extant and only known from seventeenth-century copies. The interpolation must have been made before 1210, because this is when significant parts of Janik's diploma, including this very fragment, were duplicated by Bishop Vincentius of Kraków.[7] It was possibly written in order to rectify an omission at the time the foundation charter was drawn up, or alternatively the interpolation was born from the extension of the grants in the years following 1153.[8] Consecrated by Maur before 1118, the church in Brzeźnica received tithes from seven villages and probably also from Brzeźnica, though it is unmentioned in the document. Bishop Radost added tithes from eight more villages before 1142. The Cistercians then took over a relatively well-equipped family church, with the founder also generously providing them with land.[9] The church became the convent church of the Cistercians of Burgundy, which, in the decades to come, was to be rebuilt several times. As early as in 1167, the church seems to have been reconsecrated and dedicated to the Blessed Virgin Mary and St Adalbert, being remodelled in the process in order to adapt it to the shifting needs of the monastic convent.[10] In 1210, it was replaced with a magnificent Romanesque building, a three-nave basilica, which served the Cistercians in the centuries to come.[11]

As far as other twelfth-century Cistercian abbeys are concerned, the issue of convent churches is more blurred than in the case of Jędrzejów. It may be assumed, following the research of Andrej Wyrwa, that Zbylut of the Pałuki clan donated St Peter's Church to the Cistercians. It was located in a position in the Łekno stronghold that had been previously occupied by a rotunda.[12] The fact that there was a church in the stronghold in 1153 seems to be confirmed by Łekno Abbey's foundation charter, which mentions a church dedicated to the Mother of God and St Peter.[13] It was most likely a single-nave building with a small rectangular chancel terminating in an apse.[14] Probably a little earlier, or around the same time, Zbylut donated a similar church dedicated to St James to the local Benedictine monastery at Mogilno.[15] The church

---

7 KDM, ii.380.
8 There are analogies with the Łekno foundation charter, for more detail see Dobosz, 'Dokument fundacyjny', pp. 53–83 and Chapter 15 in this volume.
9 For further detail, see Dobosz, 'Proces fundacyjny', pp. 40–79; Dobosz and Wetesko, 'Jędrzejów', in MCP ii, p. 91; Chapter 4 in this volume.
10 For discussion of the church's consecration in autumn 1167, see Dobosz, 'Proces fundacyjny'; Chapter 4 in this volume; Dobosz, *Działalność fundacyjna*, pp. 25–28. On the church architecture, see Tomaszewski, *Romańskie kościoły*, pp. 124–28; Świechowski, 'Pierwotny kształt', pp. 211–15; Lechowicz, 'Wyniki badań archeologicznych', pp. 223–32; Kwiatkowska-Kopka, Gliński and Firlet, 'Najnowsze badania archeologiczne', pp. 539–45; Dobosz and Wetesko, 'Jędrzejów', pp. 94, 97.
11 See Dobosz and Wetesko, 'Jędrzejów', pp. 95, 97.
12 For more detail, see Wyrwa, 'Łekno – Wągrowiec', pp. 240–41.
13 KDW i.18.
14 See Wyrwa, 'Łekno – Wągrowiec', p. 243, fig. 57.
15 KDW i.3.

probably did not have such early beginnings as that the one in Brzeźnica; Zbylut may have had it constructed it especially for the incoming Cistercians around the 1140s. Nothing can be said about its endowment before it was handed over to the new tenants.

A foundation charter of 1175 states that the Cistercians who settled in Lubiąż on the Oder after 1163 received the Church of St John the Evangelist's.[16] It seems that it was originally connected to the crossing of the Oder River, the Lubiąż marketplace. and the stronghold; thus it was an integral element of the local settlement complex.[17] Archaeological research failed to provide any confirmation that the church may have been related to the Benedictines who had inhabited Lubiąż before the Cistercians. Believed to date from the end of the twelfth century, the uncovered features have been interpreted as being part of a structure erected by the Cistercians.[18] The beginnings of the later Cistercian convent church were probably related to the ducal foundation. The church was, at first a significant and complementary part of the fast-developing settlement complex, later becoming the seat of the monks. It is difficult to ascertain which of the dukes may have stood behind the establishment of the church market site. Certainly, it seems that when he was returning from exile, Bolesław the Tall found a small marketplace church already in place, which suggests it had been erected by either Władysław II or Bolesław IV.[19]

It is possible that the Cistercians who were brought to Sulejów on the Pilica River by Kazimierz II also received a ready-made church. The written records are silent on this matter and only mention a mysterious St Blaise's Church, in which the monastery's foundation ceremony was held.[20] Previous historical and archaeological research has not provided a final answer to the question of where the original Cistercian church was located, whether in the immediate vicinity of the later monastery buildings or in the area of today's St Florian's Church (on a hill located on the other side of the Pilica River).[21] Likewise, there is no precise information about the original churches associated

---

16 *Lubens et attinentie eius et termini circa Oderam, videlicet ecclesia beati Hiohannis Euangeliste, forum cum omni utlitate, transitus fluvi cum circumequitatione et omnibus in ea sitis.* KDŚ i.55.
17 Bollmann was one of the first to identify the connection of the church with the market, Bollmann, *Die Säkularisation*, p. 116. According to him, the church dates from around mid-twelfth century.
18 See Harc, Harc and Łużyniecka, 'Lubiąż', pp. 203–04, 209–10, 215.
19 For economic and settlement relations in the Lubiąż region, see Wielgosz, 'Początki wielkiej własności', pp. 61–126; Wielgosz, *Wielka własność cysterska*; Trawkowski, *Gospodarka wielkiej własności*, pp. 22–34.
20 St Blaise's Church is mentioned by two well-known Sulejów forgeries: the foundation charter issued allegedly by Kazimierz II (*Acta sunt hec anno ab incarnatione domini MCLXXVI, in ecclesia s. Blassi*) and the tithe document attributed to Archbishop Piotr (*Facta sunt hec in ecclesia Blassi, anno ab incarnatione Domini M.C.LXXVI. IIII Idus Augusti*), ZDŚ i.34–35.
21 For more detail, see Dobosz, *Działalność fundacyjna*, pp. 69–70; Augustyniak, *Cysterskie opactwo*.

with the monasteries in Wąchock, Koprzywnica,Ląd, Oliwa or Kołbacz.[22] New archaeological and architectural research will, perhaps, clarify matters of the locations and construction details of the earliest churches belonging to the monasteries. The state of preservation of relevant architectural features notwithstanding, it seems certain that in all these locations the Cistercians found churches already awaiting them, whether structures founded earlier, or small single-nave churches of stone or brick constructed especially for them.

As noted, in addition to the churches that were intended to serve the convent directly, the Cistercians also received small churches and chapels with all their benefits as part of their endowment. The traces of such grants are still identifiable in the documentary record. Among earlier Cistercian foundations, Lubiąż Abbey was most generously endowed with churches from early on in the process of its foundation. In 1175, the monks from Lubiąż received the chapel with benefits and a tavern in Nabytyn, a locality identified as a suburb of Wrocław, where a St Nicholas' Church is known to have operated in 1218.[23] We can only speculate that these 'benefits' included the income from the marketplace given the market-related associations of St Nicholas. The fact that the property was located near a sizeable stronghold and that there was a tavern in Nabytyn suggests that the grant was generous, offering great prospects in economic terms. The Lubiąż foundation charter refers to a grant of the Church of St Peter and St Paul in Ostrów Tumski, Wrocław, but what this ownership was intended to entail is unknown.[24] The next sentence in the document recounts delivery of oxen by Comes Bezelin to a farm near *Brozte*. Given that *villa iuxta Protzon* granted by Comes Bezelin is mentioned under the year 1201, we can cautiously speculate that it was Bezelin who donated the church.[25]

In the course of the foundation process, Lubiąż Abbey received another church, probably from Bolesław the Tall. This was the church of St Stephen in Bytom, along with which came three villages.[26] One of these was Wierzbnice near Bytom on the Oder River; the identification of the other two remains uncertain — perhaps Brzostów and Pfafendorf near Głogów and Bytom, respectively.[27] Overall, Lubiąż Abbey received a rich endowment, which included churches with the estates and incomes that belonged to them. This probably allowed for a quick start to construction activity and the erection of

---

22   For an overview of the topic, see Walicki, ed., *Sztuka polska przedromańska* ii, pp. 702–03 (Kołbacz), pp. 704–05 (Koprzywnica), p. 725 (Ląd), p. 686 (Oliwa), pp. 773–75 (Wąchock). See also the entried in MCP iii, per note 3 above.

23   *Capella et eius attinentia et taberna in Nabitin*. KDŚ, i.55. Grünhagen, ed, *Regesten zur schlesischen Geschichte*, i.199; see also KDŚ i.55, note 14.

24   *Ecclesia beati Petri in Wrezlawe et attinentie*. KDŚ i.55, note 19.

25   *Nam Bezelinus comes tradidit ecclesie duos boves et e(qu)um et villam iuxta Brozte ex toto cum agris*. KDŚ i.55; KDŚ i.86, note 26.

26   KDŚ i.55.

27   KDŚ i.55, notes 27–29.

a new convent church at the end of the twelfth century, followed by further buildings.

The Cistercians of Sulejów likewise received an additional church in the course of their monastery's foundation. This fact is mentioned in a forged document dated 1176 that relates the abbey's foundation, including the church of Bałdrzychów and its tithe (*ecclesiam quoque de Baldrzykow cum decimis*) and is repeated in the same form in a document attributed to Archbishop Piotr on the matter of the tithe.[28] Sulejów Abbey therefore received the village of Bałdrzychów on the Ner River, along with the church and the tithes that belonged to it. Further forgeries, dated 1176, point to Kazimierz II as the benefactor in question; however, legal action brought against the monastery in 1260–1261 and 1267 by the representatives of the Gąski clan regarding rights over Bałdrzychów suggest that the donation was made by a knight named Bałdrzych.[29] Perhaps he had received this village from Kazimierz for some unknown services sometime in the mid-twelfth century and in turn donated it to the new monastery around 1176. Whether or not Bałdrzych also granted tithes for the church is difficult to conclude. Formally, they were endowed by Archbishop Piotr, but this information, as well as the idea that the village was granted by Kazimierz, may have come from a monastic forger. Perhaps there was some unspecified relationship between Bałdrzych and a significant, albeit little-known, noble named Radosław, who donated five villages on the Ner river to the Cistercians of Sulejów. Bałdrzychów and the small local church could subsequently have become the centre of a settlement complex that, after 1176, was in the hands of a single owner: Sulejów Abbey.

Not long after arriving in Poland, the Cistercians of Wąchock also received a secondary church. However, this was only recorded by a much later source, a document dated 8 March 1260 but, on the basis of monastic records, forged in the fourteenth century.[30] In the grant the Wąchock Abbey received an extensive Wierzbica estate with adjoining lands and benefits from Otto Ottonowic of the Łabędzie clan, with the consent of his closest relative, Krystyn Piotrowic (son of Piotr Wszeborowic).[31] There was also a church near the Wierzbica marketplace, possibly founded by Otto's father sometime in the late twelfth century. The donation was made in the early thirteenth century, before 1218, and probably just after 1207. The Wierzbica estate — consisting at that time

---

28 ZDŚ i.34–35.
29 See Dobosz, *Działalność fundacyjna*, pp. 19–20, 70.
30 *Item Wirbicia cum suis pertinentiis et omnibus utilitatibus, mellificio, venatione, castoribus, quam comes Otto et Cristinus filius Potriconis, frater eius dederunt. In qua dux Lestco ad petirionem dominae Grimislauae, uxoris suae, talem constituit libertatem, quod omnia iura, solutiones, quae ad eum spectabant, dicto claustro indulsit, castores datos simul et falconem remisit, forum liberum haberi ad ecclesiam instituit sub eadem libertate, qualem dominus episcopus in Tarsk et Eslza iure teutonicorum habet.* Niwiński, *Opactwo cystersów w Wąchocku*, p. 159 (a more accurate edition of the document of 8 May 1260).
31 See Chapter 6 in this volume.

of Wierzbica and probably Łęczany, Pomorzany, and Polany, as well as the aforementioned marketplace with a church and extensive benefits — also received an immunity from Leszek the White and German law for the marketplace, which profoundly bolstered the Gedko's modest foundation provisions of 1179. The endowment probably allowed the Cistercians to undertake more extensive construction activity, which was continued and developed thanks to further donations from the Leszek and the nobility.[32]

This overview has looked only at the endowments of churches in the earliest phase of the Cistercian Order in Poland, at a time when the churches were primarily an element of the grants received by the monasteries, and the estates and income belonging to them strengthened the monastic economy. In the following decades, the Gregorian reform and the progressive emancipation of the Church changed the role of those churches already granted, and the Cistercians themselves began to change their attitude to pastoral care.[33] In the lands between the Oder and the Vistula rivers, the Cistercians did not settle in sparsely inhabited territories, but rather often received highly organised estates, which brought considerable real income. This was undoubtedly the case for the settlements with churches, which were usually more than fifty years old. An integral part of the settlements, the churches were often granted along with the settlement, and not only to the Cistercians but also to other orders and church institutions operating in the early Piast period in Poland.

---

32 For more detail on the donation of the Wierzbica estate and its founders see Dobosz, 'Wokół fundatora', pp. 41–49 and Chapter 6 in this volume.
33 See Kłoczowski, 'Z zagadnień funkcji społecznych cystersów', pp. 105–26.

CHAPTER 9

The Foundation of Owińska Abbey in the Light of the Earliest Written Records*

By the thirteenth century, the Cistercian male monasteries operating in Polish territories under the control of the Piast dukes were well established. The abbeys had enjoyed uninterrupted development since the mid-twelfth century when the first Grey Monks came to Łekno (in Pałuki) and Jędrzejów (in the Sandomierz region). At the same time, Cistercian female monasteries had only just begun to function in Poland. The first Cistercian nuns were brought to Trzebnica from Bamberg by the Silesian ducal couple, Henryk I Brodaty (the Bearded) and Jadwiga (Hedwig).[1] They received a protective bull from the Pope as early as November 1202.[2] The origins of the Cistercian Order in Owińska[3] near Poznań are related to the Piasts of Wielkopolska and their involvement the foundation of monastic houses, and to the above-mentioned Trzebnica Abbey.[4]

The foundation of a monastery, however, was a process that stretched over a long period and comprised many stages that required the involvement of a host of people. First, the intention to establish the new religious institution had to be announced by the prospective founder, who would then initiate the first steps in the process: designating a site for the future monastery, determining its endowment, pledging to provide it with books and necessary liturgical items. Then the founder would ask the Ordinary of the appropriate diocese for consent to establish a foundation within his jurisdiction. After these preliminary preparations, the founder, either directly or through intermediaries, would ask the general chapter of the Cistercians to visit the site of the new foundation. At this

---

* Original publication: Józef Dobosz, 'Fundacja opactwa cysterek w Owińskach w świetle najstarszych źródeł', in *Cognitioni gestorum. Studia z dziejów średniowiecza dedykowane Profesorowi Jerzemu Strzelczykowi*, ed. by Dariusz A. Sikorski and Andrzej Marek Wyrwa (Poznań: Wydawnictwo DiG, 2006), pp. 311–31.
1 On the beginnings of Trzebnica Abbey see Zientara, *Henryk Brodaty*, pp. 139–43; Bobowski, 'Podstawy bytu konwentu trzebnickiego', pp. 61–83; Bobowski, 'Fundacja i początki', pp. 31–39. On the wider topic of Cistercian nunneries in Poland, see the essays in Wyrwa, Kiełbasa and Swastek, eds, *Cysterki w dziejach i kulturze ziem polskich*.
2 KDŚ i.92.
3 The name used here is that in current usage. In the Middle Ages it was called by various names: Ovensco, Ovensko, Ouenzk, Ouennzko, Owenzco, etc. It seems that originally the village was known as Owieńska, see T. Jurek, 'Owieńska', pp. 537–48.
4 On the medieval history of Owińska Abbey, see Ratajczak, 'Proces fundacyjny', pp. 531–48; Ratajczak, *Szkic z dziejów opactwa cysterek*, pp. 531–48.

point the initiative would be taken over by the general chapter, which appointed the inspectors — most often abbots from local Cistercian monasteries — and assuming their positive assessment of the proposal, approved the foundation and appointed the Mother Abbess. Next came the monks or nuns who took over the place of residence, appropriately arranged by the founder. The convent would then make arrangements with the founder to obtain legal approval for the foundation, most often finalised through the issuance of a foundation charter. Having settled themselves in the new location, the monks or nuns would then begin to expand the monastery, with the foundation process officially concluding with the consecration of the monastery church.[5]

Written records relating to the earliest history of Owińska Abbey are extremely modest: the text of a few documents dating to around the mid-thirteenth century, records entered under the year 1250 in the statutes of the Cistercian General Chapter, and a small note written against the year 1242 by Jan Długosz in his *Annales*. Dated 24 April 1250, the first of these documents was allegedly issued by Duke Przemysł I, and states that Dobiegniew and Osieczno were granted to the monastery at Owińska along with an immunity.[6] The text of the document has survived only in a late copy and is considered to be a mid-fourteenth century forgery. The next two documents are dated to 1252. The first was issued on 26 April, once again by Przemysł. Together his brother Bolesław Pobożny (the Pious), the Dukes endowed the Cistercian nuns with the village of Owińska with contiguities, land estates and freedoms.[7] As with the 1250 diploma, this document has not survived in its original form and is only known from a late copy (although the original was kept in the Poznań archive until as late as 1943). Scholars are in unanimous agreement that the text of this charter is authentic. The other document issued in 1252, probably dated 2 November, was again jointly issued by Dukes Przemysł and Bolesław.[8] Issued in Owińska, it confirms the donation of the village of Łęg to Gertrude, Abbess of Trzebnica.[9] This information from these sources is complemented by a brief entry under the year 1250 in the statutes of the Cistercian General Chapter, which was a response to a plea addressed to Cîteaux Abbey by an unidentified Polish duke (here called a king) regarding the establishment of a new Cistercian nunnery.[10] Finally, there is a note under the year 1242 in Jan Długosz's *Annales*, in which the chronicler reports that it was Przemysł, Duke of Wielkopolska, who founded the Cistercian female convent at Owińska.[11]

---

5 On the foundation processes of Cistercian abbeys, see Zawadzka, 'Proces fundowania opactw cysterskich', pp. 121–50, and Chapters 4 and 6 in this volume.
6 See KDW i.284.
7 See KDW i.303.
8 For the portrayals of Przemysł I and Bolesław the Pious, see Jasiński, 'Genealogia Piastów wielkopolskich', pp. 39–43.
9 For the Latin text of the document, see KDW i.308.
10 Canivez, ed., *Statuta Capitulorum Generalium* ii, pp. 347, 354.
11 Jan Długosz, *Annales*, p. 40.

Such facts as can be retrieved from these written records have become the basis for suppositions concerning the early history of Owińska Abbey put forward by historians and, in turn, the sources themselves have become objects of analysis and criticism. The first, if still very general statements about the early development of the nunnery, were made by Zenon Chodyński and Edmund Callier.[12] These show a non-critical use of the above-mentioned sources, and especially of the writings of Jan Długosz. Little more was learned from Antoni Małecki and Stanisław Kozierowski, who both mentioned the monastery in their works.[13] The first of the more serious, albeit controversial, studies came in Henryk Likowski's slightly more extensive essay, which sought to present the origins of the Cistercians at Owińska. He placed the foundation processes as occurring between 1242 and 1250, and attempted an analysis of the earliest sources relating to the nunnery.[14] It seems, however, that in both cases he fell wide of the mark. A little earlier, Witold Rubczyński had questioned the authenticity of some of the monastery documents, especially that of 1250,[15] which presented a different thesis from that of Likowski, who believed the 1250 diploma to be authentic and the 1252 endowment to be a forgery.[16] A position on the Owińska documents different from that of Likowski was also taken by German specialists in the field of medieval diplomatics, foremost among them Heinrich Appelt.[17] An extensive examination of the theses put forward by Likowski in Polish scholarship was only undertaken in the 1960s by Franciszek Sikora, who corrected all Likowski's erroneous conclusions regarding the sources. Sikora irrefutably demonstrated the inauthenticity of the 1250 document. According to him, the forgery was drawn up as late as in the mid-fourteenth century. In contrast, both documents issued in 1252 were proved indisputably authentic.[18] Sikora recognised the document of 26 April 1252 as being the legitimate foundation charter. These conclusions were accepted by Maria Bielińska in her monograph on the history of chancellery and diplomatics in thirteenth-century Wielkopolska.[19] Tomasz Jurek, the author of the extensive entry 'Owieńska' in the *Słownik historyczno-geograficzny województwa poznańskiego w średniowieczu*,[20] followed suit. Sikora's inquiries, supported by subsequent publications, probably exhaust further discussions of the legitimacy of the sources relating to the early history of the Cistercians at

---

12 Callier, 'Owińska', pp. 771–72; Chodyński, 'Cystersi w Polsce', pp. 610–11.
13 Małecki, *Z dziejów i literatury pomniejsze pisma*, p. 306; Kozierowski, *Fundacye klasztorne*, p. 30.
14 Likowski, *Początki klasztoru*.
15 Rubczyński, *Wielkopolska pod rządami*, p. 21.
16 Likowski, *Początki klasztoru*, pp. 9–25.
17 Appelt, *Die Urkundenfälschungen*, p. 131, he did not, however, know of the work of Likowski.
18 Sikora, 'Uwagi o dokumentach', pp. 61–73.
19 Bielińska, *Kancelarie i dokumenty*, pp. 246, 251–53.
20 Jurek, 'Owieńska', p. 447.

Owińska. It is worth noting that the person preparing the forgery of 1250 must have used the foundation privilege from 1252.

At this point it is worth once more examining the above-mentioned written records to see what can be reconstructed of the origins of Owińska Abbey. Chronologically, the earliest date referring to the nunnery is provided by Jan Długosz who wrote in the late fifteenth century. He states that in 1242 Przemysł I, Duke of Wielkopolska, founded a Cistercian female monastery in the ducal village of Owińska (in the text: *Owanska*), located on the Warta River. He built a church for the community dedicated to the Blessed Virgin Mary and John the Baptist, and the new nunnery was endowed with ducal villages.[21] This account was accepted by Likowski with no reservation and little critical analysis. Some decades earlier, however, Aleksander Semkowicz had subjected Długosz's work to close examination and suggested that there was a connection between the entry in the *Annales* of 1242 and the previously mentioned document dated 26 April 1252.[22] The date 1242 should probably be treated as a historian's misdating of the foundation by ten years. At that time, in 1242, the sons of Władysław Odonic were just coming to terms with other Piast rulers who controlled large areas of Wielkopolska, Bolesław II Rogatka (the Horned), and the dukes of Opole. Conflict with the Silesian Piasts continued until 1244, when an alliance was concluded and confirmed by marriage between Przemysł and Elizabeth, the daughter of Henry II Pobożny (the Pious), Duke of Silesia.[23] All of this is to suggest that before 1244 there was little opportunity for plans to be made for a religious foundation, a position that has been previously argued by Zofia Kozłowska-Budkowa. According to her, the project of establishing a new Cistercian institution could have started no earlier than 1244.[24] Likowski's hypothesis about the early foundation of the Cistercian nunnery in Owińska, based on Jan Długosz's *Annales* entry, should therefore be rejected.

In 1249, Przemysł issued a diploma to the Knights Templar of Gniezno while he was in Owińska, the document indicating that the village belonged to his mother, Duchess Jadwiga (she died on 29 December that same year).[25] Since Owińska remained in the hands of Przemysł and Bolesław the Pious' mother until the end of 1249, it should be assumed that it was only at that point when

---

21 Jan Długosz, *Annales*, p. 40.
22 Semkowicz, *Krytyczny rozbiór*, pp. 261, 39.
23 For more detail on the situation in Wielkopolska around 1242–1244, see Sikora, 'Uwagi o dokumentach', p. 72, notes 77–78. See Topolski, *Dzieje Wielkopolski*; Jasiński, 'Studia nad wielkopolskim', pp. 161–201. For information on the marriage of Przemysł I and Elżbieta see Balzer, *Genealogia Piastów*, pp. 130–31, cf. Jasiński, 'Genealogia Piastów wielkopolskich', pp. 40–41.
24 Kozłowska-Budkowa, 'Gertruda', p. 408.
25 Ulanowski, 'Dokumenty kujawskie i mazowieckie', p. 352. On Jadwiga, wife of Władysław Odonic, see Balzer, *Genealogia Piastów*, pp. 222–23; Jasiński, 'Genealogia Piastów wielkopolskich', pp. 38–39, cf. Rymar, 'Czy Jadwiga żona Władysława Odonica', pp. 35–59.

the idea of founding a monastery there was born. Perhaps Jadwiga, who was already sick, commended her sons to establish a new Cistercian institution in her village. Certainly, Sikora suspects that this may have been the purpose of Przemysł's visit to Owińska.[26] The entry in the statutes of the Cistercian General Chapter under the year 1250, in which a Polish duke asked to send a monk to assist in the establishment of an abbey for Cistercian nuns, could therefore have been an echo of the efforts of the Dukes of Wielkopolska.[27] The answer to this petition, which most probably came from Przemysł, was positive. A little later in the statutes of the Cistercian General Chapter, we read that the general chapter commissioned the abbots of the Cistercian monasteries in Jędrzejów and Lubiąż to visit the prospective foundation.[28] The move toward founding the abbey must have developed quickly, and the Duke of Wielkopolska easily won the favour of the general chapter of the Cistercians. Subsequent events indicate that the visitors were satisfied with the conditions offered to the new monastic congregation.

Soon after the appointment of the inspectors, the foundation must have received the go-ahead and Trzebnica in Silesia was confirmed as the mother monastery. This can be concluded from the foundation charter issued by Przemysł in Gniezno with the collaboration of his brother Bolesław, dated 26 April 1252.[29] Until the end of World War II, this diploma had been preserved in its original form, though the editor of *Kodeks dyplomatyczny Wielkopolski* knew it only from a copy. In June 1943 the document was moved to the archives in Poznań along with other documents in the possession of the von Treskow family relating to Owińska. However, it went missing after the war. According to the content of the diploma, there had originally been four seals attached to the document, including two ducal seals, but in 1943 only that of Przemysł was still in place. The seal of Bolesław the Pious had to be torn off the document before 1612, just like the seals of Pełka, Archbishop of Gniezno, and Boguchwał, Bishop of Poznań.[30] The recipient of the foundation privilege was Gertruda, Abbess of Trzebnica, and it included the land endowment, tithes, and an immunity. Thus, the Cistercian nuns of Owińska received sixteen villages with tithes: Owińska as the seat of the convent; Bolechowo, Radojewo, Marszowice, and Wierzenica within the Owińska settlement complex; Chludowo, Samołęż, Dobiegniew, Olesno, Golina Czasławowa, Głuchów,

---

26 Sikora, 'Uwagi o dokumentach', p. 67.
27 *Petitio domini regis Poloniae [sic!] de habendo unum monachum de ordine ad dandum consilium et auxilium abbatiae monialium quam ipse construxit exauditur*, Canivez, ed., Statuta Capitulorum Generalium ii, p. 347.
28 *Inspectio abbatiae monialium de Claustro Trebniciensis quam petit Ordini incorporari noblilis vir dux Poloniae, de Andreo et de Lubes abbatibus in plenaria Ordinis potestate committitur qui ad locum*, Canivez, ed., Statuta Capitulorum Generalium ii, p. 354.
29 KDW i.303.
30 Sikora has demonstrated the document's authenticity, Sikora, 'Uwagi o dokumentach', pp. 66–73 (the seals are described on p. 69).

Sienno, and Rokietnica; and the lost settlements of Tmienich, Milkowice, and Raskowicze. In addition, the dukes added thirty *grzywnas*, probably in silver coin, from the mint in Poznań to pay for the nuns' garments, and twelve wax and thirty tallow stones for candles, which were to be used during services. In addition, the nuns of Owińska came into possession of both banks of the Warta River in the vicinity of their estate with all their benefits (forests, fish, beavers, mills, and so on), and they also received the privilege of settling newcomers from Germany in their property without restriction. The new monastery also received an extensive economic and judicial immunity. The Duke also decreed that, in less important cases, the abbess had the right to appoint a judge for the trial of associated clergy, though in more serious cases they were to be brought before the ducal court. The nuns of Owińska were exempted from subjection to numerous tributes, dues, and services resultant from the *ius ducale*: *stróża* (the provision of cereal or money for fortresses); *podwód* (the provision of horses and transport); *powóz* (the provision of carts); *stan* (the provision of board and lodging); *podworowe* (the manorial tribute, most often paid in cereals); *kłodnicze* (the obligation to put wire entanglements on the animal's paths from fallen trunks, from behind which the hunter could more easily reach the animal); *powołowe* (the 'ox-penny'); as well as the exemption from fortress construction and military expeditions (with the exception of the defensive war).[31]

The establishment and endowment of the Cistercian nunnery in Owińska, carried out by Przemysł and confirmed by the document issued in Gniezno, took place in the presence of both the hierarchs of the Church in Poland and the most outstanding secular dignitaries of Wielkopolska. The foundation charter lists the witnesses of this event: Boguchwał, Bishop of Poznań and Chancellor of Duke Przemysł; Isaiah, Chancellor of Kalisz; Marcin, Provost of Santok and Governor Bogumił; Domarat, the Duke's judge; Przedpełk, Castellan of Poznań; Dzierżykraj, Castellan of Gniezno; Arkembold, Castellan of Kalisz; Jarosz, Castellan of Ruda; Przecław, Castellan of Biechów; Boguta, Castellan of Drzeń; Gerward, Castellan of Śrem; Bogusz, Voivode of Kujawy; Bodzęta, Pantler of Gniezno; Bogusza, the Duke's chamberlain; and Henryk, the Duke's steward. Pełka, Archbishop of Gniezno, is also mentioned as one who co-sealed the document.[32]

In light of the above document, we can assume that the process of establishing a new Cistercian monastery was concluded by April 1252. The village of Owińska was designated as its seat, with its economy being based on the noted grants: villages, tithes, and immunity. The foundation charter

---

31 KDW i, pp. 268–69. For the endowments contained therein, see Jurek, 'Owieńska', p. 540, and for the immunity, see Matuszewski, *Immunitet ekonomiczny*, pp. 395–96; Kaczmarczyk, *Immunitet sądowy i jurysdykcja poimmunitetowa*, pp. 247–48.

32 KDW i, pp. 269–70. For analysis of the witness list, see Sikora, 'Uwagi o dokumentach', from p. 68. For discussion of the lay witnesses, see also Bielińska, Gąsiorowski and Łojko, *Urzędnicy wielkopolscy XII–XV wieku*.

does not provide information as to whether any buildings were erected in Owińska, nor does it report the arrival of the convent. The name of the first superior of the local convent is also missing. These gaps are filled by other thirteenth-century documents. At the beginning of November 1252, the Dukes Przemysł and Bolesław stayed in Owińska. It was then that, at the request of Gertrude the Abbess of Trzebnica, they issued a diploma in which they confirm that the village of Łęg had been granted by Władysław Odonic to Trzebnica Abbey. Issued under the year 1252, the document gives a date inconsistent with the Roman calendar. The document reads *anno Domini M.CC.LII. septimo Nonas Novembris*.[33] This may simply be a spelling mistake introduced at the stage of preparing the fair copy, as had been suggested by Jurek. If the writer had misread the draft document as stating VII rather than IIII, then the date *quatro Nonas Novembris* would be 2 November 1252.[34] Since Przemysł and Bolesław also issued another document in Owińska on exactly that day (in that instance for the Cistercians of the monastery at Henryków in Silesia[35]), it seems likely that the confirmation for the Cistercians of Trzebnica could have been issued at the same time. The diploma for Abbess Gertrude contains one more item of information of great importance to this discussion, namely that it was issued eighteen days after the convent's arrival in Owińska.[36] Assuming that the document was issued on 2 November, the nuns must have entered the new nunnery on 16 October 1252. Thus, it can be suggested that, sometime in mid-October 1252, the Cistercian nuns arrived in Owińska to find at the very least temporary monastery buildings and a church. Whether at this stage this had been fabricated from burnt brick, as Jan Długosz claims, is difficult to ascertain.[37]

Owińska Abbey is mentioned in one further document, dated 24 April 1250 and issued again by Przemysł. This grant provided the monastery the villages of Dobiegniew and Osieczno with contiguities, immunity, and the privilege of settlement under German law.[38] This document is known to be a fourteenth-century forgery, largely based on the foundation charter.[39] The forgery mentions Jadwiga, Abbess of Owińska, as the recipient of grants and privileges.[40] Likowski recognised her as the first superior of the female Cistercian convent in Owińska.[41] As the document was forged as late as in the fourteenth century, it is difficult to accept that Jadwiga was the first abbess of the Owińska nunnery without questioning the identification. Semkowicz,

---

33 KDW i.308.
34 Cf. Jurek, 'Owieńska', p. 547.
35 See KDW i.307.
36 KDW i.308.
37 Jan Długosz, *Annales*, p. 40.
38 KDW i.284.
39 KDW i.284.
40 KDW i.284.
41 Likowski, *Początki klasztoru*, p. 62.

who edited an edition of *Żywot świętej Jadwigi*, pointed to the presence in that text of Racława, Abbess of Owińska, and saw in her the abbey's first abbess.[42] This was also the conclusion of Sikora, who identified Racława, a sacristan from Trzebnica and a foster child of Abbess Gertrude, as the first superior of Owińska.[43]

To summarise, from what is known of the beginnings of the Cistercian nunnery in Owińska, it can be said that the idea for a new foundation was conceived around the mid-thirteenth century by members of the Wielkopolska branch of the Piast dynasty. The contacts between the descendants of Władysław Odonic and the Silesian Piasts, the founders and guardians of the first Cistercian foundation in Polish lands in Trzebnica, could have played a role in this undertaking, most notably in the 1244 marriage between Przemysł I and Elizabeth, the daughter of Henry II. There is no doubt that the abbey was founded by Przemysł in cooperation with his brother Bolesław, although the idea may have been that of their mother, Jadwiga. Sometime around 1250, Przemysł petitioned the general chapter of the Cistercians to help establish the new abbey. In 1250, the chapter took up the initiative and appointed the site inspectors for the foundation of the new institution: the abbots from Jędrzejów and Lubiąż. The visit must have been a success, since in 1252 the dukes of Wielkopolska issued a foundation charter and granted rich endowment, tithes, and extensive immunity to the nunnery. Around mid-October 1252, the first Cistercian convent arrived in Owińska from Trzebnica, which demonstrates that some buildings had already been constructed at the site, intended for the seat of the monastery and prepared for God's service. As far as the process of establishing a Cistercian monastery is concerned, as outlined above, the sources do not hint at when the consent for the foundation was granted by the relevant bishop or when the monastery church was consecrated. As to the former, however, we can conclude that the very fact that the Bishop of Poznań co-sealed the foundation charter implies his acceptance of Przemysł's for the foundation. It seems therefore that the idea to found the convent was quickly implemented, within two to three years, and in the next period, both the representatives of the Piast dynasty and the higher clergy of Wielkopolska expressed an avid interest in the Cistercian nunnery at Owińska, providing the nuns with goods, income, and care.[44]

---

42 *Vita sanctae Hedwigis*, MPH iv, pp. 552–53.
43 Sikora, 'Uwagi o dokumentach', pp. 72–73. Similarly, Jurek, 'Owieńska', pp. 543, 547.
44 Endowments for the nunnery were given or confirmed by Przemysł II; Władysław I Łokietek (the Elbow-High); Elisabeth of Poland (daughter of Władysław I, Queen of Hungary); Kazimierz III; Andrzej Zaremba, Bishop of Poznań; Janisław, Archbishop of Gniezno; Arkembold, Voivode of Kalisz. See Jurek, 'Owieńska', p. 540; Ratajczak, 'Proces fundacyjny', pp. 640–43.

Part II

Documents

CHAPTER 10

The Written Document in Medieval Poland*

The origins of the chancellery document in the lands ruled by the Piasts in the tenth century are lost to history. After the formation of the state and its adoption of Christianity, various elements of what we now call 'Western culture' were introduced into Poland by increments, hence the region's slow yet gradual transition from orality to literacy. In as far as contacts and correspondence between states was concerned, the diploma or letter probably came into use upon the formation of the state structure and the adoption of Christianity along the Warta, Oder and Vistula rivers, especially at the level of the ruler's court and the ecclesiastic hierarchy.[1] It is most unfortunate that there are no extant examples of this type of literature predating the late eleventh century. The only exception is the famous summary dated to c. 1080 that begins with the words *Dagome iudex*, found in a register compiled during the papacy of Gregory VII. This, however, is not a product of a Polish chancellery but a late summary of a document entrusting *Civitas Schinesghe* to the Pope. As the full content of the *Dagome iudex* remains unknown, and the register itself contains several puzzling phrases, it has been the subject of a number of heated scholarly debates. The most hotly debated are the use and meaning of the titles of *iudex* and *senatrix* ascribed in the document to the Polish ducal couple Mieszko I and Oda, an evident lack of familiarity with regional nomenclature, and Mieszko's naming as Dagome.[2] The most important thing here, however, is that the so-called *Dagome iudex* provides evidence for the existence of some form of written communication between the realm of Mieszko I, perhaps the duke himself or his family circle, and the Holy See.

A greater number of written documents survive from the eleventh century. Mieszko's grandson, King Mieszko II appears as the addressee of

---

* Original publication: Józef Dobosz, 'Dokument na ziemiach polskich w wiekach średnich', in Ars scribendi. O sztuce pisania w średniowiecznej Polsce, ed. by Leszek Wetesko (Gniezno: Muzeum Początków Państwa Polskiego, 2008), pp. 37–49.
1 This has been addressed by various scholars, see for example Kętrzyński, *Zarys nauki o dokumencie*, pp. 83–84, 90. Cf. ZDŚ i, pp. 57–72; RPD i, pp. 1–19, 141, which identifies only fifteen tenth-century documents connected to the history of Poland.
2 For more detail, see RPD i.2; Kürbis, '*Dagome iudex*', pp. 9–87, which includes the text with Polish translation at pp. 46–50. The text has also been printed in Labuda, *Słowiańszczyzna starożytna*, pp. 159–61. Additional analysis can be found in Łowmiański, *Początki Polski* v, pp. 595–618; Labuda, 'Akt *Dagome iudex*', pp. 17–24.

a letter composed by Matilda of Lorraine (Swabia) around 1028.[3] This letter has been the subject of various analyses by Florentine Mütherich, Jerzy Pietrusiński and, most importantly, Brygida Kürbis.[4] It is one of the few known examples of written correspondence between 'older' and 'younger' Europe dating from this time. The well-known letter of Pope Gregory VII dated 20 April 1075 and sent to Duke Bolesław II Śmiały (the Bold), holds similar significance.[5] In addition, it provides broader context for the ecclesiastical and political situation in Polish lands, emphasising the lack of a metropolitan, an insufficient number of bishops and priests, and touching upon the threads of a policy toward the Rus'.[6] Several eleventh-century examples also demonstrate that the Poles also issued such documents. Lambert, Bishop of Kraków, sent a letter to King Vratislav of Bohemia some time before the end of January 1092.[7] In turn, there is an extant diploma concerning donations to Bamberg Cathedral, issued by Duke Władysław I Herman and preserved in the original, which dates to the end of the eleventh century or the very beginning of the twelfth.[8] This modest collection also included a few forgeries, mentions of at least two acts provided by Gallus Anonymous, and documents — imperial and papal — relating to the boundaries of the Prague bishopric.

Among the forged documents, the Magdeburg forgery is the most prominent, repeatedly discussed and used in a variety of studies on the history of the Church in Poland.[9] Of somewhat lesser importance is the note found in *Vita maior sancti Stanislai*, which summarises an alleged document by Pope Benedict IX, dated in Cologne in 1046, purporting to establish the archbishopric of Kraków for eternity.[10] Similar is the diploma forged in the name of Lambert, Bishop of Kraków, which sanctions tithes for the church

---

3 RPD i.5. The letter has also been published with critical apparatus as *Epistola Mathildis Suevae*, in Kürbis et al., eds, *Kodeks Matyldy*, pp. 139–40.
4 Mütherich, '*Epistola Mathildis Suevae*', pp. 73–78; Pietrusiński, '*Epistola Mathildis Suevae*', pp. 53–72; Kürbis, 'Studia nad Kodeksem Matyldy', pp. 125–49; cf. Kürbis et al., eds, *Kodeks Matyldy*, pp. 49–83; Kürbis, 'Die *Epistola Mathildis Suevae*', pp. 318–38.
5 MPH i, pp. 367–71. The letter has been published in numerous other editions, although it has not been preserved in its original form, RPD i.9.
6 MPH i, pp. 367–68. For more detail on the events mentioned by Pope Gregory VII, see Dobosz, *Monarcha i możni*, from p. 124. A comprehensive analysis of the letter can be found in Skwierczyński, *Recepcja idei gregoriańskich*, pp. 42–56.
7 MPH i, pp. 372–73, here wrongly dated to 1079–1082; RPD i.13. This letter is not known from the original; a copy, once kept in St Emmeram's Abbey at Regensburg, is missing.
8 Krzyżanowski, ed., *Album palaeographicum* 1, pp. 1–2. RPD i.14.
9 KDW i.1; cf. Israel, ed., *Urkundenbuch des Erzstifts Magdeburg*, p. 185. See also, Kehr, *Das Erzbistum Magdeburg*, from p. 53; RPD i.3; Labuda, *Studia*, pp. 431–32, 471; Abraham, *Organizacja Kościoła w Polsce*, pp. 163–67.
10 It must be assumed that an authentic document issued in 1046 never existed, and that the *Vita* author was working from a forgery, see RPD i.6, pp. 7–8. The text of the summary is provided in MPH iv, p. 383, while the relevant forged fragment is given in MPH i, pp. 358–59.

in Kazimierza Mała in 1063. This is a late fourteenth-century document that holds no significance for research on either early Polish diplomatics or the history of the eleventh century.[11] On the other hand, another forgery, the alleged foundation charter of the Benedictine monastery at Mogilno, dated 11 April 1065 in Płock, is very important indeed.[12] Drawn up in the second half of the thirteenth century, the text contains several older layers synthesised into a whole, and it likely serves quite well to preserve information on the early history of Mogilno Abbey.[13]

On the basis of the chronicle written by Gallus Anonymous, Zofia Kozłowska-Budkowa indicates the possible existence of two more documents. In 1000, Pope Sylvester II purportedly issued a bull confirming an agreement between Bolesław I and Emperor Otto III concluded in Gniezno.[14] In 1085 Władysław Herman and his consort, Judith, allegedly sent a request for prayers that they be blessed with a child and heir to Odilon, Abbot of St Giles Abbey, duly accompanied by appropriate intercessory gifts.[15] While it may be accepted that a papal bull was issued in 1000 and that the abbot of the monastery at St Giles received a letter, it must be emphasised that, apart from the references in Gallus' work, no other trace of these documents can be found. There is also an important 1086 document issued by Emperor Henry for Gebhard-Jaromir, Bishop of Prague, sanctioning the boundaries of his diocese as established by Pope Benedict and Emperor Otto I. However, though this connects to the history of the Polish state and Church to some degree, the diploma does not belong to Polish diplomatics.[16]

In summary, there is a mere handful of documents issued by the Polish state or Church that somehow relate to the tenth and eleventh centuries. The only original document among them is the so-called Bamberg document of Władysław Herman. Any speculation about possible missing diplomas aside, it suffices to conclude that, in this early phase, the period of constructing and consolidating the foundations of statehood and shaping the structure of the Church, the advantage of orality over literacy was so great that the latter seemed unnecessary in internal relations. It was used sparingly and only in an 'international' context. Hence, in the wider Polish territories, the twelfth and thirteenth centuries in fact represent the earliest stage of the reception of the written document, yet not as a witness to *memoria* of past times and

---

11   The forgery has been published in Semkowicz, 'Przyczynki dyplomatyczne', p. 46; RPD i.7.
12   KDW i, p. 3. The document was preserved in a forged transumpt of Mieszko III dated 5 September 1103, see RPD i.8, 15.
13   Research on this topic has been surveyed in Kürbis, 'Najstarsze dokumenty', pp. 27–61; Płocha, *Najdawniejsze dzieje*, pp. 78–103; Dobosz, *Monarcha i możni*, pp. 140–47.
14   MPH ii, pp. 19–20; RPD i.4.
15   MPH ii, p. 58; RPD i.10.
16   This document has been preserved in a twelfth-century copy and in Cosmas of Prague's *Chronica Boemorum*, see RPD i.11; cf. RPD i.1, 12. On Cosmas' *Chronica*, see also Labuda, *Studia*, pp. 228–37.

events, but primarily as a means of evidence in the case of trial.[17] Therefore, the pragmatic side of the diploma comes to the fore, and the document itself is written according to patterns and chancellery forms well known and established in the West. The twelfth century saw the beginning of their gradual introduction into common practice, which probably brought about not only the evolution of their form and structure, but also the initial phases in establishing the chancellery institution, followed by its rapid development in the thirteenth century.[18]

Disputes about the origins of the Polish chancellery document and its stages of reception at the courts of early medieval Poland are as old as modern historical science in Poland, which had its beginnings in complex circumstances and out of a variety of traditions during the partitions of the nineteenth century.[19] It remains beyond dispute that the reception of the document was significantly influenced by various ecclesiastical institutions, the intensive development of which can be observed in the lands ruled by the Piasts in the twelfth century.[20] At that time, around 1124, the network of dioceses subordinate to metropolitan Gniezno significantly expanded[21] and, closer to the middle of the century, new orders appeared, mainly Cistercians and various orders of canons regular, headed by the Premonstratensians, further expanding in the following decades.[22] The exchange of correspondence and information with the Holy See — and with other church centres beyond the Elbe and the Empire — was also becoming more frequent. This primarily

---

17 See Kętrzyński, *Zarys nauki o dokumencie*, pp. 81–128, though cf. the extensive review of this still basic textbook on Polish diplomatics by Władysław Semkowicz. Debate in Poland regarding the beginnings of the chancellery document began with the publication of Wojciech Kętrzyński's *Studia nad dokumentami XII w.*, in 1891. For overviews of the ongoing discussion, see Stanisław Kętrzyński, *Zarys nauki o dokumencie*, pp. 463–72; Dymmel, *Bibliografia*, pp. 131–39, 165–71; Adamska, 'Bibliographie', pp. 275–336.

18 For further detail, see Kętrzyński, *Zarys nauki o dokumencie*, pp. 90–128, 129–205; Maleczyński, *Zarys dyplomatyki*, pp. 57–240; Dobosz, 'Badania nad dokumentami', pp. 137–48; Chapter 10 in this volume.

19 For an overview of the beginnings of Polish historical science, building its modern foundations in the nineteenth century, see Grabski, *Zarys historii historiografii polskiej*; cf, Wierzbicki, *Historiografia polska doby romantyzmu*. The growth of Polish diplomatics was a parallel development, beginning with the publication of Joachim Lelewel's dissertation on the study of historical sources in 1822, and maturing over subsequent centuries as generations of scholars published and analysed source texts. On this, see Maleczyński, *Zarys dyplomatyki polskiej*, pp. 39–56; Kętrzyński, *Zarys nauki o dokumencie*, from p. 463; Szymański, *Sto lat przemian metodologicznych*, pp. 35–47.

20 Kętrzyński, *Zarys nauki o dokumencie*, pp. 96–97. For the development of church institutions in the lands under Piast rule in the twelfth century, see Dobosz, *Monarcha i możni*, pp. 171–438.

21 Labuda, 'Początki organizacji kościelnej', pp. 19–60; Dobosz, *Monarcha i możni*, pp. 202–20.

22 For the development of early forms of communal life and the emergence of new orders on Polish soil, see Kłoczowski, 'Zakony na ziemiach polskich', pp. 373–582. On the Benedictines, see Derwich, *Monastycyzm benedyktyński*; on the Cistercians see Wyrwa, 'Powstanie zakonu cystersów', pp. 37–51; see also Part 1 of this volume. No community of canons regular

resulted from the specific situation in Poland: the ecclesiastical arguments between Gniezno and Magdeburg (1133–1136); the removal from the throne of Władysław II in the spring of 1146 and his departure from the country; the 1177 coup in Kraków and its consequences, including the acquisition of the relics of St Florian in 1184; and later papal legacies and bulls concerning the early days of the Gregorian reform.[23] This period probably saw a gradual transformation of the basic court 'writing' institution, the ducal *capella*, into an institution similar to the later chancellery and *scriptoria*, in the broadest sense of the term, without any artificial division into, for example, book *scriptoria* and document *scriptoria*. This resulted in monasteries and bishoprics gaining importance as a place for copying — though there are no hints as to what this looked like in Poland — and perhaps for storing liturgical books, but also for the creation of memorandum notes such as obituaries, fraternity books, inventories, later also annals and chronicles and, of course, administrative documents.[24] It is not certain that the thesis that this period saw the evolution of such documents from the so-called *notitia* to the seal-certified document is justifiable.[25] It seems that both forms were produced simultaneously, but this is probably a separate research issue, and one difficult to settle considering the scarcity of sources.

It is of note that the development of research and debate over the origins of the Polish chancellery document overlapped with heated disputes over forgeries: their form, scope, and causes. A brief look over the work done by Kozłowska-Budkowa in her *Repertorjum polskich dokumentów doby piastowskiej* shows that she identified slightly more than 150 documents and letters as dating to before the end of the twelfth century, including several known only as very late copies or mentioned in other sources, and some produced outside Poland. Of these, she considered as many as thirty-five to

---

in the lands ruled by the Piasts prior to the thirteenth century has been the subject of a comprehensive study, though see Dobosz, 'Piastowie wobec premonstratensów', pp. 6–9 and Chapter 1 of this volume.

23 On the Polish state and church during this period, see Dobosz, *Monarcha i możni*, pp. 222–26, 294–366, 433–38. For the Gregorian reforms in Poland, see Skwierczyński, *Recepcja idei gregoriańskich*, and on its most important advocate, Archbishop Henryk Kietlicz, see Baran-Kozłowski, *Arcybiskup gnieźnieński*. For the events of 1144–1146 and 1177 in Poland, see Bieniak, 'Polska elita polityczna XII wieku, Part III B', pp. 11–44; Bieniak, 'Polska elita polityczna XII wieku, Part III C', pp. 9–66; Bieniak, 'Polska elita polityczna XII wieku, Part III D', pp. 9–53. Further detail on the bringing of St Florian's relics to Kraków can be found in Dobosz, *Działalność fundacyjna*, pp. 86–90, and for the papal legacies to Poland in the late twelfth century, see Dobosz, *Monarcha i możni*, pp. 433–36; Baran-Kozłowski, *Arcybiskup gnieźnieński*, pp. 47–48.

24 On court *capella*, see Maleczyński, *Zarys dyplomatyki polskiej*, pp. 88–98; cf. Kętrzyński, *Zarys nauki o dokumencie*, p. 81. For analysis of scriptoria, see Dobosz, 'Badania nad dokumentami', pp. 137–49; Chapter 10 in this volume; cf. Wałkówski, *Skryptoria cystersów*.

25 For relations between *notitia* and *carta*, see Kętrzyński, *Zarys nauki o dokumencie*, from p. 111; cf. Maleczyński – *Zarys dyplomatyki polskiej*, from p. 68.

be evident forgeries and another nine as interpolated or suspicious.[26] That is, about thirty percent of the collection of the oldest Polish documents known to us today, including those from Pomerania, should be considered at least doubtful even assuming a hypercritical approach to the texts from Kozłowska-Budkowa.[27]

While the twelfth century was undoubtedly a turning point in the reception of the document in the area governed by the Piast dynasty, the thirteenth century represents a significant quantitative breakthrough: the number of issued and forged documents exceeds the scale known from early centuries many times over. It is difficult to cite any specific numbers, but there are hundreds of diplomas of various contents and forms issued for various recipients by different issuers. The subject of disputes being resolved with the help of such administrative documentation is also much broader: the endowments or foundations of various ecclesiastical institutions or their confirmation no longer dominate. There are more and more exchanges of villages; purchase and sale transactions; additional adjudications of various disputes; and, above all, villages and towns began to be founded on German law.[28]

The deepening fragmentation of Poland, coupled with the accompanying rise in the number of ducal courts, undoubtedly brought about a substantial increase in the number of chancelleries which issued diplomas. There was no longer a single centre of power. Instead, there were a dozen or so, and perhaps even more, at the peak of this phenomenon. This multiplication of issuers may well have affected the number of documents issued. The thirteenth century witnessed the development of a number of chancelleries under the control of regional dukes, a fact strongly emphasised by Karol Maleczyński in his textbook on Polish diplomatics.[29] Some of these chancelleries have been the focus of monographs analysing them in quite some depth, while others are still waiting to become the subjects of more comprehensive studies.[30] The main recipient of the royal privileges until then, the Church, lost its dominant position,[31] but its various institutions (bishops, chapters, monasteries) began to issue

---

26 RPD.
27 See Maleczyński's review of RPD, pp. 573–83.
28 On the matter of the expansion of German law, see for example Tyc, *Początki kolonizacji wiejskiej*; A. Gąsiorowski, 'Ze studiów nad szerzeniem', pp. 123–70; Kuraś, *Przywileje prawa niemieckiego*.
29 Maleczyński, *Zarys dyplomatyki*, from p. 99.
30 One of the earliest publications of this type is Krzyżanowski, *Dyplomy i kancelaria Przemysła II*, pp. 122–92. See also Maleczyński, *Studia nad dyplomami*; Bobowski, 'Ze studiów nad dokumentami', pp. 29–66; Bobowski, *Dokumenty i kancelarie na Pomorzu*; M. Bielińska, *Kancelarie i dokumenty*; Sikora, *Dokumenty i kancelaria Przemysła I*; Mazur, *Studia nad kancelarią*; Mitkowski, *Kancelaria Kazimierza Konradowica*; Trelińska, *Kancelaria i dokumenty*; Żerelik, 'Dokumenty i kancelaria Henryka III', pp. 3–99; Suchodolska, *Kancelarie na Mazowszu*.
31 Kętrzyński, *Zarys nauki o dokumencie*, pp. 154–63, suggests that a ducal diploma alone had authoritative value as a charter.

documents on their own.[32] The gradual emancipation of the Church in Poland starting from the second half of the twelfth century and the intensification of its contacts with the West, mainly the Holy See, perhaps acted as an accelerating factor in this. By the thirteenth century there was a marked tendency (better known in the centuries to come) among various ecclesiastical institutions, especially monasteries, to copy their own documentary resources.[33] Gradually, *scriptoria* that roughly conformed to the classical type were formed, which dealt not only with copying books but also with preparing diplomas.[34] Since the judicial monopoly of witnesses was broken in favour of the document,[35] not only the clergy but also the laity reached for the written word. All of this was probably related to the development of immunities,[36] with increasing settlement density prompting disputes over land and income, and the final shaping of knightly law.[37] The emergence of towns also contributed to an increase in the number of diplomas issued, although probably at first not by town chancelleries; initially towns were the recipients of privileges, mainly from ducal sources.[38]

To conclude, the twelfth and thirteenth centuries brought a significant growth of the document as a legal tool, and thus the gradual but still clear development and multiplication of dedicated writing institutions: chancelleries and *scriptoria*. This time also saw the development of the formulary of these documents and the significant expansion of the circle of their recipients, growing to include numerous monasteries and churches, secular nobles (with time, the entire knighthood), and the towns that were progressively establishing themselves in the local economic and social landscape. The increasing number of forged documents was probably not accidental; the spread of this practice indicates the growing ubiquity of the chancellery document as an effective means of evidence in court proceedings.[39] The following centuries

---

32 Kętrzyński, *Zarys nauki o dokumencie*, from p. 163. See also Mieszkowski, *Studia nad dokumentami katedry krakowskiej*; Żerelik, *Kancelaria biskupów wrocławskich*; Rybicka-Adamska, 'Dokument i kancelaria biskupa krakowskiego', pp. 77–142.

33 On Silesian cartularies, see Wałkówski, *Skryptoria cystersów*; a comprehensive analysis of the oldest Henryków cartulary can be found in Bruder, *Najstarszy kopiarz*; the cartulary of Lubiń Abbey has been examined in Wałkówski, 'Najstarszy kopiarz lubiąski', pp. 163–221.

34 See Wałkówski, *Skryptoria cystersów*; cf. Dobosz, 'Badania nad dokumentami', pp. 137–48; Chapter 10 in this volume.

35 Kętrzyński, *Zarys nauki o dokumencie*, from p. 129.

36 For the origins of the immunity, see Grodecki, *Początki immunitetu w Polsce*; Wojciechowski, 'Początki immunitetu w Polsce', pp. 349–66; Matuszewski, *Immunitet ekonomiczny*; Kaczmarczyk, *Immunitet sądowy i jurysdykcja poimmunitetowa*.

37 On knightly law, see Z. Wojciechowski, *Prawo rycerskie*. His opinion that this phenomenon developed as late as in the thirteenth century is hard to maintain and its origins are probably linked to the first land grants and immunity. See Łowmiański, *Początki Polski* vi, pp. 617–34, and also pp. 234–398 for discussion on the beginnings of knightly rule over land in Poland.

38 Unlike church institutions, cities were not co-creators of such documents, Maleczyński, Bielińska and Gąsiorowski, *Dyplomatyka wieków średnich*, p. 320.

39 Dobosz, 'Legitymizacja falsyfikatów dokumentów', pp. 43–54; Chapter 12 in this volume.

witnessed the intensified growth of all the above-mentioned elements and, due to the rapidly growing number of issued documents, the emergence of new phenomena, previously unheard of on Polish soil.

It can probably be said without too much exaggeration that, in the era of the united Piast monarchy and subsequently the great Jagiellon monarchy, the written record became relatively common. It was no longer the sole domain of the recipient, who collected any written certificates of possession, purchase, exchange or donation of movable and immovable property. The royal chancellery[40] and the court chancelleries (*terrestria* and *castrensia*)[41] were established in order that each of them would introduce controls over issued documents through document registers.[42] At the central level, in the royal chancellery (the chancellery of the Kingdom of Poland, then the Crown Chancellery), the foundations for the Crown Record were created (the oldest surviving book dates from 1447). *Judicia castrensia* and *terrestria*, established during the first half of the fourteenth century, also introduced registers toward the end of that century, and initially made all entries in one book. From early modern times, series of these books began to appear in *judicia castrensia*. Document registers became the foundational element of activities undertaken by church (bishop, consistory, chapter house, parish) and town chancelleries (*acta advocatia, scabinalia, consularia*).[43]

The late Middle Ages saw a considerable growth in the number of chancelleries — be they state, church or municipal — and in the number of the staff serving officials,[44] which may have further contributed to the dissemination of written testimonies. It was then that the institution of public notary began to form in Poland. The origins of the notary date back to the thirteenth century, but its major development was observed from the middle of the fourteenth. Reaching its apogee in Poland in the fifteenth century, the public notary was primarily used in Church institutions and gained full evidential force in courts.[45]

The first few centuries of the reception and development of the written document in Poland brought about the consolidation of this type of testimony in at least three groups of society of that time: secular elites, clergy, and bourgeoisie. At that time, the foundations of the chancellery systems

---

40 Important works on royal chancelleries in the fourteenth and fifteenth centuries include Kętrzyński, 'Uwagi o początkach', pp. 1–30; Kętrzyński, *Zarys nauki o dokumencie*, pp. 464–65; Sułkowska-Kurasiowa, *Polska kancelaria królewska*; Krzyżaniakowa, *Kancelaria królewska Władysława Jagiełły*.

41 On such chancelleries, see Perzanowski, *Dokument i kancelaria*.

42 For general information about registers see Szymański, *Nauki pomocnicze historii*, pp. 397–403; Kętrzyński, *Zarys nauki o dokumencie*, pp. 401–61.

43 Radtke, *Kancelaria miasta Poznania*; Skupieński, 'Klasztory a początki', pp. 93–102.

44 Nawrocki, *Rozwój form kancelaryjnych*.

45 On notaries in Poland, see Mikucki, 'Początki notariatu publicznego', pp. 10–26; Kętrzyński, *Zarys nauki o dokumencie*, pp. 230–45; Skupieński, *Notariat publiczny*; Gąsiorowski, *Notariusze publiczni w Wielkopolsce*.

were laid, continuing long after the fifteenth century, and the chancellery document was introduced as a means of evidence in the court proceedings. This undoubtedly meant that the document gradually ceased to fulfil purely elitist and commemorative functions. It became somewhat more common and was used in pragmatics. And yet, all this time, the diploma remained the domain of a relatively small group of people who learned to write and not only had a command of Latin, but were also skilled in the principles of document production.

Attempts to unveil the secrets of medieval documents have been undertaken by scholars in the modern subdiscipline of history called diplomatics. In Poland, such attempts have been undertaken for only two centuries and, therefore, a comprehensive overview of achievements in research on medieval documents is not possible at this point. It need only be emphasised that the medieval diplomas, writs, and charters of Poland have been analysed by many of the most outstanding Polish medievalists. The publication of collections of acts drawn up in medieval Poland, various in form and content, has probably been the most remarkable achievement of the Polish diplomatics. That said, much was done already in the nineteenth century when the so-called diplomatic codices were quite extensively published, and the most outstanding editors of those times should be acknowledged: August Bielowski, Antoni Z. Helcel, Józef Bartoszewicz, Antoni Muczkowski, Franciszek Piekosiński, Stanisław Krzyżanowski, Stanisław Smolka, Bolesław Ulanowski, Ignacy Zakrzewski, and Michał Bobrzyński. Their work was continued in the following years by Władysław Semkowicz, Karol Maleczyński, Jan K. Kochanowski, Zofia Kozłowska-Budkowa, and Józef Mitkowski, and then by Brygida Kürbis, Irena Sułkowska-Kurasiowa, Stanisław Kuraś, Antoni Gąsiorowski, and Tomasz Jasiński.[46] It is beyond the scope of this book to point out which problematic issues of diplomatics have been solved by Polish scholars. After all, diplomatics deals not only with the traditional matters, such as *ductus* and *dictatus*, formularies of individual documents, writers' hands, a variety of chancelleries, lists of witnesses, the public notary or *scriptoria*, and so on, but also seeks to emphasise the pragmatic side of medieval documents, their culture-forming role, their embeddedness in literary culture, and their social significance.[47] There is still much work left to be done by contemporary specialists: the editions of documents dating from the second half of the fifteenth century, extensive late-medieval chancelleries, and the role of the script in societies that were otherwise largely illiterate is still pending research.

---

46 The most important achievements of Polish diplomatics include the publication of the six-volume edition of KDW (Poznań 1982–1999); two volumes of *Nowy kodeks dyplomatyczny Mazowsza* (Wrocław 1989 and Warszawa 2000); and the ongoing publication of *Bullarium Poloniae*.

47 See the available bibliographical works, Dymmel, *Bibliografia*, pp. 131–39, 165–71; Adamska, *Bibliographie*, pp. 275–336; Gąsiorowski, 'Staropolski dokument', pp. 53–62.

CHAPTER 11

Research on the Documents and Scriptoria of the Polish Cistercians*

The documents of the Polish Cistercians have never been a subject of focused analysis. There are some diplomatic and palaeographic examinations of diplomas drawn up in individual monasteries but, most often, comment on the topic has been made on the margins of other issues related to the history of the Cistercian Order. Despite Kazimierz Bobowski's exhortation that Cistercian documentary scriptoria needed to be investigated, the issue has never received wide attention outside the Wrocław research centre.[1] Certainly, no overview of research on Cistercian documents or documents issued for the Cistercians (the so-called recipient's archive) has been produced. However, such a study would allow for the identification of shortcomings and the setting out of further directions for the examination of the Cistercian document. This chapter, therefore, aims to provide just such an overview of the research to date — at times purposeful and advanced, at others incidental and accidental — on Cistercian documents and scriptoria.

Diplomatic and palaeographic studies, which have been analytical fields for almost one and a half centuries, began in earnest with the printing of diplomatic codices around the mid-nineteenth century. These drew attention to the Cistercian communities, who were well-represented in the documentary material of the Polish Middle Ages. These publications used both the original documents and their copies, certified copies, transumpts, and cartularies prepared in monasteries. A fairly thorough search was, therefore, carried out in archives and libraries, and some collections of medieval documents of certain Cistercian monasteries were even published as separate monographs.[2] The documents of the Krzeszów Abbey were printed as a non-critical edition as early as in the eighteenth century.[3] In the early nineteenth century, Johann Büsching published a volume on the documentary heritage of Lubiąż Abbey, while the documents of the Cistercian monasteries in Rudy Raciborskie and Jemielnica were published in the mid-nineteenth century by W. Wattenbach

---

* Original publication: Józef Dobosz, 'Badania nad dokumentami i skryptoriami polskich cystersów', in *Monasticon Cisterciense Poloniae*, ed. by Andrzej Marek Wyrwa, Jerzy Strzelczyk and Krzysztof Kaczmarek, vol. 1 (Poznań: WP, 1999), pp. 137–48.
1 Bobowski, 'O potrzebie badań', pp. 55–62.
2 For example, Smolka, 'Archiwa w W. X. Poznańskim', pp. 170–464.
3 *Diplomatarium Grissoviensene Silesiae coenobii Cisterciensis*, pp. 369–536.

as part of the second volume of the *Kodeks dyplomatyczny Śląska*.[4] In turn, in the late nineteenth century Eugeniusz Janota published the preserved documents of Mogiła Abbey, and Paul Pfotenhauer the medieval diplomas of the Cistercian monastery at Kamieniec Ząbkowicki.[5] Work toward publishing a diplomatic codex of the Cistercian monasteries in Wielkopolska (Ląd, Obra, Łekno) was undertaken by Heinrich Hockenbeck, though the project never came to full fruition. The material collected by Hockenbeck is currently stored in the State Archives in Poznań.[6] Thus, through publication, a significant number of medieval documents of Cistercian monasteries were made available to scholars, which necessitated their critical evaluation. In this way, Cistercian documents, among other things, became subjects in the late nineteenth-century debates about the beginnings of Polish diplomatics and the ensuing long-lasting controversies of the authenticity of some diplomas.

This discussion was initiated by Wojciech Kętrzyński with his classic treatise on the written document of the twelfth century, in which he devoted much space to the earliest documents concerning Polish Cistercian monasteries. Not only did Kętrzyński carefully analyse the two oldest diplomas issued for the monks from Jędrzejów and Łekno in 1153, but also diplomas for other Cistercian institutions established in the twelfth century. Kętrzyński's approach led to critical — perhaps even hypercritical — perspectives on the diplomatic legacy of the twelfth century and, to some extent, this informed the development of the research methods of modern diplomatics. Meticulous analyses of the documents issued for monasteries in Sulejów, Jędrzejów, Łekno, and Lubiąż led Kętrzyński to the conclusion that the majority of them, especially those from the foundation period, were forgeries produced as late as around the mid-thirteenth century. This is how he assessed, among others, the Sulejów foundation charters series of 1176 and 1178, as well as the entire series of documents allegedly issued in the twelfth century for the monastery at Ląd. However, Kętrzyński emphasised that many of the documents have reliable foundations, having been based on earlier monastic records which he called 'protocols'.[7] A significant part of the theses formulated by Kętrzyński in relation to the Cistercian documents is accurate and, with only slight modifications, commonly accepted by historians.

An attempt to refine Kętrzyński's theories on the beginnings of Polish diplomatics, and of his views on forgeries, was undertaken by Stanisław Krzyżanowski. Krzyżanowski sought to soften Kętrzyński's criticism,

---

4 Büsching, *Die Urkunden des Klosters Leubus*; Wattenbach, ed., *Urkunden der Klöster Rauden*.
5 Janota, ed., *Zbiór dokumentów klasztoru mogilskiego* (includes parchment documents from the thirteenth through to the early sixteenth centuries); Pfotenhauer, ed., *Die Urkunden des Klosters Kamenz*.
6 Poznań, State Archives, *Spuścizny osób i rodzin – Hockenbeck-2*, folder II, years 1145–1400, s. 23, no. 1.
7 Kętrzyński, *Studia nad dokumentami XII w.*, pp. 201–313.

especially of the twelfth-century documents he considered to be forgeries.[8] Kętrzyński, however, stood firm on the accuracy of nearly all his statements.[9] However, this was only the beginning of the debates surrounding the origins of Polish diplomatics and the authenticity of the oldest documents. The discussion was soon joined by Antoni Małecki, who, in his valuable dissertation, focused on the issues related to false documents connected to the twelfth century. As part of this, he expressed several original thoughts on the forgeries prepared by the Cistercians (from Sulejów, Jędrzejów, Ląd, Mogiła, Lubiąż, and Łekno).[10] Many of his most impressive arguments, however, can scarcely be considered as valid in detail. The next phase of the debate began with Krzyżanowski's publication of *Monumenta Poloniae paleographica* and *Album paleographicum*, which contained representations of several documents, including those issued for the Cistercians. Extensive and thorough reviews of the works for some time exhausted debate on the origins the written document in Poland, and the place and importance of the Cistercians in its adoption.[11]

This era of the history of Polish diplomatics was closed by Stanisław Kętrzyński who, in 1934, published the first modern textbook on the topic. He also made some comment about the Cistercians, expressing appreciation for their contribution to the reception of the document in Poland.[12] Władysław Semkowicz's extensive article, published around the same time and returning to the discussion on the beginnings of the written document, echoed Kętrzyński's publication.[13] However, disputes over the authenticity of the oldest documents of the Cistercian monasteries in Sulejów, Jędrzejów, Ląd or Lubiąż did not die out, and the publication of *Repertorjum polskich dokumentów doby piastowskiej* by Zofia Kozłowska-Budkowa reopened the discussion with redoubled strength. The author carried out a thorough analysis of the documents over which Wojciech Kętrzyński and Krzyżanowski had disagreed. Her research once again confirmed that numerous Cistercian documents with twelfth-century dates were the products of the subsequent century. Kozłowska-Budkowa pointed out that the majority of these false documents were the so-called diplomatic forgeries, securely grounded in the monastery records, which were the basic material at the disposal of forgers. However, she noticed some traces of factual forgeries, especially in immunity clauses, and sometimes also regarding donations or tithes.[14] Not

---

8   Krzyżanowski, 'Początki dyplomatyki polskiej', pp. 781–820.
9   Kętrzyński, 'O początkach dyplomatyki polskiej', pp. 16–49.
10 Małecki, 'W kwestii fałszerstwa dokumentów', pp. 1–17, 411–80.
11 Semkowicz, review of Kętrzyński, MPP, pp. 385–400; von Ottenthal, review of Kętrzyński, MPP, p. 338.
12 Kętrzyński, *Zarys nauki o dokumencie*.
13 Semkowicz, 'Uwagi o początkach dokumentu polskiego', pp. 1–55.
14 RPD.

entirely agreeing with Kozłowska-Budkowa's assertions, Karol Maleczyński defended the authenticity of the oldest Sulejów documents, among others.[15]

Cistercian documents (and documents issued for the Cistercians) were also widely quoted by Karol Maleczyński in his textbook on Polish diplomatics, by Semkowicz in his study on the history of Latin palaeography, and by the authors of the 1971 textbook on medieval diplomatics, *Dyplomatyka wieków średnich*.[16] The above review shows that 'Cistercian diplomatics' was embedded in the mainstream of the field of research. The Cistercians and their diplomatic legacy were simply one element within the wider disputes and scholarly discussions of the period when modern Polish diplomatics was born and developed. At the same time, detailed studies of the documents from individual monasteries or even individual diplomas were also carried out. Semkowicz, for example, examined and analysed two unknown diplomas allegedly issued by Mieszko III and Kazimierz II for the convent in Jędrzejów. His analysis demonstrated that these were in fact thirteenth-century forgeries.[17] Maleczyński identified new charters dating from the thirteenth century for this monastery in the archives, which he subsequently published.[18] Kozłowska-Budkowa undertook a brief analysis of the documents of the Cistercians of Kamieniec Ząbkowicki, while the previously unknown documents of Leszek the White, issued for the Cistercians of Sulejów, were published by Józef Mitkowski with commentary.[19] The oldest documents from Trzebnica were investigated by Helena Polaczkówna, who examined the testimonies in the 1208 privilege of Henryk I.[20] Heinrich Appelt also took an interest in Trzebnica Abbey, analysing its foundation charter and the abbey's forgeries.[21] Years later, Kazimierz Tymieniecki returned to the question of the interpretation of the earliest Trzebnica documents, but he focused instead on their importance for the research on the economic processes of ducal law.[22] The matter of the chancellery origin of the foundation charters of Krzeszów Abbey was taken up by Andrzej Wałkówski, with Wojciech Kętrzyński undertaking a dedicated analysis of the abbey's 1262 charter.[23] Kętrzyński has also made a number of

---

15 Maleczyński, review of RPD in *Kwartalnik Historyczny* 51 (1937), pp. 573–83.
16 Maleczyński, *Zarys dyplomatyki polskiej*; Semkowicz, *Paleografia łacińska*; Maleczyński, Bielińska and Gąsiorowski, *Dyplomatyka wieków średnich*.
17 Semkowicz, 'Nieznane nadania', pp. 66–97.
18 Maleczyński, 'Dwa nieznane dokumenty', pp. 456–59.
19 Kozłowska-Budkowa, 'Przyczynki do krytyki dokumentów', pp. 1–19; Mitkowski, 'Nieznane dokumenty Leszka Białego', pp. 645–58.
20 Polaczkówna, 'Roty przywileju Henryka I Brodatego', pp. 429–53.
21 Appelt, 'Vorarbeiten zum Schlesischen Urkundenbuch', pp. 1–56 and Appelt, *Die Urkundenfälschungen*.
22 Tymieniecki, 'O interpretację dokumentów trzebnickich', pp. 143–71. See also, Tymieniecki, 'Społeczeństwo śląskie', pp. 319–42; Tymieniecki, 'Najdawniejsza polska ustawa dworska', pp. 21–44.
23 Wałkówski, 'Pochodzenie kancelaryjne pierwszych dokumentów', pp. 44–60; Kętrzyński, 'Eine unechte Trebnitzer Urkunde', pp. 357–60.

assertions about the foundation privilege of Jędrzejów Abbey, while Brygida Kürbis has discussed it within a broader context, juxtaposing it with the foundation charter of the monastery at Łekno and the letter from Bishop Mateusz and Piotr Włostowic to St Bernard of Clairvaux.[24] In the 1990s, I returned to the discussion of the documents published by Semkowicz, alongside several previously known documents of Jędrzejów Abbey from 1166/67. My claim is that these were forgeries based on the monastery records, and thus I rejected the hypothesis that they contained elements of factual forgery, and dated the described events to 1167.[25] I also devoted much attention to the oldest documents of Sulejów Abbey, retaining most of the observations formulated by Kozłowska-Budkowa and Mitkowski, but also being able to present some fresh findings regarding the documents.[26]

The foundation charter of Łekno Abbey is, without doubt, one of the most thoroughly explored and discussed Cistercian documents, and thus was analysed not only as part of the investigations into the early Polish diplomatics, but was subject to several independent studies.[27] Maleczyński analysed its *ductus* as it related to cultural ties with Leodium on the Meuse River.[28] It was also discussed by Kürbis against the background of broader twelfth-century cultural phenomena in Poland, while I have elsewhere summarised the research on the document.[29]

Max Perlbach showed great interest in the archival materials of Ląd Abbey deposited in the archives of the city of Cologne.[30] Brief remarks on one of the Ląd forgeries, currently also stored in the Cologne city archives, were made by Tadeusz Przykowski.[31] Other German scholars analysed the oldest foundation charter of the Cistercian monastery at Lubiąż. Numerous important observations were made in an extensive article by Colmar Grünhagen on the foundation of the monastery in light of criticisms of its foundation documents.[32] Erich Missalek, Hans Krupicka, Adolf Moepert and Victor

---

24 Kętrzyński, 'O przywileju Jana Arcybiskupa', pp. 865–73; Kürbis, 'Cystersi w kulturze polskiego', pp. 321–42.
25 Dobosz, 'Najstarsze świadectwa', pp. 69–71; Dobosz, *Działalność fundacyjna*, pp. 25–28; Dobosz, 'Trzynastowieczne falsyfikaty', pp. 226–29, 236; Chapters 2 and 13 in this volume.
26 Dobosz, 'Najstarsze świadectwa', pp. 66–68; Dobosz, *Działalność fundacyjna*, pp. 19–23 and Dobosz, 'Trzynastowieczne falsyfikaty', pp. 229–33, 237; Chapters 2 and 13 in this volume.
27 Research on this document has been compiled in Dobosz, 'Dokument fundacyjny', pp. 53–83 and in Chapter 15 in this volume, with the charter text. See also Wyrwa, *Procesy fundacyjne*, pp. 53–64.
28 Maleczyński, 'O wpływie szkoły pisarskiej leodyjskiej', pp. 367–80.
29 Kürbis, 'Cystersi w kulturze polskiego', pp. 328–40 (in comparison with the Łekno foundation charter); Dobosz, 'Dokument fundacyjny', pp. 56–57; Chapter 15 in this volume.
30 Perlbach, 'Die Cistercienser Abtei Lond', pp. 71–127.
31 Przypkowski, 'Przywieszenie pieczęci Mieszka Starego', pp. 89–93.
32 Grünhagen, 'Über die Zeit der Gründung von Kloster Leubus', pp. 193–221.

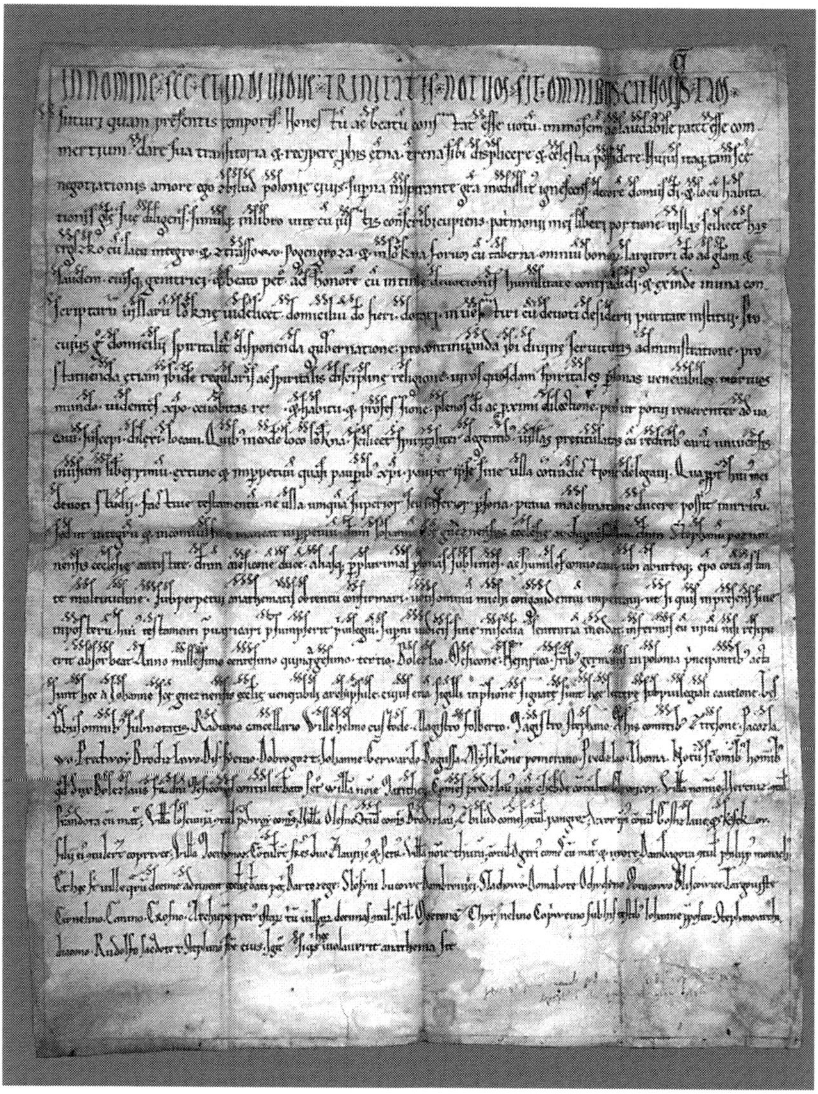

Figure 3. Late twelfth-century copy of the foundation charter of Łekno Abbey. AAG, ref. Dipl. Gn. 4. From the collection of the Cistercians. Photo P. Namiota.

Seidel have all also commented on the Lubiąż charter of 1175.[33] In addition, Konstanty K. Jażdżewski devoted a few remarks to this source, while Andrzej

---

33 Missalek, 'Zur Leubuser Urkunde', pp. 401–04; Krupicka, 'Die sogenannte Leubuser Stiftungsurkunde', pp. 63–110; Moepert, 'Die Echtheit der Leubuser Stiftungsurkunde', pp. 42–3; Seidel, 'Zur Beurteilung', pp. 20–8. See also Tymieniecki, 'Die sogenannte' (review of Krupicka).

Wałkówski attempted to evaluate the development of the script of the Lubiąż documents.[34] Finally, Olgierd Górka's extensive statement on the documentary heritage of Lubiąż should also be acknowledged.[35]

Certain documents of the Cistercian Wąchock Abbey have been the subject of separate considerations. Mieczysław Niwiński devoted some space to the diplomas issued by Władysław I for the estates of the Wąchock community that were located in the Łęczyca region.[36] Zygmunt Wdowiszewski discovered and published several unknown documents related to the history of Wąchock Abbey.[37] The oldest privileges issued for Szczyrzyc Abbey were also widely debated and an extensive commentary was provided by Krzyżanowski.[38] The documents of Pomeranian monasteries were dealt with by German historians, one of whom, Richard Koebner, devoted attention to the history of Oliwa Abbey and its documents from 1178–1342.[39] Heinz Lingenberg raised the matter of the Oliwa documents in his discussion of the monastery's history, while Paul von Nießen undertook some analysis of the documents of Kołbacz Abbey.[40] Among Polish scholars, Józef Spors shared some reflections on Sambor I's diploma for Oliwa, and Klemens Bruski drew attention to the charter issued by Sambor II for the same monastery.[41] Bruski, along with Wiesław Długokęcki, located two documents from 1314 and 1315 in the Pelplin cartulary, which relate to Pelpin Abbey, and printed them with a commentary.[42] Similarly, Stella Maria Szacherska located two unknown documents of the Cistercian monastery at Szpetal, and published them accompanied by detailed analysis.[43] Franciszek Sikora has made numerous comments relating to the documents of the Cistercian nunnery in Owińska.[44]

This perhaps still incomplete overview shows that studies of particular Cistercian convents often included painstaking research on single documents. As a result, the body of scholarship does not constitute a comprehensive survey of documentary heritage but rather is comprised of in-depth analyses of foundation charters or the publication of new source materials complemented with discussion. In addition to this research, over a hundred years of scholarship on the Polish Cistercians produced several monograph-like

---

34 Jażdżewski, 'Poglądy średniowiecza', pp. 67–8. Wałkówski, 'Zarys rozwoju', pp. 15–31; cf. Jażdżewski, 'Jeszcze o lubiąskiej', pp. 203–05; Jażdżewski, 'Dzieła kaligraficzne', pp. 18–24.
35 Górka, 'Przyczynki do dyplomatyki polskiej', pp. 363–428.
36 Niwiński, 'Dokumenty Łokietka', pp. 371–77.
37 Wdowiszewski, 'Nieznane dyplomy średniowieczne', pp. 39–46.
38 Krzyżanowski, 'Przywileje szczyrzyckie', pp. 193–209.
39 Koebner, 'Urkundenstudien zur Geschichte', pp. 5–85.
40 Lingenberg, *Die älteste Olivaer Geschichtsschreibung*; von Nießen, 'Ueber die Echtheit', pp. 108–09.
41 Spors, 'Dokument fundacyjny Sambora I', pp. 111–24; Bruski, 'Sprawa autentyczności dokumentów', pp. 5–20.
42 Bruski and Długokęcki, 'Dwa dokumenty krzyżackie', pp. 245–56, with the text of both documents on pp. 251–56.
43 Szacherska, 'Z dziejów kancelarii', pp. 1–23.
44 Sikora, 'Uwagi o dokumentach', pp. 61–73.

studies on the history of individual Cistercian congregations. At least some of their authors devoted considerable attention to the source heritage, including the documents of individual abbeys.

As far as the monasteries of Pomerania are concerned, some comment on the documentary heritage of Pelplin Abbey was made in the late-nineteenth century by Ernst Strehlke in his dissertation on Doberan Abbey and its branches.[45] Some information on the Oliwa documents was also provided by Kazimierz Dąbrowski in his monograph on the abbey.[46] We can also find some remarks on the documents of Cistercian monasteries in Silesia in several monographs. Franciszek Lenczowski drew attention to those of the monastery at Kamieniec Ząbkowicki, and Ambrosius Rose analysed the diplomas of Krzeszów Abbey.[47] In his work on the Cistercians of Rudy, Stanisław Rybandt included an entire chapter on the monastic scriptorium and the activity of the chancellery, albeit with the latter issue considered but briefly.[48] In his extensive considerations on the history of Lubiąż Abbey, Jażdżewski devoted much space to the cultural activity of the local Cistercians, but he paid particular attention to the library and books produced in the monastery. The scriptorium was discussed in detail in the context of the codices produced in the abbey, though the author also occasionally referenced chancellery documents.[49] Some discussion of the documents of Henryków Abbey can be found in the works of Heinrich Grüger, Hans Goetting and Wilhelm Schulte.[50]

The monasteries located in Wielkopolska have been the subject of several monographic studies, which also included matters concerning the documents relating to individual institutions. Critical analyses of monastic documents can be found in earlier German studies, which provide for a more accurate representation of the abbeys' history. Łekno Abbey and its documentary heritage were explored by Heinrich Hockenbeck, the monastery at Paradyż by Teodor Warmiński, and Obra Abbey by L. Petzelt.[51] In the first chapter of his extensive monograph on Łekno Abbey, Józef Krasoń carried out a detailed analysis of the oldest foundation-related documents (drawn up between 1231 and 1238) and published five of them.[52] His findings were thoroughly re-analysed by Mitkowski, and Andrzej M. Wyrwa has also commented on this subject at length.[53]

---

45 Strehlke, 'Doberan und Neu-Doberan' with, for example, the Pelpin cartulary detailed on pp. 23–24.
46 Dąbrowski, *Opactwo cystersów w Oliwie*; cf. Dąbrowski, *Działalność gospodarcza, społeczna*.
47 Lenczowski, 'Zarys dziejów klasztoru cystersów', 61–103; Rose, *Kloster Grüssau*.
48 Rybandt, *Średniowieczne opactwo cystersów*, pp. 148–62, especially pp. 161–62.
49 Jażdżewski, *Lubiąż*, pp. 174–240 on both the scriptorium and the practices of book making.
50 Grüger, *Heinrichau*; Goetting, 'Urkundenstudien zur Frühgeschichte', pp. 59–86; Schulte, 'Das Heinrichauer Gründungsbuch', 34 (1900), pp. 343–70.
51 Hockenbeck, *Beiträge zur Geschichte*; Petzelt, 'Urkundliches über die ältere Geschichte', pp. 193–97; Warmiński, *Urkundliche Geschichte*.
52 Krasoń, *Uposażenie klasztoru cystersów*, pp. 4–35, 167–69.
53 Mitkowski, review of Krasoń, *Uposażenie klasztoru* cystersów, pp. 304–12; Wyrwa, *Procesy fundacyjne*, pp. 127–35.

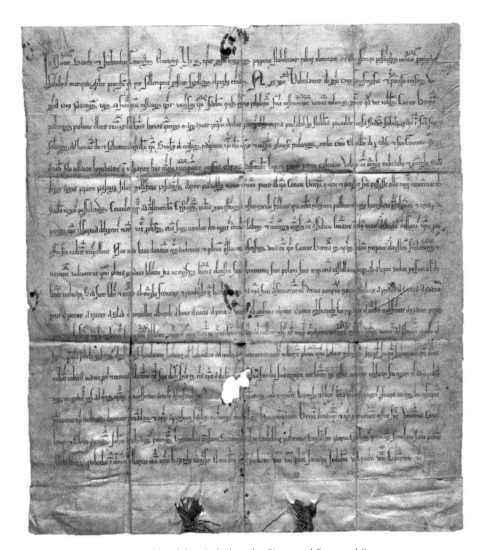

Figure 4. The charter issued by dukes Bolesław the Pious and Przemysł II on 6 January 1278 to confirm Voivode Benjamin's endowment for the Cistercian monastery at Paradyż. APP, Cystersi Paradyż ref. D.I. From the collection of the Cistercians Photo P. Namiota.

There are many valuable book-length studies on the Cistercians of Małopolska, the authors of which occasionally undertook fairly detailed analyses of the documentary heritage of individual institutions. In his monograph on Jędrzejów Abbey, Antoni Z. Helcel devoted some attention to the documents, especially the 1153 foundation charter issued by Archbishop

Jan.[54] In his study on the history of the Szczyrzyc foundation, Stanisław Zakrzewski gave a thorough analysis of the oldest privileges of the abbey, which provoked a response from Krzyżanowski.[55] Niwiński wrote a study of another Cistercian monastery at Małopolska, namely Wąchock, focusing on the abbey's economic history. At the beginning of that volume, Niwiński presented his views about the most important sources for the history of the monastery. Those observations included discussion of two documents forged in the name of Bolesław V (dated 1260 and 1271), an overview of other chancellery documents, and a small section about the monastery's cartulary. At the end of his work, Niwiński also published the 1260 forgery.[56] Mitkowski presented an extensive but partial monograph of the Cistercian Abbey at Sulejów, covering its history until the end of the thirteenth century. Mitkowski devoted a relatively large amount of space to an in-depth analysis of the documents prepared in the local scriptorium, as well as those created in other chancelleries and addressed to the monastery. He paid special attention to the forgeries drawn up by the monks of Sulejów, mainly in the thirteenth century, and especially to the series of documents referring to the foundation of the abbey and to the documents concerning the disputes over the village of Łęczno. Mitkowski also made a thorough analysis of the *dictatus* and *ductus* of the Sulejów diplomas, provided sample script and, in the appendix, a register of the thirteenth-century documents. Additionally, Mikowski included an extensive selection of the Sulejów documents from the twelfth through to the fifteen centuries, some previous published with errors, others not yet published — forty documents in total. The description and analysis of the seventeenth-century monastery cartulary is an important addition.[57] Mitkowski's book is deserving of this slightly more extensive summary because, from the point of view of source analysis, it is the finest monograph ever written about a Cistercian monastery in Poland. In regards the research methods and erudition, it remains an unmatched model for contemporary experts in Cistercian issues.

Some commentary on the documents of the monastery at Szpetal has been made, albeit very briefly, by Józef Nowacki and Szacherska.[58] A detailed list of the documents related to Mogiła Abbey and stored in large numbers in the local archives was put together by Gerard Kowalski and Kazimierz Kaczmarczyk just after World War I. It included 309 documents dating between 1220 and

---

54 Helcel, 'O klasztorze jędrzejowskim', pp. 125–228.
55 Zakrzewski, *Najdawniejsze dzieje klasztoru*, pp. 1–75; Krzyżanowski, 'Przywileje szczyrzyckie', pp. 193–209.
56 Niwiński, *Opactwo cystersów w Wąchocku*, pp. 6–20, see also pp. 158–63 for the text of the document of Bolesław V dated 8 May 1260.
57 Mitkowski, *Początki klasztoru cystersów*, pp. 1–132, with transcriptions and copes of the documents on pp. 301–71.
58 Nowacki, *Opactwo św. Gotarda*, pp. 15–22; Szacherska, *Opactwo cysterskie w Szpetalu*, pp. 8–10.

1886.[59] A register of the documents of Kołbacz Abbey was also prepared by Barbara Popielas-Szultka.[60] Among a considerable number of monographs of individual Cistercian monasteries in Poland, there are several in which the analysis of sources, including the documents, was treated as a side issue. The authors focused on using the content of the written accounts, and either postponed their detailed analyses or were content with existing studies on the subject. The works by Mitkowski and, to a lesser extent, by Zakrzewski, Niwiński, and Rybandt are a few notable exceptions.

Cistercian documents and documents issued for the Cistercians were also inspected in services of other issues, both in the field of diplomatics and the history of individual Cistercian communities. A lot of information about the documentary legacy of Pomeranian monasteries (mainly Kołbacz, Oliwa and Pelplin) can be found in the works of nineteenth- and early twentieth-century German scholars. Examples include Heinrich Giesebrecht's largely outdated work on the chronology of the oldest Pomeranian documents, Max Perlbach's still valuable Prussian-Polish study, and Friedrich Salis' article on West Pomerania documents of the twelfth and thirteenth centuries.[61] Hermann Hoogeweg also published numerous comments on the documents of Cistercian monasteries in Western Pomerania.[62]

In the course of studying the diplomatics of individual districts of Poland, some scholars have remarked on regionalism in the shaping and reception of the document in Poland. Gerard Labuda investigated the oldest documents of Gdańsk Pomerania, devoting much attention to the Oliwa diplomas issued by Sambor and Świętopełek.[63] In Maria Bielińska's study dedicated to the thirteenth-century documents and chancelleries of Wielkopolska, she made some remark on the documents addressed by the dukes of Wielkopolska and church hierarchs from Poznań and Gniezno to individual Cistercian monasteries.[64] Information on the documents issued by Przemysł I and Bolesław the Pious for the monastery at Obra and other Cistercian institutions in Wielkopolska can be found in Sikora's works, while Przemysł II's relations with the Cistercians are addressed in Krzyżanowski's now-classic monograph devoted Przemysł's diplomas and chancellery.[65] The offices of Władysław Odonic and Władysław III have been thoroughly investigated by Maleczyński, who

---

59 Kaczmarczyk and Kowalski, eds, *Katalog archiwum opactwa cystersów*, pp. 1–104.
60 Popielas-Szultka, 'Regesty dokumentów', pp. 5–37; cf. Piskorski, 'Z najnowszych badań', pp. 176–79.
61 Giesebrecht, 'Zur Chronologie', pp. 165–83; Perlbach, *Preussisch-polnische Studien*; Salis, 'Untersuchungen zum Pommerschen Urkundenwesen', pp. 129–30.
62 Hoogeweg, *Die Stifter und Klöster*.
63 Labuda, 'Ze studiów nad najstarszymi dokumentami', pp. 113–35; cf. Jasiński, 'Kilka uwag o najstarszych dokumentach', pp. 147–53.
64 Bielińska, *Kancelarie i dokumenty*, and see Jasiński's review of the work.
65 Sikora, *Dokumenty i kancelaria Przemysła*; Sikora, 'Krytyka autentyczności', pp. 139–79; Krzyżanowski, *Dyplomy i kancelaria Przemysława II*, pp. 122–92.

Figure 5. Charter of Kazimierz III from 12 October 1334 for the Cistercian Abbey at Mogiła. Archive of the Cistercian Abbey at Mogiła, ref. 67. From the collection of the Cistercians. Photo P. Namiota.

also noted their contacts with the Cistercians of Wielkopolska.[66] Maleczyński has also looked at the Cistercian documents in his shorter works.[67]

The Cistercian documents have been discussed by Górka, Nowacki, Wdowiszewski, and Roman Grodecki on the margin of other issues.[68] In his analysis of written records regarding the history of the Bogoria family, Wdowiszewski raised the issue of their ancestral foundation in Koprzywnica and printed a 1277 document issued for the Cistercians by Bolesław V.[69] Krzysztof Skupieński has made some comments about Cistercian monasteries from Małopolska as the recipients of decisions in private legal matters, drawing

---

66 Maleczyński, *Studia nad dyplomami*, and see Kozłowska-Budkowa's review of the work.
67 Maleczyński, *Stanowisko dokumentu*; Maleczyński, 'Wpływy obce na dokument Polski', pp. 1–35; Maleczyński, 'Kilka nieznanych dokumentów', pp. 185–96.
68 Górka, *Studia nad dziejami Śląska*; Grodecki, 'Książęca włość trzebnicka', pp. 433–75 (1912) pp. 1–66 (1913); Nowacki, 'Arcybiskup gnieźnieński Janusz', pp. 355–69.
69 Wdowiszewski, 'Ród Bogoriów', pp. 2–3; 83–86; cf. Kozłowska-Budkowa and Szczur, 'Dzieje opactwa cystersów', pp. 71–73.

attention to examples connected to the Cistercian communities at Sulejów, Jędrzejów, Mogiła, and Szczyrzyc.[70]

The cartularies prepared by the Polish Cistercians from the mid-thirteenth century until the dissolution of the order in the nineteenth is a separate research issue. A large number of them have survived to date in Polish archives and libraries, often constituting the only basis for publishing Cistercian-related documents. The research on the cartularies remains underdeveloped, in most cases being limited to references in monographs devoted to the history of particular Cistercian communities.[71] Only Mitkowski has paid more than passing attention to the seventeenth-century cartulary from Sulejów. He prepared its description, analysed both the script and the writing material on which the cartulary was made, examined its content, and determined the time of its creation.[72] The Pelplin cartulary dating from the early fifteenth century (1418–1421) was inspected by Bruski and Długokęcki, who also identified another cartulary from Pelpin dating from the mid-fifteenth century.[73] The oldest known cartulary, a mid-thirteenth-century codex from Lubiąż, was analysed by Wałkówski,[74] while the oldest Henryków cartulary was the subject of a fairly extensive monograph by Artur Bruder.[75] This type of source, like scriptoria, has not been very popular among specialists in the field of diplomatics, specialists in sources or, more broadly, among historians. Despite Bobowski's above-mentioned exhortation that the scriptoria of Cistercian monasteries were deserving of comprehensive studies, a mere handful of relevant publications have thus far appeared in print. Bobowski examined a documentary scriptorium of the Cistercian monastery at Dragun, an institution located outside Poland.[76] He also devoted some attention to the documentary scriptorium of the Cistercian convent in Szczecin, while

---

70 Skupieński, *Funkcje małopolskich dokumentów*, pp. 65–71, and see Mularczyk's review of the work.
71 Some remarks on the seventeenth-century cartulary of Wąchock Abbey are made in Niwiński, *Opactwo cystersw w Wąchocku*, pp. 23–25, while comment on the fifteenth-century Kołbacz cartulary and can be found in Chłopocka, *Powstanie i rozwój*, p. 10. The cartularies of Koprzywnica Abbey are briefly discussed in Kozłowska-Budkowa and Szczur, 'Dzieje opactwa cystersów', pp. 6–7. The sixteenth- and seventeenth-century cartularies of the Cistercian monastery at Żarnowiec are noted in K. Dąbrowski, *Rozwój wielkiej własności*, pp. 8, 148. Similar sources have also been preserved for other Cistercian monasteries. For example: two cartularies of Jędrzejów Abbey, both dating from the early seventeenth century; a cartulary of the monastery at Byszewo-Koronowo, from the end of the seventeenth century; a copy of the seventeenth-century Obra Abbey cartulary that was used by the editors of the KDW; an eighteenth-century cartulary of Ląd Abbey in the State Archives in Poznań; and a fifteenth-century cartulary of Ląd Abbey in the archives of the city of Cologne.
72 Mitkowski, *Początki klasztoru cystersów*, pp. 288–301.
73 Bruski and Długokęcki, 'Kopiarz dokumentów klasztoru cystersów', pp. 295–302.
74 Wałkówski, 'Z badań nad najstarszym kopiarzem', pp. 445–52; Wałkówski, 'Najstarszy kopiarz lubiąski', pp. 163–221; Wałkówski, 'Transumowanie ogólnocysterskich bulli papieskich', pp. 115–21.
75 Bruder, *Najstarszy kopiarz*.
76 Bobowski, *Skryptorium dokumentowe*.

Wałkówski has analysed the relations between the scriptoria of the monasteries in Pforta and Lubiąż and other colonies of Pforta Abbey established in Silesia (Henryków, Kamieniec Ząbkowicki, Krzeszów, Trzebnica).[77] Karl Rother had, many years early, undertaken research into the scriptorium of Henryków Abbey.[78] The topic of Cistercian scriptoria was raised once more in a 1993 symposium in Dąbrowa Niemodlińska entitled 'The monastery in medieval Polish culture'. Here Marek L. Wójcik undertook a close analysis of the scriptorium of the monastery at Rudy Raciborskie, and Wałkówski again discussed the Cistercian monastery at Kamieniec Ząbkowicki.[79] It is also worth noting Rościsław Żerelik's research on the people working in the monastery scriptoria of Silesia, and the work of the German scholar Konrad Wutke in the interwar period, who studied medieval formularies from Silesia, extending to Cistercian monasteries.[80] All the above-mentioned authors, with the exception of Wutke, looked at the topic of the documentary scriptorium in a relatively narrow chronological range, basically limiting their analyses to the thirteenth century. Rybandt discussed the scriptorium of the monastery at Rudy in a wider chronological framework, but most of his analysis concerned the books written in that location.[81] The same is true of the valuable analysis of the literary activity of the Cistercians of Lubiąż by Jażdżewski.[82]

The research on the documents related to the Polish Cistercian monasteries, which has been going on for over a hundred years, has produced erudite conclusions, and in many cases provided the starting point for monographs on individual Cistercian communities. In light of these still merely partial investigations, the Cistercians may be perceived as vitally interested in the document as a means of evidence in court proceedings and as a method of legally securing their property. Cistercian monks were competent and effective users of documents in disputes over property. This is evidenced by, for example, the thirteenth-century trials of Sulejów Abbey and the forgeries drawn up in the monastery scriptorium, as well as court trials conducted by Jędrzejów Abbey with ducal officials.[83] Concern for the monastic property also pushed the Polish Cistercians to forge documents. This is particularly true of the abbeys in Sulejów, Lubiąż, and Ląd, but other institutions also partook

---

77 Bobowski, 'Aktywność skryptorium dokumentowego', pp. 7–19; Wałkówski, 'Wpływy skryptorium klasztoru cystersów', pp. 203–47; Wałkówski, 'Wpływy lubiąskie na skryptorium dokumentowe', pp. 189–221; Wałkówski, *Skryptoria cystersów*.
78 Rother, 'Aus Schreibstube und Bücherei', pp. 44–80.
79 Wójcik, 'Początki skryptorium', pp. 263–77; Wałkówski, 'Skryptorium dokumentowe klasztoru cystersów', pp. 239–61.
80 Żerelik, 'Urzędnicy skryptoriów klasztornych', pp. 557–70; Wutke, *Über schlesische Formelbücher*, pp. 30–31.
81 Rybandt, *Średniowieczne opactwo cystersów w Rudach*, pp. 148–62.
82 Jażdżewski, *Lubiąż*, pp. 174–89.
83 For the processes of Sulejów Abbey, see Mitkowski, *Początki klasztoru cystersów*, pp. 1–85; for Sulejów and Jędrzejów, see Dobosz, 'Trzynastowieczne falsyfikaty', pp. 225–26 and Chapter 13 in this volume.

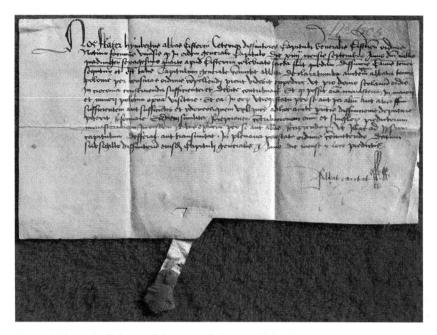

Figure 6. The 1464 diploma of the general chapter of the Cistercians to the Abbot of Mogiła authorising him to engage other Polish abbots in the construction of a house for the students of the monastery. Archive of the Cistercian Abbey at Mogiła, ref. 6. From the collection of the Cistercians. Photo P. Namiota.

of the practice. Upon their arrival in Poland in the mid-twelfth century, the Cistercians seemed to acknowledge the importance of written testimony, hence their probable demands for the issuance of foundation charters, for example at Łekno, Jędrzejów, and Lubiąż. This concern for written testimonies regarding grants and their use in court proceedings before castellan or ducal courts significantly contributed to the reception of the document in Poland, and consequently to the development of legal culture. The fact that the Cistercians began registering the documents in cartularies, in addition to storing genuine diplomas, demonstrates their profound appreciation of the significance of the written document. This phenomenon is observed throughout the entire period of the order's development in Poland, though a marked rise is seen at the start of the Early Modern period. Thanks to this practice, many documents (their content, not form) have survived to this day, and cartularies were used by the publishers of sources from the nineteenth century.

The question of the mutual contacts between the Cistercian monasteries and the transfer of writing patterns within them (*ductus* and *dictatus*) is a separate research problem. It is known, for example, that the document formulary of Lubiąż Abbey was used in Ląd and that is how it got to Gdańsk Pomerania.

Dictatus known from the Sulejów documents found its way to Byszewo. These influences most often spread along the filiation lines of individual monasteries, such as Pforta and Lubiąż, but this is a matter pending further research. The long-observed fact that the monks of some monasteries were called ducal chaplains, such as the monks of Sulejów in the documents of Kazimierz II or Leszek the White, is another vital issue for future research. Maleczyński and, for example, Tadeusz Wasilewski, were inclined to see them as actual members of the ducal *capella* and believed that they fulfilled office functions. Mitkowski was more sceptical, and his position should probably be accepted.[84] The title of ducal chaplain was probably purely prestigious, given only to monks from monasteries associated with the rulers, yet research on this problem should be resumed in a wider context (monks under other rules also bore such titles in the thirteenth century). Further extensive work needs to be done on Cistercian documents, both monographs on individual abbeys and general analyses of Cistercian diplomatics need to be undertaken. The investigations already ongoing on Cistercian scriptoria should, without doubt, be continued. Above all, a comprehensive study of Cistercian culture should be undertaken, in particular a study of the literary culture, perhaps without artificial divisions into documentary scriptoria, book scriptoria or the issue of monastic libraries. Only a holistic view of these issues will show us the Cistercians who dwelt in the Polish monasteries as both the creators and the consumers of culture.

---

84   Mitkowski, *Początki klasztoru cystersów*, pp. 160–61.

CHAPTER 12

Forgeries as a Subject of Research of Polish Diplomatics of the Middle Ages*

Almost forty years ago, the grand *Monumenta Germaniae Historica* conference on forgery in the Middle Ages was held in Munich. Six volumes on various types of forgeries followed in 1988, including two bulky volumes of over 700 pages each devoted to various types of diplomatic forgeries.[1] These, however, contain no significant information on Polish forgeries, even though two Polish authors gave extensive presentations. Gerard Labuda dealt with forged copies of thirteenth-century documents of the Teutonic Knights that, while related to matters in Poland, were produced in foreign offices. Labuda considered eleven documents allegedly or actually issued by Emperor Frederick II, Pope Gregory IX, Prussian Bishop Christian, Konrad I of Mazovia, Gunter, Bishop of Płock, and others.[2] Kazimierz Bobowski analysed West Pomeranian documents dated prior to the end of the thirteenth century, though the principalities should be treated as a 'near-foreign country'.[3] They were beyond the reach of the Piast family and, ruled by their own dynasty, effectively emancipated themselves (although this at times generated other ties of dependence). Some matters related to Polish diplomatics were also taken up by the German scholar Heinrich Appelt, who prepared an extensive dissertation on document forgery in Silesia.[4] Although the material undoubtedly had broad connection to the Piast era, there is little said about Polish research in this case. All in all, it is regrettable that at this important congress, the Poles did not make their voice heard in regard to diplomatic forgery in the Poland of the Piasts and then of the Jagiellons, and the basis and scale of the phenomenon.

Generally speaking, there remains a need for a broader understanding of the phenomenon of document forgery in the Polish Middle Ages. In the course of almost two hundred years of research on various forged documents, the credibility of the document, its authenticity, interpolations, the scope of forgery, and other issues have been considered. The terms *formal (diplomatic)*

---

* Original publication: Józef Dobosz, 'Falsyfikaty jako przedmiot badań polskiej dyplomatyki średniowiecznej', in *Belliculum diplomaticum IV Thorunense. Dyplomatyka staropolska – stan obecny i perspektywy badań*, ed. by Waldemar Chorążyczewski and Janusz Tandecki (Toruń: Uniwersytet Mikołaja Kopernika, 2011), pp. 11–22.
1 *Fälschungen im Mittelalter* (MGH Schriften 33, iii–iv).
2 Labuda, 'Über die angeblichen', pp. 499–521. See also, Labuda, 'Epilog dyskusji', pp. 271–98.
3 Bobowski, 'Zur Frage der Echtheit', pp. 523–30.
4 Appelt, *Die Urkundenfälschungen*, pp. 531–73.

forgery and *factual forgery* were introduced, while several contributions were written regarding forgeries from different regions of Poland and their various issuers. Although these issues became subjects of truly fierce scholarly battles, any summary of these debates and their conclusions is still pending.[5] The intent here is to go some way to filling that gap by sketching a broad picture of the main trends in the research on forgeries undertaken so far in Polish historiography.

The fact that the authenticity of at least some chancellery documents could be questioned to some degree was already noticed back in the Middle Ages,[6] particularly from the end of the twelfth century, when the diploma attained great importance as a means of evidence in court proceedings.[7] It was also identified that the forgers took interest not only in the text of the document itself, but also in the seals that authenticated it.[8] Nonetheless, medieval forgeries only really gained the attention of historians as a research problem in the nineteenth century, when the basic canon of research methods for the discipline was formed. Research considerably accelerated with the large-scale publication of Polish medieval documentary heritage, which began around the mid-nineteenth century. Scholars editing the diplomatic material certainly paid attention to various doubts about the authenticity of their sources that arose during the preparation for printing of items from individual archives and libraries. Quasi-discussions on the credibility and authenticity of the published documents often appeared in footnotes. Franciszek Piekosiński (*Kodeks dyplomatyczny Małopolski* and *Kodeks dyplomatyczny katedry krakowskiej*), and later Jan Karol Kochanowski (*Zbiór ogólny przywilejów i spominków mazowieckich*), excelled in this, as did Antoni Z. Helcel, Bolesław Ulanowski, Ignacy Zakrzewski, and others. It is in the circle of such distinguished nineteenth-century source editors that the first genuine researchers of medieval diplomatic forgery can be found. Stanisław Smolka was already aware of the substantial scale of the phenomenon when, in 1874, he visited and described the archives in Wielkopolska on behalf of the Polska Akademia Umiejętności.[9] From there, study of forgeries grew to be more dynamic, driven at least in part by the publication in 1875 of *Kodeks dyplomatyczny klasztoru tynieckiego* by Smolka and Wojciech Kętrzyński, which included the famous Tyniec document of Cardinal Gilo. This charter, at the time considered the

---

5   See Dobosz, 'Legitymizacja falsyfikatów dokumentów', pp. 43–54; Chapter 12 in this volume; though this intervention should not be read as a conclusion.
6   Mikucki, *Badanie autentyczności dokumentów*.
7   These matters have been most fully analysed in S. Kętrzyński, *Zarys nauki o dokumencie*, pp. 113–78.
8   The thirteenth-century statutes of the general chapter of the Cistercians made seal forgery a punishable offence; in 1247 the general chapter ordered that Friar Jakub of Paradyż Abbey, commonly regarded as a forger of the seal, be captured and imprisoned. Canivez, ed., *Statuta Capitulorum Generalium* ii, pp. 15, 317.
9   Smolka, 'Archiwa w W. X. Poznańskim', pp. 170–464.

oldest Polish document and equally often erroneously dated to 1105, became the subject of countless debates.

In the last quarter of the nineteenth century, some considerable literature arose around the Tyniec forgery, which was largely due to its state of preservation. For a long time, it was known only from copies or transumpts: the transumpt of Bolesław V from 1275, two extracts in the Tyniec cartulary from 1634, and in another monastic cartulary from the seventeenth century.[10] In the context of his research for *Kodeks dyplomatyczny klasztoru tynieckiego*, Kętrzyński devoted an extensive article to the forged documents of Tyniec Abbey as well as a separate paper to Cardinal Gilo's charter, both published in 1874.[11] Kętrzyński would return to the subject fifteen years later, providing a revised analysis of the Tyniec forgery.[12] Other scholars quickly followed in his footsteps, resulting in a fairly extensive list of publications devoted to this allegedly genuine diploma. It must, however, be admitted that the whole discussion was somewhat artificial, as most of its participants agreed on the basic fact that the document was false, and thus primarily argued about minor details of secondary importance. The document was also analysed by Franciszek Piekosiński, who defended the authenticity of the 1275 transumpt, though he considered the document text itself to be a forgery.[13] Other notable scholars who passed some comment on the charter include Fryderyk Papée, Stanisław Krzyżanowski, Antoni Małecki, Władysław Semkowicz, Aleksander Hirschberg, Stanisław Kętrzyński, Zofia Kozłowska-Budkowa, and, on the margins of other works, Tadeusz Wojciechowski, S. Smolka, Władysław Abraham, Karol Potkański, Karol Maleczyński, and Stanisław Taszycki.[14] This multi-threaded and often very detailed discussion brought the following results: the identification of the handwritten basis; the recognition of the document as a forgery; the determination of the scope of factual forgery; the identification of personal and geographical names; the recognition of the dependencies and relations between the preserved copies and the alleged original; and a conclusion that an authentic charter of Cardinal Gilo must have once existed, albeit in a more modest form. The breakthrough came with Krzyżanowski's discovery of the alleged original document in a Viennese antique shop in 1903/04.[15] Later discussion focused only on the content of the forgery, its suitability for research into economic and social relations in Poland at the turn of the twelfth century, or the employed terminology.

10 RPD i.26.
11 W. Kętrzyński, 'Podrobione dyplomata tynieckie', pp. 161–86; Kętrzyński, 'O podrobionym przywileju', pp. 81–97, and see Piekosiński's review of the work.
12 Kętrzyński, 'O przywileju kardynała Idziego', pp. 316–30.
13 Piekosiński, 'Jeszcze słowo o dokumencie legata', pp. 49–74; Piekosiński, *Jeszcze słowo o dokumencie legata*, pp. xvii–xix.
14 Papée, *Najstarszy dokument polski*, pp. 268–312, and for a list of other literature, see RPD i.26.
15 This discovery was detailed by Krzyżanowski in 'Sprawozdania z Czynności i Posiedzeń Akademii Umiejętności', 9 (1904), p. 9.

The multi-faceted discussion of the Tyniec document soon turned out to be just one link in a broader debate about the documents forged in Piast Poland, especially various diplomas bearing twelfth-century dates. The dispute became part of another multi-threaded discussion: the debate about the origins of Polish diplomatics. This had been smouldering since the first critical publication of medieval sources around the mid-nineteenth century, but it entered its main phase when W. Kętrzyński published his ground-breaking dissertation on the earliest Polish documentary sources.[16] Kętrzyński carried out a thorough diplomatic and historical analysis of all documents dated to the twelfth century, including those known as genuine documents, copies, or simply mentioned in other written accounts (slightly more than 100 in total). He concluded that a considerable number of them were forgeries to varying degrees, from slight interpolations to full forgeries in terms of content and form. He pointed to entire cycles of forgeries, such as the documents of the monasteries in Ląd or Sulejów, as well as many other forged acts bearing twelfth-century dates deriving from the monasteries in Trzemeszno, Mogilno, Lubiąż, and Lubiń, among others. In his view, the scale and extent of the forgeries varied from case to case, and many of the forged documents had genuine foundations with minimal recourse to factual forgery. He employed the concept of protocols, or categories of records, which in many cases provided the theoretical basis for forgeries. This was not limited to the so-called notations or objective records, but more broadly all records concerning grants, foundations, and the like connected to various church institutions. In general, Kętrzyński's investigations showed that forgeries were primarily associated with economic matters, sometimes with prestige, and they were created in the thirteenth and fourteenth centuries by various church institutions as need dictated.

Kętrzyński's quite unequivocal position as to the quality of the oldest collection of Polish documents, described by his opponents as hypercritical, sparked one of the most interesting polemics in the history of research on Polish diplomatics. Although, in general, this was apparently a discussion about the beginnings of the document in Poland, forgeries were at the core of this debate. Kętrzyński's *Studia nad dokumentami XII w.* provoked a response from one of the greatest authorities in the field of diplomatics at that time, Stanisław Krzyżanowski. In his extensive 1892 article, Krzyżanowski argued that a significant number of Kętrzyński's conclusions regarding forged documents were exaggerated, and he vigorously defended the authenticity of the earliest documents of Sulejów Abbey.[17] Kętrzyński responded to this lengthy dissertation with an equally expansive article the following year, maintaining his position, yet without putting forward any new arguments or

---

16 Kętrzyński, *Studia nad dokumentami XII w.*
17 Krzyżanowski, 'Początki dyplomatyki polskiej', pp. 781–820.

evidence.[18] Krzyżanowski followed with yet another response, but by this stage both authors were probably beyond being able to arrive at any consensus.[19] The discourse turned from initially stimulating to quite barren as the debaters stiffened their positions.

The following years did not bring any significant progress either in the discussion on the beginnings of the written document in Poland or on documentary forgeries. The research on the latter did, however, expand somewhat to include other examples of questionable diplomas, such as, the alleged 1203 diploma of Konrad of Mazovia, showing an endowment to the Płock bishopric. Its publication in 1888 by Kętrzyński in the fifth volume of MPH, using as his base a fourteenth-century manuscript, triggered yet another debate.[20] Kętrzyński considered it to be a forgery.[21] And yet, despite the perceived contradictions that include inconsistency between witnesses and date, Bishop Gunter being the recipient, and an evidently inappropriate seal, Bolesław Ulanowski went on to argue that such deficiencies could result from negligent copying.[22] Kętrzyński's view that Konrad's diploma, although based on authentic grounds, had most likely been forged in the fourteenth century, was eventually commonly adopted.[23] In his turn, Stanisław Zakrzewski undertook critical examination of documents from the Cistercian monastery at Szczyrzyc,[24] and almost simultaneously opened a critical inquiry into the Gniezno bull of 1136.[25]

Antoni Małecki was perhaps the only historian to adopt a broader perspective on the problem of document forgery in the early twelfth century. In an attempt to provide an overview of the ten-year-long discussion on the oldest Polish diplomas, Małecki wrote an extensive paper, fairly ground-breaking at the time in 1904, in which he sought to place the analysed forgeries in a wider historical context.[26] At the same time, a large-scale publication of Polish

---

18 Kętrzyński, 'O początkach dyplomatyki polskiej', pp. 16–49.
19 Krzyżanowski, 'Jeszcze o początkach', pp. 192–95.
20 MPH v, pp. 419–43. This text is, in fact, a fourteenth-century inventory of the estate of the bishopric of Płock. Konrad's supposed document itself was most accurately published in Kochanowski, ed., *Codex diplomaticus*, pp. 342–46.
21 See Kętrzyński, 'Założenie i uposażenie', pp. 385–92; Kętrzyński, 'Dokument księcia Konrada Mazowieckiego', pp. 289–98, 385–94. Both publications predate the printing of the Płock inventory in MPH.
22 Ulanowski, O *uposażeniu biskupstwa płockiego*, pp. 1–48.
23 Piekosiński, review of Kętrzyński, 'Dokument księcia Konrada Mazowieckiego', pp. 503–12; Kozłowska-Budkowa, 'Pieczęć Konrada Mazowieckiego', pp. 292–95. A more complete discussion can also be found in Łowmiański, *Początki Polski* vi, pp. 355–61. See also Łodyński, *Falsyfikaty wśród dokumentów*, pp. 148–91.
24 Zakrzewski, *Najdawniejsze dzieje*, pp. 3–19; Krzyżanowski, 'Przywileje szczyrzyckie', pp. 193–209.
25 Zakrzewski, *Ze studiów nad bullą*, pp. 1–80. The bull in its present form is considered to be a chancellery copy, see RPD i.31. See also Dobosz, 'Bulla z 1136 roku', p. 130; Maleczyński, *W sprawie autentyczności* (who argued the document was a forgery).
26 Małecki, 'W kwestii fałszerstwa dokumentów', pp. 1–17, 411–80.

documentary resources, or at least the oldest ones, was undertaken.[27] These projects, however, neither stimulated discussion on forgeries nor pushed it in new directions. In the interwar period, the problem of document forgery was essentially dealt with on the margin of other studies, for example during work on the history of ducal chancelleries. Only Zofia Kozłowska-Budkowa, an alumna of Władysław Semkowicz's school who undertook to compile a repertory of the documents dating from the Piast era, had need to fully engage with the issue of forgeries. Taking on a task that presented an enormous challenge, Kozłowska-Budkowa prepared the first issue of this publication in 1937. Extremely thorough in her approach, she compiled more than 150 documents preserved in various formats, including originals, copies, and mentions. The adoption of two main research principles — an overview of the state of research and the examination of the preserved relics of diplomatics — arrived at the following conclusion: from among the analysed collection, she considered over 30 per cent of the documents to be forged, interpolated or uncertain.[28] This led to the establishment of a certain *status quo* with regard to the credibility of the oldest Polish diplomas, although, as with Kętrzyński, Kozłowska-Budkowa did not avoid accusations of hypercriticism.[29]

The *Repertorjum* prepared by Kozłowska-Budkowa did not, however, close the discussion on the forgeries of Poland's oldest documents, even if it never again reached the temperature of the debates of the late-nineteenth century. Olga Łaszczyńska prepared another edition of the bull of 1136,[30] while Maleczyński returned to the topic of its authenticity, arguing that the document was a fake.[31] In turn, while preparing his doctoral dissertation on the earliest history of Sulejów Abbey, Józef Mitkowski returned to the dispute over the foundation cycle Sulejów forgeries, to which Kętrzyński, Krzyżanowski and Małecki had devoted so much attention a half century earlier. In essence, Mitkowski maintained the position of Kętrzyński and Kozłowska-Budkowa, although he located them within the wider context of the history of the monastery and constructed a complementary vision of their origin. Indeed he offered a sophisticated criticism of chancellery documents, by offering analysis of the *ductus*, *dictatus*, content, state of preservation and historical context of the charters. It can even be argued that Mitkowski closed an important phase in the history of Polish diplomatics, ending the disputes of the old schools on the origins of the document in Poland.

The following years brought many interesting contributions, and even raised important and interesting disputes, but it seems that Polish diplomatics slowly lost interest in the great scholarly conflicts. Debate around forgeries

---

27 MPP; Krzyżanowski, ed., *Album palaeographicum*.
28 RPD.
29 Maleczyński, review of RPD, pp. 573–83.
30 Łaszczyńska, ed., *Najstarsze papieskie*, and see Grodecki's review of the work.
31 Maleczyński, *W sprawie autentyczności*.

returned occasionally only on the margins of other major projects. This, for example, occurred when the oldest history of the Benedictine abbey at Mogilno was compiled in the 1960s, causing historians to suddenly recall the Mogilno forgery dated 1065. At that time, Brygida Kürbis provided a new analysis of the document and, in his monograph on the monastery, Józef Płocha attempted to expand on that analysis.[32] In turn, the 1967 publication of an overview of thirteenth-century documents from Wielkopolska by Maria Bielińska prompted a response from Franciszek Sikora.[33] Debate over the authenticity of the oldest Teutonic documents, especially the Kruszwica document, has also been quite heated. Labuda had sought to summarise these discussions, as had Tomasz Jasiński, Dariusz A. Sikorski, and several other Polish scholars before him.[34] The debate on the authenticity of the Kruszwica document, or the bull of Frederick II, forms part of the ongoing research into the origins of *Ordensstaat* in Prussia, and necessarily draws German historians into its orbit. In this case, the historical and sometimes even political context plays the most important role.

Several other minor papers have been written on forgeries, prompted by other projects related to diplomatics and, while it is impossible to list them all here, some are certainly noteworthy. In connection with the publication of the new Masovian Codex, an interesting article was published by Jan Piętka, who looked at various forgeries from Mazovia in the first half of the thirteenth century.[35] Authors of books focusing on the chancelleries of individual district dukes or bishops too often wrote about forgeries on the margins of their works.[36] There was an interesting short-term dispute around the authenticity of the Krewo act, which was questioned by the Lithuanian scholar Jonas Dainauskas and successfully defended by Maria Koczerska and Lidia Korczak.[37] The extensive statement by Tomasz Jurek on the will of Henryk Probus should receive similar treatment.[38] From my point of view, the most interesting of these debates is that regarding the oldest documents of the monastery at Ląd, conducted by Tomasz Jurek and Tomasz Ginter,[39] alongside a brief paper by Krzysztof Mosingiewicz and Błażej Śliwiński on the late forgery of a document allegedly issued by Kazimierz II around 1182.[40] Without going into the details of the debate, it should be noted that

---

32 Kürbis, 'Najstarsze dokumenty', pp. 27–61; Płocha, *Najdawniejsze dzieje*.
33 Bielińska, *Kancelarie i dokumenty*; Sikora, 'Krytyka autentyczności', pp. 139–79; Sikora, 'Przywileje rycerskie', pp. 9–47. On the debate sparked by this latter work, see the review by Gąsiorowski and the response, Sikora, 'Jeszcze o przywilejach rycerskich', pp. 181–97.
34 Labuda, 'Epilog dyskusji', pp. 271–98.
35 Piętka, 'Fałszywe, niepewne i podejrzane', pp. 289–315.
36 Mieszkowski, 'Krytyka autentyczności dokumentów', pp. 147–58.
37 Dainauskas, 'Autentyczność aktu krewskiego', pp. 125–42; Koczerska, 'Autentyczność dokumentu', pp. 59–80 and Korczak, 'O akcie krewskim', pp. 473–79.
38 Jurek, 'Testament Henryka Probusa', pp. 79–99.
39 Jurek, 'Dokumenty fundacyjne', pp. 7–52; Ginter, *Działalność fundacyjna*.
40 Mosingiewicz and Śliwiński, 'Rycerstwo polskie', pp. 713–22.

it can only be settled via a full diplomatic and historiographic examination of the Cistercian abbey's extant documents. Finally, it is worth mentioning that Bobowski, Śliwiński, Klemens Bruski, Edward Rymar, and Józef Spors have all dealt with Pomeranian forgeries to some degree, while the forgeries of Silesia documents have received the attentions of Wacław Korta and Anna Pobóg-Lenartowicz.[41]

Textbooks on Polish diplomatics of the Middle Ages occupy a separate space in the disputes and discussions on the forging of documents. Providing basic theoretical information, they do not enter into disputes about the credibility or authenticity of individual diplomas. Today, there are essentially three studies on Polish diplomatics of the Middle Ages that can be defined as textbooks. Further to these are Semkowicz's *Encyklopedią nauk pomocniczych historii* and *Paleografia łacińska*, and Józef Szymański's textbook for auxiliary sciences of history. Chronologically, the earliest is Semkowicz's *Encyklopedia* from 1923, which includes a chapter on diplomatics.[42] Concluding his reflections on medieval documents, Semkowicz made quite extensive remarks on forgeries. While this does not allow for specific inquiries related to the falsification of Polish medieval documents, Semkowicz gave a basic overview on the causes of document forgeries and their forms, pointing to their general typology-that is: converting objective notes into diplomas; creating diplomas from private notes; interpolations; interference with 'counterfeiting'; rewriting the content of a document; and pure forgery prepared 'from scratch'.[43] On the other hand, the author of the first textbook of Polish diplomatics, S. Kętrzyński does not talk separately about falsifications, although he quotes many of them in the pages of his work. He quite clearly defines what comprises a forgery but also draws attention to the difficulties in classifying such creations.[44] Maleczyński was another scholar to offer a definition of a forgery in the field of diplomatics, in which he largely followed Semkowicz, or rather Harry Bresslau: 'all the constituent features of the original are the result of the knowledge and will of the issuer; at least in theory'. A forgery is a document that does not have these features, and the intention of which is also to pass for something other than what it really is'.[45] He further divided the forgeries into formal and factual. Referring to specific issues, Maleczyński held to his former views from the period of polemics with Kozłowska-Budkowa, and criticised Mitkowski's findings regarding the Sulejów documents.[46]

The conclusions of the above analysis are as follows:
1. Particularly intensive production of forgeries is noticeable from the twelfth to early-fourteenth centuries, which on the one hand most likely results

---

41 For an overview, see Dymmel, *Bibliografia*, from p. 131.
42 Semkowicz, *Encyklopedia*, pp. 47–96.
43 Semkowicz, *Encyklopedia*, pp. 91–96; cf. Semkowicz, *Paleografia łacińska*.
44 Kętrzyński, *Zarys nauki o dokumencie*, pp. 61–63, note 50.
45 Maleczyński, *Zarys dyplomatyki*, pp. 16–17.
46 Maleczyński, *Zarys dyplomatyki*, pp. 16–17, 89–90.

from weaker control of the diplomas and, on the other, from the desire of some recipients such as church institutions to make up for the lack of documentation regarding existing rights.
2. The above has also sparked the intensification of research on the forgeries of the oldest Polish documents.
3. Each forgery for the early period of Polish history is of immense importance due to the scarcity and enigmatic nature of the source base, a fact already underlined by Stanisław Kutrzeba, followed by S. Kętrzyński, Mosingiewicz and Śliwiński.
4. The analysis of forgeries is of great significance for historical and legal research.
5. Regardless of S. Kętrzyński's reluctance to classify forgeries, we should acknowledge that their range, both in terms of form and subject matter, was fairly extensive.
6. It is necessary to emphasise the evolving nature of research into forgeries, from the initially formal approach (evaluation of the *ductus* and *dictatus*), to the search for the causes of forgeries, through to placing them in a broader historical and cultural context — that is, the hunt for motives and circumstances behind their production and their scope for usefulness in formulating general historical conclusions.
7. Any assessment of the scale and quality of research on forgeries to date is necessarily ambiguous, if only because the focus has so far been on the earliest period. What draws attention is the sometimes quite accidental research on specific documents, often a single diploma, while a broader plane of reference is neglected. Generally speaking, much has been done in the field of research on forgeries, or at least enough as to warrant the summarising of its previous achievements.
8. Finally, an exhortation that has already been put forward many times but is still unfulfilled: Kozłowska-Budkowa's work should be continued, an undertaking which would finally make it possible to estimate the scale of document forgery in the Polish Middle Ages.

CHAPTER 13

Legitimisation of Forged Documents in Twelfth- and Thirteenth-Century Poland*

The twelfth and thirteenth centuries witnessed the earliest stages of the inception and reception of the written document in the lands of the Poles. The document was understood not as a witness to the *memorii* of past times and events, but above all as a means of evidence in court proceedings.[1] Therefore, its pragmatic side came to the fore, and the document itself was written according to patterns and text formulas well known and established in the West. In the early Piast dynasty, the diploma or letter was most likely to have been used in the context of contact and correspondence with foreign realms, especially at the level of the ruler's court and the ecclesiastic hierarchy.[2] However, it was in the twelfth century that the written document began to be introduced into common practice. This likely caused not only the form and structure of the written documents to evolve but also led to the foundation of the chancellery and that institution's rapid development in the thirteenth century.[3]

The fact that chancellery documents (indeed, frequently entire cycles of documents) were forged, especially by Church institutions in Poland, is no longer a matter of debate, and discussion on that topic seems redundant. Likewise, there is little controversy in the conclusion that monasteries or other ecclesiastical institutions were the first to engage in this practice, primarily in the thirteenth and early fourteenth centuries, because they were better acquainted with the models of Western culture, including legal culture, and held something of a monopoly on writing. Secular people, especially knightly and noble families, were a little late to adopt forgery as a means of legitimation, and their discovery of the practice came along with the construction of their

---

* Original publication: Józef Dobosz, 'Legitymizacja falsyfikatów dokumentów w XII–XIII-wiecznej Polsce', in Pragmatické písemnosti v kontextu právním a správním, ed. by Zdeněk Hojda and Hana Pátková (Praha: Togga, 2008), pp. 43–54.
1 See Kętrzyński, *Zarys nauki o dokumencie*, pp. 81–128, and the extensive review of this work by Władysław Semkowicz. See also Chapters 9 and 11 in this volume.
2 Kętrzyński, *Zarys nauki o dokumencie*, pp. 83–84, 90–91. See also RPD i, pp. 1–19, 141, which registers only fifteen documents connected with the history of Poland for the tenth to eleventh centuries (including obvious forgeries drawn up in the thirteenth century), but rarely from Polish issuers.
3 On Polish diplomatics, see Chapters 9 and 10 in this volume as well as Kętrzyński, *Zarys nauki o dokumencie*, pp. 90–205; Maleczyński, *Zarys dyplomatyki polskiej*, pp. 57–240; Dobosz, 'Badania nad dokumentami', pp. 137–48; Chapter 10 in this volume.

own family, group, and legal identity.[4] Thus, when speaking of forgeries in this early period of document production in Poland, it is the Church that requires the most attention as the main producer and recipient of forgeries. As the study of forgery has grown as a research field, new avenues of inquiry have been opening up for specialists in diplomatics. Formal inquiries such as *ductus*, *dictatus*, the scope of forgery, and so on, can largely be abandoned in favour of more extensive research on the motives behind forgeries, the circumstances in which they were produced, the means by which they were put into circulation, and how they were used for legitimisation. Study of these 'fakes', therefore, should be revived and their wider social, legal (especially the brand-new legal culture of the twelfth and thirteenth centuries), and political contexts emphasised.[5] Behind these forgeries were, after all, people who, with varying degrees of success, introduced other people, places, and phenomena onto the historical stage through their actions.

For obvious reasons, a broader discussion of the motives and circumstances behind Polish document forgeries is omitted here, as this context is extremely complex. Yet, it is worth noting a list of the greatest 'culprits' in this regard and point first of all to the Cistercian monasteries in Ląd, Sulejów, Jędrzejów, and Lubiąż, which produced the greatest number of forgeries among those identified by Kozłowska-Budkowa. Ląd was undoubtedly the leader in this field, all nine potential documents dated to the twelfth century are forgeries.[6] Sulejów Abbey, however, was the most fascinating forger.[7] The list also includes the Benedictines, although they did not engage in this practice to the extent of their younger cousins, the Cistercians. The monasteries in Tyniec near Kraków (document of Cardinal Gilo),[8] in Lubiń (document dated 1181),[9] and especially in Mogilno (document dated 11 April 1065),[10] warrant

---

4   For discussion on this phase in the development of the Polish nobility and knighthood, see Bieniak, 'Rody rycerskie', pp. 161–200; Bieniak, 'Knight Clans in Medieval Poland', pp. 123–76; Bieniak, 'Jeszcze w sprawie genezy rodów rycerskich', pp. 45–55. See also Gąsiorowski, 'Research into Medieval Polish Nobility', pp. 7–20.

5   This was the approach of Brigida Kürbis in her extensive analysis of the Mogilno forgery dated 1065: Kürbis, 'Najstarsze dokumenty', pp. 27–61. See also, Jasiński, 'Uwagi o autentyczności', pp. 226–39; Jasiński, 'Złota bulla Fryderyka II', pp. 107–53; Sikorski, *Przywilej kruszwicki*; Labuda, 'Studia źródłoznawcze', pp. 189–270, which discusses the forgeries of the Teutonic Knights in connection with their seizure of Chełmno and Prussian lands.

6   RPD i.39–41, i.52, i.71, i.73, i.99, i.111, i.117. An exception in this string of forgeries is found in the statutes of the Cistercian General Chapter, which report in 1193 that Ląd Abbey should not be abolished, Canivez, ed., *Statuta Capitulorum Generalium* i, p. 168). This contrasts with as statute of 1191, which indicates the outpost in Ląd was to be closed down, Canivez, ed., *Statuta Capitulorum Generalium* i, p. 137. Cf. Jurek, 'Dokumenty fundacyjne', pp. 7–51.

7   See RPD i.80–81, i.91; cf. Dobosz, 'Trzynastowieczne falsyfikaty', pp. 225–37; Dobosz, 'Najstarsze świadectwa', pp. 66–68; Chapters 2 and 13 in this volume.

8   RPD i.26; cf. Labuda, 'Klasztor Benedyktynów w Tyńcu', pp. 247–76, in which can be found a detailed analysis of the document of Cardinal-Legate Gilo of Tusculum.

9   RPD i.104.

10 RPD i.8; cf. Kürbis, 'Najstarsze dokumenty'; Dobosz, *Monarcha i możni*, pp. 140–47.

especial mention, and the various orders of canons regular are not free from suspicion, especially those abbeys in Trzemeszno[11] or Wrocław,[12] nor are any other Church institutions.

Generally speaking, the purpose of fabricating documents was to protect one's own property. The production of forgeries was most frequently based on various types of memorandum notes, possibly some kind of inventory of goods or books of benefactors, and the factual scope of forgeries was usually modest, limited to the formal aspect. It was, therefore, a question of fabricating evidence for legally acquired movable and immovable wealth, to give it written substantiation. From time to time, some zealot may have attempted to shape reality in their own way or introduced anachronism by 'adjusting' actual grants to their own vision, and even by adding donations acquired later than the date of the alleged original document. This is how the elements of factual forgery were born, all in the interests of the Church, which often urgently needed such legal evidence.

It seems that a few of the forgeries were not created solely and exclusively out of a desire to fill the gaps in a church or monastery 'archive', even though those were probably severe in the case of the older Church institutions founded in the twelfth century and earlier. Foundations and endowments addressed to them most often happened within the framework of the phenomenon referred to as 'orature', that is they were given orally at rallies, court or foundation conventions or on the occasion of the consecration of churches.[13] Consequently, forgers had to ensure that the documents had the credible form and content, and quickly make them certified by political and ecclesiastical dignitaries. Initially, Church institutions in Poland sought to make up for the gaps in the documents, especially those concerning foundation, by obtaining protective bulls confirming their property (mainly immovable wealth) from the Holy See. Examples likely include the Gniezno archbishopric,[14] which was followed by the monastery of regular canons in Trzemeszno in 1147,[15] the Kujawy bishopric in 1148,[16] and the Wrocław bishopric and the abbey of canons

---

11   For the premier forgery fabricated in the monastery in Trzemeszno, a document in the name of Mieszko the Old and dated 28 April 1145, see RPD i.42; cf. Dobosz, 'Dokument Mieszka III Starego', pp. 87–106.
12   Kozłowska-Budkowa considers the Ołbin diploma of Bolesław IV for the Benedictine Abbey in June 1149 to be false, RPD i.49. So too the charter of Bishop Walter of Wrocław from around 1150 for the monastery of canons regular on Piasek, RPD i.51. Cf. Korta, *Tajemnice góry Ślęży*, from p. 260.
13   Kętrzyński, *Zarys nauki o dokumencie*, pp. 86, 107. Cf. Maleczyński, *Zarys dyplomatyki polskiej*, from p. 59.
14   The Gniezno bull of 7 July 1136, RPD i.31. Kozłowska-Budkowa considered the diploma to be a 'chancellery copy', while Maleczyński was convinced that it was a forgery, Maleczyński, *W sprawie autentyczności*. See also Dobosz, 'Bulla z 1136 roku', p. 130.
15   RPD i.46; Kozłowska-Budkowa mentions the Parish Archive in Trzemeszno as the place where this document is stored, but today it is kept in the Archdiocesan Archive in Gniezno, Dypl. Tr 2.
16   RPD i.47.

regular in Czerwińsk, both in 1155.[17] Initially, such a procedure for obtaining approval of ownership from the realm was effective and, thus, in the first quarter of the thirteenth century — especially during the pontificate of Innocent III, Honorius III and Gregory IX — it became widespread.[18] However, it quickly turned out to be futile. This was because these bulls did not always contain a precise enumeration of the grants in conjunction with their benefactors, and thus could not stand as relevant evidence in court proceedings. Starting from the thirteenth century, disputes grew between Church institutions about property (especially tithes), and between Church institutions and lay nobles about the boundaries of property and the retraction of certain estates. In 1198, the Canons of the Holy Sepulchre at Miechów managed to obtain an effective document from the Patriarch of Jerusalem, Monachus: not a simple list of property, but a full register with benefactors.[19] It was probably the last successful attempt of this kind. It was, therefore, necessary to find a more reliable method of providing evidence than recourse to the often-enigmatic papal documents, especially as the potential witnesses of the foundation or donation were usually long dead.

It was at this point that the forgeries entered onto the stage on a larger scale, serving then to fill the above-mentioned severe gaps in the archives. Yet before they were drafted and introduced into legal circulation, an interesting method of legitimising the grants for which they had no written evidence was used by the Cistercians of Łekno. They had the original copy of the foundation charter of Comes Zbylut from 1153, probably prepared in the court of Archbishop Jan and sealed by him, but listing only the grants provided by the founder himself before 1153.[20] At the end of the twelfth century — thanks to the Piast dukes, the lay nobility, and clergy — the monastic property was much more extensive. The monks from Łekno noticed that they had no written evidence to prove their ownership, but there was still considerable space left on the genuine document below the text and around the seal of Archbishop Jan, which was pressed directly on the parchment. This is the so-called the Poznań copy, named for the place where it is currently stored in the State Archives in Poznań. A monk, trained in the art of writing letters, wrote a few lines of the text, skilfully imitating the original script, and made the most of the space around the seal.[21] This annotation included later grants from the years after

---

17 RPD i.57–58. For information about the bull for the bishoprics of Wrocław, see also KDŚ i, pp. 84–102; Korta, *Rozwój wielkiej własności feudalnej*, pp. 58–64.

18 Sułkowska-Kuraś and Kuraś, *Bullarium Poloniae*, from p. 18.

19 RPD i.143 (the so-called *Album Patriarchale*), i.144 (document of the Patriarch of Jerusalem, Monachus). See also Dobosz, *Monarcha i możni*, p. 372, note 441.

20 For the foundation charter of the Cistercian monastery at Łekno see Z. Kozłowska-Budkowa, *Repertorjum*, no. 53, pp. 58–60; Dobosz, 'Dokument fundacyjny', pp. 53–83; Wyrwa and Strzelecka, *Dokument fundacyjny*; cf. Kürbis, 'Cystersi w kulturze polskiego', pp. 228–39.

21 See Dobosz, 'Dokument fundacyjny', pp. 63–65 for discussion of the annotation on the Poznań copy of the charter, and p. 55 for the text of the annotation.

1153 to around 1190, and thus tried to legitimise them. Therefore, it is not a forgery or an interpolation of the text in the literal sense of the term. After successive endowments from Archbishop Piotr, before 1198, the Cistercians of Łekno made a copy of the 1153 document with yet further additions, this copy kept today in the Archdiocese Archives in Gniezno, but whether it was used in legal practice is unknown.[22]

Produced fairly regularly in later times, classical forgeries were sometimes carefully examined at the ducal courts, thus their form was carefully prepared. That said, it was not always realised that twelfth-century documents often had a different shape, a different way of sealing, alongside variations in script, composition (*dictatus*) and content. Some Church institutions prepared forgeries with full corroboration formulas and even tried to attach fake seals; others were content with substitutes, such as hanging strings or strips of parchment, claiming the original seals were destroyed in 'historical storms'. The practice of counterfeiting seals must have become very common in the thirteenth century, especially among the Cistercians, since in the statutes of the Cistercian General Chapter there are references and orders to prosecute stamp forgers from Poland.[23] An even more sophisticated form of legitimising counterfeits was to submit them for ratification (transumpt; *vidimus*) either to monastic authorities or, less frequently, the Holy See, as well as to the reigning ruler, preferably a descendant of the founder if possible. After such legitimisation, the alleged original was usually lost.

The case of the Sulejów privilege for the Cistercians, apparently issued in 1176, is a particularly flamboyant example of such a type of the certification of forgeries. The document appeared around 1260 in the face of attempts to retract the village of Bałdrzychów by the Silesian Gąski family.[24] Earlier, the monastery had applied for a protective bull of Pope Honorius III in 1218 and Gregory IX in 1229 and 1234.[25] When, in 1260/61, the dispute over the village of Bałdrzychów was resolved in front of the court of the descendant of the founder of the monastery, Kazimierz Duke of Kujawy, the ruler considered this evidence in the form of the bull of Honorius III insufficient, because it did not provide the name of the donor. Time was set for Sulejów Abbey to provide more reliable evidence. In February 1261, the trial was resumed, and Abbot Piotr submitted a foundation charter, which indicated in black and white

---

22 Dobosz, 'Dokument fundacyjny', pp. 63–65.
23 This recalls again the Friar Jakub of the monastery at Paradyż, known as a forger of seals. See Chapter 11, note 8.
24 RPD i.80; Kętrzyński, *Zarys nauki o dokumencie*, pp. 145–46, and later by Mitkowski, *Początki klasztoru cystersów*, pp. 3–14, with an edition of the document on pp. 313–14. See also Dobosz, 'Najstarsze świadectwa', pp. 66–67; Dobosz, 'Trzynastowieczne falsyfikaty'; Chapters 2 and 13 in this volume.
25 Mitkowski, *Początki klasztoru cystersów*, pp. 317–18 (the bull of Honorius III), pp. 321–26 (successive bulls of Pope Gregory IX of 1234 – six in total); KDM ii.398 (bull of Gregory IX of 1229).

that Bałdrzychów had been granted by the monastery's founder, Kazimierz II, in 1176.[26] It is easy to guess how this conflict before the ducal court ended for the Gąski family and what sentence was passed, but more importantly, the same foundation charter was submitted by the same Abbot Piotr in 1262 to another descendant of the founder, Duke Bolesław V, who ratified it.[27] Then the alleged foundation charter disappeared and never again resurfaced, the Cistercians making exclusively use of the transumpt. The documentary gap was thus resolved, and the false document was fully certified by the dignity of the authority of the Duke and, at the same time, the heir of the founder.

The Cistercians of Sulejów followed a similar path in the case of a document on tithing dated 10 August 1176 and attributed to Archbishop Piotr, which they forged in the form of a transumpt of Archbishop Pełka (with the date 1232), and then submitted in 1289 to the Cistercian abbot and obtained his *vidimus*.[28] Needless to say, Pełka's purported transumpt was immediately lost. They did the same for a forged document in the name of Konrad of Masovia, dated 23 October 1242, which was transumed in 1279 by Duke Leszek the Black.[29]

The Benedictines of Tyniec also transumed their flagship — though forged — charter of Cardinal-Legate Gilo of Tusculum, the ratification being provided by Bolesław V in 1275. In this case, the alleged original has been preserved today in the State Archives in Kraków.[30] In turn, the purported foundation charter of the Benedictines in Mogilno, dated 11 April 1065, is known only from a transumpt, and the transumption is forged, thus making it a similar situation to the Archbishop Piotr's charter granting tithes to the Cistercians of Sulejów.[31] In the alleged original, however, a document dated April 28 1145 has been preserved, forged in the name of Mieszko III, for the monastery of canons regular in Trzemeszno. In this case, the forgery, neatly produced in terms of external features, has survived and today resides in the Archdiocese Archives in Gniezno.[32] Only a careful analysis of the content demonstrates the scale and multi-layered nature of the forgery. The same was probably the case with the whole series of Jędrzejów forgeries describing the events of the autumn of 1167 but forged just before 1245.[33] This, however, cannot be verified, as the alleged authentic documents have vanished, and their content is known only from late, seventeenth-century copies. The Cistercians of Lubiąż probably acted differently from the Cistercians of Sulejów or Jędrzejów and

---

26 These events are described by the document of Duke Kazimierz of Kujawy of 6 February 1261, KDP i.49, note 35.
27 KDP i.50, transcription of Bolesław V of 30 September 1262.
28 See KDW i.587 (21a); RPD i.81, note 35.
29 KDP i.31 (charter of Konrad of Mazovia), i.61 (transumpt of Duke Leszek the White). See Mitkowski, *Początki klasztoru cystersów*, pp. 14–24.
30 RPD i.26. See also note 19 above and Krzyżanowski, ed., *Album palaeographicum*, 18, p. 35.
31 RPD i.8, which lists the editions of the Mogilno forgery. See also note 20.
32 KDW i.11. See also note 22.
33 RPD i.63–67. See also Dobosz, 'Trzynastowieczne falsyfikaty'; Chapter 13 in this volume.

retained their forged documents.[34] The above-mentioned forgeries from Ląd are a separate research issue. Their mutual relations, the motivations leading to their fabrication, and the very circumstances that accompanied it should all be subject to further investigation, especially since most of them have survived in late copies. This is in spite of the efforts of Tomasz Jurek, who probably strives to see something more than can be actually read from them.[35]

This short and necessarily incomplete overview of the oldest Polish forgeries leads to a simple conclusion: despite being forgeries, they played an important role in the reception of not only the document, but also of legal culture in Poland. The often minor extent of factual forgery allows them to be used as valuable resources for the reconstruction of the origins of various Church institutions. Their legitimisation would have been cause for worry even at the time of their production, and it was probably realised that the truth could come out, and thus the development of the entire systems of producing transumpts, *vidimuses*, or copies followed. Today, these documents represent an additional and fascinating research source, not just for specialists in diplomatics, but also for historians of law, culture, and customs.

---

34 RPD i.75–77. See also Jażdżewski, *Lubiąż*, pp. 25–28.
35 Jurek, 'Dokumenty fundacyjne'. See the position of Labuda, *Szkice historyczne X–XI wieku*, p. 392, note 103; cf. Dobosz, 'Założenie klasztoru w Łeknie', pp. 77–78; Chapter 3 in this volume.

CHAPTER 14

The False Thirteenth-Century Documents of the Cistercian Abbeys at Sulejów and Jędrzejów*

The monasteries at Jędrzejów and Sulejów were among the earliest Cistercian communities in Poland. Established during the first stage of the Cistercian expansion into the lands ruled by the dukes of the Piast dynasty, they were founded between *c.* 1140–1167 (Jędrzejów) and 1176–1191 (Sulejów). Jędrzejów Abbey was founded by Janik, who initiated the foundation as a parish priest in Gniezno and Wrocław, and concluded his work as Archbishop of Gniezno.[1] The matter of bringing the Cistercian monks to Sulejów and the granting of their endowments was undertaken by Kazimierz II, then Duke of Sandomierz, who was assisted by his trusted associates. Kazimierz probably followed the pattern he was acquainted with through the foundation of Jędrzejów Abbey.[2] Both monasteries came directly from Morimond, Burgundy, and their early days on Polish soil are illuminated by certain forged documents that were produced in the thirteenth century. In the case of Jędrzejów, these were acts associated with the convention held on the occasion of the consecration of the first monastery church and the grants that the abbey received as part of this event, while the Sulejów forgeries consist of a series of documents concerning the foundation process of Sulejów Abbey.

The Jędrzejów forgeries comprise two diplomas issued by Mieszko III and Kazimierz II, and one issued by Bishops Janik and Gedko. None of them has survived in their original form, and are known from relatively late sixteenth and seventeenth-century copies.[3] Analysis of the Jędrzejów documents has been undertaken by, among others, Wojciech Kętrzyński, Franciszek Piekosiński, Antoni Małecki, and Władysław Semkowicz,[4] while

---

* Original publication: Józef Dobosz, 'Trzynastowieczne falsyfikaty z Sulejowa i Jędrzejowa – motywy i okoliczności powstania', in *Klasztor w kulturze średniowiecznej Polski*, ed. by Anna Pobóg-Lenartowicz and Marek Derwich (Opole: Wydawnictwo Św. Krzyża, 1995), pp. 225–37.
1 For the foundation process of the Cistercian monastery at Jędrzejów, see Chapter 4 in this volume.
2 For the beginnings of Sulejów Abbey, see Chapter 5 in this volume. See also Mitkowski, *Początki klasztoru cystersów*; Dobosz, 'Casimir le Juste', pp. 243–56.
3 The copies are preserved in two seventeenth-century monastic cartularies and in *Metrica Regni Poloniae*, see RPD i.63–67.
4 W. Kętrzyński, *Studia nad dokumentami XII w.*, pp. 229–30; ZDŚ i.32; KDM ii.3741; Małecki, 'W kwestii fałszerstwa dokumentów', pp. 3–4; Semkowicz, 'Nieznane nadania', pp. 66–97.

Zofia Kozłowska-Budkowa has compiled and summarised the results of this research. Ultimately, she considered all the above-mentioned documents as forgeries based on monastery records. In addition, Kozłowska-Budkowa noticed a factual forgery in the ducal diplomas which, she alleged, concerns the immunity clause.[5]

The Sulejów forgeries comprise three documents: a charter of Kazimierz II dated 1176, the so-called foundation charter; another charter of Kazimierz II dated 1178; and the diploma of Archbishop Piotr on tithing dated 1176.[6] Any analysis should also include their transumpts and the various acts that reference these documents.[7] Kozłowska-Budkowa and Józef Mitkowski both reviewed the research on the Sulejów documents and concluded that they were forgeries, though based on reliable grounds, which exhibit some accrual of factual forgery, mainly regarding the monastery's immunity.[8]

Unfortunately, not all of the statements that have been made in the course of the debate on the forgeries of Jędrzejów and Sulejów are fully substantiated. As such, it is worth taking a fresh look at the documents. There are some specific issues that need to be carefully considered: first, the dating of the Jędrzejów congress; second, the date on which tithes were granted to Sulejów; and finally, the scope of forgery in both document cycles. The circumstances and motives behind their preparation should also be considered, and the question of the role of the Cistercian Order in the adoption of the written document in Piast Poland — or, more broadly, about its culture-forming role — needs reappraisal.

On the first matter, the series of Jędrzejów forgeries serve to illuminate the events that unfolded at the solemn convention on the occasion of the consecration of the monastery church. The ducal documents assert that the issuers confirmed the monastery's freedom from the ducal law as granted by their predecessors, and further state that the dukes provided the abbey with salt grants.[9] In turn, the bishops' document provides information about land donations and tithes granted by Janik and Gedko.[10] The date of the congress is generally understood to have been around the turn of 1166 and 1167, and so this point serves as a good place from which to begin considerations.[11]

It has previously been assumed that the Jędrzejów convention must have taken place after 18 October 1166, at which time Gedko may have taken

---

5   RPD i.63–67.
6   See Mitkowski, *Początki klasztoru cystersów*, pp. 313–16; KDW i.587 (21a).
7   Their complete documentation is provided in Mitkowski, *Początki klasztoru cystersów*, pp. 3–4, 308, 310–11.
8   A summary of this research can be found in RPD i.80–81, 91. Mitkowski outlined his own reflections in *Początki klasztoru cystersów*, pp. 3–4.
9   Semkowicz, 'Nieznane nadania', pp. 69–70.
10 ZDŚ i.32; KDM ii.380.
11 Semkowicz, 'Nieznane nadania', pp. 73–78; RPD i.63–67, which supports Semkowicz's position. This dating has been widely accepted with little debate.

over the bishop's seat in Kraków, and before 2 March 1167, the date on which Kazimierz Kazimierzowic died.[12] I would argue, however, that this is not correct. While Gedko, Bishop of Kraków, granted numerous tithes for Jędrzejów, his elevation to the see of Kraków was only confirmed on 19 June 1167, the feast of St Gervasius and St Protasius.[13] Thus, the question should be asked, could the convention have been held, and his tithes issued, before he became Bishop of Kraków? It should also be noted that the Jędrzejów Cistercian Church was dedicated to St Adalbert, in which can be seen the influence of the founder, Janik, Archbishop of Gniezno. From the twelfth century, the *Translatio sancti Adalberti* feast was celebrated in the majority of Polish dioceses, including Gniezno and Kraków.[14] Adalbert's *translatio* is observed on 20 October and thus, with all these facts taken together, it seems most likely that the convention took place on 20 October 1167.[15]

The second issue to be considered is the allegation of factual forgery that was made by Kozłowska-Budkowa in regard to the documents bearing the names of the dukes.[16] Semkowicz, passionately defended the Jędrzejów forgeries, firmly convinced of their credibility, and his argument has much to merit it. The misunderstanding would seemingly arise from treating these forgeries as describing events that happened simultaneously. Some of the ducal grants listed in the forgery were certainly done at the congress of 20 October 1167, such as the salt grants,[17] but the records confirming the immunity come from the following years. The exemption was probably granted by Bolesław IV between 1153 and 1173, and his successors on the Kraków throne confirmed it, first Mieszko III between 1173 and 1177 and, after 1177, Kazimierz II. Thus, the ducal documents have two chronological layers within them, which a forger, using undated monastic notes, merged into a single event.

---

12   Gedko took over the bishopric of Kraków after Mateusz's death on 18 October 1166, ZDŚ i.27. The date of the death of the first-born son of Kazimierz II, also bearing the name Kazimierz, is given as 1 March by *Kalendarz katedry krakowskiej*, MPH v, p. 128. The year of his death is found in *Rocznik Traski* (1167) and *Rocznik krakowski* (1168), MPH ii, p. 834. Following Balzer, *Genealogia Piastów*, pp. 261–62, Semkowicz and Kozłowska-Budkowa identified the information provided by *Rocznik Traski* to be the more reliable, and so determined the year of the convention as 1166/67. Bieniak, however, holds a different opinion, dating the Jędrzejów convention to 1168. See Bieniak, 'Polska elita polityczna XII w.', Part III A', p. 49; Bieniak, 'Obóz obrońców', pp. 29–30.
13   Jan Długosz, *Annales*, p. 82. The same date is given by *Rocznik kapituły krakowskiej*, MPH v, p. 62, and other sources (mostly catalogues of the bishops of Kraków).
14   *Kalendarz katedry krakowskiej*, MPH v, p. 179. See also Włodarski, ed., *Chronologia polska*, pp. 139, 153, 168, 174, 221; Gustaw, ed., *Hagiografia polska*, p. 586; Likowski, 'Geneza święta', pp. 53–80.
15   I have also suggested that the convention could have been held on 14 September 1167, the Elevation of the Cross, a holiday important for the Cistercians, see Chapter 2 in this volume, and Dobosz, 'Najstarsze świadectwo', pp. 70–71.
16   RPD i.63–64.
17   The authenticity of these grants was defended with much conviction in Semkowicz, 'Nieznane nadania', pp. 71–72. Cf. Grzesiowski and Piotrowcz, 'Sól małopolska w nadaniach', pp. 71–189; Keckowa, *Saliny ziemi krakowskiej*.

Similarly, it seems unlikely that any signs of factual forgery may be observed in the Bishops' document, although it should be noted that there are three known extant versions of it. The first, identified by Piekosiński with the number 2 relates a smaller number of granted villages and tithes, and contains a witness list that correlates with the subscriptions of the ducal documents, though being slightly shorter. The second version is identified in Piekosiński's edition with the number 1, while the third version, lacking Janik's grants, was included in a forged document dated 1210 and attributed to Bishop Vincentius of Kraków. They relate subsequent changes in the monastery's immovable wealth, which occurred as a result of the intensification of settlement processes, and perhaps also the exchange of properties and tithes. The first version should be considered the oldest one, reflecting the state of the monastery's possessions closest to 1167. The third version, in which the forger took only Bishop Gedko's endowments into account and inserted them into the false transumpt of Bishop Vincentius, was probably the latest.[18]

Sulejów's forgeries relate to the foundation process of the monastery; without them, the reconstruction of its initial history would hardly be possible. The two forged documents in the name of Kazimierz II are dated to 1176 (the foundation charter) and 1178, but clearly exceed these dates in their content. The first document is an amalgam of monastic records, the chronology of which goes back to the years around 1176–1191. The year 1176 probably marks the date of Kazimierz's decision to establish a new community and his promise of an initial endowment. In the following years, his foundation initiative was supported by various of his associates: Radosław and Bałdrzych; then Gedko and Pełka, Bishops of Kraków; and, in 1191, Archbishop Piotr, who granted tithes and Mieszko III, who endowed the monastery with some lands.

The immunity clause in the foundation charter is at odds with the twelfth-century formulas and, as it seems, originally it was closer to the wording of the Jędrzejów forgeries, which included the entry confirming the grant of the villages and settlers, and the market-place of the church, previously granted together with various immunities and freedoms.[19] Following from this, it must surely be accepted that, in the form known from the alleged foundation charter, the document is a thirteenth-century forgery.[20]

The only diploma preserved as the apparently original copy, the document dated 1178, is also a fabrication made up of several chronological layers. The year 1178 relates to the exchange of some villages between the duke and the monastery, which took place after the monks' arrival in Sulejów. Yet, Mieszko was unable to make any grants at the time because he was on bad terms

---

18 KDM ii.380. See also Mieszkowski, 'Krytyka autentyczności dokumentów', from p. 147.
19 *Confirmo etiam villis, et colonis, et foro ipsius Ecclesie, quam predecessores mei contulerunt immunitatem et omnis pensionis atque tributarie seruitutis libertatem*. Semkowicz, 'Nieznane nadania', pp. 69–70.
20 See Mitkowski, *Początki klasztoru cystersów*, pp. 197–98, which summarises the state of the research.

with Kazimierz and was very likely abroad. However, Mieszko's exile came about only in 1191, following his unsuccessful attempt to seize Kraków. When Archbishop Piotr brought about reconciliation between the brothers, Mieszko supported his younger brother's favourite foundation as a token of consent.[21]

The third forgery, listing the tithes, was also based on monastic records, and the forger mistakenly linked the year of the abbey's foundation to the date the tithes were granted, hence 10 August 1176. This date is, of course, unacceptable, as the tithing donation actually took place on 10 August 1191. At that time, Archbishop Piotr, who was going to Małopolska, consecrated the original monastery church and — at the request of Kazimierz and Pełka, Bishop of Kraków — provided the monks of Sulejów with tithes.

Both the Jędrzejów and Sulejów forgeries resemble objective notes, although they contain the *invocatio*, the *intitulatio*, the *arenga* or the *sanctio*, in some cases extensive witness lists (documents of Mieszko and Kazimierz), and the *corroboratio*. It is hardly difficult to identify the formulary similarities between them, while those parts of Kazimierz's charters concerning the salt grants for both abbeys — his diploma for Jędrzejów and the foundation charter for Sulejów — would indicate that Jędrzejów forgeries served as a model for the slightly later Sulejów documents. It seems, however, that the Cistercians of Sulejów went a bit further than that, introducing creative developments to both the formulary and the system of transuming the resulting false documents.

It is reasonable at this point to turn to the matter of when the forgeries were actually produced. As far as the documents purportedly issued by Mieszko and Kazimierz are concerned, the clues are contained in two documents issued by their successors. The first document, issued by Duchess Grzymisława in 1228, refers to the endowments of Kazimierz and Leszek the White for the monastery at Jędrzejów but fails to mention the existence of the documents issued by the dukes.[22] However, the other diploma, that of Bolesław V, does cite the documents of Kazimierz and Leszek, which has been submitted to arbitration by Michał, Castellan of Kraków. Having investigated the grievance, the Bolesław judged the documents to be genuine. The case was resolved on 16 May 1245 at a convention in Chrobrze.[23] Seemingly, the alleged document of Kazimierz, and probably also that of Mieszko, was created shortly before 16 May 1245. The bishops' document was likely produced at the same time, and certainly after 1221, when the tithes given by Janik were approved by Vincent, Archbishop of Gniezno, who failed to mention the existence of other related documents.[24]

The Sulejów diplomas were written a little later than those concerning Jędrzejów. A detailed analysis by Mitkowski showed that the document dated

---

21 See Chapter 5 in this volume.
22 KDM i.2.
23 KDM iii.24.
24 KDM ii.386. See Mieszkowski, 'Krytyka autentyczności dokumentów', pp. 149–50.

1178 could only have been created after 1237 at the earliest, and probably around the mid-thirteen century.[25] The date of the alleged foundation charter can be specified in more detail. This issue is resolved by the existence of a document by Kazimierz of Kujawy from February 1261, in which the Duke resolves a dispute over Bałdrzychów. It shows that the foundation charter of Sulejów only made an appearance in the context of a trial before the ducal court in January–February 1261 (or slightly earlier).[26] Finally, the third of the Sulejów forgeries surfaced only in the late thirteenth century, between 1285 and 1289, a fact convincingly demonstrated by Mitkowski.[27]

At this point, it is necessary to consider the circumstances surrounding the production of the forgeries in question and the reasons for their creation. The most important factor is undeniably common to both groups of forgeries: twelfth-century monasteries often found themselves in need of written legitimation for their ownership of property. This is true not only of the Jędrzejów and Sulejów communities but also other establishments of monks and the canons regular. The rapid spread of the written document as a means of evidence in court proceedings in Poland during the thirteenth century put these institutions in a rather precarious situation. They were in possession of numerous endowments, obtained from rulers, knights, and clergy, for which they were unable to provide evidence. In the new legal environment, these deficiencies were resolved by the skilful preparation of forged documentation. Having a foundation charter at their disposal, the monks of Jędrzejów were undoubtedly better off than the monks of Sulejów, who did not obtain any such certificates for the grants received in the twelfth century. Although both abbeys had records of the foundations and endowments, they were of no use in the new legal environment. It was, nonetheless, these records that served as a basis for forgeries.

Other, more detailed circumstances surrounding the fabrications of the monks of Jędrzejów are suggested in the previously mentioned 1245 document of Bolesław V. Here a dispute between Michał, Castellan of Kraków, and the monastery at Jędrzejów is detailed, which relates to the exercise of certain powers vested in the Castellan under the ducal law in the monastic estates. In the course of the disagreement, Castellan Michał questioned the authenticity of Kazimierz and Leszek the White's documents confirming the immunity exemptions. However, Bolesław finally dismissed his official's claims and found the contentious diplomas to be authentic.[28] It seems, therefore, that the forgery was created in response to concerns about losing rights to monastic immunity. The whole legal dispute unfolded during three gatherings, in Piasek, Kraków, and Chrobrze, likely all held in 1245. It is possible that the

---

25 Mitkowski, *Początki klasztoru cystersów*, pp. 35–49.
26 KDP i.49.
27 Mitkowski, *Początki klasztoru cystersów*, pp. 32–35.
28 KDP i.24.

monks of Jędrzejów also forged the document in the name of Mieszko III at this time and perhaps also the first version of the bishops' document. The latter forgery likely arose out of the concern for the monastic tithes, the rights to which were endowed to the abbey by Janik and Gedko. The first version of the bishops' document, as noted, reflects the complete state of monastic ownership in the twelfth century. It appears that the successive editions were an attempt at providing legal substantiation for the alternations in the endowments that ensued mainly as a result of exchanges and settlement processes. They are a little later than the first version, having perhaps been drawn up around 1250.

Apart from the above-mentioned factors, the Cistercians of Sulejów were driven to forgery by the disputes they had between local knights about the village of Łęczno and the threat of rights over their other village, Bałdrzychów, being rescinded. The mid-thirteenth century witnessed increasing pressure from the knighthood to recover previously owned estates from monasteries. It seems that the victorious trials for Łęczno and Bałdrzychów were the swan song of Sulejów Abbey under the resilient rule of the abbots of Willelm and then Piotr. Soon, the Cistercians of Sulejów were overwhelmed by the management of vast estates scattered across Małopolska, Kujawy, Wielkopolska, and Pomerania, resulting in a crisis in the 1280s that necessitated the intervention of the general chapter.[29] In the case of monastic tithes, this forgery was provoked by the 1285 statute of Archbishop Jakub Świnka, whereby a seal-certified document confirming endowments was required.[30] The monks of Sulejów were probably also concerned about their immunity, which they received from the founder in an undefined form and scope, and which was probably extended by his successors. This forced the forger to significantly expand the immunity clause in the alleged foundation charter, significantly exceeding its original wording.

While on the topic of the Sulejów forgeries, it is impossible to ignore how quickly they were transumed. The foundation charter was transumed shortly after its preparation by Bolesław V in 1262.[31] In turn, the document listing the tithes was immediately prepared as a transumpt from Archbishop Pełka dated 1232 from its inception, and this false transumpt was legalised by Cistercian abbots in 1289.[32] It should be emphasised that the alleged originals disappeared immediately after the documents were transumed. It should also be added that the monastery quickly obtained protection bulls from Honorius III (1218) and then from Gregory IX (1234).[33] A document

---

29 See Sikora, 'Upadek fundacji cysterskiej', pp. 6–35.
30 Mitkowski, *Początki klasztoru cystersów*, pp. 34–35.
31 KDP i50.
32 This document has never been printed in its entirety, see Mitkowski, *Początki klasztoru cystersów*, pp. 305, 311.
33 Mitkowski, *Początki klasztoru cystersów*, pp. 317–18 (bull of Honorius III), pp. 324–25 (bull of Gregory IX).

confirming all previous endowments was also forged in the name of Konrad of Masovia. This diploma, dated 23 October 1242, was drawn up around 1279 and promptly transumed.[34] It is therefore clear that the monks went to a great deal of effort to secure the monastic property and that these measures were effective.

In summary, the oldest Sulejów and Jędrzejów documents are two cycles of fairly well-prepared forgeries, which were essentially based on earlier credible monastery records. Their purpose was to certify the foundations and endowments, and the scope of factual forgery was minor. Resembling objective records, the forgeries are modest in content and form, and similar to one another. It should be noted that they are fundamental sources for the early history of the monasteries in Jędrzejów and Sulejów, and their detailed analysis and new attempts at interpretation may lead to a more complete understanding of the origins of the Cistercians in Poland.

It is worth emphasising that the analysed examples of forgeries point to the Cistercian interest in the written document as a new means of evidence in court proceedings. This confirms the previously expressed opinion that the Cistercians constituted an important link in the reception and development of the document in Piast Poland, and that they were among the first to identify its legal utility.[35] It is possible, therefore, to claim that the Cistercians to some extent contributed to the development of Polish legal culture, despite their role in the development of architecture and art having been more vividly accentuated to date. There is, of course more that could be said. The question of transferring the formulary in the documents drawn up by various Cistercian abbeys requires more research, though is addressed to some degree in Chapter 10. The matter of the scriptoria in the Cistercian monasteries of Małopolska must necessarily be left for future investigation. The list of witnesses mentioned in the Jędrzejów forgeries, certainly reliable and providing much information about the political and social elites of the twelfth century, also requires future analysis. Lastly, research on the forgeries produced by the monastery at Ląd, may lead to a satisfactory resolution of the dispute about the origins of this Cistercian institution. However, this short analysis has focused on the forgeries of Jędrzejów and Sulejów and will, hopefully, provide impetus and direction for the work that is yet to be done.

---

34 KDP i.31. For more information about the document and transumpt, see Mitkowski, *Początki klasztoru cystersów*, pp. 14–24.
35 This has been previously suggested by S. Kętrzyński, *Zarys nauki o dokumencie*, p. 96.

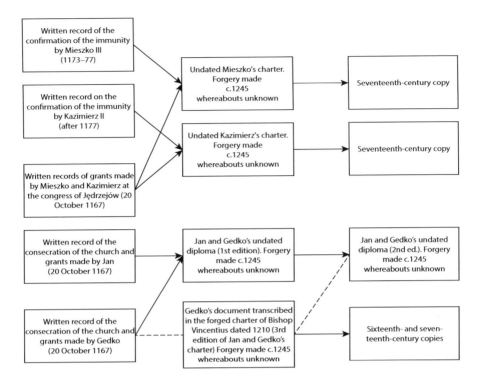

Figure 7. The Scheme of the Production of the Jędrzejów Forgeries.

CHAPTER 14

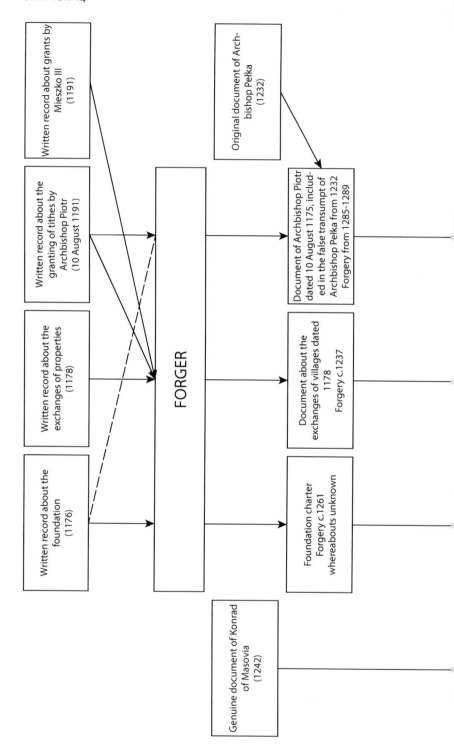

THE FALSE THIRTEENTH-CENTURY DOCUMENTS OF THE CISTERCIAN ABBEYS 217

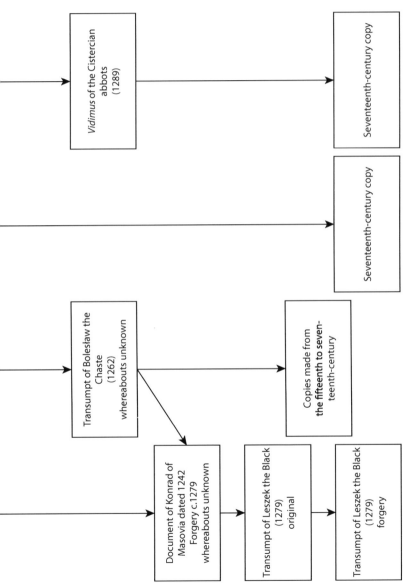

Figure 8. The Scheme of the Production of the Sulejów Forgeries.

CHAPTER 15

The Diploma of Mieszko III for the Canons Regular in Trzemeszno (28 April 1145)*

The earliest history of the convent of canons regular in Trzemeszno has received much attention from historians, archaeologists, and art historians. Relying on the fragmentary documentary record and on late tradition, its origins were traced back to St Adalbert or even to the first Polish Christian couple, Dobrawa and Mieszko. Research to this point has suggested that the canonry of Trzemeszno could have been established as early as the mid-eleventh century, having been founded either by Kazimierz I or Bolesław II.[1] The end of the eleventh century brought about the destruction of the convent, possibly in the aftermath of the Pomeranian invasions or the power struggles between Bolesław III and Zbigniew.

A new period in the canon's history began with the renewal of its activities and the settling of canons regular, who enjoyed considerable popularity in the twelfth century. They were probably brought to Trzemeszno by Bolesław III. These events are evidenced in the earliest written testimonies concerning the canonical institution in Trzemeszno, its twelfth-century documents. This chapter aims to analyse the document of primary significance for the reconstruction of the early history of the monastery, a diploma of Mieszko III dated 28 April 1145.[2]

Mieszko's diploma has been examined by several historians who have attached fundamental importance to questions about its authenticity and reliability. The document served as a basis for the reconstruction of the endowment received by the canons of Trzemeszno; its usefulness for research on the social and political elite of the mid-twelfth century has been considered comparatively less often. Zofia Kozłowska-Budkowa provided an overview of early critical analysis of the Trzemeszno document, in the

---

* Original publication: Józef Dobosz, 'Dokument Mieszka III Starego dla kanoników regularnych w Trzemesznie (28 kwietnia 1145 r.)', in *Gniezno. Studia i materiały historyczne*, vol. 4 (Warszawa-Poznań: PWN, 1995), pp. 87–106.
1 For the origins of the Trzemeszno canonry, see Kürbis, 'O początkach kanonii w Trzemesznie', pp. 327–43; Kürbis, 'Pogranicze Wielkopolski i Kujaw', pp. 85–99. See also Gieysztor and Głubiew-Lotyszowa, 'Trzemeszno', pp. 191–96. For information on the monastic architecture, see Józefowiczówna. 'Trzy romańskie klasztory', pp. 165–207; Chudziakowa, 'Z badań nad architekturą', pp. 9–20.
2 The alleged original of this document is currently stored in the Archdiocesan Archives in Gnieźnie, ref. Dypl. Tr 1. For copies and editions, see RPD i.42.

course of which she determined it to be a forgery. She argued that the false document was produced in the mid-thirteenth century based on monastery records copied from the calendar, foundation book or album, which in turn relied on Cardinal Hubaldus's 1146 privilege for Trzemeszno. In her examination, Kozłowska-Budkowa recognised the *dictatus* of Chancellor Janusz, who would later become Archbishop of Gniezno.[3] From this point, research on the Trzemeszno forgery was abandoned for some time and Kozłowska-Budkowa's findings were generally accepted without question.[4] However, new attempts have been made to evaluate the document. Brygida Kürbis confirmed the fact that it was forged in the thirteenth century and pointed to its authentic foundations by arguing that the bull of Eugene III from 1147 and the diploma of Hubaldus could serve as a test of historicity. She also undertook the most comprehensive analysis of the endowment of the Trzemeszno canonry to date, as presented in the forgery.[5] Mieszko's charter for Trzemeszno has also been inspected by Józef Spors in the course of his analysis of the district divisions in Poland in the mid-twelfth century, and by Henryk Łowmiański.[6] Taking the position that the act was a forgery, Łowmiański nevertheless confirmed the credibility of the information it contained. Łowmiański saw the origins of the monastery during the reign of Bolesław II, whom he considered to be the founder, in his opinion an evident conclusion based on the diploma's opening passages.[7] The last historian to deal with Mieszko's Trzemeszno act was Jarosław Wenta, who decided that some of its fragments had to have been copied directly from Hubaldus's document. At the same time, Wenta rejected the date given in the document as unreliable, seeing it as a random contribution of the forger.[8]

While all these scholars are in agreement on the most important issue — that the document is a twelfth-century forgery — they differ in their identifications of the grounds for forging the Trzemeszno diploma, and on the date it bears. The aim of this study, therefore, is to determine when, why and on what basis the act of Mieszko was drawn up and to show its importance for research on the economy and society of twelfth-century Poland.

Turning first to the analysis of the form of the document, it opens with an invocation that precedes a fairly extensive *arenga*, mixed with the inscription and address, naming both those to whom the document is directed and the sender. The multi-layered disposition opens with an

---

[3] RPD i.42.
[4] See for example Sczaniecki, *Nadania na rzecz rycerzy*, p. 112; Wolfarth, *Ascripticii w Polsce*, p. 49; Zajączkowski, 'O posiadłościach klasztoru', p. 53.
[5] Kürbis, 'Pogranicze Wielkopolski i Kujaw', pp. 95–96, 98; cf. Kürbis, 'O początkach kanonii w Trzemesznie', pp. 339–43.
[6] Spors, *Podział dzielnicowy Polski*, pp. 95–96.
[7] Łowmiański, *Początki Polski* vi, pp. 324–29.
[8] Wenta, 'Na marginesie dokumentu', pp. 106–11.

immunity clause, and then the text relays information about the original endowment received by the canonry. The next part of the *dispositio* lists the endowments granted by Bolesław III, his wife Salomea, four younger sons, and several nobles. The final protocol consists of the witness list, the *corroboratio*, and the date of issue.

In terms of composition, this alleged act of Mieszko III resembles other well-known and widely discussed documents, such as those for the Benedictines of Mogilno (dated 11 April 1065) and of Tyniec (from 1123/24).[9] It seems that the similarities in formulary resulted from the analogous circumstances of their issuance, as well as the motives and grounds behind the forgery. Neither the Benedictine abbeys in Tyniec and Mogilno nor the monastery of canons regular in Trzemeszno had foundation charters signed by the members of the ruling dynasty. The latter received a protective bull from Eugene III, and the Benedictines of Tyniec had a document allegedly issued by Cardinal-Legate Gilo, but they did not fully protect all monastic properties (if only because of the laconic description of the acquisition of certain estates). In the early thirteenth century, the written document became more widespread and its role in the judicial process increased, which is probably why this period saw a steep rise in the number of interpolations and falsifications of ducal endowment and confirmation documents. It seems probable that the three diplomas mentioned above must have been part of this cycle of falsifications and interpolations. The Canons of the Holy Sepulchre in Miechów took a different path. In 1198, they received a charter issued by Patriarch Monachus confirming their possessions.[10] As with the three charters mentioned above, the enumeration of estates again begins with ducal donations, and these are followed by grants from the nobility. The canons of Miechów, therefore, received confirmation of their grants earlier than the aforementioned monasteries, and without resorting to forgery. However, the question arises whether it would prove a sufficient means of evidence in judicial proceedings.

In the case of the Trzemeszno document of 28 April 1145, forged in the name of Mieszko III, it appears to have been motivated by the lack of ducal confirmation for numerous estates in the possession of the monastery. In addition, the forgery likely represents an attempt to secure some of the grants endowed by knights and rule out any potential retraction of ownership in the shifting legal environment. There is little doubt that a forgery was indeed committed in the monastery. However, its basis remains a controversial issue, and the propositions of historians have been fourfold:
1. The document was based on an authentic diploma issued by Mieszko III;
2. The document was based on monastery records;

---

9   For the texts of these documents, see ZDŚ i.26 (the Mogilno document) ZDŚ i.3. See also RPD i.8, i.26.
10 KDM ii.375.

3. The forgery was based on twelfth-century documents such as Hubaldus's privilege of 1146 and Eugene III's bull of 1147;
4. The forgery was based on the foundation charter of the monastery's founder.

The first of these propositions was enthusiastically promulgated by Karol Maleczyński and endorsed by Antoni Z. Helcel, Franciszek Piekosiński, and partly by Kürbis.[11] There is nothing, however, to indicate that a genuine document, now lost, was issued by Mieszko, and it is difficult, if not impossible, to identify such in the text of the forgery.[12] Both propositions two and three enjoyed the support of Wojciech Kętrzyński, Antoni Małecki, Teodor Tyc, Kozłowska-Budkowa, Spors, Wenta, and, to a degree, Maleczyński.[13] Kętrzyński and Tyc were convinced that the false document drew on the 1147 bull, and all were certain that it was based on Hubaldus's privilege of the previous year. Position four, advocated by Henryk Łowmiański, indicates that the forger could have relied on the foundation charter of Bolesław II, an idea that, as with the first proposition, can be rejected as unfounded.[14] The introductory formulas in Mieszko's document, and more specifically the mention of the renovation of the monastery by Bolesław III, do not permit such conclusions. Therefore, only the second and third positions remain to be considered. It seems that the bull of Eugene III can also be excluded from further consideration because it mentions far fewer granted estates and differs in the way their names are written. Moreover, some of the villages in the bull do not appear in the forgery.[15] Cardinal Hubaldus's privilege in contrast, at first glance, reveals a significant similarity with some parts of Mieszko's alleged grant:

---

11 Helcel, *List otwarty do Augusta Bielowskiego*, p. 340; ZDŚ i.10; Kürbis, 'Pogranicze Wielkopolski i Kujaw', p. 98; Maleczyński, 'Dokument Humbalda', pp. 1–29.
12 RPD i.42; Wenta, 'Na marginesie dokumentu', pp. 106–08.
13 Kętrzyński, *Studia nad dokumentami XII w.*, p. 288; Małecki, 'W kwestii fałszerstwa dokumentów', p. 473; Tyc, *Początki kolonizacji wiejskiej*, p. 120; RPD i.42; Spors, *Podział dzielnicowy Polski*, pp. 95–96; Wenta, 'Na marginesie dokumentu', p. 106; Maleczyński, 'Dokument Humbalda', pp. 1–29.
14 Łowmiański, *Początki Polski* vi, pp. 327–28.
15 RPD i.42. See also the below table.

The document of Hubaldus	Forgery dated 28 April 1145
Ideoque notum fieri uolumus presentibus et futuris, quoniam dum apud Genezen ciuitatem essemus, Bolesclauus et Misico duces et fratres eorum Henricus atque Kazimierzus, filij quondam Bolesclaui ducis, cappellam sancte Marie apud Lonciziam in monte sitam, pro remedio anime sue eorumque parentum ecclesie sancti Adhalberti, que est in loco, qui dicitur Sciremusine, cum omnibus redditibus ad eam pertinentibus, perpetuo contulerunt...	Dum vero apud Gnezden ciuitatem essemus, Mesco et Boleslaus et fratres nostri Henricus et Kazimirus duces, capellam sancte Marie apud Lanciciam in monte sitam, cum uilla ipsius montis et uilla in Lubnice cum hominibus Zaclodnici et uilla Ostrou, insuper molendium per medium et foralia et theloneum post quinque fora, omnes uero thabernam in castro preter decimam ebdomandam, examina uomerum, aque et caldarij, atque manulae ferrum et capam in Cracouia ad Magnum Salem decimamque vrnam celarij nostri in Sarnov pro remedio anime nostre nostrorumque parentum dicte ecclesie iure hereditario ac perpetuo contulimus possidenda...
...forum quoque Quetisougue, quod idem Bolesclauus et Misico duces...	Cum uero nos et frater noster Boleslaus dux Mazouie et Cuiauie conuentum celebrassemus in Quecisou pro parcium terminis, frater noster prefatus Quecisou sue dicionj cedere uolebat, nosque nostro dominio redigere uolebamus eandem; tunc ducissa Salome a nobis filijs suis utrisque prece obtinuit, ut sibi eam conferremus, quod et fecimus quam protinus ecclesie nominate contulit et duas sortes ej adiacentes, scilicet Oseycouo et Pustuino, uillam Cebar cum foro ei accumulauit...
	[further text of the immunity clause regarding Kwieciszewo]
...et forum Wasnoe, quod Salome ducissa predicte ecclesie sancti Adhalberti contulerunt...	Salome quoque ducissa contulit Wasnou forum cum thabernis et ecclesia ad supplementum salis ecclesie predicte...[16]

The forgery contains all the information provided by Hubaldus, and some phrases are repeated in both sources. What draws attention here, however, is the different

---

16   ZDŚ i.10–12.

spelling of the names and, above all, the more extensive and detailed information provided in the forgery. If the counterfeiter used Hubaldus's diploma, it could not have been his primary source. It seems more likely that both the forged document of Mieszko and the Cardinal's act drew information from the monastic records. This was probably the so-called objective record, which, next to the benefactors and the list of their donations, also perhaps included the names of the nobles present at the event. This brings the discussion to the forger's basic source of information: the monastic records. From these, the canons, as Kozłowska-Budkowa has argued, compiled an inventory of goods in the thirteenth century (between 1216 and 1223).[17] Sometime later, it formed the basis for the preparation of the forged act of Mieszko. The content of the latter allows for the distinguishing of individual elements of the grants, which were probably registered as separate records, and for an attempt to determine their chronology.

Any attempt to distinguish the content of such records from the forged text must necessarily begin with an analysis of the document's introduction. Neither the *arenga* nor the text containing the immunity exemption fits stylistically or materially within twelfth-century diplomatic conventions.[18] The broad privileges indicated in the document were acquired by the canons for their property between the mid-twelfth and mid-thirteenth centuries, and they are one of the few elements of factual forgery in Mieszko's act. After the exemption, the diploma enumerates a number of grants from dukes and nobles. The first part lists the early eleventh-century endowment of the Trzemeszno canonry. Just who granted the original endowment to Trzemeszno is difficult to say. It can be hypothesised that this may have happened as early as the reign of Kazimierz I, though Łowmiański may be right in identifying Bolesław II as the benefactor.[19] The monastic legacy probably contained some records reporting this event. These must have been used when the inventory of the monastery's property was compiled, and thus found their way into the forgery. The 1147 bull contains the names of two additional settlements, Młodojewo and Chomiąża, which left the hands of the monastery in the early thirteenth century, and thus were not included in the inventory of the property and were consequently omitted by the forger.[20] The next section concerns the grants received directly from the restorer of the canonry, Bolesław III. The bull of Eugene III fails to mention them, most likely because the papal confirmation was limited to listing specific grants of estates, lakes, and markets, while ignoring the donations of income. Bolesław III donated St Giles' Church with villages and income from the crossings over the Pilica River as a supplement to the grants of his predecessors. This occurred on the occasion of the renewal of the canonry before 1138, and the donation was scrupulously recorded by the monastic scribe.

---

17 RPD i.42.
18 RPD i.42; Kürbis, 'Pogranicze Wielkopolski i Kujaw', p. 96.
19 Łowmiański, *Początki Polski* vi, p. 324.
20 ZDŚ i.13; cf. RPD i.42.

The next part of the *dispositio* concerns the donations of the successors of Duke Bolesław III. It lists Kwieciszewo (with immunity); Zbar, a settlement complex near Łęczyca (with incomes); and Waśniów, the estates granted by Salomea and her sons. They were all probably included in a single entry made in 1145, certainly after 27 July 1144 and before 2 March 1146, which summarised the entire cycle of grants. The record contained a list of endowments, a date, and perhaps witness list. The date of 28 April 1145 was commonly linked with the convention at which the canons of Trzemeszno were given a settlement complex in the vicinity of Łęczyca. However, this assumption has been questioned by J. Wenta who, based on an analysis of the acts of Hubaldus and Mieszko, connected these events with a family reunion on the occasion of Salomea's funeral in August 1144 in Płock. The grants were to be confirmed the same year at the congress in Gniezno.[21] Wenta's argument that the entry *pro remedio anime sue eorumque parentum* proves that the affairs of the deceased mother were arranged on the occasion of her funeral is clearly exaggerated. Similar passages are found in numerous documents dating from the period. They rather manifest the duke-founders' solicitude for their own and their loved ones' salvation, although on this instance the wording itself could have been taken from another document. Neither does the list of witnesses indicate that the convention was family-oriented or took place in Płock. The witness lists of Mieszko's and Hubaldus's documents are as follows:

Mieszko's document	Hubaldus document
Mesco	… … …
Boleslaus	… … …
Henricus	… … …
Kasimirus	… … …
Iacobus archiepiscopus	… … …
Alexander Plocensis episcopus	Alexander uidelicet Plocensis episcopus
Iohannes et Peianus cancelarij	Iohannes et Peanus cancelarij
comes Odolanus	Odolanus comes
Schebor	Shebor
Saulus	Saulus
Dirsicaraus	Dirsichraus
Zbiluth	Zbiluta
Bogumilus	Bogomil
Degno	… … …
Montinus	Montinus
Pacoslaus	Bacosclaus comes
Sspithigneus	Spitagneuus
et alij quam plures	et alij plures[22]

---

21 Wenta, 'Na marginesie dokumentu', from p. 106.
22 ZDŚ i.10–12.

There are only slight differences in the subscriptions of both documents. As the dukes appear as the issuers of Hubaldus's diploma, only Archbishop Jakub and Comes Degnon are missing when compared to the forgery. Based on these witness lists, a political party supporting the younger Piasts in the civil war of 1144–1146 — specifically its leaders — can be reconstructed. The faction probably formed during the life of Salomea, as evidenced by the document issued by her before 1144.[23] Most of the nobles mentioned in both documents are known from their activities around the mid-twelfth century, mainly in Wielkopolska extending to its border with Kujawy, or in the central districts such as Zbylut, Dzierżykraj, Wszebor, Pakosław, and Degno. Zbylut, Degno, and Wszebor had previously supported Salomea.[24] The convention at which the mentioned witnesses were present was related to the political events that unfolded fairly quickly after the Duchess' death. The camp of the younger Piasts was closing ranks, trying to retain old supporters and win new ones. At one of the numerous conventions and rallies held at that time, new grants were approved and old grants were ratified for the benefit of the canons of Trzemeszno. A reasonably precise record was then composed, which Provost Bernard (a supporter of Salomea and, later, her sons) took to Rome and, at the turn of spring 1146, submitted to Cardinal Hubaldus, who had been a papal legate in Poland from 1145. Based on the record, Cardinal Hubaldus prepared a document dated 2 March 1146. It seems that, in the face of the civil war and its unknown outcome, Bernard feared that the canons might lose their monastic properties. In the event of Władysław's victory, the act issued by the legate provided much-welcomed protection. Perhaps the fact that Hubaldus's diploma was drawn up in Rome accounts for the differences in the number of witnesses in the documents and the spelling of some names. This might also explain the fact that Archbishop Jakub and Degnon were left out (as may a careless copyist).

The next portion of the *dispositio* of the forgery concerns the donations granted by nobles. First, individual grants are listed, followed by information about the construction of St John the Evangelist's Church by Comes Janusz. The document states that Janusz donated the church, along with its property and income, to the monastery, with Archbishop Jakub adding tithes. These facts are not included in the bull of Eugene III of 31 May 1147, leading to the conclusion that the grants may have been endowed by the nobles around this date. Mieszko's act adds the detail that St John the Evangelist's Church was consecrated by Archbishop Jakub in the presence of the dukes and knights on 24 April of an unknown year. Only the dates 24 April 1147 or 24 April 1148 would fit with the year of Archbishop Jakub's death, though individual nobles might have offered their grants later.

The dating recorded in the forgery, and the correlation between the forgery's witness list and the document issued by Hubaldus, have already

---

23 Wenta, 'Na marginesie dokumentu, p. 47.
24 Ibid.

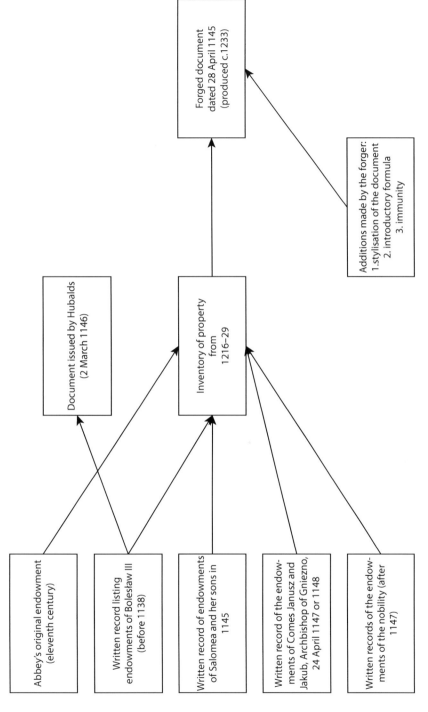

Figure 9. The Origin of the Trzemeszno Forgery (28 April 1145).

Table 4. The Economic Foundations of the Monastery in Trzemeszno (considering the forgery of 28 April 1145, bull of Eugene III of 31 May 1147, diploma of Hubaldus of 2 March 1146)[25]

No.	Endowments acc. to the 1145 forgery	Benefactor	Time of endowment	In the 1147 bull	In Hubaldus's document
1.	Trzemeszno with people and benefits	?	?	Listed	-
2.	Immunity for the monastic estates (thirteenth century in form)	?	Took shape between the mid-twelfth and mid-thirteenth centuries	-	-
3.	Palędzie with lakes and benefits	Bolesław II or Kazimierz I	Second half of the eleventh century	Palenda	-
4.	Popielewo with a lake (formerly Lake Lubień, now Lake Popielewskie)	as above	as above	Luben cum lacu	-
5.	Wylatowo with Lake Wylatowskie and three plots of land: Siedlikowo (today Siedluchna), Robakowo and Myślątkowo	as above	as above	Velatov cum lacu	-
6.	Lake Kamienieckie with two adjoining villages (most probably including Kamieniec)	as above	as above	As in forgery	-
7.	St Giles Church in Inowłodz, with two unnamed villages, income from taverns and duty (customs chambers when crossing the Pilica River: Inowłódz, Sulejów, Przedbórz)	Bolesław III	Before 1138	-	-

---

25   Many of the locations mentioned in this table are given by Jan Łaski's *Liber beneficiorum archidyecezyi gnieźnieńskiej*. Much of the work of identifying particular villages and towns was undertaken by Stanisław Kozierowski, for example Kozierowski, *Pierwotne osiedlenie*; Kozierowski, *Badania nazw topograficznych*; Kozierowski, 'Pierwotne osiedlenie pojezierza Gopła', pp. 6–54. Kürbis, 'Pogranicze Wielkopolski i Kujaw', pp. 96–98 provides data on the distribution of monastic properties. See also Kamińska, *Nazwy miejscowe*; Zajączkowski and Zajączkowski, *Materiały do słownika geograficzno-historycznego*. The latest data is contained in *Kartoteka Słownika Historyczno-Geograficznego Wielkopolski* stored at the Department of the Institute of History of the Polish Academy of Sciences in Poznań.

No.	Endowments acc. to the 1145 forgery	Benefactor	Time of endowment	In the 1147 bull	In Hubaldus's document
8.	Kwieciszewo with immunity	Bolesław IV and Mieszko II (at Salomea's request); Kazimierz II participated in the granting of immunity	Donation of the village before 1144, immunity after 1166	Villa Quetisou cum foro	forum quoque Quetisougue
9.	Zbar with a marketplace, two plots of land: Osiekowo and Pustwino	Salomea	1138–1144	in Zbar forum cum villa	-
10.	Chapel in Góra Małgorzaty near Łęczyca with emolument; villages of Góra, Łubnice, Zachłodzice with people; Ostrów with half of the income from the mill; fees from every fifth marketplace; the tavern in Łęczyca (without tithes) and court fees from *judicium Dei*	Bolesław IV, Mieszko III, Henryk and Kazimierz II	1145	Capella in Lonsitia cum omnibus ad eam pertinentibus	capellam Sancte Marie apud Lonciziam in monte sitam (with benefits)
11.	Salina in Wieliczka and the tenth jug from the ducal cellar in Żarnów	as above	1145	-	-
12.	Church, marketplace and taverns in Waśniów (with salt)	Salomea	1138–1144	Wasnov forum cum villa	forum Wasnoe
13.	Church in Korczyn with two villages and adjoining areas	Wszebor	After 1147	-	-
14.	Stojsławie (village Stojsława)	Stojsław	as above	-	-
15.	Jeżewo (near Waśniów)	Mikora	as above	-	-
16.	Prawastów (Prawęcice? upon the Bzura River)	Niemir	as above	-	-
17.	Gąsawa and Konratowo with Lake Gosale and benefits	Dzierżykraj	as above	-	-
18.	Oćwieka with three lakes	Degno	as above	-	-
19.	Szelejewo (Żelewo)	Bernard	as above	-	-
20.	Jabłowo and Załachów with duty and benefits	Zdzisław	as above	-	-
21.	Brzyskorzystew with benefits	Wincenty, Canon of Gniezno	Thirteenth century	-	-
22.	Grabonowo and Pikutkowo	Trojan	After 1147	-	-

CHAPTER 15

No.	Endowments acc. to the 1145 forgery	Benefactor	Time of endowment	In the 1147 bull	In Hubaldus's document
23.	Strzelno (rather Strzelce) with benefits	Janusz	as above	-	-
24.	Włostowo with part of Lake Gopło	Włost	as above	-	-
25.	Tithe from Końskie	Szaweł	as above	-	-
26.	St John the Evangelist's Church in Trzemeszno (build and given to the abbey)	Janusz	24 April 1147 or 1148	-	-
27.	Tithes from Żelisławice, Sieraków, Mirosławice and Ostrowite	Archbishop Jakub	as above	-	-
28.	Sierakowo, Ostrowite, Januszowo, Chorzelino	Janusz	as above	-	-
29.	Income from inns, markets, and chambers in the town of Wyszogród and the village of Łoskuń (with income)	Janusz with his wife Sulisława	as above	-	-
				Additionally: Młodojewo, Chomiąża and Węgłowo	

been noted. Admittedly, the question of the source of the date of 28 April 1145 remains open. It seems, however, that this is not an arbitrary addition by the forger, but a piece of information rooted in monastic records. At this point, however, the *dispositio* of the Trzemeszno forgery draws attention, and the detail it provides on the economic foundations of the Trzemeszno canonry require analysis.

The listed grants were endowed by the Polish dukes and the noble elite. The forged Mieszko document illustrates the endowments that the monastery in Trzemeszno received over a span of 150 years, from around the mid-eleventh century to its economic stabilisation sometime in the first quarter of the thirteenth century. The vast majority of donations were owed to the generosity of Bolesław III; his wife Salomea; and their sons Bolesław IV, Mieszko III, Henryk, and Kazimierz II; as well as the noble circles of the four brothers. The period from the beginning of the reign of Bolesław III to about the mid-twelfth century saw the greatest economic expansion of the Trzemeszno monastery. It was then that the monastic holdings grew, and the monastery itself acquired sufficient economic foundation for unrestricted activity. This development likely derived from Provost Bernard's consistent support for the younger Piasts in the 1144–1146 war with Władysław, as well as his earlier connections to the court of Bolesław III and Salomea. In total, the canonry managed to gather around forty villages and plots of land prior to the mid-twelfth century; at least nine lakes or parts thereof; five churches and chapels; tithes from four villages and people settled there; income from markets, crossings, customs, taverns, strongholds, and trials by ordeal; salt grants; and immunity. The exemption in the form shown in the forgery could not have been granted before the thirteenth century.[25]

The monastic estates must have enjoyed some freedoms prior to this, but their scope is impossible to reconstruct. Mieszko III is a likely benefactor, and his successors probably extended the freedoms he provided to the extent known from the document. This is evidenced by the details concerning the immunity for Kwieciszewo, which was granted jointly by Bolesław, Mieszko, and Kazimierz. Here, too, doubts have arisen over the rather broad exemptions purportedly granted to the monastery.[26] It seems unlikely that the exact list of exemptions from ducal law would have been composed in the mid-twelfth century. Even more doubtful is the exemption from the *narzaz* obligation, a tribute to the duke paid in non-horned animals, though sometimes also in cattle and sheep, which is mentioned in documents from only the early thirteenth century.[27] Despite certain reservations, it should be noted that a similar immunity clause is contained in the Zagość 1173–1175 document of Kazimierz II.[28] The fact that only three of the brothers — Bolesław, Mieszko, and Kazimierz — were present when Kwieciszewo was granted indicates that, unless the forger simply left out Henry, this legal action took place after 1166 (the year in which year Henry died) and before 1172, with Bolesław meeting his fate in January 1173.[29]

The monastic estates were concentrated in a few clusters scattered around Wielkopolska, Kujawy, and the central districts, though the canonry also possessed several peripheral estates in the Sandomierz territory. The abbey also received salt grants from the mines near Kraków (Wieliczka). The original endowment of the canonry was located in Wielkopolska; Trzemeszno and the villages located in its immediate vicinity; Palędzie, Popielewo, Wylatowo, and Kamieniec (with lakes); as well as Młodojewo, which was lost in the early thirteenth century. Gąsawa, Konratowo, Oćwieka, Szelejewo, Jabłowo, Załachów, and Brzysotykew were located in Pałuki. The villages of Zbar (Wiśniewo?), Kwieciszewo, Pustwino, Osiekowo, Ostrowite, Januszowo, and Chrzelino,

---

25 Wojciechowski, 'Zagadnienie immunitetu sądowego', p. 168, note 2; Wojciechowski, 'Początki immunitetu w Polsce', p. 356. Wojciechowski rejected Mieszko's document as being useless for analysis of the immunity. Kaczmarczyk, *Immunitet sądowy i jurysdykcja poimmunitetowa*, pp. 236–38; Matuszewski, *Immunitet ekonomiczny*, pp. 409–13; Grodecki, *Początki immunitetu w Polsce*, pp. 49–50, 66 all used the thirteenth-century forgery in their research on immunity, though emphasising its late origins.

26 *Nos quoque duces Mesco, Boleslaus, Kasimirus, hominibus in Quecisou degentibus omnem libertatem contulimus, eos ab omnibus tributis absoluentes, videlicet a strosa, a poduoroue, a naraz, a pouoloue, a castri edificacione nec non expedicione.* ZDŚ i.10.

27 See Balzer, *Narzaz w systemie*.

28 ZDŚ i.29.

29 Cf. Grodecki, *Początki immunitetu w Polsce*, pp. 49–50.

as well as Chomiąża and Węgłowo (lost before 1113), were also located in Wielkopolska. Włostowo and Sierakowo were on Lake Gopło, while Góra Małgorzata, Ostrów, Łubnica, and Zachłodzice were located in the immediate vicinity of Łęczyca. On the Vistula and Brda, within the borders of Kujawy, the monastery owned Łoskuń, Pikutkowo, Grabonowo, a stronghold in Wyszogród, and most likely Strzelce. On the Pilica River there was Inowłódz with St Giles' Church, two villages, and the crossings in Sulejów and Przedbórz. In the Sandomierz territories, the monastery received grants in Waśniów, Żarnów, Korczyn, Końskie, and Jeżewo.[30]

While the circumstances underlying the creation of the Trzemeszno forgery constitute an important research problem in their own right, the Trzemeszno forgery also offers insights into yet another research field. The considerable number of people listed in the document make it an indispensable source of information about the of mid-twelfth century Poland. Furthermore, the document provides grounds for the reconstruction of the political camp centred around the younger Piasts on the eve of the war with their half-brother Władysław. It mentions twenty-three names of nobles: fourteen in the list of witnesses (some also appearing as benefactors) and a further nine in the list of benefactors (including one listed with his wife). The witness list is opened by Jakub, Archbishop of Gniezno, who held this title between 1127 and 1148, and probably came from the Pałuki clan.[31] Second is another church dignitary, Alexander of Malonne, Bishop of Płock.[32] Behind the hierarchs of the Church in Poland are two chancellors of the younger Piasts: first Jan, Chancellor of Bolesław IV, then Pean, who performed an analogous function alongside Mieszko III.[33] Among secular nobles, Odolan of Wielkopolska, bearing the title of *comes*,[34] is mentioned first, followed by Wszebor, probably the later voivode of younger Piasts

---

30 Cf. Kürbis, 'Pogranicze Wielkopolski i Kujaw', pp. 96–98.
31 Listed in the document issued by Duchess Salomea (before 27 July 1144), ZDŚ i.7, and in *Księga bracka opactwa Panny Marii w Lubiniu*, MPH ix, p. 6, note 19. Semkowicz argued that he was a member of the Pałuki clan, Semkowicz, *Ród Pałuków*. See also PSB x, pp. 371–72; Bieniak, 'Polska elita polityczna XII wieku, Part II', p. 64.
32 See Gębarowicz, 'Aleksander', in PSB i, pp. 65–66; Deptuła, 'Krąg kościelny płocki', pp. 5–122.
33 Pean, the more famous of the two, became Bishop of Poznań, see Gąsiorowski, 'Pean', in PSB xxv, p. 534. See also Maleczyński, 'O kanclerzach polskich XII wieku', pp. 9–10; Maleczyński, *Zarys dyplomatyki polskiej*, pp. 83–87, 95–96, in which argues that Chancellor Jan of the Mogilno forgery (ZDŚ, i.12), was the same person as Jan of the Gryfici clan, Bishop of Wrocław, later Archbishop of Gniezno. Cf. Kozłowska-Budkowa, 'Jan', in PSB x, pp. 428–30, who is doubtful about this identification.
34 In addition to the Trzemeszno forgery and the Hubaldus document, it was entered in the *Księga bracka lubińska* and the Obituary of Lubiń Abbey. The editor of the former wrongly identified the nobleman, considering that *Hodalanus* listed there had lived several decades earlier, p. 5, note 9. *Hodalanus* is also mentioned on p. 95 under 31 August. See Bieniak, 'Odolan', in PSB xxii, pp. 537–38; Bieniak, 'Polska elita polityczna XII wieku, Part II', p. 70.

in the war with Władysław.[35] Next comes Comes Szaweł of the Odrowąż family, who granted the tithe from Końskie.[36] Next there are two nobles from Wielkopolska: Dzierżykraj of the Nałęcz family, who was also the benefactor to the abbey,[37] and Zbylut, one of the first known representatives of the Pałuki clan.[38] Behind them comes Comes Bogumił, whom Władysław Semkowicz identified with Bogusza mentioned in the Łekno document and with Archbishop Bogumił (which seems unlikely), believing that he had been a member of the Pałuki clan.[39] Comes Degno, who is known from the document of Duchess Salomea (before 1144), was probably a noble from Wielkopolska, a previous associate of the Duchess and then of her son Mieszko III.[40] The mysterious Montinus who follows Degnon is known only from Hubaldus's document. Perhaps Mantina (with brothers), a witness from a document issued in 1161 for Czerwińsk, is the same person.[41] Unlike several of the other subscribers, Pakosław Awdaniec is a well-known figure. The youngest son of Skarbimir, Voivode of Bolesław III, he held office in the territories under the control of Mieszko III, probably as the castellan.[42] The witness list is completed with an unknown Spicygnev.[43]

Several witnesses of the document were also listed as the benefactors of the canonry: Wszebor, Szaweł, Dzierżykraj, and Degno. Among other benefactors, Wincenty, Canon of Gniezno, was entered rather by accident. He was a benefactor to the canonry who lived in the twelfth century. The counterfeiter must have accidentally rewritten his name and donation from

---

35 He is also mentioned in the Mogilno forgery (ZDŚ i.26), a document issued by Salomea before 27 July 1144 ZDŚ i.7) and Hubaldus document (ZDŚ i.12). His son Piotr witnessed a diploma of Mieszko III from 1176 (ZDŚ i.36) and is mentioned in *Księga bracka lubińska*, p. 13, notes 59–60. In this fraternity book we also find *Suebor* (p. 8) but whether he can be identified with the prominent nobleman is unclear. See also Kürbis, 'Pogranicze Wielkopolski i Kujaw', p. 97, who argues that Wszebor was a relative of Piotr Włostowic. Cf. Bieniak, 'Dyskusja i podsumowanie obrad', pp. 123–24.
36 Also in Hubaldus document, ZDŚ i.12, p. 64. See Górski, 'Ród Odrowążów', pp. 69–70; Kürbis, 'Pogranicze Wielkopolski i Kujaw', pp. 97–98.
37 For the portrayal of this nobleman see Dobosz, 'Dokument fundacyjny', pp. 76–77.
38 See Dobosz, 'Dokument fundacyjny', pp. 70–72.
39 Semkowicz, *Ród Pałuków*, pp. 253–54. Bogumił is listed as a witness in Hubaldus diploma and the Jędrzejów foundation charter (ZDŚ i.12, i.20) and it seems that he was a nobleman from Wielkopolska. The name is mentioned several times in the *Księga bracka lubińska* (pp. 5–8), but it is difficult to say which one of them is the same as Comes Bogumił from the Trzemeszno forgeries. In the documents, Bogumił is always mentioned along with Zbylut of the Pałuki clan.
40 See ZDŚ i.7. He is also mentioned in the *Księga bracka lubińska*, p. 5, note 11, in which the issuer is incorrectly identified. His son Szymon was a witness to the 1176 document of Mieszko (ZDŚ i.36) and was included in *Księga bracka lubińska* (p. 13) under the same year.
41 ZDŚ i.12, i.24.
42 See Bieniak, 'Pakosław', in PSB xxv, pp. 37–38; Dobosz, 'Dokument fundacyjny', pp. 75–76.
43 He was mentioned as a witness in Hubaldus document, ZDŚ i.12.

the inventory of goods.[44] Donators Włast[45] and Mikora[46] were members of the Łabędzie clan, closely related to Piotr Włostowic. Sons of Wojsław and the nobles of Mazovia-Kujawy-Sandomierz, Janusz and Trojan represented the Powała clan.[47] The group of benefactors of the monastery finishes with the lesser-known Niemir (Niemierza?), Stojsław, Bernard, and Comes Zdzisław.

The Trzemeszno forgery relates directly to the turbulent times of the civil war between Władysław and the younger Piasts, sons of Salomea, and some of the endowments listed therein can be directly associated with these events, especially those of young dukes. Other donations, mainly from the nobles, were granted between 1147 and 1148 right after the younger Piasts took power. Some parts of the document come from the forger and concern later grants in the early thirteenth century, which is particularly true of the immunity. The forgery itself was produced in the monastery around 1233 on the basis of genuine monastery records, probably because the canons did not have a ducal document confirming the grants they received. Obtaining a written substantiation of grants became a necessity as the written document became more popular in court proceedings and the knighthood put greater pressure on the recovery of goods previously granted to the Church. Containing only faint traces of factual forgery, the false document of Trzemeszno should be considered a reliable and valuable source for the study of the property relations of the canonry, the scope of knightly property around the mid-twelfth century, and the social connections of that time, mainly of the political and social elite.

---

44 Cf. Kürbis, 'Pogranicze Wielkopolski i Kujaw', p. 97, note 123.
45 Probably Piotr Włostowic's brother or cousin (son of his father's brother), see Bieniak, 'Polska elita polityczna XII wieku, Part II', pp. 72–73.
46 Known from numerous twelfth-century documents, he also appears in the *Księga bracka lubińska*, p. 5, note 14, where the issuer is incorrectly identified. See Bieniak, 'Polska elita polityczna XII wieku, Part II', p. 73; Trawkowski, 'Mikora', in PSB xxi, pp. 157–59.
47 Semkowicz, 'Ród Powałów', pp. 19–20; Bieniak, 'Polska elita polityczna XII wieku, Part II', from p. 19.

CHAPTER 16

The Foundation Charter of the Cistercian Abbey at Łekno

The 1153 foundation charter of the Cistercian abbey at Łekno is one of the most interesting documents of medieval culture that have been preserved in Poland. Both its remarkable importance for the reconstruction of Poland's twelfth-century history and its literary value, taken alongside the archaeological research undertaken at Łekno, have necessitated another edition of the document, duly supplemented with extensive commentary.

Historical scholarship is replete with extensive and diverse studies on Zbylut's document for Łekno.[1] In addition to its importance to the reconstruction twelfth-century history and its outstanding literary value, much attention has derived from the fact that it is the earliest extant authentic monastic foundation charter in Poland, and it has survived in three copies.[2]

The document was made available to a wider group of historians when it was printed in *Kodeks dyplomatyczny Polski*.[3] A few years later, Antoni Helcel passed some brief comment on Zbylut's charter in his discussion of the 1153 document issued by Archbishop Janik (Jan) for Jędrzejów.[4] After this, the document did not draw attention for some time. It was not until 1874, when Stanisław Smolka travelled to the archives of the Grand Duchy of Poznań and located copies of the document that a description was published.[5] A few years later, when the *Kodeks dyplomatyczny Wielkopolski* was published, the first volume included Zbylut's charter with a short commentary.[6] This publication prompted an immediate response among medieval historians, including a review by Franciszek Piekosiński, in which he devoted some space to the Łekno foundation charter.[7] The next stage of research on the document came with the study of the monastery and the town of Wągrowiec, carried out by Heinrich Hockenbeck, who provided a description of the document and

---

1 The spelling of the name of Zbylut, the founder of Łekno Abbey follows: Taszycki, 'Najdawniejsze polskie imiona osobowe', p. 134.
2 See RPD i.53, pp. 58–60; Semkowicz, *Paleografia łacińska*, p. 334.
3 KDP i.2, edition based on the Gniezno original.
4 Helcel, 'O klasztorze jędrzejowskim', p. 133.
5 Smolka, 'Archiwa w W. X. Poznańskim', pp. 170–464.
6 KDW i.18, pp. 23–24, based on the Poznań original with the annotation on Copy 1 on pp. 577–78.
7 Piekosiński, review of KDW i, p. 454.

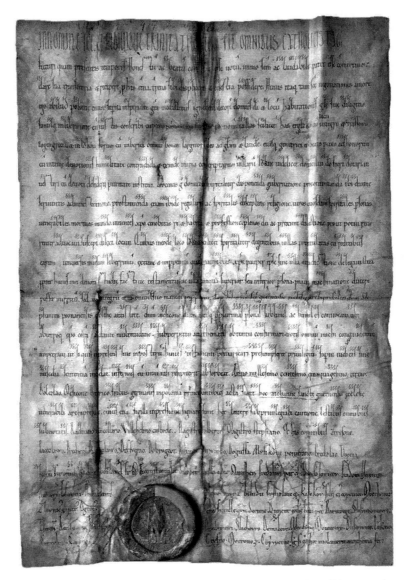

Figure 10. Poznań foundation charter of Łekno Abbey (end of twelfth century). Photo P. Namiota (MPP, table vi).

its translation into German.[8] The late nineteenth century brought a critical and valuable treatise on twelfth-century Polish documents by Wojciech

---

8 Hockenbeck, *Beiträge zur Geschichte* i, pp. 12–16. This research was later used in Depdolla, *Geschichte des Klosters Lekno*, pp. 15–16.

Kętrzyński. He devoted much attention to the mystery of the Łekno document, and his findings remain, to a large extent, current today.[9] Kętrzyński's study brought a response from another well-known specialist in diplomatic issues, Stanisław Krzyżanowski, who argued with Kętrzyński on many issues in an extensive dissertation on the beginnings of Polish diplomatics. The Łekno document was one of the thornier issues.[10] Krzyżanowski's work, naturally, provoked a response from Kętrzyński who, after accusations levelled again him by others, composed a response on the subject of Zbylut's charter.[11] The debate between these scholars comprised an unparalleled contribution to the discussion about the earliest Polish documents and opened up new avenues of research for their successors.

Research on the Łekno document entered its next phase with its third publication, this time with a fairly extensive commentary by Piekosiński.[12] In the early twentieth century, the foundation charter was also inspected by Antoni Małecki, another well-known researcher on the Polish Middle Ages, who provided his own views about the document.[13] Finally, in 1907, a faithful copy of the document was published by Krzyżanowski.[14] This publication garnered a strong response from researchers and was reviewed by renowned scholars such as Emil von Ottenthal and Władysław Semkowicz.[15] The latter also discussed the document as a part of the history of the Pałuki clan.[16] In the following years, Zbylut's charter was discussed by Karol Maleczyński, who presented its diplomatic and palaeographic aspects in three dissertations, at the same time drawing attention to the literary aspects of the document.[17] Around the same time, Semkowicz took up the issue of the document once more,[18] this time as a part of a debate with the author of the first modern textbook on diplomatics, Stanisław Kętrzyński,[19] correcting many errors made by the latter in the process. Earlier, I. Błażkiewiczówna prepared a minor study about the monastery at Łekno, referring briefly to the document issued by Zbylut.[20] Ultimately, the discussion on the Łekno foundation charter was

---

9   Kętrzyński, *Studia nad dokumentami XII w.*, pp. 210–14.
10 Krzyżanowski, 'Początki dyplomatyki polskiej', pp. 797–99.
11 Kętrzyński, 'O początkach dyplomatyki polskiej', pp. 25–26.
12 ZDŚ, pp. 76–81.
13 Małecki, 'W kwestii fałszerstwa dokumentów', pp. 430–33.
14 MPP tabl. 4–6. See also Krzyżanowski, ed., *Album paleographicum*, table 2 (according to original 2).
15 Semkowicz, review of Kętrzyński, MPP, pp. 385–400; von Ottenthal, review of Kętrzyński, MPP, p. 338.
16 Semkowicz, 'Ród Pałuków', pp. 206–07.
17 Maleczyński, 'O kanclerzach polskich XII wieku', pp. 42–44; Maleczyński, 'O wpływie szkoły pisarskiej leodyjskiej', pp. 77–88; Maleczyński, 'Wpływy obce na dokument polski', pp. 109–11.
18 Semkowicz, 'Uwagi o początkach dokumentu polskiego', pp. 30, 36–38, 41.
19 Kętrzyński, *Zarys nauki o dokumencie polskim*, pp. 134, 156, 198.
20 Błażkiewiczówna, 'Fundacja i pierwotne uposażenie', pp. 89–93.

largely concluded by Zofia Kozłowska-Budkowa, who recapitulated the state of research and added her own observations.[21] This is how research on the foundation charter of Łekno developed prior to 1939. After the war, several works were published on the subject of Zbylut's document, but most of them accepted Kozłowska-Budkowa's findings. Particularly noteworthy, however, are two works published in 1951: Semkowicz's *Paleografia łacińska*,[22] and Maleczyński's *Zarys dyplomatyki polskiej wieków średnich*.[23] Finally, it is worth mentioning Tadeusz Przybysz's study of the foundation of Łekno Abbey, which cites extensive references on the issue,[24] and Brygida Kürbis's comparative analysis of the Łekno foundation charter and its Jędrzejów parallel of 1153.[25]

It follows from the above that the Łekno foundation charter has been a subject of scrupulous historical studies. Some researchers dealt with its editorial aspects, others focused on diplomatic matters, while other historians explored the palaeography of the document. In view of the enormous quantity of historiographic material, it is necessary to present the final results of this expansive research on the Łekno document in an orderly manner.

The authenticity of the document has never been questioned, and yet many problems arising from the fact that it has been preserved in three copies. A copy stored in the State Archives in Poznań was drawn up on a fairly large sheet of parchment. It carries the seal of Archbishop Jan (Figure 13), around which some annotations were added. This is termed here Copy 1. The second copy, kept in the Archdiocesan Archives in Gniezno, is written on a sheet of parchment smaller than Copy 1. The archbishop's seal has not been preserved but some traces of an oval wax seal are still visible. There is no annotation corresponding to the that of Copy 1. This document will be referred to as Copy 2. The third copy, also kept in the Archdiocesan Archives in Gniezno, was prepared on a large sheet of parchment and does not carry a seal. This copy contains an annotation, an extended version of that added around the seal on Copy 1. It is referred to as Copy 3.

A variety of statements and hypotheses have been put forward to explain the interconnectedness of the three copies of Zbylut's document. Smolka mistakenly assumed that there must have been four copies of the foundation charter. His ultimate conclusion was that Copies 1 and 2 are the originals, while Copy 3 is nothing but a reproduction of Copy 1.[26] The editor of *Kodeks dyplomatyczny Wielkopolski* established that there were two original documents (Copies 1 and 2) written by one hand, and he considered Copy 3 to be a slightly later

---

21 RPD i.53, 149, 150.
22 Semkowicz, *Paleografia łacińska*, pp. 336–42.
23 Maleczyński, *Zarys dyplomatyki polskiej*, pp. 36, 74–77, 86, 93.
24 Przybysz, 'Fundacja i pierwotne', pp. 60. See also Krzyżaniakowa, 'Rozwój kultury', pp. 328–40, where Zbylut's document is discussed in the context of the cultural development of Wielkopolska.
25 Kürbis, 'Cystersi w kulturze polskiego', pp. 328–40.
26 Smolka, 'Archiwa w W. X. Poznańskim', pp. 238, 240, 343–45.

copy.[27] Wojciech Kętrzyński perceived the script on all copies to be similar. In his opinion, the annotation on Copy 1 was not added by the person who prepared Copies 1 and 2. The script on Copy 3 differs from the originals and dates from the last decade of the twelfth century. Finally, he came to the conclusion that Copy 1 was the original document and Copy 2 was a rough draft.[28] Krzyżanowski disputed Kętrzyński's findings, and stated that Copy 2 was actually the original document, while Copy 1 was written by the same hand and that, as an authentic endowment of Zbylut, it should still be treated as an original. Krzyżanowski believed that Copy 3 was uniformly prepared at the end of the twelfth century. The script on Copies 1 and 3 are closer to each other than Copy 2, because Copy 3 is an exact redraw of Copy 1.[29] The distinguished editor Piekosiński also took his position on the documents. Following Krzyżanowski, Piekosiński considered Copy 2 to be the primary original. In his opinion, Copy 1 was produced when further endowments were granted to the monastery but there was no space left to add them on Copy 2. This is when Copy 2 was made and an annotation added. When the monastery received the tithes from Archbishop Piotr, Copy 3 was drawn up as a uniform document.[30] Małecki, on the other hand, considered Copy 2 to be the original and Copy 1 to be the original duplicate, both written with different hands, yet coetaneous, with Copy 3 being created slightly later than them. According to Małecki, the annotation from Copy 3 was primarily in relation to the annotation from Copy 1 and constituted a separate entity until around 1210. Copy 3 itself was produced for the ratification of a whole series of later endowments.[31]

In the course of his research on the genealogy of the Pałuki clan, Semkowicz also presented some discussions of the charter but, in his considerations, followed the erroneous path laid out by Piekosiński. He therefore considered Copy 2 to be the original. He argued that Copy 1 was produced between 1153 and 1173, and Copy 3 in the last decade of the twelfth century.[32] Semkowicz did not, however, maintain this position. When reviewing *Monumenta Poloniae paleographica*, he considered the script of Copies 1 and 2 to have been produced by one hand, with the annotation on Copy 1 being added slightly later and written by a different hand. He considered Copy 3 to be an imitation of Copy 1, a product of a different hand than the one that produced Copies 1 and 2. Both originals (Copes 1 and 2) were drawn up by the recipient. Copy 1 was given to the monastery, and Copy 2 to the Archbishop of Gniezno, while Copy 3

---

27 KDW i.18.
28 Kętrzyński, *Studia nad dokumentami*, pp. 210–14.
29 Krzyżanowski, 'Początki dyplomatyki polskiej', pp. 797–99. See also Kętrzyński's reply, 'O początkach dyplomatyki polskiej', pp. 25–26.
30 ZDŚ i.19.
31 Małecki, 'W kwestii fałszerstwa dokumentów', pp. 430–33.
32 Semkowicz, *Ród Pałuków*, p. 206, note 10.

was prepared after an annotation was made on Copy 1.[33] Although the theses presented by Semkowicz seemed to be clear and very plausible, discussion of Zbylut's document continued unabated. Maleczyński expressed his views on this subject and stated that Copies 1, 2, and 3 were all written by different hands, but from the same writing school. He stated that the annotation on Copy 1 and the entirety of Copy 3 reveal later features and some Gothic influences and thus come from the early thirteenth century (after 1208, or maybe after 1213), and that Copy 3 is an imitation copy. According to Maleczyński, Copies 1 and 2 were given to the monastery.[34]

The state of research on the Łekno foundation charter was then summarised by Kozłowska-Budkowa who, based on the consistency of the text, the contemporaneity of the script, and the presence of the same seal, recognised Copies 1 and 2 as equal originals. Both originals were received by the recipient and, as Kozłowska-Budkowa indisputably established, both were kept in the monastery in the eighteenth century (Copy 2 was only moved to Gniezno in the nineteenth century). In Kozłowska-Budkowa's opinion, Copies 1 and 2 were written by the same hand, while Copy 3 and the annotation on Copy 1 were composed with a different hand. The fact that these two hands were related can hardly be regarded as proven and it is difficult to settle this problem definitively. Kozłowska-Budkowa also emphasised that it was difficult to determine whether Copies 1 and 2 were written by the recipient (a Cistercian monk) or a cleric in the service of Archbishop Jan. In her consideration, the annotation on Copy 1 was written with a different hand from that used for the text of Copy 1, just a little earlier than Copy 3. She believed that Copy 3, which she considered to be an imitation copy of Copy 1, was drawn up between 1181 and 1199, and that the annotation of Copy 1 and Copy 3 were probably authored by a monk from Łekno.[35]

In light of research carried out to date, the interconnectedness of the three copies of Zbylut's document can be summarised as follows: the Poznań copy (Copy 1) and the smaller Gniezno copy (Copy 2) are two equal originals, written with the same hand, while the larger Gniezno copy (Copy 3) is an imitation. The two original documents were drawn up concurrently around 1153, the annotation on Copy 1 was added by a different hand from the originals. It is difficult to determine when the annotation was made. According to Kozłowska-Budkowa, it was made between 1181 and 1199. It seems that the annotation was compiled from earlier written monastic records concerning grants and, as Kozłowska-Budkowa rightly suggests, its author was a monk from Łekno.[36] An imitation copy of the Poznań document (Copy 1), the

---

33 Semkowicz, review of Kętrzyński, MPP, pp. 395–96.
34 Maleczyński, 'O wpływie szkoły pisarskiej leodyjskiej', pp. 79–80.
35 RPD i.53, 149, 150. In historical literature, this problem is encountered several more times, see Semkowicz, *Paleografia łacińska*, pp. 334–35; Przybysz, 'Fundacja i pierwotne', p. 60; Domański, 'Dokumenty fundacyjne'.
36 RPD i.149.

larger Gniezno copy (Copy 3) was also written by a different hand from the originals, after an annotation was added to Copy 1.[37] The primary indicator of the preparation date of Copy 3 is the tenure of Piotr as archbishop. According to the extended version of the annotation, he provided Łekno Abbey the right to receive tithes from three villages.[38] Kozłowska-Budkowa assumed that this happened between 1181 and 1199,[39] but it seems that this period can be slightly narrowed. Piotr appears in the sources for the first time in 1191 and, as suggested by Stanisław Trawkowski, he was enthroned as archbishop around 1190.[40] Obituaries report that Piotr died on 20 or 21 August and, since Henryk Kietlicz was enthroned as Archbishop of Gniezno by March 1199, Piotr's death must have taken place in 1198.[41] Hence the conclusion that the tithes were granted (and perhaps the document prepared) sometime between 1190 and 1198. Thus, this is the proposed relationship between the copies of the Łekno foundation charter put forward here:

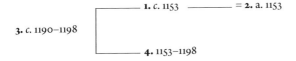

1. the Poznań original; 2. the Gniezno original; 3. imitation copy from the late twelfth century; 4. annotation on Copy 1.

The underlying intent of the annotation on Copy 1, and the drawing up of Copy 3, is difficult to ascertain. It seems likely that the monks of Łekno were driven by the desire to provide the endowments that the monastery received with documentary legitimacy; until this point, these had likely been scrupulously noted in the monastic records. The purpose of preparing two editions of the original document remains unexplained. The authors of the *Dyplomatyka wieków średnich* argued that each copy of Zbylut's original document was stored in a separate archive as a means of recording and controlling the content of the charter.[42] However, this position can be safely rejected given that both copies were kept in the monastery archive until the eighteenth century.[43]

The handwriting in the Łekno foundation charter is very interesting. Its first but brief description was made by Smolka.[44] W. Kętrzyński also pointed out

---

37 The idea put forward in Maleczyński, 'O wpływie szkoły pisarskiej leodyjskiej', p. 80, whereby 1 and 3 originated after 1208, cannot be sustained. See RPD i.150.
38 KDW i, pp. 577–78: *Archiepiscopus Petrus istarum trium villarum decimas contulit, scilicet Mocronoz, Chyrnelino, Copriwcino.*
39 RPD i.150.
40 KDM i.2 (the Sandomierz record).
41 Trawkowski, 'Piotr', pp. 361–62.
42 Maleczyński, Bielińska and Gąsiorowski, *Dyplomatyka wieków średnich*, p. 119.
43 RPD i.53.
44 Smolka, 'Archiwa w W. X. Poznańskim', p. 239.

several characteristics of the handwriting in Zbylut's document.[45] However, the most complete descriptions were given by Semkowicz, Maleczyński, and finally Kozłowska-Budkowa, who summed up the discussion. The first lines in Copies 1 and 2 were written using an uncial script; other lines using round minuscule. Maleczyński concluded that neither original contains traces of Gothic script. The stems on letters m, n, i, and u; the lower terminals on l and t; and the softly rounded bowls of b and h are all characteristic of a Romanesque hand. In comparison, Copy 3, the imitation copy, and the annotation on Copy 1 do show some Gothic features, such as the sharp terminals on m, n, t, and i and the descenders cutting across the s stems. The handwriting of Copy 1 is of a large size and thicker than that of Copy 2, and some letters are formed differently. Moreover, Maleczyński identified the most characteristic feature of all copies of the charter: that is, the fact that the upper terminals in the letters s, 1, and h (and often in d and b) start from a series of (vertical) loops running parallel to the line of writing. Looking for the provenance of the script, Maleczyński compared the documents with those of the Bishops of Liège and determined that the handwriting comes from the Liège school.[46]

While inspecting the script of the document, Semkowicz came to slightly different conclusions. He stated that both copies of the original were written in diplomatic script that could compete in terms of appearance with the then imperial documents. Although it still retains Romanesque features as a rounded minuscule, the Gothic influence is already visible in the pointed arches of e, o and in all the letter bowls, and in the sharp lower terminals of i, m, n, and u. Moreover, while he recognised certain features of the Liège script in the documents' scripts, these were not the most typical. As such, he defined them as the recipient's script, though an Altenberg monk trained in Liège script could have stayed in Łekno.[47] Kozłowska-Budkowa drew attention to other details of the handwriting in the Łekno documents. She assumed that it was not possible to determine whether it was the recipient's or issuer's script. Both the recipient-monk and the cleric in Archbishop Jan's service may have learned to write somewhere on the Rhine, perhaps even Liège. The most important thing is that the writer was a foreigner, as indicated by two local names noted in the wrong grammatical case: Panigródź-Pogengroza (Panigrodzia) and, instead of Łekno or in Łeknie-Lokna, in Lökna (Łekna). The same applies to the spelling of Ergelzko instead of Rgielsko, which recalls Ergles-Zglesz from a document by Henryk, Duke of Sandomierz for Zagość, also written by a foreigner. The orthography also shows some German features: Heinricus, ö in Lökna, Mysiköne.[48] Ultimately, the script should be considered similar to that found in the diplomas of the Bishops of Liège, and it may be assumed

---

45   Kętrzyński, *Studia nad dokumentami*, p. 212.
46   Maleczyński, 'O wpływie szkoły pisarskiej leodyjskiej', pp. 79–87.
47   Semkowicz, *Paleografia łacińska*, pp. 334–36, 342.
48   RPD i.53.

Figure 11. Characteristics of the script of the foundation charter of Łekno Abbey. Fragment of the Poznań original. Photo P. Namiota (MPP, table iv).

Figure 12. Script in the original Poznań foundation charter of Łekno Abbey. Photo P. Namiota (MPP, table iv).

that the documents were written by a foreigner, though it cannot be said whether this was the issuer or the recipient. It generally shows the features of a Romanesque minuscule but contains some Gothic elements. The script of the annotation and Copy 3 is of a later date and contains clearer traces of Gothic script, though also imitating the original script.

Attached to the bottom of Copy 1 is a well-preserved wax seal, while Copy 2 contains only the trace of a seal.[49] It is commonly noted that the seal was neither Zbylut's nor Duke Mieszko III's, but Jan's, Archbishop of Gniezno, who was asked by the issuer to affix a seal to the document.[50] The round seal was impressed in wax spilled directly on the parchment, a common practice in the first half of the twelfth century. The seal depicts an enthroned bishop, and the throne terminates in sculptures of animal heads and paws. The archbishop is dressed in ecclesiastical vestments with a mitre. He is holding a crosier in his right hand and an open book in his left hand. A minuscule inscription on the rim reads: *SIGILLUM. JOHANNIS. ARCHIEPISCOPI POLONIE*.[51]

---

49 The trace of the seal on the smaller Gniezno copy sparked a fairly lively debate. The seal was described in KDP i.2, noted in Smolka, 'Archiwa w W. X. Poznańskim', p. 238), and in KDW i.18. According to Kętrzyński, *Studia nad dokumentami*, p. 214, the document did not originally carry a seal because it was a draft, the seal was attached later. Krzyżanowski, 'Początki dyplomatyki polskiej', pp. 797–98 argued against this position, though Kętrzyński remained resolute, Kętrzyński, 'O początkach dyplomatyki polskiej', p. 26. Piekosiński, *Pieczęcie* i.8 and RPD i.53 maintained that both original copies were sealed by Archbishop Janik and this is the position taken here.

50 Maleczyński, Bielińska and Gąsiorowski, *Dyplomatyka wieków średnich*, pp. 118, 125; Maleczyński, *Zarys dyplomatyki polskiej*, p. 74.

51 Descriptions of the seal can be found in Smolka, 'Archiwa w W. X. Poznańskim', p. 344; Małecki, *Studia heraldyczne* i, pp. 286–87; Gumowski, Haisig, and Mikucki, *Sfragistyka*, p. 211; Karwasińska, 'Archiepiscopus Polonie-Archiepiscopus Gneznensis', p. 35; KDW iv.1; Piekosiński, *Pieczęcie* i.8.

Figure 13. Seal of Archbishop Janik. Photo P. Namiota.

The seal is considered the oldest extant Polish episcopal seal. In formal and legal terms, attaching an archbishop's seal to the document did not diminish its significance; in the West too it was a *sigillum authenticum*.[52]

The elaborate formulary of the Łekno document and its resemblance to the formulary of the Jędrzejów foundation charter quickly attracted the attention of researchers. It was first noticed by Helcel, who recognised Archbishop Jan as the issuer of both documents.[53] W. Kętrzyński and Maleczyński followed the same path.[54] Kozłowska-Budkowa similarly emphasises the formulary similarities of the two documents, yet states that there are more possible authors: perhaps someone from Jan's circle or a Cistercian monk from Jędrzejów or Łekno.[55] Kürbis undertook to resolve the matter of the formulary of the Łekno and Jędrzejów foundation charters, and her comprehensive analysis concluded that both documents were authored by Archbishop Jan, who was perhaps assisted by two witnesses of the Łekno document: Magister Folbert and Magister Stefan.[56]

The formulary composition of the Łekno document consists of the following elements: the invocation, the notification (*promulgatio*), the *arenga*,

---

52 See Semkowicz, 'Uwagi o początkach dokumentu polskiego', pp. 36–38; RPD i.53.
53 Helcel, 'O klasztorze jędrzejowskim', p. 133.
54 Kętrzyński, 'O początkach dyplomatyki polskiej', p. 43; Maleczyński, 'O kanclerzach polskich XII wieku', p. 42; Maleczyński, 'O wpływie szkoły pisarskiej leodyjskiej', p. 78. See also KDP i.2; KDM ii.372.
55 RPD i.53.
56 Kürbis, 'Cystersi w kulturze polskiego', pp. 333–38.

the *narratio*, the *dispositio* with a perpetual formula, information about the convocation of the assembly and the legal decree of enactment, the *sanctio*, dating, the *corroboratio*, and witness list.

The invocation *In nomine sancte et individue trinitatis* is common in twelfth-century documents, and it is often seen in chancellery practice. The Łekno charter also contains a promulgation, though seemingly truncated, while the *arenga* too is short if compared to, for example, that of the Jędrzejów charter. In the *narratio*, the issuer presents himself to us as a devout person and Zbylut is raised to the rank of a clergyman.[57] Apart from the endowments granted to the new monastery, the *dispositio* also includes a perpetual formula and a laudation of the issuer and the recipient. Then the document informs of the convocation of the congregation and the legal action taken, starting from the words *Qua propter huius mei deuoti* to *personas sublimes ac humiles conuocaui*. The formula is directly followed by the *sanctio*: *ubi ab utroque episcopo — nisi resipuerit, absorbeat*, a threat of an eternal curse and the vision of the powers of hell consuming anyone daring to violate the enactment. The document gives both the year 1153 and the reigning dukes: Bolesław IV, Mieszko III and Henry. According to Kozłowska-Budkowa, the year is according to the Pisan calendar.[58] However, it is difficult to narrow down the date. The *corroboratio* contains information that Archbishop Jan sealed the document. The list of witnesses first includes four clergymen — the ducal chancellor, custodian, two magisters — and then twelve lay names of individuals, as indicated in the document.[59]

The style of the document, like the language, is uniform, sophisticated, and very solemn, although some examples of vulgar Latin can be found, such as *spiritales* instead of *spirituales*.[60] The literary uniqueness of this document, like the Jędrzejów charter, is marked by the fact that is written in a rhyming prose embellished with *cursus*. It contains forty-one rhyming lines, and the form of the poetry is very elaborate. The poem contains monosyllabic and trisyllabic rhymes, and is not limited to paired rhymes, but contains triple rhymes, and in one case even intersecting rhymes. Internal rhymes are also frequent.[61] Oswald Balzer pointed to the occurrence of Roman legal vocabulary in the document (*civis, testamentum*), which would suggest that someone who participated in its composition was familiar with Roman law.[62]

The public-law value of Zbylut's document has aroused some controversy among scholars. It should be assumed that it differs from the standards established later, because it is the known example of a document being certified with the

---

57 See Michałowski, 'Święta moc fundatora klasztoru', pp. 3–24.
58 RPD i.53. According to this calendar, the year began on 25 March, in this case 1152.
59 The formulary of the document was described after: B. Kürbis, *Cystersi w kulturze*, pp. 333–38.
60 See RPD i.53. Cf. Kürbis, 'Cystersi w kulturze polskiego', p. 338.
61 Maleczyński, 'Wpływy obce na dokument polski', pp. 109–11. The work quotes all instances of verse and compares the charter with the Jędrzejów document.
62 Balzer, 'Studyum o Kadłubku', p. 128.

seal of a sitting archbishop (in this case Jan) as opposed to the Duke present at the congress (here Mieszko III). However, this fact does not deprive the document of its status. It seems to have the character of a public dispositive document and as such one that could be used as legal evidence.[63] This sums up the state of research conducted over the course of over a hundred years on the foundation charter of the Cistercian monastery at Łekno.

The identification of people appearing in the Łekno document is a separate issue. There are not many extant written records for the twelfth century, and a common view among scholars is that genealogical relations among the Polish nobility can only really be examined from the turn of the thirteenth century.[64] For the earlier period, genealogical data should be treated as largely hypothetical with some, but not many, notable exceptions, and literature on the subject, which in this regard is not always able to meet the requirements of contemporary source criticism, should be referred to with caution.

It seems proper to first examine the founder of Łekno Abbey, the noble Zbylut of Wielkopolska. The historical record furnishes little information about Zbylut. Not surprisingly, we are unable to determine the date of his birth or death, though he can certainly be identified as the first known representative of the Pałuki clan.[65] He makes recurring appearances in documents between 1140 and 1153, particularly in the witness lists of, for example, the diploma of Duchess Salomea for Mogilno,[66] the 1145 charter of Mieszko III for the monastery of canons regular in Trzemeszno,[67] and the 1146 document of the papal legate Hubaldus, also for Trzemeszno.[68] In the well-known Mogilno forgery of 1065, Zbylut is not just listed as a witness but as a benefactor of the Benedictine abbey. The document mentions him as the first of six knights who endowed the monastery and reports his donations to Mogilno Abbey: St James' Church in Mogilno and the village of Bogusino (today Baba).[69] In addition, he is among the witnesses enumerated in the 1153 foundation charter of Jędrzejów Abbey,[70] which seems understandable considering that he was also the founder of the monastery.

---

63 Krzyżanowski, 'Początki dyplomatyki polskiej', p. 798 considered the document to be private, but W. Kętrzyński, *Studia nad dokumentami*, p. 210 advocated the idea that it was a public document, sealed and containing a corroboration. The formal and legal aspects of Zbylut's document were most fiercely attacked in S. Kętrzyński, *Zarys dyplomatyki*, pp. 134, 156, 198, though his mistaken conclusions were corrected in Semkowicz, 'Uwagi o początkach dokumentu polskiego', pp. 36–38.
64 Bieniak, 'Rody rycerskie', p. 179.
65 Semkowicz, *Ród Pałuków*, p. 206; for further discussion of the Pałuki clan, see Anyszko, 'Ród Pałuków'.
66 KDW i.9. The document is dated to 1138–1144.
67 KDW i.11.
68 KDW i.12.
69 KDW i.3: *ecclesiam sancti Jacobi in Mogilna, quam fundavit Sbyluth miles, addens eidem ecclesie hereditatem Bogussino cum consensu amicorum suorum*.
70 KDW ii.372.

Further, Zbylut is found in another Mogilno forgery, again listed as a witness, this dated by the *Kodeks dyplomatyczny Wielkopolski* editor to the year 1100.[71] His name is also mentioned in two well-known medieval obituaries. The obituary of the Benedictine monastery at Lubiń mentions *Sbiluti comitis* under 28 March and,[72] the editor contends, this can be identified as Zbylut, the founder of Łekno, who lived around the mid-twelfth century.[73] The other obituary, *Nekrolog opactwa św. Wincentego*, states under 24 November: *Sbilut comes*.[74] Both possible dates of death exclude the possibility that they report the demise of the same person. It seems that the entry in the Obituary of Lubiń refers to the Zbylut of the Łekno foundation charter, if only because he came from Wielkopolska and, apart from one case, his name is found only in documents from Wielkopolska. He was also well known in Wielkopolska for his engagement in the foundation and support of ecclesiastical houses. The entry in the obituary of St Vincent's Abbey may refer to an unknown Silesian noble, most probably active in the thirteenth century. This is what the sources tell us about Zbylut. The obituary and the forgery for Mogilno of 1100 mention him along with the title of *comes*; the Mogilno forgery, that of 1065, bestows the title *miles* upon him, unusual as for the mid-twelfth century. Whether or not Zbylut was a *comes* is hard to guess; if he were, it would suggest that he must have held some office, perhaps as the leader of the stronghold. In the Łekno foundation charter, he identifies himself as *Polonie ciuis*, which, rhetoric notwithstanding, would prove that he was aware of his high social position. In truth, while Zbylut was obviously a representative of the twelfth-century nobility, as evidenced by the endowments he granted to the monasteries in Łekno and Mogilno, it seems unlikely that he should have been entitled to the title of *comes*.[75] As to his family relations, it can be said that he was married with sons, for these contributed to the enhancement of the Łekno foundation, though their names are unknown. In addition, the annotation made on Copy 1 of the Łekno charter mentions the brothers Sławnik and Piotr, who were Zbylut's nephews. Semkowicz's assertion that Zbylut may have been the nephew or son of Jakub of Żnin finds no support in written records.

This much can be said about the founder of Łekno Abbey in light of written records. In addition, the documents mention two clergymen: Jan, Archbishop of Gniezno, and Stefan, Bishop of Poznań. There is substantial literature on Jan, who is well known to medieval historians,[76] but there is still considerable controversy surrounding Stefan, Bishop of Poznań. This is

---

71　KDW i.36. According to RPD i.15, the list of witnesses of this document was prepared on the basis of Salomea's diploma.
72　*Nekrolog opactwa Panny Marii w Lubiniu*, MPH ix, p. 48.
73　Ibid., p. 48, note 112.
74　*Nekrolog opactwa św. Wincentego we Wrocławiu*, MPH ix, p. 87, note 788.
75　On the title of *comes* see Bogucki, *Komes w polskich źródłach średniowiecznych*.
76　See Kozłowska-Budkowa, 'Jan', pp. 428–30 and Chapter 17 in this volume.

due to the incorrect information provided by Jan Długosz, who confused the order and dates of the twelfth-century bishops of Poznań. He established that Stefan become Bishop in 1154 and registered his death under the year 1156, similarly to *Rocznik kapitulny krakowski*.[77] Completely different information about Bishop Stefan was provided by the *Rocznik lubiński*, which reads under 1152: *Peanus episcopus Poznaniensis obiit, Stephanus succedit* and under 1159: *Stephanus episcopus Poznaniensis obiit, Bernardus succedit*.[78] This suggests that Stefan was Bishop of Poznań between 1152 and 1159 and was the time frame adopted by Stanisław Karwowski and the editors of *Rocznik lubiński*.[79] The exact date of Stefan's death also raises some controversy. In the old edition of *Nekrolog lubiński*, two dates are provided for the bishop's death: 2 March and 3 September,[80] while the newest edition mentions his name only under the first date.[81] The editors of *Rocznik lubiński* cautiously espoused 3 September,[82] while those of *Nekrolog lubiński* were inclined to accepted 2 March as the date of his death.[83] In view of the comments of the *Nekrolog lubiński* editors, the date of 2 March appears to be more plausible.[84]

The document contains references to Duke Mieszko III and his brother, Duke Bolesław IV (in the annotation). So much has already been said in the historiography of medieval Poland about these two that it suffices to refer readers to the relevant subject literature.[85]

The list of the witnesses to the document begins with Radwan, who was the ducal chancellor at the time the document was drawn up. Maleczyński was unable to define unequivocally whose chancellor Radwan was, but supposed that he was the chancellor of Mieszko III and the successor to Pean, who became Bishop of Poznań.[86] This is beyond doubt, taking into account the fact that Mieszko was the only duke to attend the ceremonial foundation convention. There is also no doubt that the same Radwan later took over the bishopric of Poznań, yet the exact period when he held episcopal office is hard to determine, again because of Jan Długosz and the imprecise

---

77 Jan Długosz, *Annales*, p. 49, which states under year 1151: *Piano episcopo Posnaniensi succedit Stephanus*. Długosz reports Stefan's death under the year 1156, p. 57. Also, Jan Długosz, *Vitae episcoporum Poloniae*, pp. 488–89. *Rocznik kapitulny krakowski*, MPH ii, p. 798. See also Semkowicz, *Krytyczny rozbiór*, pp. 177–78.
78 *Rocznik lubiński*, MPH vi, p. 113.
79 Karwowski, *Biskupi poznańscy*, p. 119; *Rocznik lubiński*, MPH vi, p. 117, note 10. This matter is also discussed in the critical edition *Nekrolog lubiński*, MPH v, p. 36, note 5, though clear position is not taken. Cf. Nowacki, *Dzieje archidiecezji poznańskiej*, p. 49.
80 *Nekrolog lubiński*, MPH v, pp. 613, 638.
81 *Nekrolog lubiński*, MPH v, p. 36: *Comemeracio Stephani et Cunradi episcoporum*.
82 *Rocznik lubiński*, MPH vi, p. 117.
83 *Nekrolog lubiński*, MPH v, p. 36, note 5.
84 Ibid.
85 See relevant biographies in PSB; Balzer, *Genealogia Piastów*, pp. 155–61, 161–69; Smolka, *Mieszko Stary i jego wiek*.
86 Maleczyński, 'O kanclerzach polskich XII wieku', p. 44.

information in *Rocznik lubiński*. In his *Annales*, Długosz notes under 1156 that *Stephano Poznaniensis episcopo succedit Radwanus*, and reports Radwan's death in 1162.[87] However, in his 1170 entry he mentions that Radwan was still alive, though above this, in the same year, he also states that Bernard was Bishop of Poznań.[88] That Długosz had serious problems with establishing the chronology of the bishops of Poznań is therefore evident. The information he provides in his *Katalog biskupów poznańskich* is identical to that found in *Annales*.[89] *Rocznik lubiński* in comparison provides the following information under 1172: *Cherubinus episcopus Poznaniensis obiit Raduanus succedit*.[90] Karwowski was unable to find a way out of this tangle of dates, and recognised Radwan as sitting on the bishop's throne between 1159 and 1162.[91] It seems, however, that the problem of Radwan's rule was finally resolved by Semkowicz, who stated that Radwan was Bishop of Poznań between 1164 and 1172.[92] Semkowicz's position has since achieved a broad consensus.[93]

The next person on the list of witnesses is Wilhelm, who is registered as the *custos*. In contrast to the above discussed individuals, barely anything can be said about him. He was not mentioned in any twelfth-century documents, unless it is accepted that the *Villechelmus* from Salomea's document of 1138–1144, who is referred to as the chaplain of St Peter's,[94] was the later *custos* (probably of the Poznań chapter). It seems possible in terms of chronology, although with such a poor source base such unambiguous conclusions are unwarranted.

Two magisters appear next: Folbert and Stefan. However, the historical record furnishes no further information about the two. There has been a proposition that this Stefan could have been Stefan, Chancellor of Kazimierz II, mentioned in the well-known Jędrzejów documents of Mieszko and Kazimierz from 1166/67,[95] though this seems unlikely. Balzer probably came closer to the truth in pointing out the possible alignment between the two magisters and Archbishop Jan.[96] Jan Korytkowski even assumed that they were the canons of Gniezno.[97] Kürbis has put forward the interesting hypothesis that Folbert and Stefan were perhaps scholastics at the cathedrals of Poznań or Gniezno, thus

---

87 Jan Długosz, *Annales*, pp. 57, 73, 374; Semkowicz, *Krytyczny rozbiór*, pp. 178–79, 182.
88 Jan Długosz, *Annales*, pp. 95–96.
89 Jan Długosz, *Vitae episcoporum Poloniae*, p. 489.
90 *Rocznik lubiński*, MPH vi, p. 114.
91 Karwowski, *Biskupi poznańscy*, pp. 119–21.
92 Semkowicz, 'Nieznane nadania', p. 84.
93 See *Rocznik lubiński*, MPH vi, p. 119, note 26; Maleczyński, 'O kanclerzach polskich XII wieku', p. 44; Sappok, *Die Anfänge des Bistums Posen*, pp. 87–88. See also Gąsiorowski in PSB xxx, p. 19. Only Nowacki has expressed a different opinion, Nowacki, *Dzieje archidiecezji poznańskiej*, p. 49.
94 KDW i.9.
95 Maleczyński, 'O kanclerzach polskich XII wieku', p. 44, though cf. Semkowicz, 'Nieznane nadania', pp. 90–91. See also Chapter 4 in this volume.
96 Balzer, 'Studyum o Kadłubku', pp. 15–17.
97 Korytkowski, *Prałaci i kanonicy*, p. 27.

providing additional arguments to strengthen the thesis of their purported affiliation with Archbishop Jan.[98] This proposition seems the most probable.

Folbert and Stefan close the list of clergy witnesses, and the group of lay witnesses starts with Strasz (Strzesz, Strzeżysław), on whom historical sources provide little information. The name appears in *Księga bracka lubińska*,[99] and in the 1175 document of Bolesław the Tall for Lubiąż.[100] According to Piekosiński, the witness from Zbylut's document is the same as the *Ztreso* of the Lubiąż document, who belongs to the Czewoja clan.[101] Marek Cetwiński is of a similar opinion, although he rejects the hypothesis about Strasz's affiliation with the Czewoja clan.[102] Semkowicz saw Strasz as a member of the Pałuki clan of Zbylut's generation,[103] an opinion endorsed by Stanisław Kozierowski.[104] It is indeed probable that Strasz was a member of the Pałuki clan and that the entry in *Księga bracka lubińska* refers to him.[105]

The identification of the next two people among the witnesses of the Łekno foundation charter should not raise any doubts. Pakosław appears on a fairly regular basis in twelfth-century sources. He is a witness to the documents for the monastery in Trzemeszno, those of Mieszko III and of Cardinal Hubaldus, issued in 1145 and 1146, respectively.[106] He is also presented as a benefactor to the monastery of St Vincent and the Blessed Virgin Mary in Wrocław.[107] In addition, his name is found in the *Księga bracka lubińska*.[108] In the historical record, Pakosław is consistently referred to as Awdaniec. According to Janusz Bieniak, he was the youngest son of Skarbimir, voivode of Bolesław III, and the title of *comes* indicates that he was a castellan somewhere in Mieszko III's district. He is considered to be the forebear of the Awdaniec clan of Małopolska and died after 1152.[109] Scholars also usually identify Przedwój, who follows Pakosław on the list of witnesses, as a member of the Awdaniec clan.[110] Semkowicz understood him to be Pakosław's brother,[111] but Bieniak has since proved that Przedwój from the Łekno document was probably Pakosław's nephew, because he comes after

---

98 Kürbis, 'Cystersi w kulturze', pp. 330, 338.
99 *Księga bracka lubińska*, MPH ix, p. 6.
100 KDŚ i.55; KDW i.21.
101 Piekosiński, *Rycerstwo polskie*, p. 274.
102 Cetwiński, *Rycerstwo śląskie*, pp. 19–20.
103 Semkowicz, *Ród Pałuków*, p. 206.
104 Kozierowski, *Fundacye klasztorne*, p. 18.
105 The Strasz from the Lubiąż document and this Strasz cannot be understood to be the same person, both because of the considerable gap between the two events (22 years) and the fact that he is first noble witness in Zbylut's document, but sixth in the Lubiąż diploma.
106 KDW i.11 (*Pacoslaus*); KDW i.12 (*Bacosclaus comes*).
107 KDW i.25: *In montibus Pachozlaus villam dedit et molendinum in Dobra*.
108 *Księga bracka lubińska*, MPH ix, p. 4.
109 Bieniak, 'Polska elita polityczna XII w., Part II', pp. 68–69. See also Bieniak, 'Pakosław', pp. 37–38.
110 Semkowicz, *Ród Awdańców*, p. 179; Sczaniecki, *Nadania na rzecz rycerzy*, p. 113; Bieniak, 'Pakosław', pp. 37–38; Bieniak, 'Polska elita polityczna XII w., Part II', p. 68.
111 Semkowicz, *Ród Awdańców*, p. 179.

him on the list of witnesses.[112] Both Semkowicz and Bieniak point out that the Przedwój listed in the annotation on Copy 1, and who granted Łoskuń to the monastery, is the same as the one who witnessed this document.

Then comes Brodzisław on the list of witnesses. It is impossible to identify this noble, probably of Wielkopolska, because he is mentioned in no other twelfth-century document. On the basis of his name, Kozierowski identified him as a member of the Grzymała clan,[113] and Michał Sczaniecki accepted this hypothesis.[114] In addition to the witness list, one Brodzisław is found in the annotation, where he is mentioned as the person who granted Olesno. It is difficult to draw any broader conclusions from such meagre information. A little more can be said of the next three witnesses from Zbylut's document: Dzierżykraj, Dobrogost, and Jan. Dzierżykraj is found in several mid-twelfth century documents. In the document of Mieszko III for Trzemeszno he is named *Dirsicraus*,[115] while in Hubaldus's document he is mentioned as *Dirsichraus*.[116] Cetwiński suggested Dzierżykraj was the same as Krajek from the 1149 document of Bolesław IV, although he did not exclude the possibility of his affiliation with the Nałęcz clan.[117] However, contrary to Cetwiński's opinion, it seems that the Dzierżykrajowice clan that he reconstructed did not originate with the Dzierżykraj who witnessed the Łekno charter, and Dzierżykraj and Krajek cannot be understood as the same person. Jan Pakulski, however, seems to be correct in identifying Dzierżykraj as a member of the Nałęcz clan, the eldest son of Dobrogost Stary,[118] in agreement with previous scholarship.[119] The Dobrogost listed in the Łekno foundation charter was also a member of the Nałęcz clan, most likely the younger brother of Dzierżykraj.[120] Unfortunately, he appears in no other twelfth-century documents, though he may also be the Dobrogost mentioned in *Księga bracka lubińska*.[121] The third of the above-mentioned, Jan, is also found only in the Łekno charter and in *Księga bracka lubińska*.[122] He too is believed to have been a member of the Nałęcz clan, the brother of Dzierżykraj and Dobrogost.[123]

Another witness to the Łekno foundation charter, Gerward, is not mentioned in any other contemporary sources. Kozierowski included him within the

---

112 Bieniak, 'Pakosław', pp. 37–38; Bieniak, 'Polska elita polityczna XII w.', Part II', p. 68.
113 Kozierowski, *Pierwotne osiedlenie*, p. 49.
114 Sczaniecki, *Nadania na rzecz rycerzy*, p. 113.
115 KDW i.11. He is also mentioned here as having granted two villages (Gąsawa and Komratowo) and part of Lake Golse to the monastery of the canons regular in Trzemeszno.
116 KDW i.12.
117 Cetwiński, *Rycerstwo śląskie*, p. 8.
118 Pakulski, *Nałęcze wielkopolscy*, pp. 212.
119 See Semkowicz, *Ród Pałuków*, p. 242; Kozierowski, *Fundacye klasztorne*, pp. 21–22; Sczaniecki, *Nadania na rzecz rycerzy*, p. 112.
120 Pakulski, *Nałęcze wielkopolscy*, pp. 21–23.
121 *Księga bracka lubińska*, MPH ix, p. 6: Thomas. Dobrogost. Iohannes.
122 Ibid.
123 Pakulski, *Nałęcze wielkopolscy*, pp. 21, 23.

Leszczyce clan, but it seems that this identification should be approached with caution. Kozierowski also claimed that another witness to Zbylut's diploma, Bogusza, was a member of the Leszczyce clan.[124] Semkowicz, on the other hand, identified Bogusza with Comes Bogumił mentioned in the 1145 document of Mieszko III for Trzemeszno and the foundation charter of Jędrzejów, who was perhaps the same as Archbishop Bogumił.[125] This thesis, however, seems too fantastic to be true. The name does not otherwise appear in twelfth-century documents. *Księga bracka lubińska* contains the entry *Bogussa cum uxore* and, although this record may apply to our Bogusza, there is no way we can be certain about this.[126] Mieszko, referred to as the Pomeranian, who comes next in the list of witnesses, unfortunately does not appear in any sources; the only thing that may be said is that he was possibly from Pomerania. The next witness, Przecław, likely appears on Mieszko III's forgery dated 1103 (*Predeslaus*),[127] and possibly also in a document of 1161 (*Przeczslao*).[128] In the annotation to Zbylut's charter, he is seemingly cited as the person who endowed the village of Głojkowo to the abbey. Kozierowski, and Sczaniecki after him, considered Przecław to be a Pomian.[129] This name appears twice in *Księga bracka lubińska* among those entries chronologically consistent with the Łekno foundation charter.[130] Whether any of them can be identified with Przecław is hard to tell. He should most likely be included in a later generation and was possibly a contemporary of Przedwoj Awdaniec, as evidenced by the grants that they both made for Łekno Abbey after 1153 and before 1198. The list of witnesses to the Łekno document is completed with Tomasz, who is mentioned in no other twelfth-century written records, unless he can be identified among the several men bearing that name in *Księga bracka lubińska*.[131] The most fitting of these is the Tomasz who appears next to the two previously mentioned members of the Nałęcz clan, Dobrogost and Jan,[132] but it may as well be that the Tomasz who witnessed the Łekno charter was an entirely different person.

A few more people are listed in the annotations made on the Łekno document. Zbylut's wife, his sons, and two nephews have already been noted and, since their identification does not pose any problems, it is worth moving the discussion on to other people. According to the annotation on Zbylut's charter, Turza was endowed by Ogierz, who is also mentioned in a document

---

124 Kozierowski, *Leszczyce i ich plemiennik*, pp. 20, 31.
125 Semkowicz, *Ród Pałuków*, pp. 253–4.
126 *Księga bracka lubińska*, MPH ix, p. 6.
127 KDW i.33.
128 KDW ii.373.
129 Kozierowski, *Pierwotne osiedlenie*, pp. 45, 90; Sczaniecki, *Nadania na rzecz rycerzy*, p. 113.
130 *Księga bracka lubińska*, MPH ix, pp. 5–6.
131 Tomasz appears in *Księga bracka lubińska*, MPH ix, p. 6 (*Thomas. Dobrogost. Iohannes*), again on this page (*Borizlaus. Thoma. Margareta*) and on p. 8 (*Godefridus decanus. Thoma. Stephanus*). See also *Nekrolog lubiński*, MPH v, pp. 98–103 (dates 21 September, 2 October, 20 October).
132 *Księga bracka lubińska*, MPH ix, p. 6.

from 1208 according to which Duke Władysław confirmed Ogierz's earlier grants with his son's consent.[133] According to Semkowicz, he belonged to the Niałkowie-Jelenie clan,[134] but following the name criterion, Kozierowski included him in the Poraj-Różyce clan,[135] with Sczaniecki following this latter position.[136] Filip, who granted Dębogóra, was probably a monk of Łekno, known elsewhere as Boguchwał, and a member of the Pałuki clan.[137] Wierzenica was endowed to Łekno Abbey by Prędota, probably the same as the one who appears under 30 January in *Nekrolog św. Wincentego*.[138] He was probably a member of the Odrowąż clan, a son or relative of its progenitor, Prędota Stary.[139] The above-mentioned persons appear in the annotation added to Copy 1, while the annotation in Copy 3 contains additional grants endowed by Archbishop Piotr. In view of the controversy that arose around him in Polish historiography, it is worth taking a closer look at Piotr.

Various views have been put forward in the historical literature about who Archbishop Piotr was and when he was in office. This, however, is given some consideration in Chapter 17 of this volume, and it will suffice here to provide some bibliographical references in order to focus instead on written records.[140] In *Annales*, Jan Długosz dates the beginning of the reign of Archbishop Piotr as Jan's successor to 1165 and stresses that he came from the Śreniawa clan. Długosz

---

133   KDW i.63.
134   Semkowicz, *Ród Pałuków*, p. 207, note 6. In Semkowicz's opinion, Ogierz's wife was a member of the Pałuki clan and Turza was her dowry.
135   Kozierowski, *Ród Porajów-Różyców*, p. 100; Kozierowski, *Pierwotne osiedlenie*, pp. 45, 57, 60. See also Piekosiński, *Rycerstwo polskie*, pp. 272–73.
136   Sczaniecki, *Nadania na rzecz rycerzy*, p. 113.
137   Semkowicz, *Ród Pałuków*, pp. 207–08, 237; Kozłowska-Budkowa, 'Bogumił', PSB ii, p. 199.
138   *Nekrolog św. Wincentego*, MPH ix, p. 12.
139   Górski, 'Ród Odrowążów', p. 13; Kozierowski, *Pierwotne osiedlenie*, pp. 45, 66; Sczaniecki, *Nadania na rzecz rycerzy*, p. 113.
140   See Trawkowski, 'Piotr', pp. 361–62, who considers him to be the grandson of Piotr Włostowic, and that he became archbishop between 1180 and 1190, likely dying in 1198. See also Semkowicz, *Ród Pałuków*, pp. 244–63, which suggests Piotr was archbishop between 1187 and 1199, commensurate with Blessed Bogumił, a member of the Pałuki clan; Korytkowski, *Arcybiskupi gnieźnieńscy*, p. 299, who states Piotr took archbishopric after Zdzisław, in 1180 at the latest, and that he belonged to the Śreniawici clan; Kozierowski, *Leszczyce i ich plemiennik*, pp. 31–64 argues that Blessed Bogumił was the same as Archbishop Piotr II and was of the Leszczyc clan; Kozłowska-Budkowa, 'Bogumił', p. 200 separates the figures of Archbishops Peter and Bogumił, considering the former to have been a member of the Łabędzie clan; Nowacki, 'Bogumił-Piotr II', pp. 147–55, which recognises Piotr as a member of the Leszczyce clan and identifies him with Bogumił; Deptuła, 'Wokół postaci arcybiskupa', pp. 37–47, which states Piotr was probably the grandson of Piotr Włostowic, and the son of Świętosław, identical to Comes Piotr listed in the 1193 bull of Celestine III; Cetwiński, *Rycerstwo śląskie*, pp. 17–18 opposes Deptuła's identification and does not count Piotr among the Łabędzie clan); Kürbis, 'Introduction', *Chronica Polonorum*, pp. xviii–xx, suggesting Piotr was perhaps the Chancellor Piotr of the Opatów document, he took over the archbishopric as an ally of Kazimierz II in 1191; Łowmiański, *Początki Polski*, pp. 267–68, who rejects the claim that Piotr belongs to the Leszczyce clan. Finally, see Chapter 17 in this volume.

mentions Piotr's death under the year 1182.[141] He gives almost identical details in the *Katalog arcybiskupów gnieźnieńskich*, and Długosz's successors followed in his footsteps.[142] Regrettably, the imprecise pieces of information these preserve raise serious doubts regarding their credibility. The fact that Piotr was not Jan's successor, but Zdzisław's, is obvious. More difficult, however, is the task of establishing when he came into the position of archbishop. He is mentioned in the documentary record for the first time in 1191 and,[143] as Trawkowski probably rightly concluded, he had become the archbishop not long before, sometime around 1190.[144] The date of the archbishop's death was registered by as many as four sources. Under 20 August, *Nekrolog św. Wincentego* records: *Obiit Petrus archiepiscopus*.[145] The same date is given by Jan Długosz, while the Kraków calendar notes 19 August.[146] *Nekrolog lubiński*, in contrast, records Piotr's death on 21 August.[147] The year of the archbishop's death is nowhere to be found. Since Henryk Kietlicz was Archbishop of Gniezno on 23 March 1199, Piotr must have died on 20 or 21 August 1198.[148] References to Archbishop Piotr are found in several twelfth-century documents and he is also mentioned by Vincentius, Bishop of Kraków. The hypothesis stating that Piotr belonged to the Łabędzie clan has gained popularity over time, while suggestions that Piotr was the same person as Blessed Bogumił and a member of the Pałuki or Leszczyce clan should be rejected. The hypothesis is based mainly on the information from a 1219 document, according to which the Benedictine monks from Ołbin were removed and replaced with Premonstratensians *ad instanciam Petri archiepiscopi patroni*.[149] This thesis is undermined by Cetwiński, who claims that the term *patroni* here refers to archbishop because of his office, not hereditary rights.[150] It seems that the preserved records cannot unravel the mystery of Archbishop Piotr's origin, and his purported affiliation with the Łabędzie clan is poorly substantiated. It is perhaps once more best to follow the path suggested by Kürbis,[151] or at the very least to subject Archbishop Piotr to new analysis.

There has been considerable discussion among scholars about the foundation of the Cistercian monastery at Łekno.[152] This does not require recapitulation and is addressed in Chapter 3 of this volume. It is, nonetheless, worth drawing

---

141 Jan Długosz, *Annales*, pp. 80, 129.
142 Jan Długosz, *Catalogus archiepiscoporum Gnesnensium*, p. 349; Paprocki, *Herby rycerstwa polskiego*, pp. 116, 197.
143 KDM i.2.
144 Trawkowski, 'Piotr', pp. 361–62.
145 *Nekrolog św. Wincentego*, MPH ix, p. 64, note 593.
146 *Kalendarz katedry krakowskiej*, MPH v, p. 163, which reads under 19 August: *Petrus archiepiscopus obiit*.
147 *Nekrolog lubiński*, MPH v, p. 92, which reads under 21 August: *Comemoracio Petri archiepiscopi*.
148 Trawkowski, 'Piotr', pp. 361–62.
149 KDŚ ii.221.
150 Cetwiński, *Rycerstwo śląskie*, p. 18.
151 Kürbis, 'Introduction', pp. xviii–xx.
152 See Przybysz, 'Fundacja i pierwotne', pp. 57–72.

attention to the fact that the foundation of the monastery was not a one-off act, but a process extended over time, consisting of the following stages as outlined in Chapter 4:
1. Arriving at the decision to found an abbey;
2. Obtaining the approval of the bishop or archbishop;
3. Efforts to establish a convent by an existing Cistercian abbey or general chapter,
4. Visit to the foundation site;
5. Arrival of the convent;
6. Commencement of the construction of the church and monastery;
7. Issuing a foundation charter;
8. Consecration of the church.[153]

It is most unfortunate that due to the very limited sources, these individual stages cannot be elaborated in the case of Łekno Abbey. The idea to establish a monastery was probably taken in the 1140s or perhaps the end of the 1130s. Whether Archbishop Jakub, called Jakub of Żnin, had any part in it, is difficult to say. It seems that the founder had the decisive vote here, and Jakub's role was limited to granting consent for the foundation. Perhaps he also participated in negotiations with the general chapter on the bringing of the convent. When exactly this happened is unknown, neither is there any information about the visit to the site by Cistercian surveyors. It has been relatively easy for the researchers to determine the date of bringing the convent, which occurred in the period after 1142. There is still considerable uncertainty as to the erecting of the first buildings at the site of the foundation. The least problematic is the question of when the foundation charter was issued, which happened around 1153. The consecration of the church is a greater source of concern because the foundation charter's wording suggests that at the time the charter was issued, a consecrated monastic church had already been functioning in Łekno. Conversely, this was perhaps the original church, the dedication of which was later taken over by the Cistercians after they constructed a new church. Its consecration would have taken place after the foundation charter had been issued, and on the occasion of this ceremony the monastery received rich tithes, listed in the annotation to Copies 1 and 3, and perhaps also some of the grants mentioned therein. This, in a nutshell, is the foundation process of the Cistercian abbey at Łekno, as a result of which the Cistercians received the estates listed in Table 5 below, which shows the ownership status of Łekno Abbey until the end of the twelfth century. The initial endowment granted by Zbylut was relatively modest, while the increases brought about by later grants can be described as average at best.[154]

---

153 Zawadzka, 'Proces fundowania opactw cysterskich', pp. 121–50. See also Chapter 4 in this volume.
154 Compare, for example, the Sulejów grants, which are listed in: Dobosz, 'Uwagi o fundacji opactwa cystersów', p. 90 (table).

The name of an Abbot of Łekno makes a fairly early appearance in the historical record; around 1166/67, the Jędrzejów documents mention *Simon abbas de Lukna*.[155] Whether he was the first abbot is difficult to say as there is no other information to corroborate the supposition. The reasons underlying the foundation is another matter and it seems a range of factors were at work here (devotional, economic, political, cultural), but the most important is that the Cistercians desired to come to Poland and there found welcome.

This concludes the discussion of the problems related to the foundation charter of the Cistercian monastery at Łekno. It has focused mainly on presenting the state of research on the document itself and the identification of people involved in it, treating the rest of the issues as marginal. Despite some shortcomings, my sincere hope is that this study will be useful for further research, both on the history of Łekno Abbey and the written document in Poland.

Table 5. Twelfth-century grants for Łekno Abbey[156]

	No.	Name of village/town	Benefactor	Date of endowment	Ref to the document (see the note below)
Land grants	1	Rgielsko	Zbylut	c. 1153	1, 2, 3
	2	Straszewo	as above	as above	as above
	3	Panigródź	as above	as above	as above
	4	Mątwy	Bolesław IV	1153–1173	3, 4
	5	Głojkowo	Przecław	1153–1198	as above
	6	Wierzenica	Prędota	as above	as above
	7	Łoskuń	Przedwoj	as above	as above
	8	Olesno	Brodzisław	as above	as above
	9	Gościeszyn	Zbylut's wife	as above	as above
	10	Kaczkowo	as above	as above	as above
	11	Pokrzywno	Zbylut's sons	as above	as above
	12	Mokronosy	Sławnik and Piotr	as above	as above
	13	Turza	Ogierz	as above	as above
	14	Dębogóra	Filip	as above	as above

---

155 Semkowicz, 'Nieznane nadania', pp. 69–70; KDM ii.374.
156 Przybysz, 'Fundacja i pierwotne', pp. 56–72. Studies on the identification of villages: Kozierowski, *Badania nazw topograficznych gnieźnieńskiej*; Kozierowski, *Badania nazw topograficznych*; Kozierowski, *Pierwotne osiedlenie*; Chmielewski et al, eds, *Słownik historyczno-geograficzny województwa poznańskiego*. See also Śliwiński, *Rozwój uposażenia ziemskiego*; Leśny, 'Ze studiów nad osadnictwem', pp. 123–76.

	No.	Name of village/ town	Benefactor	Date of endowment	Ref to the document (see the note below)
Tithes	1	Bartodzieje	Archbishop Jan or Zdzisław? (rather Jan)	1153-c. 1190	3, 4
	2	Słosim	as above	as above	as above
	3	Bukowie	as above	as above	as above
	4	Dąbrowa	as above	as above	as above
	5	Zalachowo	as above	as above	as above
	6	Donaborz	as above	as above	as above
	7	Ochodza	as above	as above	as above
	8	Morakowo	as above	as above	as above
	9	Bliżyce	as above	as above	as above
	10	Targowiste	as above	as above	as above
	11	Koninek	as above	as above	as above
	12	Krosno	as above	as above	as above
	13	Mokronosy	Archbishop Piotr	c. 1190–1198	3
	14	Pokrzywno	as above	as above	as above
	15	Czerlin	as above	as above	as above
Other	1	Marketplace and a tavern in Łekno	Zbylut	c. 1153	1, 2, 3

Note: 1 – Poznań original, 2 – Gniezno original, 3 – late twelfth-century imitation copy, 4 – annotation on the Poznań original.

Text of the charter:

1153
Zbylut founds and endows a Cistercian abbey at Łekno with a part of his free patrimony

Original document   1. State Archives in Poznań, sygn. kl. Łekno A 1;
2. Archdiocesan Archives in Gniezno, sygn. Dypl. Gn. 3;

Copy
1. Archdiocesan Archives in Gniezno, sygn. Dypl. Gn. 4;
2. Archdiocesan Archives in Gniezno, sygn. Dypl. Gn. 1237 a, (transumpt of Sigismundus II Augustus of 1 July 1570).

Other copies are listed in: Błażkiewiczówna, 'Fundacja i pierwotne uposażenie', pp. 8–93; Maleczyński, 'O wpływie szkoły pisarskiej leodyjskiej', pp. 78–79.

Printed editions
1. MPP, tables iv, v, vi (acc. to original documents 1 and 2 and copy 1);
2. Krzyżanowski, ed., *Album palaeographicum*, table ii (acc. to original document 2);

Publications
1. KDP i.2 (acc. to the original document 2);
2. KDW i (acc. to original document 1);
3. ZDŚ i.19 (acc. to the original document 1);
4. Kürbis, 'Cystersi w kulturze polskiego', pp. 330–33, in comparison with the foundation charter of Jędrzejów;
5. Incomplete edition in Maleczyński, 'Wpływy obce na dokument polski', pp. 109–11.

In addition, annotations on original document 1 and copy 1 can be found in: Małecki, 'W kwestii fałszerstwa dokumentów', p. 431; Kętrzyński, *Studia nad dokumentami XII w.*, p. 213; KDW i, pp. 577–78; ZDŚ i, pp. 78–79; Smolka, 'Archiwa w W. X. Poznańskim', pp. 239–40, 344–45.

Text of original document 1 from the State Archives in Poznań, sygn. kl. Łekno A 1:

In nomine sancte et indiuidue Trinitatis. Notum sit omnibus catholicis tam futuri quam presentis temporis. Honestum ac beatum constat esse uotum, immo sanctum ac laudabile patet esse commertium, dare sua transitoria et recipere pro his eterna, terrena sibi displicere et celestia possidere. Huius itaque tam sancte negotiationis amore ego Zbilud Polonie ciuis superna inspirante gratia medullitus ignescens, decorem domus Dei et locum habitationis glorie sue diligens, simulque in libro uite cum iustis conscribi cupiens, patrimonii mei liberi portionem, uillas scilicet has: Ergelzko cum lacu integro et Ztrassowo, Pogengroza et in Lökna forum cum taberna, omnium bonorum largitori Deo ad gloriam et laudem eiusque genitrici et beato Petro ad honorem cum intime deuotionis humilitate contradidi et exinde in una conscriptarum uillarum, Lökne uidelicet, domicilium Deo fieri, dotari, inuestiri cum deuoti desiderii puritate institui. Pro cuius ergo domicilii spiritaliter disponenda gubernatione, pro continuanda ibi diuine seruitutis administratione, pro statuenda etiam ibidem regularis ac discipline religione, uiros quosdam spiritales, personas uenerabiles, mortuos mundo, uiuentes Christo, cenobitas re et habitu et professione, plenos Dei ac proximi dilectione, prout potui reuerender aduocaui, suscepi, dilexi, locaui. Quibus in eodem loco Lökna scilicet spiritaliter degentibus, uillas pretitulatas cum reditibus earum uniuersis in usum liberrimum extunc et in perpetuum quasi pauperibus Christi pauper ipse sine ulla contraditione delegaui. Quapropter huius mei deuoti studii factiue testamentum, ne ulla um quam superior seu inferior persona praua machinatione ducere possit inirritum, sed ut integrum et inconuulsum maneat in perpetuum, dominum Iohannem sancte Gneznensis ecclesie archipresulem, dominum Stephanum Poznanensis ecclesie antistitem, dominum Mesiconem ducem aliasque per plurimas personas sublimes ac humiles conuocaui, ubi ab utroque episcopo coram astante multitudine sub perpetui anathematis obtentu confirmari uotis omnium michi congaudentium impetraui, ut si quis in presens siue in posterum huius testamenti preuaricari presumpserit priuilegium, superni iudicis sine misericordia sententiam incidat, infernus eum uiuum, nisi resipuerit, absorbeat. Anno millesimo centesimo quinquagesimo tertio, Bolezlao, Mesicone, Heinrico fratribus germanis in Polonia principatibus, acta sunt hec a Iohanne sancte Gneznensis ecclesie uenerabili archipresule, cuius etiam sigilli inpressione signate sunt hec littere sub priuilegiali cautione, testibus omnibus subnotatis: Raduano cancellario, Willehelmo custode, magistro Folberto, magistro Stephano, et his comitibus: Ztresone, Pacozlawo, Predwoy, Brodizlawo, Dirsycrao, Dobrogozt, Iohanne, Gerwardo, Bogussa, Mysicone Pomerano, Predzlao, Thoma.

There are minimal differences between original documents 1 and 2:

Original document 1	Original document 2
integro et Ztrassowo	integro, Ztrassowo
beato Petro	sancto Petro
Mesiconem	Mesikonem
Mesicone	Mesikone
Willehelmo	Wilhelmo
Mysiköne	Mysyköne
Brodizlawo	Brodyslawo
Dirsycrao	Dyrsycrao
Anno millesimo centesimo quinquagesimo tertio.	Anno M.C.L.III.

Annotation on original document 1 from the State Archives in Poznań, sygn. kl. Łekno A 1:

Notum sit omnibus, quod dux Bolezlaws frater Mesiconis contulit beato Petro uillam nomine Manthev, Predzlavs pater Chebde Glovicov, Pradota Uereniz, Predwoy Loscuniam, Brodizlaws Olesno, uxor Zbiludi Gostizlaue et Kasckov, filii eius Copriuce, Mocrhonoz Zlavnicus et Petrus, Ogerius Thuram, Dambagoram Phillipus. Et hec sunt uille quarum decime adtinent ecclesie beati Petri: Bartozege, Slosym, Bucowe, Dambrouici, Slachowo, Domabore, Ochvclyno, Moracowo, Bliscowice, Loknö, Cirnelino, Canino, Crosno, Mocronoz, Copriwcino. Igitur si quis hec uiolauerit, anathema sit.

Extended version of the above annotation from document 2 from Archdiocesan Archives in Gniezno, sygn. Dypl. Gn. 3.

Notum sit omnibus hominibus, quod dux Bolezlaus frater domini Mesiconis contulit beato Petro willam nomine Mantheu. Comes Predzlaus pater Chebde contulit Glowicov, villam nomine Uereniz contulit Prandota cum matre, villam Loscuniam contulit Predwoy comes, uillam Olesno contulit comes Brodizlaus, Zbilud comes contulit Pangroz, vxor ipsius contulit Gostizlaue et Kasckov, filii eius contulerunt Coprivce, villam Mocrhonoz contulerunt fratres duo Zlaunicus et Petrus, villam nomine Thuram contulit Ogerius comes cum matre et uxore, Dambagora contulit Phillypus monachus. Et hęc sunt uille quarum decime adtinent ęcclesię beati Petri: Bartozege, Slosym, Bucowe, Dambrouici, Slachowo, Domabore, Ochvclyno, Moracowo, Bliscowice, Targouiste, Cirnelino, Canino, Crosno. Archiepiscoups Petrus istarum trium uillarum decimas contulit, scilicet: Mocronoz, Chyrnelino, Coprivcino sub his testibus: Iohanne preposito, Stephano archidiacono, Rudolfo sacredote et Stephano fratre eius. Igitur si quis hęc uiolauerit, anathema sit.

Part III

People

CHAPTER 17

Maur, Bishop of Kraków*

The early days of the reign of Bolesław III heralded considerable activity in ecclesiastical politics. No sooner had the young Duke taken power after his father's death in 1102 than a feud started within the Church in Poland that saw the removal of two bishops from their posts. One of them was probably Czasław, mentioned in the inventory of the treasury of Kraków Cathedral from 1101, who was replaced by Baldwin, a nominee of Bolesław III.[1] In 1103, the papal legate Galo (Walo), Bishop of Beauvais. came to Poland and it was likely then that the work of reforming the developing chapter circles, initiated by Władysław I Herman, was completed.[2] Once the situation was stabilised, the power in the Kraków diocese rested in the hands of the aforementioned Baldwin, a foreign yet trusted associate of Bolesław.[3] After the short-lived reign of the hierarch and his death on 7 September 1109,[4] the Duke appointed Maur as Baldwin's successor. His origin is hard to determine,[5] although Jan Długosz described him as an Italian of noble family.[6]

There are some sources for the life of Maur, mostly reporting his rise to the bishopric of Kraków and his death, but his activities are less often recounted in the written records. Maur is mentioned by Gallus Anonymous

---

* Original publication: Józef Dobosz, 'Biskup krakowski Maur', in *Scriptura custos memoriae. Prace historyczne*, ed. by Danuta Zydorek (Poznań: UAM, 2001), pp. 49–55.
1 *Spisy dawne skarbca i biblioteki kapitulnej krakowskiej*, MPH i, p. 376.
2 For more details on these events see Maleczyński, *Bolesław III*, from p. 253; Szymański, 'Krakowski rękopis reguły', pp. 39–52; Szymański, *Kanonikat świecki w Małopolsce*, p. 15.
3 MPH ii, p. 90, the chronicle of Gallus Anonymous which recounts that it was Baldwin who arranged the papal dispensation relating to Bolesław's marriage to an unnamed duchess [Zbysława].
4 For Bishop Baldwin's date of death, see *Rocznik kapituły krakowskiej*, MPH v, p. 54 (for the year), and *Kalendarz katedry krakowskiej*, MPH v, p. 168 (for the day and month).
5 Maur's origin is uncertain, though he is thought to have been French or Italian by birth, a view advocated in Swoboda, 'Maur', 185–86. Kozłowska-Budkowa, 'Maur', pp. 261–62, suggest he came from northern France. A more precise identification of Maur was attempted by Danuta Borawska, who identified him with the deacon Jan Maur, chosen as Bishop of Torcello (Italy) but later removed from that post. Borawska, 'Gallus Anonim', pp. 111–19, cf. Kozłowska-Budkowa, 'Maur', p. 261, which disputes this identification.
6 'Vir genere Italus, Romanus, ex familia nobili ducens genus', Jan Długosz, *Annales*, p. 225 (1109). The chronicler repeated this information in his *Katalog biskupów krakowskich*, MPH x, p. 152. Similarly, *Katalogi biskupów krakowskich*, Wiślica Edition, MPH x, p. 287 (here: *Maurus, natione Romanus*); the Franciscan Edition, p. 296, suggests a French origin (here: *Maurus Gallus*), as does the Jędrzejów Edition, p. 304.

among the Polish bishops in the opening sentences of his *Gesta*.[7] The various Polish annals specify the time frame of his pontificate, in most cases defining it quite precisely. *Rocznik kapituły krakowskiej* records his succession to Baldwin in 1109 and Maur's death in 1118.[8] Similar information is given in *Rocznik krótki*;[9] *Annals Sandivogii*, which dates Maur's pontificate between 1110 and 1118;[10] and *Rocznik Traski* and *Rocznik krakowski* record only the year of his death, 1118.[11] The various copies of *Rocznik małopolski* provide slightly different details. The codices of Kuropatnicki and Lubiń note the beginning of Maur's pontificate under the year 1110, and his death under 1118.[12] The Codex of Königsberg, on the other hand, reports that Maur became Bishop of Kraków after 1111, and the Codex of Szamotuły ignores the event. Both codices do, however, date Bishop Maur's death to 1118.[13] Virtually all editions of the catalogues of the bishops of Kraków,[14] Jan Długosz,[15] and the late *Rocznik Krasińskich*[16] give similar time frames of Maur's episcopate, 1108–1117 in the case of the latter. The only different information is provided by *Rocznik świętokrzyski*, the author of which incorrectly recorded the death of Baldwin and Maur's succession as Bishop of Kraków under the year 1138, with the death of the latter dated to 1153.[17] Ultimately, the consensus within the historical record is that Maur held the position of Bishop of Kraków between 1110 and 1118.[18]

Such a conclusion seems logical given that Baldwin died on 7 September 1109, and it took some time to fill the abandoned bishop's seat. It does not contradict the information provided by *Rocznik kapituły krakowskiej* which, in the first instance, records the death of Baldwin under the year 1109, only adding the information about Maur's succession later within the sequence of events. The

---

7 MPH ii, p. 1.
8 MPH v, pp. 54–56.
9 *Rocznik krótki*, MPH v, p. 237.
10 *Rocznik Sędziwoja*, MPH ii, p. 874.
11 *Rocznik krakowski*, MPH ii, p. 831; *Rocznik Traski*, MPH ii, p. 831.
12 *Rocznik małopolski*, MPH iii, pp. 150, 152.
13 *Rocznik małopolski*, MPH iii, pp. 151, 153.
14 *Katalogi biskupów krakowskich*, Edition I, MPH x, p. 24, undated; Edition II, MPH x, pp. 31, 1108 and nine years of pontificate; Edition III, MPH x, pp. 46, 1109, died in 1118; Świętokrzyska Edition IV, MPH x, pp. 56, 1109–1118); Dominican Edition V, MPH x, pp. 86, 1108–1118); Lublin Edition, MPH x, pp. 110, 1109–1118; Wiślica Edition, MPH x, p. 287, seven years of pontificate and died in 1117; Franciscan Edition, MPH x, pp. 296, 1109–1118; Jędrzejów Edition, MPH x, pp. 304, 1109–1118).
15 Jan Długosz, *Annales*, p. 255 (1109, Baldwin's death and Maur's succession), p. 283 (1117, Maur's death); Jan Długosz, *Katalog biskupów krakowskich*, MPH x, pp. 151–52 (1110–1117).
16 *Rocznik Krasińskich*, MPH iii, p. 131.
17 Rocznik świętokrzyski, MPH xii, p. 22.
18 Swoboda, 'Maur', pp. 185–86 assumes the period 1109–1118; cf. Kozłowska-Budkowa, 'Maur', pp. 261–62, which justifies the dating 1110–1118. See also *Spisy dawne skarbca i biblioteki kapitulnej krakowskiej*, MPH i, p. 377, where Bishop Maur's reign is reported as beginning in 1110.

exact date of the bishop's death, as given by *Kalendarz katedry krakowskiej*, 5 March, was later replicated by Jan Długosz.[19] Almost all the above-mentioned editions of the catalogues of the bishops of Kraków point to Kraków Cathedral as the place of Maur's burial,[20] which has since been confirmed by an inscription found in a tomb in St Leonard's crypt.[21]

The activities of Bishop Maur, as noted, are poorly evidenced in the written records. It seems that he was fairy actively engaged in the life of the diocese, as suggested by his consecration of new churches and granting them the rights to tithes. Bishop Maur granted tithes from seven villages and one plot of land to St Martin's Church in Pacanów, most likely on the occasion of its dedication on 25–31 August at some time between the years 1110 and 1117. These villages were Pacanów, Żabiec, Zgórsko, Niegosławice, Górowo, Gorzakiew, Szczeglin, and Kwasów. Maur confirmed the tithes in fish, calves, lambs, piglets, and cheese, as well as a tavern given by the founder, Comes Siemian of the Nagodzice family.[22] This event was also noted by Jan Długosz in *Liber beneficiorum* of the Kraków diocese,[23] possibly drawing on a transumpt of 15 August 1219 of Iwo Odrowąż, Bishop of Kraków.[24] A similar event was recorded for Brzeźnica (later Jędrzejów), in the lands of the Gryfici, where Maur also consecrated the church, most likely dedicated to St Andrew, in the ancestral seat of the magnate.[25] An account of this event was initially passed on in the Jędrzejów foundation charter of 1153, in which it is also recounted

---

19 *Kalendarz katedry krakowskiej*, MPH v, p. 129; Jan Długosz, *Annales*, p. 283; Jan Długosz, *Katalog biskupów krakowskich*, pp. 151–52.

20 *Katalogi biskupów krakowskich* (all from Edition III), MPH x, pp. 46, 56, 86, 110, Franciscan Edition, p. 296, Jędrzejów Edition, p. 304. Also Jan Długosz, *Katalog biskupów krakowskich*, p. 152 and Jan Długosz, *Annales*, p. 283.

21 In 1938, the tomb of Bishop Maur was found in St Leonard's Crypt in St Wenceslas' Cathedral, Wawel, and a lead plaque bearing the date of the bishop's death, 5 March 1118, was recovered. For more detail, see Bochnak, 'Grób biskupa Maura', pp. 239–48. For the inscription with the incomplete text of the *credo*, allegedly testifying to Mauro's links with the Cathar heresy see David, 'Un credo cathare?', pp. 756–61.

22 ZDK i.3. For the Pacanów document, see RPD i.21. Paweł Sczaniecki dates Maur's grant to the dedication of the church of the Nagodzice family, Sczaniecki, *Sacramentum dedicationis*, p. 74. In his article on the Nagodzice family, Karol Potkański, argues that Siemian was not a representative of the family, and claimed that he was rather a member of the Awdaniec clan. Potkański, 'Ród Nagodziców', pp. 209–39, especially 212–13); his genealogical findings were corrected in Semkowicz, *Ród Awdańców*, pp. 15–22.

23 LB ii, p. 422.

24 ZDK i.4. When, around 1317, Jan Muskata approved the tithes for the Pacanów church, he did not mention Maur's document or Iwon's transumpt, so probably did not know of them, ZDK i.28. Długosz, however, did have access to these sources and used them in his historical work, though this was not noted in either his *Annales* or his *Katalog biskupów krakowskich*.

25 Sczaniecki, *Sacramentum dedicationis*, p. 76, who argues, after RPD i.55, that it is possible that Maur consecrated the church. For the invocation of the church in Brzeźnica see Dobosz, 'Proces fundacyjny', p. 56, note 82; Chapter 4 in this volume.

that Maur added tithes from eight villages for the church.[26] This information is repeated in a forged document of Bishop Vincentius of Kraków, dated 1210,[27] and by Jan Długosz.[28] Although that part of the charter relating to the granting of tithes to Jędrzejów Abbey has been judged to be an interpolation,[29] it was most likely a formal interpolation introduced between 1210 and *c.* 1153, designed to rectify a deficiency in the Cistercian monastery's ownership records. Thus, Bishop Maur consecrated at least two churches in estates owned by the nobility and distributed generous tithes amounting to around fifteen villages and a plot of land in the above cases, all of which were important elements of his duties. It is worth noting that these activities came to fruition when Bolesław III committed himself to the conquest of Pomerania and pursued an active policy in the south.

Bishop Maur's activity, as recorded in the historical sources, was not limited to the consecration of new private churches and the distribution of tithes. He continued the work initiated by his predecessors in the Kraków bishopric, Lambert and Baldwin, building the Romanesque cathedral at Wawel. Jan Długosz noted that Maur consecrated the new cathedral in Kraków on 20 April[30] and most likely used the thirteenth-century *Kalendarz katedry krakowskiej* as his source.[31] This assertion that Kraków Cathedral was consecrated when Maur was in office, however, contradicts the accounts of other sources that claim this happened during the pontificate of Bishop Robert I, most likely in 1142.[32] Tadeusz Wojciechowski offered a different interpretation and argued

---

26 KDM ii.1, which states: *preterea episcopus bone memorie Maurus, qui eandem ecclesiam consecrauit, et Radosth successor suus, decimas super villas has addiderunt sub anathemates: Osarowici, Preneslawe, Konare, Michowo, Bechlowo, Borowa, Prekopa, Linowo omnium bonorum largitori*. For the document, see RPD i.55; Kürbis, 'Cystersi w kulturze polskiego', pp. 321–42.

27 KDM ii.380.

28 The content of the Jędrzejów foundation charter was recounted in some detail by Jan Długosz who included information on the activities of Bishop Maur, LB iii, pp. 361–75. See also Jan Długosz, *Katalog biskupów krakowskich*, p. 152, which reads: *Hic ecclesie et cenobio Andrzeouiensi nondum fundato et dotato, fabricato tamen in consecratione ecclesie cenobialis per ipsum factae contulit decimas manipulares mense sue Cracouiensis in villis Marowicze, Przenÿeslawÿe, Conari, Michowo, et Wieglowo*; cf. Jan Długosz, *Annales*, p. 283, where an identical entry was made under 1117 (the death of Maur and the bishopric taken over by Radost). The chronicler here conflated two events that were clearly separate within the Jędrzejów foundation charter: the consecration of the church in Brzeźnica by Maur, which happened before 1118, and the founding of Jędrzejów Abbey, which took place after 1140. For more detail on the foundation of Jędrzejów Abbey and the identification of the mentioned places, see Chapter 4 in this volume; Dobosz, 'Proces fundacyjny', pp. 40–79.

29 Krzyżanowski, 'Początki dyplomatyki polskiej', p. 788; cf. RPD i.55.

30 'Hic Maurus episcopus ecclesiam maiorem Cracouiensem sub tempore regiminis sui XII Calendas Maij dedicauit'. Jan Długosz, *Katalog biskupów krakowskich*, p. 152. Długosz did not record this information in his *Annales*.

31 *Kalendarz katedry krakowskiej*, MPH v, p. 141.

32 See *Rocznik małopolski*, MPH iii, pp. 154–55; *Rocznik Traski*, MPH ii, p. 833; *Rocznik krakowski*, MPH ii, p. 833; *Rocznik Sędziwoja*, MPH ii, p. 875; *Rocznik Krasińskich*, MPH iii, p. 131.

that the record refers to the consecration of Kraków Cathedral during the reign of Bolesław I, on 20 April 1001,[33] thus rejecting Długosz's statement regarding Maur's participation in these important events. A more sensible solution was adopted by Zofia Kozłowska-Budkowa, who assumed that Długosz's information refers to the consecration of the cathedral by Robert in 1142, when Easter Monday fell on 20 April.[34] The question arises whether Jan Długosz's statement should be categorically rejected, or if there is some grain of truth in it. Perhaps the date recorded by the chronicler refers only to 1142, but this does not exclude some liturgical function around the consecration of Kraków Cathedral, or some part of it, in Maur's time. According to Jerzy Pietrusiński, the new construction functioned at least partially before 1118, a theory for which he cites a handful of evidence, including St Leonard's crypt and the unearthed grave in the crypt: that of Bishop Maur.[35] It can be hypothetically assumed that some part of the church was completed during Maur's episcopate and that dedication ceremonies were carried out, but that Długosz confused these events with the celebrations related to the completion of the cathedral in 1142.

Maur's episcopate brought another important event: it was most likely on the order of Maur that the second inventory of the treasury and the cathedral library in Kraków was compiled in 1110. The inventory was prepared after Bishop Baldwin's death[36] and, as Długosz emphasises, this happened in the very first year of Maur's episcopate.[37] The inventory enumerates expensive liturgical items, such as vestments[38] and books (library),[39] and lists several benefactors: Wojsław, Szczedrzyk, Cześcibor/Cieszybor(?), Michał, Milej, and Doezdoua.[40]

Certain researchers have linked Maur with unspecified followers of the Cathar heresy in Kraków. Adam Bochnak's excavations in Leonard's crypt

---

33 Wojciechowski, *Kościół katedralny w Krakowie*, pp. 57–60.
34 Kozłowska-Budkowa, 'Który Bolesław?', from p. 87.
35 Pietrusiński, 'Krakowska katedra romańska', pp. 43–93.
36 Spisy dawne skarbca i biblioteki kapitulnej krakowskiej, MPH i, p. 377: *Anno dominice incarnationis MCX, defuncto reuerentissimo praesule Balduino, successit in locum eius uenerabilis pontifex Maurus.*
37 Jan Długosz, *Katalog biskupów krakowskich*, p. 152.
38 There are twenty-two items listed in this part of the inventory, including chasubles, capes, coats, dalmatics, chalices, candlesticks, vats, reliquary boxes, crosses, wine dishes, a flag and others, and even two ostrich eggs — Spisy dawne skarbca i biblioteki kapitulnej krakowskiej, MPH i, p. 377.
39 Ibid., p. 377. Only the inventory of 1110 contains the list of books. Among several dozen volumes gathered in the library are found works of ancient authors, theological treatises, book concerning grammar and law, and a large number of liturgical volumes; it is also worth noting some of the authors listed, who include, among others, Isidore, St Paul, Boetius, Ovid, Salustius and Terence.
40 Ibid. Wojsław donated two complete liturgical vestments, Cześcibor (Cieszybor?) a coat, Szczedrzyk a chasuble, Michał priestly garments, Milej, Doezdoua one *plenarium*. The identification of this group of people has been considered in Bieniak, 'Polska elita polityczna XII w., Part II', pp. 13–74.

at Wawel uncovered a lead plaque in a tomb that turned out to be Maur's. The plaque contained the date of the bishop's death and the text of the *credo*, which omitted the dogma on the resurrection of the body. This sufficed to allow for hypotheses about Bishop Maur's potential connections with the Cathars.[41] Kozłowska-Budkowa immediately questioned this supposition and linked the lack of the above-mentioned dogma with medieval asceticism, and especially with its deep contempt for the body (corporeality).[42] A more careful analysis of the Cathar doctrine demonstrates that its adherents did not deny the resurrection of the body.[43] Maur was neither a supporter nor a follower of Catharism, and the short rule of this newcomer from the south in the Kraków bishopric appears to have been relatively fruitful. He participated in the life of the diocese, consecrated churches, took some role in building the cathedral in Kraków, where he rested after his death, and gave away tithes. Maur's activity was focused on his diocese, while Bolesław pursued active political gains in the north-west. This is most likely why the Bishop of Kraków did not participate in political affairs alongside his duke. The occasional voiced opinion that Maur did not play a significant political role in the state seems to be an unfair assessment,[44] insufficiently corroborated by the preserved written records.

The episcopal reign of Maur seems to have represented a continuation of the activities of his predecessors, Lambert and Baldwin, although sources are largely silent on this subject. It is unlikely that it will ever be known how Maur reformed the canonical circles, yet the consecration and tithing of private churches with small groups of clergy suggest an attempt to construct new church structures in the Kraków diocese. The list of questions relating to the Bishop of Kraków would, no doubt, be much longer than the answers to them, but even the insignificant amount of information furnished by the written records indicates that studies of such persons as Maur, Baldwin, and other Polish bishops of that period should cover more than mere biography. The bishops' contribution to the development of the Church in Poland is an issue worthy of further research.

---

41 See Bochnak, 'Grób biskupa Maura', pp. 239–48; David, 'Un credo cathare?', pp. 756–61.
42 Kozłowska-Budkowa, Zofia, review of Bochnak, 'Grób biskupa Maura', pp. 85–88; cf. Semkowicz, *Paleografia łacińska*, pp. 538–40.
43 For more detail, see Swoboda, 'Początki herezji', pp. 385–87.
44 Szczur, 'Biskupi krakowscy', p. 13.

CHAPTER 18

Archbishop Janik and His Successors: Preparation for the Reform of Henryk Kietlicz*

The second half of the twelfth century brought significant changes to the Polish monarchy and Church. The gradual weakening of the central power led to an increase in the power of the nobility and set the Church in Poland on the path to emancipation. In the history of the divided monarchy, this period was marked not only by the gradual deepening of political fragmentation, but also by the economic and organisational solidification of church structures. The dukes found political partners not only in eminent lay nobles but also among the representatives of the Church, who were so abundant in the twelfth century. The political setting for the Polish ecclesiastical hierarchy of the second half of the twelfth century was established by Archbishop Jakub, called Jakub of Żnin, who defended the independence of the Polish ecclesiastical province from the designs of Magdeburg. Considering the events of 1146, it seems reasonable to assume that Jakub was in political liaison with the younger Piasts. He should certainly be credited with the economic stabilisation of the Gniezno archbishopric.[1] Jakub's work was taken up by his successors and augmented in the following years. These archbishops were, in turn, Jan (Janik) Gryfita, then Zdzisław and Piotr from the Łabędzie clan. It is hypothetically presumed that between the episcopates of Zdzisław and Piotr, there was one more archbishop (Blessed Bogumił).[2] The three or four archbishops had their seats in Gniezno between 1149 and 1198, laying the groundwork for the reforms carried out in the Gregorian idiom by their successor, Henryk Kietlicz.

There is no doubt that Archbishop Janik was one of the most fascinating people of his period. While he has received some attention in Polish historiography — mainly in the context of the Cistercian monastery at Jędrzejów,

---

* Original publication: Józef Dobosz, 'Arcybiskup Janik i jego następcy. Przygotowanie do reformy Henryka Kietlicza', in *1000 lat Archidiecezji Gnieźnieńskiej*, ed. by Jerzy Strzelczyk and Janusz Górny (Gniezno: Gaudentinum, 2000), pp. 81–96.

1 Jakub lacks detailed biographical study, though see Korytkowski, *Arcybiskupi gnieźnieńscy*, pp. 223–45; Labuda, 'Jakub zwany ze Żnina', in PSB x, pp. 371–72; Gąsiorowski, 'Jakub ze Żnina II', p. 278.

2 Trawkowski, 'Piotr', in PSB xxvi, p. 361; Labuda, 'Prusy rodzime', p. 85; Labuda, 'Święty Wojciech', pp. 89–92.

which he founded — Janik has never been a subject of a comprehensive study.³ When the medieval historical record is considered, the greatest amount of information about Janik was furnished by Jan Długosz, who portrayed him not only in his *Katalog arcybiskupów gnieźnieńskich*, but also in his *Annales*, and even in the *Liber beneficiorium* of the Kraków diocese.⁴ Information surrounding the earliest period of Polish history as provided by Długosz, especially concerning Wielkopolska, is notably vague. In *Katalog*, Janik is the twelfth name on Długosz's list of archbishops. He reports that Janik was a member of the Gryfici clan from the village of Brzeźnica, and emphasises that he was previously Bishop of Wrocław, then transferred to Gniezno by Pope Eugene III in 1148. According to information Długosz provides, Janik sat on the archbishop's seat for seventeen years before dying near Żnin in 1165 and being buried in Gniezno Cathedral. Długosz calls him a devout man of religion, intent on the growth of the Church in Poland, extending to the establishment and endowment of Jędrzejów Abbey at 1154.⁵ The information contained in Długosz's other works do not broaden our knowledge of Janik. With such meagre accounts, it is difficult to sketch a more complete portrayal of Janik. Later catalogues of Archbishop of Gniezno are of no use either, given that they either omit him or contain even more imprecise information.

Nonetheless, one further attempt may be made to take a closer look at Janik through the prism of historical sources. It is possible to reconstruct the early days of his life. In accordance with preserved written records, it can be said with some confidence that he belonged to the Gryfici clan.⁶ From the fact that the Jędrzejów foundation charter mentions his brother Klemens,⁷ it can be concluded that Janik was younger and as such, was destined for a spiritual career. Nonetheless, he was provided with some part of his patrimony, which is revealed by the foundation charter's statement that he passed it onto the Cistercians.⁸ His parents' names (Klemens and Anna) are given by Długosz, but these could be debatable.⁹ There are some hints that would allow the presumption that Janik was among those who received the best education in Poland. He is reported to have studied abroad, somewhere in the Romance countries,¹⁰ and there is little reason to doubt this, as Vincentius of Kraków made Jan the interlocutor of Mateusz in the dialogue part of his chronicle

---

3 Korytkowski, *Arcybiskupi gnieźnieńscy*, pp. 246–61; Kozłowska-Budkowa, 'Jan', in PSB x, pp. 428–30; Gąsiorowski, 'Jan', p. 285; Gąsiorowski, 'Janik (Jan)', p. 319.
4 Jan Długosz, *Catalogus archiepiscoporum Gnesnensium*, pp. 348–49; Jan Długosz, *Annales*, p. 45; LB iii, from p. 261.
5 Jan Długosz, *Catalogus archiepiscoporum Gnesnensium*, pp. 348–49; Jan Długosz, *Catalogus episcoporum Wratislauiensium*, pp. 455–56: *Vir devotus et religiosus, et ad augendas res divinas plurimum intentus.*
6 See Wójcik, *Ród Gryfitów*, pp. 25–28.
7 KDM ii.372.
8 Ibid: *patrimoni mei liberam portionem.*
9 Jan Długosz, *Catalogus episcoporum Wratislaviensium*, p. 455.
10 See Kozłowska-Budkowa, 'Jan', p. 428; cf. Kürbis, 'Cystersi w kulturze polskiego', pp. 329–30.

(books I–III). Both give a scholarly, erudite commentary on various events in the history of Poland.[11] The beginnings of the spiritual career of the future archbishop are similarly veiled in mystery. Karol Maleczyński suggested that these need to be sought in the ducal chancellery. In his opinion, Jan was Chancellor of Bolesław IV,[12] who is mentioned in the document of Cardinal Hubaldus from 1146,[13] and in the two thirteenth-century forgeries known as the Mogilno document[14] and the Trzemeszno document.[15] Finding this difficult to prove in light of historical sources, Zofia Kozłowska-Budkowa questioned Maleczyński's basis for this hypothesis.[16] She rejected Maleczyński's position based on the date when Janik assumed the bishopric of Wrocław. Written records report that in the early 1240s, after Radost's death, Bishop Robert was transferred from Wrocław to Kraków. Most sources put this event in 1142,[17] others in 1143,[18] while Długosz places it in 1141.[19] Only the date provided by *Rocznik świętokrzyski* considerably differs from others, registering Radost's death and Robert's succession in 1158.[20] It should be assumed that Robert was transferred to the Kraków bishopric in 1142. However, Robert was not immediately succeeded by Janik but Konrad, who held the Wrocław bishopric between 1142 and 1146.[21] It follows then that Janik took over Wrocław Cathedral only in 1146, and the possibility of an earlier chancellery career should be acknowledged, although whether he can be identified with Chancellor of Bolesław IV is unresolvable. The uncertainty results from difficulties with the exact dating of, above all, the Mogilno forgery.

---

11   *Chronica Polonorum*.
12   Maleczyński, 'O kanclerzach polskich XII wieku', pp. 9–10; Maleczyński, *Zarys dyplomatyki polskiej*, pp. 83–87, 95–96.
13   KDW i.12. For Hubaldus document, see Wenta, 'Na marginesie dokumentu', pp. 106–11. Cf. von Güttner-Sporzyński, *Poland, Holy War, and the Piast Monarchy* pp. 72, 180–81.
14   KDW i.3. For more detail on this forgery, see RPD i.8; Kürbis, 'Najstarsze dokumenty', pp. 27–59.
15   KDW i.11. See also Dobosz, 'Dokument Mieszka III Starego', pp. 87–106; Chapter 14 in this volume.
16   Kozłowska-Budkowa, 'Jan', p. 428.
17   Robert was transferred to Kraków in 1142, *Rocznik kapituły krakowskiej*, MPH v, p. 58; *Rocznik krótki*, MPH v, p. 237; *Rocznik małopolski*, MPH iii, pp. 154–55 (Kodeks Kuropatnickiego and Kodeks lubiński); *Rocznik Traski*, MPH ii, p. 833; *Rocznik Sędziwoja*, MPH ii, p. 875; *Rocznik Krasińskich*. MPH iii, p. 131. Similar information is provided by most editions of the *Katalogi biskupów krakowskich*, MPH x, pp. 47, 56, 87, 110, 296, 304.
18   Robert's *translatio* in 1143 is recorded in *Roczniki wielkopolskie* (Rocznik lubiński), MPH vi, p. 113; *Rocznik krakowski*, MPH ii, p. 833; *Katalogi biskupów krakowskich*, Edition II, MPH x, p. 32.
19   Jan Długosz, *Katalog biskupów krakowskich*, MPH x, p. 154; Jan Długosz, *Catalogus episcoporum Wratislaviensium*, p. 453.
20   *Rocznik świętokrzyski*, MPH xii, p. 23.
21   For more information on Bishop Konrad and the gap between 1140 and 1146 in the catalogues of the bishops of Wrocław, see Jurek, 'Zagadka biskupa', pp, 1–11. Cf. Wójcik, *Ród Gryfitów*, p. 26; Korta, *Tajemnice góry Ślęży*, pp. 263–7.

What ecclesiastical dignities Janik achieved before his promotion to Bishop of Wrocław is hard to determine. Such information as can be found was again provided by Jan Długosz, who in his *Katalog biskupów wrocławskich* referred to him as *Jan of Brzeźnica, called Janik, also known Janislaus the provost of Wrocław and canon of Gniezno and Kraków*.[22] No such information was registered in other catalogues of the bishops of Wrocław, and in the six editions prepared between the thirteenth and fifteenth centuries, it is only stated that he was the seventh or eighth Bishop of Wrocław and held his office in the years 1146–1148, 1146–1147, or 1147–1148.[23] Only the period set out by the Henryków catalogue differs.[24] Very little is known about Janik's activity in Silesia between 1146 and 1149. He was, it seems, a nominee of Bolesław IV but there is no information about his contacts with the duke. In a document dated 22 June 1149, Janik is mentioned as Bishop of Wrocław and the benefactor to St Vincent's Abbey, to which he was granted the rights; he also consecrated the local church founded by Palatine Piotr Włostowic and was placed first on the witness list, before Mateusz, Bishop of Kraków.[25] For some researchers, this is the evidence of close cooperation between a leading magnate and the bishop.[26] Before leaving for Silesia, Janik most likely transferred his support to the younger Piasts and established a close liaison with Archbishop Jakub. At that time, he was already working on his own independent initiative to bring the Cistercians to his family estate, which was successfully completed in stages in the following years.[27] The extent of his participation in these endeavours with Archbishop Jakub — or, earlier, with Władysław II as sometimes suggested in the literature — must remain pure speculation.

In light of the document of 22 June 1149,[28] it should be assumed Janik was nominated to the archbishopric of Gniezno sometime after that date. In a letter of 23 January 1150, addressed to the Polish clergy by Pope Eugene III regarding their failure to respect the curse cast by Cardinal Guido on the opponents of Władysław II, there is reference to an unnamed Polish archbishop.[29] It was Janik, who took over the legacy of Jakub in a fairly turbulent period, when the disruptions of the recent civil war of 1144–1146 were still noticeable, and, what is more, in the face of the curse cast by the papal legate on the supporters of the younger Piasts.[30] This happened during

---

22 Jan Długosz, Catalogus episcoporum Wratislaviensium, p. 455: *Iohannem de Brzesznicza, qui et Ianik, alias Ianislaum Praepositum Wratislaviensem et Canonicum Gnesensem et Cracoviensem*.
23 *Katalogi biskupów wrocławskich*, MPH vi, pp. 561, 567 (the Lubiąż and Głogów editions).
24 *Katalog henrykowski*, MPH vi, p. 558.
25 KDŚ i.25.
26 For example, Kozłowska-Budkowa, 'Jan', p. 428.
27 Dobosz, 'Proces fundacyjny', pp. 40–79; Chapter 4 in this volume.
28 KDŚ i.25.
29 *List Eugeniusza III*, MPH ii, p. 18.
30 See *List Gwidona do króla Konrada III*, MPH ii, p. 17.

the first days of 1150 and the Polish clergy, headed by the Archbishop of Gniezno, thus became the subject of the above-mentioned papal remarks. However, the diplomatic efforts of the German king Konrad III, the papal legate and the pope himself, were of no avail. It seems that not only did many of the nobles and knights take the side of the younger Piasts, so too did the Church hierarchy, led by Janik, which was faithful to the political positions of Archbishop Jakub.

Once he took the archbishop's seat, Janik began to finalise his earlier foundation with redoubled energy and brought the Cistercian monks from Morimond to his native Brzeźnica in the Sandomierz territories. Soon after, in 1153, he issued a foundation charter, securing the foundation legal and economic status and, in 1167, he organised a convention in Jędrzejów, during which the rebuilt monastery church was solemnly consecrated.[31] At the same time, Janik endorsed an analogous initiative of Zbylut of the Pałuki clan, a noble from Wielkopolska, who founded the Cistercian monastery at Łekno. Janik participated in the foundation convention, dictating and subscribing the 1153 document.[32] The independent foundational activity of the Archbishop of Gniezno and his support for other foundations indicate that he was a vigorous guardian of the Church. This is particularly evident in the impressive collegiate church in Tum near Łęczyca, consecrated on 21 May 1161.[33] Though the initiative may have come from Jakub, the construction of this splendid Romanesque building should be attributed to his immediate successor.[34] In contrast, Janik's participation in Mieszko III's foundation in Kalisz is uncertain. Jan Długosz alone mentions this fact under the year 1155 referring to Janik's encouragement of the duke in the foundation of the Collegiate Church of St Paul.[35] However, this information is not corroborated by any other sources,[36] and the construction was certainly completed in the late twelfth century, when the body of Mieszko the Younger was buried there in 1193. The collegiate church itself is cautiously dated to the third quarter of the twelfth century.[37] The comparison of Długosz's information and the entry in *Kronika wielkopolska* on the foundation of the Collegiate Church of

---

31 For the foundation of Jędrzejów Abbey, see Chapter 4 in this volume. For the foundation charter of 1153, see KDM ii.372; RPD i.55; Kürbis, 'Cystersi w kulturze polskiego', pp. 328–40. See also Dobosz, *Działalność fundacyjna*, pp. 25–28; Dobosz, 'Trzynastowieczne falsyfikaty', pp. 225–29; Chapter 13 in this volume.
32 KDW i.18.
33 KDM ii.373.
34 See Walicki, ed., *Sztuka polska przedromańska* ii, p. 699.
35 Jan Długosz, *Annales*, p. 56: *sed etiam Iohannis archiepiscopi incitabatur persuasione, qui ad cultum Dei propensius in diebus suis augendum estuabat*.
36 Although Mieszko III's foundation of the Collegiate Church of St Paul in Kalisz is confirmed by *Kronika wielkopolska*, MPH viii, p. 55, it does not mention Jan. It does record that Mieszko III and his son Mieszko Młodszy (the Younger) were interred there.
37 See Walicki, ed., *Sztuka polska przedromańska* ii, pp. 731–32.

St Paul suggests that Długosz made use of the source but added Archbishop Janik's participation in this important act himself.[38]

Janik was one of the better educated people of his time. He himself dictated documents, which may be indicative of his chancellery past. The formulary of the documents he drew up suggest a great proficiency in this area, coupled with a working knowledge of Roman law. The fact that he was recognised by Vincentius of Kraków shows Janik as a man who moved in the intellectual circles of the time and thus likely connected to the so-called twelfth-century Renaissance. In Church matters, Janik continued the work of Jakub through his engagement in founding religious houses, and in his support for the cult of St Adalbert. It was probably Janik who sought to introduce the cult in the Sandomierz and Kraków regions, as evidenced in the act in which St Adalbert was added as the patron saint of the monastery church in Jędrzejów in the autumn of 1167. Some researchers believe that he was also responsible for the commissioning of the bronze Gniezno Doors, but since they date sometime in the second half of the twelfth century, they may equally well be attributed to his successors.[39] Admittedly, such an initiative would be another step in the process of strengthening the position of St Adalbert as the patron saint of Poland.

To what extent Archbishop Janik was involved in political activities, apart from the support given to the younger Piasts at the beginning of his pontificate, is unclear. Bolesław IV was absent from the convention Janik organised on the occasion of the consecration of the Jędrzejów church, which was probably a consequence of the defeat of the 1166 Prussian expedition. However, Mieszko III and Kazimierz II attended the meeting. Some scholars connect this fact with Vincentius' account of the plot against Bolesław IV which he describes as being headed by Świętosław Piotrowic and Jaksa of Miechów, both of whom were also present at the Jędrzejów convention.[40] A final answer to the question of whether Janik was involved in this possible conspiracy is difficult to give, especially since Kazimierz, as a favoured successor to Bolesław, rejected the proposal and the project failed. No other sources confirm the existence of the conspiracy, and it will probably remain another unsolved mystery of Polish history.

The Jędrzejów convention in the autumn of 1167 is the last fact from the life of Archbishop Janik reported by historical sources. The written records failed to register the year of Janik's death, so only the day is known. This was

---

38 Jan Długosz, *Annales*, p. 56: *In opido insuper Kalish Gneznensis dioecesis ecclesia ex dolatis lapidibus in honorem doctoris Divini Pauli fabricans, prepositum et aliquot canonicorum numerum in ea constituit et dote sufficienti providit*; *Kronika wielkopolska*, MPH viii, p. 55: *In Kalisz vero ecclesiam in honorem Sancti Pauli de lapidibus dolatis fundavit et construxit, in qua prepositurum et aliquot prebendas instituit et dotavit*.
39 See Walicki, ed., *Sztuka polska przedromańska* ii, pp. 690–91.
40 *Chronica Polonorum* iv.17; Deptuła, 'Wokół postaci arcybiskupa', pp. 37–47; Dobosz, *Działalność fundacyjna*, pp. 194–95.

recorded by the Lubiń obituary as 11 March,[41] the obituary of St Vincent in Wrocław as 12 March,[42] and the Jędrzejów obituary as 13 March. The latter source reports the death of Janik's brother, Klemens, and his relative Śmił on 16 March.[43] Janik's successor, Zdzisław, appeared on a diploma of Mieszko III dated 26 April 1177,[44] hence it should be assumed that Jan died on 11 March between 1168 and 1176.

Much less again is known about Janik's successor. Zdzisław's life is not so brightly illuminated by the historical sources, and his activity was probably much more modest than that of his predecessor.[45] In his *Katalog arcybiskupów*, Jan Długosz placed him between Piotr II and Henryk Kietlicz, stating that his pontificate lasted 17 years, between 1183 and 1199. He purportedly came from the Koźlerogi family and, before having been elected archbishop, he was allegedly Canon of Gniezno. The chronicler described him as *animosus bonorum ecclesiae defensor*.[46] There is no mention of Zdzisław in the catalogue of Maciej of Pełczyn, while the post-Długosz catalogues list him as the fourteenth archbishop, also placing him between Piotr II and Henryk Kietlicz. They unanimously report the years of his pontificate as between 1171 and 1187 and call him *vir modestus et industriosus*.[47] However, all the authors of the catalogues confused the order of the archbishops who lived in the second half of the twelfth century; Zdzisław was Janik's immediate successor. He was probably nominated by Mieszko III, although because the date of his predecessor's death is unknown, Bolesław IV might have placed him on the archbishop's throne. On 26 April 1177, he appeared as a witness on Mieszko's charter for the Cistercian monastery at Lubiąż, issued in Gniezno.[48]

However, it is difficult to assess his relations with the princeps. In 1180, he turned out for the Łęczyca convention with the entire Church hierarchy of that time, accepting Kazimierz II's guarantees of privileges for the Church in Poland.[49] The oldest Miechów documents tell that on Easter of an unspecified year, Zdzisław, alongside Kazimierz, partook in the Świerże Górne convention, during which the Duke endowed the Canons of the Holy Sepulchre convent in Miechów. Lupus, Bishop of Płock, who fulfilled chancellery duties by the

---

41 *Nekrolog opactwa Panny Marii w Lubiniu*, MPH ix, p. 41.
42 *Nekrolog opactwa św. Wincentego we Wrocławiu*, MPH ix, p. 26.
43 *Nekrolog jędrzejowski*, MPH v, p. 779.
44 KDW i.22.
45 See Korytkowski, *Arcybiskupi gnieźnieńscy*, pp. 278–98.
46 Jan Długosz, *Catalogus archiepiscoporum Gnesnensium*, pp. 349–50; Długosz places the pontificate of Zdzisław in 1182, *Annales*, p. 129.
47 *Archiepiscopi Ecclesiae Metropolitanae Gnesnensis*, MPH iii, p. 406; Bolz, ed., *Nieznany katalog*, pp. 271–81. See also Damalewicz, *Series archiepiscoporum Gnesnensium*; Bużeński, *Żywoty arcybiskupów* gnieźnieńskich.
48 KDW i.22.
49 The participation of Zdzisław in the Łęczyca convention is confirmed in *Chronica Polonorum*, p, 204, and later by *Kronika wielkopolska* MPH viii, p. 59; Henryk of Góra, *Tractatus contra cruciferos*, MPH iv, p. 189; Jan Długosz, *Annales*, p. 121.

duke at the time,[50] also participated in this undertaking. These events were cautiously dated sometime between 1170 and 1187, based on various sources' attestations of Bishop Lupus and his successor Wit.[51] It is worth positing some causative link between these two important congresses, the grants for the Canons of the Holy Sepulchre being of rather secondary importance here. As archbishop, Zdzisław had to take care of the interests of the Church, and the contacts with the princeps, even if not entirely legal, were necessary. It seems likely, therefore, that the congress in Świerże should be read in relation to the convention in Łęczyca, probably as a sort of run-up to that event, and perhaps also the first meeting between the Archbishop of Gniezno and Duke Kazimierz after the events of 1177–1179. This means it must have taken place around 1180.[52] Additionally, the archbishop appears several times in Długosz's *Annales*: under 1189, when he consecrated Mrokota, Bishop of Poznań; under 1191, on the occasion of Mieszko's attempt to seize Kraków, the chronicler assigning him the role of Archbishop Piotr; under 1196, on the occasion of the consecration of Filip, Bishop of Poznań; and, finally, under 1198, on the occasion of the consecration of Jarosław, Bishop of Wrocław.[53] The latter event is also mentioned in the *Kronika śląska skrócona*.[54] All these, however, are to some extent the arbitrary interpolations and interpretations of chroniclers in response to the above-mentioned confusion of the order of the archbishops of Gniezno.

Zdzisław held the archbishopric in Gniezno for at least several years during a particularly difficult period for the Polish monarchy: the rebellions of the nobility of Kraków, Odon, and Kazimierz, and the changes the *princeps* in Kraków. The period of his service as Archbishop of Gniezno also witnessed an intensified manoeuvring in Kraków for a stronger position in the Church in Poland and the acquisition of the relics of St Florian in 1184, probably in opposition to St Adalbert.[55] It is to Zdzisław that the Church probably owes the guarantee of important privileges that it received in Łęczyca in 1180, Gniezno's undiminished position on the ecclesiastical map of Poland, and the development of the cult of St Adalbert. These were important elements in the Church in Poland's struggle for emancipation from the power of dukes and nobles, which had begun long before the arrival of the main proponent in the fight, Archbishop Henryk Kietlicz. The question of when Zdzisław died must remain unanswered, because neither the year nor date of his death are reported by reliable sources, though Długosz places it in 1187.

50 KDM ii.375.
51 RPD, pp. 110–11.
52 Dobosz, *Działalność fundacyjna*, pp. 109, 202–03.
53 Długosz, *Annales*, pp. 140, 151, 166, 172.
54 *Kronika śląska skrócona*, MPH iii, p. 724.
55 Dobosz, *Działalność fundacyjna*, pp. 86–90, 149–50; cf. Śliwiński, 'Na marginesie fundacyjnej', pp. 174–78.

It is equally difficult to determine who succeeded Zdzisław on the archbishops' throne. A widely held view is that it was Archbishop Piotr, but it has also been suggested that it was Blessed Bogumił who held authority in Gniezno between Zdzisław and Piotr.[56] This Bogumił seems to be the most mysterious figure among all the twelfth-century archbishops of Gniezno, and he is not listed in any of the catalogues. He appears in only one document, that issued by Władysław Odonic on 29 June 1232, which reports that he donated the Dobrowo settlement complex to the Cistercians.[57] Aside from this, he is only known from late fifteenth- and seventeenth-century records related to his beatification,[58] and a forgery dated 23 April 1234, in the name of Archbishop Pełka.[59] In *Rocznik świętokrzyski dawny* an entry under the year 1092 reads: *Bogumylus archiepiscopus obit*.[60] This meagre set of sources has caused quite a stir regarding the person of Archbishop Bogumił, granted that documents are mutually exlusive. Several theories have appeared in historiography attempting to solve this puzzle: (a) there were two archbishops, one living in the late eleventh century and the other in the late twelfth century: Bogumił-Piotr I and Piotr II;[61] (b) there was only one Archbishop Bogumił, who lived in the late twelfth century and is identified with Archbishop Piotr II;[62] (c) there was only one Archbishop Bogumił, who lived in the late eleventh century;[63] (d) Archbishop Bogumił lived in the second half of the twelfth century and ruled in Gniezno between Zdzisław and Piotr II; (e) Bogumił was a hermit at the turn of the thirteenth century and was never an archbishop.[64]

The most sensible position seems to be that Bogumił was Archbishop of Gniezno, probably in the mid-1280s, then renounced his position and found seclusion in a hermitage. He also granted the sizeable Dobrowo settlement complex to the Cistercians. Speculations identifying Archbishop Bogumił with Piotr II, especially those of Józef Nowacki, should be rejected as improbable.

---

56   For more information on Bogumił, see also Korytkowski, *Arcybiskupi gnieźnieńscy*, pp. 262–77.
57   KDW i.136, pp. 120–21. For more details about the Dobrowo settlement complex see Kozłowski, *Rozwój uposażenia klasztoru cystersów*, pp. 191–242; Zielińska-Melkowska, 'Klucz dobrowski', pp. 207–20. Odonic's document has been considered to be false, see Kozłowska-Budkowa, 'Bogumił', pp. 200–01; Łowmiański, *Początki Polski* vi, p. 268; Likowski, *W sprawie żywota bł. Bogumiła*. However, the authenticity of the document was convincingly defended by Maleczyński, *Studia nad dyplomami*, pp. 40–45.
58   These are discussed by Bolz, 'Proces beatyfikacyjny', pp. 28–40; cf. Semkowicz, *Ród Pałuków*, p. 95.
59   KDW i.165, pp. 142–43. See Maleczyński, *Studia nad dyplomami*, p. 43; Łowmiański, *Początki Polski* vi, p. 268.
60   *Rocznik świętokrzyski dawny*, MPH ii, p. 773; cf. Semkowicz, *Rocznik Świętokrzyski dawny*, p. 228; *Rocznik dawny*, MPH v, p. 11.
61   Wojciechowski, *Szkice historyczne XI wieku*, pp. 97–144.
62   Semkowicz, *Ród Pałukow*, pp. 94–112; cf. Kozierowski, *Leszczyce i ich plemiennik*; Nowacki, 'Bogumił-Piotr II', pp. 112–13.
63   Kozłowska-Budkowa, 'Bogumił', p. 200.
64   Gieysztor, 'Drzwi gnieźnieńskie', p. 18.

Particularly absurd is the statement, based on unreliable seventeenth-century sources, that Piotr II was a Cistercian.[65]

The family affiliation of Bogumił has sparked equally intense debates. Three stances can be distinguished: (a) a late tradition that claimed he was a member of the Poraje-Różyce family;[66] (b) his inclusion among the Pałuki clan the inclusion by Władysław Semkowicz;[67] (c) a hypothesis that assumed his affiliation with the Leszczyce clan, which latter has turned out to be best grounded.[68] It can, therefore, be assumed that after 1180, the archbishopric of Gniezno was taken by Blessed Bogumił of the Leszczyce clan, who around 1190 renounced his dignity as the archbishop and became a hermit. It is a historical fact that he handed Dobrowo over to the Cistercians. However, nothing certain is known about his ecclesiastical activity beyond the fantastic inventions, speculations, and conjectures woven by historians, based on the uncertain and late tradition of Byszewo Abbey and other Cistercian monasteries. The date of hermit Bogumił's death is unknown and, again, it can only be hypothetically assumed that Bogumił died sometime in the early thirteenth century.[69]

Bogumił was succeeded by Piotr, who was frequently identified with him. Although the sources furnish some more reliable information about Piotr,[70] Archbishop of Gniezno, he too aroused controversy among historians, particularly concerning his ancestral affiliation. Following his identification with Blessed Bogumił, he was believed to have been the member of the Pałuki, the Poraje-Różyce, or the Leszczyce family. Attempts have been made to link him with Kazimierz II or Piotr, Kazimierz's deputy chancellor mentioned in the Opatów document of 1189.[71] Jan Długosz considered him to be a representative of the Śreniawici family,[72] but the basis for this is unknown. Ultimately, Piotr is most often counted as a member of the prominent Łabędzie clan, which seems to be the most sensible solution.[73] Thus, it is assumed that Piotr was a descendant of this noble family, a grandson of Piotr Włostowic, and the son of Konstantyn or Świętosław. He was probably enthroned as archbishop around

---

65 Nowacki, *Bogumił-Piotr II*, pp. 113–17.
66 Bolz, 'Proces beatyfikacyjny', p. 40.
67 Semkowicz, *Ród Pałuków*, from p. 94.
68 Kozierowski, *Leszczyce i ich plemiennik*, identifies Bogumił as a member of the Leszczyce family. See also Nowacki, 'Bogumił-Piotr II', p. 113; Bieniak, 'Autor Rocznika dawnego', pp. 433–35.
69 Sixteenth- and seventeenth-century tradition most often reports his death as 1182, with the suggestion that he was buried in Dobrowo. See Bolz, ed., *Proces beatyfikacyjny*, pp. 33–40; Nowacki 'Bogumił-Piotr II', p. 112, assumes that he died around 1203/04.
70 For information on Piotr in earlier literature, see Korytkowski, *Arcybiskupi gnieźnieńscy*, pp. 299–312.
71 Kürbis, 'Introduction', *Chronica Polonorum*, p. xxvi.
72 Jan Długosz, *Catalogus archiepiscoporum Gnesnesium*, p. 349; Jan Długosz, *Annales*, p. 80.
73 Trawkowski, 'Wprowadzenie zwyczajów arrowezyjskich', pp. 111–16; Deptuła, 'Wokół postaci arcybiskupa', pp. 37–47. See also Grzesik, 'Piotr', pp. 512–13; cf. Dobosz, *Działalność fundacyjna*, pp. 178–86; Trawkowski, 'Piotr', p. 361.

1190, although the catalogues of archbishops move this date further back. Jan Długosz called him *vir modestus et frugi, bonorum amator* and stated that he took over Gniezno Cathedral in 1166, ruled for 22 years, and died in 1182.[74] Other catalogues report that Piotr ruled in Gniezno Cathedral between 1149 and 1171.[75] Piotr was likely born around the mid-twelfth century, but neither the early days of his life nor the beginning of his ecclesiastical activities are illuminated by the historical record.[76] He was probably educated, as Vincentius seems to suggest in his panegyric assessment of the archbishop.[77] Following this lead, Stanisław Trawkowski found the conjecture about Piotr's education justified, although he believed that it covered only the *trivium*.[78] When, where, and under what circumstances Piotr received his education is unclear. The sources are similarly vague as to when Piotr was consecrated as Archbishop of Gniezno. As already observed, it is impossible to rely on Długosz or post-Długosz catalogues for this information. A suggestion that it occurred around 1190,[79] and that Piotr was appointed to this position by Mieszko III is probably correct. The newly enthroned archbishop first appears in the historical record only in the summer and early autumn of 1191. At that time he was likely acting as an intermediary between Mieszko III and Kazimierz II after the former's unsuccessful attempt to seize Kraków.[80] Regulating relations between the two dukes was, it seems, the primary purpose of the archbishop's journey to Małopolska. On 8 September 1191, he also consecrated one of Kazimierz's most important foundations, the Collegiate Church of the Blessed Virgin Mary in Sandomierz.[81] A connection with his stay in Kraków and Sandomierz in 1191 can also be observed in Piotr's acceptance as a member of the confraternity of the Canons of the Holy Sepulchre in Miechów, perhaps together with Pełka, Bishop of Kraków.[82] It also seems that on the way to Kraków and Sandomierz, on 10 August 1191, at Kazimierz and Bishop Pełka's request, Piotr granted rights to extensive tithes to the duke's favourite foundation, the Cistercian monastery at Sulejów.[83]

Once the relations between the dukes had been settled, Piotr was able to deal with intra-Church matters. He is credited with the reform of St Vincent's

---

74 Jan Długosz, *Catalogus archiepiscoporum Gnesnensium*, p. 349.
75 *Archiepiscopi Ecclesiae Metropolitanae Gnesnensis*, MPH iii, p. 406; Bolz, ed., *Nieznany katalog*, p. 281 (as Petrus II); *Catalogus reverendissimorum patrum dominorum Gnesnensium archiepiscoporum*, MPH iii, p. 392, places Piotr I between Stefan and Marcin, but provides the death day of Piotr II.
76 Deptuła, 'Wokół postaci arcybiskupa', pp. 41–42, dates his birth to early 1147.
77 *Chronicon Polonorum* iv.17. Cf. Kürbis, 'Introduction', pp. xxv–xxvi.
78 Trawkowski, 'Piotr', p. 361.
79 Ibid.
80 *Chronica Polonorum* iv.17. Cf. *Kronika wielkopolska*, MPH viii, p. 64.
81 This is reported in the Sandomierz record, KDM i.2.
82 Both Church dignitaries are named in the *Album patriarchale*, KDM ii.376.
83 The document about tithes is a thirteenth-century forgery dated 10 August 1176, KDW i.587 [21a].

Abbey at Ołbin, from whence the Benedictines were removed to be replaced with the Premonstratensians,[84] and the introduction of Arrouaisian *observance* in another foundation of Piotr Włostowic, the convent of the Blessed Virgin Mary on Piasek Island in Wrocław. These events date back to around 1191, and certainly before 1193.[85] Furthermore, Archbishop Piotr was somehow connected to the introduction of the Premonstratensian observance in the convent of canonesses in Strzelno by Stefan, Bishop of Poznań,[86] as well as the renovation of Ląd Abbey in the 1190s with the participation of Mieszko III. Perhaps as a compensation for giving estates up to Ląd, Piotr also granted the Cistercians of Łekno rights to receive tithes from three villages.[87] Again, it has been conjectured that Piotr might have participated in the creation of the Gniezno Doors.[88] The end of his life is completely unknown; Piotr's possible involvement in the compromise concluded after the bloody Battle of the Mozgawa in 1195 remains mere speculation.[89] The Archbishop of Gniezno passed away soon after these events, and he was succeeded by Henryk Kietlicz, who held this position by 23 March 1199.[90] The day of Piotr's death was recorded by some obituaries, with *Petrus archiepiscopus Gnesnensis* being written against the entry for 20 August (St Hubert and Bernard's day) in the *Nekrolog strzelneński*.[91] A similar entry can be found in the *Nekrolog lubiński*, but on 21 August.[92] The *Nekrolog św. Wincentego na Ołbinie* also recorded his death on 21 August,[93] while the *Kalendarz katedry krakowskiej* places it on 19 August.[94] Ultimately, it can be assumed that Piotr died between 19 and 21 August 1198.[95]

The half-century that saw what was likely four successive archbishops of Gniezno take that title abounded in numerous and important political events, in which the Church hierarchy was often involved. Janik and his predecessor, Jakub, supported the younger Piasts, contributing both to the overthrowing of Władysław II and Bolesław IV's continuance on the Kraków throne. Zdzisław, and especially Piotr, were arbitrators in disputes between the younger sons of Bolesław III. The gradual decentralisation of the state opened the way for

---

84 The 1219 document, KDŚ ii.221. For more detail, see Trawkowski, 'Wprowadzenie zwyczajów arrowezyjskich'; Deptuła, 'Wokół postaci arcybiskupa'.
85 See Trawkowski, 'Piotr', pp. 361–62.
86 Ibid.
87 The Łekno document from 1153 (late twelfth-century copy), KDW i.18; Dobosz, 'Dokument fundacyjny', from p. 53; Chapter 15 in this volume.
88 Trawkowski, 'Piotr', p. 362.
89 Ibid.
90 See Dobosz, 'Dokument fundacyjny', p. 80; Trawkowski, 'Piotr', p. 362; Chapter 15 in this volume.
91 *Nekrolog strzelneński*, MPH v, p. 749.
92 *Nekrolog opactwa Panny Marii w Lubiniu*, MPH ix, 92.
93 *Nekrolog opactwa św. Wincentego we Wrocławiu*, MPH ix, p. 64.
94 *Kalendarz katedry krakowskiej*, MPH v, p. 163.
95 See Dobosz, *Działalność fundacyjna*, p. 178; Trawkowski, 'Piotr', p. 362; Grzesik, 'Piotr', pp. 512–13.

the Church in Poland to abandon its dependence on royal authority. This path probably began with the relatively independent activity of Archbishop Janik, who stands at the forefront of outstanding bishop-founders, next to Alexander, Bishop of Płock.[96] Janik issued independent diplomas not only for his ancestral foundation in Jędrzejów, but also for Łekno, sealing them with his own archbishop's seal. Other Polish bishops, such as Gedko, Pełka, Wit, and Piotr, quickly followed in the footsteps of Janik and Alexander. The second half of the twelfth century witnessed the commencement of the construction of the organisational framework of the Church in Poland by the gradual introduction of archdeaconries or provosts. Many Church establishments, especially bishoprics and large abbeys, received protection bulls from popes. This period also saw the emerging right of patronage in Church institutions, which was gradually replacing the right of ownership. During this period, the Church in Poland managed to build adequate economic foundations for independent function and was ready to emancipate itself from the economic inconveniences of the ducal law, and ultimately to commence a battle for full independence from secular authority in the first years of the thirteenth century.

All this took place in parallel with the struggle within the Church for primacy between Kraków and Gniezno. Various arguments were used in this dispute, the cult of St Adalbert was revived, the relics of St Florian were brought to Kraków, and support was sought in the papacy or in certain representatives of the dynasty. Ultimately, with a bull of 1186, Pełka, Bishop of Kraków secured himself second place after the archbishop among the hierarchs of the Church in Poland.[97] The rivalry did not weaken the position of the Church; instead, it boosted the development of its structures, strengthened contacts with Rome, and indirectly contributed to the initiation of Gregorian reforms. The second half of the twelfth century saw at least four papal legations to the lands ruled by the Piast dukes. The first, Cardinal Guido's in the early 1150s, concerned purely political matters, mainly Władysław II's exile from the throne.[98] The three later legates dealt directly with ecclesiastical matters and were probably connected with synods, with the last two being observed by Polish annalists. At the time when Gedko was Bishop of Kraków, before 1185, Legate Rajnald (Reinaldus) stayed in Poland, as evidenced by a document dated 13 January, issued in Jeżów without year.[99] When exactly the synod of Jeżów was held is hard to settle. Perhaps it was somehow related to the Łęczyca convention, in which case, it would have been held in 1180. Perhaps what is seen here is the triangle of Świerże Górne — Łęczyca — Jeżów, although it could also be hypothesised that the purpose of the Jeżów convention was to discuss the matter of obtaining the relics of St Florian. Under 1189, the Polish

---

96 On Alexander of Malonne, see Drzymała, 'Działalność fundacyjna biskupa', pp. 37–69.
97 KKK i.3.
98 MPH ii, p. 17.
99 KKK i.2; RPD i.107.

annals concordantly register the legation of Cardinal Jan Malabrank,[100] the representative of Pope Clement III.[101] That legation may have taken place as early as the reign of Archbishop Piotr, or maybe even Bogumił. The last known legation undoubtedly occurred in the period when Piotr was Archbishop of Gniezno, as the annals clearly indicate the year 1197.[102] Having stayed in Prague since March, Cardinal Pierre de Capuano, the papal legate, arrived in May 1197.[103] During the synods held in Kraków and Lubcza, according to Długosz,[104] the cardinal dealt with issues directly related to the Gregorian reform, particularly sacramental marriages and the celibacy of priests.

The Polish clergy gathered at synods not only on the occasion of the presence of papal legates. Many representatives of the Church hierarchy also met on the occasion of important Church and state events, at least some of which were accompanied by synods. Such conventions often coincided with the consecration of important Church institutions — for example, in 1161 in Łęczyca, when the local collegiate church was consecrated,[105] or 1191 in Sandomierz at the consecration of Collegiate Church of the Blessed Virgin Mary,[106] to name just the largest. The Łęczyca congress of 1180, which basically legitimised the 1177 coup, is another matter.

There is no doubt that the second half of the twelfth century laid the ground for a different Church in Poland, which was internally reforming itself in the Gregorian spirit. It was then that its economic and organisational foundations were laid and, at the same time, new relations were gradually established between the Church and the monarchy. Poland was entering a new phase that deepened the processes of Christianisation. The Church owed all this to its outstanding representatives, among whom the archbishops — such as Janik, Zdzisław, Bogumił, and Piotr — should be highly ranked. They came from the local noble elite and hence their political actions were characterised by deep realism. Thorough education and probable journeys to the West brought awareness of the problems within the Church, which in the near future would lead to the introduction of the Gregorian ideal in Poland. The greatest contributions to both the Church and the Piast monarchy in its difficult moments were made by Janik and Piotr. It is to them that such outstanding people as Kietlicz, Vincentius, and Iwo Odrowąż owe their appearance in the history of Poland.

---

100 *Rocznik Traski*, MPH ii, p. 835; *Rocznik Sędziwoja*, MPH ii, p. 876; *Rocznik kapituły krakowskiej*, MPH v, p. 66. See also Jan Długosz, *Annales*, p. 146.
101 For this legation see *Rocznik kapituły krakowskiej*, MPH v, p. 66, note 218.
102 *Rocznik Traski*, MPH ii, p. 836; *Rocznik krakowski*, p. 836; *Rocznik Sędziwoja*, MPH ii, p. 876; *Rocznik małopolski* (The Codex of Kuropatnicki and the Codex of Lubiń), MPH iii, pp. 162–63 (the Codex of Königsberg incorrectly under 1216); *Rocznik kapituły krakowskiej*, MPH v, p. 67. The same information is given by Jan Długosz, *Annales*, pp. 166–67.
103 See *Rocznik kapituły krakowskiej*, MPH v, p. 67.
104 Jan Długosz, *Annales*, p. 167.
105 KDM ii. 373.
106 KDM i.2.

CHAPTER 19

Thirteenth-Century Abbots of the Cistercian Abbey at Wąchock*

This chapter is dedicated to the memory of Reverend Father Dr Eugeniusz Gerard Kocik, President of the Polish Cistercian Congregation and successor of the earlier abbots of Wąchock.

The Cistercian abbey at Wąchock is one of Poland's earlier Cistercian monasteries, established in the late-twelfth century. It was founded by Gedko, Bishop of Kraków, a member of the Wojsławice-Powała clan,[1] and it is generally accepted that this foundation dates to 1179.[2] The origins of this Cistercian institution — its endowment, benefactors, medieval history, and the controversies surrounding it — have been widely discussed in scholarship.[3] Nonetheless, a complete history of the Cistercians of Wąchock is still pending, with a survey of the full period of the abbey's operations between the late twelfth century and the early nineteenth century yet to be undertaken.[4] In this period, Wąchock Abbey was not only an important component of the historical and cultural mosaic of its immediate region, but also of Poland more broadly and even, to some extent, of wider Europe. Among the important, yet underdeveloped, issues related to the abbey is the complete and critical reconstruction of the catalogue of local abbots. Although a catalogue of the superiors of the local community was compiled in the seventeenth century, and subsequent abbots were scrupulously registered until 1737,[5] this cannot serve as a basis for medieval studies. The reason for this is simple: it appears that the writer who undertook the task of compiling the list of abbots in the early seventeenth century had

---

* Original publication: Józef Dobosz, 'Trzynastowieczni opaci klasztoru cystersów w Wąchocku', in *Ingenio et humanitate. Studia z dziejów zakonu cystersów i Kościoła na ziemiach polskich*, ed. by Andrzej Marek Wyrwa (Katowice: Biblioteka Śląska, 2007), pp. 61–70.
1 See Chapter 6 in this volume and Dobosz, 'Wokół fundatora', pp. 37–49.
2 See Niwiński, *Opactwo cystersów w Wąchocku*, pp. 27–28; Dobosz, 'Wokół fundatora', pp. 41–42; Chapter 6 in this volume.
3 For a summary of earlier research in this field, see Niwiński, *Opactwo cystersów w Wąchocku*. See also Massalski and Olszewski, eds, *Z dziejów opactwa cystersów w Wąchocku*; Dobosz and Wetesko, 'Wąchock', pp. 328–40.
4 The time from the beginning of the foundation until the dissolution of the monastery encompasses the period 1179–1819.
5 For the description of this manuscript catalogue, see Niwiński, 'Średniowieczni opaci klasztoru wąchockiego', pp. 34–36.

no access to the pertinent historical sources. As such, the catalogue's record of medieval abbots derives from the writer's own hypotheses and conjectures rather than the actual state of affairs. For the period from the beginning of the history of the abbey until 1501, twenty-nine names of abbots are listed in the catalogue, with accompanying information about the year of each abbot's death and the duration of his administration of the monastery. From this group, as Mieczysław Niwiński has established, only four are real figures, mainly of the fifteenth-century.[6] For the thirteenth century, the catalogue lists the following names of ten *abbates* of Wąchock: Haymo (1212, twenty-three years), Lambert (1227, fifteen years), Ignacy (1236, nine years), Walerian (1250, fourteen years), Gotard (1255, five years), Pankracy (1264, nine years), Rudolf (1275, eleven years), Melchiades (1284, nine years), Nazar (1289, five years) and Remigiusz (1301, twelve years).[7] This list clearly shows that Haymo must have been the first superior of Wąchock Abbey. Accordingly, Haymo should have arrived with the first convent around 1179. However, the writer indicates he died in 1212 and held the office for twenty-three years, the calculation of which indicates that Haymo would have arrived in 1189. This is probably an error on the part of the writer. In noting that this information did not coincide with the analysis of medieval sources, Niwiński rejected almost the entire list of thirteenth-century abbots, with reservations only about the first of them, Haymo.[8] Nevertheless, the task at hand is to follow the sources and reconstruct as complete a list of the earliest abbots of Wąchock as possible.

A survey of the earliest historical sources containing references to the Wąchock Cistercians reveals information about the names of the abbots who ruled the monastery in the twelfth century. The first of them, *abbas de Camina Guido* appears only in the diplomas of Leszek the White dated 1206 and 1208.[9] The pages of a handwritten catalogue make no mention of him, nor does he appear in other written records. Niwiński's suggestion that he may have participated in the 1210 congress held on the occasion of the consecration of the Cistercian monastery church in Jędrzejów by Vincentius, Bishop of Kraków, is partially confirmed by a forged document issued by the bishop.[10] An unidentified *abbas de Cavnna* is listed as a witness to the tithes granted to Jędrzejów Abbey by Vincentius.[11] This is most likely the abbot *de Camina* (Kamienna), or rather of Wąchock, because it is how the sources dubbed him in the early days of his reign,[12] but whether it was Guido is unclear. It may be worth risking a hypothesis that he was the first abbot of Wąchock

---

6 See Niwiński, 'Średniowieczni opaci klasztoru wąchockiego', p. 35, note 1.
7 Ibid.
8 Ibid., p. 33.
9 MPP tabl. 38–39; KDM i.4.
10 Niwiński, 'Średniowieczni opaci klasztoru wąchockiego', p. 4.
11 KDM ii.380. For discussion of the document see Mieszkowski, *Studia nad dokumentami katedry krakowskiej*, pp. 105–06.
12 Niwiński, *Opactwo cystersów w Wąchocku*, pp. 28–34.

and that he died sometime around 1210; several dozen years of administering the community was certainly not unusual at the time, as is addressed below. He perhaps arrived at the head of the first convent shortly after 1179,[13] and went about performing the duties of the superior of the community for thirty years. Such a solution seems closer to reality than any attempt to legitimise the apocryphal Abbot Haymo from the manuscript catalogue as Niwiński seemed to suggest.[14]

Another abbot of Wąchock is mentioned by name in a document issued on 18 October 1219 in Wiślica, concerning the settlement of the dispute between the Premonstratensians and the Benedictines over St Vincent's Abbey at Wrocław. Among the witnesses of this event is found Hugo, Abbot *de Vancoz*.[15] This is the only record that reveals the name of this abbot. He was, perhaps, succeeded by Walo who, on 11 May 1234, exchanged the tithes from the villages of Mikorek and Wielice for Łęcznia and Modrzany with Henryk, Provost of the canonry at Miechów. Not only did the abbey document issued on this occasion provide the name of the abbot, but also the composition of almost the entire convent in Wąchock: it lists Prior Wiardus, Subprior Piotr, Treasurer Martyr, *Custos* Adam, Cantor Bogusław, Subcellarius Teobald, Infirmarian Jan, bailiff Wilhelm, and friars Gerard, Maurycy, and Jan.[16] In total, twelve monks from Wąchock are listed, including the abbot. This is the only record from this period that gives such precise information about the composition of the convent.

Generally, there are few challenges to interpreting the written records that record the names of the next abbots of Wąchock Abbey. Niwiński determined the succession of two superiors of the community named Markusz and Marcin.[17] A forgery dated 8 May 1260, which contains a list of monastic estates, states that the Lisów estate along with another village was purchased for the Cistercians of Wąchock by *Marcussius abbas de Wanchock*,[18] and a similar statement can be found in Jan Długosz's *Liber benecifiorum*.[19] These are the only references to this abbot; other references to the abbots of Wąchock from this time are to Abbot Marcin. According to Niwiński,

---

13 The date of the foundation of Wąchock Abbey is arbitrarily set to 1179, though to which point in the complicated foundation process this refers is unknown. See Dobosz, 'Wokół fundatora', from p. 41; Chapter 6 in this volume.
14 Niwiński, 'Średniowieczni opaci klasztoru wąchockiego', pp. 4, 33.
15 KDW i.106; Niwiński suggests that Hugo was not only a witness but also a judge in the dispute, 'Średniowieczni opaci klasztoru wąchockiego', p. 5. However, judging from the content and composition of the document, it seems that Hugo was only a witness of the events that took place in Wiślica in October 1219, clearly indicated by his position in the witness list, the naming of eight individual judges, and the phrase that precedes the names of Hugo and Bishop Iwo: *in presentia*.
16 KDM ii.410.
17 Niwiński, 'Średniowieczni opaci klasztoru wąchockiego', pp. 6, 33.
18 Niwiński, *Opactwo cystersów w Wąchocku*, p. 161.
19 LB iii, p, 409.

Marcin is mentioned for the first time as late as in 1250, as a witness in one of the documents of Bolesław V. Niwiński dates his administration to the years 1250–1274.[20] However, in Bolesław V's diploma concerning the exchange of some villages between the Cistercians of Wąchock and the collegiate church in Sandomierz, issued together with his mother Duchess Grzymisława on 20 March 1243, there is mention of *Martinus abbas claustri prefati* (of Wąchock).[21] Thus, it seems that it was in Sandomierz in 1243 that Abbot Marcin first appears, and his name recurs in several other documents. He is mentioned as a witness in diplomas relating to the grants for the Cistercians of Mogiła. First, he is named in a charter of Duke Bolesław V issued on St Urban's day in 1250 at a rally in Kraków regarding the granting of rights to a farmstead in Czyżyny.[22] Second, in the same year, he appears in a charter of Wacław, chaplain of St Adalbert's Church in Kraków, regarding the sale of a farmstead in the village of Czyżyny then held by a monastery of the Dominicans of Kraków, together with the abbots of Koprzywnica, Jędrzejów, and Lubiąż.[23] Marcin is referred to twice in the 1260 forgery, both when he purchased land from the brothers Florian and Wolisz, and then in the case of Dołuszyce.[24] In addition, his name is found in a document of 1254,[25] in another of 17 April 1255 in Zawichost,[26] and in a diploma of Bolesław V dated 8 May 1274.[27] Earlier, on 8 May 1271, in Kraków, Abbot N. gained permission from Bolesław to apply German law to monastic villages,[28] but this record probably also refers to Marcin, as Niwiński rightly assumed.[29]

Only these references to the abbots Markusz and Marcin have been preserved, and it follows from them that the former was probably the direct successor of Walon. Since Marcin appeared for the first time in 1243, Markusz must have been active in 1230/40s, and at the time he probably purchased the

---

20 Niwiński, 'Średniowieczni opaci klasztoru wąchockiego', pp. 6–7, 33.
21 *Zbiór dokumentów małopolskich* iv.875.
22 Janota, ed., *Zbiór dyplomów klasztoru mogilskiego* 22.
23 Janota, ed., *Zbiór dyplomów klasztoru mogilskiego* 23, 25. The latter document from August 1250 is a certification of legal action from the previous document.
24 Niwiński, *Opactwo cystersów w Wąchocku*, p. 161. See also LB iii, pp. 409–10, in which the conflation of abbots Markusz and Marcin proves that Jan Długosz accessed the Wąchock forgery dated 8 May 1260.
25 KDP i.43, in which Legate Opizo appoints him as guardian of the abbey of the canons regular in Czerwińsk (next to Archbishop of Gniezno).
26 KKK i.42.
27 KDM ii.480, in which Bolesław IV certifies the acquisition of the village of Pakosławice (Pękosławice) by Wąchock Abbey.
28 KDM ii.477. The document has been identified as a forgery, Niwiński, *Opactwo cystersów w Wąchocku*, pp. 17–20.
29 Niwiński, 'Średniowieczni opaci klasztoru wąchockiego', p. 6, note 6. The 1271 document is known only from the copy included in the seventeenth-century Wąchock cartulary; the monastic copyist used the transumpt of King Sigismund August from 1550. See KDM ii.477, p. 131; Niwiński, *Opactwo cystersów w Wąchocku*, pp. 17–18.

village of Lisów for the monastery.³⁰ The period of Marcin's administration of the abbey looks more impressive and probably covers over 30 years, from at least 1243 to 1274. The administration of this abbot is of particular importance for the Cistercians of Wąchock, as it was he who most likely restored the monastery following the destruction caused by the Tatar invasions of 1241 and 1259–1260.³¹ He also managed to convince Duke Bolesław V to grant the right to a number of privileges to the monastery, and was a frequent witness to documents issued by this duke and other leading men. Unfortunately, the date of the death of Abbot Marcin cannot be determined, so it is not known who went before the duke to supplicate for the confirmation of the entire monastic property, which Bolesław issued in Stopnica on 11 June 1275.³² A privilege of a similar nature, issued on 22 January 1284 in Osiek by Duke Leszek the Black, mentions Abbot Szymon,³³ probably the direct successor of Marcin. This is the only mention of him that has been identified from extant sources. It seems that he was a only short-term abbot in Wąchock, since in the following year Jan is found fulfilling this function.

Jan's rule in Wąchock also turned out to be short-lived as, in 1285, following some unspecified 'scandal', a visitation was organised to Sulejów Abbey. Jan, as the abbot, was appointed as one of the inspectors by the Cistercian general chapter, and was supposed to resolve the issue together with the abbots of Koprzywnica, Szczyrzyc, and Byszewo.³⁴ The inspection took place at the turn of winter and spring 1285 and, on 10 March the same year, the commission (composed of the abbots Jan of Wąchock, Stefan of Koprzywnica, Baldwin of Szczyrzyc, and Mikołaj of Byszewo) issued a special ordinance on the reform of the property of Sulejów Abbey. As a result, the property was divided into two parts, and the Sulejów monks had to move to Byszewo or Szpetal.³⁵ These decisions were soon approved on 23 June by Hugo, Abbot of Morimond,

---

30 Niwiński does not provide a chronology of the acquisition of Lisów in his analysis of the monastery's oldest endowment. Judging from the 1260 forgery, it can be concluded that this estate was most likely acquired in the late 1230s. See Niwiński, *Opactwo cystersów w Wąchocku*, pp. 45–61, 158–63.

31 For more information on these events, see Ulanowski, *Drugi napad Tatarów na Polskę*, pp. 282–313; Krakowski, *Polska w walce*. The consequences of the second Tartar invasion for the Cistercian abbeys in Małopolska (Koprzywnica, Jędrzejów, Wąchock, Sulejów, Mogiła, and Ludźmierz) were described by the abbot of the Cistercian monastery at Rudy in a letter to the abbot of Velehrad. He wrote not only of the destruction of Cistercian property, but the deaths of around fifty monks. KDM ii.457.

32 KDM ii.481.

33 KDM ii.498.

34 The general chapter issued a decision to visit Sulejów Abbey around the autumn of 1284, Canivez, ed., *Statuta Capitulorum Generalium Ordinis Cisterciensis* iii, p. 232; Winter, *Die Cistercienser* iii, p. 243.

35 The content of the ordinance is reproduced in a document issued by the inspectors, KDW iii.2034 (553a); Ulanowski, 'Dokumenty kujawskie i mazowieckie', p. 218. For a description of these events and their circumstances, see Dobosz, 'Kryzys w opactwie cysterskim', pp. 133–46.

as the mother-abbot of Sulejów.³⁶ Further events unfolded quickly. On 15 August 1285, Hugo's document and decisions were validated by Jakub Świnka, Archbishop of Gniezno, and just slightly earlier, new monks from nearby Wąchock, headed by Abbot Jan, moved to Sulejów.³⁷ The new abbot renewed the agreement with the outgoing convent, and eventually the monks who came from Wąchock became the tenants of Sulejów Abbey.³⁸ Jan, therefore, administered Wąchock Abbey for only a few months or about a year. What is primarily learned from these events is that the Wąchock convent was strong enough to maintain so large and important a post as Sulejów.³⁹

Jan's successor was probably Idzi, who is mentioned in a diploma dated 25 May 1288, on the occasion of the exchange of a village with Duke Władysław I Łokietek (the elbow-high).⁴⁰ His presence was recorded again on 13 October 1289 in Lubiąż, where Cistercian abbots ratified the charter attributed to Pełka, Archbishop of Gniezno, for Sulejów Abbey.⁴¹ There are no further references to the abbots of Wąchock in the thirteenth-century written record. Thus there are eight of them in total, and it seems that they form a fairly coherent list, although it is entirely feasible that the name of some thirteenth-century superior of the Wąchock community has been lost somewhere in the darkness of history.

The position of Wąchock Abbey in the hierarchy of the Church in Poland must have been relatively high during the rule of these eight abbots. This assessment does not rest on the number of properties the monastery accumulated alone.⁴² The abbots of Wąchock were often appointed as mediators of various internal disputes, and the general chapter of the Cistercians entrusted them quite regularly with visiting tasks in other Cistercian institutions. This testifies to their personal merits, as well as the role of the monastery managed by them. Finally, the local abbey was strong enough to join the processes of establishing and settling new Cistercian outposts. However, the first reference to the abbots of Wąchock in the statutes of the Cistercian General Chapter, given under 1214, does not extol or detail the merits or tasks assigned to Wąchock Abbey. Rather, it provides an anecdote of an abbot who went to Rome and was assaulted and robbed on his return journey, and, for this very reason his absence from the annual general chapter was excused.⁴³ Unfortunately, it is not possible to identify whether the unlucky man was Guido or perhaps his successor Hugo.

---

36 KDW i.328; Ulanowski, 'Dokumenty kujawskie i mazowieckie', pp. 219–20.
37 KDW i.558. See also Dobosz, 'Kryzys w opactwie cysterskim', pp. 142–45.
38 Ulanowski, 'Dokumenty kujawskie i mazowieckie', pp. 220–21.
39 Niwiński, 'Średniowieczni opaci klasztoru wąchockiego', pp. 7–9.
40 For this document and another issued by Duke Władysław I, see Niwiński, *Opactwo cystersów w Wąchocku*, pp. 7, 76–77.
41 KDW i.593.
42 For the study of the economic development of Wąchock Abbey in the thirteenth century, see Niwiński, *Opactwo cystersów w Wąchocku*, pp. 35–118; Dobosz and Wetesko, 'Wąchock'.
43 Canivez, ed., *Statuta Capitulorum Generalium Ordinis Cisterciensis* i, p. 420. The abbot of Wąchock was also obliged to appear at the next chapter and to offer a personal explanation.

Another entry in the statutes of the Cistercian General Chapter, noted under 1220, refers to the Abbot of Wąchock being assigned to visit the site for the planned abbey at Mogiła near Kraków (or perhaps in Kacice or Prandocin?).[44] This mention certainly refers to Abbot Hugo, who, as noted, appeared in 1219 as a witness in the clash between the Benedictines and the Premonstratensians over St Vincent's Abbey. Hugo may also have been the Abbot of Wąchock who was appointed on 26 May 1218 by Pope Honorius III to a committee tasked with settling the conflict between Henryk I and Władysław Odonic over Kalisz.[45] It is also possible that it was under the reign of Abbot Hugo that the first daughter-house of Wąchock Abbey was established. This is suggested by the request registered under the year 1223 in the statutes of the Cistercian General Chapter to inspect the conditions of the prospective Cistercian foundation in Spisz.[46] Wąchock was to later become the mother-house of that Cistercian mission. Further decisions of the general chapter concerning the appointment of the Wąchock abbot as the inspector of the new foundation which was to be established in Podhale (later Szczyrzyc), date back to 1235.[47]

In 1243, an abbot of Wąchock, perhaps already Marcin, was appointed a mission of a different character. The abbot was obliged to settle a dispute between the monasteries in Paradyż and Lehnin, to report on this undertaking to the general chapter, and also resolve the conflict between a nunnery in the Meissen Diocese and its visitator, the Abbot of the Monastery of *Vallis s. Aegida*.[48] He played a similar role a year later, and this time the general chapter ordered him, together with the Abbot of Lubiąż, to resolve the otherwise unknown dispute between the abbots of Jędrzejów, who had brought a complaint to the general chapter, and Koprzywnica.[49] This was the last entry in the files of the general chapter from the first half of the thirteenth century, and the next reference to an abbot of Wąchock did not occur for another thirty-five years. In 1279, the general chapter recommended the Abbot of Wąchock, together with his Jędrzejów counterpart, visit the site of a future

---

44 Canivez, ed., *Statuta Capitulorum Generalium Ordinis Cisterciensis* i, p. 528. Here Iwo Odrowąż, Bishop of Kraków, requests the foundation of a new monastery with the site to be visited by the abbots of Lubiąż and *Camencium* (Kamieniec or Kamienna?). There can be no doubt that this was not about the Silesian Kamieniec, but about a monastery called in Latin *Camina* (or *Camina Minor*), that is Wąchock. See Ziętara, 'Opactwo wąchockie', pp. 52–53.
45 KDW i.99.
46 Canivez, ed., *Statuta Capitulorum Generalium Ordinis Cisterciensis* ii, p. 28. The abbey is known as Schawnik (formely, Szepesz), see Hervay, *Repertorium historicum*, pp. 172–80; Dobosz and Wetesko, 'Wąchock', p. 339; Ziętara, 'Opactwo wąchockie', p. 53.
47 See Canivez, ed., *Statuta Capitulorum Generalium Ordinis Cisterciensis* ii, p. 150; Ziętara, 'Opactwo wąchockie', pp. 53–54. As conjectured in Niwiński, 'Średniowieczni opaci klasztoru wąchockiego', p. 6, Walo was the abbot at the time.
48 Canivez, ed., *Statuta Capitulorum Generalium Ordinis Cisterciensis* ii, pp. 272. Neither Walo nor Markusz could have been the abbot at the time, see Ziętara, 'Opactwo wąchockie', p. 54.
49 Canivez, ed., *Statuta Capitulorum Generalium Ordinis Cisterciensis* ii, p. 287.

Cistercian foundation that was to be established by an unknown duke of Rus' (*Rusciae*).[50] Unfortunately, nothing definitive can be said of this project, and it most likely did not come to fruition. It is also impossible to determine which of the Wąchock abbots was in charge of the monastery at that time, whether Marcin or Szymon, if the abbacy had passed to him. The last entry in the statutes of the Cistercian General Chapter concerning the abbots of Wąchock was that mentioned above from 1284, regarding the visit to Sulejów Abbey. All in all, the materials collected in the files of the general chapter of the Cistercians reveal an interesting picture of the role and activities of the abbots of Wąchock and the Cistercian community under their administration. The missions they were appointed to were twofold: they included visits to the sites of prospective foundations, and the settlement of disputes and mediation between the opposing parties. They must have fulfilled them well, especially in the first half of the thirteenth century, and were often involved in matters concerning other Cistercian communities in north eastern Europe. In the second half of the century, their activities were relatively less intensive, but this was probably due to the destruction of monastic property and the need to focus on its reconstruction and internal matters. Once the most urgent problems had been resolved and new privileges obtained, the abbots of Wąchock were back in their former role (1279 and 1284–1285).

The approximately hundred-year rule of the first abbots of Wąchock resulted in the construction of an independent and large abbey that had been founded on a rather modest primary endowment.[51] The abbots quickly gained a stable political position among the Polish thirteenth-century clergy, which manifested itself in their participation in the resolution of intra-Church and state disputes. Above all, however, they were excellent hosts, a fact observable on two levels: construction (erection of the conventual church and monastery buildings in the thirteenth century) or, more broadly, cultural;[52] and the accumulation and consolidation of the property, and the efficient acquisition of privileges,[53] which led to the strengthening of the economic position of Wąchock Abbey. In addition, the monastery's abbots had to contend with historical adversities, especially with the Tatar invasions, although it seems that only Marcin, the longest-serving superior of thirteenth century Wąchock Abbey, was able to distinguish himself in this area. The final measure of their successes, however, was not only their visit and mediation in the Sulejów 'scandal' of 1285, but the fact that they took control of Sulejów Abbey after that community had been moved to Byszewo.

---

50 Canivez, ed., *Statuta Capitulorum Generalium Ordinis Cisterciensis* iii, p. 150.
51 See Niwiński, *Opactwo cystersów w Wąchocku*, pp. 35–38; Dobosz, 'Wokół fundatora', pp. 46–48; Chapter 6 in this volume.
52 For more detail, see Dobosz and Wetesko, 'Wąchock', pp. 334–36; Dobosz, 'Cystersi małopolscy', pp. 52–54; Chapter 19 in this volume.
53 See Niwiński, *Opactwo cystersów w Wąchocku*, p. 6; Dobosz, 'Wokół fundatora', pp. 331–33; Chapter 6 in this volume.

CHAPTER 20

The Cistercians in Małopolska and their Position in the Economy and Culture of Thirteenth-Century Poland*

The Cistercians first arrived on Polish soil around the mid-twelfth century, a congregation that had emerged from the Benedictine Order in the late eleventh century and undergone rapid development.[1] The order attracted the interest of members of both the ruling dynasty and Polish nobility. Its outposts in Łekno — Pałuki and Jędrzejów, the Sandomierz territories — were the earliest Cistercian communities on the Vistula, Oder, and Warta rivers.[2] In the following decades, Grey Monks dispersed to all districts of the Piast realm and, at the end of the thirteenth century, there were almost thirty male convents and a handful of nunneries in Poland.

For the past 150 years, Polish historians have investigated both the Cistercian as an order within Poland, and their individual monasteries.[3] The Cistercian communities of Małopolska, or more precisely of the Kraków and Sandomierz regions, have always occupied a special place in this research, probably because of their size and importance, but also because it was here that the Polish branch of the Cistercian Order best survived the period of monastic dissolution. Historians have thoroughly investigated the origins of the six Cistercian monasteries in Małopolska founded in the twelfth–thirteenth centuries, with most of the abbeys being

---

* Original publication: Józef Dobosz, 'Cystersi małopolscy, ich miejsce w gospodarce i kulturze Polski XIII wieku', *Rocznik Bocheński*, 5 (2001), 49–56.
1 For the origins and organisational structure of the order see Wyrwa, 'Cystersi. Geneza, duchowość, organizacja', pp. 11–39; Wyrwa, 'Rozprzestrzenianie się cystersów', pp. 25–43.
2 Excavations carried out in the area of the former monastery at Łekno provided information about the abbey's origins, see Wyrwa, 'Łekno', pp. 417–21; Wyrwa, *Procesy fundacyjne*, pp. 53–82. Cf. Dobosz, 'Dokument fundacyjny', pp. 53–83 and Chapter 3 in this volume. For the beginnings of Jędrzejów Abbey see Dobosz, 'Proces fundacyjny', pp. 40–79; Chapter 4 in this volume.
3 Research on the Cistercians in Poland has been summarised in Chłopocka, 'Fundacje cysterskie w Polsce', pp. 7–23. Materials from four Cistercian symposiums that took place in 1985 (Błażejewko), 1987 (Gniezno), 1993 (Poznań) and 1998 (Kraków-Mogiła) have also appeared in print: Strzelczyk, ed., *Historia i kultura cystersów*; Strzelczyk, ed., *Cystersi w kulturze średniowiecznej Europy*; Strzelczyk, ed., *Dzieje, kultura artystyczna*; Wyrwa and Dobosz, eds, *Cystersi w społeczeństwie Europy Środkowej*. These publications partially summarise research on various threads of the history of the Polish Cistercians, while a more complete 'state of the field' overview can be found in the two volumes of MCP.

the subjects of monographs.[4] Scholars have also showed significant interest in the economic processes taking place within the estates of individual institutions, especially the endowment of lands, regalia, immunities, tithes, and so on.[5] The fields of art and architectural studies have taken a robust interest in the Polish Cistercians and can boast enormous critical and erudite achievements. Much commentary has been produced on the architecture of the churches and monasteries in Jędrzejów, Sulejów, Koprzywnica, Wąchock or Mogiła, with only Szczyrzyc seeming to have been generally neglected by researchers.[6] Various studies have also been written on the role of the Cistercians in Poland in the cultural sphere, extending to their activities in Małopolska,[7] although on this topic many questions are yet to be answered. Yet for all the questions that have been resolved in relation to the Cistercians of Małopolska, it should be noted that there are still no studies that can be considered to provide a comprehensive portrayal of this important congregation. Moreover, many issues need to be revisited and their study resumed, while, in the case of some structures, complex archaeological and architectural research seems to be necessary that may shed new light on their history.

The Cistercians came to Poland when the fragmentation of the region was still in its early stages, and as far as Małopolska is concerned, the order first settled in Jędrzejów. The exact date of the monastery's foundation is unknown, but the entire foundation process unfolded between around 1140 and 1167. The abbey was founded by one of the most outstanding archbishops of Gniezno of his time, Janik Gryfita, whose initiative was probably supported by the entire clan, first among them Janik's brother, Klemens. It seems important that the new outpost of Grey Monks was located in their ancestral village of Brzeźnica, which was granted along with the church and its endowment to the abbey. Jędrzejów Abbey was among the best-endowed religious communities in Poland: by the end of the twelfth century, it had received forty-two villages, tithes from more than forty others, as well as extensive immunity and regalia.[8]

---

4   On the history of Jędrzejów Abbey, see Helcel, 'O klasztorze jędrzejowskim', pp. 125–228; Olszewski, ed., *Cystersi w Polsce*, and Chapter 4 in this volume. For Wąchock Abbey, see Niwiński, *Opactwo cystersów w Wąchocku*, pp. 1–164; Massalski and Olszewski, eds, *Z dziejów opactwa cystersów*, and Chapters 6 and 18 in this volume. For Sulejów Abbey, see Mitkowski, *Początki klasztoru cystersów*, and Chapter 5 in this volume. On Koprzywnica Abbey, see Kozłowska-Budkowa and Szczur, 'Dzieje opactwa cystersów', pp. 5–76. For the monasteries of Mogiła and Szczyrzyc, see the relevent chapters of MCP.
5   See for example, Matuszewski, *Immunitet ekonomiczny*; Kaczmarczyk, *Immunitet sądowy i jurysdykcja poimmunitetowa*; R. Grodecki, *Początki immunitetu w Polsce*.
6   For an overview of the substantial literature on this topic, see Splitt, 'Stan badań archeologiczno-architektonicznych', pp. 225–48; Kubica, 'Katalog zabytków wczesnośredniowiecznej', pp. 131–89.
7   For example, Dunin-Wąsowicz, 'Rola cystersów', pp. 9–23; MCP.
8   Dobosz, 'Proces fundacyjny', pp. 56–79.

Soon, both the dukes of the Piast dynasty and their leading magnates began emulating the initiative launched by Janik in Małopolska and his contemporary, Zbylut of the Pałuki clan, in Wielkopolska. As early as 1176, Kazimierz II, then Duke of Sandomierz, began the process of establishing and endowing the monastery at Sulejów, which was completed sometime prior to 1191. The Cistercians settled on the border of his realm along the Pilica River, near the old river crossing and the customs house.[9] In turn, in the years prior to 1179, Gedko, Bishop of Kraków, undertook to establish a Cistercian monastery in his episcopal estates, an initiative that Kazimierz soon endorsed. Around the same time, the monks from Morimond who had previously settled outposts in Jędrzejów and Sulejów arrived at Wąchock, located on the edge of the Świętokrzyskie Mountains.[10] Finally, the foundation of Koprzywnica Abbey is believed to date from 1185, although to which point in the foundation process this date refers cannot be ascertained.[11] Koprzywnica was founded by Mikołaj Bogoria and endowed with family estates.

The foundation of Koprzywnica marked the end of the establishment and endowment of new Cistercian outposts in Kraków and Sandomierz for several dozen years. This was mostly driven by two concerns. The first was the need to ensure that the already existing Cistercian foundations were well established and prepared for their future function. The second was the growth of decentralisation processes and the weakening of the principate, which led to the dukes and nobility focusing their attention and resources on the struggle for Kraków.

Sometime before 1218, the Odrowąż clan endeavoured to establish a monastery of Grey Monks in their estates. Originally, one of the representatives of this clan, Wisław, wanted to settle them in Prandocin or Kacice in the vicinity of one of the major clan abodes. Ultimately, however, the initiative was taken over by Iwo, Bishop of Kraków, who settled the Cistercians brought from Lubiąż in the village of Mogiła near Kraków, on the Vistula River. The foundation process was quite complicated and stretched over the period 1218–1225, although the foundation charter was issued by Bishop Iwo in 1222.[12]

There was one further Cistercian institution in Małopolska: Szczyrzyc Abbey. The abbey was founded in the 1230s, again by a noble clan, in this case the Gryfici. Teodor, Voivode of Kraków, is commonly believed to be its founder. The origins of the abbey are shrouded in mystery; although Ludźmierz was originally allocated as the site for the foundation, the monks were eventually settled in Szczyrzyc.[13]

---

9 Dobosz, 'Okoliczności i motywy fundacji', pp. 177–78.
10 Dobosz, 'Wokół fundatora', pp. 37–49. See also Dobosz, *Działalność fundacyjna*, pp. 74–77; cf. Niwiński, *Opactwo cystersów w Wąchocku*, pp. 25–35.
11 See Kozłowska-Budkowa and Szczur, 'Dzieje opactwa cystersów'; Dobosz, *Działalność fundacyjna*, pp. 77–78.
12 Janota, ed., *Zbiór dokumentów klasztoru mogilskiego* 3.
13 On the beginnings of the Szczyrzc foundation, see Zakrzewski, *Najdawniejsze dzieje*, pp. 1–2.

Figure 14. The interior of the Cistercian monastery at Wąchock. Photo P. Namiota.

Initially supported by both the founders and dukes (Kazimierz II, Leszek the White, Grzymisława), the Cistercians who settled in Małopolska gradually established the basis for an independent existence. Typically, upon arrival, a Cistercian would find a church and some makeshift buildings in the site allocated for their abode. This was certainly the case in Jędrzejów and Mogiła;[14] in other cases, archaeological research has not provided conclusive evidence for the location of the original monastery church.[15] The Cistercians devoted the first years of their residence to preparing the facilities required for *officium divinum* and securing all the economic needs of their institution. The donated churches were thus embellished; land holdings began to be consolidated; and the dukes, bishops, and nobility were earnestly and humbly asked for further grants (mainly immunities, tithes, regalia). Once their institutions were bolstered, the Cistercians began to erect new, more magnificent monastic churches and other buildings. The oldest monastery at Małopolska, Jędrzejów Abbey, completed the construction of a three-nave Romanesque basilica as early as 1210. It was

---

14 See Dobosz, 'Proces fundacyjny', pp. 46–50; Lechowicz, 'Wyniki badań archeologicznych', pp. 223–32.

15 This is particularly unclear in the case of Wąchock. See Pianowski, 'W sprawie domniemanej rezydencji', pp. 57–66; Dobosz, *Wokół fundatora*, pp. 37–49, and Chapter 6 in this volume. The same can be said of Sulejów and Koprzywnica Abbeys, though see respectively, Świechowski, *Opactwo sulejowskie*; Polanowski, 'Architektura klasztoru pocysterskiego', pp. 201–20.

consecrated by Vincentius, Bishop of Kraków.[16] The construction of the Koprzywnica church was completed soon after, around the year 1217, and the church in Sulejów, dedicated to St Tomasz Becket, was consecrated in 1232.[17] The church in Wąchock was finished at a point prior to the Tatar invasion of 1241.[18]

All these churches looked impressive, and their architecture mimicked the classical architectural patterns used by Cistercians all over Europe.[19] It was in this area that the Grey Monks revealed their culture-forming role, with Władysław Łuszczkiewicz going so far as to describe them as 'the pioneers of Gothicism in Poland'.[20] These outstanding construction initiatives of the first half of the thirteenth century would not have been not possible if it had not been for the importation of technical expertise, both in terms of planning and engineering, through links with mother abbeys. At the same time, this could not have happened without the considerable economic assistance of Polish dukes and nobility. Thus, it is around this time that numerous grants begin to appear in the documentary record that offered quick and often long-term profits (beavers, salt, mills, the right to mint coins).

The Cistercians, therefore, significantly contributed to the development of architecture in Poland. At the same time, by supplicating for documents validating foundations and endowments from dukes and bishops in the twelfth and thirteenth centuries, they also played a role in legitimating the written document as a means of evidence in court proceedings, and thereby in its dissemination. As addressed elsewhere in this volume, this extended to the Cistercians' production of documents in their own scriptoria, and quite often to the fabrication of the so-called formal forgeries wherever they lacked written evidence for their property holdings (particularly true of the monasteries in Sulejów, Jędrzejów, and Wąchock).[21] As such, it will not be an exaggeration to say that the Cistercians contributed to the reception of the document in Poland and, at the same time, improved a legal culture that had previously been based on oral decisions; the foundation and endowment of Church institutions were rarely documented before the mid-twelfth century. Previously established monastic houses, such as those of the Benedictines, did not initially demand charters as confirmation of foundation or of grants; however, the Cistercians who came into Poland from the mid-twelfth century were well aware of the significance of the written document, an innovation already quite common in the West. The chancellery functions fulfilled by the Cistercians is an interesting aspect of their introducing the written document

---

16 KDM ii.380.
17 See Mitkowski, *Początki klasztoru cystersów*, pp. 157–59, 319–20.
18 Dobosz, *Wokół fundatora*, pp. 37–49.
19 For more detail on the architecture of the Polish Cistercians see MCP.
20 Łuszczkiewicz, 'Pionierowie gotycyzmu w Polsce', pp. 112–35, 342–64.
21 See Dobosz, 'Trzynastowieczne falsyfikaty', pp. 225–37; Niwiński, *Opactwo cystersów w Wąchocku*, pp. 7–17, and Chapter 7 in this volume.

into the legal culture of Poland. In thirteenth-century sources, references to the Cistercians as ducal chaplains can be found,[22] although today it is thought that the office was merely titular, rather than being directly related to work in ducal chancelleries.

The most outstanding Polish intellectuals of the twelfth and thirteenth centuries were also variously associated with the Cistercians. They had a faithful advocate in Janik Gryfita, Archbishop of Gniezno; Mateusz, Bishop of Kraków, corresponded with Bernard of Clairvaux; Vincentius, the chronicler and Bishop of Kraków was a resident of the convent in Jędrzejów. Iwo Odrowąż, Bishop of Kraków, also established close contacts with the Cistercians, a fact that requires further research, as he is most often associated with the intellectual mendicant circle.

The Cistercians also left their mark on the economic life of the thirteenth century. Previous scholarship, especially German, saw them as pioneers of culture and economy in Poland.[23] More recently, such theses have been seriously modified, especially with regard to the Cistercians' economic impacts. When they came to Poland, the Cistercians received estates that were already firmly embedded within the local economic landscape. These were usually well-developed and populated complexes of land estates, heavily buttressed by immunity exemptions, markets, regalia, salt grants, and tithes. The fate of the monasteries was close the heart of the founders, their descendants, and the members of the ruling dynasty. The monks were not settled *in cruda radice* but in areas boasting centuries-old settlement traditions, though with Wąchock Abbey serving to some degree as an exception. Individual monasteries usually obtained economic independence some decades after their foundation, and it was then that they began the above-mentioned large-scale construction projects. In the case of the Małopolska abbeys, this happened between the end of the twelfth century and the 1270s. This process was to some extent shaken by the Tatar invasions, but thanks to the support of the patrons and Duke Bolesław V, those effects were short-lived. In the thirteenth century, most monasteries in the Kraków and Sandomierz regions carried out numerous transactions of purchase and sale of villages or other properties. Estates were also exchanged in an attempt to dispose of lands that failed to bring the expected benefits, and to consolidate villages into complexes. In this, it was likely that the Cistercian communities in Poland were looking to the organisational principles and centralist models of their order. All the best features of this centralisation of the congregation and the ordinances of the general chapter were employed to create thriving, economically independent institutions. It can be said without hyperbole that the Cistercians used all the finest features of their order to organise the estates they received in Małopolska into the best possible support structures.

22   Dobosz, *Działalność fundacyjna*, pp. 153–55.
23   For an overview of this research, see MCP.

Another matter than should be raised is the salt economy of individual Cistercian institutions in the Sandomierz and Kraków regions. Cistercian convents frequently received salt grants upon their foundation. This happened in the case of Sulejów and Jędrzejów, which were granted the right to receive thirteen carts of Rus' salt annually from the customs house in Sandomierz. In addition, Sulejów received a saltern in Kraków, probably in Wieliczka.[24] Mogiła Abbey received salt from Iwo Odrowąż.[25] Koprzywnica and Wąchock received rights to salt grants from salt deposits near Kraków, most likely from Leszek the White.[26] However, apart from Wąchock Abbey, none of the Cistercian institutions showed any greater initiative in the practice of salt mining. They were rather passive recipients of ducal privileges in this regard until the great salt reform of Bolesław V around 1277.[27]

For unknown reasons, Wąchock Abbey became involved in mining activity, not only in relation to salt, but also to various types of metal ores. The Cistercians of Wąchock only developed metallurgical activity on a large scale by the turn of the Middle Ages and early modern times, opening smelters and *fabrica ferii* in Bzin and Starachowice, and using fossil resources from the Świętokrzyskie Mountains. However, their involvement in this area goes back to a privilege issued to the monastery in 1249 by Bolesław V, whereby Wąchock Abbey received extensive rights allowing the mining and prospecting of gold, silver, lead, and tin. In terms of salt, the Cistercians were granted the right to search for salt in Bolesław's principality in Kraków and Sandomierz, and to re-establish the productivity of previously discovered salt springs which had been destroyed. The monastery was also granted the right to sell salt and, after the renovation of the damaged salt spring in Bochnia, the right to its entire production for a year, and then to one third of its production.[28]

Why Wąchock Abbey received this type of privilege from Duke Bolesław is hard to say. The Bochnia salt grant was explained by a 1249 document that emphasised that the site, from which the monastery took 1/10 of production, was destroyed by a landslide.[29] The initial privilege was probably granted by Leszek the White during the construction of the church. Bolesław thus allowed the monastery to restore the salt spring and transferred a significant part of the income to the abbey, likely as compensation for the loss. This, however, does not explain why the monastery was granted permission to search for precious and non-ferrous metals. It seems that the Cistercians of Wąchock distinguished themselves in this area in some way in their estates located on

---

24 Mitkowski, *Początki klasztoru cystersów*, pp. 313–14.
25 Janota, ed., *Zbiór dokumentów klasztoru mogilskiego* 2.
26 Niwiński, *Opactwo cystersów w Wąchocku*, p. 159 (document issued by Bolesław IV dated 8 May 1260).
27 For Bolesław IV's salt reform of *c.* 1277 see Grzesiowski and Piotrowicz, 'Sól małopolska w nadaniach', pp. 133–35.
28 KDP i.
29 Ibid.

the northern edge of the Świętokrzyskie Mountains, which were a reservoir of various types of minerals. These skills were probably brought by monks from the West which, as Jan Długosz suggests, came to Wąchock from Italy.[30] What these skills consisted of and what successes were in the thirteenth century, apart from the renovation the Bochnia salt spring, is unclear.

This very general and brief overview shows that the Cistercians performed a key economic and culture-forming role in thirteenth-century Małopolska. The Cistercians had close contacts with the ducal court in Kraków, and with the courts of particular bishops of Kraków, most notably Pełka and Iwo Odrowąż. They often appeared as witnesses in documents issued by both dukes and bishops. The close ties between the Cistercians and the twelfth-and thirteenth-century intellectual elite are also worth noting, as is the Cistercians' participation in the reception and shaping of the Polish document and, indirectly, the chancellery, leading to the construction of a new legal culture. It is necessary to emphasise once again their notable participation in the introduction and final formation of architectural patterns that are still visible in the cultural landscape of Małopolska. Rather than bringing models of a new economy, however, the Cistercians brought excellent organisational principles to their estates, expertly integrating those into the existing environment. The thirteenth century undoubtedly saw the apogee of the successes of the Cistercian monasteries in Małopolska. All of them prospered economically, built churches and residences, and skilfully participated in the shaping of settlement processes. The 1285 crisis in Sulejów Abbey, which was resolved thanks to the intervention of the general chapter of the Cistercians, was a small flaw in this picture.[31] However, despite their close liaison with the Piast dukes — mainly the rulers of Kraków, Sandomierz, and Mazovia — the Cistercians were not active in politics until the end of the thirteenth century. It is only at the turn of the fourteenth century that they became more visible in that area. Most Cistercians supported Władysław I, who fought for the unification of Polish lands under his rule and granted them rights to several privileges.

30 Jan Długosz, *Annales*, p. 119.
31 See Mitkowski, *Początki klasztoru cystersów*, pp. 202–74.

Bibliography

Archival Sources

Gniezno, Archdiocesan Archives, sygn. Dypl. Tr 2.
Gniezno, Archdiocesan Archives, sygn. Dypl. Gn. 3
Gniezno, Archdiocesan Archives, sygn. Dypl. Gn. 4
Gniezno, Archdiocesan Archives, sygn. Dypl. Gn. 1237
Kartoteka Słownika Historyczno-Geograficznego Wielkopolski, Oddział IH PAN w Poznaniu
Poznań, State Archives, *Spuścizny osób i rodzin – Hockenbeck-2*, folder II, years 1145–1400, s. 23, no. 1.
Poznań, State Archives, sygn. kl. Łekno A 1

Primary Sources

Bolz, Bogdan, 'Nieznany katalog arcybiskupów gnieźnieńskich', *Archiwa, Biblioteki i Muzea Kościelne*, 11 (1954), 271–85
Büsching, J. G. G., *Die Urkunden des Klosters Leubus* (Breslau: Verein für Schlesische Geschichte, 1821)
Bużeński, Stanisław, *Żywoty arcybiskupów gnieźnieńskich, prymasów Korony Polskiej i Wielkiego Księstwa Litewskiego, od Wilibalda do Andrzeja Olszowskiego włącznie*, trans. by Michał Bohusz-Szyszko (Wilno: Nakładem R. Rafałowicza, 1860)
Callier, Edmund, *Kronika żałobna utraconej w granicach W. X. Poznańskiego ziemi polskiej. Powiat wągrowiecki* (Poznań: Drukarnia Dziennika Poznańskiego, 1894)
Canivez, Joseph-Marie, *Statuta Capitulorum Generalium Ordinis Cisterciensis ab anno 1116 ad annum 1786*, 2 vols (Louvain: Bureaux de la Revue, 1933)
Damalewicz, Stefan, *Series archiepiscoporum Gnesnensium* (Warszawa: [n. pub.], 1649)
Grünhagen, Colmar, *Regesten zur schlesischen Geschichte*, vol. 1 (Breslau: Josef Max, 1866)
Israel, Friedrich, ed., *Urkundenbuch des Erzstifts Magdeburg*, vol. 1 (Magdeburg: Landesgeschichtlichen Forschungsatelle, 1937)
Jan Długosz, *Annales seu cronicae incliti Regni Poloniae*, liber 5–6 (Warszawa: PWN, 1973)

Jan Długosz, *Catalogus archiepiscoporum Gnesnensium*, in *Opera omnia*, ed. by Ignacy Polkowski and Żegota Pauli, vol. 1 (Kraków: [n. pub.], 1887), pp. 343–79

Jan Długosz, *Catalogus episcoporum Wratislauiensium*, in *Opera omnia*, ed. by Ignacy Polkowski and Żegota Pauli, vol. 1 (Kraków: [n. pub.], 1887), pp. 439–77

Jan Długosz, *Liber beneficiorum dioecesis Cracoviensis*, ed. by A. Przeździecki, 3 vols (Kraków: Kirchmajeriana, 1863–1864)

Jan Długosz, *Vitae episcoporum Poloniae. Catalogus archiepiscoporum gnesnensium*, in *Opera omnia*, ed. by Ignacy Polkowski and Żegota Pauli, vol. 1 (Kraków: [n. pub.], 1887), pp. 337–78

Jan Łaski, *Liber beneficiorum archidyecezyi gnieźnieńskiej*, ed. by Jan Łukowski and Jan Korytkowski, 2 vols (Gniezno: Lange, 1880–1881)

Janota, Eugeniusz, ed., *Zbiór dokumentów klasztoru mogilskiego*, part 2 of *Monografia opactwa cystersów we wsi Mogile* (Kraków: Drukarnia Uniwersytetu Jagiellońskiego, 1867)

Janota, Eugeniusz, ed., *Zbiór dyplomów klasztoru mogilskiego przy Krakowie* (Kraków: Drukarnia Uniwersytetu Jagiellońskiego, 1865)

Kochanowski, Jan K., ed., *Codex diplomaticus et commemorationum Masoviae generalis*, vol. 1 (Warszawa: Towarzystwo Naukowe, 1919)

Kochanowski, Jan K., ed., *Zbiór ogólny przywilejów i spominków mazowieckich*, vol. 1 (Warszawa: Towarzystwo Naukowe, 1919)

Konopka, Marek, 'List do Redakcji', *Biuletyn Historii Sztuki*, 45 (1983), pp. 245–47

Kozłowska-Budkowa, Zofia, ed., *Repertorjum polskich dokumentów doby piastowskiej*, vol. 1: *Do końca wieku XII* (Kraków: PAU, 1937)

Krzyżanowski, Stanisław, ed., *Album palaeographicum Tabularum I–XXXI textus*, revised by Władysław Semkowicz and Zofia Kozłowska-Budkowa, 2nd edn (Kraków: Nakładem Uniwersytetu Jagiellońskiego, 1960)

Krzyżanowski, Stanisław, ed., *Monumenta Poloniae paleographica* (Kraków: [n. pub.], 1907).

Kuraś, Stanisław, *Przywileje prawa niemieckiego miast i wsi małopolskich XIV–XV wieku* (Wrocław: ZNO, 1971)

Kuraś, Stanisław, ed., *Zbiór dokumentów katedry i diecezji krakowskiej*, vol. 1 (Lublin: Towarzystwo Naukowe Katolickiego Uniwersytetu Lubelskiego, 1965)

Kuraś, Stanisław, and Irena Sułkowska-Kuraś, eds, *Zbiór dokumentów małopolskich*, Part IV: *Dokumenty z lat 1211–1400* (Wrocław: ZNO, 1969)

Kürbis, Brygida, Bogdan Bolz, Bogusław Nadolski, and Danuta Zydorek, eds, *Kodeks Matyldy. Księga obrzędów z kartami dedykacyjnymi* (Kraków: PAU, 2000)

Maleczyński, Karol, ed., *Kodeks dyplomatyczny Śląska*, vol. 1 (Wrocław: Wrocławskie Towarzystwo Miłośników Historii, 1956)

Mistrz Wincenty (tzw. Kadłubek), *Kronika polska (Chronica polonorum)*, ed. and trans. by Brygida Kürbis (Wrocław: ZNO, 1992)

Monumenta Poloniae Historica, various editors, 13 vols (1864–1888, 1962–2017)

Perlbach, Max, ed., *Pommerellisches Urkundenbuch* (Danzig: [n. pub.], 1882)

Pfotenhauer, Paul, ed., *Die Urkunden des Klosters Kamenz* (Breslau: Josef Max, 1881)

Piekosiński, Franciszek, ed., *Kodeks dyplomatyczny Małopolski*, 2 vols (Kraków: AU, 1878–1886)

Piekosiński, Franciszek, ed., *Kodeks dyplomatyczny katedry krakowskiej św. Wacława* (Kraków: AU, 1874)

Piekosiński, Franciszek, ed., *Zbiór dokumentów średniowiecznych do objaśniania prawa polskiego ziemskiego służących* (Kraków: [n. pub.], 1897)

Reliquiae manuscriptorum omnis aevi diplomatum ac monumentarum. Diplomatarium Grissoviensene Silesiae coenobii Cisterciensis ab 1240 ad an. 1399, vol. 5 (Frankfurt and Leipzig: [n. pub.], 1723)

Rzyszczewski, Leon, Antoni Muczkowski, and Antoni Zygmunt Helcel, eds, *Kodeks dyplomatyczny Polski*, 3 vols (Varsaviae: Typis Stanislai Strąbski, 1847–1858)

Smolka, Stanisław, and Wojciech Kętrzyński, eds, *Kodeks dyplomatyczny klasztoru tynieckiego*, Part I: *1105–1399*, 2 vols (Lwów: ZNO, 1875)

Sułkowska-Kuraś, Irena, and Stanisław Kuraś, ed., *Bullarium Poloniae*, vol. 1 (Rome: École Française de Rome, 1982)

Thietmar Merseburgensis, *Chronicon*, ed. by Robert Holzamann, *MGH Scriptores NS* 9, reprint (Munich: MGH, 1996 [1935])

Ulanowski, Bolesław, ed., 'Dokumenty kujawskie i mazowieckie przeważnie z XIII wieku', *Archiwum Komisji Historycznej*, 4 (1888), 115–534

Wattenbach, W., ed., *Urkunden der Klöster Rauden und Himmelwitz, der Dominicaner und Dominicanerinnen in der Stadt Ratibor*, vol. 2 (Breslau: Josef Max, 1859)

Zakrzewski, Ignacy, *Kodeks dyplomatyczny Wielkopolski*, vol. 1 (Poznań: PTPN, 1877)

Secondary Works

Abraham, Władysław, *Organizacja Kościoła w Polsce do połowy XII w.*, 3rd edn (Poznań: Pallotinum, 1962)

Adamska, Anna, 'Bibliographie de la diplomatique polonaise 1956–1996', *Archiv für Diplomatik, Schriftgeschichte, Siegel- und Wappenkunde*, 44 (1998), 275–336

Anyszko, Małgorzata, 'Ród Pałuków w świetle nowszych badań' (unpublished master's thesis, UAM, 1983)

Appelt, Heinrich, *Die Urkundenfälschungen des Klosters Trebnitz* (Breslau: Priebatschs Buchh, 1940)

Appelt, Heinrich, 'Vorarbeiten zum Schlesischen Urkundenbuch. Die Echtheit der Trebnitzer Gründungsurkunden (1201/18)', *Zeitschrift des Vereins für Geschichte Schlesiens*, 71 (1937), 1–56

Augustyniak, Jerzy, *Cysterskie opactwo w Sulejowie. Rozwój przestrzenny do końca XVI wieku w świetle badań archeologiczno-architektonicznych w latach 1989–2003* (Łódź: Muzeum Archeologiczne i Etnograficzne, 2005)

Augustyniak, Jerzy, Andrzej Grzybkowski, and Robert Kunkel, 'Marginalia Suleioviana', in *Cystersi w kulturze średniowiecznej Europy*, ed. by Jerzy Strzelczyk (Poznań UAM, 1992), pp. 351–62

Bachulski, Aleksy, 'Założenie klasztoru kanoników regularnych w Czerwińsku', in *Księga pamiątkowa ku uczczeniu dwudziestopięcioletniej działalności naukowej prof. Marcelego Handelsmana* (Warszawa: [n. pub.], 1929), pp. 51–76

Balzer, Oswald, *Genealogia Piastów* (Kraków: PAU, 1895)

Balzer, Oswald, *Narzaz w systemie danin książęcych pierwotnej Polski* (Lwów: Drukarnia Uniwersytetu Jagiellońskiego, 1928)

Balzer, Oswald, 'Studyum o Kadłubku', *Pisma pośmiertne*, vol. 1 (Lwów: Towarzystwo Naukowe, 1934)

Baran-Kozłowski, Wojciech, *Arcybiskup gnieźnieński Henryk Kietlicz (1199–1219). Działalność kościelna i polityczna* (Poznań: WP, 2005)

Bardach, Juliusz, *Historia państwa i prawa Polski*, vol. I: *do połowy XV wieku* (Warszawa: PWN, 1964)

Białoskórska, Krystyna, 'Kilka uwag na marginesie dyskusji o przedcysterskich budowlach odkrytych w Wąchocku', *Biuletyn Historii Sztuki*, 45 (1983), pp. 256–57

Białoskórska, Krystyna, 'Opactwo cysterskie w Wąchocku w świetle najnowszych badań archeologicznych i architektonicznych', in *V Konferencja naukowa w Busku Zdroju i w Wiślicy 19–20 maja 1966*, ed. by Włodzimierz Antoniewicz and Piotr Biegański (Warszawa: PWN, 1968), pp. 65–82

Białoskórska, Krystyna, 'Problem relacji polsko-włoskich w XIII wieku – zagadnienie mecenatu Iwona Odrowąża i małopolskich opactw cysterskich', *Sprawozdania z Posiedzeń Komisji – Polska Akademia Nauk Oddział w Krakowie*, 7 (1963), 249–57

Białoskórska, Krystyna, 'Uwagi o "Głosie w dyskusji" w sprawie przedcysterskiego Wąchocka', in *Klasztor w kulturze Polski średniowiecznej*, ed. by Anna Pobóg-Lenartowicz and Marek Derwich (Opole: [n. pub.], 1995), pp. 393–418

Białoskórska, Krystyna, 'W związku z pismem w sprawie artykułu o wczesnopiastowskiej rezydencji w Wąchocku', *Biuletyn Historii Sztuki*, 43 (1981), 103–10

Białoskórska, Krystyna, *Wąchock. Opactwo cystersów* (Warszawa: Arkady, 1960)

Białoskórska, Krystyna, 'Wąchocka rezydencja książęca. Nieznany epizod z dziejów Polski wczesnopiastowskiej', *Biuletyn Historii Sztuki*, 41 (1979), 135–78

Białoskórska, Krystyna, 'Wąchocki skarb brakteatów. Przyczynek do dziejów mennictwa kościelnego w Polsce w XIII stuleciu', *Wiadomości Numizmatyczne*, 29 (1985), 166–90

Bielińska, Maria, *Kancelarie i dokumenty wielkopolskie XIII wieku* (Wrocław: ZNO, 1967)

Bielińska, Maria, Antoni Gąsiorowski, and Jerzy Łojko, *Urzędnicy wielkopolscy XII–XV wieku. Spisy* (Wrocław: ZNO, 1985)

Bieniak, Janusz, 'Autor Rocznika dawnego', in *Kultura średniowieczna i staropolska. Studia ofiarowane Aleksandrowi Gieysztorowi w pięćdziesięciolecie pracy naukowej* (Warszawa: PWN, 1991), pp. 429–42

Bieniak, Janusz, 'Dyskusja i podsumowanie obrad. Rok nauki polskiej. Mistrz Wincenty Kadłubek – pierwszy uczony polski – w 750-lecie śmierci', *Studia Źródłoznawcze*, 20 (1976), pp. 123–31

Bieniak, Janusz, 'Jeszcze w sprawie genezy rodów rycerskich w Polsce', in *Społeczeństwo Polski średniowiecznej. Zbiór studiów*, vol. 5, ed. by S. K. Kuczyński (Warszawa: PWN, 1992), pp. 45–55

Bieniak, Janusz, 'Knight Clans in Medieval Poland', in *The Polish Nobility in the Middle Ages: Anthologies*, ed. by Antoni Gąsiorowski (Wrocław: ZNO, 1984), pp. 123–76

Bieniak, Janusz, 'Obóz obrońców statutu Bolesława Krzywoustego', in *Genealogia – polska elita polityczna w wiekach średnich na tle porównawczym*, ed. by Jan Wroniszewski (Toruń: Uniwersytet Mikołaja Kopernika, 1993), pp. 17–33

Bieniak, Janusz, 'Odolan', in *Polski słownik biograficzny*, vol. 22 (Wrocław: ZNO, 1977), pp. 537–38

Bieniak, Janusz, 'Pakosław', in *Polski słownik biograficzny*, vol. 25 (Wrocław: ZNO, 1980), pp. 37–38

Bieniak, Janusz, 'Polska elita polityczna XII w., Part I: Tło działalności', in *Społeczeństwo Polski średniowiecznej. Zbiór studiów*, vol. 2, ed. by S. K. Kuczyński (Warszawa: PWN, 1982), pp. 11–44.

Bieniak, Janusz, 'Polska elita polityczna XII w., Part III A: Arbitrzy książąt – krąg rodzinny Piotra Włostowica', in *Społeczeństwo Polski średniowiecznej. Zbiór studiów*, vol. 6, ed. by S. K. Kuczyński (Warszawa: PWN, 1990), pp. 1–107

Bieniak, Janusz, 'Polska elita polityczna XII w., Part III B: Arbitrzy książąt – trudne początki', in *Społeczeństwo Polski średniowiecznej. Zbiór studiów*, vol. 7, ed. by S. K. Kuczyński (Warszawa: PWN, 1996), pp. 11–44

Bieniak, Janusz, 'Polska elita polityczna XII w., Part III C: Arbitrzy książąt – pełnia władzy', in *Społeczeństwo Polski średniowiecznej. Zbiór studiów*, vol. 8, ed. by S. K. Kuczyński (Warszawa: PWN, 1996), pp. 9–66

Bieniak, Janusz, 'Polska elita polityczna XII wieku, Part III D: Arbitrzy książąt – zmierzch', in *Społeczeństwo Polski średniowiecznej. Zbiór studiów*, vol. 9, ed. by S. K. Kuczyński (Warszawa: PWN, 1996), pp. 9–53

Bieniak, Janusz, 'Ród Łabędziów', in *Genealogia. Studia nad wspólnotami krewniaczymi i terytorialnymi w Polsce średniowiecznej*, ed. by Jacek Hertel and Jan Wroniszewski (Toruń: Uniwersytet Mikołaja Kopernika, 1987), pp. 9–33

Bieniak, Janusz, 'Rody rycerskie jako czynnik struktury społecznej w Polsce XIII–XV wieku', in *Polska w okresie rozdrobnienia feudalnego*, ed. by Henryk Łowmiański (Wrocław-Gdańsk: ZNO, 1973), pp. 161–200

Biniaś-Szkopek, Magdalena, 'Kazimierz II Sprawiedliwy – księciem krakowskim' (unpublished master's thesis, UAM, 2003)

Biniaś-Szkopek, Magdalena, *Bolesław IV Kędzierzawy – książę Mazowsza i princeps*, (Poznań: WP, 2009)

Błażkiewiczówna, I., 'Fundacja i pierwotne uposażenie klasztoru cystersów w Łeknie', *Sprawozdania Poznańskiego Towarzystwa Przyjaciół Nauk*, 8 (1934), 8–93

Bobowski, Kazimierz, 'Aktywność skryptorium dokumentowego klasztoru cysterek w Szczecinie do końca XIII wieku (w zakresie "ars dictandi" i "ars moriendi")', *Przegląd Zachodniopomorski*, 35 (1991), 7–19

Bobowski, Kazimierz, 'Fundacja i początki klasztoru cysterek w Trzebnicy', in *Studia historyczne. Ustrój, Kościół, militaria*, ed. by Kazimierz Bobowski (Wrocław: WUW, 1993), pp. 319

Bobowski, Kazimierz, *Dokumenty i kancelarie na Pomorzu Zachodnim do końca XIII w.* (Wrocław: WUW, 1988)

Bobowski, Kazimierz, 'O potrzebie badań nad skryptoriami dokumentowymi cystersów na ziemiach polskich w okresie średniowiecza. Stan i propozycje metod badawczych', in *Cystersi kulturze średniowiecznej Europy*, ed. by Jerzy Strzelczyk (Poznań: UAM, 1992), pp. 55–62

Bobowski, Kazimierz, 'Podstawy bytu konwentu trzebnickiego', in *Księga Jadwiżańska*, ed. by Michał Kaczmarek and Marek L. Wójcik (Wrocław: WUW, 1995), pp. 61–83

Bobowski, Kazimierz, *Skryptorium dokumentowe klasztoru cystersów w Dargunie do końca XIII wieku* (Wrocław: WUW, 1991)

Bobowski, Kazimierz, 'Ze studiów nad dokumentami i kancelarią Bolesława Wstydliwego', *Acta Universitatis Wratislaviensis. Historia*, 36 (1965), 29–66

Bobowski, Kazimierz, 'Zur Frage der Echtheit westpommerscher Urkunden bis zum Ende des 13. Jahrhunderts', in *Fälschungen im Mittelalter*, MGH Schriften 33, iv (Hanover: Hansche, 1988) pp. 523–30

Bochnak, Adam, 'Grób biskupa Maura w krypcie św. Leonarda na Wawelu', *Rocznik Krakowski*, 30 (1938), 239–48

Bogucki, Ambroży, *Komes w polskich źródłach średniowiecznych* (Warszawa–Poznań: PWN, 1971)

Bollmann, Aloysius, *Die Säkularisation der Zisterzienserstiftes Leubus* (Breslau: Ostdeutsche Verlagsanstalt, 1932)

Bolz, Bogdan, *Proces beatyfikacyjny i kanonizacyjny arcybiskupa Bogumiła w XVII wieku według rękopisu Ossolineum 220 II* (Poznań: Księgarnia św. Wojciecha, 1982)

Borawska, Danuta, 'Gallus Anonim czy Italus Anonim', *Przegląd Historyczny*, 56 (1965), 111–19

Brociek, W. R., 'Czy cystersi wąchoccy wybijali własną monetę?', *Nummus. Ostrowieckie zapiski numizmatyczne*, 3 (1993), 3–11

Bruder, Artur, *Najstarszy kopiarz klasztoru cystersów w Henrykowie* (Wrocław: WUW, 1992)

Bruski, Klemens, 'Sprawa autentyczności dokumentów Sambora II dla cystersów oliwskich', *Zeszyty Naukowe Wydziału Humanistycznego Uniwersytetu Gdańskiego. Historia*, 15 (1985), 5–20

Bruski, Klemens, and Wiesław Długokęcki, 'Dwa dokumenty krzyżackie dla klasztoru cystersów w Pelplinie z lat 1314–1315', in *Ludzie, władza, posiadłości*, ed. by Jan Powierski and Błażej Śliwiński (Gdańsk: Uniwersytet Gdański, 1994), pp. 245–56

Bruski, Klemens, and Wiesław Długokęcki, 'Kopiarz dokumentów klasztoru cystersów w Pelplinie z lat 1418–1421', *Nasza Przeszłość*, 83 (1994), 295–302

Buczek, Karol, 'Jeszcze o testamencie Bolesława Krzywoustego', *Przegląd Historyczny*, 60 (1969), 621–39

Callier, Edmund, 'Owińska', in *Słownik geograficzny Królestwa Polskiego i innych krajów słowiańskich*, vol. 7, ed. by Bronisław Chlebowski and Władysław Walewski (Warszawa: Filip Sulimierski and Władysław Walewski, 1886), pp. 771–72

Cetwiński, Marek, *Rycerstwo śląskie do końca XIII w. Biogramy i rodowody* (Wrocław: ZNO, 1982)

Chlebowski, Bronisław, and Władysław Walewski, eds, *Słownik geograficzny Królestwa Polskiego i innych krajów słowiańskich*, 15 vols (Warszawa: Filip Sulimierski and Władysław Walewski, 1880–1914)

Chłopocka, Helena, 'Fundacje cysterskie w Polsce średniowiecznej w poglądach historiografii polskiej', in *Historia i kultura cystersów w dawnej Polsce i ich europejskie związki*, ed. by Jerzy Strzelczyk (Poznań: UAM, 1987), pp. 7–23

Chłopocka, Helena, *Powstanie i rozwój wielkiej własności ziemskiej opactwa cystersów w Kołbaczu* (Poznań: PTPN, 1953)

Chmielewski, Stefan et al, eds, *Słownik historyczno-geograficzny województwa poznańskiego w średniowieczu*, 4 vols (Wrocław: ZNO, 1982–1995)

Chodyński, Zenon, 'Cystersi w Polsce', in *Encyklopedja kościelna*, vol. 3, ed. by Michał Nowodworski (Warszawa: Drukarnia Czerwińskiego, 1874), pp. 610–11

Chudziakowa, Jadwiga, 'Kościół opacki w Trzemesznie – próba rekonstrukcji faz rozwojowych', *Archaeologia Historica Polona*, 2 (1995), 133–44

Chudziakowa, Jadwiga, 'Romański kościół Kanoników Regularnych w Trzemesznie', in *Ars sine scientia nihil est. Księga ofiarowana Profesorowi Zygmuntowi Świechowskiemu*, ed. by Joanna Olenderek (Warszawa: Dom Wydawniczy ARS, 1997), pp. 55–60

Chudziakowa, Jadwiga, 'Z badań nad architekturą sakralną w Trzemesznie (z lat 1987–1988)', *Acta Universitatis Nicolai Copernici*, 20 (1992), 9–20

Dąbrowski, Franciszek, *Studia nad organizacją kasztelańską Polski XIII wieku* (Warszawa: Neriton, 2007)

Dąbrowski, Kazimierz, *Opactwo cystersów w Oliwie od XII do XVI wieku* (Gdańsk: ZNO, 1975)

Dąbrowski, Kazimierz, *Działalność gospodarcza, społeczna i kulturalna cystersów oliwskich, XII–XVI wiek* (Pelplin: [Nakładem Autora], 1972)

Dąbrowski, Kazimierz, *Rozwój wielkiej własności ziemskiej klasztoru cysterek w Żarnowcu od XIII do XVII wieku* (Gdańsk: ZNO, 1970)

Dainauskas, Jonas, 'Autentyczność aktu krewskiego', *Lituano-Slavica Posnaniensia*, 2 (1987), 125–42

David, Pierre, 'Un credo cathare?', *Revue d'histoire ecclesiastique*, 35 (1939), 756–61

Dekański, Dariusz A., and Leszek Wetesko, 'Oliwa', in *Monasticon Cisterciense Poloniae*, ed. by Andrzej Marek Wyrwa, Jerzy Strzelczyk, and Krzysztof Kaczmarek, vol. 2 (Poznań: WP, 1999), pp. 268–80

Depdolla, Wilhelm, *Geschichte des Klosters Lekno – Wongrowitz* (Lekno: Selbstverl, 1917)

Deptuła, Czesław, 'Krąg kościelny płocki w połowie XII wieku', *Roczniki Humanistyczne*, 8 (1959), 5–122

Deptuła, Czesław, 'Monasterium Bethleem: Wokół misji Henryka Zdika i początki opactwa w Brzesku', *Roczniki Humanistyczne*, 18 (1970), 27–44

Deptuła, Czesław, 'O niektórych źródłach do historii zakonu premonstrateńskiego w Polsce XII i XIII wieku', *Archiwa Biblioteki i Muzea Kościelne*, 22 (1971), 187–222

Deptuła, Czesław, 'Przyczynek do dziejów Ślęży i jej opactwa', *Roczniki Humanistyczne*, 15 (1967), 17–35

Deptuła, Czesław, 'Wokół postaci arcybiskupa Piotra Łabędzia', *Roczniki Humanistyczne*, 15 (1967), 36–47

Derwich, Marek, *Benedyktyński klasztor św. Krzyża na Łysej Górze w średniowieczu* (Warszawa–Wrocław, PWN, 1992)

Derwich, Marek, 'Die Prämonstratenserorden im mittelalterlichen Polen. Seine Rolle in Kirche und Gesellschaft', in *Studien zum Prämonstratenserorden*, ed. by Irene Crusius and Helmut Flachenecker (Göttingen: Vandenhoeck & Ruprecht, 2003), pp. 311–47

Derwich, Marek, 'Fundacja lubińska na tle rozwoju monastycyzmu benedyktyńskiego w Polsce', in *Opactwo Benedyktynów w Lubiniu. Pierwsze wieki istnienia*, ed. by Zofia Kurnatowska (Poznań: UAM, 1996), pp. 12–23

Derwich, Marek, *Monastycyzm benedyktyński w średniowiecznej Europie i Polsce. Wybrane problemy* (Wrocław: WUW, 1998)

Derwich, Marek, 'Studia nad początkami monastycyzmu na ziemiach polskich. Pierwsze opactwa i ich funkcje', *Kwartalnik Historyczny*, 107 (2000), 77–105

Derwich, Marek, 'Testament Bolesława Krzywoustego w polskiej historiografii średniowiecznej', *Acta Universitatis Wratislaviensis, Historia*, 33 (1980), 113–52

Derwich, Marek, 'Zarys dziejów benedyktynów i benedyktynek na Śląsku', *Śląski Kwartalnik Historyczny Sobótka*, 53 (1998), 435–56

Dobosz, Józef, 'Arcybiskup Janik i jego następcy. Przygotowanie do reformy Henryka Kietlicza', in *1000 lat Archidiecezji Gnieźnieńskiej*, ed. by Jerzy Strzelczyk and Janusz Górny (Gniezno: Gaudentinum, 2000), pp. 81–96

Dobosz, Józef, 'Badania nad dokumentami i skryptoriami polskich cystersów', in *Monasticon Cisterciense Poloniae*, ed. by Andrzej Marek Wyrwa, Jerzy Strzelczyk, and Krzysztof Kaczmarek, vol. 1 (Poznań: WP, 1999), pp. 137–48

Dobosz, Józef, 'Bulla z 1136 roku', in *Gniezno. Pierwsza stolica Polski, miasto świętego Wojciecha* (Gniezno: Muzeum Archidiecezjalne w Gnieźnie, 1995), p. 130.

Dobosz, Józef, 'Casimir le Juste et les fondations d'abbayes cisterciennes en Petite Pologne au XIIe siecle', *Cîteaux. Commentarii cistercienses*, 46 (1995), 243–56

Dobosz, Józef, 'Cystersi małopolscy, ich miejsce w gospodarce i kulturze Polski XIII wieku', *Rocznik Bocheński*, 5 (2001), 49–56

Dobosz, Józef, 'Dokument fundacyjny klasztoru cystersów w Łeknie', in *Studia i materiały do dziejów Pałuk*, vol. I: *Osadnictwo i architektura w rejonie Łekna we wczesnym średniowieczu*, ed. by Andrzej Marek Wyrwa (Poznań: UAM, 1989), pp. 53–83

Dobosz, Józef, 'Dokument Mieszka III Starego dla kanoników regularnych w Trzemesznie (28 kwietnia 1145 r.)', in *Gniezno. Studia i materiały historyczne*, vol. 4 (Warszawa–Poznań: PWN, 1995), pp. 87–106

Dobosz, Józef, 'Dokumenty', in *Cystersi w średniowiecznej Polsce. Kultura i sztuka. Katalog wystawy* (Warszawa–Poznań: PWN, 1991), pp. 16–48

Dobosz, Józef, *Działalność fundacyjna Kazimierza Sprawiedliwego* (Poznań: UAM, 1995)

Dobosz, Józef, *Kazimierz II Sprawiedliwy* (Poznań: WP, 2011)

Dobosz, Józef, 'Kościół jako element uposażenia klasztorów cysterskich w Polsce w XII i początkach XIII wieku', in *Nihil superfluum esse. Studia z dziejów średniowiecza ofiarowane Jadwidze Krzyżaniakowej*, ed. by Jerzy Strzelczyk and Józef Dobosz (Poznań: UAM, 2000), pp. 187–93

Dobosz, Józef, 'Kryzys w opactwie cysterskim w Sulejowie w drugiej połowie XIII w.', in *Docendo discimus. Studia historyczne ofiarowane Profesorowi Zbigniewowi Wielgoszowi w siedemdziesiątą rocznicę urodzin*, ed. by Krzysztof Kaczmarek and Jarosław Nikodem (Poznań: UAM, 2000), pp. 133–46

Dobosz, Józef, 'Legitymizacja falsyfikatów dokumentów w XII–XIII-wiecznej Polsce', in *Pragmatické písemnosti v kontextu právním a správním*, ed. by Zdeněk Hojda and Hana Pátková (Praha: Togga, 2008), pp. 43–54

Dobosz, Józef, *Monarcha i możni wobec Kościoła w Polsce do początku XIII wieku* (Poznań: WP, 2002)

Dobosz, Józef, 'Najstarsze świadectwa działalności fundacyjnej Kazimierza Sprawiedliwego', *Studia Źródłoznawcze*, 35 (1994), 65–77

Dobosz, Józef, 'Okoliczności i motywy fundacji klasztoru cystersów w Sulejowie', in *Dzieje, kultura artystyczna i umysłowa polskich cystersów od średniowiecza do końca XVIII wieku.*, ed. by Jerzy Strzelczyk (Kraków: Instytut Wydawniczy Księży Misjonarzy, 1994), pp. 177–87

Dobosz, Józef, 'Piastowie wobec premonstratensów i innych form kanonikatu regularnego w XII wieku', in *Premonstratensi na ziemiach polskich w średniowieczu i epoce nowożytnej*, ed. by Jerzy Rajman (Kraków: Wydawnictwo Naukowe Akademii Pedagogicznej, 2007), pp. 6–18

Dobosz, Józef, 'Proces fundacyjny i pierwotne uposażenie opactwa cystersów w Jędrzejowie', in *Cystersi w Polsce. W 850-lecie fundacji opactwa jędrzejowskiego*, ed. by Daniela Olszewski (Kielce: Wydawnictwo Jedność, 1990), pp. 40–79

Dobosz, Józef, 'Trzynastowieczne falsyfikaty z Sulejowa i Jędrzejowa – motywy i okoliczności powstania', in *Klasztor w kulturze średniowiecznej Polski*, ed. by Anna Pobóg-Lenartowicz and Marek Derwich (Opole: Wydawnictwo Św. Krzyża, 1995), pp. 225–37

Dobosz, Józef, 'Uwagi o fundacji opactwa cystersów w Sulejowie', *Sprawozdania Poznańskiego Towarzystwa Przyjaciół Nauk. Wydział Nauk o Sztuce*, 100 (1982), 77–91

Dobosz, Józef, 'Wokół fundatora i początków klasztoru cystersów w Wąchocku', *Scripta Minora*, 2 (1998), 37–49

Dobosz, Józef, 'Założenie klasztoru w Łeknie na tle dwunastowiecznych fundacji cysterskich na ziemiach polskich', in *Cystersi łekneńscy w krajobrazie kulturowym* ziem polskich w 850-lecie fundacji opactwa cysterskiego w Łeknie. 1153–2003, ed. by Andrzej Marek Wyrwa (Łekno–Wągrowiec–Poznań: UAM, 2004), pp. 69–81

Dobosz, Józef, and Tomasz Jurek, eds, *Polonia coepit habere episcopum: The origin of the Poznań bishopric in the light of the latest research* (Poznań: UAM, 2019)

Dobosz, Józef, Marzena Matla, and Jerzy Strzelczyk, eds, *Chrystianizacja 'Młodszej Europy'* (Poznań: UAM, 2016)

Dobosz, Józef, Marzena Matla, and Jerzy Strzelczyk, eds, *Chrzest Mieszka I i chrystianizacja państwa Piastów* (Poznań: UAM, 2017)

Dobosz, Józef, and Jerzy Strzelczyk, eds, *Chrystianizacja Europy. Kościół na przełomie I i II tysiąclecia* (Poznań: UAM, 2014)

Dobosz, Józef, and Leszek Wetesko, 'Jędrzejów', in *Monasticon Cisterciense Poloniae*, ed. by Andrzej Marek Wyrwa, Jerzy Strzelczyk, and Krzysztof Kaczmarek, vol. 2 (Poznań: WP, 1999), pp. 90–97

Dobosz, Józef, and Leszek Wetesko, 'Koprzywnica', in *Monasticon Cisterciense Poloniae*, ed. by Andrzej Marek Wyrwa, Jerzy Strzelczyk, and Krzysztof Kaczmarek, vol. 2 (Poznań: WP, 1999), pp. 149–57

Dobosz, Józef, and Leszek Wetesko, 'Wąchock', in *Monasticon Cisterciense Poloniae*, ed. by Andrzej Marek Wyrwa, Jerzy Strzelczyk, and Krzysztof Kaczmarek, vol. 2 (Poznań: WP, 1999), pp. 328–40

Dobosz, Józef, and Andrzej Marek Wyrwa, 'Działalność gospodarcza cystersów na ziemiach polskich – zarys problemu', in *Monasticon Cisterciense Poloniae*, ed. by Andrzej Marek Wyrwa, Jerzy Strzelczyk, and Krzysztof Kaczmarek, vol. 1 (Poznań: WP, 1999), pp. 189–212

Domański, S., 'Dokumenty fundacyjne i rozwój uposażenia klasztoru cystersów w Łeknie do końca XIII w.' (unpublished master's thesis, UAM, 1967)

Dumézil, Bruno, *Chrześcijańskie korzenie Europy. Konwersja i wolność w królestwa barbarzyńskich o V do VIII wieku*, trans. Piotr Rak (Kęty: Wydawnictwo Marek Derewiecki, 2008)

Dunin-Wąsowicz, Teresa, 'Rola cystersów w rozwoju kultury materialnej w Polsce wczesnośredniowiecznej', in *Cystersi w kulturze średniowiecznej Europy*, ed. by Jerzy Strzelczyk (Poznań: UAM, 1992), pp. 9–23

Dunin-Wąsowicz, Teresa, 'Kilka uwag w sprawie działalności misyjnej cystersów na Rusi w XII–XIII wieku', in *Społeczeństwo Polski średniowiecznej. Zbiór studiów*, vol. 5, ed. by S. K. Kuczyński (Warszawa: Warszawa: PWN, 1992), pp. 353–64

Drzymała, Jerzy, 'Działalność fundacyjna biskupa Aleksandra z Malonne', *Nasze Historie*, 3 (1998), 37–69

Dworsatschek, Mariusz, *Władysław II Wygnaniec* (Wrocław: Przyjaciół Ossolineum, 1998)

Dymmel, Piotr, *Bibliografia edytorstwa źródeł historycznych w Polsce. Historia – krytyka tekstu – metodyka i technika wydawnicza* (Lublin: Uniwersytet Marii Curie-Skłodowskiej, 2001)

Fälschungen im Mittelalter. International Kongress der Monumenta Germaniae Historica, München, 16.-19. September 1986, vols III–IV: *Diplomatische Fälschungen*, MGH Schriften, 33, iii–iv (Hanover: Hansche, 1988)

Gartkiewicz, Przemysław, Andrzej Grzybkowski, Robert Kunkel, and Jarosław Widawski, 'Do redakcji Biuletynu Historii Sztuki', *Biuletyn Historii Sztuki*, 43 (1981), 98–102

Gąsiorowski, Antoni, 'Jakub ze Żnina II', in *Wielkopolski słownik biograficzny* (Poznań: PWN, 1981), p. 278

Gąsiorowski, Antoni, 'Jan', in *Wielkopolski słownik biograficzny* (Poznań: PWN, 1981), p. 285

Gąsiorowski, Antoni, 'Janik (Jan)', in *Słownik starożytności słowiańskich. Encyklopedyczny zarys kultury Słowian od czasów najdawniejszych*, ed. by Władysław Kowalenko, Gerard Labuda, and Tadeusz Lehr-Spławiński, vol. 2 (Wrocław: ZNO, 1965), p. 319

Gąsiorowski, Antoni, *Notariusze publiczni w Wielkopolsce schyłku wieków średnich* (Poznań: Towarzystwo Przyjaciół Nauk, 1993)

Gąsiorowski, Antoni, 'Pean', in *Polski słownik biograficzny*, vol. 25 (Wrocław: ZNO, 1980), p. 543

Gąsiorowski, Antoni, 'Research into Medieval Polish Nobility: Introduction', in *The Polish Nobility in the Middle Ages: Anthologies*, ed. by Antoni Gąsiorowski (Wrocław: ZNO, 1984), pp. 7–20

Gąsiorowski, Antoni, review of Sikora, 'Przywileje rycerskie synów Władysława Odonica', *Studia Źródłoznawcze*, 14 (1969), 212–13

Gąsiorowski, Antoni, 'Spory o polskie rozbicie dzielnicowe', in *Badania nad historią gospodarczo-społeczną w Polsce (problemy i metody)*, ed. by Władysław Rusiński (Warszawa – Poznań: PWN, 1978), pp. 115–22

Gąsiorowski, Antoni, 'Staropolski dokument i kancelaria jako przedmiot badań historycznych', in *Nauki pomocnicze historii na XI Powszechnym Zjeździe Historyków Polskich w Toruniu*, ed. by Andrzej Tomczak (Warszawa–Łódź: PWN, 1976), pp. 53–62

Gąsiorowski, Antoni, 'Ze studiów nad szerzeniem się tzw. prawa niemieckiego we wsiach ziemi krakowskiej i sandomierskiej (do roku 1333)', *Roczniki Historyczne*, 26 (1960), 123–70

Gąssowski, Jerzy, and Zbigniew Lechowicz, 'Jędrzejów, woj. kieleckie. Opactwo oo. Cystersów', *Informator Archeologiczny: Badania*, 11 (1977), 169

Gawlas, Sławomir, *O kształt zjednoczonego Królestwa. Niemieckie władztwo terytorialne a geneza społeczno-ustrojowej odrębności Polski* (Warszawa: Wydawnictwo DiG, 1996)

Gębarowicz, Mieczysław, 'Aleksander', in *Polski słownik biograficzny*, vol. 1 (Kraków: PAU 1935), pp. 65–66

Gębarowicz, Mieczysław, 'Mogilno – Płock – Czerwińsk: Studia nad organizacją Kościoła na Mazowszu w XI i XII wieku', in *Prace historyczne w 30-lecie działalności profesorskiej Stanisława Zakrzewskiego* (Lwów: [n. pub.], 1934), pp. 112–74

Giesebrecht, Heinrich Ludwig, 'Zur Chronologie der ältesten Pommerschen Urkunden', *Baltische Studien*, 9 (1843), 165–83

Gieysztor, Aleksander, 'Drzwi gnieźnieńskie jako wyraz polskiej świadomości narodowej', in *Drzwi gnieźnieńskie*, ed. by Michał Walicki, vol. 1 (Warszawa: ZNO, 1956), pp. 16–19

Gieysztor, Aleksander, and Głubiew-Lotyszowa, 'Trzemeszno', in *Słownik starożytności słowiańskich. Encyklopedyczny zarys kultury Słowian od czasów najdawniejszych do schyłku wieku XII*, ed. by Władysław Kowalenko, Gerard Labuda, and Tadeusz Lehr-Spławiński, vol. 6 (Wrocław: ZNO, 1977), pp. 191–96

Ginter, Tomasz, *Działalność fundacyjna księcia Mieszka III Starego* (Kraków: Societas Vistulana, 2008)

Goetting, Hans, 'Urkundenstudien zur Frühgeschichte des Klosters Heinrichau', *Zeitschrift des Vereins für Geschichte Schlesiens*, 73 (1939), 59–86

Góra, Mieczysław, 'Poszukiwania najstarszego Sulejowa', *Z Otchłani Wieków*, 47 (1981), 53–55

Górka, Olgierd, 'Przyczynki do dyplomatyki polskiej XII wieku', *Kwartalnik Historyczny*, 25 (1911), pp. 363–428

Górka, Olgierd, *Studia nad dziejami Śląska. Najstarsza tradycja opactwa cystersów w Lubiążu* (Lwów: Towarzystwo Naukowe, 1911)

Górski, Karol, *Ród Odrowążów w wiekach średnich* (Lwów: Polskie Towarzystwo Heraldyczne, 1928)

Grabski, Andrzej Feliks, *Zarys historii historiografii polskiej* (Poznań: WP, 2000)

Grodecki, Roman, 'Gedko, biskup krakowski', in *Polski słownik biograficzny*, vol. 7 (Wrocław: ZNO, 1958), pp. 366–67

Grodecki, Roman, 'Książęca włość trzebnicka na tle organizacji majątków książęcych w Polsce XII wieku', *Kwartalnik Historyczny*, 26 (1912), 433–75; 27 (1913), 1–66

Grodecki, Roman, *Początki immunitetu w Polsce* (Lwów: Instytut Popierania Polskiej Twórczości Naukowej, 1930)

Grodecki, Roman, review of Łaszczyńska, *Najstarsze papieskie bulle protekcyjne dla biskupstw polskich*, *Kwartalnik Historyczny*, 55 (1948), 216–24

Grüger, Heinrich, *Heinrichau. Geschichte eines schlesischen Zisterzienserklosters 1227–1977* (Köln: Böhlau, 1978)

Grünhagen, Colmar, 'Über die Zeit der Gründung von Kloster Leubus. Ein Beitrag zur Kritik der ältesten Leubuser Urkunden. Vom Provinzial-Achivar', *Zeitschrift des Vereins für Geschichte und Alterthum Schlesiens*, 5 (1863), 193–221

Grzesik, 'Piotr', in *Słownik starożytności słowiańskich. Encyklopedyczny zarys kultury Słowian od czasów najdawniejszych*, ed. by Władysław Kowalenko, Gerard Labuda, and Tadeusz Lehr-Spławiński, vol. 8 (Wrocław: ZNO, 1996), pp. 512–13

Grzesiowski, Jósef, and Jósef Piotrowicz, 'Sól małopolska w nadaniach i przywilejach dla klasztorów (do początku XVI wieku)', in *Krakowskie żupy solne na tle 1000-lecia dziejów Polski*, ed. by Alfons Długosz (Wieliczka: Muzeum Żup Krakowskich, 1965), pp. 71–187

Gumowski, Marian, Marian Haisig, and Sylwiusz Mikucki, *Sfragistyka* (Warszawa: Instytut Historii Polskiej Akademii Nauk, 1960)

Gustaw, Romuald, *Hagiografia polska. Słownik biobibliograficzny*, vol. 2 (Warszawa–Poznań–Lublin: Księgarnia Św. Wojciecha, 1972)

Harc, Artur, Lucyna Harc, and Ewa Łużyniecka, 'Lubiąż', in *Monasticon Cisterciense Poloniae*, ed. by Andrzej Marek Wyrwa, Jerzy Strzelczyk, and Krzysztof Kaczmarek, vol. 2 (Poznań: WP, 1999), pp. 202–17

Helcel, Antoni Zygmunt, *List otwarty do Augusta Bielowskiego o najdawniejszych znanych nadaniach klasztoru benedyktynów w Mogilnie* (Lwów: ZNO, 1865)

Helcel, Antoni Zygmunt, 'O klasztorze jędrzejowskim i będącym tam nagrobku Pakosława kasztelana krakowskiego', *Rocznik Towarzystwa Naukowego Krakowskiego z Uniwersytetem Jagiellońskim Złączonego. Oddział Sztuk i Archeologii*, 1 (1852), 125–228

Hervay, Ferenc L., *Repertorium historicum ordinis cisterciensis in Hungaria* (Roma: Bibliotheca Cisterciensis, 1984)

Hockenbeck, Heinrich, *Beiträge zur Geschichte des Klosters und der Stadt Wongrowitz*, 3 vols (Leipzig: B. G. Teubner, 1879–1883)

Holas, Aleksander, 'Dwie bazyliki romańskie w Trzemesznie', in *Gniezno: Studia i materiały historyczne*, vol. 4 (Warszawa–Poznań: PWN, 1987), pp. 107–28

Hoogeweg, Hermann, *Die Stifter und Klöster der Provinz Pommern*, 2 vols (Stettin: I. Böhlau, 1924–1925)

Janauschek, Leopold, *Originum cisterciensium*, vol. 1 (Vienna: Alfred Hoelder, 1877)

Jarzewicz, Jarosław, and Edward Rymar, 'Kołbacz', in *Monasticon Cisterciense Poloniae*, ed. by Andrzej Marek Wyrwa, Jerzy Strzelczyk, and Krzysztof Kaczmarek, vol. 2 (Poznań: WP, 1999), pp. 135–48

Jasiński, Kazimierz, 'Genealogia Piastów wielkopolskich. Potomstwo Władysława Odonica', *Kronika Miasta Poznania*, 2 (1995), 39–43

Jasiński, Kazimierz, 'Kilka uwag o najstarszych dokumentach Pomorza Gdańskiego', *Studia Źródłoznawcze*, 29 (1959), 147–53

Jasiński, Kazimierz, 'Nekrolog klasztoru norbertanek w Strzelnie. Uwagi krytyczno-erudycyjne', in *Prace wybrane z nauk pomocniczych historii*, ed. by Kazimierz Jasiński (Toruń: UMK, 1996), pp. 7–44

Jasiński, Kazimierz, 'Studia nad wielkopolskim stronnictwem książęcym w połowie XIII w. Współpracownicy Przemysła I do 1253 r.', in *Społeczeństwo Polski średniowiecznej. Zbiór studiów*, vol. 2, ed. by S. K. Kuczyński (Warszawa: PWN, 1981), pp. 161–201

Jasiński, Kazimierz, review of Bielińska, *Kancelarie i dokumenty*, *Przegląd Historyczny*, 59 (1968), 164–67

Jasiński, Kazimierz, review of Kozłowska-Budkowa, 'Który Bolesław?', *Studia Źródłoznawcze*, 7 (1962), 182–84

Jasiński, Tomasz, 'Uwagi o autentyczności przywileju kruszwickiego z czerwca 1230 roku', in *Personae. Colligationes. Facta*, ed. by Janusz Bieniak et al. (Toruń: Uniwersytet Mikołaja Kopernika, 1991), pp. 226–39

Jasiński, Tomasz, 'Złota bulla Fryderyka II dla Zakonu Krzyżackiego z roku rzekomo 1226', *Roczniki Historyczne*, 60 (1994), 107–53

Jażdżewski, Konstanty Klemens, 'Dzieła kaligraficzne mnicha Jakuba, kopisty skryptorium cysterskiego w Lubiążu z pierwszej ćwierci XIII wieku', *Studia Źródłoznawcze*, 21 (1976), 18–24

Jażdżewski, Konstanty Klemens, 'Jeszcze o lubiąskiej tradycji kaligraficznej a rozwidlonego', *Studia Źródłoznawcze*, 28 (1983), 203–05

Jażdżewski, Konstanty Klemens, *Lubiąż. Losy i kultura umysłowa śląskiego opactwa cystersów (1165–1642)* (Wrocław: WUW, 1992)

Jażdżewski, Konstanty Klemens, 'Poglądy średniowiecza na fałszowanie dokumentów. (W związku z czterema falsyfikatami przywileju fundacyjnego dla cystersów w Lubiążu z 1175 roku). Komunikat', *Sprawozdania Wrocławskiego Towarzystwa Naukowego. A*, 33 (1978), 66–71

Józefowiczówna, Krystyna, *Trzemeszno. Klasztor św. Wojciecha w dwu pierwszych wiekach istnienia* (Warszawa: PWN, 1978)

Józefowiczówna, Krystyna, 'Trzy klasztory romańskie', in *Studia z dziejów ziemi mogileńskiej*, ed. by Czesław Łuczak (Poznań: UAM, 1978), pp. 165–207

Jurek, Tomasz, 'Dokumenty fundacyjne opactwa w Lądzie', *Roczniki Historyczne*, 66 (2000), 7–51

Jurek, Tomasz, 'Nowsze badania historyków nad dziejami Polski w XII i XIII wieku', *Fontes Archaeologici Posnanienses*, 51 (2015), 7–19

Jurek, Tomasz, 'Owieńska', in *Słownik historyczno-geograficzny województwa poznańskiego w średniowieczu*, Issue 3: *Oporowo – Pniewo*, ed. by Antoni Gąsiorowski (Poznań: PTPN, 1997), pp. 537–48

Jurek, Tomasz, 'Testament Henryka Probusa. Autentyk czy falsyfikat?', *Studia Źródłoznawcze*, 35 (1994), 79–99

Jurek, Tomasz, 'Zagadka biskupa wrocławskiego Roberta', *Śląski Kwartalnik Historyczny Sobótka*, 45 (1990), pp. 1–11

Kaczmarczyk, Kazimierz, and Gerard Kowalski, eds, *Katalog archiwum opactwa cystersów w Mogile* (Kraków: Drukarnia Uniwersytetu Jagiellońskiego, 1919)

Kaczmarczyk, Zdzisław, *Immunitet sądowy i jurysdykcja poimmunitetowa w dobrach Kościoła w Polsce do końca XIV wieku* (Poznań: PTPN, 1936)

Kamińska, Maria *Nazwy miejscowe dawnego województwa sandomierskiego*, 2 vols (Wrocław: ZNO, 1964)

Karczewski, Dariusz, *Dzieje klasztoru norbertanek w Strzelnie do początku XVI wieku* (Wrocław: Polskie Towarzystwo Historyczne, 2001)

Karwasińska, Jadwiga, 'Archiepiscopus Polonie-Archiepiscopus Gneznensis. O adresacie bulli Paschalisa II', *Studia Źródłoznawcze* 28 (1983)

Karwowski, Stanisław, *Biskupi poznańscy z XII i początku XIII wieku* (Poznań: PTPN, 1911)

Keckowa, Antonina, *Saliny ziemi krakowskiej do końca XIII wieku* (Wrocław: ZNO, 1965)

Kehr, Paul Fridolin, *Das Erzbistum Magdeburg und die erste Organisation der christlichen Kirche in Polen* (Berlin: Verlag der Akademie der Wissenschaften, 1920)

Kętrzyński, Stanisław, 'Uwagi o początkach Metryki Koronnej i jej charakterze w XV w.', *Archeion*, 2 (1927), 1–30

Kętrzyński, Stanisław, *Zarys nauki o dokumencie polskim wieków średnich* (Warszawa: Drukarnia Artystyczna, 1934)

Kętrzyński, Wojciech, *Biblioteka hr. Raczyńskich w Rogalinie* (Lwów: ZNO, 1905)

Kętrzyński, Wojciech, 'Dokument księcia Konrada Mazowieckiego z r. 1203', *Przewodnik Naukowy i Literacki*, 15 (1887), 289–98, 385–94

Kętrzyński, Wojciech, 'O początkach dyplomatyki polskiej', *Kwartalnik Historyczny*, 7 (1893), 16–49

Kętrzyński, Wojciech, 'O podrobionym przywileju Idziego kardynała z r. 1105', *Przewodnik Naukowy i Literacki*, 2 (1874), 81–97

Kętrzyński, Wojciech, 'O przywileju Jana Arcybiskupa gnieźnieńskiego', *Przewodnik Naukowy i Literacki*, 8 (1890), 865–73

Kętrzyński, 'O przywileju kardynała Idziego z roku 1105', *Przewodnik Naukowy i Literacki*, 17 (1889), 316–30

Kętrzyński, Wojciech, 'Podrobione dyplomata tynieckie', *Przewodnik Naukowy i Literacki*, 2 (1874), 161–86

Kętrzyński, Wojciech, *Studia nad dokumentami XII w.* (Kraków: AU, 1891)

Kętrzyński, Wojciech, 'Eine unechte Trebnitzer Urkunde vom Jahre 1262', *Zeitschrift des Vereins für Geschichte und Alterthum Schlesiens*, 24 (1890), 357–60

Kętrzyński, Wojciech, 'Założenie i uposażenie biskupstwa płockiego', *Przewodnik Naukowy i Literacki*, 14 (1886), 385–92

Kłoczowski, Jerzy, *Chrystianizacja Litwy* (Krakow: Społeczny Instytut Wydawniczy Znak, 1987)

Kłoczowski, Jerzy, ed., *Chrześcijaństwo w Polsce. Zarys przemian 966–1979* (Lublin Uniwersytet Lubelski, 1992)

Kłoczowski, Jerzy, *Dzieje chrześcijaństwa polskiego. Wydanie uzupełnione* (Warszawa: Świat Książki, 2007)

Kłoczowski, Jerzy, 'Z zagadnień funkcji społecznych cystersów w Polsce średniowiecznej', in *Opuscula Casimiro Tymieniecki septuagenario dedicata* (Poznań: PTPN, 1959), pp. 105–26

Kłoczowski, Jerzy, 'Zakony na ziemiach polskich w wiekach średnich', in *Kościół w Polsce*, vol. I: *Średniowiecze*, ed. by Jerzy Kłoczowski (Kraków: Znak, 1966)

Koczerska, Maria, 'Autentyczność dokumentu unii krewskiej 1385 roku', *Kwartalnik Historyczny*, 99 (1992), 59–80

Koebner, Richard, 'Urkundenstudien zur Geschichte Danzigs und Olivas von 1178 bis 1342', *Zeitschrift des Westpreussischen Geschichtsvereins*, 71 (1934), 5–85

Korczak, Lidia, 'O akcie krewskim raz jeszcze na marginesie rozprawy Jonasa Dainauskasa', *Studia Historyczne*, 34 (1991), 473–79

Korta, Wacław, *Rozwój wielkiej własności feudalnej na Śląsku do połowy XIII wieku* (Wrocław: ZNO, 1964)

Korta, Wacław, *Tajemnice góry Ślęży* (Katowice: Śląski Instytut Naukowy, 1988)

Korytkowski, Jan, *Arcybiskupi gnieźnieńscy, prymasowie i metropolici polscy od roku 1000 aż do roku 1821, czyli do połączenia arcybiskupstwa gnieźnieńskiego z biskupstwem poznańskiém*, vol. 1 (Poznań: Kuryer Poznański, 1888)

Korytkowski, Jan, *Prałaci i kanonicy katedry metropolitalnej gnieźnieńskiej*, vol. 2 (Gniezno: J. B. Langiego, 1883)

Kowalska, Elżbieta, 'Dokument Humbalda, kardynała, legata papieskiego, wystawiony dla Trzemeszna w dniu 2 marca 1146 roku', in *Gniezno. Studia i materiały historyczne*, vol. 1 (Warszawa–Poznań: PWN, 1984), pp. 27–47

Kozierowski, Stanisław, *Badania nazw topograficznych dzisiejszej archidiecezji gnieźnieńskiej*, 4 vols (Poznań: Dziennik Poznański, 1911–1913)

Kozierowski, Stanisław *Badania nazw topograficznych na obszarze dawnej wschodniej Wielkopolski*, 2 vols (Poznań: Krajowy Instytut Wydawniczy, 1926–1928)

Kozierowski, Stanisław, *Fundacye klasztorne rodów rycerskich zachodniej Wielkopolski w dobie piastowskiej* (Poznań: Drukarnia Pracy, 1914)

Kozierowski, Stanisław, *Leszczyce i ich plemiennik arcybiskup gnieźnieński św. Bogumił z Dobrowa* (Poznań: Księgarnia św. Wojciecha, 1926)

Kozierowski, Stanisław, 'Pierwotne osiedlenie pojezierza Gopła', *Slavia Occidentalis* (1922), 3–54

Kozierowski, Stanisław, *Pierwotne osiedlenie ziemi gnieźnieńskiej wraz z Pałukami w świetle nazw geograficznych i charakterystycznych imion rycerskich* (Poznań: UAM, 1924)

Kozierowski, Stanisław, *Ród Porajów-Różyców* (Kraków: Polskie Towarzystwo Heraldyczne, 1930)

Kozłowska-Budkowa, 'Bogumił', in *Polski słownik biograficzny*, vol. 2 (Kraków: PAU, 1936), pp. 200–01

Kozłowska-Budkowa, Zofia, 'Gertruda', in *Polski słownik biograficzny*, vol. 7 (Wrocław: ZNO, 1948–1958), pp. 405–08

Kozłowska-Budkowa, Zofia, 'Jan', in *Polski słownik biograficzny*, vol. 10 (Wrocław: ZNO, 1962–1964), pp. 428–30

Kozłowska-Budkowa, Zofia, 'Który Bolesław?', in *Prace z dziejów Polski feudalnej ofiarowane Romanowi Grodeckiem w 70. rocznicę urodzin* (Warszawa: PWN, 1960), pp. 81–89

Kozłowska-Budkowa, Zofia, 'Maur', in *Polski słownik biograficzny*, vol. 20 (Wrocław: ZNO, 1975), pp. 261–62

Kozłowska-Budkowa, Zofia, 'Pieczęć Konrada Mazowieckiego z r. 1223 i jej falsyfikat', *Wiadomości Numizmatyczno-Archeologiczne*, 20 (1938), 292–95

Kozłowska-Budkowa, Zofia, 'Przyczynki do krytyki dokumentów śląskich z XII/XIII wieku', in *Studja z historji społecznej i gospodarczej poświęcone prof. dr. Franciszkowi Bujakowi* (Lwów: Drukarnia Naukowa, 1931), pp. 1–19

Kozłowska-Budkowa, Zofia, review of Bochnak, 'Grób biskupa Maura', *Kwartalnik Historyczny*, 53 (1939), 85–88

Kozłowska-Budkowa, Zofia, review of Maleczyński, *Studia nad dyplomami i kancelarią Odonica i Laskonogiego*, *Kwartalnik Historyczny*, 43 (1929), 46–61

Kozłowska-Budkowa, Zofia, 'Rodost', in *Polski słownik biograficzny*, vol. 29 (Wrocław: ZNO, 1986), p. 747

Kozłowska-Budkowa, Zofia, and Stanisław Szczur, 'Dzieje opactwa cystersów w Koprzywnicy do końca XIV wieku', *Nasza Przeszłość*, 60 (1983), 1–72

Kozłowski, Ryszard, *Rozwój uposażenia klasztoru cystersów w Byszewie (Koronowie)* (Poznań: PWN, 1973)

Krakowski, Stefan, *Polska w walce z najazdami tatarskimi w XIII wieku* (Warszawa: Ministerstwo Obrony Narodowej, 1956)

Krasoń, Józef, *Uposażenie klasztoru cystersów w Obrze w wiekach średnich* (Poznań: PTPN, 1950)

Krupicka, Hanns, 'Die sogenannte Leubuser Stiftungsurkunde von 1175. Ein Beitrag zur Beurteilung der Echtheitsfrage', *Zeitschrift des Vereins für Geschichte Schlesiens*, 70 (1936), 63–110

Krzyżaniakowej, Jadwiga, *Kancelaria królewska Władysława Jagiełły. Studium z dziejów kultury politycznej Polski w XV wieku*, 2 vols (Poznań: UAM, 1972–1979)

Krzyżanowski, Stanisław, *Dyplomy i kancelaria Przemysła II. Studium z dyplomatyki polskiej XIII w.* (Kraków: Drukarnia Uniwersytetu Jagiellońskiego, 1890)

Krzyżanowski, Stanisław, 'Jeszcze o początkach dyplomatyki polskiej', *Kwartalnik Historyczny*, 7 (1893), 192–95

Krzyżanowski, Stanisław, 'Początki dyplomatyki polskiej', *Kwartalnik Historyczny*, 6 (1892), 781–820

Krzyżanowski, Stanisław, 'Przywileje szczyrzyckie', *Kwartalnik Historyczny*, 18 (1904), 193–209

Kubica, Ewa, 'Katalog zabytków wczesnośredniowiecznej architektury monumentalnej Małopolski, Rusi Halickiej i Wołynia', *Materiały i Sprawozdania Rzeszowskiego Ośrodka Archeologicznego*, 17 (1996), 131–89

Kürbis, Brygida, 'Cystersi w kulturze polskiego średniowiecza. Trzy świadectwa z XII wieku', in *Historia i kultura cystersów w dawnej Polsce i ich europejskie związki*, ed. by Jerzy Strzelczyk (Poznań: UAM, 1987), pp. 221–41

Kürbis, Brygida, '*Dagome iudex* – studium krytyczne', in *Na progach historii II. O świadectwach do dziejów kultury Polski średniowiecznej* (Poznań: WP, 2001), pp. 9–87

Kürbis, Brygida, 'Die *Epistola Mathildis Suevae* an Mieszko II. in neure Sicht. Ein Forschungsbericht', *Frühmittelalterliche Studien*, 23 (1989), 318–38

Kürbis, Brygida, 'Najstarsze dokumenty opactwa benedyktynów w Mogilnie (XI–XII w.)', *Studia Źródłoznawcze*, 13 (1968), 27–61

Kürbis, Brygida, 'O początkach kanonii w Trzemesznie', in *Europa – Słowiańszczyzna – Polska. Studia ku uczczeniu Prof. Kazimierza Tymienieckiego*, ed. by Juliusz Bardach (Poznań: UAM, 1970), pp. 337–43

Kürbis, Brygida, 'Pogranicze Wielkopolski i Kujaw w X–XII wieku', in *Studia z dziejów ziemi mogileńskiej*, ed. by Czesław Łuczak (Poznań: UAM, 1978), pp. 65–111

Kürbis, Brygida, 'Studia nad Kodeksem Matyldy, III: List księżnej Matyldy do Mieszka II', *Studia Źródłoznawcze*, 30 (1987), 125–49

Kurnatowska, Zofia, 'Głos w dyskusji na temat odkryć w Wąchocku', in *Klasztor w kulturze Polski średniowiecznej*, ed. by Anna Pobóg-Lenartowicz and Marek Derwich (Opole: Wydawnictwo Św. Krzyża, 1995), pp. 525–27

Kwiatkowska-Kopka, Beata, Waldemar Gliński, and Janusz Firlet, 'Najnowsze badania archeologiczne w obrębie opactwa ojców cystersów w Jędrzejowie', in *Klasztor w społeczeństwie średniowiecznym i nowożytnym*, ed. by Marek Derwich and Anna Pobóg-Lenartowicz (Opole-Wrocław: WUW, 1996), pp. 539–45

Krzyżaniakowa, Jadwiga, 'Rozwój kultury w XII–XV wieku', in *Dzieje Wielkopolski*, T. I., ed. by Jerzy Topolski (Poznań: WP, 1969), pp. 328–40

Labuda, Gerard, 'Akt *Dagome iudex* – pierwsza "konkordatowa" umowa między Polską a Stolicą Apostolską z czasów papieża Jana XV (985–996)', *Pamiętnik Biblioteki Kórnickiej*, 25 (2001), 17–24

Labuda, Gerard. 'Epilog dyskusji o początkach Zakonu Krzyżackiego w ziemi chełmińskiej i w Prusach', in *Studia krytyczne o początkach Zakonu Krzyżackiego w Prusach i na Pomorzu. Pisma wybrane* (Poznań: WP, 2007) pp. 271–98

Labuda, Gerard, 'Jakub zwany ze Żnina', in *Polski słownik biograficzny*, vol. 10 (Wrocław: ZNO, 1962–1964), pp. 371–72

Labuda, Gerard, 'Klasztor Benedyktynów w Tyńcu', in *Szkice historyczne X–XI wieku. Z dziejów organizacji Kościoła w Polsce we wczesnym średniowieczu*, ed. by Gerard Labuda, reprint (Poznań: WP, 2004), pp. 247–76

Labuda, Gerard, 'Najstarsze klasztory w Polsce', in *Szkice historyczne X–XI wieku. Z dziejów organizacji Kościoła w Polsce we wczesnym średniowieczu*, ed. by Gerard Labuda, reprint (Poznań: WP, 2004), pp. 187–93

Labuda, Gerard, *Początki organizacji kościelnej na Pomorzu i Kujawach w XI i XII wieku, Zapiski Historyczne*, 33 (1968), 19–60

Labuda, Gerard, 'Prusy rodzime', in *Dzieje Zakonu Krzyżackiego w Prusach. Gospodarka – społeczeństwo – państwo – ideologia*, ed. by Marian Biskup and Gerard Labuda (Gdańsk: Wydawnictwo Morskie, 1986), p. 85

Labuda, Gerard, *Słowiańszczyzna starożytna i wczesnośredniowieczna. Antologia tekstów źródłowych* (Poznań: Towarzystwo Przyjaciół Nauk, 1999)

Labuda, Gerard, *Studia nad początkami państwa polskiego*, vol. 2 (Poznań: UAM, 1988)

Labuda, Gerard, 'Studia źródłoznawcze', in *Studia krytyczne o początkach Zakonu Krzyżackiego w Prusach i na Pomorzu. Pisma wybrane* (Poznań: WP, 2007) pp. 189–270

Labuda, Gerard, 'Święty Wojciech w tradycji, w działaniu i w legendzie', in *Święty Wojciech w tradycji i kulturze europejskiej*, ed. by Kazimierz Śmigiel (Gniezno: Gaudentinum, 1992), pp. 89–92

Labuda, Gerard, 'Szkice historyczne XI wieku I. Najstarsze klasztory w Polsce', in *Z badań nad dziejami klasztorów w Polsce*, ed. by Jerzy Olczak (Toruń: Wydawnictwo Uniwersytetu Mikołaja Kopernika, 1995), pp. 7–73

Labuda, Gerard, 'Testament Bolesława Krzywoustego', in *Opuscula Casimiro Tymieniecki septuagenario dedicata* (Poznań: Towarzystwo Przyjaciół Nauk, 1959), pp. 171–94

Labuda, Gerard, 'Über die angeblichen und vermuteren Fälschungen des Deutschen Ordens in Preussen', in *Fälschungen im Mittelalter*, MGH Schriften 33, iv (Hanover: Hansche, 1988) pp. 499–521

Labuda, Gerard, 'W sprawie osoby fundatora i daty powstania najstarszych (przedcysterskich) budowli sakralno-pałacowych w Wąchocku', *Biuletyn Historii Sztuki*, 45 (1983), 251–55

Labuda, Gerard, 'Zabiegi o utrzymanie jedności państwa polskiego w latach 1138–1146', *Kwartalnik Historyczny*, 66 (1959), 1147–1167

Labuda, Gerard, 'Ze studiów nad najstarszymi dokumentami Pomorza
 Gdańskiego', *Zapiski Towarzystwa Naukowego w Toruniu*, 18 (1952), 105–55
Lalik, Tadeusz, 'Organizacja grodowo-prowincjonalna w Polsce XI i początków
 XII wieku', *Studia z Dziejów Osadnictwa*, 5 (1967), 5–51
Łaszczyńska, Olga, ed., *Najstarsze papieskie bulle protekcyjne dla biskupstw polskich*,
 Part I: *Bulla gnieźnieńska z r. 1136* (Poznań: Księgarnia Akademicka, 1947)
Lechowicz, Zbigniew, 'Wyniki badań archeologicznych w zespole klasztornym
 cystersów w Jędrzejowie', *Sprawozdania Archeologiczne*, 34 (1982), 223–32
Lejawa, Jerzy, 'Historia i stan badań archeologicznych na terenie opactwa
 cystersów w Wąchocku', in *Z dziejów opactwa cystersów w Wąchocku*, ed. by
 Adam Massalski and Daniel Olszewski (Kielce: Towarzystwo Naukowe, 1993),
 pp. 153–58
Lenczowski, Franciszek, 'Zarys dziejów klasztoru cystersów w Kamieńcu
 Ząbkowickim na Śląsku w wiekach średnich', *Nasza Przeszłość*, 19 (1964), 61–103
Leśny, Jan, 'Ze studiów nad osadnictwem i dziejami ziemi pałuckiej we wczesnym
 średniowieczu', *Slavia Antiqua*, 22 (1975), 123–76
Likowski, Henryk, 'Geneza święta Translationis S. Adalberti w Kościele polskim',
 Kwartalnik Teologiczny Wileński, 1 (1923), 53–80
Likowski, Henryk, *Początki klasztoru cysterek w Owińskach (1242–1250)* (Poznań:
 Fiszer i Majewski Księgarnia Uniwersytecka, 1924)
Likowski, Henryk, 'W sprawie żywota bł. Bogumiła', *Kurier Poznański*, 20 (1925)
Lingenberg, Heinz, *Die älteste Olivaer Geschichtsschreibung (bis etwa 1350) und die
 Gründung des Klosters Oliva* (Lübeck: Unser Danzig, 1994)
Lipińska, Olga, 'Badania archeologiczne w klasztorze cystersów w Wąchocku, pow.
 Iłża, w 1962 i 1963 roku', in *IV Konferencja Naukowa w Kielcach 5 kwietnia 1963
 roku*, ed. by Włodzimierz Antoniewicz and Piotr Biegński (Warszawa: PWN,
 1965), pp. 94–97
Lipińska, Olga, *Rola 'włości wierzbickiej' i jej pierwszych właścicieli w najdawniejszych
 dziejach klasztoru Cystersów w Wąchocku*, in *Z dziejów opactwa cystersów w
 Wąchocku*, ed. by Adam Massalski and Daniel Olszewski (Kielce: Towarzystwo
 Naukowe, 1993), pp. 341–73
Łodyński, Marian, *Falsyfikaty wśród dokumentów biskupstwa płockiego w XIII w.*
 (Kraków: AU, 1916)
Łowmiański, Henryk, 'Rozdrobnienie feudalne Polski w historiografii naukowej',
 in *Polska w okresie rozdrobnienia feudalnego*, ed. by Henryk Łowmiański
 (Wrocław-Gdańsk: ZNO, 1973), pp. 7–34
Łowmiański, Henryk, *Początki Polski. Politczyne i społeczne procesy kształtowania się
 narodu do początku wieku XIV*, vols 5 & 6 (Warszawa: PWN, 1973, 1985)
Łuszczkiewicz, Władysław, 'Pionierowie gotycyzmu w Polsce. Architektura
 cysterska i wpływ jej pomników na gotycyzm krakowski', *Ateneum*, 2 (1882),
 112–35, 342–64
Łuszczkiewicz, Władysław, 'Romańska architektura w Wąchocku, kościół i reszty
 cysterskiego klasztoru', *Sprawozdania Komisji do Badania Historii Sztuki w
 Polsce*, 5 (1896), 49–71

Maleczyński, Karol, *Bolesław III Krzywousty* (Wrocław: ZNO, 1975)
Maleczyński, Karol, 'Dokument Humbalda kardynała legata papieskiego dla klasztoru w Trzemesznie opatrzony datą 2 marca 1146', *Roczniki Historyczne*, 4 (1928), 1–29
Maleczyński, Karol, 'Dwa nieznane dokumenty jędrzejowskie z XIII wieku', *Kwartalnik Historyczny*, 38 (1924), 456–9
Maleczyński, Karol, 'Kilka nieznanych dokumentów z XIII wieku przeważnie z archiwów poznańskich', *Kwartalnik Historyczny*, 40 (1926), 185–96
Maleczyński, Karol, 'O kanclerzach polskich XII wieku', *Kwartalnik Historyczny*, 42 (1928), 29–58
Maleczyński, Karol, 'O wpływie szkoły pisarskiej leodyjskiej na dukt dokumentów łekneńskich', in *Księga pamiątkowa ku czci Władysława Abrahama*, vol. 1 (Lwów: Gubrynowicz i Syn, 1930), pp. 367–80
Maleczyński, Karol, review of Kozłowska-Budkowa, *Repertorjum polskich dokumentów doby piastowskiej*, *Kwartalnik Historyczny*, 52 (1937), 578–83
Maleczyński, Karol, *Stanowisko dokumentu w polskim prawie prywatnym i przewodzie sądowym do połowy XIII wieku* (Lwów: Lwowskie Towarzystwo Naukowe, 1935)
Maleczyński, Karol, *Studia nad dyplomami i kancelarią Odonica i Laskonogiego* (Lwów: Towarzystwo Naukowego, 1928)
Maleczyński, Karol, *W sprawie autentyczności bulli gnieźnieńskiej* (Wrocław: Nakładem Wrocławskiego Towarzystwo Naukowego, 1947)
Maleczyński, Karol, 'Wpływy obce na dokument Polski w XII wieku', *Kwartalnik Historyczny*, 46 (1932), 1–35
Maleczyński, Karol, *Zarys dyplomatyki polskiej wieków średnich* (Wrocław: Towarzystwo Naukowe, 1951)
Maleczyński, Karol, Maria Bielińska, and Antoni Gąsiorowski, *Dyplomatyka wieków średnich* (Warszawa: PWN, 1971)
Małecki, Antoni, *Studia heraldyczne*, vol. 1 (Lwów: ZNO, 1890)
Małecki, Antoni, 'W kwestii fałszerstwa dokumentów', *Kwartalnik Historyczny*, 18 (1904), 1–17, 411–80
Małecki, Antoni, *Z dziejów i literatury pomniejsze pisma* (Lwów: Księgarnia Hermana Altenberga, 1896)
Manikowska, Halina, 'Princeps fundator w przedlokacyjnym Wrocławiu. Od Piotra Włostowica do Henryka Brodatego', in *Fundacje i fundatorzy w średniowieczu i epoce nowożytnej*, ed. by Edward Opaliński and Tomasz Wiślicz (Warszawa: Neriton, 2000), pp. 37–57
Manteuffel, Tadeusz, *Papiestwo i cystersi ze szczególnym uwzględnieniem ich roli w Polsce na przełomie XII i XIII wieku* (Warszawa: PWN, 1955)
Massalski, Adam, and Daniela Olszewski, eds, *Z dziejów opactwa cystersów w Wąchocku* (Kielce: Towarzystwo Naukowe, 1993)
Matuszewski, Józef, *Annales seu cronicae Jana Długosza w oczach Aleksandra Semkowicza* (Wrocław: ZNO, 1987)
Matuszewski, Józef, *Immunitet ekonomiczny w dobrach Kościoła w Polsce do r. 1381* (Poznań: PTPN, 1936)

Matuszewski, Józef, 'Jeszcze o treści dokumentu lubiąskiego 1175 r.', *Czasopismo Prawno-Historyczne*, 47 (1995), 171–85

Mazur, Zygmunt, *Studia nad kancelarią księcia Leszka Czarnego* (Wrocław: ZNO, 1975)

Michałowski, Roman, *Princeps-fundator. Studium z dziejów kultury politycznej w Polsce X–XIII w.* (Warszawa: Zamek Królewski w Warszawie, 1993)

Michałowski, Roman, 'Święta moc fundatora klasztoru (Niemcy XI-XII w.)', *Kwartalnik Historyczny*, 91 (1984), 3–24

Mieszkowski, Karol, 'Krytyka autentyczności dokumentów biskupów krakowskich XIII wieku', *Przegląd Historyczny*, 65 (1974), pp, 147–58

Mieszkowski, Karol, *Studia nad dokumentami katedry krakowskiej XIII wieku. Początki kancelarii biskupiej* (Wrocław: ZNO, 1974)

Mikucki, Sylwiusz, *Badanie autentyczności dokumentów w praktyce kancelarii monarszej i sądów polskich w wiekach średnich* (Kraków: PAU, 1934)

Mikucki, Sylwiusz, 'Początki notariatu publicznego w Polsce', *Przegląd Historyczny*, 34 (1938), 10–26

Missalek, Erich, 'Zur Leubuser Urkunde von 1175', *Zeitschrift für Osteuropäische Geschichte*, 4 (1914), 401–04

Mitkowski, Józef, *Kancelaria Kazimierza Konradowica, księcia kujawsko-łęczyckiego (1233–1267)* (Wrocław: ZNO, 1968)

Mitkowski, Józef, 'Nieznane dokumenty Leszka Białego z lat 1217, 1222', *Kwartalnik Historyczny*, 52 (1938), 645–58

Mitkowski, Józef, *Początki klasztoru cystersów w Sulejowie. Studia nad dokumentami, fundacją i rozwojem uposażenia do końca XIII wieku* (Poznań: PTPN, 1949)

Mitkowski, Józef, review of Krasoń, *Uposażenie klasztoru cystersów*, *Roczniki Dziejów Społecznych i Gospodarczych*, 13 (1951), 304–12

Moepert, Adolf, 'Die Echtheit der Leubuser Stiftungsurkunde in sprachwissenschaftlicher Beleuchtung', *Zeitschrift des Vereins für Geschichte Schlesiens*, 73 (1939), 42–58

Mosingiewicz, Krzysztof, and Błażej Śliwiński, 'Rycerstwo polskie z końca XII wieku w falsyfikacie Kazimierza Sprawiedliwego', *Kwartalnik Historyczny*, 88 (1981), 713–22

Mrozowicz, Wojciech, 'Kanonicy regularni św. Augustyna (augustianie) na Śląsku', *Śląski Kwartalnik Historyczny Sobótka*, 53 (1998), 401–13

Mularczyk, Jerzy, review of Skupieński, *Funkcje małopolskich dokumentów w oprawach prywatnoprawnych do roku 1306*, *Studia Historyczne*, 35 (1992), 431–33

Mütherich, Florentine, 'Epistola Mathildis Suevae. Eine wiederaufgefundene Handschrift', *Studia Źródłoznawcze*, 26 (1981), 73–78

Nawrocki, Stanisław, *Rozwój form kancelaryjnych* (Poznań: UAM, 1997)

Niwiński, Mieczysław, 'Dokumenty Łokietka dla dóbr łęczyckich opactwa wąchockiego', *Kwartalnik Historyczny*, 46 (1932), 371–77

Niwiński, Mieczysław, *Opactwo cystersów w Wąchocku. Fundacja i dzieje uposażenia do końca wieków średnich* (Kraków: PAU, 1930)

Niwiński, Mieczysław, 'Ród panów na Wierzbicy', *Miesięcznik Heraldycznym*, 10 (1931), 29–35

Niwiński, Mieczysław, 'Średniowieczni opaci klasztoru wąchockiego', *Przegląd Powszechny*, 48 (1931), 329–43

Nowacki, Józef, 'Arcybiskup gnieźnieński Janusz i nieznany synod prowincjonalny roku 1258. Part 1: Nieznany dokument elekta gnieźnieńskiego Janusza z 1258 r.', *Collectanea Theologica*, 13 (1932), 355–69

Nowacki, Józef, 'Bogumił-Piotr II', in *Nasi święci. Słownik hagiograficzny*, ed. by Aleksandra Witkowska (Poznań: Księgarnia św. Wojciecha, 1995), pp. 112–13

Nowacki, Józef, *Dzieje archidiecezji poznańskiej*, vol. 2 (Poznań: Księgarnia Św. Wojciecha, 1964)

Nowacki, Józef, *Opactwo św. Gotarda w Szpetalu pod Włocławkiem Zakonu Cysterskiego (ok. 1228/1285–1358). Przyczynek do misji pruskiej biskupa Chrystjana* (Gniezno: Studia Gnesnensia, 1934)

Oblizajek, Wojciech, 'Najstarsze dokumenty bożogrobców miechowskich (1198)', *Studia Źródłoznawcze*, 24 (1979), 97–108

Olszewski, Daniel, ed., *Cystersi w Polsce. W 850-lecie fundacji opactwa jędrzejowskiego* (Kielce: Wydawnictwo Jedność, 1990)

Pakulski, Jan, *Nałęcze wielkopolscy w średniowieczu. Genealogia, uposażenie i rola polityczna w XII–XIV w.* (Warszawa: PWN, 1982)

Paliński, Piotr, *Powiat wągrowiecki* (Wągrowiec: Walenty Masłowski and J. Czajkowski, 1932)

Papée, Fryderyk, *Najstarszy dokument polski* (Kraków: AU, 1888)

Paprocki, Bartosz, *Herby rycerstwa polskiego* (Kraków: Biblioteka Polska, 1858)

Pauk, Marcin R., 'Początki Kościoła na Pomorzu', in *Europa sięga po Bałtyk. Polska i Pomorze w kształtowaniu cywilizacji europejskiej (X–XII wiek)*, ed. by Stanisław Rosik (Wrocław: Uniwersytet Wrocławski, 2020), pp. 403–70

Perlbach, Max, 'Die Cistercienser Abtei Lond im Stadtkolnischen Archiv', *Mitteilungen aus dem Stadtarchiv von Köln*, 2 (1884), 71–127

Perlbach, Max, *Preussisch-polnische Studien zur Geschichte des Mittelalters* (Halle: M. Niemeyer, 1886)

Perzanowski, Zbigniew, *Dokument i kancelaria sądu ziemskiego krakowskiego do połowy XV wieku* (Kraków: Uniwersytet Jagielloński, 1968)

Petzelt, L., 'Urkundliches über die ältere Geschichte der ehemaligen Cistercienser Abtei Obra bei Wollstein, Prov. Posen', *Cistercienser Chronik*, 23 (1911), 193–97

Pianowski, Zbigniew, 'Głos w dyskusji o przedcysterskich budowlach w Wąchocku', in *Klasztor w kulturze Polski średniowiecznej*, ed. by Anna Pobóg-Lenartowicz and Marek Derwich (Opole: [n. pub.], 1995), pp. 389–92

Pianowski, Zbigniew, *Sedes regni principales. Wawel i inne rezydencje piastowskie do połowy XIII wieku* (Kraków: Politechnika Krakowska, 1994)

Pianowski, Zbigniew, 'W sprawie domniemanej rezydencji wczesnopiastowskiej w Wąchocku', *Kwartalnik Architektury i Urbanistyki*, 36 (1991), 57–66

Pęckowski, Zbigniew, *Miechów: Studia z dziejów miasta i ziemi miechowskiej do r. 1914* (Kraków: Wydawnictwo Literackie, 1967)

Piechowicz, Michał, 'Działalność fundacyjno-donacyjna Mieszka III Starego' (unpublished master's thesis, UAM, 2001)

Piekosiński, Franciszek, *Jeszcze słowo o dokumencie legata Idziego dla Tyńca* (Kraków: AU, 1888)
Piekosiński, Franciszek, 'Jeszcze słowo o dokumencie legata Idziego dla Tyńca', *Kwartalnik Historyczny*, 3 (1889), 49–74
Piekosiński, Franciszek, *Pieczęcie polskie wieków średnich*, vol. 1: *Doba piastowska* (Kraków: Nakładem Własnym, 1888)
Piekosiński, Franciszek, review of Kętrzyński, 'Dokument księcia Konrada Mazowieckiego', *Kwartalnik Historyczny*, 1 (1887), 503–12
Piekosiński, Franciszek, review of Kętrzyński, 'Podrobione dyplomata tynieckie', *Przegląd Krytyczny* (1876), 404–21
Piekosiński, Franciszek, review of Zakrzewski, *Kodeks dyplomatyczny Wielkopolski* vol. 1, *Przegląd Krytyczny* (1877), 454
Piekosiński, Franciszek, *Rycerstwo polskie wieków średnich*, vol. 2 (Kraków: AU, 1896)
Piętka, Jan, 'Fałszywe, niepewne i podejrzane dokumenty mazowieckie z pierwszej połowy XIII wieku', *Przegląd Historyczny*, 88 (1997), 289–315
Pietrusiński, Jerzy, '*Epistola Mathildis Suevae*. O zaginionej miniaturze', *Studia Źródłoznawcze*, 26 (1981), 53–72
Pietrusiński, Jerzy, 'Krakowska katedra romańska fundacji króla Bolesława II Szczodrego', in *Katedra krakowska w średniowieczu. Materiały sesji Oddziału Krakowskiego Stowarzyszenia Historyków Sztuki, Kraków, kwiecień 1994*, ed. by Joanna Daranowska-Łukaszewska and Kazimierz Kuczman (Kraków: Oddział Krakowski SHS, 1996), pp. 43–93
Piłat, Zbigniew, 'Fundator i fundacja klasztoru Bożogrobców w Miechowie', in *Bożogrobcy w Polsce. Praca zbiorowa* (Miechów–Warszawa: Instytut Wydawniczy Pax, 1999), pp. 11–43
Piskorski, Jan M., 'Z najnowszych badań nad historią klasztorów zachodniopomorskich w średniowieczu', *Roczniki Historyczne*, 53 (1987), 176–79
Plenkiewicz, Roman, 'Opactwo Cystersów w Wąchocku', *Przegląd Historyczny*, 6 (1908), 13–32
Plezia, Marian, 'List biskupa Mateusza do św. Bernarda', in *Prace z dziejów Polski feudalnej ofiarowane Romanowi Grodeckiemu w 70. rocznicę urodzin* (Warszawa: PWN, 1960), pp. 123–40
Płocha, Józef, *Najdawniejsze dzieje opactwa benedyktynów w Mogilnie* (Wrocław: ZNO, 1969)
Pobóg-Lenartowicz, Anna, *Kanonicy regularni na Śląsku. Życie konwentów w śląskich klasztorach kanoników regularnych w średniowieczu* (Opole: Uniwersytet Opolski, 1999)
Pobóg-Lenartowicz, Anna, *Uposażenie i działalność gospodarcza klasztoru kanoników regularnych NMP na Piasku we Wrocławiu do początku XVI wieku* (Opole: Uniwersytet Opolski, 1994)
Polaczkówna, Helena, 'Roty przywileju Henryka I Brodatego dla Trzebnicy z 1208 roku', in *Księga pamiątkowa ku czci Władysława Abrahama*, vol. 1 (Lwów: Gubrynowicz i Syn, 1930), pp. 429–53

Polanowski, Leszek, 'Architektura klasztoru pocysterskiego w Koprzywnicy. Wyniki badań archeologicznych', *Materiały i Sprawozdania Rzeszowskiego Ośrodka Archeologicznego*, 17 (1996), 201–20

Popielas-Szultka, Barbara, 'Regesty dokumentów klasztoru cystersów w Kołbaczu', *Informator Archiwalny Archiwum Państwowego w Szczecinie*, 12 (1983), 5–37

Potkański, Karol, 'Ród Nagodziców', in *Pisma pośmiertne*, vol. 2 (Kraków: PAU, 1924), pp. 209–39

Przybył, Maciej, *Mieszko III Stary* (Poznań: Wydawnictwo WBP, 2002)

Przybysz, Tadeusz, 'Fundacja i pierwotne uposażenie klasztoru cystersów w Łeknie', *Rocznik Nadnotecki*, 7 (1976), 56–72

Przypkowski, Tadeusz, *Katalog zabytków sztuki w Polsce*, vol. III: *Powiat jędrzejowski* (Warszawa: Panstwowy Instytut Sztuki, 1957)

Przypkowski, Tadeusz, 'Przywieszenie pieczęci Mieszka Starego u falsyfikatu lądzkiego w Kolonii', *Wiadomości Numizmatyczno-Archeologiczne*, 12 (1930), 89–93

Ptakówna, Wanda, 'Kazimierz Sprawiedliwy (1138–1194)', in *Polski słownik biograficzny*, vol. 12 (Wrocław: ZNO, 1966–1967), pp. 263–64

Radtke, Irena, *Kancelaria miasta Poznania do r. 1570* (Warszawa: PWN, 1967)

Radzimiński, Andrzej, *Duchowieństwo kapituł katedralnych w Polsce XIV i XV w. na tle porównawczym. Studium nad rekrutacją i drogami awansu* (Toruń: Uniwersytet Mikołaja Kopernika, 1995)

Rajman, Jerzy, *Klasztor norbertanek na Zwierzyńcu w wiekach średnich* (Kraków: Secesja, 1993)

Rajman, Jerzy, 'Nadanie dóbr skowieszyńskich klasztorowi na Zwierzyńcu pod Krakowem', in *Problemy dziejów i konserwacji miast zabytkowych*, ed. by Ryszard Szczygieł (Radom–Kazimierz Dolny: Radomskie Towarzystwo Naukowe, 1990), pp. 23–33

Rajman, Jerzy, 'Norbertanie polscy XII wieku. Możni wobec ordinis novi', in *Społeczeństwo Polski średniowiecznej. Zbiór studiów*, vol. 7, ed. by S. K. Kuczyński (Warszawa: PWN, 1996), pp. 71–105

Rajman, Jerzy, 'The Origins of the Polish Praemonstratensian Circary', *Analecta Praemonstratensia*, 66 (1990), 203–19

Rajman, Jerzy, 'Średniowieczne zapiski w nekrologu klasztoru norbertanek na Zwierzyńcu', *Nasza Przeszłość*, 77 (1992), 33–55

Ratajczak, Krzysztof, 'Proces fundacyjny klasztoru cysterek w Owińskach i zarys jego średniowiecznych dziejów', in *Cysterki w dziejach i kulturze ziem polskich*, ed. by Andrzej Marek Wyrwa, Antoni Kiełbasa, and Józef Swastek (Poznań: WP, 2004), pp. 634–47

Ratajczak, Krzysztof, 'Szkic z dziejów opactwa cysterek w Owińskach. 750. rocznica fundacji', *Nasza Przeszłość*, 98 (2002), 531–48

Rose, Ambrosius, *Kloster Grüssau* (Stuttgart-Aalen: Theiss, 1974)

Rosik, Stanisław, *Bolesław Krzywousty* (Wrocław: Chronicon, 2013)

Rother, Karl Heinrich, 'Aus Schreibstube und Bücherei des ehemaligen Zisterzienserklosters Heinrichau', *Zeitschrift des Vereins für Geschichte Schlesiens*, 61 (1927), 44–80

Rubczyński, Witold, *Wielkopolska pod rządami synów Władysława Odonicza (1239–1279)* (Kraków: Drukarnia Uniwersytetu Jagiellońskiego, 1886)
Rybandt, Stanisław, *Średniowieczne opactwo cystersów w Rudach* (Wrocław: ZNO, 1977)
Rybicka-Adamska, 'Dokument i kancelaria biskupa krakowskiego Jana Grota (1326–1347)', *Roczniki Humanistyczne*, 37 (1989), 77–142
Rymar, Edward, 'Czy Jadwiga żona Władysława Odonica była księżniczką pomorską?', *Studia i Materiały do Dziejów Wielkopolski i Pomorza*, 13 (1980), 35–59
Rymut, Kazimierz, *Patronimiczne nazwy miejscowe w Małopolsce* (Wrocław: ZNO, 1971)
Salis, Friedrich, 'Untersuchungen zum Pommerschen Urkundenwesen im XII und XIII Jh.', *Baltische Studien*, 13 (1911), 128–97
Sappok, Gerhard, *Die Anfänge des Bistums Posen und die Reihe seiner Bischöfe von 968–1498* (Leipzig: Hirzel, 1937)
Schulte, Wilhelm, 'Das Heinrichauer Gründungsbuch nach seiner Bedeutung für die Geschichte des Urkundenwesens in Schlesien', *Zeitschrift des Vereins für Geschichte Schlesiens*, 34 (1900), 343–70
Sczaniecki, Michał, *Nadania na rzecz rycerzy w Polsce do końca XIII wieku* (Poznań: PTPN, 1938)
Sczaniecki, Paweł, *Sacramentum dedicationis. Obrzęd poświęcenia kościoła i jego znaczenie w dziedzinie religijnej, obyczajowej i kulturalnej na podstawie źródeł polskich z XII wieku* (Lublin: Katolicki Uniwersytet Lubelski, 1979)
Seidel, Viktor, 'Zur Beurteilung der Leubuser Stiftungsurkunde', *Archiv für Schlesische Kirchengeschichte*, 3 (1938), 20–28
Semkowicz, Aleksander, *Krytyczny rozbiór Dziejów polskich Jana Długosza (do roku 1384)* (Kraków: NAU, 1887)
Semkowicz, Władysław, *Encyklopedia nauk pomocniczych historii*, ed. by Bożena Wyrozumska (Kraków: TAiWPN, 1999)
Semkowicz, Władysław, 'Nieznane nadania na rzecz opactwa jędrzejowskiego w XII w.', *Kwartalnik Historyczny*, 24 (1910), 70–97
Semkowicz, Władysław, *Paleografia łacińska* (Kraków: PAU, 1951)
Semkowicz, Władysław, 'Przyczynki dyplomatyczne z wieków średnich', in *Księga pamiątkowa ku uczczeniu 250-tej rocznicy założenia Uniwersytetu Lwowskiego przez króla Jana Kazimierza r. 1661*, vol. 2 (Lwów: Uniwersytet Lwowski, 1912), pp. 1–52
Semkowicz, Władysław, review of Krzyżanowski, *Monumenta Poloniae paleographica*, *Kwartalnik Historyczny*, 23 (1909), 385–400
Semkowicz, Władysław, *Rocznik Świętokrzyski dawny* (Kraków: AU, 1910)
Semkowicz, Władysław, *Ród Awdańców w wiekach średnich* (Poznań: PTPN, 1920)
Semkowicz, Władysław, *Ród Pałuków* (Kraków: AU, 1907)
Semkowicz, Władysław, 'Ród Powałów', *Sprawozdania z Czynności i Posiedzeń Akademii Umiejętności w Krakowie*, 19 (1914), 1–23
Semkowicz, Władysław, 'Uwagi o początkach dokumentu polskiego', *Kwartalnik Historyczny*, 49 (1935), 1–55 (review of Kętrzyński, *Zarys nauki o dokumencie polskim wieków średnich*)

Sikora, Franciszek, *Dokumenty i kancelaria Przemysła I i Bolesława Pobożnego 1239–1279 na tle współczesnej dyplomatyki wielkopolskiej* (Wrocław: ZNO, 1969)

Sikora, Franciszek, 'Jeszcze o przywilejach rycerskich synów Odonica', *Studia Źródłoznawcze*, 16 (1971), 181–97

Sikora, Franciszek, 'Krytyka autentyczności dokumentów Przemysła I', *Studia Historyczne*, 11 (1968), 139–79

Sikora, Franciszek, 'Przywileje rycerskie synów Władysława Odonica', *Roczniki Historyczne*, 34 (1968), 9–47

Sikora, Franciszek, 'Upadek fundacji cysterskiej w Szpetalu i początki odnowionego klasztoru byszewskiego', *Zapiski Historyczne*, 40 (1975), 6–35

Sikora, Franciszek, 'Uwagi o dokumentach klasztoru cysterek w Owińskach', *Studia Źródłoznawcze*, 9 (1964), 61–73

Sikorski, Dariusz Andrzej, *Kościół w Polsce za Mieszka I i Bolesława Chrobrego. Rozważania nad granicami poznania historycznego*, 2nd edn (Poznań: UAM, 2013)

Sikorski, Dariusz Adam, *Przywilej kruszwicki. Studium wczesnych dziejów Zakonu Niemieckiego w Prusach* (Warszawa: Trio, 2001)

Skierska, Irena, and Antoni Gąsiorowski, 'Średniowieczna monarchia objazdowa: władca w centralnych ośrodkach państwa', in *Sedes regni principales. Materiały z konferencji, Sandomierz 20–21 października 1997 r.*, ed. by Barbara Trelińska (Sandomierz: Studium Generale Sandomiriense, 1999), pp. 67–80

Skupieński, Krzysztof, *Funkcje małopolskich dokumentów w oprawach prywatnoprawnych do roku 1306* (Lublin: Uniwersytet Marii Curie-Skłodowskiej, 1990)

Skupieński, Krzysztof, 'Klasztory a początki dokumentu miejskiego w Polsce', in *Klasztor w mieście średniowiecznym i nowożytnym*, ed. by Marek Derwich and Anna Pobóg-Lenartowicz (Wrocław–Opole: WUW, 2000), pp. 93–102

Skupieński, Krzysztof, *Notariat publiczny w średniowiecznej Polsce* (Lublin: Uniwersytet Marii Curie-Skłodowskiej, 1997)

Skwierczyński, Krzysztof, *Recepcja idei gregoriańskich w Polsce do początku XIII wieku* (Wrocław: Uniwersytet Mikołaja Kopernika, 2005)

Śliwiński, Błażej, 'Na marginesie fundacyjnej działalności Kazimierza Sprawiedliwego – książę krakowski a kulty św. Wojciecha i św. Floriana', *Roczniki Historyczne*, 61 (1995), 174–78

Śliwiński, Józef, *Rozwój uposażenia ziemskiego opactwa cystersów w Łeknie do końca XIV wieku* (Olsztyn: WSP, 1981)

Smolka, Stanisław, 'Archiwa w W. X. Poznańskim i w Prusiech Wschodnich i Zachodnich. Sprawozdanie z podróży odbytej z polecenia Komisji Historyczne, w lecie 1874 r.', *Rozprawy i Sprawozdania z Posiedzeń Wydziału Historyczno-Filozoficznego Akademii Umiejętności*, 4 (1875), 170–464

Smolka, Stanisław, *Mieszko Stary i jego wiek* (Warszawa: Nakładem Gebethnera i Wolffa, 1881)

Snoch, Bogdan, *Synowie Krzywoustego. Opowieść o początkach rozbicia dzielnicowego w Polsce* (Warszawa: Wydawnictwa Szkolne i Pedagogiczne, 1987)

Splitt, Jerzy A., 'Stan badań archeologiczno-architektonicznych nad męskimi opactwami cysterskimi w Polsce', in *Historia i kultura cystersów w dawnej Polsce i ich europejskie związki*, ed. by Jerzy Strzelczyk (Poznań: UAM, 1987), pp. 225–49

Spors, Józef, 'Dokument fundacyjny Sambora I dla Oliwy z roku 1178', *Studia Źródłoznawcze*, 22 (1977), 111–24

Spors, Józef, *Podział dzielnicowy Polski według statutu Bolesława Krzywoustego* (Słupsk: WSP, 1978)

Strehlke, Ernst, 'Doberan und Neu-Doberan', *Jahrbücher des Vereins für Mecklenburgische Geschichte und Altertumskunde*, 34 (1869), 20–54

Strzelczyk, Jerzy, ed., *Cystersi w kulturze średniowiecznej Europy* (Poznań: UAM, 1992)

Strzelczyk, Jerzy, ed., *Dzieje, kultura artystyczna i umysłowa polskich cystersów od średniowiecza do końca XVIII wieku* (Kraków: Instytut Wydawczniczy Księży Mansjonarzy "Nasza Przeszłość", 1994)

Strzelczyk, Jerzy, ed., *Historia i kultura cystersów w dawnej Polsce i ich europejskie związki* (Poznań: UAM, 1987)

Suchodolska, Ewa, *Kancelarie na Mazowszu w latach 1248–1345. Ośrodki zarządzania i kultury* (Warszawa: PWN, 1977)

Suchodolski, Stanisław, *Moneta możnowładcza i kościelna w Polsce wczesnośredniowiecznej* (Wrocław: ZNO, 1987)

Sułkowska-Kurasiowa, Irena, *Polska kancelaria królewska w latach 1447–1506* (Wrocław: ZNO, 1967)

Świechowska, Ewa, and Wojciech Mischke, *Architektura romańska w Polsce: Bibliografia* (Warszawa: Wydawnictwo DiG, 2001)

Świechowski, Zygmunt, *Architektura romańska w Polsce* (Warszawa: Wydawnictwo DiG, 2000)

Świechowski, Zygmunt, *Budownictwo romańskie w Polsce. Katalog zabytków* (Wrocław: ZNO, 1963)

Świechowski, Zygmunt, *Opactwo sulejowskie. Monografia architektoniczna* (Poznań: PWN, 1954)

Świechowski, Zygmunt, 'Pierwotny kształt i chronologia kościoła grodowego w Prandocinie', *Kwartalnik Architektury i Urbanistyki*, 33 (1988), 211–16

Świechowski, Zygmunt, 'Romańskie bazyliki Wielkopolski północno-wschodniej w świetle najnowszych badań', *Archaeologia Historica Polona*, 2 (1995), 105–14

Świechowski, Zygmunt, 'Znaczenie kościoła w Prandocinie', *Kwartalnik Architektury i Urbanistyki*, 1 (1956), 13–26

Swoboda, Wincenty, 'Maur', in *Słownik starożytności słowiańskich. Encyklopedyczny zarys kultury Słowian od czasów najdawniejszych*, ed. by Władysław Kowalenko, Gerard Labuda, and Tadeusz Lehr-Spławiński, vol. 3 (Wrocław: ZNO, 1967), pp. 185–86

Swoboda, Wincenty, 'Początki herezji na ziemiach polskich', in *Europa – Słowiańszczyzna – Polska. Studia ku uczczeniu Prof. Kazimierza Tymienieckiego*, ed. by Juliusz Bardach (Poznań: UAM, 1970), pp. 385–96

Szacherska, Stella Maria, *Opactwo cysterskie w Szpetalu a misja pruska* (Warszawa: PWN, 1960)

Szacherska, Stella Maria, 'Z dziejów kancelarii książąt kujawskich w XIII wieku. Dwa nieznane dokumenty szpetalskie', *Studia Źródłoznawcze*, 5 (1960), 1–23

Szczur, Stanisław, 'Biskupi krakowscy w Polsce piastowskiej. Między tronem a ołtarzem', in *Katedra krakowska w średniowieczu. Materiały sesji Oddziału Krakowskiego Stowarzyszenia Historyków Sztuki, Kraków, kwiecień 1994*, ed. by Joanna Daranowska-Łukaszewska and Kazimierz Kuczman (Kraków: Oddział Krakowski SHS, 1996), pp. 9–24

Sztolcman, Władysław, 'Nieznane zabytki romańszczyzny i gotyku w dawnym opactwie cystersów w Wąchocku', *Architekt*, 8 (1907), 34–39

Szydłowski, Tadeusz, 'Architektoniczny palimpsest jędrzejowski', *Sztuki Piękne*, 3 (1926–1927), 229–34

Szydłowski, Tadeusz, 'O cysterskich budowlach z początku XIII wieku w Wąchocku, Koprzywnicy, Sulejowie i Jędrzejowie oraz odkryciu absydy pierwotnego romańskiego kościoła w Jędrzejowie', *Prace Komisji Historii Sztuki*, 4 (1930), lxvii–lx

Szydłowski, Tadeusz, *Pomniki architektury epoki piastowskiej, we województwach krakowskiem i kieleckiem* (Kraków: Gebethner i Wolff, 1928)

Szymański, Józef, 'Kanonicy opatowscy w planach polityki ruskiej z przełomu XII i XIII wieku', *Przegląd Historyczny*, 56 (1965), pp. 388–96

Szymański, Józef, 'Kanonikat' in *Słownik starożytności słowiańskich. Encyklopedyczny zarys kultury Słowian od czasów najdawniejszych*, ed. by Władysław Kowalenko, Gerard Labuda, and Tadeusz Lehr-Spławiński, vol. 2 (Wrocław: ZNO, 1964), pp. 356–59

Szymański, Józef, *Kanonikat świecki w Małopolsce od końca XI do połowy XIII wieku* (Lublin: Agencja Wydawniczo-Handlowa, 1995)

Szymański, Józef, 'Krakowski rękopis reguły akwizgrańskiej z około 1103 roku', *Studia Źródłoznawcze*, 11 (1966), 39–52

Szymański, Józef, *Nauki pomocnicze historii od schyłku IV do końca XVIII w.* (Warszawa: PWN, 1976)

Szymański, Józef, 'Sto lat przemian metodologicznych nauk pomocniczych historii w Polsce', in *Tradycje i perspektywy nauk pomocniczych historii w Polsce*, ed. by Mieczysław Rokosz (Kraków: Uniwersytet Jagielloński, 1995), pp. 35–47

Taszycki, Witold, 'Najdawniejsze polskie imiona osobowe', in Witold Taszycki, *Rozprawy i studia polonistyczne*, vol. I: *Onomastyka* (Wrocław: ZNO, 1958)

Teterycz, Agnieszka, 'Rządy księcia Henryka, syna Bolesława Krzywoustego w ziemi sandomierskiej', in *Mazowsze, Pomorze, Prusy*, ed. by Błażej Śliwiński (Gdańsk: Officina Ferebriana, 2000), pp. 245–70

Teterycz-Puzio, Agnieszka, *Henryk Sandomierski (1126/1133–18 X 1166)* (Kraków: Avalon, 2009)

Tomala, Janusz, 'Krótkie podsumowanie wyników badań archeologicznych opactwa cysterskiego w Sulejowie', *Kwartalnik Historii Kultury Materialnej*, 38 (1990), 249–60

Tomaszewski, Andrzej, *Romańskie kościoły z emporami zachodnimi na obszarze Polski, Czech i Węgier* (Wrocław: ZNO, 1974)
Topolski, Jerzy, ed., *Dzieje Wielkopolski*, vol. 1 (Poznań: WP, 1969)
Trawkowski, Stanisław, *Gospodarka wielkiej własności cysterskiej na Dolnym Śląsku w XIII wieku* (Warszawa: PWN, 1959)
Trawkowski, Stanisław, 'Mikora', in *Polski słownik biograficzny*, vol. 21 (Wrocław: ZNO, 1976), pp. 157–59
Trawkowski, Stanisław, 'Otto z Wierzbicy', in *Polski słownik biograficzny*, vol. 26 (Wrocław: ZNO - WPAN, 1981), pp. 335–37
Trawkowski, Stanisław, 'Piotr', in *Polski słownik biograficzny*, vol. 26 (Wrocław: ZNO - WPAN, 1981), pp. 361–62
Trawkowski, Stanisław, 'Młyny wodne w Polsce XII w.', *Kwartalnik Historii Kultury Materialnej*, 7 (1959), 62–86
Trawkowski, Stanisław, 'Wprowadzenie zwyczajów arrowezyjskich we wrocławskim klasztorze na Piasku', in *Wieki średnie. Medium aevum. Prace ofiarowane Tadeuszowi Manteufflowi w 60. rocznicę urodzin* (Warszawa: PWN 1962), 111–16
Trelińska, Barbara, *Kancelaria i dokumenty książąt cieszyńskich 1290–1573* (Warszawa–Łódź: PWN, 1983)
Tyc, Teodor, *Początki kolonizacji wiejskiej na prawie niemieckim w Wielkopolsce (1200–1333)* (Poznań: Drukiem K. Miarki, 1924)
Tymieniecki, Kazimierz, 'Najdawniejsza polska ustawa dworska', in *Studja z historji społecznej i gospodarczej poświęcone prof. dr. Franciszkowi Bujakowi* (Lwów: Drukarnia Naukowa, 1931), pp 21–44
Tymieniecki, Kazimierz, 'O interpretację dokumentów trzebnickich', *Roczniki Historyczne*, 25 (1959), 143–71
Tymieniecki, Kazimierz, review of Manteuffel, *Papiestwo i cystersi*, *Kwartalnik Historyczny*, 63 (1956), 167–73
Tymieniecki, Kazimierz, review of Manteuffel, 'Rola cystersów w Polsce XII wieku', *Roczniki Historyczne*, 63 (1956), 214–20
Tymieniecki, Kazimierz, 'Die sogenannte', *Roczniki Dziejów Społecznych i Gospodarczych*, 6 (1937), 381–87 (review of Krupicka, 'Die sogenannte Leubuser Stiftungsurkunde')
Tymieniecki, Kazimierz, 'Majętność książęca w Zagościu i pierwotne uposażenie klasztoru joannitów na tle osadnictwa dorzecza dolnej Nidy. Studium z dziejów gospodarczych XII w.', in Kazimierz Tymieniecki, *Pisma wybrane* (Warszawa: PWN, 1956)
Tymieniecki, Kazimierz, 'Społeczeństwo śląskie na podstawie dokumentów trzebnickich z lat 1203, 1204 i 1208. Studia społeczne i gospodarcze', in *Studja społeczne i gospodarcze. Księga jubileuszowa dla uczczenia 40-lecia pracy naukowej Ludwika Krzywickiego* (Warszawa: Księgarnia F. Hoesicka, 1925), pp. 319–42
Ulanowski, Bolesław, *Drugi napad Tatarów na Polskę* (Kraków: Drukarnia Uniwersytetu Jagiellońskiego, 1885)

Ulanowski, Bolesław, *O uposażeniu biskupstwa płockiego* (Kraków: Drukarnia Uniwersytetu Jagiellońskiego, 1888)

von Güttner-Sporzyński, Darius, *Poland, Holy War, and the Piast Monarchy, 1100–1230* (Turnhout: Brepols, 2014)

von Nießen, Paul, 'Ueber die Echtheit einiger Urkunden zur Geschichte von Colbatz', *Monatsblätter*, 2 (1888), 108–09, 121–24

von Ottenthal, Emil, review of Krzyżanowski, *Monumenta Poloniae paleographica*, *Mitteilungen des österreichischen Instituts für Geschichtsforschung*, 38 (1920), 338

Walicki, Michał, ed., *Sztuka polska przedromańska i romańska do schyłku XIII wieku*, Part 2: *Katalog* (Warszawa: PWN, 1971)

Wałkówski, Andrzej, 'Najstarszy kopiarz lubiąski', *Acta Universitatis Wratislaviensis. Historia*, 50 (1985), 163–221

Wałkówski, Andrzej, 'Pochodzenie kancelaryjne pierwszych dokumentów fundacyjnych opactwa cystersów w Krzeszowie', in *Krzeszów uświęcony łaską*, ed. by Henryk Dziurla and Kazimierz Bobowski (Wrocław: WUW, 1997), pp. 44–60

Wałkówski, Andrzej, *Skryptoria cystersów filiacji portyjskiej na Śląsku do końca XIII wieku* (Zielona Góra–Wrocław: Wydawnictwo Wyższej Szkoły Pedagogicznej, 1996)

Wałkówski, Andrzej, 'Skryptorium dokumentowe klasztoru cystersów w Kamieńcu Ząbkowickim do końca XIII wieku. Zarys dziejów', *Klasztor w kulturze średniowiecznej Polski*, ed. by Anna Pobóg-Lenartowicz and Marek Derwich (Opole: Wydawnictwo Św. Krzyża, 1995), pp. 239–61

Wałkówski, Andrzej, 'Transumowanie ogólnocysterskich bulli papieskich 27 I 1234 – IX 1234 w świetle najstarszego kopiarza lubiąskiego', in *Źródłoznawstwo i studia historyczne*, ed. by Kazimierz Bobowski (Wrocław: WUW, 1989), pp. 115–21

Wałkówski, Andrzej, 'Wpływy lubiąskie na skryptorium dokumentowe klasztoru cysterek w Trzebnicy', in *Księga jadwiżańska*, ed. by Michał Kaczmarek and Marek L. Wójcik (Wrocław: WUW, 1995), pp. 189–221

Wałkówski, Andrzej, 'Wpływy skryptorium klasztoru cystersów w Pforcie na dokument lubiąski do końca XIII wieku', *Nasza Przeszłość*, 83 (1994), 203–47

Wałkówski, Andrzej, 'Z badań nad najstarszym kopiarzem lubiąskim', in *Historia i kultura cystersów w dawnej Polsce i ich europejskie związki*, ed. by Jerzy Strzelczyk (Poznań: UAM, 1987), pp. 445–52

Wałkówski, Andrzej, 'Zarys rozwoju pisma dokumentów lubiąskich do połowy XIII wieku', in *Kultura średniowieczna Śląska. Pierwiastki rodzime i obce. Zbiór studiów*, ed. by Kazimierz Bobowski (Wrocław: WUW, 1993), pp. 15–31

Waraczewski, Henryk, 'Proces fundacyjny klasztoru cystersów w Lądzie nad Wartą', *Nasza Przeszłość*, 83 (1994), 151–68

Warmiński, Teodor, *Urkundliche Geschichte des ehemaligen Cistercienser-Klosters zu Paradies* (Meseritz: R. Wild, 1886)

Wasilewski, Tadeusz, 'Helena księżniczka znojemska, żona Kazimierza Sprawiedliwego. Przyczynek do dziejów stosunków polsko-czeskich w XII–XIII w.', *Przegląd Historyczny*, 69 (1978), 115–20

Wasilewski, Tadeusz, 'Kazimierz II Sprawiedliwy', in *Poczet królów i książąt polskich*, ed. by Andrzej Garlicki (Warszawa: Spółdzielnia Wydawnicza Czytelnik, 1984), pp. 122–30

Wdowiszewski, Zygmunt, 'Nieznane dyplomy średniowieczne do dziejów opactwa cystersów w Wąchocku', *Archeion*, 16 (1938–1939), 39–46

Wdowiszewski, Zygmunt, 'Ród Bogoriów w wiekach średnich', *Rocznik Polskiego Towarzystwa Heraldycznego we Lwowie*, 9 (1928–1929), 1–96

Wędzki, Andrzej, 'Jędrzejów', in *Słownik starożytności słowiańskich. Encyklopedyczny zarys kultury Słowian od czasów najdawniejszych do schyłku wieku XII*, ed. by Władysław Kowalenko, Gerard Labuda, and Tadeusz Lehr-Spławiński, vol. 2 (Wrocław: ZNO, 1964), pp. 335

Wędzki, Andrzej, 'Wąchock', in *Słownik starożytności słowiańskich. Encyklopedyczny zarys kultury Słowian od czasów najdawniejszych do schyłku wieku XII*, ed. by Władysław Kowalenko, Gerard Labuda, and Tadeusz Lehr-Spławiński, vol. 6 (Wrocław: ZNO, 1980), pp. 349–53

Wenta, Jarosław, 'Na marginesie dokumentu legata Humbalda z 2 marca 1146 roku dla Trzemeszna', *Roczniki Historyczne*, 53 (1987), 101–14

Wetesko, Leszek, *Historyczne konteksty monarszych fundacji artystycznych w Wielkopolsce do początku XIII wieku* (Poznań: WP, 2009)

Wetesko, Leszek, *W służbie państwa i Kościoła. Historyczne konteksty monarszych fundacji artystycznych w Wielkopolsce do początku XIII wieku* (Poznań: WP, 2007)

Wielgosz, Zbigniew, 'Początki wielkiej własności klasztornej cystersów w Lubiążu', *Roczniki Historyczne*, 22 (1955–1956), 61–124

Wielgosz, Zbigniew, *Wielka własność cysterska w osadnictwie pogranicza Śląska i Wielkopolski* (Poznań: PTPN, 1964)

Wierzbicki, Andrzej, *Historiografia polska doby romantyzmu* (Wrocław: Funna, 1999)

Winter, Franz, *Die Cistercienser des nordöstlichen Deutschlands. Ein Beitrag zur Kirchen- und Culturgeschichte des deutschen Mittelalters*, 2 vols (Gotha: Scientia Verlag, 1868)

Wiśniewski, Jan, *Dekanat iłżecki* (Radom: J. K. Trzebiński, 1911)

Wiszewski, Przemysław, 'Piąte koło i złoty dzban, czyli profetyczna wizja w Kronice Kadłubka (III, 26)', in *Causa creandi. O pragmatyce źródła historycznego*, ed. by Stanisław Rosik and Przemysław Wiszewski (Wrocław: WUW, 2005), pp. 479–95

Włodarski, Bronisław, ed., *Chronologia polska* (Warszawa: PWN, 1957)

Wojciechowski, Tadeusz, *Kościół katedralny w Krakowie* (Kraków: AU, 1900)

Wojciechowski, Tadeusz, *Szkice historyczne jedynastego wieku*, 5th edn., ed. by Gerard Labuda (Poznań: WP, 2004)

Wojciechowski, Zygmunt, 'Początki immunitetu w Polsce', *Przewodnik Historyczno-Prawny*, 1 (1930), 349–66

Wojciechowski, Zygmunt, *Prawo rycerskie w Polsce przed Statutami Kazimierza Wielkiego* (Poznań: PTPN, 1928)

Wojciechowski, Zygmunt, 'Zagadnienie immunitetu sądowego w Polsce XII wieku', in *Księga pamiątkowa ku czci Władysława Abrahama*, vol. 2 (Lwów: Gubrynowicz i Syn, 1931), pp. 167–86

Wójcik, Andrzej, 'Sulejów-Podklasztorze, gm. Mniszków, woj. Piotrkowskie', *Informator Archeologiczny. Badania*, 9 (1975), 296–97

Wójcik, Andrzej, 'Sulejów-Podklasztorze, pow. Opoczno', *Informator Archeologiczny. Badania*, 8 (1974), 287

Wójcik, Marek L., 'Początki skryptorium dokumentowego klasztoru cystersów w Rudach', in *Klasztor w kulturze średniowiecznej Polski*, ed. by Anna Pobóg-Lenartowicz and Marek Derwich (Opole: Wydawnictwo Św. Krzyża, 1995), pp. 263–77

Wójcik, Marek L., *Ród Gryfitów do końca XIII wieku. Pochodzenie – genealogia – rozsiedlenie* (Wrocław: WUW, 1993)

Wolfarth, Włodzimierz, *Ascripticii w Polsce* (Wrocław: ZNO, 1959)

Wutke, Konrad, *Über schlesische Formelbücher des Mittelalter* (Breslau: F. Hirt, 1919)

Wykaz urzędowych nazw miejscowości w Polsce, 3 vols (Warszawa: Wydawnictwa Akcydensowe, 1980–1982)

Wyrozumski, Jerzy *Państwowa gospodarka solna w Polsce do schyłku XIV wieku* (Kraków: Nakładem Uniwersytetu Jagiellońskiego, 1968)

Wyrwa, Andrzej Marek, 'Badania archeologiczno-architektoniczne w łekneńskim kompleksie osadniczym w świetle najnowszych badań', in *Osadnictwo i architektura ziem polskich w dobie zjazdu gnieźnieńskiego*, ed. by Andrzej Buko and Zygmunt Świechowski (Warszawa: Letter Quality, 2000), pp. 1–52

Wyrwa, Andrzej Marek, 'Cystersi. Geneza, duchowość, organizacja życia w zakonie (do XV wieku) i początki fundacji na ziemiach polskich. Zarys', in *Cystersi w Polsce. W 850-lecie fundacji opactwa jędrzejowskiego*, ed. by Daniel Olszewski (Kielce: Wydawnictwo Jedność, 1990), pp. 11–39

Wyrwa, Andrzej Marek, 'Ląd', in *Monasticon Cisterciense Poloniae*, ed. by Andrzej Marek Wyrwa, Jerzy Strzelczyk, and Krzysztof Kaczmarek, vol. 2 (Poznań: WP, 1999), pp. 189–201

Wyrwa, Andrzej Marek, 'Łekno', in *Słownik starożytności słowiańskich. Encyklopedyczny zarys kultury Słowian od czasów najdawniejszych*, ed. by Władysław Kowalenko, Gerard Labuda, and Tadeusz Lehr-Spławiński, vol. 8 (Wrocław: ZNO, 1996), pp. 417–21

Wyrwa, Andrzej Marek, 'Łekno-Wągrowiec', in *Monasticon Cisterciense Poloniae*, ed. by Andrzej Marek Wyrwa, Jerzy Strzelczyk, and Krzysztof Kaczmarek, vol. 2 (Poznań: WP, 1999), pp. 230–50

Wyrwa, Andrzej Marek, 'Powstanie zakonu cystersów i jego rozwój na ziemiach polskich w średniowieczu', in *Monasticon Cisterciense Poloniae*, ed. by Andrzej Marek Wyrwa, Jerzy Strzelczyk, and Krzysztof Kaczmarek, vol. 1 (Poznań: WP, 1999), pp. 25–74

Wyrwa, Andrzej Marek, *Procesy fundacyjne wielkopolskich klasztorów cysterskich linii altenberskiej. Łekno – Ląd – Obra* (Poznań: Uniwersytet im. Adama Mickiewicza, 1995)

Wyrwa, Andrzej Marek, 'Rozprzestrzenianie się cystersów w Europie Zachodniej i na ziemiach polskich', in *Cystersi kulturze średniowiecznej Europy*, ed. by Jerzy Strzelczyk (Poznań: UAM, 1992), pp. 25–54

Wyrwa, Andrzej Marek, and Józef Dobosz, ed., *Cystersi w społeczeństwie Europy Środkowej. Materiały z konferencji naukowej odbytej w klasztorze oo. Cystersów w Krakowie Mogile z okazji 900. rocznicy powstania Zakonu Ojców Cystersów* (Poznań: WP, 2000)

Wyrwa, Andrzej Marek, Antoni Kiełbasa, and Józef Swastek, ed., *Cysterki w dziejach i kulturze ziem polskich, dawnej Rzeczypospolitej i Europy Środkowej. Materiały z siódmej Międzynarodowej Konferencji Cystersologów odbytej z okazji 800. rocznicy fundacji opactwa cysterek w Trzebnicy. Trzebnica 18–21 września 2002 r.* (Poznań: WP, 2004)

Wyrwa, Andrzej Marek, ed., and Anna Strzelecka, trans., *Dokument fundacyjny klasztoru cysterskiego w Łeknie z roku 1153* (Poznań: Uniwersytet im. Adama Mickiewicza, 2003)

Wyrwa, Andrzej Marek, Jerzy Strzelczyk, and Krzysztof Kaczmarek, ed., *Monasticon Cisterciense Poloniae*, 2 vols (Poznań: WP, 1999)

Zachorowski, Stanisław, 'Colloquia w Polsce od w. XII do XIV', in *Studia z historii prawa kościelnego i polskiego*, ed. by Stanisław Zachorowski (Kraków: AU 1917), pp. 3–78

Zachorowski, Stanisław, review of Plenkiewicz, 'Opactwo Cystersów w Wąchocku', *Kwartalnik Historyczny*, 24 (1910), 283–89

Zahajkiewicz, Marek T., ed., *Chrzest Litwy. Geneza – Przebieg – Konsekwencje* (Lublin: Katolicki Uniwersytet Lubelski, 1990)

Zajączkowski, Stanisław, 'O posiadłościach klasztoru trzemeszeńskiego w Łęczyckiem w XII wieku na tle początków Łęczycy', *Roczniki Historyczne*, 30 (1964), 53–85

Zajączkowski, Stanisław, 'Uwagi nad terytorialnym ustrojem Polski XII w.', *Czasopismo Prawno-Historyczne*, 7 (1955), 285–323

Zajączkowski, Stanisław, and Stanisław Marian Zajączkowski, *Materiały do słownika geograficzno-historycznego dawnych ziem łęczyckiej i sieradzkiej do 1400 roku*, 2 vols (Łódź: Łódzkie Towarzystwo Naukowe, 1966–1970)

Zakrzewski, Stanisław, *Najdawniejsze dzieje klasztoru cystersów w Szczyrzycu (1258–1582). Przyczynek do dziejów osadnictwa na Podhalu* (Kraków: AU, 1901)

Zakrzewski, Stanisław, *Ze studiów nad bullą z r. 1136* (Kraków: AU, 1903)

Zawadzka, Józefa, 'Procesy fundowania opactw cysterskich w XII i XIII wieku', *Roczniki Humanistyczne* 7 (1958), 121–50

Zdanek, Maciej, 'Pierwsze opactwo cystersów w Polsce: Łekno czy Jędrzejów?', *Studenckie Zeszyty Naukowe Uniwersytetu Jagiellońskiego*, 13 (2000), 27–34

Żebrowski, Tadeusz, 'Kościół (X–XIII w.)', in *Dzieje Mazowsza do 1526 roku*, ed. by Aleksander Gieysztor and Henryk Samsonowicz (Warszawa: PWN, 1994), pp. 132–62

Żerelik, Rościsław, 'Dokumenty i kancelaria Henryka III księcia głogowskiego', *Acta Universitatis Wratislaviensis. Historia*, 42 (1984), 3–99

Żerelik, Rościsław, *Kancelaria biskupów wrocławskich do 1301 roku* (Wrocław: WUW, 1991)

Żerelik, Rościsław, 'Urzędnicy skryptoriów klasztornych na Śląsku do końca I połowy XIV wieku. Ze studiów nad działalnością dyplomatyczną klasztorów śląskich', *Śląski Kwartalnik Historyczny Sobótka*, 44 (1989), 557–70

Zielińska-Melkowska, Krystyna, 'Klucz dobrowski w uposażeniu misji pruskiej', in *Nihil superfluum esse. Studia z dziejów średniowiecza ofiarowane Jadwidze Krzyżaniakowej*, ed. by Jerzy Strzelczyk and Józef Dobosz (Poznań: UAM, 2000), pp. 207–20

Zientara, Benedykt, *Henryk Brodaty i jego czasy*, 2nd edn (Warszawa: Trio, 1997)

Ziętara, Baldwin, 'Opactwo wąchockie na Kapitułach Generalnych Cystersów w Cîteaux', in *Z dziejów opactwa cystersów w Wąchocku*, ed. by Adam Massalski and Daniel Olszewski (Kielce: Towarzystwo Naukowe, 1993), pp. 51–60

Index

Aaron, Bishop of Kraków: 25
Abraham, Władysław: 191
Achardus (Achard), Master: 76, 99, 101
Adalbert of Prague, Bishop of Prague, saint: 22–24, 28, 274
Adalbert, Bishop of Wolin: 29
Adam, Custos of Wąchock Abbey: 285
Agnes of Austria, wife of Władysław II: 76, 145
Alexander of Malonne, Bishop of Płock: 47–49, 52, 225, 232, 281
Alexander III, Pope: 65
Altenberg: 85
Anna, mother of Jan Archbishop of Gniezno: 270
Appelt, Heinrich: 155, 176, 189
Arkembold, Castellan of Kalisz: 158
Arnold, Abbot of Sieciechów: 100
Augustyniak, Jerzy: 123
Awdańcy, clan: 78, 126, 250
Baldwin, Abbot of Szczyrzyc Abbey: 287
Baldwin, Bishop of Kraków: 263–68
Balzer, Oswald: 63, 65, 245, 249
Bałdrzych, knight: 58, 62, 73, 83, 126, 150, 210
Bałdrzychów, village: 58–59, 83, 150, 203, 204, 212–13
Bamberg: 28, 153, 164
Bartodzieje, village: 79, 259–60
Bartoszewicz, Józef: 171
Bąków, village: 142
Bechlowo, village: 102, 146, 266
Benedict IX, Pope 164, 165
Bernard of Clairvaux, saint: 76, 98–99, 177, 296

Bernard the Spaniard, missionary in Pomerania: 29
Bernard, Bishop of Poznań: 249
Bernard, comes: 234
Bernard, Provost of Trzemeszno: 45, 48, 226, 230
Bezelin, comes: 149
Bezprym, Prince of Poland, son of Bolesław I the Brave: 23
Białoskórska, Krystyna: 133, 135
Bielińska, Maria: 155, 183, 195
Bielowski, August: 171
Bieniak, Janusz: 37, 65, 139, 250–51
Bliskowice, village 79, 259–60
Błażkiewiczówna, I.: 237, 258
Bobowski, Kazimierz; 173, 185, 189, 196
Bobrzyński, Michał: 171
Bochnak, Adam: 267
Bochnia, town: 297–98
Bodzęta, knight: 105
Bodzęta, Pantler of Gniezno: 158
Bogoria, Clan: 184
Boguchwał I, Bishop of Poznań: 48
Boguchwał II, Bishop of Poznań: 157–58
Boguchwał Pałuka, knight: 253
Bogumił II, Archbishop of Gniezno: 79, 233, 252, 254, 269, 277–78, 282
Bogumił, comes: 225, 233
Bogusław I, Duke of West Pomerania: 8
Bogusław, Cantor of Wąchock Abbey: 285
Bogusz, voivode of Kujawy: 158
Bogusza = Bogumił?, comes: 233, 252, 259

Bogusza, the duke's Chamberlain: 158
Boguszyno (dzisiaj Baba?), village: 77, 246
Boguta, Castellan of Drzeń: 158
Bohemia (Czechy): 19, 25, 138
Bolechowo, village: 157
Boleslav I, Duke of Bohemia: 19
Bolesław I Chrobry (the Brave), Duke then King of Poland: 21–23, 25, 28, 31–33, 165, 267
Bolesław I Wysoki (the Tall), Duke of Silesia: 54, 81–82, 85, 148–49, 250
Bolesław II Rogatka (the Horned), Duke of Silesia: 156
Bolesław II Śmiały (the Bold), Duke then King of Poland: 25, 28, 47, 164, 219, 222, 224
Bolesław III Krzywousty (the Wrymouth), Duke of Poland: 12, 13, 28, 29, 30–35, 37, 39, 46–49, 52, 54, 68, 77, 81, 84, 139, 219, 221–25, 230, 233, 250, 263, 266, 280
Bolesław IV Kędzierzawy (the Curly), Duke of Mazovia and princeps: 34–35, 37, 39, 48, 51–55, 62–64, 69–70, 78–81, 100, 109–10, 130, 148, 209, 223, 225, 230–32, 245, 248, 259–60, 271–72, 274–75, 280
Bolesław Konradowic, Duke of Mazovia, son of Konrad I: 51, 61
Bolesław Pobożny (the Pious), Duke of Wielkopolska: 154, 156, 159–60, 183
Bolesław V Wstydliwy (the Chaste), Duke of Kraków and Sandomierz: 59, 63–64, 67, 70–71, 73, 109, 140, 143, 182, 185, 191, 204, 211, 213, 286–87, 296–97
Bolesław, son of Mieszko III Stary: 50–51, 100
Borowa (Borowo), village: 102, 146, 266
Bożen, knight: 138

Branichia, village 108
Brda, river: 232
Bresslau, Harry: 196
Břetislav I, Duke of Bohemia: 23, 39
Brodzisław, comes: 78, 251, 259–60
Bronów, village: 143
Bruder, Artur: 185
Bruno of Querfurt, Benedictine monk and missionary Bishop: 23
Bruski, Klemens: 178, 185, 196
Brzesko-Hebdów, Premonstratensian Monastery: 49
Brzezie, village: 143
Brzeźnica [= Abbey of Jędrzejów], village: 77, 80, 92, 94, 98–99, 101–03, 109–10, 126, 148, 265, 273
Brzostów near Głogów, village: 149
Brzyskorzystew, village: 231
Buczek, Karol: 37
Bukowiec, village: 79, 259–60
Burgundy 83, 124, 147, 207
Büsching, Johann: 173
Buszków, village: 67
Byczyna, village: 126
Byszewo, Cistercian Abbey 278, 287, 290
Bytom, castle: 149
Bzin, village: 142, 297

Callier, Edmund: 155
Cebar see Zbar
Celestine III, Pope: 50–51, 54
Cetwiński, Marek: 250–51, 254
Cherubin z Wysokiej, knight: 143
Cherubin, chancellor of Mieszko III the Old than the Bishop of Poznań: 100, 232, 249
Chludowo, village: 157
Chodyński, Zenon: 155
Chomiąża, village: 224, 232
Chorzelino, village: 231
Chorzewa, village: 102, 146
Chrobrze, village: 211–12
Chronów, village: 143
Chropy, district: 28, 66, 136

Chrystian, Bishop of Prussia: 189
Cienia, village: 126–27
Ciepła, village: 142
Citeaux, Cistercian Abbey: 154
Clement III, Pope: 282
Cologne: 85, 164, 177
Czasław, Bishop of Kraków: 263
Czerlin, village: 79, 259–60
Czerwińsk, monastery of Canon Regular: 11, 46, 49, 52–53, 54–55, 70, 72, 202, 233
Cześcibor (Cieszybor?), comes: 267
Czewoja, clan: 250
Czyżyny, village (part of Kraków today): 286

Dainauskas, Jonas: 195
Damian, peasant: 126
Danabórz, village: 79
Dąbrowa Niemodlińska: 186
Dąbrowa, village: 79, 126, 259–60
Dąbrowice, village: 259–60
Dąbrowski, Kazimierz: 180
Degno (Dzięgień), comes: 225–26, 233
Denmark: 86
Deptuła, Czesław: 49
Dębogóra, village: 78, 253, 259–60
Długokęcki, Wiesław: 178, 185
Długosz Jan, polish chronicler, Canon of Kraków: 66, 90–96, 101, 103, 105, 108, 123, 126, 135, 137–38, 140–43, 154–56, 159, 248–49, 253–54, 263–67, 270–76, 278–79, 282, 285, 298
Doberan, Cistercian Abbey: 180
Dobiechna, Wife of Wojsław: 54
Dobiegniew, town: 154, 157, 159
Dobrawa, Duchess of Poland: 19–21, 219
Dobrogost Stary, comes: 251
Dobrogost, of Nałęcz clan, comes: 251–52, 259
Dobrowo, village: 79, 277–78
Doezdoua, knight: 267

Dołuszyce, village: 286
Domarat, duke's judge: 158
Dragun, Cistercian Abbey: 185
Dunin-Wąsowicz, Teresa: 134
Dzierżek, of Janina clan: 55
Dzierżykraj, Castellan of Gniezno: 158
Dzierżykraj, of Nałęcz clan, comes: 225–26, 233, 251, 259
Dzierżykrajowice, clan: 251
Dzięgień see Degno

Elbe, river: 29, 88, 166
Elżbieta (Elisabeth), Wife of Przemysł I: 156, 160
Emmeram, comes: 100
Empire: 166
Eudoxia, wife of Mieszko III Stary: 52
Eugene III, Pope: 220–22, 224, 226, 270, 272

Filip, Bishop of Poznań: 276
Filip, Monk of Łekno Abbey: 78, 259–60, 253
Five Martyred Brother: 23–24
Folbert, magister: 244, 249–50, 259
France: 263
Fryderyk II, Emperor: 189, 195

Gallus Anonymous, Polish chronicler: 22, 24–25, 28, 164–65, 263
Galo (Walo), Bishop of Beauvaix: 263
Gąsawa, village: 231
Gąsiorowski, Antoni: 171
Gąski, family: 150, 203–04
Gebhard-Jaromir, Bishop of Prague: 165
Gedko, Bishop of Kraków: 31, 62, 65–66, 69, 71, 73, 80–81, 85–86, 91, 100, 103, 105, 108, 110, 135, 137–38, 140–44, 207–10, 213, 281, 283, 293
Gerard, friar of Wąchock Abbey: 285

Germany: 23, 158, 236
Gertruda, Abbess of Trzebnica: 154, 157, 159–60
Gerward, Castellan of Śrem: 158
Gerward, comes: 251, 259
Giecz, stroghold: 21, 23
Giesebrecht, Heinrich: 183
Gilo of Tousy, Cardinal, Bishop of Tusculum: 29, 190–91, 200, 204, 221
Ginter, Tomasz: 13, 195
Głojkowo, village: 78, 252, 259–60
Głuchów, village: 157
Gniewomir, comes: 100
Gniezno (city, castle, archbishopric, cathedral church): 13, 19–25, 28–32, 50, 60, 68, 77, 141, 157, 165–67, 183, 201, 207, 209, 223, 225, 238, 240, 249, 269–70, 272, 274–81, 292
Goetting, Hans: 180
Golina Czasławowa, village: 157
Gopło, lake: 232
Gorzakiew, village: 265
Gościsław, village: 78, 259–60
Gotard, Abbot of Wąchock: 284
Gozdawit, clan: 138
Góra Małgorzaty near Łęczyca, village: 53, 67–68, 232
Góra, village: 126
Górka, Olgierd: 178, 184
Górowo, village: 265
Grabonowo, village: 232
Grambalow, village: 108
Gregory IX, Pope: 71, 189, 202–03, 213
Gregory VII, Pope: 163–64
Grodecki, Roman: 109, 184
Grodzisk, villae: 52
Grüger, Heinrich: 180
Grünhagen, Colmar: 177
Gryffin, dynasty: 29, 87
Gryfici, clan: 77, 80–81, 95, 98–99, 101–03, 140, 145, 265, 270, 293
Grzybowo, village: 2

Grzymała, clan: 251
Grzymisława, Duchess of Kraków, wife of Leszek Biały: 64, 109, 140, 143, 211, 286, 294
Guido, Abbot of Wąchock: 284, 288
Guido, Cardinal: 272, 281
Gunter, Bishop of Płock: 189, 193
Guzów, village: 142

Hadrian IV, Pope: 52
Haymo, Abbot of Wąchock: 284–85
Helcel, Antoni Zygmunt: 93, 171, 81, 190, 222, 235, 244
Helena, wife of Kazimierz II: 55
Henry IV, Emperor: 165
Henryk I Brodaty (the Bearded), Duke of Silesia 13, 153, 176
Henryk (Henry) II Pobożny (the Pious), Duke of Silesia: 156, 160
Henryk IV Probus, Duke of Wrocław: 195
Henryk Kietlicz, Archbishop of Gniezno: 13, 241, 254, 269, 275–76, 280, 282
Henryk Kietlicz, Castellan of Kraków: 127
Henryk Sandomierski (Henry), Duke of Sandomierz: 34, 35, 37, 39, 52–53, 62, 65, 73, 125, 130, 223, 225, 231, 242, 245, 259
Henryk, duke's Steward: 158
Henryk, Prevost of Miechów: 285
Henryków, Cistercian Abbey: 159, 180, 185–86
Herman II, Archbishop of Cologne: 25
Hildebrand, Abbot of Tyniec: 100
Hirschberg, Aleksander: 191
Hockenbeck, Heinrich: 174, 180, 235
Holosisze, village: 102
Holy See: 30–31, 127, 163, 166, 169, 201, 203
Honoriusz III, Pope: 58, 202–03, 213, 289
Hoogeweg Hermann 183

Hubaldus, Cardinal: 68–69, 99, 220, 222–23, 225–26, 233, 246, 250, 271
Hugo, Abbot of Morimond: 287–88
Hugo, Abbot of Wąchock: 285, 288–89
Humbert, Canon of Sandomierz: 143

Idzi, Abbot of Wąchock: 288
Ignacy, Abbot of Wąchock: 284
Innocent II, Pope: 29
Innocent III, Pope: 67, 71, 202
Inowłódz, village: 31, 47, 126, 232
Inowrocław, town: 51
Isaiah, Chancellor of Kalisz: 158
Italy: 263, 298
Iwo Odrowąż, Bishop of Kraków, Chancellor of Leszek Biały: 140, 143, 265, 282, 289, 293, 296–98

Jabłonica, village: 143
Jabłowo, village 231
Jadwiga, Abbess of Owińska: 159
Jadwiga St., Duchess of Silesia, wife of Henryk I Brodaty: 153
Jadwiga, wife of Władysław Odonic: 156–57, 160
Jagiellon monarchy: 170
Jaksa of Miechów, comes: 31, 51, 53–55, 62–63, 75, 100, 274
Jakub of Żnin, Archbishop of Gniezno: 48, 77, 145, 225, 226, 232, 247, 255, 269, 272–74
Jakub Świnka, Archbishop of Gniezno: 60, 213, 288
Jan (Janik), Archbishop of Gniezno: 67, 70, 76–77, 79–81, 91–95, 98–100–03, 105, 108, 110–11, 125, 130, 145–47, 182, 202, 207–11, 213, 220, 225, 232, 235, 238, 242–45, 247, 249–50, 253–54, 259, 269–75, 280–82, 292–93, 296
Jan Malabrank, cardinal: 282
Jan Maur, Bishop of Torcello: 263
Jan, Abbot of Wąchock and Sulejów: 287–88

Jan, Chancellor of Bolesław IV see Jan, Archbishop of Gniezno
Jan, friar of Wąchock Abbey: 285
Jan, Infirmarian of Wąchock Abbey: 285
Jan, comes: 251–52, 259
Jan, Provost of Gniezno: 260
Janauschek, Leopold: 125, 133
Janik, of Gryfita clan, comes: 93, 95, 100
Janina, clan: 55
Jankowice, village: 142
Janota, Eugeniusz: 174
Janusz, of Powała clan, comes: 141, 226, 234
Januszowo, village: 231
Jarosław, Bishop of Wrocław: 276
Jarosz, Castellan of Ruda: 158
Jasiński, Kazimierz: 63
Jasiński, Tomasz: 171, 195
Jaworzec, village: 53
Jażdżewski, Konstanty K.: 178–79, 186
Jemielnica, Cistercian Abbey: 173
Jeżewo, village: 232
Jeżów, village: 281
Jędrzejów (village, Cistercian Abbey): 12–13, 59–60, 63–66, 70–73, 76, 79–82, 84, 87–96, 98–104, 108–11, 124–25, 127, 130, 140, 145, 147, 153, 160, 174–75, 177, 181, 185–87, 200, 204, 207–08, 211–12, 214, 235, 238, 244, 246, 265–66, 269–70, 273–74, 281, 284, 286, 289, 292–96
John, Bishop of Wrocław: 22
Jordan, Bishop of Poland: 20–22
Judith of Bohemia, wife of Władysław I Herman: 28, 165
Judith of Swabia (Judyta Maria), wife of Władysław I Herman: 28, 135
Jurek, Tomasz: 84, 159, 195, 205

Kacice, village: 289, 293
Kaczkowo, village: 78, 259–60

INDEX

Kaczmarczyk, Kazimierz: 182
Kalina, village: 66
Kalisz, city: 273–74, 289
Kałdus, village: 23
Kamieniec Ząbkowicki, Cistercian Abbey: 174, 176, 180, 186, 289
Kamieniec, village: 231
Kamienna (see Wąchock), village: 142
Kamienna, river: 140
Kamień, village: 29
Karwowski, Stanisław: 248–49
Kazimierz Dolny, town: 53
Kazimierz I Odnowiciel (the Restorer), Duke of Poland: 23, 25, 28, 135, 219, 224
Kazimierz II Sprawiedliwy (the Just), Duke of Sandomierz, Kraków, princeps: 12, 34–35, 37, 39, 51–55, 57–58, 61–65–64, 66–67, 69–73, 80–83, 85–87, 91, 100, 103–05, 108–10, 124–31, 138, 140, 142, 144, 148, 150, 176, 188, 195, 204, 207–10–212, 223, 225, 230–31, 249, 274–76, 278–79, 293–94
Kazimierz Kazimierzowic, son of Kazimierz II: 65, 100, 209
Kazimierz of Kujawy, Duke of Kujawy: 71, 203–04, 212
Kazimierza Mała, village: 165
Kępa, village: 126
Kętrzyński, Stanisław: 175, 191, 196–19
Kętrzyński, Wojciech: 58, 94, 174–76, 191–94, 207, 222, 237, 239, 241, 244, 258
Kielce, city: 76
Klemens, father of Jan Archbishop of Gniezno: 270
Klemens, of Gryfita clan, comes: 93, 95, 100–02, 270, 275, 292
Kleparz, part of Kraków today: 66
Kłodawa, village: 51
Kochanowski, Jan K.: 171, 190
Koczerska, Maria: 195

Koebner, Richard: 178
Kołbacz, Cistercian Abbey: 87, 133, 145, 149, 178, 183
Kołobrzeg, strongold and bishopric: 22–23
Konare, village: 102, 146, 266
Koninek, village: 79, 259–60
Konrad I, Duke of Mazovia: 51, 52, 53, 70–71, 73, 189, 192, 204, 214
Konrad III, King of Germany: 273
Konstantyn, son of Piotr Włostowic: 278
Końskie, village: 232–33
Koprzywnica, Cistercian Abbey: 86, 88, 145, 149, 184, 286, 289, 292–93, 295, 297
Korczak, Lidia: 195
Korczyn, village: 232
Kornatowo, village 231
Korta, Wacław: 196
Korytkowski, Jan: 93, 249
Kościelna Wieś, village near Kalisz: 49, 50, 54
Kowalski, Gerard: 182
Kozierowski, Stanisław: 155, 251–53
Kozłowska-Budkowa Zofia: 58, 62–64, 66, 68, 94, 127, 156, 167–68, 171, 175–77, 191, 194, 196–97, 200, 208–09, 219–20, 222, 224, 238, 240–42, 244–45, 267–68, 271
Koźlerogi, family: 275
Krajek, knight: 143
Krajków, village: 143
Kraków (city, castle, bishopric, cathedral church, Wawel Hill) 12–13, 22, 25, 28, 31–32, 34–35, 39, 54, 57, 61, 64, 66, 70, 72, 82, 85–86, 92, 102, 109, 127, 135–37, 141–42, 144, 164, 167, 209, 211–12, 223, 263, 265–68, 271, 274, 276, 279, 281–82, 286, 291, 293, 296–98
Kramarówka, village: 108
Krasoń, Józef: 180
Krewo, town in the Grand Duch of Lithuaania: 195

Krępa, village: 53
Krosno, village: 79, 259–60
Krupicka, Hans: 177
Kruszwica, stronghold, collegiate: 29, 51, 195
Krystyn, comes: 138–40
Krystyn, son of Piotr Stary Wszeborowic: 139–40, 144, 150
Krzcencino, village: 105, 108
Krzeszów, Cistercian Abbey: 173, 176, 180, 186
Krzysz, knight: 143
Krzyżanowski, Stanisław: 58, 171, 174, 178, 182–83, 191–94, 237, 239, 258
Księże Wielkie, village: 50
Kuraś, Stanisław: 66, 171
Kürbis, Brygida: 68, 164, 171, 177, 195, 220, 222, 238, 244, 249, 254, 258
Kutrzeba, Stanisław: 197
Kuyavia/Kujawy: 29, 32, 34–35, 37, 39, 51, 201, 213, 226, 231–32, 234
Kwasów, village: 265
Kwieciszewo, village: 48, 51, 68, 223, 225, 231

Labuda, Gerard: 33, 35, 134–35, 189, 193, 195
Lambert, Abbot of Wąchock: 284
Lambert, Bishop of Kraków: 164, 266, 268
Lambert, knight: 143
Lanche, village: 105
Lantczyno, village: 102, 146
Ląd, Cistercian Abbey: 72, 84–85, 88, 130, 133, 145, 149, 174–75, 177, 186, 192, 195, 200, 205, 214, 280
Lechowicz, Zbigniew: 95, 97
Lehnin, Cistercian Abbey: 289
Lelewel, Joachim: 33
Lenczowski, Franciszek: 180
Leonard, son of Piotr Włostowic: 100
Leszczyce, clan: 252, 254, 278
Leszek Biały (the White), Duke of Kraków: 54, 64, 71, 73, 109, 129, 140, 142–43, 151, 176, 188, 211–12, 294, 297
Leszek Czarny (the Black), Duke of Sieradz and Kraków: 71, 204, 287
Leszek, son of Bolesław IV: 62
Liege (Leodium), bishopric: 177, 242
Likowski, Henryk: 155–56, 159
Lingenberg, Heinz: 178
Linowo, village: 102, 146, 266
Lipińska, Olga: 133
Lisów, village: 287
Lubcza, village: 282
Lubiąż, Cistercian Abbey: 81–82, 87–88, 130, 133, 145, 148–49, 160, 173–75, 177–78, 180, 185–88, 192, 200, 204, 250, 275, 286, 289
Lubiń, Benedictine Abbey: 28, 192, 200, 247, 275
Lubusz, stronhold, bishopric: 19, 20, 29, 31–32
Ludźmierz, village: 293
Lupus, Bishop of Płock: 62, 67, 69, 73. 275–76
Lusowo, village: 84
Lutogniew, village: 143
Lyszakowo, village: 102, 146
Łabędzie, clan: 77, 139, 150, 234, 254, 278
Łagów, village: 136
Łaszczyńska, Olga: 194
Łekneńskie, lake: 78
Łekno, Cistercian Abbey: 12–13, 72, 75–6, 78–80, 83–84, 85, 88, 99–100, 103, 110, 145, 147, 153, 174–75, 177, 180, 187, 202–03, 233, 235, 237–38, 240–42, 244–47, 250–59, 273, 281, 291
Łęczany, village: 143, 151
Łęcznia, village: 285
Łęczno, village: 182, 213
Łęczyca, city, stronghold, region: 20, 35, 37, 48, 52, 68–69, 73, 138, 141, 178, 223, 225, 232, 275–76, 281–82
Łęg, village: 154, 159

Łomna, village: 52–53, 70
Łoskuń, villlage: 78, 232, 259–60
Łowmiański, Henryk: 33, 68, 220, 222, 224
Łubnica, village: 223, 232
Łukawa, village: 143
Łuszczkiewicz, Władysław: 133, 295

Maciej of Pełczyn, knight: 275
Magdeburg, city, archbishopric: 19, 164, 167, 269
Mainz: 2
Maleczyński, Karol: 102, 168, 171, 176–77, 184, 188, 191, 194, 196, 222, 237–38, 240, 242, 244, 248, 258, 271
Małecki, Antoni: 94, 109, 155, 175, 191, 193–94, 207, 222, 237, 239, 258
Małopolska: 13, 25, 35, 85–88, 110, 127–28, 141, 143, 181–82, 184, 211, 213–14, 250, 279, 291–94, 296, 298
Manikowska, Halina: 13
Manteuffel, Tadeusz: 94, 110, 124, 128–29, 134
Marcin, Abbot of Wąchock: 285–87, 289–90
Marcin, Provost of Santok: 158
Marek, of Gryfici clan, comes: 143
Maria Dobroniega, wife of Kazimierz I Odnowiciel: 25
Markusz, Abbot of Wąchock: 285–86
Markusz, comes: 143
Marszowice, village: 157
Martyr, treasurer of Wąchock Abbey: 285
Mateusz, Bishop of Kraków: 65, 98, 177, 270, 272, 296
Matilda of Lorraine (Swabia), Duchess of Upper Lorraine: 164
Matuszewski, Józef: 109
Maur, Bishop of Kraków: 91–93, 95–98, 100, 102–03, 146–47, 263–68
Maurycy, friar of Wąchock Abbey: 285

Mazovia: 20, 25, 34–35, 37, 39, 47, 53, 70, 195, 234, 298
Mątwy, village: 51, 78, 259–60
Meissen, bishopric: 289
Melachides, Abbot of Wąchock: 284
Meuse, river: 177
Mianów, village 126
Michał, Castellan of Kraków: 64, 211–12
Michał, comes: 267
Michałowski, Roman: 12
Michowo, village: 102, 146, 266
Miechów, monastery of the Canons of St. Grave: 47, 51–53, 55, 66–69, 71–72, 127, 139, 141–42, 202, 221, 279, 285
Miecław, cupbearer of Mieszko II: 25
Mieszko [IV] Plątonogi (the Tanglefoot), Duke of Racibórz and Kraków: 50
Mieszko I, Duke of Poland: 17, 19–22, 33, 163, 219
Mieszko II, King of Poland: 23, 25, 163
Mieszko III Stary (the Old), Duke of Wielkopolska, princeps: 13, 34–35, 37, 39, 46, 48–50–53, 55, 57, 61–63, 67–68, 72, 80, 82–85, 91, 100, 103, 105, 108, 110, 127–30, 176, 201, 204, 207, 209–11, 213, 220–26, 230–33, 243, 245–46, 248–50, 259, 273–76, 279–80
Mieszko Pomeranian, comes: 252, 259
Mieszko, son of Mieszko III: 100, 273
Międzyrzecz, stronghold: 23
Mikołaj of the Bogoria: 86, 293
Mikołaj Repczol, Chancellor of Leszek Biały: 143
Mikołaj, Abbot of Byszewo: 287
Mikołaj, voivode of Kraków: 100, 143
Mikora, comes: 234
Mikorek, village: 285
Milej, knight: 267

Milej, peasant: 128
Milejów, village: 61, 83, 128
Milica, village: 62–63, 67
Milkowice, village: 158
Milvanus, Abbot of Clavo Monte: 100
Miraue, village: 105
Mirzec, settlement: 142
Missalek, Erich: 177
Mitkowski, Józef: 58, 71, 123–25, 127–28, 130, 171, 176–77, 180, 182–83, 185, 188, 194, 196, 208, 212
Młodocin, village: 142
Młodojewo, village: 224, 231
Modrzany, village: 285
Moepert, Adolf: 177
Mogilno, Benedictine Abbey: 25, 48, 77, 147, 165, 192, 195, 200, 204, 221, 246–47, 271
Mogiła near Kraków (part of Kraków today), Cistercian Abbey: 174–75, 182, 185, 286, 289, 292–94, 297
Mokronosy, village: 78–79, 259–60
Monachus, Patriarch of Jerozolima: 66–69, 221
Montinus/Mantina (Męcina), comes: 225, 233
Morakowo, village: 79, 259–60
Moravia: 138
Morimond, Cistercian Abbey: 83, 86, 88, 94, 99–101, 124, 130, 134, 207, 273, 293
Mosingiewicz, Krzysztof: 195, 197
Mozgawa, village: 280
Mrokota, Bishop of Poznań: 276
Muczkowski, Antoni: 171
Munich: 189
Mütterich, Florentine: 164

Nabytyn, village: 149
Nagodzice, clan: 265
Nałęcze, clan: 251
Nazar, Abbot of Wąchock: 284
Ner, river: 83, 126, 150

Niałkowie–Jelenie (Niałek–Jeleń), clan: 78, 253
Niegosławice, village: 67, 265
Niemir (Niemierza?), comes: 229, 234
Niessen von, Paul: 178
Niwiński Mieczysław 70, 133, 135, 138–40, 178, 182–83, 284–86
Norbert, Archbishop of Magdeburg: 29
Nowacki, Józef: 182, 184, 277

Obra, Cistercian Abbey: 174, 180, 183
Ochodza, village: 79, 231, 259–60
Oda, wife of Mieszko I: 21, 163
Oder, river: 29, 46, 133, 145, 148–49, 151, 163, 291
Odilo, Abbot of the Abbey of Saint Gilles in Provence: 28, 165
Odolan, comes: 225, 232
Odon, son of Mieszko III: 276
Odrowąż, clan: 78, 232, 293
Ogierz, comes: 78, 252, 259–60
Olesno (Oleszno), village: 78, 157, 251, 259–60
Oliwa (part of Gdańsk today), Cistercian Abbey: 87, 145, 149, 178–79, 183
Olomouc (town in Bohemia): 22
Ołbin (part of Wrocław today, island on the Oder), Benedictine Abbey: 49, 50, 54, 254, 280
Opatkowo (Opatkowice), village: 108
Opatów, town: 12, 66, 129, 278
Orońsk, village: 142
Osarowici (Ożarowice), village: 102, 146, 266
Osieczno, village: 154, 159
Osiek, village: 287
Osiekowo, village: 223, 231
Osobłoga, river: 82
Ostrowite, village: 231
Ostrów Lednicki, stronghold: 19–21
Ostrów Tumski (part of Poznań today), island on the Warta River: 21

Ostrów Tumski (part of Wrocław today), island on the Oder River: 149
Ostrów, village: 223, 232
Ottenthal von, Emil: 237
Otto I, Emperor: 20, 165
Otto III, Emperor: 21, 165
Otto of Bamberg, Bishop of Bamberg 29
Otto of Wierzbica 138–40
Otto, son of Otton z Wierzbicy: 139–40, 143, 150
Owińska, Cistercians Abbey: 12, 153–60, 178

Pacanów, village: 265
Pakosław, of Awdańcy clan, comes: 225–26, 233, 250–59
Pakulski, Jan: 251
Palędzie, village: 231
Pałuki, clan: 77, 81, 145, 232–33, 237, 246, 250, 253–54, 278, 293
Pałuki, region: 76, 79, 153, 231, 191
Panigródź, village: 78, 242, 258–60
Pankracy, Abbot of Wąchock: 284
Paradyż, Cistercian Abbey: 180, 289
Pean, Chancellor of Mieszko III, then Bishop of Poznań: 225, 248
Pelplin, Cistercian Abbey: 178, 180, 183, 185
Pełka, Archbishop of Gniezno: 157–58, 204, 213, 277, 288
Pełka, Bishop of Kraków: 59–62, 66–67, 86, 127, 210–11, 279, 281, 298
Pełknice, village: 105
Perlbach, Max: 177, 183
Petzelt, L.: 180
Pfafendorf near Bytom, village: 149
Pforta, Cistercian Abbey: 81, 186, 188
Pfotenhauer, Paul: 174
Pianowski, Zbigniew: 134–36
Piasek, island on the Oder River (Wrocław): 49, 212, 280
Piast dynasty and Piast monarchy: 11–13, 15, 17–26, 29–34, 35, 37, 39, 41, 45, 46–48, 51, 53–57, 69, 75–77, 80–81, 83–84, 86–88, 98, 130, 138, 141, 145, 151, 153, 156, 160, 163, 166–68, 170, 189, 192, 199, 202, 207, 208, 214, 226, 230, 232, 234, 269, 272–74, 280–82, 291, 293, 298
Piekosiński, Franciszek: 93, 171, 190–91, 207, 210, 222, 235, 237, 239, 250
Pierre de Capuano, Cardinal: 282
Pictrusiński, Jerzy: 164, 267
Piętka, Jan: 195
Pikutkowo, village: 232
Pilica, river: 47, 82–83, 124, 126–27, 130, 136, 148, 224, 232, 293
Piotr Pałuka, knight: 78, 239, 247, 259–60
Piotr Włostowic, voivode of Poland: 13, 31, 37, 49, 55, 75, 77, 80, 98, 127, 177, 234, 253, 272, 278, 280
Piotr Wszeborowic, comes: 55, 150, 233
Piotr, Abbot in Sulejów: 58, 203–04, 213
Piotr, Archbishop of Gniezno: 58–62, 79, 83, 85, 127–28, 150, 203–04, 208, 210–11, 233, 241, 253–54, 260, 269, 275–82
Piotr, subprior of Wąchock Abbey: 285
Piotrów, village: 126
Pisa: 29
Plenkiewicz, Roman: 133
Plezia, Marian: 99
Płocha, Józef: 195
Płock, city, stronghold, bishopric: 25, 54, 68–69, 135, 165, 192, 225
Pobóg-Lenartowicz, Anna: 196
Podhale, region: 289
Podkarpacie Region: 86
Pokrzywnica, village: 78–79, 259–60
Polaczkówna Helena 176
Polany, village: 143, 151
Pomerania: 19, 29, 35, 86, 168, 178, 180, 213, 252, 266

Pomerania East (Gdańsk): 20, 29, 87, 183, 187
Pomerania West: 20, 23, 29, 183, 189
Pomian, clan: 78, 252
Pomorzany, village: 143, 151
Popielas-Szultka, Barbara: 183
Popielewo, village: 231
Poppo, Bishop of Kraków: 22
Poraje-Różyce, clan: 278, 53, 278
Pothok, village: 102, 146
Potkański, Karol: 191
Powała, clan: 85, 141, 234, 283
Poznań, city, stronghold, bishopric: 19–21, 24–25, 31–32, 84, 157–58, 183, 235, 238, 240, 248–49
Prague, city, bishopric: 19, 22, 24, 164, 282
Prandocin, village: 94–95, 126, 289, 293
Prekopa, village: 102, 146, 266
Přemyslid, dynasty: 19
Preneslawe, village: 102, 146, 266
Prędota Stary, comes: 253
Prędota, comes of Odrowąż clan: 78, 253, 259–60
Prusinowice, village: 143
Prussia: 22, 29, 79, 195
Przecław, Castellan of Biechów: 158
Przecław, Chebda's father: 259–60
Przecław, knight: 78, 252, 259
Przedbórz, village: 47, 232
Przedpełk, Castellan of Poznań: 158
Przedwój/Przedwoj, comes: 78, 250–52, 259, 260
Przemysł I, Duke of Wielkopolska: 154, 156–57, 159–60, 183
Przemysł II, Duke of Wielkopolska: 183
Przybysz, Tadeusz: 238
Przypkowski, Tadeusz: 177
Puczniew, village: 126
Pustwino, village: 223, 231

Racława, Abbess of Owińska: 160
Radim Gaudentius, Archbishop of Gniezno: 22, 24
Radojewo, village: 157
Radom Forest: 86
Radosław, comes: 59, 62, 69, 73, 83, 126, 150, 210
Radost, Bishop of Kraków: 81, 91–93, 97–98, 101–03, 110, 147, 266, 271
Radwan, Bishop of Poznań: 248, 249, 259
Radziejów Stary, village: 77
Rajnald (Reinaldus), cardinal, papal legate: 281
Rakoszyno, village: 102, 146
Rakowo, village: 102, 146
Raskowicze, village: 158
Regensburg: 19
Reinbern, Bishop of Kolberg: 22
Remigiusz, Abbot of Wąchock: 284
Rgielskie, lake: 78
Rgielsko, village: 78, 242
Rhine, river: 242
Richeza of Lotharingia, Queen of Poland: 23
Robert I, Bishop of Kraków: 266, 267, 271
Rokietnica, village: 158
Rome: 69, 226, 281, 288
Rose, Ambrosius: 180
Rother, Karl: 186
Ruda, village: 142
Rudolf, Abbot of Wąchock: 284
Rudolf, priest: 260
Rudy Raciborskie, Cistercian Abbey: 173, 180, 186
Rus': 57, 110, 124, 128–29, 164, 290, 297
Rybandt, Stanisław: 180, 183, 186
Rymar, Edward: 196
Rzeczyca, village: 53

Salis, Friedrich: 183
Salomea of Berg, wife of Bolesław III: 33, 35, 37, 48, 51, 54, 68, 77, 130, 221, 223, 225–26, 230, 233–34, 246

Sambor I, Duke of East Pomerania: 87, 178, 183
Sambor II, Duke of East Pomerania: 178
Samołęż, village: 157
Sandomierz (Zandemir), city, stronghold, region: 34, 35, 54, 60–61, 63, 70, 72, 80–83, 86, 88, 108, 124–25, 127, 153, 232–31, 234, 273–74, 279, 282, 286, 291, 293, 296–98
Sarbick, village: 51
Schulte, Wilhelm: 180
Sczaniecki, Michał: 251–53
Semkowicz, Aleksander: 156, 159
Semkowicz, Władysław: 58, 63–65, 77, 102, 104, 171, 175–77, 191, 194, 196, 207, 209, 233, 237–40, 242, 247, 249–51, 253, 278
Sgimir Coquelic, peasant: 126
Siemian, knight: 265
Sienno, village: 158
Sieradz, region, stronghold: 20, 35, 37
Sierakowo, village: 232
Sikora, Franciszek: 155–57, 160, 178, 183, 195
Sikorski, Dariusz Adam: 195
Silesia: 24–25, 34–35, 37, 39, 82, 88, 157, 159, 186, 189, 272
Skarbimir, voivode of Poland: 233, 250
Skaryszew, village 51, 66–67, 69
Skarżysko Kamienna, town: 142
Skąpice (Skąpe), village: 82, 127
Skotniki, village: 105
Skowieszyn, village: 53
Skupieński, Krzysztof: 185
Sławnik Pałuka, knight: 78, 247, 259–60
Słosim (Słosin), village: 79, 259–60
Smolka, Stanisław: 33, 171, 190–91, 235, 237–38, 241, 258
Sobieslawowice, dynasty of East Pomerania: 87

Sobiesław I, Duke of East Pomerania: 87
Spicygniew/Spitygniew, comes: 225, 233
Spisz, region: 289
Spors, Józef: 196, 178, 220, 222
Stanisław, Bishop of Kraków and saint: 28, 33
Starachowice, town: 297
Stefan form Lis clan: 100
Stefan, Abbot of Koprzywnica: 287
Stefan, Archdeacon of Gniezno: 260
Stefan, Bishop of Poznań: 247, 248, 259, 280
Stefan, magister, Chancellor of Kazimierz II: 100, 244, 249–50, 259
Stefan, son of Mieszko III: 100
Stefanów, village: 126
Stojsław, knight: 234
Stopnica, village: 140, 287
Stradunia, river: 82
Strasz, comes: 250, 259
Straszewo, village: 78, 258
Straszów, village: 82, 127
Strehlke, Ernst: 180
Strzegomie, Clan: 55
Strzelce, village: 126, 232
Strzelno, Norbertine Monastery: 49, 51, 280
Suemingala, peasant: 128
Sulejów, Cistercian Abbey: 12–13, 47, 58–63, 70–73, 82–83, 87–88, 108–10, 123–31, 133, 136, 140, 142, 145, 148, 150, 175–77, 182, 185–88, 192, 196, 200, 203–04, 207, 210–14, 232, 279, 287–88, 290, 292–93, 295, 297–98
Sułkowska-Kurasiowa, Irena: 171
Sylvester II, Pope: 165
Szacherska, Stella Maria: 178, 182
Szaweł, Chancellor of Leszek Biały: 143
Szaweł, comes: 225, 233
Szczecin, city: 19, 29, 185

Szczedrzyk, comes: 267
Szczeglin, village: 265
Szczyrzyc, Cistercian Abbey: 178, 182, 185, 193, 289, 292–93
Szelejewo, village: 231
Szpetal, village: 178, 182, 287
Szydłowski, Tadeusz: 94, 97
Szymański, Józef: 124, 129, 196
Szymon, Abbot of Łekno: 79, 100, 256
Szymon, Abbot of Wąchock: 287, 290
Śliwiński, Błażej: 195–97
Śmił (Smile), comes: 105, 275
Śreniawa/Śreniawici, clan: 253, 278
Św. Krzyż, Monastery in Świętokrzyskie Mountains: 30
Świechowski Zygmunt 94, 96, 123, 126
Świerczek, village: 142
Świerże Górne, village: 69, 73, 275–76, 281
Świętokrzyskie Mountain: 136–37, 293, 297–98
Świętopełk I, Duke of Gdańsk Pomerania: 183
Świętosław Piotrowic, son of Piotr Włostowic: 54, 100, 274, 278
Świniów, village: 142

Targowiste, village: 260
Tarszawa (Tharszawa), village: 67, 70, 73, 102, 146
Taszycki, Witold: 191
Tądów, village: 126–27
Teobald, *subcellarius* of Wąchock Abbey: 285
Teodor, voivode of Kraków: 293
Thietmar of Merseburg, chronicler: 21, 23
Tmienich, village: 158
Tomasz, of the Nałęcz clan, comes: 252, 259
Tomaszewski, Andrzej: 95
Tomisławice, village: 82, 127

Toporczyk, clan: 146
Trawkowski, Stanisław: 135, 138–39, 241, 254, 279
Treskow, family: 157
Trojan Powała, comes: 141, 234
Trojanów, village: 52, 70
Trzebnica, Cistercians Abbey: 153, 157, 159–60, 176, 186
Trzemeszno, Monastery of Canons Regular: 11, 13, 46–49, 52–55, 67–70, 72, 84, 141, 192, 201, 204, 219–25, 230, 232, 234, 250–52
Tum near Łęczyca, village: 95, 273
Turza, village: 78, 252, 259, 260
Tyc, Teodor: 222
Tymieniecki, Kazimierz: 128, 176
Tyniec near Kraków (part of Kraków today), Benedictine Abbey: 25, 28, 191–92, 200, 204, 221

Ulanowski, Bolesław: 171, 190, 193
Unger, Bishop of Poland (Poznań): 21–22
Utrosza, peasant: 126
Uxor Zbylut see wife of Zbylut

Valdemar I, King of Denmark: 86
Vincent, Archbishop of Gniezno: 211
Vincentius, bishop of Kraków, chronicler: 34–35, 39, 57, 62, 91–92, 96, 98, 103, 105, 108, 127, 129–30, 147, 210, 254, 266, 270, 274, 279, 284, 295–96
Vistula, river: 25, 29, 46, 53, 88, 133, 145, 151, 163, 232, 291, 293
Vratislav II, King of Bohemia: 164

Walerian, Abbot of Wąchock: 284
Walicki, Michał: 95
Walo, Abbot of Wąchock: 285–86
Wałkówski, Andrzej: 176, 185–86
Warmiński, Teodor: 180
Warta, river: 29, 46, 84, 145, 156, 158, 163, 291

Wasilewski, Tadeusz: 188
Waśniów, village: 223, 225, 232
Wattenbach, Wilhelm: 173
Wawrzyszów, village: 143
Wąchock, Cistercian Abbey: 12, 13, 70–73, 86, 88, 133–42, 144–45, 149–50, 178, 182, 283–90, 292, 295–98
Wągrowiec, town: 235
Wdowiszewski, Zygmunt: 178, 184
Wenta, Jarosław: 68–69, 220, 222, 225
Wetesko, Leszek: 13
Wędzki, Andrzej: 94
Węgierce, village: 51
Węgłowo, village: 232
Wiardus, Prior of Wąchock Abbey: 285
Wichman II the Younger, Count of the Billung family: 20
Wielice, village: 285
Wieliczka near Kraków (Magnum Salem): 81, 83, 108, 223, 231, 297
Wielka Wieś, village: 142
Wielkopolska: 13, 20, 24, 34–35, 37, 46–47, 50–52, 85, 88, 99, 103, 153, 156, 160, 174, 183–84, 190, 195, 213, 226, 231–33, 247, 251, 270, 293
Wierzbica, village 139–40, 143–44, 150, 151
Wierzbnice near Bytom, village 149
Wierzenica, village: 78, 157, 253, 259–60
Wietrzna Góra, village: 53
Wife of Zbylut (unknown by name, maybe Zofia?): 43, 78, 245, 252, 259–60
Wilczkowice, village: 143
Wilhelm, Abbot of Sulejów: 213
Wilhelm, Bailiff of Wąchock Abbey: 285
Wilhelm, Custos 249, 259
Wincenty, Canon of Gniezno: 233
Winter, Franz: 93, 125, 133
Wisław Odrowąż, comes: 293

Wiślica, stronghold, district: 12, 53, 57, 65, 125, 285
Wit, Bishop of Płock: 276, 281
Wit, comes of Janina clan: 55
Witów, village: 61
Władysław I Herman, Duke of Poland: 25, 28, 46, 135, 164–65, 263
Władysław I Łokietek, Duke then King of Poland: 288, 298
Władysław II Wygnaniec (the Exile), Duke of Silesia, princeps: 34, 35, 37, 48, 49, 69, 75, 77, 81, 139, 145, 148, 178, 226, 232–34, 272, 280–81
Władysław III Laskonogi, Duke of Wielkopolska and Kraków: 100, 183, 253
Władysław Odonic, Duke of Wielkopolska: 156, 159–60, 183, 277, 289
Włast, comes 234
Włocławek, city: 29
Włostowo, village: 232
Wojciechowski, Tadeusz: 33, 35, 37, 191, 266
Wojsław, brother of Gedko the Bishop of Kraków: 141, 234
Wojsław, comes, guardian of Bolesław III: 141, 267
Wojszyn, village: 53
Wolin, bishopric: 19, 29, 31–32
Wójcik, Marek L.: 186
Wratislaw II, Duke of West Pomerania: 87
Wrocław, stronghold, city, bishopric: 22, 25, 31–32, 46, 49, 102, 149, 173, 201, 207, 250, 271, 275, 285
Wszebor, son of Krystyn Piotrowic: 143
Wszebor, voivode: 138–39, 225–26, 232–33
Wutke, Konrad: 186
Wylatowo, village: 231
Wyrwa, Andrzej M.: 84, 147, 180

Wysocko, village: 142
Wysoka, village: 142
Wyszogród, stronghold: 232

Yaroslav the Wise, Grand Duke of Kyiv: 25

Zachłodzice, village: 223, 232
Zagość, commandery of the Order of Saint John: 62, 64, 67, 72, 142, 231, 242
Zakrzewski, Ignacy: 171, 190
Zakrzewski, Stanisław: 182–83, 193
Załachowo/Załachów (Salachowo), village: 79, 231, 259–60
Zawadzka, Józefa: 89, 96, 137
Zawichost, town: 286
Zbar, village: 223, 225, 231
Zbigniew, Prince of Poland: 219
Zbylut, comes: 76–78, 80, 84, 103, 145, 147–48, 202, 225–26, 233, 235–37, 239–40, 246–47, 255, 257–58, 260, 273, 293

Zbysława, wife of Bolesław III: 34
Zdeccze, village: 105, 108
Zdziechowice, village: 142
Zdziechów, village: 142
Zdziechówek, village: 142
Zdzisław, Archbishop of Gniezno: 60, 69, 79, 127, 254, 269, 275–77, 280, 282
Zdzisław, comes 234
Zerczicze, village: 105
Zesie, village: 105
Zgórsko, village: 265
Ziemakowice, village: 142
Zofia see wife of Zbylut
Zuzela, village: 52
Zwierzyniec near Kraków (part of Kraków today): 12, 53, 55
Żabiec, village: 265
Żarnów (Sarnov), stronghold, village: 223, 232
Żerelik, Rościsław: 186
Żyra, voivode of Mazovia: 141
Żyrcin, village: 143